PLATINUM EDITION

3

Series Director: Diane Larsen-Freeman

GRAMMAR DIMENSIONS

TEACHER'S EDITION

Stephen H. Thewlis

Center for International Programs
Saint Mary's College of California

W9-APH-201

HH Heinle & Heinle
Thomson Learning

Australia • Canada • Denmark • Japan • Mexico • New Zealand
Philippines • Puerto Rico • Singapore • Spain • United Kingdom • United States

Acquisitions Editor: Eric Bredenberg
Senior Developmental Editor: Amy Lawler
Production Editor: Michael Burggren
Senior Marketing Manager: Charlotte Sturdy
Manufacturing Coordinator: Mary Beth Hennebury
Composition/Project Management: The PRD Group, Inc.
Text Design: Sue Gerould, Perspectives
Cover Design: Hannus Design Associates
Printer: Phoenix Color

For permission to use material from this text, contact us:
web   www.thomsonrights.com
fax   1-800-730-2215
phone   1-800-730-2214

Heinle & Heinle Publishers
20 Park Plaza
Boston, MA 02116

UK/EUROPE/MIDDLE EAST:
Thomson Learning
Berkshire House
168-173 High Holborn
London, WC1V 7AA, United Kingdom

ASIA (excluding Japan):
Thomson Learning
60 Albert Street #15-01
Albert Complex
Singapore 189969

AUSTRALIA/NEW ZEALAND:
Nelson/Thomson Learning
102 Dodds Street
South Melbourne
Victoria 3205 Australia

LATIN AMERICA:
Thomson Learning
Seneca, 53
Colonia Polanco
11560 México D.F. México

JAPAN:
Thomson Learning
Palaceside Building, 5F
1-1-1 Hitotsubashi, Chiyoda-ku
Tokyo 100 0003, Japan

CANADA:
Nelson/Thomson Learning
1120 Birchmount Road
Scarborough, Ontario
Canada M1K 5G4

SPAIN:
Thomson Learning
Calle Magallanes, 25
28015-Madrid
Espana

ISBN: 0-8384-0285-2

 This book is printed on acid-free recycled paper.

Printed in the United States of America
2 3 4 5 6 7 8 9 04 03 02 01 00

Teacher's Edition Contents

Contents

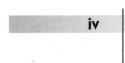

CONTENTS   **vii**

Introduction

A Word from Diane Larsen-Freeman, Series Director

Before **Grammar Dimensions** was published, teachers would always ask me, "What is the role of grammar in a communicative approach?" These teachers recognized the importance of teaching grammar, but they associated grammar with form and communication with meaning, and thus could not see how the two easily fit together. **Grammar Dimensions** was created to help teachers and students appreciate the fact that grammar is not just about form. While grammar does indeed involve form, in order to communicate, language users also need to know the meaning of the forms and when to use them appropriately. In fact, it is sometimes not the form, but the *meaning* or *appropriate use* of a grammatical structure that represents the greatest long-term learning challenge for students. For instance, learning when it is appropriate to use the present perfect tense instead of the past tense, or being able to use two-word or phrasal verbs meaningfully, represent formidable challenges for ESL students.

The three dimensions of form, meaning, and use can be depicted in a pie chart with their interrelationship illustrated by the three arrows:

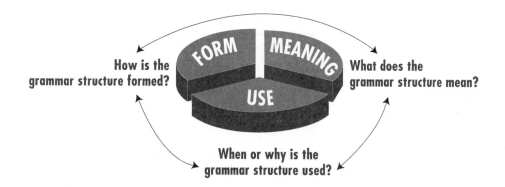

Helping students learn to use grammatical structures accurately, meaningfully, and appropriately is the fundamental goal of **Grammar Dimensions.** It is consistent with the goal of helping students to communicate meaningfully in English, and one that recognizes the undeniable interdependence of grammar and communication.

Enjoy the Platinum Edition!

To learn more about form, meaning, and use, read **The Grammar Book: An ESL/EFL Teacher's Course,** Second Edition, by Marianne Celce-Murcia and Diane Larsen-Freeman, also from Heinle & Heinle. It helps both prospective and practicing teachers of ESL/EFL enhance their understanding of English grammar, expand their skills in linguistic analysis, and develop a pedagogical approach to teaching English grammar that builds on the three dimensions. ISBN: 0-8384-4725-2.

Welcome to Grammar Dimensions, Platinum Edition!

The most comprehensive communicative grammar series available.

Updated and revised, *Grammar Dimensions, Platinum Edition,* makes teaching grammar easy and more effective than ever. Clear grammar explanations, a wealth of exercises, lively communicative activities, technology resources, and fully annotated Teacher's Editions help both beginning and experienced teachers give their students the practice and skills they need to communicate accurately, meaningfully, and appropriately.

Grammar Dimensions, Platinum Edition is:

Communicative	• Students practice the **form, meaning,** and **use** of each grammar structure. • **Improved! A variety of communicative activities** helps students practice grammar and communication in tandem, eliciting self-expression and personalized practice. • Students learn to communicate accurately, meaningfully, and appropriately.
Comprehensive	• **Improved!** Grammar is presented in **clear charts.** • **A wealth of exercises** helps students practice and master their new language. • **The Workbook** provides extra practice and helps students prepare for the TOEFL® Test. • **Engaging listening activities** on audiocassette further reinforce the target structure. • **New! Enclosed CD-ROM** includes over 500 activities and gives students even more practice in mastering grammar and its use in language. **FREE!**
Clear	• **Improved! Simplified grammar explanations** help both students and teachers easily understand and comprehend each language structure. • **Improved! A fresh new design** makes each activity engaging. • **New! Communicative activities** ("the Purple Pages") are now labeled with the skill being practiced. • **New!** The Teacher's Edition has **page references** for the Student Book and Workbook, minimizing extra preparation time.

User Friendly for Students	• **Contextualized grammar explanations and examples** help students understand the target language.
	• **New! Goals** at the beginning of each unit focus students' attention on the learning they will do.
	• **Sample phrases and sentences** model the appropriate use of the structure.
User Friendly for Teachers	• **New!** Teacher's Edition now contains answers, tests, tape scripts, and complete, **step-by-step teaching suggestions** for every activity.
	• **New!** "Purple Page" activities are now labeled with the skill.
	• **Improved! A tight integration** among the Student Book, the Workbook, and the Teacher's Edition make extension activities easy to do.
Flexible	• Instructors can use the units in order or as set by their curriculum.
	• Exercises can be used in order or as needed by the students.
	• "Purple Page" activities can be used at the end of the unit or interspersed throughout the unit.
Effective	Students who learn the form, meaning, and use of each grammar structure will be able to communicate more accurately, meaningfully, and appropriately.

Grammar Dimensions, Platinum Edition

In *Grammar Dimensions, Platinum Edition,* students progress from the sentence level to the discourse level, and learn to communicate appropriately at all levels.

| Grammar Dimensions Book 1 | Grammar Dimensions Book 2 | Grammar Dimensions Book 3 | Grammar Dimensions Book 4 |

Sentence level → **Discourse level**

	Grammar Dimensions, Book 1	Grammar Dimensions, Book 2	Grammar Dimensions, Book 3	Grammar Dimensions, Book 4
Level	High beginning	Intermediate	High intermediate	Advanced
Grammar level	Sentence and subsentence level	Sentence and subsentence level	Discourse level	Discourse level
Primary language and communication focus	Semantic notions such as *time* and *place*	Social functions, such as *making requests* and *seeking permission*	Cohesion and coherence at the discourse level	Academic and technical discourse
Major skill focus	Listening and speaking	Listening and speaking	Reading and writing	Reading and writing
Outcome	Students form accurate, meaningful, and appropriate structures at the sentence level.	Students form accurate, meaningful, and appropriate structures at the sentence level.	Students learn how accurate, meaningful, and appropriate grammatical structures contribute to the organization of language above the simple	Students learn how accurate, meaningful, and appropriate grammatical structures contribute to the organization of language above the simple sentence.

Unit Organization

Used with or without the Workbook and the *Grammar 3D* CD-ROM, ***Grammar Dimensions*** Student Book units are designed to be clear, comprehensive, flexible, and communicative.

Goals	• **Focus students' attention** on the learning they will do in each chapter.
Opening Task	• **Contextualizes** the target grammatical structure. • **Enables teachers to diagnose** their students' performance and identify the aspect of the structure with which their students have the most difficulty. • **Provides a roadmap** for the grammar points students need to work on in that unit.
Focus Boxes	• **Present the form, meaning,** or **use** of a particular grammatical structure. • **Focus students' attention** to a particular feature of the target structure. Each rule or explanation is preceded by examples, so teachers can have students work inductively to try to discover the rule on their own.
Exercises	• Provide a wealth of opportunity to **practice** the form and meaning of the grammar structures. • Help students develop the skill of **"grammaring"**—the ability to use structures accurately, meaningfully, and appropriately. • Are varied, thematically coherent, but purposeful. • Give students many opportunities to personalize and own the language.
Communicative Activities ("The Purple Pages")	• Help students practice **grammar and communication in tandem.** • **Are engaging!** • Encourage students to **use their new language** both inside and outside the classroom. • Provide an opportunity to **practice reading, writing, listening, and speaking skills,** helping students realize the communicative value of the grammar they are learning.

About the Teacher's Edition

The Teacher's Edition includes the following:

- General suggestions for teaching with *Grammar Dimensions Platinum.*
- Detailed teaching suggestions and answer keys for each unit in the Student Book. The following icons appear in this section:

-  This icon signals a time when you could present a grammar point on the board.

-  The pairwork icon appears when an exercise can be done in pairs.

- The groupwork icon appears when an exercise can be done in a group.

- This icon appears when a corresponding Workbook exercise or exercises can be assigned. The exercise and page number(s) in the Workbook are supplied next to the icon. The answers for the Workbook exercises appear in the Workbook Answer Key section of this Teacher's Edition. The page number for the answers to each exercise appear as part of each Workbook anno.

- This icon and an accompanying anno appear in the "Use Your English" section when there is an audio activity.

- Tests. A 15-minute test is included for each unit. You can administer it after each unit or combine with other units to create longer tests. You are welcome to photocopy the tests for student use. This icon appears when a test can be given.

- Answer key for the tests.
- Answer key for Workbook exercises.
- Tapescripts for the Listening Activities that appear in the "Use Your English" communicative activities section (purple pages) for each unit of the Student Book.

General Teaching Suggestions

OPENING TASK

Our time with our students is very precious. We must seek ways to put it to their best advantage. In order to do this, you need to learn what your students know and don't know how to do. This will allow you to target what you teach to what your students don't know, and therefore, need to learn. This is the major purpose of the opening task. You should be able to obtain invaluable information about your students' learning needs from "reading" (closely observing) your students as they go about doing the task. Each task has been constructed so that students will need to use the target structures in order to complete it.

As the students are focused on completing the task, you are freed to learn as much as you can about your students' learning needs. It will probably be best if after you have introduced the task (making sure students know what they are being asked to do), you have the students carry out as much of the task as they can by themselves. This will allow you to more closely observe your students' performance.

One way of doing this is to circulate in the classroom and "eavesdrop" on small group discussions. Take mental or written notes on your observations. Pay particular attention to how accurate, meaningful, and appropriate your students' use of the target structures is. Hold up the form, meaning, and use pie chart in your mind and see if you can determine where they have been successful, and where they need help. At this point, it is probably better if you refrain from any error correction. The tasks are supposed to encourage students to work meaningfully without concern that they will be interrupted, evaluated, or corrected. The only exception might be the need to remind students to work in English if they are using another language.

Sometimes the tasks involve individual written performances. When this is the case, study carefully what your students write. It, too, can provide valuable clues about what they can and cannot do. In many cases, students will want to hear each other's solutions to the questions or problems posed in the task. This provides yet another excellent opportunity for you to listen to your students and learn what has been easy for them and what has been difficult.

Of course, as with anything, different difficulties are likely to arise for different students. To cope with differing learning needs, you may consider grouping students with similar problems in class and giving each group different exercises to work through and/or different homework assignments. Another possibility is to group students in such a way that students who already know certain aspects of the target structure are grouped with other students who don't. In this way, students can learn from one another as they work through the focus boxes and exercises. If you do group students in this manner, however, it is important that each student be given a role in the group, so that students who are struggling with the content can still be contributing members of the group. For example, give these students the assignment of recording the group's answers, or reporting them to another group or to the whole class.

Obviously, if students demonstrate no ability to use the target structures required in completing the task, you will need to work systematically through the unit. It may be the case, though, that you will discover that students do not need to attend to all the focus boxes or do all the exercises; this makes your teaching more efficient.

Don't hesitate to alter tasks to fit your timetable. For example, have your students do only part of the task, or have them do one of the communicative activities at the end of the unit, if you feel that the opening task would not work as well. Other teachers have found it helpful to have students do the task twice—first for diagnostic purposes and second after students have worked through a unit in order to determine how much they have progressed.

All in all, what we are trying to achieve is an optimal use of the time we have available by identifying teachable moments when the students need to and are ready to learn.

FOCUS BOXES

The focus boxes feature the form, meaning, and use facts concerning the target structure that are appropriate for students at a given level of instruction. By treating one aspect of the structure at a time, followed by exercises providing practice, the focus boxes allow students to develop step-by-step a better understanding of, and an ability to use, the structure accurately, meaningfully, and appropriately.

Use student performance on the opening task as a bridge to the focus boxes. One way to do this is to write students' responses to the task on the blackboard, eliciting or supplying the target structures as they are needed. By going back and pointing out the target structures and asking questions about their form, meaning, or use, you may be able to induce the rules in the focus boxes

(not all at once, of course). At this point, you may want students to consult the relevant focus box in order to confirm the generalizations they have just made. On the other hand, if the students have arrived at the generalizations you feel they need to know, you may simply want to call their attention to the appropriate focus boxes for them to refer to for homework or when needed.

If you prefer a more deductive approach, you could go right to the first or appropriate focus box after the students have completed the task. You could present it orally to students or read it while they listen or read along silently with you. Alternatively, you could have the students read the focus boxes for homework or silently in class. You could help them when they do not understand something. You could check their understanding by asking students to come up with additional examples to supplement the ones in the focus box or asking them to compare how the material in this focus box differs from one earlier in the unit or from those in a related unit that they have completed.

A variation on this is to ask students individually or in pairs to present the information in a focus box to another pair of students, or even to the whole class, adding a few new examples of their own. Teaching something to others is a great way to learn!

Another possible way of teaching the focus boxes is not to present them at all, but rather to assign students the exercises that go along with them. The focus boxes can be used for reference purposes as the students work their way through the exercises. In this way, the material becomes more meaningful to students because they will need to access and understand it in order to do something with it.

EXERCISES

At least one exercise follows each focus box. There is a wide variety of exercises in *Grammar Dimensions*. There are both comprehension and production exercises. Comprehension exercises work on students' awareness and understanding. Production exercises develop students' skill in using the structures.

There are exercises that are consistent with the theme of the task and ones that introduce students to new themes and vocabulary in order to provide variety and to foster students' ability to transfer their learning to new contexts. There are personalized exercises, in which students use their own background knowledge or opinions to answer questions, and ones where students use the information that is supplied in order to complete the exercise.

Then, too, although general directions are provided for each exercise, there is a great deal of flexibility in how the exercises can be handled. Some exercises, such as information gaps, call for pairwork. Others are amenable to many different student configurations: individual, pair, small group, whole class; so you will need to decide what works best for a particular exercise and particular group of students. For instance, some students prefer to work individually at first and then get together with others to go over their answers. The variety of possible student configurations that the exercises permit allows students' differing learning styles to be catered to.

Sometimes you can choose freely whether to have students do an exercise orally or in writing. At other times, an exercise will work better in one modality than another because of the modality in which the structure normally occurs. Some exercises may be done in class, others for homework, and still others skipped all together. Don't forget to consult the Workbook for additional exercises.

There are also many options for how exercise answers can be checked. For example:

1. You can circulate while students are doing an exercise in class and spot-check.
2. You can go over the exercise afterwards as a whole class with each student being called on to supply an answer.

3. Exercises can be done individually and then pairs of students can get together to check their answers with each other. Where a difference of opinion occurs, you (or another pair of students) can act as a referee.
4. Different students, pairs, or groups of students can be assigned different parts of an exercise. For example, the first group does #'s 1–5, the second group does #6–10, etc. The groups post their answers on newsprint or butcher block paper and everyone circulates at the end noting the answers and asking questions.
5. A variation of #4 is to have one student from each group get together and present to the other students the exercise answers that his or her group came up with.
6. You can prepare a handout with the answers, and each student corrects his or her answers individually.
7. You can collect the written work, and make a list of common errors. You can put the errors on an overhead transparency and show it to the students during the next class and have them correct the errors together.

There are both closed and open-ended answers to questions. With closed questions, there is a single right answer. This is the most common type of question in Books 1 and 2. In Books 3 and 4, while closed questions still prevail, sometimes open-ended questions, for which there are no definitive answers, are used. Nuances of the language and contextual differences are such that it is sometimes difficult to say definitively what the single best answer is. The point is that students should understand that they have choices, but they also need to understand the consequences of their choices, i.e., they should be able to explain why they have chosen a particular answer. In many of these cases a "most likely" interpretation (based on English native speaker responses) has been indicated in the answer key, but no feasible opinion offered by your students should be discounted. Giving students an opportunity to defend their answers encourages students to form their own hypotheses about the appropriate use of certain grammar structures and to test these hypotheses through continued observation and analysis.

"USE YOUR ENGLISH" ACTIVITIES

In the "Use Your English" activities section of each unit (the purple pages), students can apply the language discussed in the unit to wider contexts and integrate it with the language they already know. Many activities give students more control over what they want to say or write than the exercises, and offer them more opportunities to express their own points of view across a range of topics. Most of the activities are quite open-ended in that they lend themselves to being done with structures covered in the unit, but they do not absolutely require their use.

The activities section is also designed to give instructors a variety of options. Since time is limited, you probably will not be able to have students do all the activities. You might choose two to do or ask your students to choose ones that they would prefer. Perhaps different groups of students could do different activities and then report on their experience to the whole class. Like the exercises, the activities can be adapted for use with different group configurations and different modalities.

If you are teaching in a program that is skill-based, you might want to collaborate with your colleagues and distribute the activities among yourselves. For example, the writing teacher could assign the activities that involve a written report, the teacher of listening could work on the listening activities during his or her class periods, or the teacher of speaking could work with students on activities where students are supposed to make an oral presentation.

Although the activities are meant to be culminating, it is also possible to intersperse them among the exercises. Sometimes an activity provides a particularly useful follow-up to an exercise. And we have already mentioned that certain activities might work well in place of the recommended opening task. Also, it may be useful to go back to a previous unit and do an activity for review purposes. This is especially useful at the beginning of a new, but related, unit.

The activities are an integral part of each unit because they not only provide students with opportunities to stretch their language use, but as with the opening task, they also provide you with the opportunity to observe your students' language use in action. In this way, activities can be informal holistic assessment measures encouraging students to show you how well they can use the target structures communicatively. Any persistent problems that still exist at this point can be noted for follow-up at a later time when students are more ready to deal with them.

As you can see, *Grammar Dimensions* is meant to provide you with a great deal of flexibility so that you can provide quality instruction appropriate for your class. We encourage you to experiment with different aspects of the material in order to best meet the needs of your unique group of students.

Unit 1

UNIT OVERVIEW

Unit 1 and Unit 2 provide a broad review and overview of the basic relationship between tense, time, and aspect. They can be used to diagnose whether or not certain other units (13, 14, 15, and 23) need to be covered in detail as well.

UNIT GOALS

Review the goals listed on this page so students (Ss) understand what they should be able to know by the end of the unit.

OPENING TASK

Note: The **Opening Task** allows Ss to try using the target structures and allows teachers to notice what kinds of help they may need. For a more complete discussion of the Opening Task, see p. xix of this Teachers' Edition. The purpose of this particular task is to create a context in which Ss discuss situations that use all three time frames. The Ss' attention will most likely be focused on meaning, not on form, so you will be able to see to what extent they can produce correct verb forms spontaneously. Answers will vary, depending on how Ss describe the lives of the three people.

Step 1

Pair up Ss according to different backgrounds, or let them choose their own partners, with the instruction that they should work with someone they don't already know. Listen in on pairs to monitor how well they distinguish between present and past time frames.

ⓤ N I T **1**

OVERVIEW OF THE ENGLISH VERB SYSTEM

Time and Tense

UNIT GOALS:

- To review the English verb system
- To keep tenses in the same time frame
- To change the time frame correctly within a passage

▶ OPENING TASK
Comparing Past, Present, and Future

STEP 1 Work with a partner. Student A, look at the following information about Bob Lee, a typical American college student. Student B, look at the information on the next page about Bob's grandfather, Robert Lee. Student A, tell Student B about Bob's life. Student B, tell Student A about Robert's life.

BOB LEE

Born: 1981

Family: Two brothers and one sister, living with mother; parents divorced; Bob lives in a college dorm

Occupation: currently a sophomore, studying biology, plans to be a doctor

Regular activities: school, part-time job in the library, time with girlfriend, visiting family some weekends and during school vacations

Hobbies or favorite sports: basketball, skiing, computers, music, TV

Visits to foreign countries: Mexico (once), Canada (twice)

Special skills or abilities: computers, university chorus

Probable activity at this moment: studying for biology midterm

ROBERT LEE

Born: 1930   **DIED:** 1992

Family: Five brothers, four sisters; only one sister and brother survived childhood; father died of tuberculosis when Robert was fourteen years old

Occupation: factory worker, never finished high school

Regular activities: Job (twelve-hour days); helping mother; family life

Hobbies or favorite sports: radio, baseball (on factory team), church

Visits to foreign countries: none

Special skills or abilities: baseball, harmonica playing

Probable activity when Bob was born: working at the factory

STEP 2   Now work together to create a story for Roberta, Bob's grand-daughter. Fill in some information below and then tell another pair of students about how you think Roberta's life will be.

ROBERTA CHONG-DAVIS

Born: 2035

Family: _____

Occupation: _____

Regular activities: _____

_____

Hobbies or favorite sports: _____

Visits to foreign countries or planets: _____

_____

Special skills or abilities: _____

Probable activity at this moment 100 years from today: _____

Step 2

Assign specific pairs to work together, or let Ss choose a pair on the other side of the room.

SUGGESTIONS

1. Have Ss write 5–10 of their responses to Step 1 and 2 in complete sentences to be handed in for you to check. Alternatively, have their partners make corrections and then you can analyze both the original responses and the corrections.

2. After the groups have shared their ideas about Roberta's life, process with the whole class by asking questions to pairs such as *"What did you predict that Roberta's hobbies will be?"* Or *"What did the other pair think Roberta's occupation will be?"* or more generic prompts such as *"What was one prediction that you all agreed on?"*

3. Finally, ask some general processing questions comparing "generations," such as *"What is one thing that you think will be the same in the lives of Robert and Roberta?"* Or *"What do you think will be the biggest difference between Bob's life and Roberta's life?"* These questions will give Ss practice at switching time frames.

1. Ask Ss how many tenses there are in English (answers will vary widely). Explain that the tense system is pretty straightforward once you have decided what general time frame you are using.
2. Have Ss compare some of their statements from the Opening Task with the example sentences listed in the appendices on pp. 417–420.
3. Ask Ss if they have any questions, and explain that in this unit they will be practicing all the tenses together.
4. Have Ss look over Focus 1 and review Appendix 1 for homework.

FOCUS **1**

▶ Overview of the English Verb System

The form of any verb in English is made up of two things: time frame and aspect.

Time frame tells **when** something took place. There are three basic time frames: **present, past,** and **future.**	**Aspect** tells **how** the verb is related to that time, or gives some other information about the quality of the action. (See Unit 2.)

There are four kinds of aspect, and each one has a basic meaning.

ASPECT	MEANING
simple	**at** that time
progressive	**in progress during** that time
perfect	**before** that time
perfect progressive	**in progress during and before** that time

When we combine the three time frames and the four aspects, we get twelve possible combinations of forms. These forms are called *tenses*, and the name of each tense tells which time frame and which aspect are being used. The charts in Appendix 1, on pages A-1 to A-4, show in more detail the three basic time frames and the tenses which are used in each.

ASPECT	SIMPLE	PROGRESSIVE	PERFECT	PERFECT PROGRESSIVE
TIME FRAME			TENSES	
Present	*simple present* study/studies give/gives	*present progressive* is/are studying is/are giving	*present perfect* has/have studied has/have given	*present perfect progressive* has/have been studying has/have been giving
Past	*simple present* studied gave	*past progressive* was/were studying was/were giving	*past perfect* had studied had given	*past perfect progressive* had been studying had been giving
Future	*simple future* will study will give	*future progressive* will be studying will be giving	*future perfect* will have studied will have given	*future perfect progressive* will have been studying will have been giving

EXERCISE 1

Read the following passages and identify the time frame of each. Is it present time, past time, or future time?

1. (a) Mac had a terrible headache. (b) His tongue was dry, and his eyes were burning. (c) He had been sneezing constantly for nearly an hour. (d) He hated springtime. (e) For most people spring meant flowers and sunshine, but for Mac it meant allergies.

2. (a) I really don't know what to do for vacation. (b) My vacation starts in three weeks, and (c) I'm trying to decide what to do. (d) I've been to Hawaii and New York. (e) It's too early in the year to go camping in the mountains. (f) I've been working hard at the office and I really need a break. (g) I've saved enough money to have a really nice trip. (h) I just can't decide where to go or what to do.

3. (a) The changing world climate will mean changes in food production. (b) Scientists think that summers throughout North America will become much hotter and drier than they are now. (c) Crops that require a lot of water will be less economical to grow. (d) Society will have to develop different energy sources, (e) since fossil fuels, such as coal and oil, may have become depleted by the end of the next century.

4. (a) "Social Darwinism" was a popular theory of the nineteenth century. (b) It compared social and economic development with biological evolution. (c) According to this theory, competition between rich people and poor people was unavoidable. (d) The poor were like dinosaurs who were dying out because they had lost the battle for survival—economic survival.

5. (a) Scientific research often has an important social impact. (b) In recent years scientists have discovered that Vitamin B can prevent certain kinds of childhood blindness. (c) As a result, programs have been established that provide education and dietary supplements to children in developing countries.

EXERCISE 2

Choose three of the passages in Exercise 1, and underline each complete verb phrase (the verb plus any auxiliary—*have, do, is,* etc.—that shows the tense of the verb). Name the tense of each verb phrase you have underlined.

EXERCISE 3

Check your knowledge of irregular verb forms by completing the chart on page 4. You may work with other students. When you finish, check your work using Appendix 6, Irregular Verbs, on page A-10.

Exercise 1

Note: The exercises following each focus box provide meaningful practice with the grammar item presented in that particular box. For a more complete discussion of how to use the exercises, see p. xxi of this Teacher's Edition.

This exercise can be done individually or as pair work.

Assign this exercise and Exercise 2 as homework to go over in class. Be sure Ss read each passage first before doing the exercise.

S U G G E S T I O N S

1. To shorten the time needed to do this exercise in class, assign individual Ss or pairs to do only one or two passages and then correct as a class.
2. If you have access to an OHP, a good way to process exercises like this is by making a transparency of this page to show to the whole class.

Exercise 2

See comments about Exercise 1. If your class has no trouble identifying and recognizing tenses, skip this exercise.

Workbook Exs. 1 & 2, pp. 1–2. Answers: TE p. 490.

Exercise 3

The complete set of irregular verbs is listed in Appendix 6. When you do this exercise, make sure Ss don't just copy the forms from that list.

Photocopy this page and use as a quiz for testing and review throughout the course.

A N S W E R   K E Y

Exercise 1

1. Past   2. Present   3. Future (Draw attention to the fact that present tense forms can also be used in Future Time.)   4. Past   5. Present

Exercise 2

1. (a) <u>had</u> (simple past) (b) His tongue <u>was</u> (simple past) <u>were burning</u>. (past progressive) (c) <u>had been sneezing</u> (past perfect progressive) (d) <u>hated</u> (simple past) (e) <u>meant</u> (simple past) <u>meant</u> (simple past)

2. (a) <u>don't know</u> (simple present) (b) <u>starts</u> (simple present) (c) <u>I'm trying</u> (present progressive) to decide what to do. (d) <u>I've been</u> (present perfect) (e) <u>It's</u> (simple present) (f) <u>I've been working</u> (present perfect progressive); <u>need</u> (simple present) (g) <u>I've saved</u> (present perfect) (h) <u>can't decide</u> (simple present(modal auxiliary))

3. (a) <u>will mean</u> (simple future) (b) <u>think</u> (simple present); <u>will become</u> (simple future); <u>are</u> (simple present). (c) <u>require</u> (simple present) <u>will be</u> (simple future) (d) <u>will have to develop</u> (simple future (phrasal modal aux.) (e) <u>may have become</u> (future perfect) depleted by the end of the next century.

4. (a) <u>was</u> (simple past) (b) <u>compared</u> (simple past) (c) <u>was</u> (simple past) (d) <u>were</u> (simple past); <u>were dying out</u> (past progressive); <u>had lost</u> (past perfect)

5. (a) <u>has</u> (simple present) (c) <u>have discovered</u> (present perfect); <u>can prevent</u> (simple present) (d) <u>have been established</u> (present perfect (passive)) <u>provide</u> (simple present)

Base form	Past tense form	Past participle
———	———	become
begin	———	———
———	bent	———
———	———	bet
bind	———	———
———	bit	———
———	———	bled
blow	———	———
———	broke	———
———	———	brought
build	———	———
———	———	bought
catch	———	———
———	chose	———
come	———	———
———	cost	———
cut	———	———
———	———	dug
do	———	———
———	drew	———
———	———	drunk
drive	———	———
———	ate	———
———	———	fallen
feed	———	———
———	felt	———
———	fought	———
find	———	———
———	fit	———
fly	———	———
forbid	———	———
forget	———	———
———	forgave	———
———	———	frozen
get	———	———
———	gave	———

Base form	Past tense form	Past participle
go	———	———
———	———	ground
———	grew	———
hang	———	———
———	had	———
hear	———	———
———	hid	———
———	hit	———
———	held	———
hurt	———	———
———	kept	———
———	———	known
lead	———	———
———	left	———
lend	———	———
———	———	let
make	———	———
———	———	meant
meet	———	———
———	put	———
———	———	quit
read	———	———
———	rode	———
———	———	rung
rise	———	———
———	ran	———
———	———	said
see	———	———
———	sought	———
———	———	sold
send	———	———
———	set	———
———	———	shaken
shine	———	———
———	shot	———
———	———	shut

Base form	Past tense form	Past participle
sing	———	———
———	sank	———
———	———	sat
sleep	———	———
———	slid	———
———	———	spoken
speed	———	———
———	spent	———
———	———	split
spread	———	———
———	sprang	———
———	———	stood
steal	———	———
———	stuck	———
———	———	stung
strike	———	———
swear	———	———
———	swept	———
———	swam	———
———	———	swung
take	———	———
———	taught	———
———	———	torn
tell	———	———
———	thought	———
———	———	thrown
understand	———	———
———	woke	———
———	———	worn
weave	———	———
———	wept	———
———	———	won
wind	———	———
———	wrote	———

FOCUS **2**

▶ **Keeping Tenses in the Same Time Frame**

In general, we choose a particular time frame and then choose from among the tenses within that time frame in order to describe events.

EXAMPLES	EXPLANATIONS
(a) My roommate **had** a dance party last Friday night. **I was working** that night, so **I didn't get** home until 10:00, and everyone **had** already **started** dancing.	Use past tenses to describe things that happened at a specific time in the past.
(b) My roommate **has** a dance party every Friday night. **I work** on Friday nights, so **I don't get** home until 10:00, and everyone **has** already **started** dancing.	Use present tenses to describe things that are happening now, are related to now, or happen again and again.
(c) My roommate **is going to have** a dance party next Friday night. **I will be working** next Friday night, so **I won't get** home until 10:00, and everyone **will** already **have started** dancing.	Use future tenses to describe events that are going to happen at some time in the future.

EXERCISE 4

Decide what time frame each of these passages should be written in, and then write the appropriate verb form in the blanks.

1. I hear we (a) _____ (be playing) games at Mike's party next week. I hope there (b) _____ (be) dancing as well! I (c) _____ (have completed) my dance class by then.

2. I (a) _____ (have) an interesting experience yesterday afternoon. As I (b) _____ (be walking) from my house to the grocery store, I (c) _____ (see) someone I (d) _____ (have gone) to high school with.

Overview of the English Verb System: Time and Tense | **5**

FOCUS 2

1. Ask Ss to read the three examples (a), (b), and (c) individually.
2. Ask Ss if they notice any similarities between the three examples. You may need to draw their attention to the progressive and perfect tenses. Explain that tenses often follow the same pattern within a basic time frame.

3. Review the uses of the three time frames described in the Explanations, and write summarizing labels such as "*past actions and events,*" "*things happening now or related to now,*" and "*future actions and events.*" Or, better, elicit these labels from the class.

Exercise 4

There are a variety of ways to do this exercise. It can be assigned as homework or done in class either individually or in pairs. Ss can be assigned to do one or two passages and then present their answers to the class, or all Ss can work on all passages, as time allows.

Workbook Exs. 3 & 4, pp. 2–3. Answers: TE p. 490.

A N S W E R   K E Y

Exercise 4
1. (Future time frame) (a) <u>we'll be/we're playing</u> (b) <u>is/will be/is going to be</u> (c) <u>will have completed</u>
2. (Past time frame) (a) <u>had</u> (b) <u>was walking</u> (c) <u>saw</u> (d) <u>had gone</u>
3. (Present time frame) (a) <u>has</u> (b) <u>is driving</u> (c) <u>gets</u> (d) <u>lives</u> (e) <u>takes</u>
4. (Past time frame) (a) <u>was</u> (b) <u>was believed</u> (c) <u>was playing</u> (d) <u>burned</u>
5. (Present time frame) (a) <u>are</u> (b) <u>is changing</u> (c) <u>believe</u> (d) <u>has resulted</u> (e) <u>are burned</u> (f) <u>increases/is increased</u> (g) <u>causes</u> (h) <u>is</u> (i) <u>has begun</u> (j) <u>have discovered</u> (k) <u>has risen</u>
6. (Future time frame) (a) <u>leaves/is leaving/will leave</u> (b) <u>is/will be staying</u> (c) <u>will find</u>

Teacher's Edition: Unit 1 **5**

3. Steve (a) _____ (have) a terrible time getting to work every day. When he (b) _____ (be driving) to work he often (c) _____ (get) caught in terrible traffic jams. Even though he only (d) _____ (live) a few miles from the office, it sometimes (e) _____ (take) nearly an hour to get to work.

4. The Imperial City of Rome (a) _____ (be) badly damaged by fire during the First Century A.D. At the time it (b) _____ (be believed) that the Emperor Nero (c) _____ (be playing) a violin while the city (d) _____ (burn) to the ground.

5. Scientists (a) _____ (be) worried that the world climate (b) _____ (be changing). They (c) _____ (believe) this change (d) _____ (have resulted) from an increase in the amount of carbon dioxide (CO_2) in the earth's atmosphere. Whenever "fossil fuels" such as coal or oil (e) _____ (be burned), the amount of CO_2 (f) _____ (increase). This (g) _____ (cause) the atmosphere to retain more heat. There (h) _____ (be) proof that this process already (i) _____ (have begun). Scientists (j) _____ (have discovered) that the average temperature of the world's oceans (k) _____ (have risen) by one degree in the last twenty years.

6. John (a) _____ (leave) for Paris on Tuesday. He (b) _____ (be staying) with a local family for the first few weeks. After that, he probably (c) _____ (find) a small apartment of his own.

FOCUS 3

Changing the Time Frame Within a Passage

Although the time frame often stays the same within a passage, an author sometimes changes the time frame.

EXAMPLES	EXPLANATIONS
(a) There **are** many examples in history of increasing military power causing a decreasing standard of living. Rome **was** unable to feed both its army and its population. Great Britain **declined** steadily from its economic position in the early part of this century.	• to move from a general statement to specific examples
(b) **One hundred years ago** the life expectancy in the United States **was** about sixty-five. **Nowadays,** it **has increased** by an average of ten years. **In the next century,** if current trends continue, people **should be able to live** until their nineties. Interestingly enough, however, **a hundred years ago** the number of people who were over one hundred **was** less than one percent of the population. That figure **has not changed** substantially, even **today.**	• to show contrast between one time and another
(c) I saw an elderly lady yesterday. **You don't see her kind much anymore.** She was wearing a black dress and she was carrying an umbrella. **Most elderly ladies I know don't carry umbrellas, and pants are more common than dresses.** As she walked down the street, I thought about how much life has changed since she was my age.	• to make a statement of general truth

EXERCISE 5

Mark the following passages with a vertical line (/) to show where the time frame changes. The first one has been done for you as an example.

1. My brother called me up yesterday. / I always know he needs to borrow money when he calls, because I never hear from him at any other time. / We spoke about this and that for a few minutes. He asked about my job and my family. We talked about his problems with his boss. / These are typical topics before he finally asks for a loan. / This phone call was no exception. He needed fifty dollars "until pay day." / Somehow, when pay-day comes he never remembers to pay back the loan.

2. I'll be really happy when the summer is over. I don't like hot weather,

---

FOCUS 3

1. Assign Focus 3 as homework to be read ahead of time.
2. Begin your discussion by reminding Ss that in Focus 2 they learned that we generally stay within a given time frame, but there are sometimes exceptions. Ask what they remember from studying that focus.

3. Review the reasons for changing time frames described in the Explanations, and write summarizing labels such as *"general statement to specific example," "time contrast," "general truth."* Or, better, elicit these labels from the class.

Exercise 5

Assign Exercise 5 as homework to go over in class. Be sure Ss read each passage before doing the exercise.

SUGGESTIONS

1. To save class time, assign individual Ss to do only one passage and then correct as a whole class.
2. If you have access to an OHP, a good way to process exercises like this is by making a transparency of this page to show to the whole class.

A N S W E R   K E Y

Exercises 5 & 6
The reasons for the changes in time frame between the two sentences (last and first words given) are shown in italics.
1. yesterday./I always (*general truth*); any other time./We spoke (*movement to specific example*); his boss. /These are typical . . . (*general truth*); a loan./This phone call was (*movement to specific example*); until pay day./Somehow, when payday comes (*general truth*) simple present

2. over./I don't like (*general truth*); in the summer. / Last summer (*clear time marker/ specific example*); were terrible!/Next year (*clear time marker*); in Antarctica./I understand (*general truth*)
3. earthquakes./The Richter Scale (*movement from general statement to specific example*); intensity./This <u>is</u> (*statement of general truth*).

and I can't stand mosquitoes. There's a lot of both of those things in the summer. Last summer I tried to escape by going on a trip to Alaska. The heat wasn't bad, but the mosquitoes were terrible! Next year I think I'll consider a vacation in Antarctica. I understand it's really cold there in July.

2. For more than fifty years scientists around the world have all used a single system to measure the strength (or "magnitude") of earthquakes. The Richter Scale was developed by Charles Richter in 1935. It was designed so scientists could compare the strength of earthquakes in different parts of the world. It was not designed to measure damage in earthquakes, but only intensity. This is because a less powerful earthquake in a heavily populated area can cause more damage than a stronger earthquake in an unpopulated area.

EXERCISE 6

Discuss each change of time frame that you found in Exercise 5 with a partner. Why did the author change the time frame? There may be more than one reason. Share your explanation with the rest of the class.

EXERCISE 7

Underline the complete verb phrases (verb plus auxiliaries) in the passages in Exercise 5 and name the tense of each verb phrase.

Use Your English

ACTIVITY 1: SPEAKING/WRITING

STEP 1 Work with a partner. Describe a typical day in your life. Tell your partner about the things you do, where you go, and how you typically spend your time. Mention at least five regular activities.

STEP 2 Next, describe a typical day in your life five years ago. Mention at least five activities that you did on a regular basis.

STEP 3 Your partner should use this information to decide what three things in your life have changed the most in the last five years, and report this information to the rest of the class. Make a similar report to the class about the changes in your partner's life.

Exercise 6

As an alternative, assign Exercise 5 in pairs and do Exercise 6 as whole-class processing of "why" the author changed the time frame.

Exercise 7

Omit Exercise 7 if Ss are not having trouble identifying verb phrases or identifying the correct name of the tense.

Workbook Exs. 5 & 6, pp. 3–4. Answers: TE p. 490.

UNIT GOAL REVIEW

Ask Ss to look at the goals on the opening page of the unit again. Help them understand how much they have accomplished in each area by asking for a summary of some of the rules they remember. Use prompts such as *"How many time frames are there in English?" "What are they?" "How many tenses are there in English?" "What are they?" "What are some reasons to change from one time frame to another within a passage?"* If Ss cannot supply explanations readily, give them a few minutes to look through the chapter and to formulate questions.

USE YOUR ENGLISH

Note: The activities on these "purple pages" at the end of each unit contain communicative activities designed to apply what students have learned and help them practice communication and grammar at the same time. For a more complete discussion of how to use the Use Your English activities, see p. xxii of this Teacher's Edition.

Activity 1

Variation: Have Ss write their Step 1 & Step 2 responses for their partner to use in Step 3. All three writing samples should be handed in for you to correct or evaluate.

ANSWER KEY

See p. 7 for Exercise 6 Answer Key

Exercise 7
1. called me up (simple past); know (simple present) needs (simple present) calls (simple present) hear (simple present); spoke (simple past) asked (simple past) talked (simple past) are (simple present) asks; was (simple past) needed (simple past); comes (simple present) ; remembers (simple present)
2. I'll be (simple future) is (simple present) don't like (simple present) can't stand (simple present). There's (simple present) tried (simple past) wasn't (simple past) were (simple past) think (simple present) I'll consider (simple future) understand (simple present) it's (simple present)
3. have all used (present perfect); was developed (simple past (passive)); was designed (simple past (passive)); could compare (simple past with modal auxiliary); was not designed (simple past (passive)) is (simple present) can cause (simple present with modal auxiliary)

8 Grammar Dimensions, Platinum Edition

ACTIVITY 2: LISTENING

Listen to these descriptions about two people—one who is no longer living and one who is still alive. Based on the time frame and verb tenses used in the descriptions, decide which person is still living and which person is deceased.

ACTIVITY 3: SPEAKING/WRITING

Congratulations! You've just won a million dollars in a contest. BUT . . . you have to spend all the money in a single week. AND . . . you can't spend more than $50,000 for any single purchase. (In other words, you can't just buy a million dollar house. You have to make at least twenty separate purchases.) If you don't spend it all, you won't get any of it.

STEP 1 What are your plans? In a brief essay, or in an oral presentation, answer this question: **How you will spend the money?**

STEP 2 It's the end of the week. How did you spend your money? Change the verb tenses of your essay or presentation to answer to this question: **How did you spend the money?**

ACTIVITY 4: WRITING/SPEAKING

Newspaper headlines represent a special kind of English. They usually omit a lot of important grammatical information. Test how well you know the basic sentence elements of English by "translating" these headlines into complete sentences. Compare your "translations" to those of another student.

▶ **EXAMPLES:** BABY FOUND IN BUS STATION

A baby has been found in the bus station.

- STOCK MARKET CRASHES
- U.S. POPULATION MOVING WEST
- NEW BUDGET TERMED "DISASTER"
- U.S. TO PROTEST NUCLEAR TESTING
- PRESIDENT TO VISIT CHINA
- DROUGHT EXPECTED TO WORSEN
- BIG WHITE HOUSE SHAKE-UP
- NEW PLAN TO IMPROVE BUS SERVICES

- TEST SCORES IMPROVING IN PUBLIC SCHOOLS
- LINK FOUND BETWEEN DIET AND HEART DISEASE
- CANCER REPORTED INCREASING
- MAJOR GROWTH IN INTERNATIONAL STUDENTS IN U.S.

Activity 2

Play textbook audio.

The tapescript for this listening appears on p. 511 of this book. Ss should not need multiple listenings if you have previewed the basic question before playing the tape.

Activity 3

Activities like this one can be done in many different ways. It can be done individually, in pairs or small groups, or as a teacher-led whole class discussion.

SUGGESTIONS

1. To do it as a whole class, record ideas and suggestions on the board. Tell Ss to be sure to use whole sentence responses such as *"We will buy a Porsche for each student in the class."* For Step 2, paraphrase the instructions and ask Ss to read what is written on the board as past tense whole sentence responses such as *"We bought a Porsche for each student in the class."*
2. Increase the diagnostic/evaluative potential of this activity by having Ss write their answers to be turned in for you to correct.

Activity 4

This activity can be done orally in pairs or small groups, or individually in written form. It can also be used to diagnose understanding of active/passive (Unit 4) and article use (Unit 19).

ANSWER KEY

Activity 2
Dr. Deborah Jones is alive. Dr. Sally Smith is dead.

Activity 4
Answers will vary slightly. Some possible paraphrases:
The stock market has crashed.
The U.S. population is moving west.
The new budget was termed a disaster.
The U.S. will protest nuclear testing.
The President will visit China.

The drought is expected to worsen.
There has been a big shakeup at the White House.
There is a new plan to improve bus services.
Test scores are improving in the public schools.
A link has been found between diet and heart disease.
Cancer is reported to be decreasing.
There has been a major growth in the number of international students in the U.S.

Activity 5

This is a useful goal-setting activity.

1. Lead the whole class through Steps 1 and 2 with Ss writing individual answers.

2. Set a ten-minute time limit for Step 3. After Ss finish brainstorming strategies, discuss the results with the whole class.

Activity 6

This activity is another important way to determine what your Ss feel they need to know. Asking them to write this information down for you will help you determine which units to focus on.

ACTIVITY 5: SPEAKING/WRITING

How are you progressing in English? Fill in this chart, following the steps listed below.

ACCOMPLISHMENTS	GOALS	STRATEGIES
1.	1.	1.
2.	2.	2.
3.	3.	3.

STEP 1 Describe how your ability to communicate in English has changed since you began your studies. What kinds of things were you able to accomplish a year ago, and what can yo do now that is different?

▶ **EXAMPLES:** 1. A year ago, I couldn't understand spoken English very well. My listening comprehension has improved a lot. I understand most things people say to me.

2. A year ago I needed to use a dictionary for almost every word. Now my vocabulary is much larger.

Think of three areas where your skills have improved. Write sentences describing those things under the column marked **Accomplishments.**

STEP 2 Next, describe some things that you still can't do, but you want to be able to do. Think of at least three things you can't or don't do now, but want to be able to do by the end of this course

▶ **EXAMPLES:** 1. I don't talk to my friends on the telephone because I have a hard time understanding them. I want to be able to talk on the telephone.

2. I can't pass the TOEFL. My scores on Part 2 are a little low. I want to get a good score on the TOEFL.

Write sentences describing those skills under the column marked **Goals.**

STEP 3 Compare your accomplishments and goals to those of other people in the class. As a group, think of three strategies for increasing your language abilities and achieving your goals, and write them under the column marked **Strategies.** Present your list of strategies to the rest of the class.

ACTIVITY 6: READING/WRITING

Now that you have finished this first unit and have some ideas about your areas of strength and weakness, look briefly through all the units of this book and the Table of Contents on pp. iv–xii in order to identify:

- one unit you would like the whole class to study
- one unit you would enjoy studying by yourself
- one unit you think you could study together with another student in the class
- one unit you feel you already understand well enough to explain to another student.

ACTIVITY 7: WRITING

Language teachers recommend that students keep a journal or language learning log to record their progress, goals, and questions. Studies have proven that students who do this learn more quickly and effectively. Here is one example of a language learning log format. Fill out this log at least once a week during this course and turn it in or discuss it with your teacher or with another student in the class.

LANGUAGE LEARNING LOG

Section 1. MISTAKES, CORRECTIONS, AND EXPLANATIONS

Write down **five mistakes** that you made in either writing or speaking in the last week. For each mistake write the correct form. In your own words, explain what was wrong with your original sentence.

▶ **EXAMPLES:**

Mistake:	I *enjoy to shop* in my free time.
Correction:	I *enjoy shopping* in my free time.
Explanation:	*enjoy* must take a gerund . . . not an infinitive.

Section 2. QUESTIONS

Write **three questions** you have about any aspect of grammar that you have read, heard, or studied in the last week. Your teacher will return your journal with an explanation of your questions.

▶ **EXAMPLES:** I don't understand the difference between <u>interesting/interested.</u>

I hear my friend say "If I <u>was</u> rich . . . " But we learned that <u>were</u> is correct. How can he say that?

Activity 7

This activity is meant to be a semester-long activity. The purpose is to get Ss to develop an analytical approach to the language they encounter in the real world. Although some students may complain that it is "a lot of work" to do, experience has proven this to be an extremely useful adjunct to any grammar course. In large classes, adjust your own workload by assigning it less frequently.

The test for this unit can be found on p. 438.
The answers are on p. 439 of this book.

Unit 2

UNIT OVERVIEW

Unit 1 and Unit 2 provide a broad review and overview of the basic relationship between tense, time, and aspect. They can be used as review and to diagnose whether or not certain other units (13, 14, 15, and 23) need to be covered in detail as well. For further reading, consult Celce-Murcia and Larsen-Freeman, *The Grammar Book, Second Edition*, Chapter 7, pp. 109–136.

UNIT GOALS

Review the goals listed on this page so students (Ss) understand what they should be able to know by the end of the unit.

OPENING TASK

The purpose of this particular task is to create a context for Ss to discuss situations that use various time relations within a given time frame. The Ss' attention will most likely be focused on meaning, not on form, so you will be able to see to what extent Ss are able to produce correct verb forms spontaneously.

UNIT 2

OVERVIEW OF THE ENGLISH VERB SYSTEM

Aspect

UNIT GOALS:

- To review aspect in English verbs
- To review the simple tenses
- To use progressive, perfect, and perfect progressive aspect appropriately

▶ OPENING TASK
A Picture Is Worth a Thousand Words

STEP 1 With a partner, discuss each of these photographs and together write sentences about them. Your sentences should answer these questions.

- What has just happened? Why do you think so?
- What is happening now? Why do you think so?
- What is going to happen next? Why do you think so?

STEP 2 Once you have described all the pictures, compare your descriptions with two other pairs of students. Do you all agree? Did you use the same verb tenses in your descriptions?

STEP 3 Report any interesting similarities and differences to the rest of the class.

Step 1
Group Ss according to different backgrounds, or let them choose their own partners; they should work with someone they don't already know well. Listen in on pairs to monitor how well they distinguish between present and past time frames in their use of verb tenses.

Step 2
Assign specific pairs to work together, or let Ss choose a pair on the other side of the room.

Step 3
As a brief processing with the whole class, focus on Ss' interpretations of the pictures, or ask Ss about their choice of verb tenses and their reasons.

V A R I A T I O N :
Ask Ss to turn in their descriptions for you to check, or focus on the follow-up discussion in Steps 2 and 3.

FOCUS 1

1. If you are teaching this unit immediately after Unit 1, start this focus by reminding Ss of the three basic time frames and how aspect is used to convey additional meanings. Point out that these additional meanings are conveyed regardless of which time frame is being used, and in general the same aspect cues are used in all three time frames.

2. Present the sentences in contrastive pairs (a & b, c & d, e & f) . Write the pairs on the board (or the alternative examples listed below) and ask these questions:

(a & b) *Which sentence describes an action that happened just once and which describes an action that happens more than once?*

(c & d) *Which sentence describes an action is finished and which describes an action that is still happening?*

(e & f) *Which sentence describes an action that is permanent and which describes an action that is temporary?*

VARIATION:

Use the following alternative sentences in your board work presentation or make up your own that refer to actual students in your class:

(a) *The students <u>laughed</u> at the teacher's joke.* (b) *The students <u>have been</u> laughing for the last hour. Their teacher must be really funny.* (c) *The students <u>are taking</u> a test.* (d) *The students <u>took</u> a test.* (e) *John <u>is living</u> with his uncle for the summer.* (f) *John <u>lives</u> with his uncle.*

3. Point out that the underlined verb contains enough information to be understood even when you remove other information from the sentence. Erase the other information from pairs a &b and e&f so that you have the following pairs to illustrate this point:

(a & b) *The students laughed. The students have been laughing.*

(e & f) *John <u>is living</u> with his uncle. John <u>lives</u> with his uncle.*

3. Have Ss read the examples in the focus box, and allow time for questions.

FOCUS **1**

▶ # Overview of Aspect

In addition to the basic aspect meanings listed in Unit 1, aspect can also be used to describe the quality of an action or situation.

EXAMPLES	EXPLANATIONS
(a) The protester **disrupted** the politician's speech.	• action happens just once
(b) Protesters **have been disrupting** politician's speeches as long as politicians **have been making** them.	• action happens continuously or repeatedly
(c) The police **are arresting** the protester, but perhaps he'll escape.	• action is still happening
(d) The police **have arrested** the protester, so he won't be able to escape.	• action is completed
(e) Shopkeepers **are storing** some of their breakable items on the floor until the threat of earthquake aftershocks has passed.	• situation is temporary
(f) Shopkeepers in earthquake areas **store** expensive, breakable items on the lower shelves in order to lessen the possibility of damage.	• situation is permanent

14   UNIT 2

EXERCISE 1

Analyze one of these paragraphs with a partner. Identify the basic time frame. Then say what meaning is contributed by the aspect in the underlined verb phrases.

1. By the time John gets on Flight 53 to Paris the day after tomorrow, he will have accomplished a great deal in a short period of time. He <u>will have moved out</u> of the apartment where he <u>has been living</u> for the last couple of years. He will have said some long, sad good-byes. He <u>will certainly be thinking</u> about all the friends he will no longer see every day.

2. When the earthquake hit San Francisco in 1989, Jeff was still at his office. He had been trying to finish a project. He <u>had been working</u> on it for over a week, and he was almost done. He <u>was just making</u> some final changes when the building started to move. When the quake started, he quickly got under his desk. He was glad that he had once read an article on what to do in earthquakes. He <u>had studied</u> the article carefully, so he knew exactly what to do.

3. Nancy is quite a stylish dresser. She thinks that it is important to be neat and well-dressed, and she always <u>wants</u> to look her best. Every morning before she leaves for work, she looks at herself in the mirror. She checks to make sure that she has combed her hair and hasn't put her makeup on too heavily. She makes sure that she <u>is wearing</u> colors that go nicely with the clothes she is wearing. She checks to see that her slip isn't showing, and if her stockings are straight. She makes sure that the shoes she <u>has chosen</u> match the color of her dress and her coat. She likes feeling confident and attractive, and feels that taking an extra minute in front of the mirror is worth the time.

Exercise 1

The purpose of the exercise is to give Ss an opportunity to note regular meaning difference typically conveyed by aspect. It can be done individually or as pair work.

SUGGESTIONS:

1. Assign pairs to do one of these paragraphs. If Ss are not having trouble identifying verb phrases, you may skip this exercise and go on to the next focus.

2. If you have access to an OHP, a good way to process exercises like this is by making a transparency of this page to show to the whole class.

Workbook Ex. 1, p. 5. Answers: TE p. 490.

ANSWER KEY

Exercise 1

The following verb phrases should be underlined. Additional meanings are listed after each verb phrase.

1. <u>will have accomplished</u> (before) <u>will have moved out</u> (before) <u>has been living</u> (before); <u>will have said</u> (before); <u>will certainly be thinking</u> (at the same time); <u>will no longer see</u> (after)

2. <u>was</u> (at the same time); <u>had been trying</u> (started before and still in progress); <u>had been working on</u> (started before and still in progress); <u>was</u> (at the same time); <u>was just making</u> (at the same time); <u>started</u> (at the same time); <u>started,</u> (at the same time); <u>got</u> (at the same time or immediately after); <u>was</u> (at the same time or immediately after) glad; <u>had once read</u> (before); <u>had studied</u> (before); <u>knew</u> (at the same time)

3. <u>is</u> (general truth); <u>thinks</u> (general truth); <u>is</u> (general truth); <u>wants</u> (habitual action); <u>leaves</u> (recurring action); <u>checks</u> (at the same time, recurring action); <u>has combed</u> (before); <u>hasn't put</u> (before); <u>makes</u> (recurring action); <u>is wearing</u> (at the same time); <u>go</u> (general relationship) <u>is wearing</u> (at the same time); <u>checks</u> (recurrent action); <u>isn't showing</u> (at the same time); <u>are</u> (at the same time); <u>makes sure</u> (recurrent action); <u>has chosen</u> (before); <u>match</u> (general relationship); <u>likes</u> (general truth); <u>feels</u> (general truth); <u>is</u> (general truth)

This focus demonstrates how simple aspect is used in all three time frames.

VARIATIONS:

1. If your class is a creative one, ask Ss to create additional examples of the basic meaning in all three time frames. Ask them to make concrete statements about their own lives and knowledge. Some other examples are:

    general ideas, truths and relationships: *Juan is from Mexico. Mexico was colonized by the Spanish. Economic development in Mexico will result in greater prosperity for its people.*

    habitual and recurrent actions: *I always brush my teeth before going to bed. My father rode his bicycle to school when he was a boy. People will have many labor-saving conveniences in the next century.*

    mental emotions and perceptions: *I love my family very much. People once thought the world was flat. In the future people will wonder why we work so hard these days.*

2. Alternatively, use Exercise 2 as a context, and ask Ss to read their sentences or write them on the board.

Exercise 2

There are a number of ways to do this exercise.

1. Assign it for homework and have Ss compare their paragraphs.
2. Ask Ss to identify sentences that are in simple aspect and explain why they chose that particular tense. Most will be in simple aspect because they are describing habitual or recurrent actions, general ideas, etc.
3. Skip this exercise and focus on presenting simple and progressive aspect in contrast. (This particular contrast is also practiced in more detail in Unit 13, (pp. 220–221.)

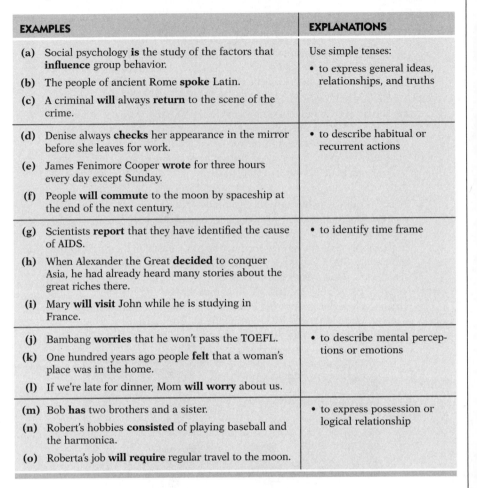

FOCUS **2**

▶ **Simple Tenses**

EXAMPLES	EXPLANATIONS
(a) Social psychology **is** the study of the factors that **influence** group behavior. (b) The people of ancient Rome **spoke** Latin. (c) A criminal **will** always **return** to the scene of the crime.	Use simple tenses: • to express general ideas, relationships, and truths
(d) Denise always **checks** her appearance in the mirror before she leaves for work. (e) James Fenimore Cooper **wrote** for three hours every day except Sunday. (f) People **will commute** to the moon by spaceship at the end of the next century.	• to describe habitual or recurrent actions
(g) Scientists **report** that they have identified the cause of AIDS. (h) When Alexander the Great **decided** to conquer Asia, he had already heard many stories about the great riches there. (i) Mary **will visit** John while he is studying in France.	• to identify time frame
(j) Bambang **worries** that he won't pass the TOEFL. (k) One hundred years ago people **felt** that a woman's place was in the home. (l) If we're late for dinner, Mom **will worry** about us.	• to describe mental perceptions or emotions
(m) Bob **has** two brothers and a sister. (n) Robert's hobbies **consisted** of playing baseball and the harmonica. (o) Roberta's job **will require** regular travel to the moon.	• to express possession or logical relationship

EXERCISE 2

Work with the same partner that you did for the Opening Task of Unit 1. But instead of describing Bob Lee and his family, describe your own lives, and those of your grandfathers and what may be true for your granddaughters. Each of you should write at least two sentences that describe the lives of each generation.

16 UNIT 2

ANSWER KEY

Exercise 2
Answers will vary. In general, sentences describing Ss' lives should be in present time frame, those describing grandparents' lives should be in past time frame, and those describing grandchildren should be in future time frame.

Progressive Aspect

USE

Progressive tenses (present progressive, past progressive, and future progressive) are made by using forms of

BE + VERB + -ING

EXAMPLES	EXPLANATIONS
(a) Other people **are** always **waiting** when Jeff **gets** to the bus stop. (They're already waiting **before** he gets there.) **(b)** Jeff **reads** the morning paper when he **gets** to the bus stop. (He reads his paper **after** he gets there.) **(c)** When I **entered** the room, the students **were studying,** but when I left the room, they **laughed.** (They were studying **before** I entered, but they laughed **after** I left.)	Use progressive aspect instead of simple aspect to describe: • actions already in progress versus actions that happen afterwards.
(d) I **teach** French, but I'm **not teaching** at the moment. **(e)** John **studied** in France for a year, but he certainly **wasn't studying** last Bastille Day.	• actions at a specific time (**now** or **then**) versus habitual or recurring actions
(f) Mary still **lives** with her parents, but she**'s staying** with friends while her parents are away.	• temporary situations versus permanent states
(g) Those students **are** always **asking** questions.	• repeated actions
(h) John **is** still **working** to perfect his French accent.	• uncompleted actions
(i) Those children **are being** very noisy, but they **are** young, so I guess it's understandable.	• actions rather than states

1. Have Ss read sentences a and b and point out how the aspect choice changes the meaning. "*Gets*" is the main verb or moment of focus, and choosing between progressive and simple aspect changes the implied sequence of activities.
2. Repeat the process with sentence c (*entered* and *left* are the focus verbs in this example). Allow Ss to ask questions before moving on to the next meaning.
   Additional examples:
   The children were watching TV when their mother came home from work. The children watched TV when they finished dinner.
3. Move on to the next meaning difference. Have Ss read sentences d & e.
   Additional examples:
   Juan speaks Spanish, but he's speaking English today in our class.
4. Sentence f illustrates a third use of progressive aspect.
   Additional examples:
   Juan lives in Jalisco, but he's living in the U.S. while he gets his MBA degree.
5. If time is short, you may wish to discuss the last three uses together under a general category of "other uses."
   Additional examples of the last three meaning differences:
   repeated actions: *Our teacher is always giving us too much homework. I'm always studying for tests instead of watching TV.*
   uncompleted actions: *I'm still studying English in order to enter the university. We're making snacks for the party, so we can't do homework right now.*
   actions rather than states: *We're having a party tomorrow. You're being rude.*
6. Make sure that all six uses of progressive aspect have been introduced before moving on to Exercise 3.

Exercise 3

This exercise can be done individually or in pairs, or as a general "whole class discussion" that extends the previous focus presentation to new sentences and asks Ss to apply their understanding to new contexts.

Exercise 4

This exercise can be assigned as homework, or done in class. If you correct the answers in class, focus the processing discussion on **why a** choice is correct by asking the Ss to identify the meaning that the aspect choice conveys.

Workbook Ex. 2, p. 6. Answers: TE p. 490.

EXERCISE 3

Why is progressive aspect used in these sentences? There may be more than one possible reason.

▶ **EXAMPLE:** He is studying for an examination now.

action in progress now, uncompleted action

1. John was reading a book when I saw him.
2. Don't call him after 10:00 because he will be sleeping.
3. They were selling candy from house to house yesterday afternoon.
4. Whenever I see John, he is always reading a book.
5. I will be visiting friends all over the country during the summer.
6. John was thinking about a solution to his problem, so I didn't interrupt him.
7. He was living with his cousin for a while.
8. I am having trouble with this assignment.
9. I will be staying at the Bates Motel during the conference.
10. I am trying to explain this, so please pay attention.

EXERCISE 4

Decide whether simple or progressive aspect should be used in these sentences. Both choices may be correct.

1. Please turn down the radio. I _____ (study) for a test.
2. Lilik _____ (read) the newspaper when the phone rang.
3. I'm afraid those students might (a) _____ (get) in trouble with Immigration because they (b) _____ (work) without official permission.
4. I still _____ (not study) as much as my parents want me to.
5. Rebecca _____ (speak) Russian. I wonder where she learned it?
6. Columbus (a) _____ (look) for a shorter route to Asia when he (b) _____ (discover) the New World by mistake.
7. When Columbus (a) _____ (reach) Cuba, he (b) _____ (think) it was India.
8. I _____ (try) to help you. Please listen carefully.
9. I (a) _____ (study) in the library, when I (b) _____ (hear) the news about Yitzhak Rabin's assassination.
10. Paolo will probably _____ (sleep) if you wait until midnight to try to call him.

ANSWER KEY

Exercise 3
1. action in progress; uncompleted action
2. action already in progress 3. repeated action 4. repeated action 5. temporary situation 6. action in progress
7. temporary situation 8. action in progress/ temporary situation 9. action happening at a specific time in the future 10. action already in progress; uncompleted action

Exercise 4
1. am studying (happening now) 2. was reading (in progress) 3. (a) get . . . (b) are working (happening now) 4. don't study/ am not studying 5. speaks (habitual/recurrent action) 6. (a) was looking . . . (action in progress) (b) discovered 7. (a) reached (b) thought 8. am trying (uncompleted action/ happening now) 9. (a) was studying . . . (action in progress) (b) heard 10. be sleeping (action in progress)

► **Perfect Aspect**

Perfect Tenses (present, perfect, past perfect, and future perfect) are made by using forms of:

HAVE + VERB-EN (past participle)

The basic meaning of the perfect aspect is this: the action described using the perfect aspect began before other action or another point in time, and it continues to have influence. We do **not** use perfect aspect to connect unrelated events.

EXAMPLES	EXPLANATIONS
(a) He **had finished** the project when I **talked** to him. (The project was finished before I talked to him.) **(b)** He **finished** the project when I **talked** to him. (I talked to him first, and then he finished the project.)	Use perfect aspect instead of simple aspect to describe actions: • that happen before another action
(c) We have an English test tomorrow. I **have reviewed** the vocabulary words, but I **haven't studied** the grammar yet.	• that focus on whether they are completed or uncompleted
(d) I **have finished** my homework so now I'm watching TV. **(e)** Anna **has** just **had** a snack, so she doesn't want dinner.	• that are related to the present moment
(f) Robert Lee **has worked** in a factory for thirty-five years. (He still works there.). **(g)** Robert Lee **worked** in a factory for thirty-five years. (He doesn't work there anymore.)	• that began in the past but still continue until now

---

FOCUS 4

Follow the same procedures as Focus 3. Introduce the meaning differences one at a time.

1. Sentence a: You may need to supply a more contrastive example such as this one:
   Juan <u>had passed</u> the TOEFL when he <u>began studying</u> business at the university. (He passed it before he began studying.) *Juan <u>passed</u> the TOEFL when he began studying English at the university.* (He passed it after he began studying.)

2. Sentence b focuses on completion. Additional examples that show this meaning difference could be presented in the following dialog or a variant:
   "Please <u>wash</u> the dishes (do your homework, take out the garbage . . .)."
   "I <u>have washed</u> the dishes." "No you <u>haven't</u>, I see some dirty ones over there by the couch."

3. Sentences c–f show ways that past events are related logically or chronologically to the present moment of focus. Unit 14 gives more practice with the "relation to now" uses exemplified by sentences c–f. (You may want to review that explanation for yourself before doing this focus. See Unit 14, especially, Focus 4, pp. 236–237.) If your preliminary discussion of this focus box indicates that Ss understand these concepts, you may be able to skip Unit 14 later. If Ss seem to be having problems, you can tell them that you will be coming back to this issue later in the course.

Additional examples:
I<u>'ve been</u> there and <u>done</u> that.
We<u>'ve studied</u> verbs, so we don't need to do this unit.
Juan<u>'s passed</u> the TOEFL, so he doesn't need to take this class anymore.

Exercises 5 and 6:

Do these exercises in a parallel fashion to Exercises 3 and 4.

Workbook Exs. 3 & 4, pp. 6–7. Answers: TE p. 491.

EXERCISE 5

Why is perfect aspect used in these sentences? There may be more than one reason.

1. Please don't take my plate. I haven't finished my dessert.
2. You are too late; the doctor has just left the office.
3. He had forgotten to leave a key, so we couldn't get into the office.
4. She will already have left before you receive her farewell letter.
5. I've done my homework for tomorrow.
6. Biff hadn't even finished high school when he joined the Army.
7. The teacher has canceled the test, so you won't need to study tonight.
8. It has rained every January for the last ten years, so I don't think it's a good idea to plan a picnic.

EXERCISE 6

Decide whether perfect or simple aspect should be used in these sentences.

1. John _____ (say) goodbye to his classmates at school when he started packing for his trip.
2. Jonas Salk _____ (conduct) many unsuccessful experiments when his efforts finally resulted in the discovery of a vaccine for polio.
3. The United States _____ (have) the same form of government for more than two hundred years.
4. Bob _____ (visit) Mexico five times so far. He really likes traveling there.
5. When Bambang (a) _____ (come) to the United States, he (b) _____ (not be) away from his parents for more than a few days.
6. By the time Roberta Chong-Davis is fifty years old, she will probably _____ (travel) to the moon several times.
7. I _____ (not sleep) well since those noisy people moved into the apartment next door.
8. Columbus (a) _____ (complete) three voyages to islands in the Caribbean when he (b) _____ (realize) that the islands (c) _____ (not be) part of India.
9. We _____ (live) in this house since 1968.
10. Lucy _____ (study) very hard for the TOEFL, so I hope she passes!

ANSWER KEY

Exercises 5

1. related to present moment 2. action happens before another event; action is related to the present moment 3. action happened before another event 4. action happens before another event 5. sentence focuses on whether the action is completed or uncompleted 6. sentence focuses on whether the action is completed or uncompleted 7. action is related to the present moment 8. action is related to the present moment

Exercise 6

1. had said/said (also possible, but with a change of meaning) 2. had conducted 3. has had 4. has visited 5. (a) came, (b) had not been 6. have traveled 7. haven't slept/don't sleep 8. had completed, realized, weren't 9. have lived 10. has studied/studied

FOCUS **5**

Perfect Progressive Aspect

Perfect progressive tenses (present perfect progressive, past perfect progressive, and future perfect progressive) are made by using forms of:

HAVE + BEEN + VERB + -ING

EXAMPLES	EXPLANATIONS
(a) Jeff **has been working** on that project all day. He still hasn't finished it. (b) Jeff **has worked** on that project for three hours. Now he can do something else.	Use perfect progressive aspect instead of perfect aspect to describe: • actions that are uncompleted (a) instead of completed (b)
(c) You **have been talking** for the last hour. Please give someone else a chance to use the phone. (d) I **have talked** to that student several times about his lack of effort.	• actions that are continuous (c) instead of repeated (d)

EXERCISE 7

Decide whether perfect or perfect progressive aspect should be used in these sentences. More than one answer may be correct.

1. It _____ (rain) ever since we got here. I wish it would stop.

2. He _____ (work) on that computer virus for nearly a year before he realized that nothing could destroy it.

3. I'm very pleased. I _____ (find) the article you mentioned in your paper.

4. Lately John _____ (find) life without Mary more and more difficult.

5. Joyce _____ (cook) all afternoon. I hope the food will be as delicious as it smells.

6. Omar (a) _____ (look) for his car keys for over an hour, when he realized that he (b) _____ (leave) them in the car.

7. I _____ (try) to solve the problem for over an hour. I give up!

FOCUS 5

1. If this focus is presented on a different day from the previous ones, start out with a general review of the previous aspect categories—at least perfect and progressive aspect. Remind Ss that it is the context and situation that determine which of these meaning differences is being communicated.

2. Ask Ss for an example of perfect aspect and progressive aspect or choose one of the sentences you used in presenting Focuses 3 and 4.

3. Discuss the use exemplified by sentences a & b first (uncompleted vs. completed). **Additional examples :** *I've been doing my homework for hours. I'll never finish it! I've done my homework. Let's party!*

4. Move on to the second use. **Additional examples:** *It's been raining for days. I wish it would stop. It's rained only three times this summer. What a dry summer!*

Exercise 7

V A R I A T I O N :

Have Ss study Focus 5 at home (after your having presented Focuses 3 and 4 in class) and do this exercise as homework for you to go over the following day, or to collect and correct.

Workbook Ex. 5, p. 7. Answers: TE p. 491.

---

8. Next January 31, Jeff and Matt _____ (live) together as room-mates for five years.

9. The Girl Scouts (a) _____ (come) to the house to sell cookies once a year ever since I (b) _____ (move) here.

10. I _____ (try) to reach him several times by phone, without success.

EXERCISE 8

Write the appropriate form for the verbs in the following paragraph. The first three have been done for you as examples.

My roommate (1) _had_ (have) a dance party last Friday night. I (2) _was working_ (work) that Friday night, so I (3) _didn't get_ (not get) home until 10:00. By the time I (4) _____ (get) there, everyone (5) _____ (start) dancing. When I (6) _____ (walk) into the room everybody (7) _____ (shout) "welcome home!" because I (8) _____ (just arrive), and they (9) _____ (keep) dancing. I (10) _____ (go) into the kitchen to find something to eat. There (11) _____ (be) several other people in the kitchen. They (12) _____ (sit) by an open window. We (13) _____ (talk) and (14) _____ (laugh) for a while. Just when I (15) _____ (be) ready to start dancing myself, there (16) _____ (be) a knock at the door. I (17) _____ (go) to answer it, and (18) _____ (discover) our neighbor, who (19) _____ (complain) about the noise. He (20) _____ (ask) us to turn the music down. We (21) _____ (obey), of course. And although the party (22) _____ (get) a little quieter, we still (23) _____ (have) fun.

Exercises 8–11

There are many ways to do Exercises 8–11.

1. They can be done individually according to the printed directions, or orally by the whole class.

2. It is a good idea to do Exercise 8 before Exercises 9 and 10, but you can divide the class into groups or work in pairs with one student or group doing Exercise 9, and the other doing Exercise 10.

3. Exercise 11 provides an opportunity for Ss to compare the verb tenses in the three passages, and can be done individually in writing or as a whole class. In most cases, the aspect choice remains the same in all three time frames. Alternative possible choices have been indicated in the Answer Key.

ANSWER KEY

Exercise 8
(1) had (2) was working (3) didn't get
(4) got (5) had started (6) walked
(7) shouted (8) had just arrived (9) kept
dancing (10) went (11) were (12) were
sitting (13) talked (14) laughed
(15) was (16) was (17) went
(18) discovered (19) was complaining
(20) asked (21) obeyed, (22) got
(23) had

EXERCISE 9

Rewrite the paragraph in Exercise 8 in a present time frame. Keep the time relations between the verbs the same by maintaining the same aspect differences as in the paragraph in Exercise 8.

My roommate (1) _has_ (have) a dance party every Friday night). I (2) _am working_ (work) Friday night these days, so I (3) _don't get_ (not get) home until 10:00. On most Fridays, by the time I (4) _____ (get) there, everyone (5) _____ (start) dancing. When I (6) _____ (walk) into the room everybody (7) _____ (shout) "welcome home!" because I (8) _____ (just arrive), and they (9) _____ (keep) dancing. I generally (10) _____ (go) into the kitchen to find something to eat. Usually, there (11) _____ (be) several other people in the kitchen. They (12 _____ (sit) by an open window. We (13) _____ (talk) and (14) _____ (laugh) for a while. Just when I (15) _____ (be) ready to start dancing myself, there (16) _____ (be) almost always a knock at the door. I (17) _____ (go) to answer it, and (18) _____ (discover) our neighbor, who (19) _____ (complain) about the noise. He (20) _____ (ask) us to turn the music down. We (21) _____ (obey), of course. And although the party (22) _____ (get) a little quieter, we generally still (23) _____ (have) fun.

ANSWER KEY

Exercise 9
(1) has (2) am working (3) don't get
(4) get (5) has started (6) walk
(7) shouts (8) have just arrived (9) keep

dancing (10) go (11) are (12) are sitting
(13) talk (14) laugh (15) am (16) is
(17) go (18) discover (19) is complaining
(20) asks (21) obey (22) gets (23) have

EXERCISE 10

Rewrite the paragraph in Exercise 8 in a future time frame. Keep the time relations between the verbs the same by maintaining the same aspect differences as in the paragraph in Exercise 8.

My roommate (1) _is going to have_ (have) a dance party next Friday night. He has done this so often that I think I know exactly what's going to happen. I (2) _will be working_ (work) next Friday night, so I (3) _won't get_ (not get) home until 10:00. By the time I (4) _____ (get) there, I'm sure that everyone (5) _____ (start) dancing already. When I (6) _____ (walk) into the room everybody (7) _____ (shout) "welcome home!" because I (8) _____ (just arrive), but they probably (9) _____ (keep) dancing. I probably (10) _____ (go) into the kitchen to find something to eat, and undoubtedly there (11) _____ (be) several other people in the kitchen. They (12) _____ (sit) by an open window. If next Friday is like most of these parties, we (13) _____ (talk) and (14) _____ (laugh) for a while, and just when I (15) _____ (be) ready to start dancing myself, there most likely (16) _____ (be) a knock at the door. I (17) _____ (go) to answer it, and (18) _____ (discover) our neighbor. He (19) _____ (complain) about the noise, and (20) _____ (ask) us to turn the music down. We (21) _____ (obey), of course. And although the party (22) _____ (get) a little quieter, we undoubtedly still (23) _____ (have) fun.

EXERCISE 11

Work with a partner. Compare the tenses you used in Exercises 8, 9, and 10. Did you use the same aspect for each verb in all three exercises? What does this tell you about how tenses work together in a particular time frame? Discuss these questions with your partner, and report your ideas to the rest of the class.

EXERCISE 12

Complete these sentences with information about yourself. Compare your answers with other students. Did you use the same verb forms?

1. Until I came to this country I . . .
2. I often think about my problems when . . .
3. I had never seen . . . before I . . .
4. The next time I see my family they . . .
5. I am usually unhappy if . . .
6. When I was growing up, I . . .
7. I have been studying English since I . . .
8. Lately I . . .
9. Once I have completed my education, I . . .
10. I have never . . . , but I plan to do it someday.

This exercise can be done as small group discussion or as a whole class review of aspect. The point is to establish that aspect markers are basically the same in all three time frames: A situation that requires progressive aspect in present time frame will typically require progressive aspect in past or future time frame as well. This important principle can "emerge" or you can point out the parallel structures. ("*Look at # 5 in Exercises 9 and 10. Is it the same aspect? What is it? Now look at # 12 in Exercises 9 and 10 . . .*) etc.

Exercise 12

You can also assign this for individual homework.

Workbook Exs. 6 & 7, pp. 8–9. Answers: TE p. 491.

UNIT GOAL REVIEW

Ask Ss to look at the goals on the opening page of the unit again. Help them understand how much they have accomplished in each area. You can use this as an opportunity to review some of the meaning distinctions you have covered in the previous focuses, or ask Ss to identify which areas they would like more practice with. Point out that these aspect differences are covered in more detail in other units of the book.

Exercise 12

Answers will vary, but tense choice should be similar to the sample answers.

1. I had never eaten hamburger. **2.** when I am homesick. **3.** snow, before I visited Colorado **4.** they will be very happy. **5.** if I don't have time to exercise. **6.** I thought babies came from a factory. **7.** since I was a student in high school. **8.** I have been worrying about the TOEFL. **9.** I will find a good job. **10.** I have never gotten 600 on TOEFL.

Activity 1

Play textbook audio.
The tapescript for this listening appears on
p. 511 of this book.

    Play each conversation three times:
1. Ss listen for the general idea.
2. Ss read the choices and then listen for answers.
3. Ss check answers, listening to one conversation at a time or all four together.

Use Your English

A C T I V I T Y 1 : L I S T E N I N G

Listen to the following conversations and put a check next to the statements which can be correctly inferred from each conversation.

Conversation 1

—— (a) Mary doesn't want a roommate.

—— (b) Mary doesn't have a roommate at the moment, but she's looking for one.

—— (c) John doesn't want a roommate.

—— (d) John doesn't have a roommate at the moment, but he's looking for one.

Conversation 2

—— (a) Peter is looking the contract over at this moment.

—— (b) Peter is not looking the contract over at this moment.

—— (c) Denise is looking the contract over at this moment.

—— (d) Denise is not looking the contract over at this moment.

Conversation 3

—— (a) The janitor finished washing the floors before Angela's arrival.

—— (b) He finished washing the floors after Angela's arrival.

—— (c) The janitor emptied the trash before Angela's arrival.

—— (d) He emptied the trash after Angela's arrival.

—— (e) The janitor finished the windows before Angela's arrival.

—— (f) He finished the windows after Angela's arrival.

Conversation 4

—— (a) Bob works at the steel mill now.

—— (b) Bob doesn't work at the steel mill now.

—— (c) Dave works at the steel mill now.

—— (d) Dave doesn't work at the steel mill now.

A N S W E R   K E Y

Activity 1
These statements can be correctly inferred from each conversation.
Conversation 1: (a) Mary doesn't want a roommate. (d) John doesn't have a roommate at the moment, but he's looking for one.
Conversation 2: (b) Peter is not looking the contract over at this moment. (c) Denise is looking the contract over at this moment.

Conversation 3: (b) He finished washing the floors after Angela's arrival (d) He emptied the trash after Angela's arrival (e) The janitor finished the windows before Angela's arrival.
Conversation 4: (b) Bob doesn't work at the steel mill now. (c) Dave works at the steel mill factory now

ACTIVITY 2: WRITING

Revise your descriptions of the photographs in the Opening Task on pages 12 and 13 by using the past time frame. Start your descriptions like this: *When this picture was taken . . .*

ACTIVITY 3: READING

Look at the front page of a newspaper. Find three examples of each of the three time frames (present, past, and future). They may be in the same article or three different articles.

ACTIVITY 4: SPEAKING

Bring in three interesting photographs from a newspaper. Make a brief presentation about these photos to the class. Describe what is happening, what has happened, and what is going to happen. Then give three reasons why you think the photo is interesting.

ACTIVITY 5: WRITING/SPEAKING

Describe a routine that you typically follow. Then describe one time when you did not follow that routine, and tell what happened. For example, perhaps you usually take the bus to school. What time do you get there? What are people on the bus doing when you get on? What happened on the day when you decided to walk to school because the bus was late, or on the day when your classmate offered to take you for a ride in his cousin's brand-new car?

Activity 2

This can be used as a testing or diagnostic activity by having Ss hand in their individual responses for you to evaluate.

Activities 3 and 4

These work best as oral presentations or follow-up warm-up/review activities before moving on to the next unit.

ACTIVITY 4 VARIATIONS:

1. Have Ss bring in magazine pictures instead of newspaper pictures.
2. If you have pictures that are subject to multiple interpretations, provide different groups with the same photo, and see what explanations they come up with.

Activity 5

This can be used as a testing or diagnostic activity by having Ss hand in their individual responses for you to evaluate. Daily routines should be described in present time frame, and the time the routine was not followed should be in past time frame.

The test for this unit can be found on p. 440.
The answers are on p. 441 of this book.

Unit 3

UNIT OVERVIEW

Unit 3 provides a review of the basic "building blocks" of grammar: words, phrases, and clauses, and an overview of adverbials.

UNIT GOALS

Review the goals listed on this page so Ss understand what they should be able to know by the end of the unit.

OPENING TASK

The purpose of this particular task is to create a context in which Ss focus on how information can be communicated by words, phrases, or clauses.

UNIT 3

ADVERBIAL PHRASES AND CLAUSES

Adverbial Phrases and Clauses

UNIT GOALS:

- To identify phrases and clauses
- To correctly position adverbs
- To correctly position adverbial phrases and clauses

OPENING TASK
Who? What? Which? Where? When? Why? How?

Ski Mask Bank Robber Strikes Again

VANCOUVER, BC

Columbia Savings and Loan was struck by a bank robber for the third time this year. An unidentified man in a blue ski mask entered the bank during the busiest time of the day and demanded money from the cashier.

Although three security officers were on duty, the thief was able to escape on foot. Bank officials estimate total losses of over ten thousand dollars. Police have been interviewing witnesses in hopes of getting a more complete description of the thief.

Similar robberies in other parts of the city have led police to suspect that the same person might be responsible for all three robberies. Authorities are concerned about the fact that robberies have increased a great deal in the last three months. As a result, bank officials say, they will begin to install metal detectors in order to prevent people from entering banks with guns.

STEP 1 Newspaper reporters say that all basic news information about people and events can be summarized by asking and answering only the seven "Universal Questions" (Who? What? Which? Where? When? Why? How?). Summarize this newspaper article by writing W*h*-questions. Write as many questions as you need to in order to summarize all the important information.

STEP 2 Give your questions to a partner. Your partner should try to reconstruct the article by writing answers to your questions. Do the same with your partner's list of questions.

STEP 3 Compare your partner's answers with your questions and with the article. Your partner should do the same with your answers. Is any important information missing from your answers? Was there anything that you did not know how to ask about? Were there questions that you could not answer?

Step 1

Follow procedures similar to the ones you used for the Opening Task in Unit 2. Group Ss according to different backgrounds, or let them choose their own partners. Listen in on pairs to monitor how well they distinguish between present and past time frames in their use of verb tenses.

Step 2

Ask Ss to turn in their descriptions for you to check, or just focus on the follow-up discussion in Steps 2 and 3.

Step 3

After the pairs have shared their summaries of the article, use Step 3 as a brief processing with the whole class.

VARIATIONS:

1. Have one summary of Step 2 written on the board or OHP for the class to correct as a whole.
2. Have Ss find their own articles from newspapers or magazines, or use ones that you have clipped and selected.

FOCUS 1

This unit is a good beginning unit, because it reviews and practices some basic grammatical concepts. It gives a good holistic review of many different kinds of sentences as well as Wh- questions.

SUGGESTIONS:

1. Explain that the ability to distinguish words, phrases, and clauses will be very helpful in understanding complex sentences and advanced written prose.

2. Write the example sentence (a–d are identical except for the highlighting) on the board and see if Ss can identify the various elements without referring to their books.
3. Move on to clauses and go over them briefly before moving on to the chart on p. 31, which contains other examples of these structures.

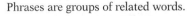

Identifying Phrases and Clauses

Phrases are groups of related words.

EXAMPLES	EXPLANATIONS
(a) **An unidentified man** in a blue ski mask has been robbing **city banks** for several months.	**Noun phrases:** noun + determiner and modifiers *Who, whom,* and *what,* ask about noun phrases.
(b) An unidentified man in a blue ski mask **has been robbing** city banks for several months.	**Verb phrases:** auxiliaries + verb *What . . . do . . .* asks about verb phrases.
(c) An unidentified man **in a blue ski mask** has been robbing city banks for several months.	**Prepositional phrases** preposition + noun phrase Adjective prepositional phrases give more information about nouns. *Which* asks about adjective phrases.
(d) An unidentified man in a blue ski mask has been robbing city banks **for several months.**	Adverbial prepositional phrases give more information about verbs. *Where, when, how,* and *why* ask about adverbial phrases.

Clauses are groups of related words that contain both a noun and a verb.

EXAMPLES	EXPLANATIONS
(e) **A man robbed the bank.**	Independent clauses can function as sentences.
(f) Have you heard **that a man robbed the bank?**	Dependent clauses cannot function as independent sentences.
(g) A man robbed the bank **that we visited yesterday.**	Adjective clauses (also called relative clauses) give more information about noun phrases.
(h) A man robbed the bank **before the police could arrive to catch him.**	Adverbial clauses give more information about verb phrases.

The following chart shows how different kinds of *Wh*-questions focus on different parts of the sentences and can be answered with either phrases or clauses.

WH-QUESTIONS		PHRASES	CLAUSES
WHO/WHOM	**Who** reported the crime to the police?	**The security manager** did.	**Whoever is responsible for security** reported it.
	Who(m) did the police arrest?	They arrested **the old man.**	They arrested the man **who they found hiding in the alley.**
WHAT	**What** have you told the reporters?	I told them **my experience.**	I told them **that the investigation is still not finished.**
WHAT . . . DO	**What did** the police **do?**	They **tried to catch the thief.**	They hoped **that they would find the criminal.**
WHICH	**Which teller** was robbed?	The teller **with the blonde hair** was.	The teller **who was interviewed by the police** was.
WHERE	**Where** did the thief go?	He went **down the street, towards the park.**	The thief went **where the police couldn't find him.**
WHEN	**When** did they finish the investigation?	They finished it **on Tuesday at 3:00.**	They finished it **when they had collected all the evidence.**
HOW	**How** did the thief get away?	He got away **on foot.**	The thief disappeared **as if he had become invisible.**
HOW _____	**How** busy was the bank yesterday?	It was **busier than usual.**	It was **so busy that nobody noticed the thief.**
HOW LONG	**How long** has that officer been on the police force?	He's been a policeman **for a long time.**	He has been a policeman **since he first moved to the city.**
HOW OFTEN	**How often** has this bank been robbed?	It's been robbed **from time to time.**	It's been robbed **as often as any other bank has been robbed.**
HOW MUCH	**How much** money did the thief take?	He took **too much to count.**	He took **so much that they haven't determined the entire amount.**
WHY	**Why** did you go to the bank?	I went **for some money.**	I went to the bank **because I needed money.**
		I went to the bank **to cash a check.**	I went to the bank **so that I could cash a check.**

4. Go over this chart briefly in class or assign it as follow-up homework for Ss to read more carefully.

V A R I A T I O N :
Photocopy the chart and cut up the various examples. They will be about the size of fortune-cookie slips. Give one to each student and have them go around the room and find the other two students who have the relevant questions and answers. (You'll end up with groups of three, who can then be used as groups for later exercises in this unit.)

Exercise 1

Intermediate Ss should be able to do Exercise 1 without having done a full-scale review of Wh-question forms, but if they are having trouble, use the examples in the first two columns of the chart on p. 31 to review.

SUGGESTIONS:

1. Make the most of the possibility of multiple correct answers by asking for possible questions from several Ss for each "answer" provided in the exercise.
2. Alternatively, assign the exercise as homework and have Ss compare their answers.
3. In more advanced classes the exercise can be done orally, or with less advanced classes as a written diagnostic of their Wh-question formation.

Workbook Ex. 1, p. 10. Answers: TE p. 491.

EXERCISE 1

There is a popular American TV quiz show called "Jeopardy." Contestants are given answers, and they must provide a question for each answer. Play Jeopardy with a partner. Here are some answers. For each answer, decide what form it is (phrase or clause) and make up a suitable question.

▶ **EXAMPLES:** by studying (phrase): *How can I get a good score on* the TOEFL?

once I get 550 on TOEFL (clause): *When will you begin your university studies?*

1. the president
2. He went to the movies.
3. I am.
4. in 1997
5. at noon
6. from Japan
7. for fun
8. after I finish school
9. because he needs money
10. because of the TOEFL
11. by studying
12. My sister can.
13. in order to learn English
14. to find a good job
15. the old man
16. until he passes the TOEFL
17. to my brother
18. a book and a pen
19. too expensive
20. as long as I am a student
21. so he can buy books

EXERCISE 2

Each of these sentences consists of two or more clauses. Put brackets around each clause, as shown in the example.

▶ **EXAMPLE:** [Although John is a little homesick], [he still plans to stay in France for at least a year].

1. Ali likes to get up early most days, but prefers to sleep late on weekends.
2. Denise has a lot of work that has to get done, so she won't consider taking a vacation.
3. Because they feel war is too destructive, many people are opposed to military solutions for international problems.
4. I once met a man who looked just like a friend of mine.
5. Bob is looking for an additional job that he can do in his spare time because he needs some extra money.
6. I know an old lady who swallowed a fly.
7. Although I have many friends, I still enjoy meeting people that I've never met before.
8. Last night after dinner I wrote to an old friend who went to school with me.

32 UNIT 3

ANSWER KEY

Exercise 1

Example questions will vary. Possible answers include:
1. noun phrase; Who is Hillary married to?
2. clause; What did John do after class?
3. clause; Who is the best student in the class?
4. phrase; When did you come to the United States? 5. phrase; When do you eat lunch?
6. phrase; Where are you from? 7. phrase; Why are you reading that comic book?
8. clause; When will you start working?
9. clause; Why is John working at night?
10. phrase; Why do you worry about your English? 11. phrase; How can I get a good score on the TOEFL? 12. clause; Who can get 500 on the TOEFL? 13. phrase; Why do you listen to English-language TV? 14. phrase; Why are you studying English? 15. phrase; Which man are you talking about? 16. clause; How long will Jose study in an intensive English program? 17. phrase; Whom did he give the message? 18. phrase; What should I bring to class? 19. phrase; How expensive is this restaurant? 20. clause; How long can you stay here on a student visa? 21. clause; Why is John going to the book store?

Exercise 2

1. [Ali likes to get up early most days], [but prefers to sleep late on weekends.]
2. [Denise has a lot of work] [that has to get done], [so she won't consider taking a vacation.] 3. [Because they feel war is too destructive], [many people are opposed to military solutions for international problems.]
4. [I once met a man] [who looked just like a friend of mine.] 5. [Bob is looking for an additional job] [that he can do in his spare time] [because he needs some extra money.]
6. [I know an old lady] [who swallowed a fly.]
7. [Although I have many friends,] [I still enjoy meeting people] [that I've never met before.]
8. [Last night after dinner I wrote to an old friend] [who went to school with me.]

FOCUS **2**

Basic Adverbial Position

Adverbials are words, phrases, and clauses that answer questions like *when, where, why, how much,* and *how often.*

EXAMPLES	EXPLANATIONS
(a) Biff **never** goes **downtown anymore.**	adverbs
(b) Biff exercises **as often as possible at the gym on Saturdays.**	adverbial phrases
(c) Biff works out **because he wants to improve his physique.**	adverbial clauses

Most adverbial information follows the verb phrase (verb + object) and usually appears in a basic order (some other variations are possible).

Verb phrase	Manner	Place	Frequency	Time	Purpose or reason
what . . . do	**how**	**where**	**how often**	**when**	**why**
(d) *Biff lifts weights*	*vigorously*	*at the gym*	*every day*	*after work*	*to fight stress.*

Some adverbs can come before the verb or between the auxiliary and the main verb.

EXAMPLES	EXPLANATIONS
(e) Gladstone **often** goes on strange diets. (f) He has **never** lost more than a few pounds.	**Adverbs of frequency:** affirmative: *always, often, usually, sometimes* negative: *seldom, rarely, hardly ever, never*
(g) He has **rigorously** avoided sweets for more than a year.	**Adverbs of manner:** *rigorously, quickly, completely,* etc.
(h) He **recently** lost fifty pounds.	**Indefinite adverbs of time:** *recently, typically, previously, finally,* etc.

FOCUS 2

1. If you are doing the entire unit in sequence (and not just the first focus on words, phrases, and clauses); start by using examples a, b, and c to link back to the previous focus. Explain that word order can be a problem with adverbials and that the rest of the unit will focus on which adverbials go in which places in the sentence.

2. Introduce the basic order by writing the basic word order (manner, place, frequency, time, purpose, or reason) on the board and then sentence d (or one of the variants listed below).

3. Lead the class in identifying the various adverbials (draw an arrow from the label to the word or words in the example sentence). Ss' books should be closed for this part of the discussion.

S U G G E S T I O N :

Repeat this process with another sentence or two. Other examples that follow the same categories and word order as sentence d are:
We study English happily in class every morning at 10:00 to improve our ability.
We do assignments carefully at home every night after dinner to prepare for the next day's lesson.

4. With books open, present the three categories of adverbs that can come before the verb and refer Ss to sentences e–h. Go over the example sentences as a whole class. Ask Ss to think of other adverbs of manner.

Exercise 3

Steps 1 and 2 are best done individually, and can be assigned as homework. Ss can then work in pairs to compare answers, or you can go over the exercise as a whole class.

SUGGESTION:

Use this exercise as an opportunity to give Ss more practice identifying phrases and clauses by asking whether the underlined units are phrases or clauses as part of your processing questions.

EXERCISE 3

Read the following passage.

1. Circle the verb phrase in every sentence.
2. Underline the adverbs and adverbial phrases.
3. Decide whether the meaning of each adverbial is frequency, manner, place, time, or reason/purpose.

The first paragraph has been done for you as an example.

Biff Bicep   *Gladstone Gulp*

Biff Bicep and Gladstone Gulp are close friends. (1) They are always trying *frequency* to change the way they look because neither one is very pleased with his appearance, (2) but they do it differently. *manner*

Biff Bicep is a serious body-builder. (3) He tries to increase the size of his muscles by lifting weights at a gym near his house. (4) He usually goes there at the same time every day. (5) He drinks special vitamin supplements to gain weight, and (6) works out vigorously twice a day—in the morning and in the afternoon. (7) He usually starts out on an exercise bike to warm up his muscles. Then he moves on to his exercises. (8) He exercises his upper body on Mondays, Wednesdays, and Fridays. (9) On Tuesdays, Thursdays, and Saturdays, he does exercises to develop the muscles of his lower body. (10) He never works out on Sundays, so his muscles can have a chance to rest.

Gladstone Gulp is a serious dieter. (11) He always seems to be trying to lose weight by going on special weight-reducing diets whenever he feels too heavy. (12) He usually drinks a special diet drink at breakfast and lunch. (13) Sometimes he doesn't eat anything after breakfast in order to save a few calories. (14) He also tries not to snack in between meals. (15) As a result, he is usually really hungry when he gets home and (16) so he often goes directly to the kitchen to find something to eat. Although he is a serious dieter, he's not a terribly successful one. (17) He has never permanently lost more than a few pounds. (18) He's always looking for a magic way to lose weight without having to diet or exercise.

34 UNIT 3

ANSWER KEY

Exercise 3

Verb phrases are in bold, adverbials are underlined, and meaning given in italics.
(3) He **tries** to increase the size of his muscles <u>by lifting weights</u> (*manner*) <u>at a gym near his house</u> (*place*). (4) He <u>usually</u> (*frequency*) **goes** <u>there</u> (*place*) <u>at the same time</u> (*time*) <u>every day</u> (*frequency*). (5) He **drinks** special vitamin supplements <u>to gain weight</u> (*reason*), and (6) **works out** <u>vigorously</u> (*manner*) <u>twice a day</u> (*frequency*)—<u>in the morning</u> (*time*) and <u>in the afternoon</u> (*time*). (7) He <u>usually</u> (*frequency*) **starts out** <u>on an exercise bike</u> (*place*) <u>to warm up his muscles</u> (*reason*). <u>Then</u> (*time*) he **moves**

<u>on to his exercises</u>. (*place*) (8) He **exercises** his upper body <u>on Mondays, Wednesdays and Fridays</u>. (*time*) (9) <u>On Tuesdays, Thursdays and Saturdays,</u> (*time*) he **does** exercises <u>to develop the muscles of his lower body.</u> (*reason*) (10) He <u>never</u> (*frequency*) **works out** <u>on Sundays,</u> (*time*) <u>so his muscles can have a chance to rest.</u> (*reason*) (11) He <u>always</u> (*frequency*) **seems to be trying** to lose weight <u>by going on special weight-reducing diets</u> (*manner*) <u>whenever he feels too heavy.</u> (*frequency*) (12) He <u>usually</u> (*frequency*) **drinks** a special diet drink <u>at breakfast and lunch.</u> (*time*) (13) <u>Sometimes</u> (*frequency*) he **doesn't eat** anything <u>after</u>

<u>breakfast</u> (*time*) <u>in order to save a few calories</u> (*reason*). (14) He <u>also</u> (*sentence adverbial*) **tries** not to snack <u>in between meals.</u> (*when*) (15) <u>As a result</u> (*sentence adverbial*), he **is** <u>usually</u> (*frequency*) really hungry <u>when he gets home,</u> (*time*) and (16) so he <u>often</u> (*frequency*) **goes** <u>directly</u> (*manner*) <u>to the kitchen</u> (*place*) <u>to find something</u> to eat. (*reason*) (17) He **has** <u>never</u> (*frequency*) <u>permanently</u> (*manner*) **lost** more than a few pounds. (18) He's <u>always</u> (*frequency*) **looking for** a magic way to lose weight <u>without having to diet or exercise.</u> (*manner*)

34 Grammar Dimensions, Platinum Edition

EXERCISE 4

Add the adverbials in parentheses to each sentence. There may be more than one possible position.

▶ **EXAMPLE:** He gains back the lost weight. (quickly) (usually)

He usually gains the lost weight back quickly.

Usually he quickly gains back the lost weight.

1. Gladstone Gulp goes on a new diet. (because he feels heavy) (every few months)

2. He uses diet pills (to increase his metabolism) (regularly)

3. He rides an exercise bicycle (occasionally) (to use up calories) (very hard)

4. He trades diet plans. (with his friend Biff) (sometimes)

5. He reads about every new diet. (in magazines) (carefully) (whenever he can)

6. He doesn't follow their directions (carefully) (always)

7. He drinks a special vitamin supplement (usually) (to make sure he gets proper nutrition)

EXERCISE 5

Interview a classmate and find out something that he or she does:

1. every day
2. for his or her health
3. very well
4. before bedtime
5. outdoors
6. occasionally
7. better than anyone else in his or her family
8. automatically
9. with considerable difficulty
10. after class

Write complete sentences about these activities and report them to the class.

Exercise 4
Allow for multiple right answers in your whole class processing.

Exercise 5
V A R I A T I O N S :

Use this exercise as a structured interview and oral report, or as a testing/diagnostic activity by collecting the sentences that Ss write about the people they have interviewed.

Workbook Ex. 2, p. 11. Answers: TE p. 491.

ANSWER KEY

Exercises 4
Answers may vary. These are all possible. In some cases there is only one correct order.
1. Every few months Gladstone Gulp goes on a new diet because he feels heavy. Gladstone Gulp goes on a new diet every few months, because he feels heavy. 2. He regularly uses diet pills to increase his metabolism. He uses diet pills regularly to increase his metabolism. To increase his metabolism, he uses diet pills regularly.
3. He occasionally rides an exercise bicycle very hard to use up calories. To use up calories, he occasionally rides an exercise bicycle very hard.

4. He sometimes trades diet plans with his friend Biff. Sometimes he trades diet plans with his friend Biff. 5. He reads carefully about every new diet in magazines whenever he can. Whenever he can, he carefully reads in magazines about every new diet. In magazines he carefully reads about every new diet whenever he can. 6. He doesn't always follow their directions carefully. 7. He usually drinks a special vitamin supplement to make sure he gets proper nutrition. To make sure he gets proper nutrition, he usually drinks a special vitamin supplement.

Exercise 5
Answers will vary. Possible answers include:
1. She goes to school every day. 2. John goes to a gym for his health. 3. He speaks English very well. 4. Joe always brushes his teeth before bedtime. 5. John plays tennis outdoors. 6. Kathy occasionally forgets to do her homework. 7. Maria sings better than anyone else in her family. 8. Steve automatically locks his car whenever he parks it. 9. Peter understands New Yorkers with considerable difficulty. 10. Jacob usually does his homework after class.

This focus can be presented in a basic straightforward way, or can be made more inductive in the following way.

1. Present this focus with books closed. Write the example sentences (a and b) on the board and point out that (a) is considered awkward or "bad style."
2. Ask Ss if they can use that information to generate their own "rules." Have them work in pairs or small groups. If you need to guide them with questions, you can use the following: *What are the adverbials in these sentences? Which adverbial is longer? Which is shorter? Which one should come first?*
3. Follow the same procedure for sentences c and d.
   What kind of adverbials are these? Manner? place? time? They're both adverbials of place. Which one is more general? Which one should come first?
4. Follow the same procedure for sentences e and f. *What's the difference between sentence e and f? How many adverbials are there? Why do you think the author moved an adverbial to the beginning of the sentence? Which kind of adverbial should we move to the beginning?*

Position and Order of Adverbial Phrases

When there is more than one adverbal phrase in a clause, the order usually follows these guidelines.

EXAMPLES	EXPLANATIONS
(a) AWKWARD: He exercise vigorously at the gym **every Monday, Wednesday, and Friday after work.** **(b)** BETTER: He exercises vigorously at the gym **after work every Monday, Wednesday, and Friday.**	Shorter adverbial phrases usually come before longer adverbial phrases. Since the frequency phrase is long, it is better to have it follow the time phrase.
(c) Many people frequently eat dinner **in neighborhood restaurants in Toronto.** **(d)** NOT: Many people frequently eat dinner **in Toronto in neighborhood restaurants.**	When there are two adverbial phrases of the same kind (place, time, etc.), the more specific adverbial phrase always comes first.
(e) AWKWARD: He washes his car **carefully in the driveway with a special soap once a week.** **(f)** BETTER: **Once a week,** he **carefully** washes his car **in the driveway with a special soap.**	It is not common to have more than two or three adverbials after the verb phrase. If there are several adverbials, then one is usually moved to the beginning of the sentence.

EXERCISE 6

Identify the meaning (place, frequency, reason, time, etc.) and form (adverb, adverb phrase, adverbial clause) of the underlined adverbials in the numbered sentences in this article. Tell why you think they appear in the order that they do. There may be several possible reasons, so discuss your ideas with a partner. The first sentence has been done for you as an example.

▶ **EXAMPLE:** (a) manner, adverb, (b) place, adverbial prepositional phrase, (c) time, adverbial clause. **Reasons:** adverbials follow general manner, place, and time order.

Exercise 6

Like many similar exercises in this book, you can assign this for homework, have Ss work on it in pairs, or go through it sentences by sentence with the whole class.

Workbook Exs. 3–5, p. 12–14. Answers: TE p. 492.

Bizarre Attack by Wild Pigs on Rampage

Buttonwillow, GA

Mary Morris is a lucky woman tonight. (1) She is resting (a) <u>comfortably</u> (b) <u>at her Buttonwillow home</u> (c) <u>after doctors released her from Buttonwillow Hospital</u> (d) <u>earlier this afternoon.</u> Early this morning she was involved in one of the strangest automobile accidents in local history. Her car was attacked by a herd of wild pigs.

(2) "I was driving (a) <u>on a dirt road</u> (b) <u>along the river,</u> (c) <u>just like I always do,</u>" she told reporters in an impromptu news conference at the hospital, (d) "<u>when I hit a muddy patch of road</u>. I got out of the car to try to push it out of the mud. (3) (a) <u>While I was doing that</u> a herd of pigs (b) <u>suddenly</u> came (c) <u>out of the bushes</u> (d) <u>to attack me.</u> There were so many of them that I was completely surrounded, but I was able to get back into the car. (4) I (a) <u>finally</u> scared them (b) <u>back into the bushes</u> (c) <u>by blowing</u> the horn. (5) Then I sat (a) <u>there</u> (b) <u>for several hours</u> (c) <u>before I felt safe enough to leave the car</u> and (d) <u>could look for some help.</u>" Ms. Morris was treated for gashes on her legs and shock. She was given a tetanus shot, and released later in the day.

Scientists are a little puzzled as to why the pigs might have attacked in the first place. Animal psychologist Dr. Lassie Kumholm suggested that it may have been because one of the females in the herd could have just given birth near where the car got stuck. (6) (a) <u>Sometimes</u> pigs can (b) <u>suddenly</u> become aggressive (c) <u>quite quickly</u> (d) <u>if their young are threatened.</u> This herd of pigs is a well-known nuisance. (7) They have (a) <u>repeatedly</u> caused minor damage (b) <u>in the area</u> (c) <u>for the last several years,</u> but this is the first time they have been known to actually attack humans. (8) (a) <u>On several occasions</u> local property owners have sent petitions (b) <u>to county offices</u> (c) <u>to complain about the problem.</u>

ANSWER KEY

Exercise 6

1. (a) manner, adverb (b) place, adverbial prepositional phrase (c) time, adverbial clause (d) time adverbial phrase **Reasons:** adverbials follow general manner, place, and time; (d) gives more information about the verb in the adverbial clause (*released*)
2. (a) place, adverbial prepositional phrase (b) place, adverbial prepositional phrase (c) manner, adverbial clause (d) time, adverbial clause **Reasons:** the adverbial prepositional phrases of place are shorter than the clauses.
3. (a) time, clause (b) manner, adverb (c) place, adverbial prepositional phrase (d) reason/purpose, infinitive phrase. **Reasons:** adverbial clause connects the sentence to the previous one. The phrases follow the general order of place before reason/purpose.
4. (a) time, adverb (b) place, adverbial prepositional phrase (c) manner, gerund phrase **Reasons:** manner comes at the end for clarity
5. (a) place, adverb (b) time, prepositional phrase (c) time, clause (d) time, clause **Reasons:** place comes before time, the shorter time adverbials come before the longer ones
6. (a) frequency, adverb (b) manner, adverb (c) manner, adverb (with intensifier) (d) reason, clause **Reasons:** these adverbials follow the usual order
7. (a) manner, adverb (b) place, prepositional phrase (c) time, prepositional phrase **Reasons:** these adverbials follow the usual order
8. (a) frequency/time, prepositional phrase (b) place, phrase (c) reason, infinitive phrase **Reasons:** these adverbials follow the usual order

FOCUS 4

1. Use the first part of this focus (sentences a–g) to give Ss a general idea of why they might choose to put adverbials at the beginning of a sentence.
2. Focus on those sentences that require "question-word order" as a follow-up presentation.

S U G G E S T I O N :

Affirmative and negative adverbs of frequency were introduced and listed in Focus 2, so you may want review them here.

FOCUS **4**

Putting Adverbial Phrases at the Beginning of a Sentence

EXAMPLES	EXPLANATIONS
(a) **Once a week,** he carefully washes his car in the driveway with a special soap. (b) **In the suitcase,** he found an extra wool sweater that had been knitted by his grandmother. (c) NOT: He found an extra wool sweater that had been knitted by his grandmother **in the suitcase.**	Most adverbials can also appear at the beginning of a clause or sentence for the following reasons. • if there are several other adverbs or adverbial phrases, or if the object of the verb phrase is very long
(d) **Carefully and slowly,** John carried the heavy tray of fragile glasses to the table.	• in order to emphasize adverbial information
(e) Berta has a beautiful apartment. **Along one wall,** there are big windows with a marvelous view. (f) Matt was born in 1965. **In 1980,** he moved to San Francisco. (g) John became quite fluent in French. **As a result,** he was able to get a job with a company that exports computer parts to West Africa.	• to show logical relationships between sentences.

Most adverbials can be placed at the beginning of the sentence without making other changes in word order, but some require a question word order when they are put at the beginning of the sentence.

EXAMPLES	EXPLANATIONS
Normal Position: (h) Gladstone **seldom loses** more than a few pounds. **Emphatic Position:** (i) **Seldom does** Gladstone **lose** more than a few pounds.	negative adverbs of frequency (*never, seldom, rarely*)

38 UNIT 3

EXERCISE 7

Make these sentences more emphatic by moving the adverbial to the beginning of the sentence. Be sure to change the word order if necessary.

1. I have rarely seen such a mess.
2. Gladstone is often so hungry that he eats an entire cake.
3. He usually doesn't lose control.
4. We will never finish this project.
5. Steve seldom feels unhappy for very long.
6. Alice typed the letter quickly and efficiently, and sent it special delivery

FOCUS **5**

Position of Adverbial Clauses

Most adverbial clauses appear after the main clause, but many can also come before the main clause.

EXAMPLES	EXPLANATIONS
(a) **As if it were the easiest thing in the world,** Mary did a triple spin and sailed off across the ice.	• to emphasize the adverbial clause
(b) **As soon as John got to the airport,** he began to have second thoughts about going to France.	
(c) **Until Jeff moved to San Francisco,** he had never seen the ocean. He had never been to a disco or eaten Chinese food. He had never even fallen in love.	• to establish a context that applies to several sentences
(d) **Whenever John thought about Mary** he began to feel guilty. He would imagine her sitting sadly at home alone, writing him long letters. He felt that he wasn't missing her as much as she was missing him.	
(e) I usually read the paper **before** I take a shower.	• to show sequence
(f) **After** I read the paper, I usually take a shower.	
(g) **If** you wash the dishes, **then** I'll dry them and put them away.	

Exercise 7

This exercise works well as a whole class follow-up to Focus 4, but can also be done in pairs or assigned as homework.

FOCUS 5

This focus can be assigned as homework, with a teacher-led review in class the next day using such questions as: "*What are some reasons to put adverbials clauses at the beginning of the sentence?*" The reasons are similar to those discussed in Focus 4.

V A R I A T I O N :

Cover both Focus 4 and 5 in class before doing Exercise 7. Then do Exercise 8 as an overall end-of-unit review

ANSWER KEY

Exercise 7
1. Rarely have I seen such a mess! 2. Often Gladstone is so hungry that he eats an entire cake. 3. Usually he doesn't lose control.
4. Never will we finish this project!
5. Seldom does Steve feel unhappy for very long! 6. Quickly and efficiently, Alice typed the letter and sent it special delivery.

Certain adverbial clauses almost always appear after the main clause.

EXAMPLES	EXPLANATIONS
(h) I shop **where** Juan shops. (i) AWKWARD: **Where** Juan shops, I shop. (j) **Wherever** he goes, Juan makes new friends and has wonderful adventures.	• adverbial clauses of place except those that begin with *wherever* or *everywhere*
(k) Dalia worked all summer **so (that) she would have enough money.** (l) AWKWARD: **So that she would have enough money,** Dalia worked all summer.	• adverbial clauses of result with *so that*
(m) I visited my grandmother **for I knew she had been sick.** (n) NOT: **For I knew she had been sick,** I visited my grandmother.	• adverbial clauses of reason with *for*

Punctuation of adverbial clauses depends on their position in a sentence.

EXAMPLES	EXPLANATIONS
(o) **After I took the examination,** I ate lunch. (p) I ate lunch **after I took the examination.**	Adverbial clauses before the main clause are followed by a comma. No extra punctuation is necessary if they appear after the main clause.
(q) **Since you don't have much money,** I'll pay for dinner. (r) I'll pay for dinner **since you don't have much money.**	

EXERCISE 8

Work with a partner to answer these questions about the sentences below. The first sentence has been done as an example.

(a) Does the adverbial clause in these sentences appear before or after the main clause? *before*

(b) Decide which of the reasons listed in Focus 5 can be used to explain why the author chose to put the adverbial clauses in this order. *to emphasize the adverbial clause*

1. Because Biff enjoys vigorous exercise, he tends to pursue sports that build up his muscles.

2. On the other hand, Gladstone practices sports like yoga because for him exercise is a means of relaxation.

3. Both Biff and Gladstone want to lose weight because they want to feel and look better.

4. Because Mary Morris may have stopped her car too close to a newborn piglet, she became the victim of a bizarre attack.

5. When the ski-mask robber entered the bank, he showed the teller a gun and demanded money.

6. Columbia Savings and Loan had already been robbed three times when the ski-mask robber appeared yesterday.

7. The bank manager told the press about the robbery so that the public would become aware of the need for more security.

8. Since he first agreed to work on the project in 1985, he has spent more than ten years trying to educate people about grammar.

Adverbial Phrases and Clauses | **41**

Exercise 8
VARIATIONS:

1. Assign different pairs of different items in this exercise to discuss and then to present to the rest of the class.

2. Assign more than one pair to each item so one pair presents their ideas, and the second pair responds to their explanation by agreeing or disagreeing and offering an alternative explanation.

Workbook Ex. 6, pp. 14–15. Answers: TE p. 492.

UNIT GOAL REVIEW

Have Ss work in pairs to look over the goals on the opening page of the unit again. Have Ss summarize their understanding of the principles involved with each goal to one another and to identify one question they still have based on this discussion. Process the questions with the whole class by asking pairs to state their question and then asking other pairs if they can answer it or explain the relevant rule in their own words.

ANSWER KEY

Exercise 8

There may be several possible explanations. Possible explanations include:
1. Before. Order expresses the logical relationship of cause and effect. **2.** After. Order emphasizes the contrast introduced by "on the other hand." **3.** After. Basic order—no special emphasis. **4.** Before. Emphasizes cause; underscores logical relation of cause and effect. **5.** Before. Follows the chronological order of events. **6.** After. Basic order—no special emphasis. **7.** After. Order expresses the logical relationship between cause and effect. **8.** Before. Follows the chronological order of events.

USE YOUR ENGLISH

Activity 1

This can be a good testing activity. Have Ss write formal "interview questions" and then record the responses of the partners they interview in complete sentences.

SUGGESTION:

If you are doing this unit later in the semester, you may wish to choose another activity, since Ss will already know each other pretty well, and the communicative need for such information will be less.

Activities 2-4

These are best done as discussion activities rather than as diagnostic activities to be written and evaluated.

Use Your English

ACTIVITY 1: SPEAKING/WRITING

STEP 1 Find out some basic information about another student in the class by asking some of the "Universal Questions" that were described in the Opening Task. Here are some suggested topics.

WHO:	name, family background
WHAT:	hobbies, special interests, plans for the future
WHERE:	home town, current living situation
WHEN:	date of birth, date of arrival in this country, date of expected completion of English studies
HOW LONG:	length of time in this country, amount of previous English study
HOW OFTEN:	regular activities, hobbies
HOW MUCH:	special skills, abilities, and interests
WHY:	reasons and goals for studying English, joining this class, leaving home

STEP 2 Report the information to the rest of the class in a short paragraph or oral presentation.

ACTIVITY 2: SPEAKING

An "ulterior motive" is a bad reason for doing a good thing. For example, helping a friend who is in trouble is a good thing to do, but if your real reason for doing it is because you want that person to lend you money later, your motive may make your action a bad one.

STEP 1 In a small group discuss the following situations. For each situation identify some "pure motives"—reasons for doing the action that would make it a good or generous act—and some "ulterior motives"—reasons that would make the act a bad or selfish one.

- loaning someone money
- not telling a friend some bad news
- being friendly and obedient to a rich relative
- working harder than anyone else at your job

STEP 2 Based on your discussion decide whether people's actions should be judged by what they do (their actions) or why they do it (their motivations). Present your opinion and your reasons to the rest of the class.

ANSWER KEY

Activity 2

Some examples of pure and ulterior motives are:

loaning someone money: (pure) because you always want to help your friends; (ulterior) because you plan to ask that person for a favor later on

not telling a friend some bad news: (pure) because you hope you can solve the problem before the friend hears about it; (ulterior) because you hope somebody else will have to do the "dirty work"

being friendly and obedient to a rich relative: (pure) because you like that person and treat all your family members that way; (ulterior) because you want that person to leave you money if he or she dies

working harder than anyone else at your job: (pure) because you love what you are doing and are excited by it; (ulterior) because you want to get ahead of your co-workers, or get them in trouble with the boss.

ACTIVITY 3: WRITING/SPEAKING

Which form of motivation is more common in your day-to-day activities: extrinsic motivation or intrinsic motivation?

Extrinsic motivation is **purpose.** You do something in order to achieve something else, such as studying business in order to get a high-paying job in the future.	Intrinsic motivation is **cause.** You do something because you like the activity itself, such as studying business because you love being a student and enjoy economic theory.

STEP 1 Decide whether your basic motivation for each of these activities is extrinsic or intrinsic, and identify two additional things you do because of intrinsic motivation. Then, in the first column in the following chart, write three things you do because of intrinsic motivation.

studying English   watching TV   cleaning the house
driving a car   reading newspapers   doing homework
cooking   exercise   shopping

STEP 2 Interview three other students in the class to find out things they do because of intrinsic motivation. Write the information in the chart below.

Your activities	Classmate 1	Classmate 2	Classmate 3
1) _____	1) _____	1) _____	1) _____
2) _____	2) _____	2) _____	2) _____
3) _____	3) _____	3) _____	3) _____

STEP 3 Form a group with two or three other students whom you did not interview and compare all the information you have gathered. As a group, decide on answers to the following question and present your ideas to the rest of the class.

What are the three most common characteristics shared by all things that people do because of intrinsic motivation? For example, do intrinsically motivated activities result in self-improvement? Are they pleasurable? Do people feel unhappy if they don't have an opportunity to pursue these activities?

ACTIVITY 4: SPEAKING

In a small group discuss the following situations. For each situation decide whether there are ever any justifiable reasons or purposes for the following actions:
- leaving your family forever
- getting married to someone against your family's wishes
- not reporting a criminal to the police
- falling in love with someone other than your spouse
- taking something that doesn't belong to you

Based on your discussion decide whether a person's actions should be determined by his or her motivations or merely by the actions themselves. Present your opinions and your reasons to the rest of the class.

ACTIVITY 5: SPEAKING

The world seems to be divided into two kinds of people: morning people (who do their best work early in the day) and night people (who are sleepy in the morning, and most productive in the late afternoon or even late at night). Which kind are you? Interview a partner to find out which kind of person he or she is.

STEP 1   Find out **how** your partner does each activity in the chart below at the time of day listed. (Some examples have been provided.) Ask about two additional activities.

STEP 2   Decide on whether your partner is a morning person or a night person, and report your findings to the rest of the class.

WHEN? WHAT?	Early morning HOW?	After lunch HOW?	Late at night HOW?
vigorous exercise	slowly	well, but not if he's hungry	easily, but it keeps him awake
balancing your checkbook			
thinking up original ideas			
relaxed reading for pleasure			
concentrated reading for work or school			
social activity and conversation			

Activity 5

EXPANSION:

Have Ss interview Ss outside of class and conduct a "poll" on whether morning people or night people are more common in given age groups.

ACTIVITY 6: LISTENING

STEP 1 Listen to the following news broadcasts. Based on what you hear write as many questions as you can with *Who, What, Where, When Why, How* about each broadcast and give them to a partner to answer. You may need to listen to the broadcasts more than once in order to ask and answer the questions.

STEP 2 Compare your questions and answers with those of another pair of students. As a group try to write a summary of one of the news stories.

Activity 6

Play textbook audio.
The tapescript for this listening appears on pp. 511–512 of this book.

EXPANSION:

A logical follow-up to this activity is to have Ss watch or listen to a newscast and bring in a summary the next day to report to the rest of the class.

The test for this unit can be found on p. 442. The answers are on p. 444 of this book.

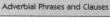

ANSWER KEY

Activity 6

Answers will vary. Here are some possible questions. You should be able to determine the correct answers from the tapescript.

Broadcast #1:

who Who toppled the government of Surinam? Who appeared on national television to announce the takeover?

what What happened in Surinam? What did the coup leaders promise?

where Where did they announce the takeover?

when When had normal holiday activities resumed? When did the coup leaders say elections would be held? When did the coup take place?

why Why did people think that Desi Bouterse is responsible for the coups? Why did the U.S. and Dutch governments condemn the coup?

how How did the coup take place? How was the change in government announced?

which Which governments condemned the takeover?

Broadcast #2:

who Who died yesterday? Who was Roosevelt Williams?

what What did Williams die from? What was Williams known for?

where Where did he do his work? Where will memorial services be held?

when When was he first diagnosed with AIDS? When will memorial services be held?

why Why was he well known? Why did some private organizations set up treatment programs?

how How successful were his efforts at AIDS education? How did he help other people with AIDS?

which Which churches will hold memorial services?

Unit 4

UNIT OVERVIEW

Unit 4 focuses on the meaning and use of passive forms. You may need to provide more practice with the form of passives if your class is encountering this for the first time. See *The Grammar Book,* Chapter 18 (pp. 343–360) for a more detailed discussion of passive voice.

UNIT GOALS

Review the goals listed on this page with your students (Ss) so they understand what they should be able to do by the end of the unit.

OPENING TASK

Ss enjoy this topic a great deal. It works well for pair or small group discussion. You can also use the task as a diagnostic activity by asking Ss to write and hand in their answers to the three unanswered questions from Step 1 and their group's opinions in Step 3, as such answers will naturally require the use of passive forms.

U N I T 4

PASSIVE VERBS

UNIT GOALS:

- To review passive form and meaning
- To know when to include the agent
- To use *get* passives
- To choose between passive and active

▶ OPENING TASK
Mysterious Places

Stonehenge is a circle of giant stones. It is located far away from anything else in the middle of a plain in southern England.

The Nazca Lines are a group of huge pictures drawn in the desert of western Peru that can only be seen from an airplane.

STEP 1 Some people believe that these places prove that beings from other planets have visited the Earth because no one can explain exactly how or why they were constructed. Read about either Stonehenge or the Nazca Lines. Develop at least one possible explanation for each of the three unanswered questions on the next page.

How were they constructed? Here are some clues.

STONEHENGE	THE NAZCA LINES
• The giant stones were transported from a great distance from an unknown place. • The stones are too heavy to be lifted upright or to be placed on top of each other. • A large number of people would probably be required to construct such a large structure, more people than were probably living in prehistoric Britain. • The distances between the stones are very precise, accurate to the millimeter	• The pictures can only be seen from the air. The people who built the designs could not actually see them. • A large number of people would be required to construct such large pictures. There definitely isn't enough water for so many people there, because it is one of the driest places on earth. • The designs are very precise. One image is a perfect spiral, accurate to the millimeter.

Why were they constructed? Here are some clues.

STONEHENGE	THE NAZCA LINES
• Some stones seem to point to certain stars. • Some stones seem to have some connection with the position of the sun at certain times of year. • Some stones may have had some connection with human sacrifices.	• Some pictures seem to have some mathematical or geometrical meaning. • Some pictures represent flowers and animals that are not found anywhere near the location of the lines. • Some designs look like symbols that are used to direct modern-day aircraft.

When were they constructed? Here are some clues.

STONEHENGE	THE NAZCA LINES
• It was already considered to be a mysterious place when Britain was occupied by the Romans in the first century B.C. • There is no historical record of its construction.	• They weren't discovered until people started flying over the area in airplanes. • They predate Inca civilization by at least 2,000 years.

STEP 2 Form a group with one student who read about the same mysterious place as you, and two students who read about the other mysterious place. Compare your answers.

STEP 3 In your group discuss this question: Are these structures proof that the Earth has been visited by beings from some other planet? Why or why not? Share your ideas with the rest of the class.

This focus assumes that Ss have had previous exposure to passive forms, and is intended as a review.

SUGGESTIONS

1. If it is clear from the Opening Task that Ss already have good control of the basic forms, you may decide to skip this focus and Exercises 1–5.
2. Alternatively, you may wish to cover it very briefly by asking Ss how to make passive sentences. Since in natural language we rarely transform active sentences into passive voice, you may want to avoid the common pedagogical practice of writing active sentences on the board and having Ss transform them. You can avoid this by starting with Exercises 3 and 4, and then coming back to this focus afterwards as a more inductive review/processing.

FOCUS **1**

▶ Review of Passive Forms

FORM

EXAMPLES	EXPLANATIONS
(a) The Nazca Lines **were discovered** by airplane pilots. **(b)** They **weren't discovered** until the 1930s. **(c)** How **were** such huge designs **built?**	*be* + **past participle** (+ *by* **phrase**) Form all passive verbs in the same way. Only the *be* auxiliary changes form. There is often no information about who or what performed the action, but when there is, it appears as a *by* phrase.
(d) Stonehenge **was** constructed of rocks that came from many miles away. **(e)** The Nazca Lines **were** made by removing soil and rocks to expose the different-colored soil underneath.	**Change *be* to indicate:** • singular or plural
(f) Stonehenge **was** constructed long before Britain **was** invaded by the armies of Rome. **(g)** The Nazca Lines **weren't** discovered until the 1930s because they **weren't** seen by people on the ground.	• affirmative or negative
(h) Mysterious structures **are** found in a number of places in the world. **(i)** Some **were discovered** this century. **(j)** Perhaps the reasons for their existence **will be** discovered with further research. **(k)** While they **were being** built, civilization was still very young. **(l)** Many theories explaining their existence **have been** proposed.	• time frame (*present, past, future*) and aspect (*simple, perfect, progressive*)
(m) The Nazca Lines **may be** destroyed, if further protection **can't be** provided. **(n)** Preservation efforts for all such mysterious structures **ought to be** started without delay. **(o)** Both Stonehenge and the Nazca Lines **might have been** used to predict astronomical events.	• modal information (*prediction, advisability, possibility,* etc.)

EXERCISE 1

Find ten examples of passive verb forms in the information provided on page 47 and underline them. Tell whether each form is:

a) singular or plural

b) affirmative or negative

c) present, past, or future time frame

d) simple, perfect, or progressive aspect

EXERCISE 2

Write the passive forms for the verbs provided below.

▶ **EXAMPLE:** construct (singular, present progressive) *is being constructed*

1. I forget (plural, past perfect)
2. establish (singular, simple past)
3. manufacture (singular, simple present)
4. obtain (singular, simple present)
5. require (plural, simple future)
6. discover (plural, present perfect)
7. make (singular, present progressive)
8. leave (plural, past perfect)
9. build (singular, simple past)
10. produce (singular, simple present)
11. send (singular, future perfect)
12. notice (plural, past progressive)
13. need (singular, simple future)
14. forget (plural, present perfect)
15. study (plural, present progressive)

Exercise 1

SUGGESTIONS

1. To increase student interest in this exercise, assign pairs and make it a contest. Who can find the most examples in a given period of time?
2. If you have access to an OHP, correct this exercise in class by making a transparency of p. 47 and underlining the passive forms as a whole class.

Exercise 2

This is a good exercise to do as a whole class. If you consider it too focused on grammatical terminology, combine it with Exercise 5 on the next page.

ANSWER KEY

Exercise 1

From p. 46: is located, be seen. From p. 47: were constructed; *Stonehenge:* were transported; to be lifted; to be placed; be required; was considered; was occupied. *The Nazca Lines:* be seen; be required; are not found; weren't discovered.

Exercise 2

1. have been forgotten 2. was established
3. is manufactured 4. is obtained 5. will be required 6. have been discovered 7. is being made 8. had been left 9. was built 10. is produced 11. will have been sent 12. were being noticed 13. will be needed 14. have been forgotten 15. are being studied.

Exercise 3

Do this exercise in a straightforward way as a whole class, or use it as a written quiz.

Exercise 4

This works well as a small group exercise. If your class is made up of a variety of cultural and language backgrounds, put Ss into single culture/language groups.

Exercise 5

If your class has a hard time coming up with creative sentences, have Ss do this in pairs. As an alternative, assign specific verbs for each student/pair to work on.

Workbook Exs. 1–5, pp. 16–18. Answers: TE p. 492.

EXERCISE 3

Use the information provided below to construct passive sentences.

▶ **EXAMPLE:** The Chinese invented gunpowder.

Gunpowder ___was invented___ in China.

1. Pakistanis speak Urdu, Punjabi, Sindhi, Baluchi, Pashtu, and English.
   Urdu, Punjabi, Sindhi, Baluchi, Pashtu, and English _____ in Pakistan.
2. The people of Sri Lanka have mined gems for centuries.
   For centuries gems _____ in Sri Lanka.
3. The French consider snails a great delicacy.
   Snails _____ a great delicacy in France.
4. People throughout Asia eat rice.
   Rice _____ throughout Asia.
5. Argentineans consume more beef per capita than in any other country.
   More beef _____ per capita in Argentina than in any other country.
6. Ancient Egyptians worshiped cats.
   Cats _____ in ancient Egypt.
7. The Japanese have developed a new system of high-resolution television.
   A new system of high-resolution television _____ in Japan.
8. Americans invented the games of baseball and basketball.
   The games of baseball and basketball both _____ in America.

EXERCISE 4

Working with a partner, make up five additional passive sentences about products or accomplishments of a national or cultural group that you are familiar with.

EXERCISE 5

Choose eight verbs from Exercise 2. Make an original sentence for each verb.

50 | UNIT 4

Passive Meaning: Agent Versus Receiver

Agent and Receiver in Active Sentences

subject	active verb	object	
agent **(a)** An employee	**action** found	**receiver** a wallet outside the office.	The **agent** is the **doer** of an action. The **receiver** is the person or thing that is affected by the action. In active sentences the agent is the subject of the sentence. The receiver is the object.

Agent and Receiver in Passive Sentences

subject	passive verb	(*by* + noun phrase)	
receiver **(b)** A wallet	**action** was found outside the office.	**(agent)**	In passive sentences the receiver is the subject and the agent is often not mentioned. When it is included, it occurs as a prepositional phrase with *by*.
(c) The wallet	was found	by an employee.	

EXERCISE 6

Read this article about the Nazca Lines. Underline all the passive constructions that you find. For each example of the passive that you can find, circle the **receiver.** If the **agent** is mentioned, draw a square around it. The first sentence of each paragraph has been done as an example.

FOCUS 2

These important concepts can best be introduced sequentially. Identify the agent and receiver first in active, then passive sentences.

Here are some simpler example sentences for your boardwork presentation of these ideas: *The carpenter hit the nail.* or *The teacher taught the students.*

ANSWER KEY

Exercise 6

The passive constructions have been underlined. *Receiver* and *agent* have been boldfaced and marked with R and A, respectively.

(1)**The Nazca Lines (R)** were not discovered until the 1930s, when **they(R)** were first noticed by airplane pilots flying over Peru's Atacama Desert(A).   (2)They consist of huge pictures, several kilometers in size, **that (R)** were drawn in the desert.   (4)**These pictures(R)** were made more than three thousand years ago by removing stones and dirt over large areas to expose the differently colored soil beneath. (5)The amazing thing about the Nazca Lines is that **none of these pictures(R)** can be seen by **people on the ground.(A)**   (6)They are so huge that **they(R)** can only be seen from a great height.   (7)**The pictures(R)** were constructed with incredible precision.   (8)**How such measurements(R)** were made(R) still hasn't been satisfactorily explained.   (9)It seems impossible that **the primitive construction techniques that existed three thousand years ago(R)** could have been used to create such gigantic, perfectly constructed designs. (10)Why were **these gigantic pictures(R)** made?   (11)Were **they(R)** intended to be used as offerings for the gods, as some people have suggested?   (12)Or, as others believe, were they (R)created as "direction signs" for visitors from other planets?   (14) **One thing (R)**is known: the reasons (R)for and methods (R)of construction have been destroyed by time(A) but the pictures (R) have been preserved for at least two thousand—and maybe even three thousand —years!

THE MYSTERY OF THE NAZCA LINES

(1) The Nazca Lines were not discovered until the 1930s, when they were first noticed by airplane pilots flying over Peru's Atacama Desert. (2) They consist of huge pictures, several kilometers in size, that were drawn in the desert. (3) They portray such things as birds, spiders, and abstract geometrical designs. (4) These pictures were made more than three thousand years ago by removing stones and dirt over large areas to expose the differently-colored soil beneath.

(5) The amazing thing about the Nazca Lines is that none of these pictures can be seen by people on the ground. (6) They are so huge that they can only be seen from a great height. (7) The pictures were constructed with amazing precision. (8) How such measurements were made still hasn't been satisfactorily explained. (9) It seems impossible that the primitive construction techniques that existed three thousand years ago could have been used to create such gigantic, perfectly-constructed designs.

(10) Why were these gigantic pictures made? (11) Were they intended as gifts for the gods, as some people have suggested? (12) Or, as others believe, were they created as "direction signs" for visitors from other planets? (13) No one knows. (14) One thing is known: The reasons and methods of their construction have been destroyed by time, but the pictures have been preserved for at least two thousand—and maybe even three thousand—years!

Exercise 7

Have students "take turns," with one student writing the passive sentences for 1, 3, & 5, and the active sentences for 2, 4, & 6, while the other student does active versions of 1, 3, & 5 and passive versions of 2, 4, & 6.

Workbook Ex. 6, p. 19. Answers: TE pp. 492–493.

EXERCISE 7

Write one active sentence and one passive sentence for each set of agent, receiver, and verb.

▶ **EXAMPLE:** **Agent:** the maid; **Receiver:** the money; **Verb:** find

active: The maid found the money.
passive: The money was found by the maid.

1. **Agent:** pilots; **Receiver:** the Nazca Lines; **Verb:** discover
2. **Agent:** Ancient Romans; **Receiver:** Stonehenge; **Verb:** can not explain
3. **Agent:** Lee Harvey Oswald; **Receiver:** John F. Kennedy; **Verb:** assassinate
4. **Agent:** beings from outer space; **Receiver:** the Earth; **Verb:** visit
5. **Agent:** parents; **Receiver:** their children; **Verb:** teach good manners
6. **Agent:** society; **Receiver:** social minorities; **Verb:** discriminate against

---

A N S W E R   K E Y

Exercise 7

Answers may vary slightly.

1. **Active:** Pilots discovered the Nazca Lines in the 1930s. **Passive:** The Nazca Lines were first discovered by pilots who flew over the area in the 1930s. 2. **Active:** Ancient Romans couldn't explain the origin of Stonehenge. **Passive:** Stonehenge couldn't be explained by the ancient Romans. 3. **Active:** Lee Harvey Oswald assassinated John F. Kennedy. **Passive:** John F. Kennedy was assassinated by Lee Harvey Oswald. 4. **Active:** Beings from outer space have visited the Earth. **Passive:** The Earth has been visited by beings from outer space. 5. **Active:** Parents should teach their children good manners. **Passive:** Children should be taught good manners by their parents. 6. **Active:** Society often discriminates against social minorities. **Passive:** Social minorities are often discriminated against by society.

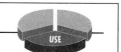

When to Include the Agent

Because we most often use passive verbs to describe situations when the agent is unknown or unimportant, we usually do not include agents (*by* + noun phrase) in passive sentences. However, sometimes it is necessary to include the agent.

EXAMPLES	EXPLANATIONS
	Include the agents:
(a) Many important scientific discoveries have been made **by women.**	• when the agent gives us additional new information.
(b) Radioactivity, for example, was discovered **by Marie Curie** in 1903.	• when information about the agent is too important to omit.
(c) This music was written **by a computer.** **(d)** That picture was painted **by a monkey.**	• when the agent is surprising or unexpected

EXERCISE 8

Identify the agent in each of these sentences and decide if it is necessary. Correct any sentences by omitting unnecessary *by* phrases.

▶ **EXAMPLE:** That symphony was written by a composer in the 19th century

Not necessary. (That symphony was written in the 19th century.)

1. The Nazca Lines were constructed by an unknown civilization approximately two thousand years ago.
2. The lesson was assigned by the teacher for next week.
3. This picture was painted by Picasso when Picasso was twelve years old.
4. My briefcase was taken by someone, but it was found and turned in to the Lost and Found Office by someone in my English class.
5. Many foreign students don't need scholarships because they are being supported by friends or relatives.
6. I would never guess that these poems were translated by children.

It is important to point out that these examples represent exceptions to the more general use of passive for situations where the agent is NOT stated. If you are pressed for time, you can skip this focus and Exercise 8, or only treat it if Ss notice and ask about examples where the agent is stated.

Exercise 8

Do this exercise as part of your presentation of Focus 3.

Workbook Exs. 7 & 8, pp. 19–20. Answers: TE p. 493.

ANSWER KEY

Exercise 8

1. *Not necessary:* The Nazca Lines were constructed approximately 2000 years ago. (*an unknown civilization* can be deleted)
2. *Not necessary:* The lesson was assigned for next week. (*teacher* can be deleted)
3. *Not necessary:* This picture was painted when Picasso was twelve years old. (*by Picasso* can be deleted)   4. *Not necessary:* My briefcase got taken, but it was found and turned in to the Lost and Found Office <u>by</u> <u>someone in my English class.</u> (second agent cannot be deleted—there is important information that the person was *someone in my English class*)   5. *Necessary:* Many foreign students don't need scholarships because they are being supported <u>by</u> <u>friends or relatives.</u> (cannot be deleted)
6. *Necessary:* I would never guess that these poems were translated <u>by children.</u> (cannot be deleted)

1. Start your discussion of this topic by asking some *get*-passive questions such as: *Who has/Have you ever gotten lost in a strange city?*
Has anyone in class ever gotten robbed?
2. Introduce the *get* passive as an informal variant of *be* passive (reviewed in Focus 1, p. 48). Contrast question and negative forms. (*Get* Passive requires *do*.)
3. Make sure Ss understand *Form* before going on to the use aspects of this structure.
4. Introduce use by explaining that sometimes we can use both forms and sometimes we can only use *be* passive.

FOCUS **4**

▶ **The Get Passive**

Forming the *Get* Passive

EXAMPLES	EXPLANATIONS
(a) John rides to work with a neighbor who works nearby. He **gets picked up** at the bus stop every morning. **(b)** John **gets dropped off** in front of his office. **(c)** He **should be getting picked up** in a few minutes.	In spoken or informal English, we can use *get* instead of *be* as the passive auxiliary
(d) **Did** John **get** picked up yesterday? **(e)** He **didn't get** dropped off at the usual place. **(f)** He **might not have gotten picked up** by the usual person.	Questions and negatives require *do* if the verb phrase does not contain a form of *be* or a model auxiliary.

Using *Get* Passive Sentences

EXAMPLES	EXPLANATIONS
(g) Kennedy **was** elected president in 1960. **(h)** He **got** elected by a very small majority. **(i)** The hospital **was built** in the 1930s. **(j)** NOT: The hospital **got built** in the 1930s.	The *get* passive is more common with animate (living) subjects, than with inanimate (nonliving) ones.
(k) Mariko **got married** last Saturday. **(l)** She **has** never **been married** before.	It emphasizes the action rather than the state.

EXERCISE 9

Decide whether *be* or *get* is more appropriate in these sentences. Sometimes either form could be correct.

▶ **EXAMPLES:** North America <u>was</u> settled by several European countries.

               John's car <u>got/was</u> damaged, so he had to take public transportation.

1. The Nazca Lines _____ discovered in the 1930s.
2. Scott _____ arrested on his way home from the football game.
3. New medicines are _____ developed that seem effective in fighting cancer.
4. That's really dangerous. If your leg _____ broken, don't blame me.
5. I don't think Luis and Karin will ever _____ married. They're too different.
6. Don't put that fish in the same aquarium with the others. It might _____ eaten by the larger ones.

Passive Verbs | **55**

Exercise 9

Do this exercise as part of your presentation of Focus 4.

Workbook Ex. 9, p. 21. Answers: TE p. 493.

ANSWER KEY

Exercise 9
1. were 2. got/was 3. being 4. get
5. get 6. get/be

This focus deals with a number of rather specific exceptions to the general use of passive. If you are pressed for time, you can simply point it out to students for their own individual study later and skip Exercise 10.

▶ **Special Cases: Verbs with No Passive Forms and Other Verbs with No Active Forms**

EXAMPLES	EXPLANATIONS
(a) Few changes **have occurred** at Stonehenge over the years. (b) The discovery of the Nazca Lines **happened** in the 1930s. (c) Some Nazca lines **seem** to be in the shape of flowers. (d) The purpose of the Nazca lines **has disappeared** under the sands of the Atacama Desert.	Some verbs don't have a passive form because they do not take direct objects. This category includes verbs such as: *collide, occur, happen, take place . . .* *appear, resemble, seem, look . . .* *emerge, disappear, appear . . .*
(e) **NOT:** A ceremonial function was had by these pictures. (f) NOT: Some animals are resembled by the pictures.	Even verbs that take objects, when they describe states, do not occur in the passive.
(g) The drawing of the Nazca lines $\begin{Bmatrix} \text{began} \\ \text{was begun} \end{Bmatrix}$ more than 2000 years ago.	Some verbs describe changes of state and can occur in the active with a passive meaning.
(h) Jeff **was born** in Kansas. (i) NOT: Jeff's mother **bore** him in Kansas.	A few passive verbs do not have active forms.
(j) The Nazca Lines **are located** (exist) in the Atacama Desert of Peru. (k) They **located** (found) the Atacama Desert on a map.	Some passive verbs have different meanings in passive and active.

Exercise 10

If your class has a hard time coming up with creative sentences, have Ss do this in pairs. As an alternative, assign specific verbs for each student/pair to work on.

Workbook Ex. 10, pp. 21–22. Answers: TE p. 493.

EXERCISE 10

Here is a list of some verbs that do not have passive forms. Choose five verbs and write a sentence for each one. Compare your sentences with those of other students.

appear	*consist of*	*seem*	*look*	*occur*
take place	*resemble*	*happen*	*have*	*emerge*
disappear	*vanish*	*collide*		

ANSWER KEY

Exercise 10

Answers will vary. These are some possible responses. 1. John **appeared** suddenly. 2. It **took place** at the party. 3. Patty **disappeared.** 4. America **consists** of 50 states. 5. Jack **resembles** his mother. 6. The bridge **vanished** in the fog. 7. This **seems** easy. 8. It **happened** at the Laundromat. 9. The car **collided** with the bus. 10. He **looks** tired. 11. A strange thing **occurred** at the party. 12. A problem **emerged.**

Choosing Passive Versus Active

As a general rule, it is usually better style to use active forms. But in some situations the passive form is preferred.

EXAMPLES	EXPLANATIONS
(a) Jan's purse **was stolen** from her locker at school.	Use passive instead of active: • if the agent is unknown
(b) The new library **was finished** about a year ago.	• if the agent is unimportant
(c) I had an accident yesterday. This other car went through a red light and hit me. My car **was** completely **destroyed.**	• if the agent is obvious from context
(d) Did you hear the news? Matt **was injured** slightly in the earthquake, but Jeff was O.K.	• to emphasize the receiver
(e) Passengers **are asked** to refrain from smoking. **(f)** The audience **will be encouraged** to participate. **(g)** Something **should be done** about the drug problem. **(h)** The present perfect tense **is used** to describe actions in the past that are related to the present in some way. **(i)** Water **is formed** by combining hydrogen and oxygen.	• to make general explanations, statements and announcements, or in scientific and technical writing.

EXERCISE 11

Why do you think the author used passive verbs in these sentences? There may be more than one possible reason.

▶ **EXAMPLE:** No one is permitted to enter the laboratory while the experiment is being conducted. *general announcement*

1. Reagan was first elected president of the United States in 1980.
2. There is a lot of controversy about the Nazca Lines, especially about why they were built and how they were constructed.

Passive Verbs **57**

FOCUS 6

Use this focus as an opportunity to remind Ss of the generalized preference for active voice in English.
Additional examples:
unknown agents:
My book bag got taken.
My bicycle got vandalized.

unimportant or obvious agents:
This room was painted last week.
We are being taught to use passive.

receiver is the most important:
Scott got arrested? Are you sure it wasn't Don?
No, I said your brother is getting married, not your mother!

Exercise 11

Do this exercise as a whole class discussion immediately following your presentation of Focus 6.

Workbook Ex. 11, pp. 22–23. Answers: TE p. 493.

ANSWER KEY

Exercise 11
1. Agent is obvious from context.   2. Agent is unknown/ to connect ideas in different clauses more clearly.   3. To emphasize receiver.
4. To emphasize receiver; agent is obvious from context.   5. Agent is unknown.

Exercise 12

S U G G E S T I O N S

1. This exercise can be assigned as homework, used as review or omitted entirely if you think that Ss have a good grasp of the reasons to use passive that they practiced in the previous exercise.
2. If you have access to an OHP, make a transparency of the passage and underline the passive constructions as part of your whole class correction.

3. They weren't even noticed until people started flying over the area in planes.
4. Was it John's brother who got arrested at the demonstration?
5. The house was broken into while the family was away.

EXERCISE 12

Read this excerpt from an introductory sociology textbook. Choose one paragraph, and underline all the passive constructions that you find. With a partner, decide why the author chose to use passive constructions.

CHAPTER 3: SOCIAL MINORITIES AND DISCRIMINATION

INTRODUCTION

(1) In most societies, certain **social minorities** are sometimes discriminated against by society as a whole. (2) Discrimination may occur because of a group's race, religion, ethnic or cultural background, sexual preference, or even the language that they speak in their homes. (3) Such groups are sometimes denied basic rights, legal protections, or access to the same facilities as the general public. (4) In many societies, discrimination is slowly being eliminated—at least in terms of legal and governmental policies. (5) But these changes have not come quickly or easily.

(6) The United States, for example, has made a great deal of progress in eliminating discrimination against some of its social minorities. (7) As recently as the 1950s blacks and whites were not allowed to get married in many southern states. (8) They were forced to use separate drinking fountains, rest rooms, and even schools and libraries. (9) However, as a result of active protest and political demonstration such discriminatory laws were changed, and segregation based on race is no longer permitted.

(10) But other groups have been less successful. (11) Women have made many gains in American society, but they are still paid less than men for the same kinds of work. (12) Gay people still face enormous legal and social discrimination. (13) They are not allowed to serve in the army or join organizations like the Boy Scouts; in many states they can be fired from their jobs if employers learn of their sexual orientation. (14) They do not have the same kind of basic legal protection for family relationships and property that the rest of society takes for granted. (15) Courts may still take children away from homosexual parents, or deny inheritance rights to lifelong partners when one partner dies.

(16) Conditions for all minorities in the United States seem to be improving, although it will be a long time before social attitudes catch up with the progress that has been made in legal protections.

A N S W E R   K E Y

Exercise 12

(1) are sometimes discriminated against
(3) are sometimes denied   (4) is slowly being eliminated   (7) were not allowed
(8) were forced   (9) were changed; is no longer permitted   (11) are still paid
(13) are not allowed; can be fired   (16) has been made

EXERCISE 13

Decide whether active or passive forms should be used in these sentences, and write the correct form in the blank. There may be more than one correct choice.

The age of pyramid-building in Egypt (1) _____ (begin) about 2900 B.C. The great pyramids (2) _____ (intend) to serve as burial places for the Pharaohs, as the kings of Egypt (3) _____ (call). Construction on the largest pyramid (4) _____ (start) around 2800 B.C. for Khufu, the King of the Fourth Dynasty, or Cheops, as he (5) _____ (refer to) by Greek historians. It (6) _____ (be) 482 feet high and 755 feet long. The Pyramids as a group (7) _____ (comprise) one of the Seven Wonders of the Ancient World. The other Six Wonders no longer (8) _____ (stand), and modern archaeologists (9) _____ (know) of them only through the descriptions that (10) _____ (write) at the time they still (11) _____ (exist).

EXERCISE 14

Decide whether active or passive forms should be used in these sentences, and write the correct form in the blank. There may be more than one correct choice.

The Taj Mahal in Agra, India, (1) _____ (build) for the Moghul Emperor Shah Jahan. It (2) _____ (design) to (3) _____

Passive Verbs | **59**

Exercises 13 & 14

These exercises practice all the focuses in this unit in an integrated fashion.

SUGGESTIONS

1. Precede these exercises with a general discussion of the photos, and make sure Ss can identify the landmarks and their location on a world map.
2. Ask Ss to name other famous landmarks. The list that they generate can be used in place of the suggested landmarks in Activity 1.

EXPANSION

Ask Ss to describe or bring in a photo of a landmark that is famous in their own country, but is perhaps not well known in the rest of the world. They can make a presentation to the rest of the class or to a partner. Examples of such landmarks are the Emerald Buddha (Thailand), the Mosque in Medina (Saudi Arabia), Borobudur (Indonesia), the Banff Hotel (Canada), The "Blue" Mosque in Mazar-i-shariff (Afghanistan).

Workbook Exs. 12–14, pp. 23–24. Answers: TE p. 493.

ANSWER KEY

Exercise 13

1. began   2. were intended   3. were called
4. started/was started   5. was referred to
6. is   7. comprise   8. stand   9. know
10. were written   11. existed

Exercise 14

1. was built   2. was designed   3. serve
4. consider   5. is made   6. intended
7. be located   8. copy   9. planned
10. consist   11. was used   12. was imprisoned   13. died   14. got
15. implement   16. was accomplished

UNIT GOAL REVIEW

1. Ask Ss to look at the goals on the opening page of the unit again.

2. Have Ss work in pairs to ask each other questions. Student 1 will keep his/her book closed while student 2 asks a question based on information in one of the focus boxes, or something more general. (Examples: *How do we form passive sentences? When/why do we use passive sentences? What's an agent? Can we use* Get *Passive?*) If student 1 cannot answer the question, student 2 must give an explanation.

3. Ss switch roles. Student 1 "finds" a question in his or her book and student 2 must try to answer it.

4. Circulate around the room and pick one or two questions to bring up to the whole class, either because you hear a lot of "wrong" explanations or because many Ss appear unable to answer it.

(serve) as a tomb for his beloved wife. Many people (4) _____ (consider) the Taj to be the most beautiful building in the world. The entire structure (5) _____ (make) of white marble and semiprecious stones. Shah Jahan originally (6) _____ (intend) for a second Taj to (7) _____ (locate) across the river from the first one. The second Taj was supposed to (8) _____ (copy) the original Taj in every detail except one: The seconed Taj, which Shah Jahan (9) _____ (plan) as his own tomb, was supposed to (10) _____ (consist) of black marble and semiprecious stones, instead of the same white marble that (11) _____ (use) for the first Taj. Shah Jahan (12) _____ (imprison) by his own son and (13) _____ (die) before he (14) _____ (get) a chance to (15) _____ (implement) his plan. His vision of two twin Taj Mahals, one white and one black, never (16) _____ (accomplish).

Use Your English

USE YOUR ENGLISH
Activity 1

ACTIVITY 1: READING/SPEAKING

The article in Exercise 12 discussed discrimination against social minorities in the United States. Share your ideas and opinions about discrimination with other students.

STEP 1 Read the article and discuss these questions with a partner or in a small group:

1. What is the main idea of this article?
2. What are some common reasons for discrimination mentioned in the article?
3. What examples does the article give of successful progress in eliminating discrimination in the United States?
4. What examples does the article provide about discrimination against women? Can you think of other examples?
5. The article discusses legalized discrimination and social discrimination. Name one example of each kind of discrimination against gay people.

STEP 2 Listed below are examples of some other social groups that sometimes face discrimination. Identify one example that you are familiar with and describe that discrimination to another student.

Koreans in Japan Turks in Germany Arabs in France Chinese in Southeast Asia Jews in Eastern Europe Hindus in Sri Lanka	Catholics in Northern Ireland people with physical disabilities people with certain political beliefs people with certain physical characteristics (fat people, short people, left-handed people)

STEP 3 With your partner think of one additional example and describe the discrimination that this group faces to the rest of the class.

STEP 4 Discuss whether there are situations in which legal or social discrimination can ever be justified. Report the results of your discussion to the rest of the class.

USE YOUR ENGLISH
Activity 1

A hot topic. Care may be needed in some classes to ensure that the discussion doesn't become too volatile. While students may feel comfortable discussing discrimination in other countries, they sometimes deny that there is discrimination in their own. Sometimes "minority" members and "mainstream" members from the same country will have very different (and heated) perspectives.

Discussions of discrimination toward gays and lesbians is another area where people have strongly held opinions. Though potentially controversial, these issues never fail to generate active discussions that involve even the quietest students in the class.

SUGGESTION

You can reduce the volatility of Step 2 by asking Ss to work with someone from another country.

Activity 2

This is a good diagnostic or testing activity.

VARIATION:

Have Ss make oral presentations to the rest of the class. See the suggestions for Exercises 13 & 14 on the previous page for other possible variations.

EXPANSION:

Use these structures as research topics for some web-based activities if you have the facilities to do so.

Activities 3 & 4

Use these as testing activities to assess student mastery of form and use of passive voice.

Activity 5

A logical carryover from the Opening Task, to be used if your class is particularly intrigued by their preliminary discussions.

EXPANSION:

Conduct a secret ballot at the end of the activity to see how many "believers" and "nonbelievers" there are in class.

ACTIVITY 2: WRITING

Write a report on the history of a famous structure or public monument. Include facts about its design, construction, and function, and why it is famous. Pick one of these examples, or choose one of your own.

The Eiffel Tower (Paris)
The Golden Gate Bridge (San Francisco)
The Statue of Liberty (New York)
Angkor Wat (Cambodia)
The Parthenon (Athens)

Latin American Tower (Mexico City)
The Imperial Palace (Tokyo)
The Temple of Heaven (Beijing)
The Chunnel (between England and France)
The Sydney Opera House (Australia)

ACTIVITY 3: WRITING

Have you ever had a day that was so unlucky that it made you wish that you had never even gotten out of bed? What happened? Was it unlucky because of what happened to you or because of something you did? Were you the "agent" or the "receiver" of your unlucky events? Write a paragraph that describes what happened on that day.

ACTIVITY 4: READING / SPEAKING / WRITING

Find out how one or more of the common items listed below are manufactured. If you prefer, you can talk about some other item you are familiar with. Report your findings to the rest of the class.

glass   molasses   silicon chips   rope   porcelain   paper

ACTIVITY 5: SPEAKING

Do you personally believe in flying saucers, UFOs, and visitors from outer space? Prepare a debate between people who believe that such things are possible and people who don't. Each side should present reasons and specific examples to support their opinions.

ACTIVITY 6: LISTENING

STEP 1 Listen to the following news broadcast and write a one-sentence summary of what the news broadcast is about.

_____

_____

STEP 2 Read the questions below and then listen to the news broadcast again. Answer the questions in complete sentences.

1. What was announced today?

_____

2. When did Velasquez probably paint the portrait?

_____

3. How did the painting get into the closet?

_____

4. Why didn't officials know about the painting's existence?

_____

5. Who authenticated the painting?

_____

6. What is being done now, as a result of this discovery?

_____

7. How much is the painting worth?

_____

STEP 3 Compare your answers with a partner's. Listen to the news broadcast a third time to check answers that you disagree on or are unsure about. Share your final answers with the rest of the class.

ACTIVITY 7: LISTENING

Listen to a national TV or radio news broadcast in English and write down five examples of passive verbs that you hear. Try to identify the receiver and the agent, if it is stated, and suggest why the passive form was used. If possible, have a partner listen independently to the same broadcast and then compare your answers.

Activity 6

Play textbook audio.
The tapescript for this listening appears on p. 512 of this book. Play the tape three times.

1. Have Ss write the summary after the first listening.
2. Have Ss read the questions before the second listening.
3. Have Ss verify their answers. For classes that have trouble with listening tasks, allow a fourth listening for Ss to focus on questions they still can't answer.

Activity 7

This activity will be challenging to students with poor listening skills. It is designed for classes that might find the previous activity too simple. For less advanced groups, you may choose not to use this activity.

The test for this unit can be found on p. 445. The answers are on p. 446 of this book.

TOEFL Test Preparation Exercises for Units 1–4 can be found on pp. 25–26 of the Workbook.
The answers are on p. 493 of this book.

ANSWER KEY

Activity 6
Answers will vary. Here are examples of probable answers:
Step 1: A previously unknown painting by Diego de Velasquez has been found in a storage closet in the Ministry of the Interior in Madrid.
Step 2: 1. A painting by Velasquez was discovered in a storage closet.   2. It was probably painted sometime between 1685 and 1700.   3. It had probably been put there during the Spanish Civil War.   4. It wasn't listed on any of the inventories of the ministry.   5. Experts at the Prado Museum authenticated the painting.   6. The ministry will do some "serious housekeeping."   7. The painting has been valued at over 1.5 million dollars.

Unit 5

UNIT OVERVIEW

Unit 5 provides a general review of one-word modal meanings and uses introduced in earlier volumes of the *Grammar Dimensions* series, and then focuses on the meaning and use of phrasal modals. Other units of this book deal with further aspects of modals in more detail. Unit 15 focuses on future time, Unit 16 on using modals to distinguish between prediction and inference. Unit 17 deals with use of modals in hypothetical constructions (also sometimes called "contrary-to-fact") ; and Unit 24 discusses other modal constructions used in past time frame. See *The Grammar Book,* Chapter 8 (pp. 137–160) for a more detailed overview of modals.

UNIT GOALS

Review the goals listed on this page so students (Ss) understand what they should be able to do by the end of the unit.

OPENING TASK

Note: The Opening Task allows Ss to try using the target structures and allows teachers to notice what kinds of help they may need. For a more complete discussion of the Opening Task, see p. xix of this Teacher's Edition.

SUGGESTIONS:

1. This particular task can be used as a diagnostic for both modals and causative verbs (which are discussed in Unit 18), by having Ss write and hand in their individual reasons and difficulties.
2. Alternatively, group lists can be generated in pairs or small groups and presented to the rest of the class.
3. If you are pressed for time, skip Step 3.

UNIT 5

ONE-WORD AND PHRASAL MODALS

UNIT GOALS:

- To review modal forms and uses
- To identify and use one-word and phrasal modals
- To understand formal and informal uses of modals

▶ OPENING TASK
Identifying the Pros and Cons of Immigration

Each year about 600,000 immigrants become new citizens of the United States. In addition to legal immigration, several thousand people enter or remain in the country illegally. For all immigrants, both legal and illegal, the move to their new country often involves a lot of difficulties.

STEP 1 Below is a list of reasons why people immigrate to a new country and a list of difficulties people sometimes face after they immigrate. Check reasons why you might immigrate to another country. Then try to add one more reason to the list.

REASONS	DIFFICULTIES
_____ People can't make enough money to feed their families.	_____ People have to learn a new language.
_____ People aren't allowed to practice their religion.	_____ People aren't able to forget their old customs.
_____ People have to serve in the army for a long time.	_____ Their children won't grow up the way they did.
_____ People are supposed to do what their parents want them to do.	_____ People have to take low-paying jobs because they can't speak the language well.
_____	_____
_____	_____

STEP 2 Check difficulties that you think you would face if you moved permanently to a new county. Then try to add one more reason to the list.

STEP 3 Discuss your responses with several classmates. Are there reasons or difficulties that everyone mentioned? Are there reasons or difficulties which apply to one particular country but not others?

Note: Focus boxes explain and give examples of each structure. For a more complete discussion of focus boxes, see p. xx of this Teacher's Edition.

This focus and Focuses 2 and 3 are intended as review. What each Ss already knows about modals may vary widely, so it's a good idea to do at least a cursory presentation of the material in these three focuses.

1. Elicit modal constructions through "real" questions. Then ask Ss how they might be transformed into negative or question forms. Some sample prompts:
   (one word modals): *Who can speak Chinese (Spanish/Lithuanian, etc.) in this class?*
   (phrasal modals): *Who is able to understand American movies? Who has to take the TOEFL this next year?*
2. Once you have elicited appropriate variants, move on to Exercise 1 and have Ss review Focus 1 as homework.

▶ Review of Modal Forms

Many one-word modals correspond to one or more phrasal modals with a similar meaning.

One-Word Modals		Phrasal Modals	
can/could	*may/might*	*be able to*	*be allowed to*
will/would	*shall/should*	*be going to*	*have to, have got to*
must		*ought to, be supposed to, had better*	

MODAL	AFFIRMATIVE STATEMENTS	NEGATIVE STATEMENTS	QUESTIONS/ SHORT ANSWERS
ONE-WORD MODALS *can/could may/might will/would shall/should must*	**(a)** Victor **can** speak Spanish. **(e)** Victor **should** speak English at school.	**(b)** He **cannot** speak it at school. **(f)** He **shouldn't** speak Spanish at school.	**(c)** Where **can** he speak it? **(d)** **Can** he speak it at home? Yes, he probably **can.** **(g)** **Should** he speak Spanish in school? No, he **shouldn't.**
PHRASAL MODALS WITH *BE* *be able to be going to be about to be supposed to be allowed to*	**(h)** Victor **is able to** speak Spanish. **(k)** Victor **was able to** speak Spanish.	**(i)** He **is not supposed to** speak Spanish at school. **(l)** He **wasn't supposed to** speak Spanish at school.	**(j)** Where **was** he **allowed to** speak it? **(m)** **Is** he **allowed to** speak it at home? Yes, he probably **is.**
PHRASAL MODALS WITHOUT *BE* *have to used to*	**(n)** Victor **has to** speak English in class. **(q)** Victor **had to** speak English in class. **(t)** He **used to** speak Spanish all the time.	**(o)** He **does not have to** speak it at home. **(r)** He **didn't have to** speak it at home. **(u)** He **didn't use to** speak English at all.	**(p)** Where **did** he **have to** speak it? **(s)** **Does** he **have to** speak it at home? No, he **doesn't.** **(v)** **Did** he **use to** speak English? No, he **didn't.**

have got to had better ought to	(w) He **has got to** speak English at home. (x) He **had better not** speak Spanish in class. (y) He **ought to** try speaking English at home, too.	These modals do not usually appear in questions or negative sentences. One-word modals are used instead.

EXERCISE 1

The forms of the modals in these sentences are incorrect. Identify the problems and write the sentences correctly.

▶ **EXAMPLE:** Has Victor to speak English?
　　　　　 Does Victor have to speak English?

1. Sunyoon hasn't to do her homework.

_____

2. Does Victor able to speak Spanish at home?

_____

3. Can Victor speak Spanish? Yes, he can speak.

_____

4. Where he is allowed to speak Spanish?

_____

5. Why he can't speak Spanish at school?

_____

6. Ought Victor to speak Spanish at school?

_____

7. Had Victor better speak English at school?

_____

8. Used Victor to speak Spanish?

_____

9. Does Victor allowed to speak Spanish in school? No, he doesn't allowed.

_____

10. Why he should speak English in school? Why he shouldn't Spanish?

_____

Exercise 1

Note: The exercises following each focus box provide meaningful practice with the grammar item presented in that particular box. For a more complete discussion of how to use the exercises, see p. xxi of this Teacher's Edition.

Workbook Ex. 1, p. 27. Answers: TE p. 493.

A N S W E R   K E Y

Exercise 1
1. Sunyoon doesn't have to do her homework.
2. Is Victor able to speak Spanish at home?
3. Can Victor speak Spanish? Yes, he can.
4. Where is he allowed to speak Spanish?
5. Why can't he speak Spanish at school?

6. Should Victor speak Spanish at school?
7. Should Victor speak English at school?
8. Did Victor use to speak Spanish? 9. Is Victor allowed to speak Spanish in school? No, he isn't. 10. Why should he speak English in school? Why shouldn't he speak Spanish?

FOCUS 2

This focus and Focuses 1 and 3 are intended as review. What each student already knows about modals may vary widely, so it's a good idea to do at least a cursory presentation of the material in these three focuses.

This particular focus reviews the "social" uses of modals that are practiced in more detail in Book 2 of the *Grammar Dimensions* series. Preface this discussion with a reminder that one particular modal form can have many different possible meanings, depending on the context.

For example:

Juan can speak Spanish (ability)
Can I help you (offer)
Can you close the door (request),
San Francisco can be cold and foggy in the summer (possibility)
You can't smoke here (prohibition)
Can you come to dinner tonight (invitation)

Social Uses of One-Word and Phrasal Modals

Modals are commonly used for many basic social interactions.

USE	ONE-WORD MODALS	EXAMPLES	PHRASAL MODALS	EXAMPLES	SPECIAL NOTES
making requests	*would*	(a) **Would** you open the window?			The one-word modals are listed in order of most polite or formal to most informal.
	could	(b) **Could** you turn down the radio?			
	will	(c) **Will** you pass the salt?			
	can	(d) **Can** you loan me a dollar?			
asking for, giving, or denying permission	*may*	(e) **May** I come in?	*be allowed to*	(h) You're **allowed to** bring a friend.	*May* is considered more polite than *can.*
	can	(f) Of course you **can!**		(i) You're **not allowed to** smoke here.	
		(g) You **can't** smoke here.			
giving invitations	*will*	(j) **Will** you come for dinner?			
	would	(k) **Would** you like to join us?			
	can	(l) **Can** you come to my party?			
making offers	*will*	(m) I'll do the dishes.	*would . . . like*	(o) **Would** you **like** me to do the dishes?	Use *shall* to make offers of action by the speaker.
	shall	(n) **Shall** I help with the dishes?			

68 Grammar Dimensions, Platinum Edition

Continued

USE	ONE-WORD MODALS	EXAMPLES	PHRASAL MODALS	EXAMPLES	SPECIAL NOTES
making promises or expressing intention	*will*	**(p)** I'll do it. **(q)** I promise I'll do it. **(r)** I'll do it, no matter what!	*be going to*	**(s)** I'm **going to** finish this, I promise. **(t)** I'm **going to** finish this whether you want me to or not.	*Be going to* expresses a stronger intention than *will*. See Unit 5, Focus 3, for more information on this difference.
making suggestions	*shall* *could* *can* *might*	**(u)** **Shall** we go out to dinner? **(v)** We **could** get Chinese food. **(w)** You **can** try that new restaurant. **(x)** Victor **might** try harder to speak English outside of class.			Use *shall* to suggest actions that involve both the speaker and the listener.
expressing advice	*could* *should*	**(y)** Victor **could** study harder. **(z)** Victor **should** study every day. **(aa)** He **shouldn't** speak Spanish at home.	*ought to* *had better* *had better not*	**(bb)** You **ought to** do your homework every night. **(cc)** You **had better** start working harder if you want to pass this class.	These forms are listed in increasing order of necessity. *Ought to* is rarely used in negative statements or questions.

One-Word and Phrasal Modals **69**

Continued

obligation, and necessity/ prohibition				USE
must	(gg) We **must** leave before 5:00. (hh) You **mustn't** tell a lie			
have to		(ii) You **have to** leave before 5:00. (jj) You **don't have to** work late if you don't want to.		*Have to* and *must* have different meanings in negative sentences: *must not* = prohibition *don't have to* = lack of necessity. *Have got to* is not used in questions or negatives.
have got to		(kk) You'**ve got to** stop spending so much money		
be supposed to			(dd) You **had better not** skip class. (ee) You'**re supposed to** do your homework every night. (ff) You'**re not supposed to** ask your roommate to help you with the homework.	*Had better* is an emphatic form. It is often used as a threat. It is used in affirmative and negative sentences, but is not used with questions. Notice that the negative form is *had better not*, NOT *hadn't better*.

EXERCISE 2

Look at the sentences below. Write the number of each sentence in the correct place in the chart to show how it is being used. Then, for each modal use, write one additional sentence of your own. Compare your completed chart to that of another student. The first three sentences have been done for you as examples.

FORM	USE
Sentences: Your Own Example: <u>Can you give me change?</u>	making requests
Sentences: #1	asking for, giving, or denying permission
Sentences: #3	giving invitations
Sentences: #2	making offers
Sentences:	making promises or expressing intention
Sentences:	making suggestions
Sentences:	expressing advice, obligation, necessity, or prohibition

1. May I have some cheese?
2. Shall I open a window?
3. Can you come to my party?
4. Would you help me?
5. Would you join us for dinner?
6. We could have Chinese food tonight.
7. We might try the Hong Kong Cafe.
8. Can you make me some coffee?
9. You mustn't forget John's birthday.
10. Aren't we allowed to watch television?
11. We don't have to study over the weekend.
12. You shouldn't stay up so late.
13. You ought to try harder in speech class.
14. Could you please turn down the radio?
15. Would you like me to help you with your homework?
16. Shall we go to Las Vegas for a vacation?
17. Shall I tell you the answer?
18. I'm going to pass the TOEFL, no matter what it takes!
19. I'll pay you back next Tuesday.
20. You'd better not leave.
21. Can you bring me a glass of water?
22. I can do that for you.
23. Victor can't speak Spanish in his English class.

One-Word and Phrasal Modals | **71**

Exercise 2

Do the exercise as directed or, alternatively, do the first part as a whole class discussion and then have Ss write other examples in pairs or small groups.

Workbook Ex. 2, pp. 28–29. Answers: TE pp. 493–494.

ANSWER KEY

Exercise 2
Examples will vary.
making requests: Sentences 4, 8, 14, 21. Can you help me? Could you turn down the radio?
asking for, giving or denying permission: Sentences 1, 10. Can I bring a friend to the party? May I come in?
giving invitations: Sentences 3, 5. Could you come to my house for dinner? Would you like to come to my party?

making offers: Sentences 2, 15, 17, 22. I could do it for you. Shall I help you?
making promises or expressing intention: Sentences 18, 19. I'll be on time. I'm going to do it for you.
making suggestions: Sentences 6, 7, 16. We could try to sing. Shall we have Chinese food?
expressing advice, obligation, necessity, or prohibition: Sentences 9, 11, 12, 13, 20, 23. You ought to study harder. You shouldn't be late for class.

This focus provides an overview of the modal forms that are focused on in Book 3. Cross-references to particular units are listed in the chart.

SUGGESTION:

1. The best way to present the focus is to have Ss close their books and for you to write example sentences on the board with meaningful, contextualized examples concerning issues familiar to the class.
   Examples:
   possibility: *Studying grammar can be very interesting.*
   impossibility: *You can't need more examples here!*
   future events: *We will have a test on Tuesday.*
   predictions: *It should be easy if you have done your homework.*
2. Then Ss suggest the meaning that is being conveyed by that particular context. It is important to introduce all possible meanings before asking Ss to do Exercise 3.

This focus and the following exercise can also serve as diagnostics to determine whether you will need to cover the other modal units in more detail.

FOCUS **3**

▲ **Common One-Word and Phrasal Modal Meanings**

Modals are also used to express important meanings.

MEANING	ONE-WORD MODALS	EXAMPLES	PHRASAL MODALS	EXAMPLES	SPECIAL NOTES
expressing general possibility	*can* *will*	(a) San Francisco **can** be foggy in the summer. (b) A good student **will** always do her homework before class starts.			See Unit 18 for more information.
expressing impossibility	*can't* *couldn't*	(c) You **can't** be telling the truth! (d) We **couldn't** be there already!			See Unit 18 for more information.
describing future activities	*will* *shall*	(e) Peter **will** be on vacation next week. (f) I **shall** pay you on Tuesday.	*be going to* *be about to*	(g) **I'm going to** spend a month in France before I start my new job. (h) **I'm about to** leave for the airport.	*Shall* is very formal in American English. *Will* is preferred. *Be going to* is discussed in Unit 15. *Be about to* is used to describe events in the immediate future.

Continued

MEANING	ONE-WORD MODALS	EXAMPLES	PHRASAL MODALS	EXAMPLES	SPECIAL NOTES
making predictions	*could* *might* *may* *should*	(i) I **could** be late. (j) I **might** be on time. (k) It **may** rain. (l) It **should** be sunny tomorrow.	*ought to*	(n) It **ought to** be sunny tomorrow.	Listed in order of increasing probability. *Ought to* is rarely used in negative statements or questions.
	will	(m) It **will** be sunny tomorrow.	*be going to*	(o) It **is going to** be sunny tomorrow.	
making logical inferences	*must*	(p) It **must** be raining, the streets are wet. (q) Bob isn't studying for the test; he **must** not be worried about his grade.	*have to*	(r) Denise **has to** be really sick because she didn't come in today.	These phrasal modals are not used in negative inferences or in questions.
			have got to	(s) Bob **has got to** be the thief. No one else had a key to the cash box.	
describing abilities	*can* *could*	(t) I **can** speak English now, but I **couldn't** do it a year ago.	*be able to*	(u) Jack **was able to** get tickets, but he **wasn't able to** go himself.	Differences in meaning and use of these forms are discussed in more detail in Unit 24.
describing habitual actions in the past	*would*	(v) When Mary was young she **would** pretend to be a fairy princess.	*used to*	(w) I **used to** speak Farsi, but I've forgotten a lot of the vocabulary.	Using *would* and *used to* implies that the situation no longer happens.

One-Word and Phrasal Modals   **73**

Exercise 3

Do the exercise as directed or, alternatively, do the first part as a whole class discussion and then have Ss write other examples in pairs or small groups.

Workbook Ex. 3, pp. 30–31. Answers: TE p. 494.

EXERCISE 3

Look at the sentences on the bottom of this page and on the next page. Write the number of each sentence in the correct place in the chart to show how it is being used. Then, for each modal use, write one additional sentence of your own. Compare your completed chart to that of another student. The first three sentences have been done for you as examples.

FORM	MEANING
Sentences: #1 Your Own Example: TOEFL questions can be very tricky.	general possibility
Sentences: #2	impossibility
Sentences:	future time
Sentences:	prediction
Sentences:	logical inference
Sentences: #3	ability
Sentences:	habitual actions in the past

1. It can be quite rainy this time of year.
2. You couldn't be hungry! You just ate.
3. I couldn't understand American TV programs a year ago.
4. I used to get frustrated when I watched TV.
5. Those naughty children will misbehave if you give them a chance.
6. I will be there at 5:00.
7. I may have to leave early.
8. Antonio got A's in all his classes. He has to be very smart.
9. I've been able to make friends in every country I've lived in.
10. It can't be midnight already! It seems like we just got here.

74 | UNIT 5

---

11. We should be there in twenty minutes unless there's a traffic jam.

12. Naomi must not have to worry about money. She buys really expensive clothes.

13. I'll graduate next June.

14. It might be too late to call John. He usually goes to bed early.

15. I would always have trouble going to sleep on the night before school started when I was a child.

EXERCISE 4

How are the modals being used in each of these sentences? Decide whether they express: request, permission, invitation, offers, promises, suggestions, advice, obligation, necessity, possibility or impossibility, future time, predictions, logical inferences, abilities, or past habitual actions.

▶ **EXAMPLES:** Can I ask you a question? ___request___

Can you speak Spanish? ___ability___

1. Will you open the door? _____

2. Will the office be open tomorrow? _____

3. I can't hear you. _____

4. You can't smoke here; it's a church. _____

5. You shouldn't smoke; it's bad for your health. _____

6. You really ought to see a doctor. _____

7. The doctor has just finished with another patient, and ought to be ready to see you in just a minute. _____

8. You walked twenty miles today? You must be tired! _____

9. You must leave at once if you don't want to miss the train. _____

10. I may be late tonight, so plan on eating dinner without me. _____

11. Can I speak to Dr. Martinez? _____

12. You may not leave before the teacher tells you to. _____

13. I'm interested in buying that car, but it could be too expensive. _____

14. Could you pass the butter? _____

15. Could you read when you were five years old? _____

EXERCISE 5

Underline the one-word and phrasal modals in this paragraph. Then identify the meaning that each modal is used to express (permission, necessity, etc.). The first sentence has been done for you as an example.

Exercise 4

This exercise reviews all the modal meanings discussed in Focuses 2 and 3, and therefore can be used as a review or as a diagnostic to see whether additional practice is necessary.

Exercise 5

If you have access to an OHP, make a transparency of the passage and underline the modals as part of your whole class processing.

ANSWER KEY

Exercise 4
1. request 2. future time 3. abilities
4. permission 5. advice
6. advice/necessity 7. predictions

8. logical inference 9. necessity
10. predictions 11. request
12. permission 13. predictions
14. request 15. abilities

► **EXAMPLE:** (1) *necessity*

(1) I'm not looking forward to this afternoon because I <u>have to</u> go to the dentist. (2) I have a broken tooth, and I can't eat anything tough. (3) I'm supposed to be there at three o'clock, and I mustn't be more than five minutes late, or they'll cancel my appointment. (4) So I guess I had better leave plenty of time to get there. (5) The bus is supposed to come every ten minutes, but it's often late. (6) I know that I ought to go to the dentist more often, but I really don't like to. (7) She's going to tell me that I have to take better care of my teeth. (8) I know I'm supposed to brush my teeth after every meal, but sometimes I just can't find the time. (9) After my appointment I won't be able to eat anything for six hours, and I'm not supposed to eat anything for three hours before my appointment, either. (10) I know I'm going to be hungry tonight!

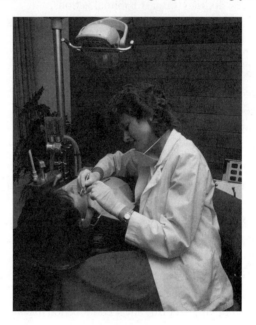

Exercise 6

If your class is not good at making up sentences "from scratch" let them work together in pairs or small groups.

EXERCISE 6

Write a sentence with a one-word modal about the topics below:

► **EXAMPLE:** an activity to avoid if you want to be healthy

You should avoid foods that are high in fat.

1. a daily responsibility

2. the best way to keep in touch with friends far away

ANSWER KEY

3. advice for a lazy student

4. something you know how to do well

5. a possible event next year

6. something that is against school rules

7. something you don't know how to do

EXERCISE 7

Work with a partner. Use the phrasal modals below to ask your partner questions about daily life and activities. For each of the phrasal modals listed below ask:

a) one *yes/no* question.

b) one *Wh-* question.

Report your partner's answers in full sentences.

The first one has been done for you as an example.

▶ **EXAMPLE:** have to: *Do you have to take the bus to get to school?*

No I don't. I get a ride with a friend.

What time do you have to leave home?

About fifteen minutes before class.

My partner doesn't have to leave her house until just before class because she gets a ride in a friend's car.

1. have to

2. be allowed to

3. be supposed to

4. be able to

5. be going to

EXERCISE 8

Restate the ideas you wrote about in Exercise 6 by using phrasal instead of one-word modals. Are there any modal meanings that cannot be expressed with phrasal modals?

▶ **EXAMPLE:** You should avoid foods that are high in fat.

You ought to avoid foods that are high in fat.

Exercise 7

This exercise should be done in pairs.

Exercise 8

To save time, do this Exercise in combination with Exercise 6.

Workbook Exs. 4 & 5, pp. 32–33. Answers: TE p. 494.

ANSWER KEY

Exercise 7

Answers will vary. Sample dialogs might be:

2. Are we allowed to smoke here? No we aren't. We can't smoke in the classrooms at all. Where can we smoke? There's a lounge on the first floor. I think we can smoke there. We aren't allowed to smoke in class, but my partner thinks that we can smoke in the lounge downstairs. **3.** Are you supposed to do any chores at your apartment? I'm supposed to take out the garbage. How often are you supposed to do that? I'm supposed to do it every day, but sometimes I forget. My

partner is supposed to take out the garbage every day, but sometimes he forgets to do it. **4.** Were you able to do the homework last night? No, I wasn't. I was too busy. Why weren't you able to do it? My uncle was visiting from Korea, and we went to a restaurant. My partner wasn't able to do her homework last night, because she had a visit from her uncle. **5.** Are you going to go anywhere on vacation? Yes, I'm going to visit Yosemite. How are you going get there? I'm going to go with a friend who has a car. My partner's going to drive to Yosemite with a friend during the vacation.

Exercise 8

Answers will vary. Possible answers include:

1. I have to make my bed. I have to go to work. **2.** You ought to write letters every month. You ought to call them on the phone if you have enough money. **3.** You had better study harder. You had better make friends with a really smart classmate. **4.** I am able to play the piano. I'm able to cook delicious bean soup. **5.** (No phrasal modals can be used to express this meaning.) I might take a vacation next summer. I could pass the TOEFL next semester. **6.** You aren't allowed to drink beer in class. You'd better not fall asleep in class. **7.** I'm not able to water ski. I'm not able to speak Lithuanian.

FOCUS 4

Use the first part of this focus as a review, especially if you are starting Focus 4 in a later class than the one that covered Focuses 1–3. Since Ss will have practiced "decoding" modal meanings in potentially ambiguous situations, show how clarifying modal meaning is a rationale for using phrasal instead of one-word modals.

1. Write sentence (l) or a class-related variant such as "*Bobo may not come to our party.*" on the board and ask for the meanings. If Ss do not suggest multiple meanings, offer prompts such as "*Yes, but can't it also mean . . .?*")

2. Introduce a context where it is necessary to have more than one modal meaning (necessity and permission or necessity and ability are good context possibilities). Elicit an incorrect one-word modal combination or provide an example such as "*I must can answer that question.*" and then have Ss correct it."

3. Ask Ss which modal meanings are being conveyed by the example sentences. (n) necessity and ability; (p) advisability and necessity; (q) possibility and ability; (r) necessity and ability; (s) advisability and ability; (t) future and necessity.

USE

Choosing One-Word Versus Phrasal Modals

Certain modal meanings and uses can only be expressed by one-word modals.

EXAMPLES	USE
(a) **Would** you help me? (b) **May** I have some cheese? (c) **Can** you turn down the radio?	Requests
(d) We **might** not have enough money. (e) We **could** fail the quiz if we don't study.	Some predictions
(f) **Can** you come to my party? (g) **Would** you join us for dinner?	Invitations
(h) We **could** have Chinese food tonight. (i) We **might** try the Hong Kong Cafe.	Suggestions
(j) A criminal **will** always return to the scene of the crime. (k) He **couldn't** have a TOEFL score of 600! He doesn't understand anything I say.	Expressions of general possibility or impossibility

In cases where both one-word and phrasal modals can be used, phrasal modals are preferred in the following situations:

To clarify modal meaning:

EXAMPLES	EXPLANATIONS
(l) Charlie **may not** bring a date	This one-word modal has two possible meanings: It's **possible** that he **won't** bring a date. He **doesn't have permission to** bring a date.
(m) Charlie **isn't allowed to** bring a date.	This phrasal modal has only one possible meaning: He **doesn't have permission to** bring a date.

To combine two modal meanings in the same verb phrase:

EXAMPLES	EXPLANATIONS
(n) A teacher **must be able to** explain things clearly. (o) NOT: She **must can** explain things clearly.	Two one-word modals cannot be combined.
(p) Poor people **shouldn't have to** pay the same taxes as rich people. (q) I **may be able to** get some extra tickets.	We can combine a one-word and phrasal modal.
(r) A firefighter **has to be able to** carry at least 250 pounds. (s) You **ought to be able to** speak French if you want a job in Paris. (t) I'm **going to have to** leave in a minute.	We can also combine two phrasal modals.

EXERCISE 9

What are the duties of citizenship? Decide whether people in society (a) **should have to do** or (b) **shouldn't have to do** these things. Add three more ideas of your own of what people should have to do and shouldn't have to do. Compare your sentences to those of a partner.

▶ **EXAMPLE:** People should have to send their children to school.

They shouldn't have to follow one particular religion.

1. send their children to school
2. follow one particular religion
3. go to work wherever the government sends them
4. work without pay on community projects
5. always obey their leaders
6. be required to vote in elections
7. report criminals to the police
8. get permission to leave the country
9. serve in the army
10. pay taxes

Exercise 9

Do this exercise as directed or use it for a small group discussion activity. Have a "recorder" write two or three of the group's answers on the board.

Exercise 10

Do this exercise as directed or use it for a small group discussion activity. Have a "recorder" write two or three of the group's answers on the board. Answers and opinions will vary.

EXERCISE 10

What does it mean to "speak another language"? Read the skills listed below and decide whether each skill is in category A or category B.

| Category A: A person **must** be able to do this in a new language in order to say that he or she "speaks the language." | Category B: A person only **should** be able to do this if he or she is a native speaker of the language. |

Write the letter of the category in the space provided, and for each category think of one more skill of your own.

1. _____ read a newspaper
2. _____ understand native speakers perfectly when they speak to each other
3. _____ understand native speakers when they speak to foreigners
4. _____ have a perfect accent
5. _____ never make mistakes
6. _____ discuss abstract philosophy
7. _____ take care of day-to-day needs
8. _____ read and understand literature and poetry
9. _____ speak correctly enough that people can understand what you mean
10. A_____
11. B_____

Based on your definition, do you consider yourself to be fluent in English? Why or why not?

Exercises 11 & 12

Do these exercises as part of your presentation of Focus 4 if your class was still having trouble with identifying modal meanings.

EXERCISE 11

What modal meanings are being expressed by the following sentences?

▶ **EXAMPLES:** Don't leave the cheese anywhere that the dog is going to be able to reach. (*future activity, ability*)

1. You're going to have to leave soon.
2. If Alicia has another cup of coffee, she's not going to be able to fall asleep.
3. The management isn't going to allow anyone to go behind the counter.
4. Most people have to be able to get a full night's sleep in order to be alert.

80 | UNIT 5

ANSWER KEY

Exercise 11
1. future activity, necessity; 2. future activity, ability; 3. future activity, permission; 4. necessity, ability; 5. necessity, permission; 6. advisability, ability; 7. advisability, permission; 8. necessity, ability

Exercise 12
Alternative possible choices have been indicated.
1. (a) must be allowed to (b) should/shouldn't be allowed to (c) should have to
2. (a) has to/has got to be able to (b) am not going to be able to (c) have to be able to (d) had better/ought to be able to

5. Horses have got to be allowed to exercise enough if they are going to stay healthy.

6. Some people feel that anyone who wants to become an American citizen ought to be able to speak English.

7. Children under sixteen years old aren't supposed to be allowed to work without their parents' permission.

8. You don't have to be able to swim in order to enjoy the beach.

EXERCISE 12
Combine the modal meanings given below.

▶ **EXAMPLE:** You <u>might be allowed to</u> bring a guest. (possibility, permission)

1. Use a one-word and phrasal modal combination:

(a) I _____ speak with the doctor. (necessity, permission)

(b) Dogs _____ ride on buses. (advisability, permission)

(c) Students _____ speak English in class. (advisability, necessity)

2. Use two phrasal modals:

(a) A firefighter _____ carry at least 250 pounds. (necessity, ability)

(b) I _____ not come to your party. (future, ability)

(c) In order for plants to be healthy, they _____ grow freely. (necessity, ability)

(d) You _____ speak French if you want a job in Paris. (advisability, ability)

EXERCISE 13
Make sentences that combine the following modal meanings. Compare your sentences with those of a partner and check your use of correct modals.

▶ **EXAMPLE:** future possibility and permission

We may be allowed to speak to the president.

1. advisability and ability

2. necessity and ability

3. future possibility and ability

4. advisability and necessity

5. necessity and permission

6. advisability and permission

One-Word and Phrasal Modals | **81**

Exercise 13

If your class has trouble creating sentences, have them do this exercise in pairs or small groups.

Workbook Ex. 5, pp. 32–33. Answers: TE p. 494.

Pronunciation:

Note: Point out the standard American pronunciation of common phrasal modals: *gonna (for going to), hafta (for have to), gotta (for have got to), and oughta (for ought to)* as part of your presentation of this focus.

Exercise 14

Omit this exercise if you are pressed for time. Alternatively, walk around and listen to pairs as they discuss. Check for common pronunciation problems (*like gonna to, have gotta to, etc.*)

Workbook Exs. 6–8, pp. 33–34. Answers: TE p. 494.

UNIT GOAL REVIEW

1. Ask Ss to look at the goals on the opening page of the unit again. Help them understand how much they have accomplished in each area by assigning each student or pair one or more modal meanings and have them write examples to share with the rest of the class.
2. Try assigning single meanings first and then, if needed, assigning double meanings (necessity and ability) . Alternatively, have them find examples of the assigned meaning from the focus examples in the unit.

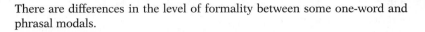

▶ # Formal and Informal Use of Modals

There are differences in the level of formality between some one-word and phrasal modals.

	MORE FORMAL	LESS FORMAL
ability *be able to/can*	**(a)** I'm **not able to** speak to you now.	**(b)** I **can't** speak to you now.
future activity *be going to/will*	**(c)** I **will** work a little longer.	**(d)** I**'m going to** work a little longer.
necessity *must/have to, have got to*	**(e)** We **must** go.	**(f)** We **have to** go. **(g)** We(**'ve**) **got to** get out of here!
advisability *should/ought to*	**(h)** You **should** tell your parents.	**(i)** You **ought to** tell your parents.

EXERCISE 14

With a partner, discuss the following topics using informal language. Compare the modals you used with those in your partner's sentences.

1. a daily responsibility
2. the best way to keep in touch with friends far away
3. advice for a lazy student
4. a possible event or occurrence next year

ANSWER KEY

Exercise 14
Answers will vary. Possible answers include:
1. You ought to do your homework. 2. You should call them every week. 3. You'd better not forget your homework. 4. We could travel somewhere.

Use Your English

USE YOUR ENGLISH

Note: The activities on these "purple pages" at the end of each unit contain communicative activities designed to apply what students have learned and help them practice communication and grammar at the same time. For a more complete discussion of how to use the Use Your English activities, see p. xxii of this Teacher's Edition.

ACTIVITY 1: SPEAKING

Below are descriptions of three people who have applied for citizenship in a new country. In a small group, pretend that you are a committee who has to decide who should be given a residence visa. Follow these steps:

STEP 1 Examine the applicants' reasons for wanting to immigrate. Decide whether they will be able to fulfill the basic duties of citizenship in the new country.

STEP 2 As a group, decide which applicant most deserves the residence visa and which one least deserves it.

STEP 3 Present your decision and your reasons to the rest of the class.

Applicant A	Applicant B	Applicant C
• belongs to a religion that is discriminated against in his or her country and will probably be imprisoned or executed because of those beliefs • plans on maintaining the family's religion and language • will not allow children of the family to go to public schools in the new country • has few job skills and may need to be supported by public welfare	• wants to earn higher wages and send the money back to relatives in the home country • has skills that are needed badly in the new country • does not intend to vote or become involved in the politics of the new country • believes in obeying the law, but will try to avoid national service	• was jailed for political activity in college and is now being threatend by the secret police • doesn't agree with the politics or government of the new country and doesn't believe in paying taxes • is engaged to someone from the new country • has skills that are badly needed in the new country

Activity 1

The priorities and reasons can be written as a diagnostic or testing activity to check understanding and use of modal forms.

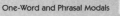

Activity 2

This activity can be done in pairs, small groups, or individually. Students may need help understanding want-ad abbreviations.

ACTIVITY 2: READING/SPEAKING

Below there are three advertisements for jobs available in clerical administration, computer programming, and sales.

STEP 1 For each job, identify

1. the things that an applicant must be able to do

2. the things he or she should be able to do (although may not be absolutely required)

3. some things that are neither required nor recommended, but are still characteristics that the "perfect candidate" might have

4. what an interested candidate has to do in order to apply for the position.

STEP 2 Would any of these jobs interest you? Why or why not? Compare your ideas to those of other students in the class.

PROGRAM ASSISTANT

Provide clerical and admin. support to five public program coord. involved in developing educational materials and providing training for hazardous waste workers.
QUALIFICATIONS: exper. operating word processing software and laser-printer hardware. Skill in establishing and maintaining master computer and paper files of program information. Interpersonal skills required to commun. with numerous instructors and staff on various university campuses. Organizational skills to estab. priorities. Related exper. working in a public service/public program atmosphere pref'd.
SALARY: $1799-2124/mo. with excel. benefits.
Send detailed resume to:
Personnel Office
Box 1012, 1066 Hastings St.
San Francisco, CA

LAW FIRM PROGRAMMER/ANALYST

Exciting opportunities exist in our office as we continue to develop, install, refine, and enhance automated solutions to law firm information processing. If you are a professional with 51years of programming experience, have a background in 4 computer languages, and have business software development exp., we'd like to hear from you. We seek individuals who strive for excellence in their work product, who prefer a challenging, fast-paced environment, and who are service oriented. Excellent communication skills are a must!
Send resume and salary history to:
Human Resources
PO Box 7880
San Francisco, CA

SALES CAREER OPPORTUNITY

College Textbook Sales McGruder-Hall Western Region Office has immediate openings for 2 Assoc. Sales Reps. These positions involve both office sales support & selling textbooks to professors on college campuses.
Qualifications include:
* 4 yr. College Degree
* Exc. Communications Skills
* Strong Organization Skills w/ Ability to Prioritize Multiple Tasks
* Desire to Move into Outside Sales Position
* Strong Motivation to Succeed
* Willingness to Travel
We offer excellent salary & benefits package. Please send resume to:
Sales Manager
McGruder-Hall Inc.
55 Francisco St., Ste. 738
SF, CA 94133
No Phone Calls Please

ACTIVITY 3: WRITING

Write your own want ads advertising the qualifications and skills necessary for these occupations. First decide on necessary and desirable qualifications, and then tell interested people what they should do in order to apply.

English teacher

firefighter

executive secretary/administrative assistant

United Nations translator

police officer

computer programmer

ACTIVITY 4: READING/SPEAKING

Look in the want ads of your local newspaper and find two examples of jobs that you think you would like. Describe the positions to the rest of the class, and tell why you think you would be a good candidate for the jobs.

ACTIVITY 5: LISTENING

STEP 1 Listen to the following conversations. Write the topic of each conversation in the chart below. Notice any modals that the speakers used and the context for using them.

STEP 2 Listen to the conversations again and list at least two examples of modals that you heard in each conversation. What meanings did these modals communicate? Write your answers in the chart

	Topic	Modals	Meaning
Conversation #1		1. 2.	1. 2.
Conversation #2		1. 2.	1. 2.

STEP 3 Compare your findings to those of other students.

- What differences in level or formality could you hear?
- Based on what you heard, think of one question you want to ask your teacher about using modals in English.

ACTIVITY 6: LISTENING

Listen to a conversation between two people. This conversation could be on television or a real-life conversation that you were able to overhear. Follow the same procedure that you used in Activity 5.

Activity 3

This activity can be done in pairs, small groups, or individually. Students may need help understanding want-ad abbreviations.

Activity 4

EXPANSION:

For certain classes (immigrants, new Americans), to give them additional information about life-skills, job hunting, etc., bring in want ads for the whole class, and have them do the activity in pairs or small groups.

Activity 5

Play textbook audio.

The tapescript for this listening appears on p. 512 of this book.

Allow for multiple listenings for each conversation.

1. Play it once for Ss to grasp the general situation.
2. The second time ask Ss to write down specific modal examples.
3. If needed play the conversation two more times, and then finally play them both together once more after both conversations have been done for Ss to check and confirm their answers.

Activity 6

SUGGESTION:

Prepare Ss by talking about "eavesdropping strategies" (pretending to read a book, writing a letter, reading something in another language, etc.) before you send them off to do this activity.

The test for this unit can be found on pp. 447–448.

The answers are on p. 449 of this book.

Unit 6

UNIT OVERVIEW

Unit 6 and Unit 7 are structured in similar ways. If you need to save time, try teaching both units—infinitives and gerunds—in an integrated fashion, following this order:

1. Focus 1, Unit 6
2. Focus 2, Unit 6
3. Focus 1, Unit 7
4. Focus 3, Unit 6
5. Focus 2, Unit 7
6. Appendix 3
7. *Alternative 1:* Focus 4, Unit 6
    Focus 3, Unit 7
    Focus 5, Unit 6
    Focus 4, Unit 7
    Focus 6, Unit 6
    Focus 5, Unit 7

Alternative 2: Many teachers prefer to present all three patterns at the same time in the following order.
    Focus 4,5,6, Unit 6
    Focus 3,4,5, Unit 7
8. Focus 8, Unit 6
9. Focus 6, Unit 7
10. Focus 7, Unit 7

UNIT GOALS

Review the goals listed on this page so students (Ss) understand what they should be able to know by the end of the unit.

OPENING TASK

SUGGESTIONS:

1. Use this task as a diagnostic by asking Ss to write full sentence answers to the discussion questions.
2. This task can also be done in small groups. Assign one question per pair/group and then do a whole class processing.

UNIT 6

INFINITIVES

UNIT GOALS:

- To review the form of infinitives and gerunds and the meaning of infinitives
- To understand and use sentences with verbs followed by infinitives
- To use infinitives as the subjects of sentences

OPENING TASK
The "To Do" List

TO DO	Check with Mary	Check with Charlie
• buy Mary a present	• Does she really	• remind about helping move
• say good-bye to Prof	understand why I'm	boxes to Mary's garage?
Montaigne	going?	• check with landlord about
• buy address book	• Is she still planning to	cleaning deposit
• buy suitcase	visit? When?	• clean the kitchen
• buy new jacket	• move boxes to her	• change name on the bill for
• get small gifts for my	parents' garage	the electric company
host family	• drive me to airport?	• get address of his old
• have farewell dinner	• have farewell	girlfriend (ballet dancer)— don't
with Mom & Dad	dinner? Where?	tell Mary!
• get traveler's checks		• get money he owes me
• reconfirm ticket and		
get seat assignment		

STEP 1 In two days John Tealhome is leaving to spend a year studying in France. On page 86 is his list of the things he needs to do before he goes, and the things that he would like his girlfriend, Mary, and his roommate, Charlie, to do for him. Look at John's "To Do" list and discuss these questions with a partner.

- What things does John still need to do?
- What things does he need Mary to do?
- What things does he want Charlie to do?
- What things does he want Charlie not to do?
- Has he forgotten to do anything?
- How ready do you think John really is?
- If he doesn't have time to get everything done, what things should he be sure to do, and what things could he decide not to do without creating problems?

STEP 2 Present your answer to the last question to the rest of the class.

If you feel your class can already identify infinitives and gerunds, try doing Exercise 1 first. Then have Ss review the focus as homework

FOCUS **1**

Overview of Infinitives and Gerunds

Infinitives and gerunds are formed from verb phrases.

EXAMPLES	EXPLANATIONS
(a) We need **to use** infinitives in certain situations.	Infinitives are formed by adding *to* before a verb (*to* + verb).
(b) Other situations require **using** gerunds.	Gerunds are formed by adding *-ing* to a verb (verb + *ing*).

Gerunds and infinitive phrases function like noun phrases.

EXAMPLES	EXPLANATIONS
(c) **Using gerunds and infinitives** can be tricky. **(d)** **To know which form is correct** requires some experience.	They can be used: • as subjects
(e) Some verbs require **using gerunds.** **(f)** With other verbs you'll need **to use infinitives.**	• as objects of verbs
(g) This unit and the following one will focus **on using** infinitives and gerunds. **(h)** By the end you should feel confident **about choosing** the correct form most of the time.	• as objects of prepositions
(i) But once you understand the principles, it's not **difficult to decide on the correct form.**	• with adjective phrases

EXERCISE 1

Underline the infinitive and gerund phrases in this passage. Tell how three of the forms you have identified are used in the sentence.

▶ **EXAMPLE:** Norman likes <u>to collect stamps</u>.

used as object of verb likes

(1) Norman likes to collect stamps. (2) He likes getting them from anywhere, but he is particularly interested in collecting stamps from Africa. (3) He has tried to get at least one stamp from every African country. (4) This hasn't always been easy to do. (5) He has tried writing to the post offices of various countries, but they haven't always responded to his request. (6) A friend suggested looking in commercial stamp-catalogs for hard-to-find stamps, and Norman has had pretty good luck finding rare or unusual stamps there. (7) He has also begun corresponding with stamp-collectors in other countries and has asked them to send him stamps when they first come out. (8) They are usually happy to do it and have urged him to do the same thing for them. (9) He enjoys learning about other countries and finds that collecting stamps is a good way to do this.

Infinitives | **89**

Exercise 1

S U G G E S T I O N :

If you have access to an OHP, a good way to process exercises like this is to make a transparency of this page to show to the whole class. Make sure Ss read the entire passage before doing the exercise.

Workbook Ex. 1, p. 35. Answers: TE p. 494.

ANSWER KEY

Exercise 1

(1) <u>to collect stamps</u> (object of verb **likes**)
(2) <u>getting them</u> (object of verb **likes**); <u>collecting stamps</u> (object of preposition)
(3) <u>to get at least one stamp</u> (object of verb **tried**)   (4) <u>to do</u> (adjective complement)
(5) <u>writing to the post offices</u> (object of verb **tried**)   (6) <u>looking in commercial stamp-catalogs</u> (object of verb **suggested**); <u>finding rare or unusual stamps</u> (noun complement)
(7) <u>corresponding with stamp-collectors</u> (object of verb **begun**); <u>to send him stamps</u> (object of verb **asked**)   (8) <u>to do it</u> (adjective complement); <u>to do the same thing</u> (object of verb **urged**)   (9) <u>learning about other countries</u> (object of verb **enjoys**); <u>collecting stamps</u> (subject of verb **is**)

1. Begin by writing **sentences k, l, & m** on the board (without the implied meaning in parentheses).
   Alternative class-related examples: *I had hoped <u>to finish</u> this project today. I had hoped <u>to have finished</u> this project yesterday. I had hoped <u>to be finishing</u> this project now.*

2. Check Ss' understanding of time relations.

3. Present other important contrasts:
   sentences c & d. Other examples:
   Students hope <u>to not have</u> homework on the weekend. Students hope <u>to have</u> free time.
   sentences f & g. Other examples:
   Students need <u>to be taught</u> grammar. Teachers need <u>to teach grammar</u> to their students.

FOCUS **2**

▶ Infinitives

EXAMPLES	EXPLANATION
(a) I want **to go to Tahiti next year.** **(b)** I am afraid **to open that door** because something bad might happen if I do.	Infinitives usually refer to the possiblity of an action occurring. The action has not yet happened.

Infinitives can contain the same information as any verb phrase.

EXAMPLES	EXPLANATIONS
(c) John decided **to go** to Paris. **(d)** Mary decided **not to go** with him. **(e)** We want **to find** another restaurant because they have asked us **not to smoke** in this one.	**Affirmative/Negative** Affirmative infinitive: *to* + verb Negative infinitive: *not to* + verb
(f) I need **to wash** my car. **(g)** My car needs **to be washed.** **(h)** Yoko intends **to become** active in student government, and hopes **to be elected** to the student council.	**Active/Passive** Active infinitive: *to* + verb Passive infinitive: *to* + *be* + past participle
(i) I would prefer **to have left** yesterday, but Lev would prefer to leave tomorrow. **(j)** We hope **to be living** in our new house by next summer.	**Perfect/Progressive Aspect** Perfect infinitive: *to* + *have* + past participle Progressive infinitive: *to* + *be* + present participle
(k) We want **to have washed** the car when he gets here. (We'll finish washing the car before he gets here.) **(l)** We want **to be washing** the car when he gets here. (We'll start washing the car before he gets here.) **(m)** We want **to wash** the car when he gets here. (We'll start washing the car after he gets here.)	Aspect tells us when the infinitive happens in relation to the main verb.

EXERCISE 2

Complete the sentences by expressing the idea in the infinitive as a verb phrase. Be sure to include all the information about time, aspect, and active or passive in your verb phrase.

▶ **EXAMPLE:** I hope **to be elected** to the student council.

I hope that I <u>will be elected to the student council.</u>

1. Morris claims **to have been born** in Russia.

   Morris claims that he _____ .

2. We expected you **to have done** the assignment already.

   We expected that you _____ .

3. The teacher reminded the students **not to forget** the homework.

   The teacher said, "_____ ."

4. We expected Hani **to be studying** when we got home.

   We expected that Hani would _____ .

5. My sister is never happy **to be left alone** on a Saturday night.

   If my sister _____ , she is never happy.

EXERCISE 3

Complete the sentences by expressing the underlined clause as an infinitive phrase. Be sure to include all the information about time, aspect, and active or passive in your infinitive phrase.

▶ **EXAMPLE:** I hope that I <u>will pass the TOEFL next month.</u>

I hope <u>to pass the TOEFL next month.</u>

1. Peter has the optimistic hope that <u>he will have finished the report by next week.</u>

   Peter hopes _____ by next week.

2. A strict teacher requires that <u>all students stop talking when class begins.</u>

   A strict teacher requires all students _____ .

3. The doctor told his patient: "<u>Don't take this medicine more than twice a day.</u>"

   The doctor reminded his patient _____ .

4. We thought that <u>the children would be sleeping</u> when we got home.

   We expected _____ when we got home.

Exercises 2 & 3

Do these exercises as part of your presentation of Focus 2 or use the answers to provide more examples of different infinitive forms.

ANSWER KEY

Exercise 2

1. was born in Russia.   2. had already done the assignment.   3. "Don't forget to do the homework."   4. be studying when we got home.   5. is left alone

Exercise 3

1. to have finished the report   2. to stop talking when class begins.   3. not to take this medicine more than twice a day.   4. the children to be sleeping.   5. being bothered while he is doing his homework.

Exercise 4

Have Ss report the partner's answers either orally to the rest of the class or in written form for you to evaluate.

Workbook Exs. 2 & 3, pp. 36–37. Answers: TE p. 494.

---

5. When <u>my brother is bothered while he is doing his homework</u>, he doesn't like it.

My brother never likes _____.

EXERCISE 4

Interview a partner to get two or three answers for each of these questions.

▶ **EXAMPLES:** What things do your teachers expect you **to do?**

They expect me to speak up in class.

What things do your teachers expect you **not to do?**

They expect me not to copy my homework from other students.

1. What things does your partner's family expect him or her **to do?**

What things do they expect him or her **not to do?**

2. How does your partner like **to treat** people he or she has just met?

How does your partner like **to be treated** by his or her teachers?

3. What things do your partner's teachers expect him or her **to do** at the beginning of class?

What things do teachers expect your partner **to have done** before the beginning of class?

4. What does your partner plan **to do** when school ends?

What does your partner plan **to be doing** when school ends?

ANSWER KEY

Exercise 4

Answers will vary. Possible answers include:
1. (a) They expect me to study hard.
(b) They expect him not to waste his time.
2. (a) I like to treat them politely.   (b) I like to be treated with respect.   3. (a) They expect me to stop talking with my friends.
(b) They expect me to have done my homework before class.   4. (a) I plan to go home for a visit.   (b) I plan to be saying good-bye to my friends and teachers.

▶ **Noun or Pronoun
Plus Infinitive**

FOCUS 3

Try doing Exercise 5 first. If your students don't have trouble, you can assign the focus for review at home. Additional examples: *Amy wants to do the work.* (She will do it.) *Amy want us to do the work.* (We will do it, not Amy.)

EXAMPLES	IMPLIED MEANING	EXPLANATIONS
(a) Norman wants **to collect foreign stamps.** **(b)** Norman want **us to collect foreign stamps.**	**Norman** will collect the stamps. **We** will collect the stamps.	Sometimes it is necessary to identify who is performing the action described by the infinitive.
(c) This question is easy **to answer.**	It's easy for everyone.	*to* + verb: The performer of the infinitive is usually the same as the subject of the main verb or "everybody."
(d) This question is easy **for experts to understand.** **(e)** The problem was difficult **for him to solve.**	It's only easy for experts; it's not easy for other people. He had difficulty, but she didn't.	*(for)* + noun phrase + *to* + verb: The performer of the infinitive can be a noun or an object pronoun (*him, us, etc.*).

EXAMPLES	EXPLANATIONS
(f) Norman **reminded us to give** him the stamps. **(g)** NOT: Norman **reminded to give** him the stamps.	Certain main verbs require using noun or pronoun + infinitive. (See Focus 5.)
(h) Infinitives are difficult **for students to understand.** **(i)** NOT: Infinitives are difficult **students to understand.**	With certain verbs (see Focus 6) and adjectives, the noun/pronoun + infinitive **must** occur with *for.*

Exercise 5

See the comments for Focus 3 about doing this exercise before presenting the focus.

Workbook Ex. 4, p. 37. Answers: TE p. 494.

EXERCISE 5

In these sentences identify who performs the action described by the highlighted infinitive.

▶ **EXAMPLES:**   We were expecting Ilana **to arrive** before now.

Ilana.

We were asked **to bring** presents to the party.

We.

1. Malcolm claims **to be speaking** for the entire class.
2. This hotel requires people **to turn** in their room keys by 11.00.
3. Wendy requested her students **to bring** their books to class.
4. My sister promised **to stay** after the party.
5. Gladstone intends **to lose** thirty pounds by Christmas.
6. The child convinced his friend **to put** a frog in the teacher's desk.
7. Norman wasn't allowed **to stay up** late when he was a child.
8. My parents encouraged all their children **to start working** part-time while they were still in high school.

ANSWER KEY

Exercise 5

1. Malcolm is speaking .   2. People turn in their room keys.   3. Her students will bring their book .   4. My sister will stay after the party.   5. Gladstone will lose 30 pounds by Christmas.   6. The friend put a frog in the teacher's desk.   7. Norman didn't stay up late.   8. The children started working.

Verbs Followed by Infinitives: Pattern 1

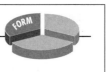

Pattern 1: Verb + Infinitive

EXAMPLES	EXPLANATION
(a) I **decided to go** shopping but I **neglected to bring** my checkbook.	With certain verbs the infinitive immediately follows the main verb.
(b) Peter **tried to help** Denise, but she **refused to accept.**	
(c) She **seemed to have** too much work, but she **was** only **pretending to be** busy.	

EXERCISE 6

There are seventeen Pattern 1 verbs in the following paragraph. Identify them and write them in the blanks.

(1) The Acme Stamp Company agreed to send Norman some stamps, but when he got them they didn't appear to be in good condition. (2) The company claimed to be reputable, but Norman still felt the stamps were bad. (3) He didn't care to pay good money for bad stamps and he felt that he deserved to get a refund. (4) So he decided to phone the company directly. (5) He demanded to speak to the manager. (6) The manager pretended to be concerned, but he hesitated to make any firm promises about refunds. (7) The company offered to exchange the stamps, but Norman refused to accept the offer. (8) All the stamps from that company seemed to be of poor quality. (9) The company also tended to be very slow in filling orders. (10) Norman has learned to make sure a company is reputable before placing a large order with them. (11) He neglected to do this with the Acme Stamp Company. (12) Norman still hopes to get a refund. (13) He is waiting to see if the company will give him one before he files a formal complaint with the post office.

1. *agree*
2. *appear*
3. _____
4. _____
5. _____
6. _____
7. _____
8. _____
9. _____
10. _____
11. _____
12. _____
13. _____
14. _____
15. _____
16. _____
17. _____

Infinitives | **95**

FOCUS 4

Most teachers choose to present Focuses 4, 5, and 6 in a similar way in the same class period. Present this pattern in a straightforward manner and then do Exercise 6.

Exercise 6

S U G G E S T I O N S :

1. Let students choose whether they want to work in pairs or individually.
2. Make the exercise a game by seeing who can find all 17 the fastest. Give prizes.

A N S W E R   K E Y

Exercise 6

1. agreed 2. appear 3. claimed
4. care 5. deserved 6. decided
7. demanded 8. pretended

9. hesitated 10. offered 11. refused
12. seemed 13. tended 14. learned
15. neglected 16. hopes 17. waiting

Exercise 7

If Ss have difficulty with creating sentences, have them do this exercise in pairs. You can shorten the time needed by having Ss work on three or four.

Exercise 8

Have Ss report the partner's answers either orally to the rest of the class or in written form for you to evaluate.

Workbook Exs. 5 & 6, pp. 38–39. Answers: TE pp. 494–495.

EXERCISE 7

Complete these sentences with infinitive phrases. Express your real opinion. Compare your answers with other students'.

▶ **EXAMPLE:** An honest person should never pretend . . .

   to be something that he or she really isn't.

1. A good parent should never neglect . . .
2. Most children in elementary school learn . . .
3. Most poor people can't afford . . .
4. The world situation today seems . . .
5. Shy students sometimes hesitate . . .
6. Selfish people rarely offer . . .
7. A good friend should never refuse . . .
8. Criminals deserve . . .
9. Most children hope . . .
10. In general, good students tend . . .
11. Most American teenagers can't wait . . .
12. Most good teachers seem . . .
13. An honest person should never agree . . .
14. Excellent athletes often appear . . .

EXERCISE 8

Interview a partner and find out about five of the following topics. Report your information to the rest of the class in full sentences.

▶ **EXAMPLE:** My partner often neglects to do her homework.

1. a responsibility he or she often neglects to do
2. something he or she learned to do in English class
3. something he or she can't afford to do
4. a kind of assistance that she or he would never hesitate to accept
5. something he or she would refuse to do, no matter how much she or he were paid to do it
6. a reward she or he thinks he or she deserves to receive
7. how he or she tends to behave in a room full of strangers
8. something he or she would pretend to do as a child
9. how people in this class appeared to be on the first day of school
10. a famous person she or he would never care to meet

ANSWER KEY

Exercise 7

Answers will vary. Possible answers include:
1. to give his child a good education/to make sure his children are healthy 2. to read and write/ to follow instructions 3. to take foreign vacations/ to buy whatever they want 4. to be getting worse and worse/to be improving 5. to raise their hands in class/to answer questions voluntarily 6. to help other people/to share their money or possessions with others 7. to help a friend in trouble/to spend time with his friends 8. to be punished for their crimes/ to get a fair trial 9. to become wealthy and famous/to live in a happy family 10. to think for themselves/to ask questions about things they don't understand 11. to become adults/to be old enough to drive a car 12. to like and respect their students/to know answers for their students' questions 13. to tell a lie/to commit a crime 14. to perform difficult actions effortlessly/to be competing against themselves

Exercise 8

Answers will vary. Possible answers include:
1. My partner often neglects to do her homework. 2. My partner learned to ask questions when she doesn't understand. 3. My partner can't afford to phone her parents very often. 4. My partner would never hesitate to accept help from a friend. 5. My partner would refuse to steal money from a friend. 6. My partner thinks he deserves to get an A in this class. 7. My partner tends to be shy in a room full of strangers. 8. My partner pretended to be invisible. 9. They appeared to be curious and friendly. 10. My partner would never care to meet Madonna.

Verbs Followed by Infinitives: Pattern 2

Pattern 2: Verb + Noun/Object Pronoun + Infinitive

EXAMPLES	EXPLANATIONS
(a) Other stamp collectors have **advised Norman to order** stamps from catalogs. (b) They **warned him not to spend** a lot of money unless he could **trust the stamp company to send** genuine stamps.	Some verbs are followed by a noun/object pronoun plus infinitive. They describe situations where the subject causes or influences someone or something else to perform the action described by the infinitive.

Verbs that occur only with this pattern are:

advise	convince	hire	persuade	tell
allow	encourage	invite	remind	trust
cause	forbid	order	require	urge
command	force	permit	teach	warn

EXERCISE 9

Create sentences using the cues given.

▶ **EXAMPLES:** (advise/study) My parents advised me to study English.

(force/cancel) The heavy fog forced the airport to cancel all flights.

1. remind/pay
2. warn/not forget
3. convince/help
4. hire/work
5. require/pay
6. forbid/marry
7. invite/join
8. teach/speak
9. allow/leave
10. order/send
11. urge/vote
12. trust/spend
13. tell/eat
14. encourage/ask
15. force/leave

Most teachers choose to present Focuses 4, 5, and 6 in a similar way in the same class period.

Exercise 9

If Ss have trouble thinking of sentences, try putting them in pairs. Make sure they know the meaning of all the listed verbs before starting. You can make this exercise easier by assigning students only two or three sentences to work on.

Workbook Ex. 7, p. 39. Answers TE p. 495.

ANSWER KEY

Exercise 9

Answers will vary widely.
1. My friend reminded me to pay him the money I owed him. 2. The doctor warned me not to forget to take my medicine. 3. John convinced Charlie to help him move his boxes. 4. We hired a secretary to work on that big project. 5. The government requires people to pay fines if they break traffic laws. 6. My parents forbid me to marry someone with a different religion. 7. Let's invite Nancy to join us at the party. 8. Our teacher taught us to speak clearly. 9. They wouldn't allow the students to leave the room until the test was finished. 10. The boss has ordered me to send this by express mail. 11. The president urged everyone to vote for him. 12. My parents trust me to spend my money wisely. 13. The doctor told me to eat less fatty foods. 14. Good teachers encourage their students to ask questions. 15. I don't want to force you to leave before you're ready.

Most teachers choose to present Focuses 4, 5, and 6 in a similar way in the same class period.

Exercise 10

Have Ss report the partner's answers either orally to the rest of the class or in written form for you to evaluate.

Workbook Exs. 8 & 9, pp. 40–42. Answers: TE p. 495.

 FOCUS **6**

Verbs Followed by Infinitives: Pattern 3

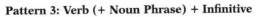

Pattern 3: Verb (+ Noun Phrase) + Infinitive

EXAMPLES	EXPLANATIONS
(a) We **expect to leave** in an hour, and we **expect you to come** with us. (b) Norman **wants to get** stamps from every country, and he **wants us to help** him.	Many verbs can be followed by either an infinitive or a noun phrase plus infinitive.
(c) Mary's father **arranged for John to get** a cheap ticket. (d) He never **intended for Mary to be** unhappy.	A few verbs of this kind must use *for* before the noun phrase. Verbs that follow this pattern are: *arrange, intend, consent, afford*.

EXERCISE 10

Interview other students in the class about one of the following topics. Report your answers in full sentences.

▶ **EXAMPLES:**   My partner likes to do the dishes, but he prefers someone else to do the cooking.

My partner needs to write a statement of purpose for her university application, but she needs a native English speaker to check over her grammar.

1. things they **like to do** versus things they **like someone else to do**
2. things they **expect to do** versus things they **expect someone else to do**
3. things they have **asked to do** versus things they have **asked someone else to do**
4. things they **need to do** versus things they **need someone else to do**
5. things they have **arranged to do** versus things they have **arranged for other people to do**

ANSWER KEY

Exercise 10

Answers will vary. Possible answers include:
1. My partner likes to cook, but he likes someone else to do the dishes.   2. My partner expects to work in the same kind of business as his uncle after he finishes school, and he expects his uncle to help him get a job.   3. My partner has asked to leave the room and he has asked me to go with him.   4. My partner needs to get a haircut, but he needs someone else to cut his hair.   5. My partner has arranged to leave on vacation right after school, and she has arranged for me to pick up her grade report.

EXERCISE 11

Combine these sentence pairs by replacing **"this"** with an infinitive phrase made from the information in the first sentence.

▶ **EXAMPLE:** John will spend a year in France. Mary doesn't want **this.**

Mary doesn't want John to spend a year in France.

1. John will write a long letter once a week. Mary has requested **this.**
2. John might postpone his trip until next year. Mary would prefer **this.**
3. She will try to visit him while he's there. She has decided **this.**
4. She was upset by the news of his plans. He didn't expect **this.**
5. John got a very cheap ticket. Mary's father arranged **this.**
6. John didn't apply for a passport. He neglected **this.**
7. John will report to the police when he arrives. French law requires **this.**
8. Mary will begin to study French herself. John has encouraged **this.**
9. Mary feels hurt that John is leaving. John never intended **this.**

Exercise 11

This exercise integrates verbs from all three patterns covered in Focuses 4–6. It is a good exercise to assign for homework for Ss to hand in.

ANSWER KEY

Exercise 11

1. Mary has requested John to write a long letter once a week.   2. Mary would prefer (for) John to postpone his trip until next year.   3. She has decided to visit him while he's there.   4. He didn't expect her to be upset by the news of his plans.   5. Mary's father arranged for John to get a very cheap ticket.   6. John neglected to apply for a passport.   7. French law requires John to report to the police when he arrives.   8. John has encouraged Mary to begin to study French herself.   9. John never intended for Mary to feel hurt that he is leaving.

You may wish to omit this Focus for lower level classes.

Other examples: *Students can be relied upon to ask a lot of questions. We were instructed to fill out the forms completely.*

Exercise 12

If Ss have trouble thinking of sentences, try putting them in pairs. You can make this exercise easier by assigning Ss only two or three sentences to work on.

Workbook Ex. 10, p. 42. Answers: TE p. 495.

FOCUS **7**

Using Infinitives with Passive Verbs

EXAMPLES	EXPLANATION
(a) **People warned Norman not to pay** a lot of money for stamps from unfamiliar companies. (b) **Norman was warned not to pay** a lot of money.	Pattern 2 and Pattern 3 verbs (except those that require *for*) can be used in passive sentences.

EXERCISE 12

Complete these sentences with infinitives. Use real information that expresses your true opinion. Compare your ideas with those of other students in the class.

1. Most people can be trusted . . .
2. Children should be allowed . . .
3. All teachers should be encouraged . . .
4. Noisy people should be told . . .
5. Teenagers should be warned . . .
6. Students should be expected . . .
7. Guests should be invited . . .
8. Rich people should be required . . .

ANSWER KEY

Exercise 12

Answers will vary widely. Possible answers include:
1. to do the right thing. 2. to ask questions about everything. 3. to help their students. 4. to be more considerate of others. 5. to say no to drugs. 6. to ask questions when they don't understand. 7. to make themselves at home. 8. to contribute to charities.

FOCUS 8

Infinitives as Subjects of a Sentence

AWKWARD	BETTER	EXPLANATION
(a) **To collect stamps** is fun.	**(b)** **It's** fun **to collect stamps.**	Infinitive phrases can be used as subjects in a sentence. We usually begin such sentences with *it* and put the infinitive phrase at the end of the sentence.
(c) **To have been introduced to you** is an honor.	**(d)** **It's** an honor **to have been introduced to you.**	
(e) **For John to study in France** is a good idea.	**(f)** **It's** a good idea **for John to study in France.**	

EXERCISE 13

Complete these sentences with ideas that express your true opinion. Compare your answers with other students'.

1. It's always a good idea . . .
2. It's enjoyable . . .
3. It's never wise . . .
4. It's every parent's dream . . .
5. It's never a teacher's responsibility . . .
6. It's sometimes difficult . . .
7. It's usually necessary . . .
8. It's seldom easy . . .

For an alternative, present this focus in contrast to Focus 6 in Unit 7, p. 116.

Exercise 13

Try doing this orally in class, asking for multiple responses to the same cue.

Workbook Ex. 11, pp. 42–43. Answers: TE p. 495.

UNIT GOAL REVIEW

1. Ask students to look at the goals on the opening page of the unit again. Help them understand how much they have accomplished in each area by reviewing the three infinitive patterns. Have students name verbs that occur with each pattern.
2. Alternatively, wait until you have finished Unit 7 and do Exercise 11 (p. 99) as a comprehensive review of both infinitives and gerunds together.

Exercise 13

Answers will vary. Possible answers include:
1. to look both ways before you cross the street.   2. to sleep late on Saturday mornings.   3. to travel without insurance.
4. to hold a grandchild in their arms.
5. to give good grades to lazy students.
6. to concentrate on homework when the sun is shining.   7. to work hard if you want to succeed.   8. to adjust to living in a new culture.

USE YOUR ENGLISH

Activity 1

Step 2 can be used as a diagnostic or testing activity by having Ss hand in their paragraphs.

Activity 2

The topic of this activity may be more appropriate for certain kinds of classes than Activity 1 (classes whose students are still living in their home country or who left their home country at a very early age). It can be used for diagnostic purposes in the same way as Activity 1.

Use Your English

ACTIVITY 1: WRITING

In the Opening Task on page 86 you examined the things on John Tealhome's mind a couple of days before his departure for a year overseas. Have you ever left for a long trip? How prepared and well-organized were you two days before your departure?

STEP 1 Make a list like John's that indicates the things you still needed to do, and some of the things that you needed other people to do for you. Compare your list and John's. Who was better organized?

STEP 2 Write a paragraph describing your experience. Did you have chance to do everything you needed or wanted to do? Was there anything you forgot to do? What advice would you give someone preparing for a similar trip?

ACTIVITY 2: SPEAKING

Do parents treat boys and girls differently?

STEP 1 Interview some classmates and find out what things children in their culture are taught to do when they are growing up.

	Boys are encouraged to . . .	Boys are encouraged not to . . .	Girls are encouraged to . . .	Girls are encouraged not to . . .
Examples	be brave defend their sisters	cry play with dolls	be neat and tidy play with dolls	play roughly get dirty
Student 1				
Student 2				
Student 3				

STEP 2 Compare the responses of the people you interviewed. What differences are there? What might be the reasons for some of these differences? What things are taught to all children regardless of their gender or culture?

ACTIVITY 3: READING/SPEAKING

STEP 1 Below is a list of some possible strategies for learning to speak English. Decide whether the listed strategy is something that language learners should **try to do** or something that they should **try not to do** in order to learn more effectively.

- Try to use new vocabulary in writing and conversation.
- Stop to look up every unfamiliar word in the dictionary.
- Be very very careful not to make any mistakes.
- Guess at the meaning of unfamiliar words by using other clues in the sentence.
- Become discouraged if you don't understand 100% of everything you hear.
- Always think of your ideas in your own language first, and then translate them word-by-word into English.
- Listen for the general idea in conversations.
- Look for opportunities to speak English as often as possible.
- Go over your mistakes on homework and try to understand why you made them.
- Go over your mistakes on homework and write the correct answer.
- Find ways to punish yourself if you make a mistake.
- Don't speak unless you are sure the answer is correct.

STEP 2 List three more strategies language learners should try to use, and three strategies they should try not to do.

STEP 3 Compare your list with several other students', and present any interesting similarities and differences to the rest of the class.

Activity 3

This activity provides opportunities for natural use of common verb+ infinitive patterns. It adapts well to whole class discussion.

Activity 4

This activity provides more explicit discussion of good strategies for independent language learning. It is appropriate to follow it up with a brief whole class discussion of the issues.

Activity 5

The presentation can be written or oral.

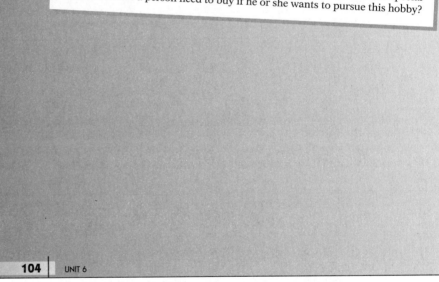

ACTIVITY 4: SPEAKING

A **superstition** is a folk belief about lucky or unlucky events. For example, in some cultures the number 13 is considered to be an unlucky number. Friday the thirteenth is supposed to be a particularly unlucky day. Some people don't want to attend a party or sit at a table where there are thirteen people. Many buildings, especially hotels, do not have a thirteenth floor. Other superstitions still affect basic manners in society. Because of an old superstition it is considered polite to say "God bless you" when someone near you sneezes, even to someone you do not know.

STEP 1 Work with other students to develop a presentation for the rest of the class about some modern superstitions and their results. Identify some things that people try to do and some things they try not to. You may wish to compare the superstitions of several different cultures. Are there any superstitions that are universal? Why do you think superstitions come into being?

STEP 2 Present your ideas to the rest of the class.

ACTIVITY 5: WRITING

Write about your favorite hobby or leisure time activity. What is it? Why do you like to do it? What skill does someone need to develop or what special equipment does a person need to buy if he or she wants to pursue this hobby?

ACTIVITY 6: LISTENING

STEP 1 Read the questions below and then listen to the following conversation for information to answer them in complete sentences.

STEP 2 Compare your answers with another student's. Listen to the conversation a second time to confirm or clarify any questions you're not sure of.

1. What information should the students expect to be tested on?

_____

2. What were they told not to study?

_____

3. What had the man been planning to do tonight?

_____

4. Why wasn't the man in class yesterday?

_____

5. What had he been told to do in order to improve his chance for graduate school?

_____

6. Why doesn't he want a paid position at the library?

_____

Play textbook audio.
The tapescript for this listening appears on pp. 512–513 of this book.
Allow for multiple listenings as needed:
1. Ss listen for the general idea.
2. Ss read the questions and then listen for answers.
3. Ss focus on listening for information they still need.
4. Ss check their answers.

The test for this unit can be found on p. 450. The answers are on p. 451 of this book

---

ANSWER KEY

Activity 6

Answers will vary. Possible versions include:
1. Anything in the second half of the book.
2. Anything in the first half of the book.
3. She had been planning on studying all night.   4. She had an appointment to be interviewed by the head librarian.   5. She had been told to try to get some practical experience.   6. She doesn't think she'd have much opportunity to get experience in all areas. The advisory board will give her a chance to learn about a variety library issues.

Unit 7

UNIT OVERVIEW

Unit 6 and Unit 7 are structured in similar ways, so as to allow teachers who want to teach the two structures together to do so. See the Unit 6 Overview on p.86 for suggestions on how to order the focuses of these two units to facilitate an integrated approach.

UNIT GOALS

Review the goals listed on this page so students (Ss) understand what they should be able to know by the end of the unit.

Opening Task

1. To use as a diagnostic activity, have Ss write their lists of the activities they enjoy doing, enjoy not doing, and don't enjoy doing as full sentences.
2. Skip Step 3 if you need to save time, and just have Ss tell the class the kinds of things they wrote in the chart.

UNIT 7

GERUNDS

UNIT GOALS:

- To understand the form and meaning of gerunds
- To understand and use sentences with verbs followed by gerunds
- To learn some basic principles about when to use an infinitive and when to use a gerund

▶ OPENING TASK
Which Kind of Person Are You?

STEP 1 Read these two definitions of different kinds of people and how they spend their free time.

DO-ERS like **doing things** during their free time. They have hobbies and activities that keep them busy. They plan their free time. A good vacation is one that lets them do many different things and have many new experiences.

BE-ERS prefer **not doing things.** They like to spend an afternoon relaxing, reading a magazine, or just doing nothing at all—sleeping, daydreaming. They don't plan their free time; they just let it happen. A good vacation is one that makes them feel relaxed.

STEP 2 In this chart, list ways you spend your free time. Two examples for each category have been provided. Add three more that are true for you.

Activities I enjoy doing in my free time (I do them, and I enjoy them).	Activities I enjoy *not* doing in my free time (*I don't do* them, and I enjoy not doing them).	Activities I don't enjoy doing in my free time (I do them, but I don't enjoy them).
1) reading the paper	1) not getting up early	1) doing chores (cleaning and laundry)
2) talking with friends	2) not driving to work	2) taking work home from the office
3) _____	3) _____	3) _____
4) _____	4) _____	4) _____
5) _____	5) _____	5) _____

STEP 3 Describe the activities in your chart to a partner. Your partner should decide whether you appear to be a do-er or a be-er. What category does your partner seem to be in? Present your findings about each other to the rest of the class.

1. Begin your presentation with writing **sentence f** on the board . Check Ss' understanding of gerunds by asking questions such as *What does he like? What does he hate?* Have Ss answer by completing these cues: *He likes the fact that... He hates the fact that...*

2. Repeat the process with **sentences g & h** (*They enjoy the fact that...*) and **j & k** (*She is nervous that... ; She was happy that...*).

3. If you are teaching gerunds and infinitives together, you can elicit "comparative" examples that show negative gerunds and infinitives in contrast, passive gerunds and infinitives, and so forth. If you feel your class can already identify infinitives and gerunds, do Exercise 1 first, and then have Ss review Focus 1 as homework.

Gerunds

EXAMPLES	EXPLANATIONS
(a) Norman enjoys **collecting stamps.** He doesn't mind **paying a lot of money** for rare ones.	Gerunds are formed by adding *-ing* to the simple form of the verb. They are used in many of the same ways that infinitives are used. In general they refer to an action that is already happening or has been completed.
(b) The librarian doesn't like **our talking.** Maybe we'd better stop.	
(c) I hate **listening** to boring lectures. I wish this class were over!	

Gerund phrases can contain the same information as any verb phrase.

EXAMPLES	EXPLANATIONS
(d) I enjoy **staying in bed** on Sunday mornings.	**Affirmative/Negative**
(e) I like **not getting up** early.	Affirmative gerund: verb + *-ing*
(f) Peter likes **having a responsible job,** but he hates **not having enough time** for his family.	Negative gerund: *not* + verb + *-ing*
(g) Matt and Jeff enjoy **inviting friends** for dinner.	**Active and Passive**
(h) Matt and Jeff enjoy **being invited** to their friends' homes for dinner.	Active gerund: verb + *-ing*
(i) Sofia likes **giving orders,** but she hates **being told** what to do.	Passive gerund: *being* + verb
(j) Ayo was nervous about **taking** tests.	**Simple/Perfect Aspect**
(k) Ayo was happy about **having gotten** a good grade on his exam.	Simple gerund: verb + *-ing*
	Perfect gerund: *having* + past participle
	We don't often use perfect gerunds, and there is no progressive gerund.

EXERCISE 1

Complete the sentences by expressing the idea in the gerund as a verb phrase.

▶ **EXAMPLE:** I enjoy **not doing** anything on Sunday mornings.

I don't do anything on Sunday , and I enjoy that.

1. We hate **being asked for** money all the time.

 When _____, we hate it.

2. I really appreciate **your having taken** such good care of my dog while I was on vacation.

 I really appreciate that _____.

3. They suspect him of **taking** the money.

 They suspect that _____.

4. We didn't plan for **their having** problems with the homework.

 We didn't plan for the fact that _____.

5. I think John resents **not being invited** to the party.

 I think John resents the fact that _____.

EXERCISE 2

Complete the sentences by expressing the underlined clause as a gerund phrase. Be sure to include all the information in the verb phrase in your gerund phrase.

▶ **EXAMPLE:** I don't ever do any homework on Saturday nights, and I enjoy that.

 I enjoy _not doing (never doing) any homework on Saturday nights._

1. When I am asked for my suggestions about ways to improve the company, I like it.

 I like _____.

2. I really appreciate that you have been so careful with this homework.

 I really appreciate your _____.

3. Mary suspected that John was planning to contact his old girlfriend.

 Mary suspected John of _____.

4. The teacher didn't plan for the fact that the students had completely forgotten the grammar rules.

 The teacher didn't plan on _____.

5. I think John is disappointed that he wasn't selected for the scholarship.

 I think that John is disappointed about _____.

Exercises 1 & 2

Do these exercises as an immediate follow-up of your presentation of Focus 1. Do them as a whole class and allow time for questions as needed.

ANSWER KEY

Exercise 1

1. we are asked for money all the time.
2. you have taken such good care of my dog while I was on vacation.   3. he took the money.   4. they would/might have problems with the homework.   5. he wasn't invited to the party.

Exercise 2

1. being asked for my suggestions about ways to improve the company.   2. having been so careful with this homework.   3. planning to contact his old girlfriend.   4. the students having completely forgotten the grammar rules.
5. not being selected for the scholarship.

Exercise 3

To use this exercise for diagnostic or testing purposes, have Ss write a paragraph based on their partners' answers to hand in for you to evaluate.

Workbook Exs. 1 & 2, pp. 44–45. Answers: TE p. 495.

EXERCISE 3

Interview a partner and find out two or three things for each of these topics.

▶ **EXAMPLE:** Things your partner enjoys doing:

  What things do you enjoy doing on Sunday mornings?
  I enjoy reading the paper.

  Things your partner enjoys not doing:

  What things do you enjoy not doing on Sunday mornings?
  I enjoy not getting up early.

1. Things your partner enjoys **doing** on the weekends.

  Things your partner enjoys **not doing** on the weekends.

2. Things your partner hates **doing**.

  Things your partner doesn't mind **other people doing**.

3. Things or services your partner likes **giving to other people**.

  Things or services your partner likes **other people giving to him or her**.

4. Things that attending a college typically requires **doing**.

  Things that attending a college typically requires **having done**.

FOCUS **2**

▶ Noun or Pronoun Plus Gerund

EXAMPLES	IMPLIED MEANING	EXPLANATIONS
(a) Denise doesn't approve of **taking** time off. **(b)** Denise doesn't approve of **Peter's taking** time off.	She doesn't like anybody's doing it. She doesn't like Peter to do it.	As with infinitives, it is sometimes necessary to identify who is performing the action described by the gerund.
(c) Peter can't understand **being** so serious about work.	He can't understand why he or anybody should do this.	verb + *-ing*: The performer of the gerund is the same as the subject of the main verb or "everybody."
(d) Peter hates **her complaining** about his absences.	Maybe he doesn't mind when other people complain; he just doesn't like it when she does it.	possessive noun phrase + gerund: The performer of the gerund is stated as a possessive noun (e.g., *Peter's* in **(b)**) or pronoun.

EXERCISE 4

In these sentences, underline the gerund and draw a line to the person who performs the action it describes.

▶ **EXAMPLES:** Is there any way we can delay taking the test?

No politician will ever admit not having a solution to the budget problem.

1. Jeff enjoys living in San Francisco.
2. I really appreciate your helping us get ready for the party.
3. Peter has considered looking for a new job.
4. Matt could never imagine leaving San Francisco.
5. Mary resents John's spending a year overseas.
6. Miss Manners will never excuse her having behaved so rudely.
7. We wanted to postpone leaving for the trip, but we didn't anticipate not being able to change our tickets.
8. We'll really miss your singing and dancing in the school talent show.

Gerunds **111**

1. If you have already done Focus 3 of Unit 6 on p. 93, review that briefly. The same concepts are useful for this focus. If your students seemed to get the principle as it applied to infinitives, they probably won't have much trouble with this focus, so try doing Exercise 4 first. If Ss don't have trouble, you can assign the focus for review at home.

2. If you have not done that focus, or Ss are still having difficulty, then present this focus explicitly by writing example sentences a and b on the board. Ask if anyone can explain the difference in meaning. Alternatively, use a class-related example such as: *Teachers approve of helping students with their homework, but they don't always approve of other students helping them.*

Exercise 4

Do this exercise to find out whether you need an explicit presentation of Focus 4 immediately following your presentation.

A N S W E R   K E Y

Exercise 4
The person who performs the action has been indicated in bold.
1. **Jeff** enjoys living in San Francisco.   2. I really appreciate **your** helping us get ready for the party.   3. **Peter** has considered looking for a new job.   4. **Matt** could never imagine leaving San Francisco.   5. Mary resents **John's** spending a year overseas.   6. **Miss Manners** will never excuse **her** having behaved so rudely.   7. **We** wanted to postpone leaving for the trip, but **we** didn't anticipate not being able to change our tickets.   8. We'll really miss **your** singing and dancing in the school talent show.

Most teachers choose to present Focuses 3, 4, and 5 in a similar way in the same class period. Present this pattern in a straightforward manner and then do Exercise 5.

Exercise 5

SUGGESTIONS:

1. Let Ss choose whether they want to work in pairs or individually. Make it a game by seeing who can find all 14 the fastest. Give prizes.

2. If you have access to an OHP, make a transparency of the passage and underline the gerunds as you go through the exercise with the class. Make sure Ss read the whole passage for understanding before they do the exercise.

Exercise 6

If Ss have trouble thinking of sentences, try putting them in pairs. Make sure they know the meaning of all the listed verbs before starting. You can make this exercise easier by assigning Ss only two or three sentences to work on.

Workbook Exs. 4 & 5, pp. 45–46. Answers: TE p. 495.

FOCUS **3**

▶ Verbs Followed by Gerunds: Pattern I

Pattern 1: Verb + Gerund

EXAMPLES	EXPLANATION
(a) Charlie **can't help falling** in love with a new woman every few weeks. (b) Mary **gave up smoking** because she knows it's bad for her health.	Some verbs are followed immediately by a gerund.

EXERCISE 5

Underline the verbs in this passage that follow Pattern 1. The first two have been done for you.

LIVING THE LOW-FAT LIFE

(1) Nutritionists <u>recommend</u> reducing the amount of fat in one's diet. (2) They <u>suggest</u> eating foods that are high in fiber and avoiding foods that are high in fat. (3) Some people deny having a high-fat diet and would never consider changing their eating habits. (4) Other people admit consuming more fat than they would really like to. (5) But nutritionists feel that everyone could benefit from the low-fat life.

(6) Most people can't help consuming a certain amount of fat, no matter how careful they are. (7) But here are a few very simple, basic changes in eating and cooking habits that will greatly decrease the amount of fat in your diet.

• (8) You can give up using rich, creamy sauces and use natural cooking juices to give your food flavor.

• (9) You should avoid consuming large amounts of red meat and quit having such foods as bacon or sausage on a regular basis.

• (10) You can practice cooking your food in different ways. (11) Such changes include not frying food in oil, but steaming or boiling it whenever possible.

(12) Initially these changes may be difficult, and you may resist changing old habits. (13) But if you keep on following the basic principles listed above, it will get easier to keep doing it.

EXERCISE 6

Use five verbs that you found in Exercise 5 to talk about some of your own health habits. Tell about things that you regularly avoid doing and things that you do regularly and intend to keep on doing.

ANSWER KEY

Exercise 5: recommend; suggest; deny; consider; admit; can't help; give up; avoid; quit; practice; include; resist; keep on; keep

Exercise 6

Answers will vary widely. Possible answers include:
recommend: I recommend following a vegetarian diet.
suggest: My personal trainer suggests lifting weights every other day.
can't help: I can't help wishing that I could eat ice cream for every meal.
includes: My new weight-reducing plan includes spending an hour a day exercising.

avoid: I avoid taking a second helping of anything but beets or celery.
keep on: I plan to keep on reading the labels of the food I buy to learn about their nutrition.
give up: If you want to lose weight, you have to give up eating between meals.
consider: In order to change your body, you have to consider changing your eating and exercise habits.
resist: I try to resist eating foods that are high in sugar or fat.
keep: It's important to keep trying, even if you sometimes don't follow your plan.

Verbs Followed by Gerunds: Pattern 2

Pattern 2: Verb + { **Gerund**
                      { **Noun Phrase + Infinitive**

EXAMPLES		EXPLANATION
Gerund (a) Doctors **advise reducing** fats in one's diet. (c) They **urge giving up** fried foods.	**Infinitive** (b) My doctor **advised me to reduce** my fat intake. (d) He **urged Peter to give up** fried foods.	Some verbs are followed by a gerund when referring to "everybody," and by an infinitive when referring to a specific person.

EXERCISE 7

For each of these Pattern 2 verbs listed below write two sentences—one with a noun phrase and one without. If you wish, you can write a single sentence that uses both patterns.

▶ **EXAMPLE:** Advise:

Most people advise taking a nice hot bath if you don't want to catch a cold, but my doctor advised me to take vitamin C instead.

1. require
2. encourage
3. urge
4. advise
5. forbid

Gerunds | **113**

FOCUS 4

Most teachers choose to present Focuses 3, 4, and 5 in a similar way in the same class period.

Exercise 7

If Ss have trouble thinking of sentences, try putting them in pairs. Make sure they know the meaning of all the listed verbs before starting. You can make this exercise easier by assigning Ss only two or three sentences to work on.

Workbook Ex. 6, p. 46. Answers: TE p. 495.

ANSWER KEY

Exercise 7

Answers will vary. Possible answers include:
1. Getting into a university usually requires passing TOEFL. Bambang's university required him to get a score of 550 on TOEFL. 2. Health experts encourage getting regular exercise. I want to encourage you to study harder. 3. Doctors urge reducing fat in one's diet. My doctor urged me to lose weight. 4. Teachers often advise keeping a journal to improve your language ability. My teacher advised me to study harder. 5. The government forbids selling drugs. My mother forbade me to stay up late when I was a child.

Exercise 8

V A R I A T I O N :

If you have done the last several exercises of this type in pairs, then vary your approach by having Ss write their answers as homework. When you assign it, do the first couple together in class to make sure their answers include gerunds.

FOCUS **5**

Verbs Followed by Gerunds: Pattern 3

Pattern 3: Verb (+ Noun Phrase) + Gerund

EXAMPLES	EXPLANATION
(a) I **don't mind borrowing** money, but I **dislike Peter's doing** it.	Many verb-gerund combinations can be used with or without noun phrases.
(b) I **dislike swimming** in cold water, but I **don't mind your doing** it.	

Common verbs that follow this pattern are:

anticipate	*delay*	*don't mind*	*imagine*	*resent*
appreciate	*deny*	*enjoy*	*miss*	*tolerate*
consider	*dislike*	*excuse*	*postpone*	*understand*

EXERCISE 8

Complete these sentences with true information. Use gerunds in your answers, and if the highlighted verb can be used with a noun phrase, try to use a noun phrase in your answer:

1. I usually **avoid** . . .
2. When I was a child I used to **imagine** . . .
3. My English teacher **recommends** . . .
4. I would like to **quit** . . .
5. I am **considering** . . .
6. Honest people shouldn't **tolerate** . . .
7. To be a good soccer player it's necessary to **practice** . . .
8. A teacher's responsibility **includes** . . .
9. Becoming a really good speaker of a foreign language **requires** . . .
10. I **appreciate** guests . . .

A N S W E R   K E Y

Exercise 8

Answers will vary. Possible answers include: 1. eating fatty foods. 2. being an astronaut. 3. reading an English newspaper for 20 minutes each day. 4. borrowing money from friends. 5. changing my major. 6. other people stealing. 7. running quickly. 8. helping students. 9. not being afraid to make mistakes. 10. helping with the dishes.

EXERCISE 9

Combine these sentence pairs by replacing "**this**" with a gerund phrase made from the first sentence.

▶ **EXAMPLE:**   John will spend a year in France. Mary resents **this**.

Mary resents John's spending a year in France.

1. John sings a funny song whenever he sees her. Mary will miss **this**.

2. He wants to become really fluent in French. Mary doesn't really understand **this**.

3. He applied to the program without consulting Mary. She resents **this**.

4. She will not have a chance to talk with him every day. She's not looking forward to **this**.

5. John is leaving in two weeks. He is quite excited about **this**.

6. John needs at least three weeks to get a passport. He didn't anticipate **this**.

7. This will make his departure even later than expected. John wanted to avoid **this**.

Exercise 9

This is a good exercise to assign for homework for Ss to write and hand in.

Workbook Exs. 7 & 8, pp. 47–48. Answers: TE p. 495.

ANSWER KEY

Exercise 9

1. Mary will miss John's singing a funny song whenever he sees her.   2. Mary doesn't really understand his wanting to become really fluent in French.   3. Mary resents his having applied/applying to the program without consulting her.   4. She's not looking forward to not having a chance to talk with him every day.   5. John is quite excited about leaving in two weeks.   6. John didn't anticipate needing at least three weeks to get a passport.
7. John wanted to avoid making his departure even later than expected.

FOCUS 6

The second part of this focus provides a useful rule for Ss about when to use a gerund instead of an infinitive. You can present it in a straightforward way by writing example sentences on the board or asking Ss to follow along as the sentences are read aloud. Ask Ss to identify the prepositions and phrasal verb particles that take the gerund complements.

Gerunds in Other Positions in a Sentence

Gerunds can be used in other places in the sentence where noun phrases normally appear.

Subjects of a sentence

EXAMPLES	EXPLANATION
Gerund Subjects (a) **Collecting stamps** is fun. (b) AWKWARD: **It's** fun **collecting stamps**. **Infinitive Subjects** (c) **It's** fun **to collect** stamps. (d) AWKWARD: **To collect stamps** is fun.	Unlike infinitive subjects, gerund subjects usually begin a sentence and are not usually used with *it* constructions.

Objects of prepositions and two-word verbs

EXAMPLES	EXPLANATION
(e) I am happy **about meeting** you. (f) This steak is too tough **for frying** in butter. (g) He is exhausted **from staying up** all night. (h) I'm **giving up smoking**. (i) I'm **looking into changing** majors.	Objects of prepositions and phrasal verbs must be expressed by nouns, pronouns, or gerunds, but never infinitives.

Exercise 10

If Ss have trouble thinking of sentences, try putting them in pairs. You can make this exercise easier by assigning Ss only two or three sentences to work on. Alternatively, do it as a whole class, asking for a variety of ways to complete the sentences.

Workbook Ex. 9, p. 49. Answers: TE p. 496.

EXERCISE 10

Complete these sentences with information that describes your true feelings about these topics. Compare your answers to those of other students in the class.

1. Talking to strangers . . .
2. Eating ice cream . . .
3. I'm nervous about . . .
4. I'm never afraid of . . .

5. My friends are concerned about . . .
6. I would like to give up . . .
7. Growing older . . .
8. I get tired of . . .

ANSWER KEY

Exercise 10

Answers will vary widely. Possible answers include:
1. is sometimes difficult.   2. is a good thing to do on a hot day.   3. making friends in this country.   4. meeting new people.   5. passing the TOEFL.   6. smoking.   7. /exercising. happens to everyone.   8. eating American food.

FOCUS **7**

Choosing Infinitives Versus Gerunds

There is a basic difference in meaning between infinitives and gerunds that can help us choose the correct form in many cases.

EXAMPLES	EXPLANATIONS
(a) I plan **to study** all weekend, so I guess I can relax this afternoon.	Infinitives usually refer to the possibility of an action occurring. The action has not happened yet.
(b) I don't enjoy **studying** all weekend, but we have a big examination on Monday.	Gerunds usually refer to an action that has already started or has already been experienced.
(c) I **want to swim** in the ocean this summer. **(d)** I **intend to take** the TOEFL at the end of the semester.	Verbs of desire (*hope, wish, plan, want,* etc.) imply that the speaker hasn't experienced the action yet, but may in the future. They are typically followed by infinitives.
(e) I **enjoy swimming** in the ocean. **(f)** I can't stand **taking** tests because they make me so nervous. **(g)** I can't stand **to take** tests because they make me so nervous.	Certain verbs of emotion (*enjoy, appreciate,* etc.) imply that the speaker has already experienced the cause of that emotion. They are typically followed by gerunds. Other verbs of emotion (*like, love, hate, can't stand*) can be followed by gerunds or infinitives without much difference in meaning.

FOCUS 7

This focus introduces the Bolinger principle (see *The Grammar Book,* pp. 648–649 for a fuller discussion). It may be a little abstract for lower-level classes; if so, refer Ss to the first part of the focus as a self-study follow-up after doing Exercises 12–14. However, it is important to make sure that even lower-level students are introduced to the semantic differences with verbs like *forget, try, stop,* etc.

Some verbs have an important difference in meaning depending on whether they are followed by an infinitive or a gerund.

VERB	EXAMPLES	IMPLIED MEANING
forget	**(h)** **I forgot to meet** her.	I didn't meet her because I forgot about our appointment.
	(i) **I forgot meeting** her.	I met her, but I didn't remember that I did.
try	**(j)** **We tried to close** the window, but it was stuck	We couldn't close it.
	(k) **We tried closing** the window, but the room was still cold.	We closed it, but that didn't make the room warmer.
remember	**(l)** John **remembered to mail** the letter.	He remembered, and then went to the mailbox.
	(m) John **remembered mailing** the letter.	He mailed the letter, and remembered it later.
stop	**(n)** John **stopped smoking** last month.	He doesn't smoke anymore.
	(o) John **stopped to smoke** because he needed a break.	John took a break and smoked.

EXERCISE 11

Review the basic patterns and common verbs in each pattern. Work with a partner and try to write as many additional verbs for each pattern as you can remember without looking back in your book. A few have been done for you.

VERBS THAT TAKE INFINITIVES			VERBS THAT TAKE GERUNDS		
Pattern 1	**Pattern 2**	**Pattern 3**	**Pattern 1**	**Pattern 2**	**Pattern 3**
appear	advise	expect	can't help	encourage	appreciate
refuse	remind	arrange	keep on	urge	anticipate
seem					dislike

EXERCISE 12

Fill in the blank with the gerund or infinitive form of the word in parentheses. There may be more than one correct answer.

1. If you want to lose weight you should try _____ (avoid) all sweets. That might be better than going on a diet.

2. I know Dimitri was at the party, but I don't remember _____ (talk) to him.

3. On her way home my mother stopped _____ (pick up) a few things at the store.

4. Suddenly all the dogs in the neighborhood began _____ (bark) at the same time.

5. My sister has never been able to quit _____ (smoke).

Gerunds | **119**

Exercise 11

1. The appendix contains a list of the verb patterns discussed in both this unit and Unit 6.

SUGGESTIONS:

1. Make sure that Ss use this exercise as a review activity, and don't just copy the answers from the back of the book.

2. Alternatively, use this activity for a Unit Goal Review activity for both Units 6 and 7.

Exercise 12

This is another exercise that combines both gerunds and infinitives. If for some reason you are doing this unit before Unit 6, wait to do this exercise until you have covered both units.

ANSWER KEY

Exercise 11

(See Appendix 3, pp. 422–423.)

Exercise 12

1. to avoid/avoiding 2. talking 3. to pick up 4. barking/to bark 5. smoking 6. to bring 7. (a) playing, (b) to prefer, (c) playing/to play 8. eating

6. Ruth couldn't watch TV because she forgot _____ (bring) her glasses with her.

7. Nowadays, children have stopped (a) _____ (play) traditional children's games and seem (b) _____ (prefer) (c) _____ (play) video games instead.

8. I'll try _____ (eat) any kind of food once.

EXERCISE 13

Fill in the blanks with the correct form of the verbs in parentheses. There may be more than one correct answer.

Before the invention of radio and television, people spent much of their leisure time (1) _____ (do) activities that required (2) _____ (do) or (3) _____ (make) something. They practiced (4) _____ (play) a musical instrument or studied (5) _____ (sing).

Most people learned (6) _____ (keep busy) by (7) _____ (try) (8) _____ (improve) their abilities in some way or by (9) _____ (practice) a skill. People who couldn't afford (10) _____ (spend) much money on hobbies often started (11) _____ (collect) simple objects, such as matchbook covers or stamps, or even things like buttons or bottle caps. Of course, most people spent a lot of time (12) _____ (read), and (13) _____ (write) letters to friends.

Children played games in which they pretended (14) _____ (be) pirates or cowboys or people they remembered (15) _____ (read about) in books. Many women were extremely clever at (16) _____ (make) and (17) _____ (decorate) articles of clothing. Men often kept busy by (18) _____ (make) toys for children or (19) _____ (carve) small sculptures out of wood.

Exercise 13

This is another exercise that combines both gerunds and infinitives. If for some reason you are doing this unit before Unit 6, then wait to do this exercise until you have covered both units.

ANSWER KEY

Exercise 13

1. doing   2. doing   3. making   4. playing
5. singing   6. to keep busy   7. trying
8. to improve   9. practicing   10. to spend
11. collecting   12. reading   13. writing
14. to be   15. reading about   16. making
17. decorating   18. making   19. carving

EXERCISE 14

Fill in the blanks with the correct form of the verbs in parentheses. There may be more than one correct answer, so be prepared to explain why you chose the answer you did.

Since the invention of radio and television, leisure-time activities have changed. Nowadays people don't find it as easy (1) _____ (fill) their time with such productive activities. Television has encouraged many people (2) _____ (stop) (3) _____ (work on) their hobbies. Children are spending more and more time (4) _____ (watch) TV or (5) _____ (play) video games. As a result, traditional children's games which have been played for hundreds of years are beginning (6) _____ (forget). Traditional skills such as embroidery, sewing, and woodcarving are failing (7) _____ (be passed on) from parent to child. People seem (8) _____ (prefer) activities that allow them (9) _____ (be) passive observers rather than active participants. If these traditional forms of recreation keep (10) _____ (disappear) at the current rate, many of the things that people used to enjoy (11) _____ (do) will only be found on television documentaries about how people tried (12) _____ (spend) their leisure time in the days before television.

Exercise 14

This is another exercise that combines both gerunds and infinitives. If for some reason you are doing this unit before Unit 6, then wait to do this exercise until you have covered both units.

Workbook Exs. 10–13, pp. 49–52. Answers: TE p. 496.

UNIT GOAL REVIEW

1. Ask Ss to look at the goals on the opening page of the unit again. Help them understand how much they have accomplished in each area by reviewing the three infinitive patterns.
2. Have Ss name verbs that occur with each pattern.
3. Alternatively, wait until you have finished Unit 7 and do Exercise 11 (p. 119) as a comprehensive review of both infinitives and gerunds together.

ANSWER KEY

Exercise 14

1. to fill/filling   2. to stop   3. working on
4. watching   5. playing   6. to be forgotten
7. to be passed on   8. to prefer   9. to be
10. disappearing   11. doing   12. to spend/spending

USE YOUR ENGLISH

The activities in this unit are designed to give Ss opportunities to use common infinitive and gerund patterns in communicative situations. By having Ss write their ideas and responses to hand in, any of these activities can be used for testing or diagnostic purposes.

Activity 1

Process Step 2 as a whole class, by recording the activities on the board and discussing differences as a whole class.

Activity 2

This activity works better as pair work without listing the surprises up on the board. If your class is shy, omit Step 2. It's also important to let Ss choose partners they want to work with for this activity.

Activity 3

Process this activity in the same way that was recommended for Activity 1. Obviously, this activity works best if it's done around New Year's time, but the discussion can take place in any season.

Use Your English

ACTIVITY 1: SPEAKING

In the Opening Task you were asked to decide whether you are a **do-er** or a **be-er** in the way that you spend your free time.

STEP 1 Form a group with other people who are in the same category as you. Together come up with a list of the five or ten best ways to spend a rainy afternoon.

STEP 2 Compare your list of activities with that of a group from the other category What does this tell you about the differences between **do-ers** and **be-ers?**

ACTIVITY 2: SPEAKING

Choose a partner that you know pretty well.

STEP 1 Describe two or three things you can't imagine him or her ever doing. Then identify two or three things you expect your partner to do on a routine basis. Explain your reasons. What is it about your partner that makes you think he or she would behave that way? Your partner should then do the same thing with you.

STEP 2 Were you or your partner surprised by any of the things you heard? For example, did your partner tell you that he couldn't imagine your doing something that you actually do quite frequently? Or perhaps your partner mentioned an expectation that you would never consider doing. Report any surprises to the rest of the class.

ACTIVITY 3: WRITING

We all have bad habits that we would like to stop doing, and things that we know we should do, but don't. New Year's Eve is a popular time to make resolutions about ways to improve our behavior.

STEP 1 Make a list of "New Year's Resolutions."

- What are some things you would like to stop doing? (For example, *watching so much TV, eating ice cream before bed, gossiping.*)
- What are some things you would like to start doing? (For example, *getting more exercise, reading for an hour every night, writing letters to friends.*)

STEP 2 Compare your New Year's Resolutions to those of other people in the class. Are there any common categories or characteristics?

ACTIVITY 4: WRITING

Write a brief paragraph on things about other people that you can't stand but many other people don't seem to mind (For example: *I can't stand friends being too serious about their work, and having no other interests in life*), and things about other people that you don't mind, but many other people can't stand (For example: *I don't mind people being late*).

ACTIVITY 5: SPEAKING

Prepare a short talk for the rest of the class on one of these topics:
- your likes and dislikes: activities that you don't mind, can't stand, love, hate, resent, and enjoy.
- your future plans: activities that you anticipate, hope, or intend to do; and things that would make you postpone or delay those activities or consider not doing them.

ACTIVITY 6: LISTENING

STEP 1 Read the questions below. Then listen for the information to answer them from the following radio program about leisure time in the United States.

1. What amount of time per week are people expected to work in the United States, Germany, and Japan?
2. What is the average amount of annual vacation for workers in the United States, Germany, and Japan?
3. What do Americans typically do on the weekend?
4. What is the third reason mentioned for the decreasing amount of free time?
5. Give two examples of "working vacations."

STEP 2 Compare your answers with a partner's, and then listen to the program again to confirm any information you're not sure of.

Gerunds **123**

Activities 4 & 5

Both activities work well as diagnostic and testing activities by having Ss write responses. Both can be used as topics for small group or whole class discussion.

Activity 6

Play textbook audio.
The tapescript for this listening appears on p. 513 of this book.
Play the tape several times, as needed.

1. Ss listen for the general idea of the topic.
2. Ss preview the questions and listen a second time for specific information.
3. Ss focus on areas they still have been unable to answer.
4. Ss check their answers.
5. A possible fifth playing will allow you to focus on the precise place in the program where the information was contained.

The test for this unit can be found on p. 452. The answers are on p. 453 of this book.

TOEFL Test Preparation Exercises for Units 5–7 can be found on pp. 53–55 of the Workbook.
The answers are on p. 496 of this book.

ANSWER KEY

Activity 6

1. Amount of time per week people are expected to work : United States 40, Germany 38, Japan 42
2. Average amount of annual vacation for workers: United States 11 holidays, 12 vacation days; Germany 10 holidays, 30 vacation days; Japan 20 holidays, 16 vacation days
3. What Americans typically do on the weekend: one full day of household chores such as shopping, laundry, housecleaning, etc.
4. The third reason mentioned for the decreasing amount of free time: Americans are increasingly using their vacations for long-term projects
5. Two examples of "working vacations": collecting and cataloging plant and animal species in national parks, going on digs at archaeological sites, participating in community development projects

Unit 8

UNIT OVERVIEW

This unit covers intensifiers and statements of degree. It is possible to study intensifiers separately (Focuses 1–5) and then come back to degree complements (Focuses 6–8) later.

UNIT GOALS

Review the goals listed on this page so students (Ss) understand what they should be able to know by the end of the unit.

OPENING TASK

This task is useful in introducing and underscoring the **very/too** distinction that many students find troublesome.

SUGGESTIONS:

1. Have Ss read the article on p. 125 as homework the night before you begin this unit and do Step 2 in pairs or small groups. The subject is one that lends itself to just relaxing and having fun.
2. One possible definition for Step 2: An *enthusiast* is someone who does something a lot and a *somethingaholic* is someone who does something too much.

UNIT 8

INTENSIFIERS (very, too, enough, etc.) AND DEGREE COMPLEMENTS (so that, such that etc.)

UNIT GOALS:

- To use intensifiers such as *very, too,* and *enough*
- To use the word *not* with intensifiers
- To correctly form *so that* and *such that* clauses
- To use *too* and *(not) enough* plus infinitive phrases

OPENING TASK
How Much Is Too Much?

STEP 1 Read the article on the next page and in your own words describe the difference between an *enthusiast* and a *somethingaholic*.

The word *workaholic* is used to describe people who like their jobs so much that they are "addicted" to them. Workaholics usually have no other important interests outside of their jobs. They often neglect other responsibilities (to their families, to their own physical health, etc.) in order to concentrate on their jobs and do them well. Another word, *enthusiast*, also describes someone who likes something a great deal. However, there is an important difference in meaning between an enthusiast and an "-aholic." An enthusiast balances that interest with other things in life. The interest is **very** important, but not **too** important.

The word *workaholic* has an interesting history. It is based on the word *alcoholic*, which is used to describe a person who is addicted to alcohol. In recent years the suffix *-aholic* has been applied to other things. Although you will not find these words in a dictionary, you may hear them in conversations or on television, or read them in popular magazines. In addition to workaholics, people can sometimes be **sportaholics** (addicted to sports), **shopaholics** (addicted to shopping), **TVaholics** (addicted to watching television), or even **chocaholics** (addicted to chocolate).

STEP 2 What other kinds of **"-aholic"** people can you think of? You have read about workaholics, TVaholics, chocaholics. Work with a partner and invent at least one other term for people who carry their enthusiasm about something too far. Present your term and definition to the rest of the class.

1. This focus is an overview of the structures covered in this unit. Point this out to students. Tell them you will be going into more depth on these structures throughout the unit.

2. As an alternative, use exercises 1 and 2 as diagnostics, to determine whether or not to omit this focus and begin with the intensifiers discussed in Focus 2.

Exercise 1

S U G G E S T I O N S :

1. Assign this for homework. Make sure Ss read the entire passage before doing the exercise.

2. If you have access to an OHP, make a transparency of this exercise and underline the intensifiers as part of your whole class discussion.

 FOCUS **1**

Describing How Much or To What Degree

We can answer *how* questions about degree or intensity with *intensifiers* or *degree complements*.

	INTENSIFIERS very, too, quite, extremely, etc.	**DEGREE COMPLEMENTS** so/such . . . that . . . too/enough . . . to . . .
How devoted is Denise?	**(a)** Denise is **extremely devoted** to her job.	**(b)** Denise is **so devoted** to her job **that** she spends her weekends at the office.
How hard a worker is she?	**(c)** She's **quite a hard worker,** and even spends her weekends at the office.	**(d)** She is **such** a hard worker **that** she has no time for a personal life outside her job.
How interested is Peter in his job?	**(e)** Peter is **slightly bored** with his job.	**(f)** Peter is **too** interested in other things **to** make his job the focus of his life.
How quickly does he work?	**(g)** He works **rather slowly.**	**(h)** Peter works steadily **enough to** avoid being fired.

EXERCISE 1

Underline the intensifiers in the folowing passage. The first sentence has been done for you.

(1) Denise Driven is a <u>very</u> dedicated employee, but she's <u>a little too</u> serious. (2) Although she's extremely hard working and quite efficient, she's also rather competitive and not very friendly. (3) She comes in to work an hour earlier than anyone else and is always the last one to leave. (4) At the end of the day she's really too tired for other activities. (5) She has no hobbies and few friends. (6) She's actually a bit dull, since she's not really interested in anything but her job. (7) Peter Principle is a rather easy-going fellow. (8) Although he works fairly hard, and is

---

ANSWER KEY

Exercise 1
(1) <u>very</u> dedicated/<u>a little too</u> serious.
(2) <u>extremely</u> hard working, and <u>quite</u> efficient/<u>rather</u> competitive, and <u>not very</u> friendly.   (4) <u>really too</u> tired (6) <u>a bit</u> dull/<u>not really</u> interested   (7) <u>rather</u> easy-

going   (8) <u>fairly</u> hard/<u>reasonably</u> serious
(9) fairly (10) <u>quite</u> (11) <u>rather</u> accomplished   (13) <u>really</u> don't get along.
(14) <u>a little</u> lazy/"<u>insufficiently</u> motivated."
(15) <u>rather</u> humorless/"not <u>very</u> nice."
(16) <u>somewhat</u> difficult

---

reasonably serious about his work, his job is not the most important thing in his life, and he likes to have time to pursue other interests. (9) He lives a fairly normal life. (10) He likes spending time with his children, and he is quite active in the Lions Club. (11) He is also a rather accomplished musician. (12) He plays the clarinet in a jazz band with some of the other people from the office. (13) Peter and Denise really don't get along. (14) She thinks he's a little lazy and "insufficiently motivated." (15) He thinks she's a rather humorless workaholic who is "not very nice." (16) It's somewhat difficult to decide who's right.

EXERCISE 2

Underline the degree complements in this paragraph. For each degree complement make a *how* question.

▶ **EXAMPLE:** Denise is <u>too serious to be able to appreciate Peter's laid-back point of view.</u>

   How question: How serious is Denise?

Denise Driven and Peter Principle still aren't getting along. (1) Denise is so rushed at work these days that she doesn't have any free time. (2) She has too little energy at the end of the workday to have any hobbies. (3) She's feeling a little lonely, but she's too busy to make any close friends. (4) Peter has suggested that she take some time off, but she always says that there's too much going on at work for her to take a vacation. (5) Nothing moves fast enough for her to feel satisfied. (6) Even her secretary types too slowly to keep up with all the letters she writes. (7) Peter, on the other hand, still works hard enough to avoid being fired. (8) But, unlike Denise, he isn't so dedicated to his job that he is willing to give up everything else in order to get ahead. (9) He loves his family enough to make their needs his most important priority. (10) He's just not competitive enough about his job for Denise to consider him a threat to her authority.

Exercise 2

See the suggestion in Focus 1 and Exercise 1 about different approaches to take with this exercise.

Workbook Ex. 1, p. 56. Answers: TE p. 496.

ANSWER KEY

Exercise 2

(1) so rushed at work these days that she doesn't have any free time. (2) too little energy at the end of the workday to have any hobbies. (3) too busy to make any close friends. (4) too much going on at work for her to take a vacation. (5) fast enough for her to feel satisfied. (6) too slowly to keep up with all the letters she writes. (7) hard enough to avoid being fired. (8) so dedicated to his job that he is willing to give up everything else in order to get ahead. (9) enough to make their needs his most important priority.

(10) not competitive enough about his job for Denise to consider him a threat to her authority.

Questions:

1. How rushed at work is Denise these days?
2. How much energy does she have at the end of the day? 3. How busy is she? 4. How much work does she say is going on? 5. How fast do things move? 6. How fast does her secretary type? 7. How hard does Peter work? 8. How dedicated is he? 9. How much does he love his family? 10. How competitive is he?

1. If you are teaching in an English-speaking environment, begin this focus with student books closed. Elicit some intensifiers from students that they have heard native English speakers using. You may need to provide a couple of contemporary examples such as *"way,"* *"totally,"* or *"hecka/hella."*
2. Have Ss generate some example sentences to put on the board.
3. Ask Ss which intensifiers are appropriate in an informal situation (with friends of family) and which are more appropriate for formal situations (with teachers, bosses, etc.).
4. Have Ss turn to the focus and make sure they are familiar with the intensifiers listed there.
5. If you are teaching overseas, or in contexts where Ss do not have an opportunity to hear native speakers on a regular basis, present this focus with books open in a straightforward way.

FOCUS **2**

FORM | USE | MEANING

▶ **Intensifiers**

MEANING	MORE FORMAL INTENSIFIERS	LESS FORMAL (CONVERSATIONAL) INTENSIFIERS
an excessive degree	(a) That's **too** expensive.	(b) She's **way too** serious.
a great degree	(c) Denise is **quite** busy. (d) She's **extremely** dedicated. (e) She works **very** hard.	(f) Denise is **really** busy. (g) She works **so** hard! (h) She's **awful(ly)** serious.
a moderate degree	(i) He's a **rather** accomplished musician. (j) It's **somewhat** difficult to decide who is right. (k) He's **fairly** hard-working. (l) He does his job **reasonably** well. (m) He works hard **enough.**	(n) Peter's **pretty** dedicated. (o) Denise is **kind of** depressed. (p) He's **sort of** easygoing.
a small degree	(q) He gets **slightly** annoyed. (r) She's **a bit** competitive. (s) Work can sometimes be **a little** monotonous.	(t) He's a **tad** lazy.
an insufficient degree	(u) He doesn't work hard **enough.**	(v) Peter doesn't get paid **near(ly) enough.**

The position of intensifiers in a sentence

EXAMPLES	EXPLANATIONS
(a) Denise works **extremely hard.** (b) Peter works **steadily enough.**	All intensifiers come before the adjective or adverb, except *enough*, which comes after.
(c) Denise is **a very dedicated** worker. (d) She is **quite a dedicated** worker.	In noun phrases, intensifiers come between the determiner (*a, the, some*, etc.) and the adjective, except for *quite*, which comes before the determiner.

128 | UNIT 8

EXERCISE 3

Use the intensifiers from Focus 2 to describe the skills and activities listed below. Make statements that are true for you.

1. **a skill you are proud of:** something you do well to a moderate degree

   ▶ **EXAMPLE:** I'm a pretty good tennis player.

2. **a favorite food:** a kind of food you like to a great degree

   ▶ **EXAMPLE:** I'm extremely fond of popcorn.

3. **something that is not enjoyable for you, but you don't hate:** an activity you dislike to a small degree

   ▶ **EXAMPLE:** Doing homework can be slightly boring.

4. **an ability you want to develop:** a skill you have in an insufficient degree

   ▶ **EXAMPLE:** I don't speak English fluently enough.

5. **a bad habit:** something you do to an excessive degree

   ▶ **EXAMPLE:** I eat too much ice cream.

6. **a special talent:** something you do well to a great degree

   ▶ **EXAMPLE:** I'm a really good musician.

Intensifiers (very, too, enough, etc.) and Degree Complements (so, so that, such that, etc.) | **129**

Exercise 3

If your Ss are not good at creating sentences, do this exercise in pairs and have Ss describe their partner's skills, favorite foods, etc.

ANSWER KEY

Exercise 3
Answers will vary. Possible answers include:
1. I'm a pretty good baseball player. I'm a rather good violinist. 2. I'm extremely fond of coke. I really like chocolate. 3. Doing homework can be slightly boring. Writing grammar books can be a little monotonous. 4. I don't speak Spanish fluently enough. I read fast enough. 5. I eat too much ice cream. I stay up too late on Saturday nights. 6. I'm a really good musician. I'm an awfully good dancer.

Exercise 4

Assign this exercise for individual homework, or do it together as a whole class discussion, allowing time for Ss to suggest alternative restatements.

Workbook Ex. 2, pp. 56–57. Answers: TE p. 496.

EXERCISE 4

Are the following sentences written in formal or informal style? If they are in informal/conversational style, change the intensifier to make the sentence more formal. If they are in formal style, change the intensifier to make the sentence less formal. There are several possible answers, so be prepared to explain why you chose the answer you did.

▶ **EXAMPLES:** That sun is so hot! *(Informal)*

More formal: _That sun is very hot._

I'm rather tired, so I won't be able to attend your party. *(Formal)*

Less formal: _I'm pretty tired . . ._

1. I'm kind of sick today.
2. I'm somewhat confused by all your questions.
3. She's really unfriendly.
4. He's quite annoyed about the broken window.
5. I'm sort of busy right now.
6. It's rather hot here, don't you think?
7. Peter works pretty hard.
8. Denise is pretty serious.
9. That man is awfully hard to understand.

FOCUS **3**

▶ *Too* Versus *Very*

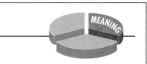

VERY—a great degree	TOO—an excessive degree (so much of something that it is not good)
(a) This car is **very** expensive, but maybe I'll buy it anyway.	**(b)** This car is **too** expensive. I can't afford it.
(c) Denise is **very** serious about her work. She's a good worker.	**(d)** Denise is **too** serious about her work. She's a workaholic.

EXERCISE 5

Complete these sentences using *too* or *very*.

1. We got there _____ late. The plane had already taken off.
2. I'm _____ busy, but I think I can finish the report for you.
3. Denise works _____ hard for her own good. She's going to get sick if she's not careful.
4. Denise works _____ hard because she's ambitious and wants to get ahead.
5. Don't bother to invite Jose to the party. He's _____ serious to have any fun!
6. The accident happened _____ quickly, but I'm _____ sure that the driver of the sports car didn't use his turn signal.
7. Children are growing up _____ quickly these days. They try to act like adults while they're still kids!
8. We arrived at the party _____ late, but there was still a little food left.
9. We arrived at the party _____ late. All the guests had left.
10. I really like Mary. I think she's _____ intelligent and has a great personality!
11. It's _____ hot. Let's forget about the tennis game.

SUGGESTION:

Write the first parts of **sentence a and b** on the board and ask Ss if they mean the same thing or different things. If possible, elicit an explanation of this difference from the class.

Exercise 5

Do this exercise as an immediate in-class follow-up of your presentation of Focus 3. Point out the contexts that communicate the notion of "too much" as opposed to "very."

Workbook Ex. 3, p. 57. Answers: TE p. 496.

ANSWER KEY

Exercises 5

1. too 2. very 3. too 4. very 5. too
6. very/too; very 7. too 8. very 9. too
10. too 11. too

Using Intensifiers with *Too*

EXAMPLES	EXPLANATION
(a) It's **way too** difficult! (b) It's **really too** hot. (c) It's **a little too** expensive. (d) It's **a bit too** late.	We use a few intensifiers with *too* to indicate how excessive something is.

EXERCISE 6

Complete these sentences, using an intensifier with *too*.

▶ **EXAMPLES:** You just missed the plane. You arrived a bit too late.

I can't reach the top shelf. It's a little too high.

1. I don't have quite that much money. It's _____.
2. I wish she would smile more. She's _____.
3. There's no way I can help you finish that report. I'm _____.
4. Only a couple of students passed the test. The test was _____.
5. The coffee needs more sugar. It's _____.

EXERCISE 7

Pick five things from the list below that you don't like. Add two other things that aren't on the list. Give reasons for your dislike, using *too* and an intensifier.

▶ **EXAMPLES:** I don't like workaholics. They're really *too* serious.

I don't like dogs. They're a little *too* friendly.

babies	workaholics	studying grammar
dogs	diamond necklaces	being away from my family
cats	summer weather	rap music
spinach	sports cars	police officers
liberals	conservatives	

FOCUS 5

▶ **U**sing Intensifiers with *Not*

These intensifiers (***too, very, so, really, quite***) can be used in negative sentences to "soften" a statement or make it more indirect or polite.

EXAMPLES	IMPLIED MEANING
(a) Tom's new dog is **not too bright**.	It's **rather stupid**.
(b) Sometimes Peter does**n't** work **very hard**.	Sometimes he's **lazy**.
(c) Please **don't** drive **so fast**.	Please drive **more slowly**.
(d) She's **not really interested** in sports.	She's **somewhat bored** with sports.
(e) I'm **not quite sure** I like that dog.	I'm **afraid of** that dog.

EXERCISE 8

Make these sentences more polite by replacing or adding intensifiers that use *not*. There may be more than one way to "soften" your comment.

▶ **EXAMPLES:** This movie's pretty boring. <u>It's not too interesting.</u>

He dances rather badly. <u>He doesn't dance too well.</u>

1. She's quite unfriendly. _____

2. Mary's somewhat unhappy with you. _____

3. I hate spinach. _____

4. Mark is a terrible cook. _____

5. Beth dislikes listening to other people's problems. _____

6. It's too crowded for me. _____

Stress the importance of softening negative statements in social situations. You can even teach the word "diplomatic" in this context.

Exercise 8

Do this exercise as a whole class. In your processing, be sure to invite more than one alternative way to soften the statements.

Workbook Exs. 5–6, pp. 58–59. Answers: TE p. 496.

ANSWER KEY

Exercises 8
Answers will vary. Possible answers include:
1. She's not too friendly./She's not very friendly. 2. Mary's not too happy with you./She's not so happy with you. 3. I'm not too fond of spinach./I don't really like spinach.

4. Mark isn't really a very good cook./Mark isn't such a great cook. 5. Beth isn't too interested in listening to other people's problems./She doesn't really enjoy listening to other people's problems. 6. I don't have quite enough room./There's not too much space.

1. With Ss books closed, write some simple contextualized "how" questions referring to real people and situations in your class on the board such as "*How fast did Juan run?*" "*How cheap were the notebooks that Ilse bought?*" and ask Ss to answer them with *too & enough* constructions.
2. Take Ss responses and rephrase them as *too & enough* structures. Answers to the questions above could be framed as "*Juan ran too slow to catch the bus.*" or "*The notebooks were cheap enough for Ilse to buy two of them.*"
3. Have Ss open their books to this page and go through the focus in a more detailed fashion. Be sure to point out the differences in word order between *too* and *enough*.

FOCUS **6**

FORM

Degree Complements with *Too* and *Enough*

Too + **infinitive phrase**

	EXAMPLES
too + adjective	**(a)** Some teenagers are **too immature** to make really wise decisions.
too + adverb	**(b)** They grow **too quickly** for clothes to fit for very long.
too much/little + noncount noun	**(c)** They have **too much pride** to ask for advice from their elders.
	(d) They have **too little patience** to wait for complete freedom.
too many/few + count noun	**(e)** They have **too many controls** to be able to feel truly independent.
	(f) They have **too few chances** to exercise responsibility.
verb + *too much/little*	**(g)** Teenagers think they **know too much** to listen to their parents and **too little** to be responsible for their actions

Enough + **infinitive phrase**

	EXAMPLES
adjective + *enough*	**(h)** Most teenagers are **responsible enough** to do a good job.
adverb + *enough*	**(i)** They work **hard enough** to get the same pay as adults.
verb + *enough*	**(j)** They have **learned enough** to make wise decisions.
enough + noun	**(k)** Parents often give their teenagers **enough responsibility** to prepare them for adult life.

134 UNIT 8

EXERCISE 9

Restate these pairs of sentences with statements of degree using *too* and *enough*.

▶ **EXAMPLES:** Denise is very serious about her career. She doesn't understand why Peter is so relaxed.

Denise is too serious about her career to understand why Peter is so relaxed.

Peter isn't terribly serious about his job. He doesn't want to spend every weekend at the office.

Peter isn't serious enough about his job to want to spend every weekend at the office.

1. Denise has lots of responsibilities. She can't take a vacation right now.
2. The pace of work is extremely hectic. Denise can't do her best work.
3. Denise's secretary types very slowly. Denise can't catch up on her correspondence.
4. Mr. Green hasn't assigned Denise much additional clerical support. Denise can't meet the contract deadline.
5. Denise is very proud. She doesn't want to ask her boss for more help.
6. Denise isn't nice to Peter. He won't offer to help her with the contract.
7. There is always a little free time. Peter spends it on his friends, his music, and his family.
8. Peter plays the clarinet quite well. He could be a professional musician.
9. He doesn't like Denise. He won't help her meet her contract deadline.
10. Work is not that important. Peter doesn't make it the focus of his life.

Exercise 9

Assign pairs to work on only two or three sentences and then process as a whole class. Ss may need help initially in deciding whether to use *too* or *enough* in their answers. You can tell them which to use.

Workbook Ex. 7, pp. 59–60. Answers: TE p. 496.

ANSWER KEY

Exercise 9

1. Denise has too many responsibilities to take a vacation right now. 2. The pace of work is too hectic for Denise to do her best work. 3. Denise's secretary types too slowly for Denise to catch up on her correspondence. 4. Mr. Green hasn't assigned Denise enough additional clerical support for her to meet the contract deadline. 5. Denise is too proud to ask her boss for more help. 6. Denise isn't nice enough to Peter for him to offer to help her with the contract. 7. There is always enough free time for Peter to spend on his friends, his music, and his family. 8. Peter plays the clarinet well enough to be a professional musician. 9. He doesn't like Denise enough to help her meet her contract deadline. 10. Work is not important enough for Peter to make it the focus of his life.

The potential ambiguity of these structures is important, but may be a little difficult for lower-level classes. You may want to skip this focus and let Ss' understanding of the implied meaning of these structures "emerge" over time.

Exercise 10

Do this exercise as a whole class or have Ss discuss in pairs first.

Workbook Ex. 8, p. 60. Answers: TE p. 496.

▶ Implied Meanings
of *Too* and *Not Enough*

The implied meaning of the infinitive phrase depends on which degree word we have chosen and the situation we are using it in.

EXAMPLES	POSSIBLE IMPLIED MEANINGS
(a) Mr. Green is **too old to worry** about losing his hair.	He doesn't worry about losing his hair. OR He worries about it, but he shouldn't.
(b) Mr. Green **is not young enough to wear** the latest fashions.	He doesn't wear the latest fashions. OR He wears those fashions, but he shouldn't.
(c) He is **wise enough to listen** to both sides in the argument.	He listens to both sides.
(d) He is **wise enough not to take sides** in the argument.	He doesn't take sides.

EXERCISE 10

Choose the correct implied meaning for these degree complements:

1. Teenagers are too young to buy alcoholic beverages.
   (a) They can buy alcoholic beverages.
   (b) They can not buy alcoholic beverages.

2. Peter does not work hard enough to be promoted.
   (a) He will be promoted.
   (b) He won't be promoted.

3. Mr. Green is wise enough to avoid taking sides in the argument.
   (a) He avoids taking sides in the argument.
   (b) He never avoids taking sides in the argument.

4. Teenagers think they are smart enough not to make mistakes.
   (a) They think they might make mistakes.
   (b) They think they won't make mistakes.

ANSWER KEY

Exercise 10

1. b **2.** b **3.** a **4.** b

EXERCISE 11

Decide whether you agree with the following statements about teenagers. Use *too* or *enough* and an infinitive to give your opinion about things that fifteen-year-olds are old enough or too young to do.

Exercise 11

Workbook Ex. 9, pp. 61–62. Answers: TE p. 497.

Fifteen-year-olds are old enough . . .

Fifteen-year-olds are too young . . .

▶ **EXAMPLES:** Fifteen-year-olds are old enough to drive.

Fifteen-year-olds are too young for their parents to let them live in their own apartments.

1. They should be able to drive.
2. They shouldn't live in their own apartments.
3. They can fall in love.
4. Schools should let them choose what classes they want to take.
5. Teachers should talk to them as adults.
6. They shouldn't be able to buy alcohol or cigarettes.
7. Their parents should give them some financial responsibility.
8. The law shouldn't treat them as adults.
9. They shouldn't be police officers or soldiers.
10. Society shouldn't give them total freedom.

Intensifiers (very, too, enough, etc.) and Degree Complements (so, so that, such that, etc.) **137**

ANSWER KEY

Exercise 11

Answers will vary. Possible answers include:
1. They are old enough to drive./They're too young to drive. 2. They're old enough for their parents to let them live in their own apartments./They're too young for their parents to let them live in their own apartments. 3. They're old enough to fall in love./They're too young to fall in love. 4. They're old enough to be allowed to choose what classes they want to take./They're too young to be allowed to choose what classes they want to take. 5. They're old enough for teachers to talk to them as adults./They're too young for teachers to talk to them as adults. 6. They're old enough to be able to buy alcohol or cigarettes./They're too young to be able to buy alcohol or cigarettes. 7. They are old enough to be given some financial responsibility./They're too young to be given some financial responsibility. 8. They're old enough for the law to treat them as adults./They're too young for the law to treat them as adults. 9. They're old enough to be police officers or soldiers./They're not old enough to be police officers or soldiers. 10. They're old enough for society to give them total freedom./They're too young to be given total freedom.

Exercise 12

Don't be reluctant to relax and let students (and yourself) have fun with this exercise. Have the class vote on the most foolish question and award a silly prize. Teach the class "duh!" as a generic response to foolish questions.

EXERCISE 12

Working with a partner, ask and answer the following "foolish" questions. Answer the question with a *yes* or *no,* and give a reason for your answer using *too.* Then try to restate your answer using *enough.* Ask your partner five more "foolish" questions of your own.

▶ **EXAMPLES:** Can you swim to Hawaii?

No. It's *too* far for someone to swim.

No. Nobody is strong *enough* to swim to Hawaii.

1. Do you have any great-great-grandchildren?
2. Can you walk 150 miles in a single day?
3. Is $50 a fair price for a cup of coffee?
4. Can dogs read?
5. Do banana trees grow wild in Russia?
6. Can one person lift a grand piano?
7. Can you learn to speak English fluently in a week?
8. Can a hundred-year-old woman still have babies?
9. Do you remember what you did on your first birthday?
10. Can you eat fifty hamburgers in a single meal?

ANSWER KEY

Exercise 12

Answers will vary. Possible answers include:
1. No, I'm too young to have any. 2. No, that's not enough time to walk that far. 3. No, that's too expensive. 4. No, they're not intelligent enough to read. 5. No, it's too cold in Russia for banana trees to grow wild. 6. No, one person isn't strong enough to lift a grand piano. 7. No, that's too little time to learn to speak English fluently. 8. No she's no longer young/ strong enough to have babies. 9. No, I was too young to remember. That was too long ago for me to remember. 10. No, that's too many for me to eat.

EXERCISE 13

Working with a partner ask and answer these questions. Give your real opinions.
Use *enough* in your answer.

▶ **EXAMPLE:** Why don't some people pass the TOEFL?

Because they don't know enough English to get a high score.

1. How much money do you need for a happy life?
2. How well do you speak English?
3. When should children move out of their parents' home?
4. When should people get married?
5. How quickly or slowly should a person drive on a turnpike or freeway?
6. What's an ideal age to retire?
7. What kind of peson should be president?
8. What is an important characteristic for a basketball player?
9. Why can't monkeys learn languages?

EXERCISE 14

Do you have all the money or all the free time you wish you had? Are there some
things you are **not** able to do because you don't have enough resources or time,
or because you have too many responsibilities?
Write sentences that describe five activities you can't do, and what keeps you
from doing them.

▶ **EXAMPLES:** I don't have enough time to read novels.

I'm too poor to take a vacation this summer.

Intensifiers (very, too, enough, etc.) and Degree Complements (so, so that, such that, etc.) | **139**

Exercise 13
This exercise can be done in small groups or
as a whole class.

Exercise 14
This is a good exercise to assign as
homework for Ss to write and hand in for you
to evaluate.

A N S W E R   K E Y

Exercise 13
Answers will vary. Possible answers include:
1. Enough to feed, clothe, and educate your
children. 2. I speak it well enough to
understand most of what I hear and read.
3. When they have enough money to live by
themselves. 4. When they are old enough to
make mature decisions. 5. Fast enough to
keep up with the rest of the traffic. 6. When
you are still young enough to enjoy your life.
7. Someone who is honest enough to be
trusted with the responsibility. 8. He or she
should be tall enough to reach the basket easily.
9. They aren't intelligent enough to do it.

Exercise 14
Answers will vary. Possible answers include:
I have too much work to take a vacation. I don't
have enough energy at the end of the day to go
to the gym. I'm too old to take up roller blading.
I'm not old enough to retire.

1. Start this focus on a day after your treatment of *too* and *enough* complements.
2. With Ss books closed, write a class-related example of each structure on the board, and then write an analogous version using *so/such + that*. (For example: "*Juan ran too slow to catch the bus.*" "*Juan ran so slow that he missed the bus.*" "*The notebooks were cheap enough for Ilse to buy two of them.*" "*They were such cheap notebooks that Ilse bought two of them.*")
3. Only after this basic presentation should you turn to the focus in the book. Don't forget to draw Ss' attention to the common deletion of *that* in these structures.

FORM

▶ Degree Complements with *So* and *Such*

So + Such + that clauses

	EXAMPLES
so + adjective	**(a)** Denise is **so serious** about her work that she rarely takes a vacation.
so + adverb	**(b)** Peter plays the clarinet **so well** that he once considered being a professional musician.
so + many/few + (count noun)	**(c)** Denise writes **so many letters** that her secretary can't type them fast enough.
	(d) She has **so few outside interests** that most people consider her rather boring.
so + much/little + (noncount noun)	**(e)** The project took **so much time** that Denise had to spend her weekend in the office.
	(f) Denise works **so much** that she never has time for friends or hobbies.
	(g) They have **so little time** to get the job done that they'll have to spend the weekend in the office.
such + (a/an) + (adjective) + noun	**(h)** The disagreement between Peter and Denise has become **such a serious problem** that they are not speaking to each other.
	(i) Denise gives her secretary **such large amounts** of work that she is thinking about quitting.

In spoken English and less formal written English the *that* in *so/such* constructions can be omitted.

(j)	I'm so happy **that** I could fly	OR **(k)**	I'm so happy, I could fly.
(l)	Denise is such a serious person **that** she probably doesn't know how to have fun.	OR **(m)**	Denise is such a serious person, she probably doesn't know how to have fun.

EXERCISE 15

Identify the degree complements in this passage by underlining the result clauses where *that* has been omitted. The first paragraph has been done for you as an example.

Tall Tales

(1) In American English we use the term *tall tale* to describe stories that are so exaggerated <u>they become funny.</u> (2) No one really believes that they're true. (3) That's part of the fun. (4) The point of a tall tale is to tell such incredible lies <u>everyone ends up laughing.</u> (5) American folklore is filled with examples of tall tales.

(6) One famous tall tale is the story of the winter when the weather was so cold everything froze. (7) Each day things got a little colder. (8) First the usual things froze: water, plants, pipes, machinery. (9) Then it got worse. (10) It was such a cold winter dogs and cats froze when they went outside, and birds fell out of the sky, frozen solid. (11) Then it got even worse. (12) It got so cold people's words froze whenever they tried to talk. (13) You couldn't hear a single sound. (14) Of course, people like to talk, no matter how cold it is. (15) So people kept talking and their words kept freezing just as soon as they came out of heir mouths.

(16) Then suddenly the cold weather came to an end. (17) One day it was so cold nobody could carry on a conversation because the words just froze right up, and the next day it was warm enough to wear shorts. (18) The change in weather was so great and so sudden everything became unfrozen all at the exact same minute. (19) All those frozen words thawed out at once, and the resulting noise was so loud everyone became deaf.

EXERCISE 16

Make statements of degree about the underlined items in these pairs of sentences by using *so* and *such*.

▶ **EXAMPLES:** There are <u>many plants</u> in the rain forest with possible medical uses. Scientists fear we may lose valuable medical resources if they are destroyed

There are <u>so many</u> plants in the rain forest with possible medical uses <u>that</u> scientists fear we may lose valuable medical resources if they are destroyed.

1. The world's forests are being destroyed at a <u>rapid rate.</u>

   We can't ignore the problem any longer.

2. The world population is growing <u>quickly.</u>

   We can't continue our old habits.

Intensifiers (very, too, enough, etc.) and Degree Complements (so, so that, such that, etc.) | **141**

Exercise 15

SUGGESTIONS:

1. Assign this exercise for homework. Make sure Ss read the entire passage before they do the exercise.
2. If you have access to an OHP, make a transparency of this exercise and underline the degree complements as part of your in-class correction of the exercise.

Exercise 16

You can make this exercise "shorter" by assigning each pair to do two, and then processing as a whole class.

ANSWER KEY

Exercise 15

(6) <u>everything froze</u> (10) <u>dogs and cats froze when they went outside, and birds fell out of the sky, frozen solid.</u> (12) <u>people's words froze whenever they tried to talk.</u> (17) <u>nobody could carry on a conversation because the words just froze right up/to wear shorts.</u> (18) <u>everything became unfrozen all at the exact same minute.</u> (19) <u>everyone became deaf.</u>

Exercise 16

1. The world's forests are being destroyed at such an alarming rate that we can't ignore the problem any longer. 2. The world population is growing so quickly that we can't continue our old habits. 3. We have so few alternative materials that we haven't stopped using trees for fuel. 4. There has been such a rapid growth in population that there are no other places for people to live except the rain forests. 5. Some countries have so few other natural resources that they are forced to use the rain forests for economic development. 6. The problems appear so impossible to solve that some countries haven't even begun to look for a solution. 7. The United Nations considers deforestation such a problem that they are trying to establish conservation programs throughout the developing world. 8. The loss of the rain forests is such a major global threat that the future of mankind may be at stake.

3. We have <u>few alternative materials.</u>

We haven't stopped using trees for fuel.

4. There has been <u>a rapid growth</u> in population.

There are no other places for people to live except the rain forests.

5. Some countries have <u>few other natural resources.</u>

They are forced to use the rain forests for economic development.

6. The problems appear <u>impossible</u> to solve.

Some countries haven't even begun to look for a solution.

7. The United Nations considers deforestation <u>a problem.</u>

They are trying to establish conservation programs throughout the developing world.

8. The loss of the rain forests is a <u>major global threat.</u>

The future of mankind may be at stake.

EXERCISE 17

Give true answers to these questions using *so/such*.

▶ **EXAMPLE:** What kind of student are you?

I'm such a good student that I always do my homework before class.

1. What kind of student are you?

2. How quickly or slowly do you walk or drive?

3. Have you ever wanted something a great deal? How badly did you want it?

4. Did you ever eat a huge amount of food? What happened?

5. How high are the Himalayan Mountains?

6. Did you have a good time on your first birthday?

7. How tall was the tallest person you've ever seen?

8. How hard is the TOEFL?

9. What happened in the most boring class you've ever been to?

10. How wonderful is your grammar teacher?

Exercise 17

You can have Ss interview and report a partner's answers to the rest of the class ("*Yanti is such a good student that she always does her homework before class.*")

Workbook Exs. 10–11, pp. 62–63. Answers: TE p. 497.

UNIT GOAL REVIEW

Ask Ss to look at the goals on the opening page of the unit again. Help them understand how much they have accomplished in each area. Have them use each of the goals to develop a description of what they learned in this unit. Examples of such statements are:

I learned that . . . intensifiers are <u>really</u> important in conversation. . . . degree complements are <u>so complicated that</u> you need to practice them a lot. . . . the difference between very and too is <u>too important to</u> ignore.

A N S W E R   K E Y

Exercise 17

Answers will vary. Possible answers include:
1. I'm such a good student that I always do my homework before class. 2. I drive so quickly that I get a speeding ticket once a week. 3. I once wanted a new bicycle so badly that I saved every penny of my allowance for over a year. 4. I once ate so much food that I got sick. 5. They're so high that climbers have to carry oxygen with them when they climb them. 6. I was so busy that I didn't celebrate it. 7. He was so tall that he had to buy his clothing at a special store 8. It's so hard that many people have to take it several times before they get a good score. 9. It was so boring that even the teacher fell asleep. 10. My grammar teacher is so wonderful that he can answer any question.

Use Your English

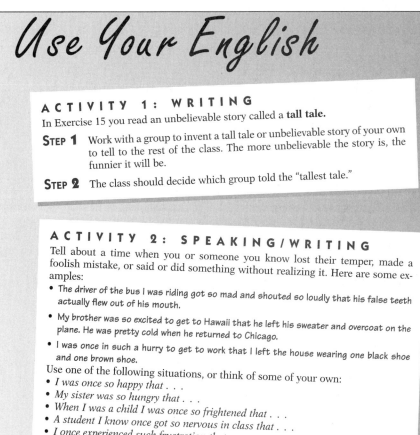

ACTIVITY 1: WRITING

In Exercise 15 you read an unbelievable story called a **tall tale.**

STEP 1 Work with a group to invent a tall tale or unbelievable story of your own to tell to the rest of the class. The more unbelievable the story is, the funnier it will be.

STEP 2 The class should decide which group told the "tallest tale."

ACTIVITY 2: SPEAKING/WRITING

Tell about a time when you or someone you know lost their temper, made a foolish mistake, or said or did something without realizing it. Here are some examples:

- The driver of the bus I was riding got so mad and shouted so loudly that his false teeth actually flew out of his mouth.
- My brother was so excited to get to Hawaii that he left his sweater and overcoat on the plane. He was pretty cold when he returned to Chicago.
- I was once in such a hurry to get to work that I left the house wearing one black shoe and one brown shoe.

Use one of the following situations, or think of some of your own:
- *I was once so happy that . . .*
- *My sister was so hungry that . . .*
- *When I was a child I was once so frightened that . . .*
- *A student I know once got so nervous in class that . . .*
- *I once experienced such frustration that . . .*
- *I was once so angry that . . .*

ACTIVITY 3: LISTENING/ SPEAKING/WRITING

When are adult children old enough to move away from home? Different cultures have different opinions about when (and if) this should happen. Interview people from three or four different countries. What is the average age at which people move away from home? What do other people think if someone leaves home at a much younger or much older age than the average? Are there different standards for men and women? Make a report on what you have discovered. It can be written report or an oral presentation to the rest of the class.

USE YOUR ENGLISH

All the activities in this unit can be used for diagnostic or testing activities by having Ss write responses.

Activities 1 & 2

These activities are best used as oral activities for fun rather than as formal assignments.

Activity 3
EXPANSION

Combine this activity with Activity 4 and have Ss interview other people outside of class.

Activity 4

Use Activity 3 as part of this activity to help Ss formulate the questions they will ask in their out-of-class interviews.

ACTIVITY 4: LISTENING/ SPEAKING/WRITING

Using this chart, interview a partner about what things he or she thinks people are old enough to do at the age of fifteen, and what things he or she thinks people are still too young to do. Then ask your partner to think of one other thing that people are old enough to do at age fifteen, and one more thing they're still too young to do. For all the things that your partner feels people are still too young to do, find out what age he or she feels is old enough for those things. Some examples have been provided for you.

ACTIVITIES	OLD ENOUGH OR TOO YOUNG?	WHY?
marry and raise a family	too young	They are not mature enough to take that responsibility. They should be in their twenties.
decide on a future career	old enough	They already know the kinds of things they like to do and the kinds of things they are good at.
fall in love		
drive a car		
go on dates without a chaperone		
make wise decisions about life		
live independently outside their parents' home		
pay taxes		
serve in the army		
get a full-time job		
get a part-time job		
take care of young children		
write poetry		
be a professional athlete		
vote in national elections		
control their own money		
become parents		
	too young	
	old enough	

ACTIVITY 5: WRITING

Write a short (one page) essay that describes how you feel about the importance of work in your life. Here are some questions you may wish to answer:
- Is work more or less important than other things in your life?
- Could you ever become a workaholic? Why or not not?
- Who would you rather work with, Denise Driven or Peter Principle? Why?

Activities 5 & 6
VARIATION

Use these activities for a small-group discussion.

ACTIVITY 6: WRITING

Write a short (one page) essay about the following topic:
There's a popular saying in America that it's not possible to be too rich, too good-looking, or too thin.
- Do you agree? Are there some qualities or characteristics that no one can have too much of? If so, what are they? Why do you feel that nobody can have too much of those qualities?
- Do you disagree? Is there a negative aspect to being extremely good-looking, wealthy, or fashionably slim?

ACTIVITY 7: LISTENING/ WRITING

STEP 1 Listen to the following lecture on the destruction of tropical rain forests. Use the outline below to organize the information from the lecture.

I. Economic impact of rapid population growth
   A.
   B.
II. Result of economic impact on rain forests
III. Problems with reforestation
IV. Primary reasons to maintain existing rainforest areas
   A.
   B.

STEP 2 Write a one or two sentence summary of the lecture.

_____

_____

_____

_____

Activity 7

Play textbook audio. The tapescript for this listening appears on pp. 513–514 of this book.

Let Ss listen for a maximum of three times: once for the general idea, once to take notes, and once to verify how they filled in the outline on the student book.

✓ The test for this unit can be found on p. 454. The answers are on p. 455 of this book.

Intensifiers (very, too, enough, etc.) and Degree Complements (so, so that, such that, etc.) | **145**

ANSWER KEY

Activity 7
Here is one version of the information from the lecture in outline and summary form.

I. Economic impact of rapid population growth
A. Developing countries need foreign exchange, which they can get by selling wood from the trees that grow in the rain forest. **(lumber for export)**
B. Developing countries need additional land for their growing populations. **(land for agriculture)**

II. Result of economic impact on rain forests
Many countries have started to develop lands that only a few years ago were uninhabited, dense tropical rain forest. This process of destruction is happening so rapidly, unless we can slow it down, <u>all</u> the world's rain forests will be completely gone in just another 20 years!

III. Problems with reforestation
Once the rain forests have been cut down, they don't just grow back. There is too little fertility in the soil of most tropical areas for the jungle to grow back again.

IV. Primary reasons to maintain existing rain forest areas
A. Rain forests contain so many plants with possible medical uses that scientists are worried that many valuable species will be destroyed before we can find out how useful they are.
B. There is a clear relationship between rain forests and the climate and weather patterns of the entire world. Rain forests are disappearing so quickly that scientists are afraid that this may already be causing changes in the atmosphere and weather of the planet.

Summary of the lecture
The destruction of the rain forests is a result of rapid population growth, which causes the need for export commodities and land for agriculture. If we can't halt the destruction of the world's rain forests, we may lose scientifically valuable plant species and forever change the world's climate.

Unit 9

UNIT OVERVIEW

This unit provides an overview of adjective word order and the often troubling topic of present and past participles used as modifiers. See *The Grammar Book,* Chapter 20 (pp. 381–400) for a more detailed discussion of these structures.

UNIT GOALS

Review the goals listed on this page so students (Ss) understand what they should be able to do by the end of the unit.

OPENING TASK

S U G G E S T I O N S :

1. Make this task more interactive by having Ss work on Steps 1 and 2 in pairs.
2. Have Ss get up and move around the room for Step 2.
3. To use this task as a diagnostic, specify that the object descriptions must be written as single-sentence descriptions, and then have Ss hand them in for your evaluation/correction.

U N I T 9

MODIFYING NOUN PHRASES

Adjectives and Participles

UNIT GOALS:

- To put adjective modifiers in the correct order
- To form and to understand the meaning of present and past participle modifiers
- To use other noun modifiers in the proper order

OPENING TASK
Going to a Flea Market

STEP 1 The objects above are all for sale at a flea market—a place where people sell things they don't want anymore. Match the objects with the descriptions.
- one slightly used, antique, blue Moroccan dish
- two interesting little wooden statues from China
- a really beautiful old Italian glass bowl
- a fascinating collection of rare, used English textbooks

STEP 2 Think of two things you own that you don't want anymore. Write a short description of each thing. Show your descriptions to your classmates. Try to find classmates who want to buy your things, and find two things you want to buy from classmates.

1. With Ss' books closed, write *We read . . . +* example g on the board. Ask Ss what the object of the verb is. They will probably say *books*, but you should underline the whole NP (all of example g) and tell them "*we are going to look at all the things that are included in noun phrases—both nouns and the things that modify them.*"

2. Ask Ss to identify the various categories in the example sentence (determiners, intensifiers, adjectives and participles, noun modifiers, and modifying phrases and clauses). It is likely that Ss won't be able to identify all these things, so be prepared to underline the relevant structures in the example sentence.

3. If necessary, repeat this process with some other complex noun phrases:

   possible choices: *We ate the extremely delicious fried meat dumplings that your mother cooked.*

   They bought my rather dirty old leather briefcase from Mexico.

4. Refer Ss to the focus on this page for further analysis or for study at home.

Word Order in Noun Phrases

A noun phrase consists of a determiner and noun plus all its modifiers.

TYPES OF NOUN PHRASES	PARTS OF NOUN PHRASES
determiner + noun (a) the books; **these** books (b) **my** books; **some** books	**Kinds of determiners** articles, demonstratives, possessives, quantifiers
determiner (+ modifiers) + noun (c) some **extremely interesting, really beautiful used** books (d) some interesting, really beautiful used **grammar** books	**Kinds of modifiers** adjectives and participles (with or without intensifiers) other nouns
determiner (+ modifiers) + noun + (modifying phrases and clauses) (e) some interesting, really beautiful used grammar books **with red covers** (f) some interesting, really beautiful used grammar books **printed in China** with red covers (g) some interesting, really beautiful used grammar books printed in China with red covers **that we studied last semester**	**Kinds of modifying phrases and clauses** prepositional phrases participle phrases relative clauses

Although it is rare to have more than three or four modifiers for a single noun phrase, this is the usual order for different categories of modifiers.

Determiner	Intensifiers	Adjectives and Participles	Noun Modifier	Noun	Modifying Phrases
the/a/an some/no my/your each/every these/those	really very slightly	old/new interesting well-known	stone university	wall campus	next to the river described in the brochure

EXERCISE 1

From the chart below, make five noun phrases that use more than one modifier. Then write a sentence for each noun phrase. Compare your sentences to the examples and those of several other students.

Determiners	Intensifiers	Adjectives and Participles	Noun Modifiers	Nouns
a	very	little	stone	teacher
some	rather	experienced	English	statue
your	extremely	cute	circus	animals
the	quite	famous	university	watch
this	wonderfully	relaxing	pocket	professor
those	really	expensive	three-week	vacation
	somewhat	good	grammar	
		pleasant		
		ugly		

▶ **EXAMPLES:** I like those really expensive pocket watches.

Only your very experienced English teachers will know the answer.

Many very famous university professors are not very good teachers.

This exercise can be done individually, in pairs, or in groups. Answers will vary widely. Check to make sure that intensifiers "match" descriptive adjectives, and determiners "match" nouns (e.g.:"*some wonderfully pleasant stone statue*" or "*this rather gold grammar animals*" would not be appropriate answers).

Workbook Ex. 1, p. 64. Answers: TE p. 497.

1. Refer back to the example sentence that you used (sentence g from Focus 1) and highlight the adjectives/participle (". . . *really beautiful used* . . .").
2. Ask Ss to supply other adjectives to add information. Prompt responses by asking questions like "big or small," "round or square." Elicit two or three more adjectives to insert.
3. Tell Ss that many times these additional modifiers must appear in a particular order and ask them to open their books to p. 150. Point out each of the categories and ask Ss if they can name one or two other adjectives in each category.

   Other examples:
   evaluation: attractive, nifty, pleasant
   appearance—size: light, huge, tiny
   shape: rectangular, oblong
   condition: filthy, spotless, shiny
   age: brand-new, modern,
   color: puce, mauve, magenta, lavender
   origin: American, Canadian
   material: bronze, steel, chiffon
4. Do Exercise 2 as an immediate follow-up.

Order of Descriptive Adjectives

Different categories of descriptive adjectives usually occur in the following order.

EVALUATION/ OPINION	APPEARANCE	AGE	COLOR	ORIGIN
good	*size/measure*	old	red	*geographical*
bad	big	young	green	French
ugly	small	new	blue	Mexican
interesting	low	antique	striped	Japanese
nice	high		bright green	*material*
intelligent	heavy		dark blue	wooden
	shape		deep purple	vegetable
	round			cotton
	square			brass
	triangular			
	condition			
	chipped			
	broken			
	rotten			

Within a category there is some possible variation.

EXAMPLES	EXPLANATIONS
(a) a **big, round, shiny** apple (b) a **big, shiny round** apple (c) a **shiny, big round** apple	Adjectives of **appearance** usually follow the order in (a): **size, shape, condition.** But other orders are also possible.
(d) a **Japanese silk** fan (e) a **silk Japanese** fan	Adjectives of **origin** usually follow the order in (d): **geographical, material.** But other orders are also possible.

EXERCISE 2

Put the descriptive adjectives in these noun phrases in the correct category in the chart below. Not every category is used in each noun phrase. The first one has been done for you as an example.

1. handsome, small, well-polished Italian leather shoes
2. a big shiny new red sports car
3. a cute little brown puppy
4. some beautiful old Thai silk pajamas
5. a round antique brass tea tray
6. a painted Japanese wooden screen
7. an interesting young French physics professor
8. a funky, broken-down old car

Assign individual Ss or groups specific items or have them do the entire exercise. Process as a whole class by asking for individual answers, and making sure that other Ss or groups agree.

CATEGORY	1	2	3	4	5	6	7	8
EVALUATION/ OPINION	handsome							
APPEARANCE size shape condition	small — well-polished							
AGE	—							
COLOR	—							
ORIGIN geographical material	Italian leather							
NOUN	shoes							

ANSWER KEY

Exercise 2

2. (size) big, (condition) shiny, (age) new, (color) red, (noun) sports car 3. (evaluation) cute, (size) little, (color) brown, (noun) puppy 4. (evaluation) beautiful, (age) old, (geog. origin) That, (material) silk , (noun) pajamas 5. (shape) round, (age) antique, (material) brass, (noun) tea tray 6. (color) painted, (geog. origin) Japanese, (material) wooden, (noun) screen 7. (evaluation) interesting, (age) young, (origin) French (noun) physics professor 8. (evaluation) funky, (condition) broken-down, (age) old, (noun) car

Exercises 3 & 4

SUGGESTIONS:

1. Do the exercises in a parallel fashion to Exercise 2: individually, in pairs, or in groups, assigning individuals or groups specific items or having the class do the entire exercise. In deciding how to assign and process these exercises take into account the basic principles of variety and efficiency described throughout this manual.

2. Process as a whole class by asking for individual answers, and making sure that other Ss or groups agree.

Workbook Ex. 2, p. 65. Answers: TE p. 497.

EXERCISE 3

Add the modifiers in the correct order to the following passages. The first one has been done for you as an example.

My friend Wolfgang is a shopaholic. Whenever he goes out of the house he returns with some (1) ___strange new___ (new, strange) "bargain." He rarely buys any (2) _____ (useful, really) items. Once he came home with some (3) _____ (bright, flannel, purple) blankets. "They match my (4) _____ (pretty, French, new) curtains," he said. But those curtains were still in their (5) _____ (plastic, original) wrappings. He was so busy shopping that he hadn't had time to hang them up.

Fortunately, Wolfgang refuses to buy anything second-hand. I can imagine all the (6) _____ (useless, incredibly ugly, antique) "art objects" he would bring home. He already has (7) _____ (brand-new, European, expensive, plenty of, brightly colored) shirts and sweaters. But that doesn't stop him from buying more. He just piles them into his (8) _____ (little, dark, bedroom, over-crowded) closet. He has some (9) _____ (Italian, nice, handmade) shoes that I have never even seen him wearing.

He's running out of space to put things. He has such a (10) _____ (new, nice) apartment with lots of storage space, but his closets look like some (11) _____ (old, poor) shopkeeper's (12) _____ (frightening, terrible) nightmare!

EXERCISE 4

Are these sentences correct or incorrect? If they are incorrect, identify the problem and correct it.

1. I bought a green, old, pretty vase at the flea market.
2. He's a university, brand-new dormitory resident.
3. It's an antique, genuine, black, old-fashioned umbrella.
4. Would you like some of these delicious, little, chocolate candies?
5. Would you like to hear about my summertime, exciting, vacation plans?

ANSWER KEY

Exercise 3
Alternative possible orders are also listed.
(1) strange, new   (2) really useful
(3) bright purple flannel   (4) pretty new French   (5) original plastic   (6) useless, incredibly ugly antique/incredibly ugly, useless antique   (7) plenty of expensive, brand-new/ brand-new expensive, brightly colored European   (8) dark, little overcrowded bedroom   (9) nice, handmade Italian
(10) nice new   (11) poor, old   (12) terrible, frightening/frightening, terrible

Exercise 4
1. incorrect: I bought a pretty, old, green vase at the flea market.   2. incorrect: He's a brand-new university dormitory resident.
3. incorrect: It's a genuine antique old-fashioned black umbrella.   4. correct
5. incorrect: Would you like to hear about my exciting summertime vacation plans?

FOCUS **3**

▶ Participle Modifiers

EXAMPLES	EXPLANATIONS
(a) **The interesting man** told wonderful stories about adventures in Sumatra.	Present and past participles can be used like descriptive adjectives to describe nouns.
(b) **The interested man** listened carefully to the wonderful stories about adventures in Sumatra.	

VERB	PRESENT PARTICIPLE	PAST PARTICIPLE	EXPLANATIONS
study	studying	studied	Present participles are formed by adding *-ing* to the verb.
forget	forgetting	forgotten	Past participles are formed by adding *-ed* to regular verbs or by using the third form (*-en* form) of irregular verbs. For a review of irregular past participle forms see Appendix 6.

1. Introduce present and past participles by writing the example sentences (a & b) on the board or asking Ss to open their books to the appropriate page. Ask questions like "*Does anybody know what a participle is?*" or "*What is the term we use to describe words like _interesting_ and _interested_?*" If Ss don't supply the answer, write it on the board.
2. Explain that many Ss have trouble understanding which form to use.
3. Verify that Ss know how to form these participles by reviewing the second half of the focus box.
4. If you need more examples, choose both regular and irregular verbs from the chart in Appendix 6 (p. 426).
5. Explain that they will now practice when to use *-ing* participles and when to use *-ed* participles.

Exercise 5

SUGGESTIONS:

1. Be sure to have Ss read the entire passage before doing the exercise. Assigning them to do this the night before is a good way to assure this happens. Start the exercise by asking Ss to summarize the main points or identify one or two things they learned.

2. There are a variety of ways to do this exercise. It can be assigned as homework (combining the structure identification with the preliminary reading assignment) or done in class either individually or in pairs. Ss can be assigned to do one or two paragraphs and then present their answers to the rest of the class, or all Ss can work on all passages, as time allows.

3. Process by asking individuals (or groups or pairs) to read the next participle that they find.

4. If you have access to an OHP, a good way to process exercises like this is by making a transparency of the whole page to mark in class as Ss read their answers.

Workbook Exs. 3–4, pp. 66–67. Answers: TE p. 497.

EXERCISE 5

Underline all the participles in the following passage, and tell what noun they describe. The first paragraph has been done as an example.

▶ **EXAMPLES:** (1) revealing—present participle, describes "information"

(2) hidden—past participle, describes "emotions"

(3) widespread—past participle, describes "reactions"

(4) exciting—present participle, describes "situations" increased—past participle, describes "heart rates"

(5) no participle modifiers in this sentence

Body Language

(1) Unconscious facial expressions and "body language" often give <u>revealing</u> information to other people. (2) Many people's "<u>hidden</u>" emotions are actually quite visible to anyone who knows how to read people's faces. (3) Some reactions are so <u>widespread</u> in all cultures that there seems to be a physical basis for them. (4) All people react in the same way to certain <u>exciting</u> situations by breathing more rapidly and experiencing <u>increased</u> heart rates. (5) Facial expressions of basic emotions, such as anger, surprise, and amusement, appear to be universal.

(6) Other reactions are not so universal. (7) Many, but not all, individuals respond to an embarrassing situation by blushing (when the face and neck turn bright red). (8) Some people show that they are bored by growing less active and becoming sleepy or inattentive. (9) Others respond to boring situations by becoming more active and showing such physical signs as jiggling feet or wiggling fingers. (10) But for other people, such reactions may be unintended indications of nervousness or anxiety, not boredom. (11) When someone experiences a confusing situation, he or she may unconsciously try to hide that confusion by smiling, thus doing what is known as "the stupid grin." (12) But another person might respond by looking angry.

(13) There are not only variations in this "silent language" between different individuals, but there are also important differences between cultures. (14) Certain kinds of "silent language" give one particular message in one culture, but a conflicting message in another culture. (15) For example, eye contact (looking directly into the eyes of the person you are speaking to) has very different meanings in different cultures. (16) In American culture, if you do not look directly into someone's eyes while talking, the listener will think that you are dishonest. (17) If someone is described as "shifty-eyed" it means that he or she cannot be trusted. (18) But in many Asian cultures, avoiding eye contact is a sign of politeness and respect, and prolonged eye contact (which indicates sincerity in American culture) means aggression or hostility, and is seen as a threatening behavior. (19) Mistaken "body language" can often result in even more misunderstanding than using the wrong word or incorrect grammar.

ANSWER KEY

Exercise 5

The following sentences have participle modifiers. Participles are underlined and the nouns they describe are bold faced.

(1) <u>revealing</u> **information** (2) <u>"hidden"</u> **emotions** (3) **reactions** are so <u>wide-spread</u> (4) <u>exciting</u> **situations**; <u>increased</u> **heart rates** (7) <u>embarrassing</u> **situation** (8) **they** are <u>bored</u> (9) <u>boring</u> **situations**; <u>jiggling</u> **feet**; <u>wiggling</u> **fingers** (10) <u>unintended</u> **indications** (11) <u>confusing</u> **situation** (14) <u>conflicting</u> **message** (17) **someone** is described as <u>"shifty-eyed"</u> (18) <u>prolonged</u> **eye contact**; <u>threatening</u> **behavior** (19) <u>Mistaken</u> **"body language"**

FOCUS **4**

Meanings of Present and Past Participles

EXAMPLES	EXPLANATIONS
(a) a **loving** mother (She loves her children.)	Present participles modify **agents.** The agents do the actions described by the participle.
(b) a **well-loved** mother (Her children love her.)	Past participles modify **receivers.** The receivers are affected by the action described by the participle.

EXERCISE 6

Paraphrase these sentences by choosing the correct participle for the cues given.

▶ **EXAMPLE:** Most of my friends enjoy reading novels.

Most of my friends are <u>interested</u> (interest) in reading novels.

Novels are <u>interesting</u> (interest) to most of my friends.

1. The audience didn't understand the lecture.

(a) The audience was _____ (confuse).

(b) The lecture was _____ (confuse).

2. The students didn't do well on the exam.

(a) The exam results were _____ (disappoint).

(b) The students were _____ (disappoint).

3. Children who watch scary movies may not be able to sleep afterwards.

(a) (Frighten) _____ children may not be able to go to sleep.

(b) (Frighten) _____ movies may keep children from sleeping.

4. That was quite a delicious snack.

(a) The snack was quite _____ (satisfy).

(b) We were quite _____ (satisfy).

5. Most students enjoy studying grammar.

(a) Most students are _____ (interest) in grammar.

(b) Grammar is _____ (interest) to most students.

FOCUS 4

1. If needed, review the concepts of agent and receiver from Unit 4.

2. Write the core sentences ("*She loves her children.*" and "*Her children love her.*") on the board and ask if anyone can turn that sentence into a participle. If they cannot, lead them through the process by pointing out that the mother is the agent in example a, and she is the receiver in example b.

3. Paraphrase the explanations in the book or have Ss read them.

Exercises 6 and 7

Follow up the initial presentation immediately by doing these exercises as a whole class, checking and refining comprehension of the terms and principles as you proceed through the exercises.

Workbook Ex. 6, p. 68. Answers TE p. 497.

ANSWER KEY

Exercise 6
1. (a) confused. (b) confusing.
2. (a) disappointing. (b) disappointed.

3. (a) Frightened (b) Frightening
4. (a) satisfying. (b) satisfied.
5. (a) interested (b) interesting

EXERCISE 7

Use present or past participles to complete these definitions.

▶ **EXAMPLE:** Information that reveals thoughts can be described as
<u>revealing</u> information.

Emotions that people hide can be described as
<u>hidden</u> emotions.

1. Situations that excite people can be described as _____ situations.

2. Interest rates that fluctuate can be described as _____ interest rates.

3. A situation that embarrasses people can be described as an _____ situation.

4. Results that people prove in experiments can be described as _____ results.

5. News that depresses people seriously can be described as _____ news.

6. Individuals whom some bad news depresses seriously can be described as _____ individuals.

7. A question that puzzles people can be described as a _____ question.

8. People that a question puzzles can be described as _____ people.

FOCUS **5**

▶ Adding Information to Participles

Noun + Participle

EXAMPLES	EXPLANATIONS
(a) a **man-eating** tiger (a tiger that eats people) **(b)** a **trend-setting** fashion (a fashion that sets a trend) **(c)** a **fire-breathing** dragon (a dragon that breathes fire)	Present participles usually describe the agent. You can also identify the receiver of the action by adding nouns.
(d) a **flea-bitten** dog (a dog that is bitten by fleas) **(e)** a **manmade** lake (a lake that was made by people) **(f)** a **male-dominated** society (a society that is dominated by males)	Past participles usually describe the receiver. You can add nouns to past participles when you want to identify the agent as well. Some noun-participle combinations appear without hyphens.

Adverb + Participle

EXAMPLES	EXPLANATIONS
(g) a **fast-moving** train (a train that moves fast) **(h)** some **homegrown** tomatoes (tomatoes that were grown at home) **(i)** a **much-visited** attraction (an attraction that is visited a lot)	You can add adverbs to both past and present participles to include important additional information to the participles. Some special cases appear without hyphens.

FOCUS 5

1. Tell Ss that you are going to look at ways to add additional information to participles.

2. Choose one of the core sentences (*"a tiger that eats people,"* etc.) from examples a–c and write it on the board. Ask students to make it into a participle phrase (*"a people-eating tiger"*).
3. If Ss supply (for example) *"an eating tiger,"* try to set a context about needing more information. A tiger that eats rabbits or ice cream is not a problem, but a tiger that eats people is.
4. Repeat steps 1–3 with a past participle example (sentences d–f).
5. Allow time for questions or discussion of **other examples**, if needed: *meat-eating animal, death-defying leap, heart-stopping discovery, moth-eaten sweater, machine-made furniture, student-centered instruction.*

E X P A N S I O N :

1. Repeat the process for examples g–h, or point information out to Ss and assign it as individual study at home.
2. Explain special cases (examples j–m) briefly in class or include as self-study.

Special Cases

EXAMPLES	EXPLANATIONS
(j) a **blue-eyed** baby (a baby with blue eyes) (k) a **long-legged** ballet dancer (a dancer with long legs)	You can make "past participles" from some adjective-noun combinations to describe certain kinds of physical characteristics.
(l) a **barely concealed** dislike (m) a **deeply depressed** individual	Some adverb-participle combinations appear without hyphens

Exercise 8

Do this as a whole class activity following your presentation of Focus 5. Call on individual Ss. Continue to explain the rationale for correct choices as needed or in answer to questions.

EXERCISE 8

Use the information in these sentences to make participles.

▶ **EXAMPLE:** The story is loved very much. It's a ___much-loved___ story.

1. In that incredible jump, Houdini defied death.

   It was a _____ jump.

2. I had to go to the store to buy this cake.

   It's a _____ cake.

3. Gladstone Gulp bought a machine to reduce his weight.

   It's a _____ machine.

4. They trained the new employee well.

   She was a _____ employee.

5. That poor kitten is starved for love.

   It's a _____ kitten.

6. They filmed the movie with a camera that they held by hand.

   It was filmed with a _____ camera.

7. Look at that man with the long hair!

   Look at that _____ man!

8. Learning grammar can consume a lot of time.

   It can be a _____ activity.

Exercise 9

Assign as homework or do in class by assigning individual Ss to write a specific answer. Be sure to allow adequate composing time if you use this second option.

EXERCISE 9

Write original sentences that describe at least five of the following.

1. the most boring teacher you have ever had
2. the most self-satisfied politician you have ever heard or read about

ANSWER KEY

Exercise 8
1. death-defying   2. store-bought
3. weight-reducing   4. a well-trained
5. love-starved   6. handheld   7. long-haired
8. time-consuming

Exercise 9
Answers will vary. Possible answers include:
1. The most boring teacher I have ever had is you.   2. The most self-satisfied politician I have ever heard or read about is Bill Clinton.
3. The most surprised reaction I have ever seen was when I finally gave my teacher my homework on time.   4. The most amazing thing I have ever seen was a huge forest fire.
5. The most worried person in my family is my sister.   6. The most modern-thinking political leader I know is Aung San Su Kyii.   7. The most bored student I have ever known actually slept in class.   8. My best friend's most irritating habit is always being late.

3. the most surprised reaction you have ever seen

4. the most amazing thing you have ever seen

5. the most worried person in your family

6. the most modern-thinking political leader you know

7. the behavior of the most bored student you have ever known

8. the most irritating habit your best friend has

EXERCISE 10

Choose the correct participle form for these sentences from the cues given. The first paragraph has been done for you as an example.

   Problems in communication can happen when some of the conscious and un-conscious actions of the (1) _nonspoken_ (non-speak) part of a language are misunderstood. There can sometimes be (2) _confusing_ (confuse) situations between teachers and students in the classroom.

   Teachers in American classrooms, for example, may often become (3) _____ (annoy) when students don't volunteer answers to general questions in class. Silence in American classrooms often means that the students are (4) _____ (bore), (5) _____ (disinterest), or (6) _____ (uninvolve) in the class activity. Similarly, teachers interpret eye contact from students as a sign that the lesson is (7) _____ (interest) and (8) _____ (involve) for them, and that they are actively (9) _____ (engage) in the learning process.

   Students are sometimes (10) _____ (confuse) about the best way to show that they are paying attention. In an American classroom, asking questions is one good way to do this, but students from other cultures may be (11) _____ (embarrass) by having to admit that they are (12) _____ (confuse). Sometimes they feel (13) _____ (worry) that asking questions may be interpreted as (14) _____ (teacher-challenge) behavior or as a somewhat (15) _____ (insult) suggestion that the teacher has not explained things clearly enough.

   The best way to solve these misunderstandings is to talk about them in class. Both American teachers and international students alike are often very (16) _____ (surprise) to find out about their sometimes (17) _____ (mistake) assumptions about what classroom behavior means in different cultures.

Modifying Noun Phrases: Adjectives and Participles **159**

Exercise 10

Assign as homework or have Ss do it in class. Either way, make sure they read the whole article before doing the exercise. For in-class activity, they can fill in the blanks individually or in pairs.

Workbook Exs. 7–9, pp. 68–70. Answers: TE pp. 497–498.

A N S W E R   K E Y

Exercise 10
(3) annoyed   (4) bored
(5) disinterested   (6) uninvolved
(7) interesting   (8) involving
(9) engaged   (10) confused
(11) embarrassed   (12) confused
(13) worried   (14) teacher-challenging
(15) insulting   (16) surprised
(17) mistaken

1. If you are pressed for time, skip this focus or assign it as homework for individual study.
2. If you present it in class, start by reviewing briefly the categories of modifiers that appear before the noun (see Focuses 1–2 at the beginning of the unit) and then introduce participle and prepositional phrases using the examples provided.
3. Use the first paragraph of Exercise 11 (where the answers have been indicated) as a follow-up if you need additional examples.

Exercise 11

1. Have Ss read the paragraph before doing the exercise.
2. Assign Ss to do one or two sentences and then present their answers to the rest of the class, or have all Ss work on the entire paragraph, as time allows.
3. Process by asking individuals (or pairs) to read the next modifying phrase that they found and what noun it refers to. Work your way through the entire exercise.

SUGGESTION:

If you have access to an OHP, a good way to process exercises like this is by making a transparency of the whole exercise to mark in class as Ss read their answers.

Workbook Ex. 10, p. 70. Answers TE p. 498.

UNIT GOAL REVIEW

Have Ss work in pairs to look over the goals on the opening page of the unit again. Have Ss summarize their understanding of the principles involved with each goal to one another and to identify one question they still have based on this discussion. Process the questions with the whole class by asking pairs to state their question and then by asking other pairs if they can answer it or explain the relevant rule in their own words.

▶ Modifiers that Follow Noun Phrases

PARTICIPLE PHRASES	PREPOSITIONAL PHRASES	EXPLANATION
(a) The man **speaking to John** told him some shocking information.	**(b)** The man **with John** told him some shocking information.	Some modifiers occur after the noun.
(c) The woman **surrounded by reporters** is a world-renowned expert on AIDS.	**(d)** The woman **next to the window** is a world-renowned expert on AIDS.	

EXAMPLES	EXPLANATIONS
(e) The man **speaking to John** told him some shocking information.	Participle phrases usually come after the noun if they identify the noun (tell which particular noun we are talking about).
(f) **Speaking to the man,** John found out some shocking information.	They can come before the noun if that noun has already been identified and the participle describes more about the noun.

EXERCISE 11

Underline the modifying phrases in this article. Draw an arrow to indicate the noun each phrase modifies. The first paragraph has been done for you as an example.

(1) One aspect of nonverbal communication <u>frequently mentioned by researchers discussing cross-cultural differences</u> is the varying size of the "conversation bubble" in each culture. (2) This bubble is the amount of physical distance <u>maintained between people engaged in different kinds of conversation.</u> (3) Americans having polite social conversations usually stand about an arm's length apart. (4) Closer distances are permitted only between people having a more intimate relationship. (5) Unless you are a very close friend or family member, moving closer than an arm's length is usually interpreted as overly aggressive (either socially or sexually). (6) People growing up in Latin cultures tend to have a smaller conversation bubble than people coming from Northern European cultures. (7) As a result, North Americans or Northern Europeans sometimes come across as a little cold or unfriendly to people raised in Latin countries such as Italy, Spain, or Latin America. (8) In general, Middle Eastern cultures tend to have the smallest conversation bubble, while North Asian and Northern European cultures tend to have the largest.

ANSWER KEY

Exercise 11

The modifying participial phrases have been underlined. The noun each phrase modifies has been boldfaced.

(1) **aspect** . . . <u>frequently mentioned by</u> <u>researchers</u> <u>discussing cross-cultural</u> <u>differences</u>,   (2) **physical distance** <u>maintained</u> <u>between</u> **people** <u>engaged in different kinds of</u> <u>conversation</u>.   (3) **Americans** <u>having polite</u> <u>social conversations</u>   (4) **people** <u>having a</u> <u>more intimate relationship.</u>   (6) **People** <u>growing up in Latin cultures</u> . . . **people** <u>coming</u> <u>from Northern European cultures.</u>   (7) **people** <u>raised in Latin countries</u>

Use Your English

USE YOUR ENGLISH

Activity 1

VARIATIONS:

Specify the number of descriptive categories (age, color, appearance, etc.) they should use to describe each object.

1. To use this as a diagnostic, ask Ss to write their responses for you to collect and evaluate.
2. Bring in objects and have the Ss write sentences that describe them.

Activity 2

This activity should be played "for fun."

VARIATION:

Increase interest by making it a tournament. Have the whole class listen to individual pairs rather than playing simultaneously. Award a prize for the pair that is able to keep playing the longest.

Activity 3

VARIATION:

Do Step 2 as a whole class discussion. Collecting written responses described in Step 3 is a good way to use this activity to evaluate Ss' command of participle forms.

Activity 4

SUGGESTION:

Use this activity as a whole class discussion by asking the questions yourself in a conversational way (for example: "*When can hiding your feelings be helpful? When can it be a disadvantage? What about expressing your emotions clearly? What are situations where this is a good thing to do? What about times where it's not a good idea?*" etc.) Responses can also be written and collected for you to evaluate/correct.

ACTIVITY 3: SPEAKING/WRITING

Examine this list of common emotions and choose two or three.

boredom   embarrassment   depression   confusion

annoyance   worry   amusement   excitement

STEP 1 For each emotion identify two or three situations that cause you to feel that emotion. Next identify two or three typical physical or psychological reactions you have when you feel each of the emotions. The first one has been done as an example.

Boring Situations:	Bored Reactions:
1) long meetings	1) I yawn, get sleepy, fidget
2) gossip about people I don't know	2) I think about other things
3) talking about things that don't interest me	3) I draw pictures in my notebook

STEP 2 Compare your responses and the situations that cause those responses with those of other students in the class. Discuss these questions:
- Are there universal reactions to certain emotions?
- Which category showed more individual variation: the reactions or the situations?
- Do some cultures express emotions more readily than others?

STEP 3 Present your ideas to the rest of the class, or write answers to the discussion questions for your teacher to read and correct.

ACTIVITY 4: SPEAKING

Some cultures value people who express their emotions easily, while others value people who can keep their feelings to themselves. What are the advantages and disadvantages to each kind of behavior?

STEP 1 Think of at least two situations where hiding your feelings can be helpful (for example, playing cards). Next, think of two situations where it is a disadvantage (for example, when trying to communicate in a language that you don't speak very well).

STEP 2 Do the same for expressing your emotions clearly.

STEP 3 Compare your answers with other students' and report any interesting similarities or differences to the rest of the class.

ACTIVITY 5: SPEAKING/WRITING

Think of three characteristics that make someone fascinating and three characteristics that make someone boring. Compare your answers with those of several other people and make a list of characteristics that everyone agrees on. Present your list to the class.

ACTIVITY 6: SPEAKING

Are facial expressions universal? This is a chart used to teach a common "vocabulary" of facial expressions to deaf students. Examine these expressions in a small group made up of people from different cultures (if possible). Are there any feelings that are expressed in your culture by different facial expressions than the ones shown? How are facial expressions different in different cultures? Present your ideas to the class.

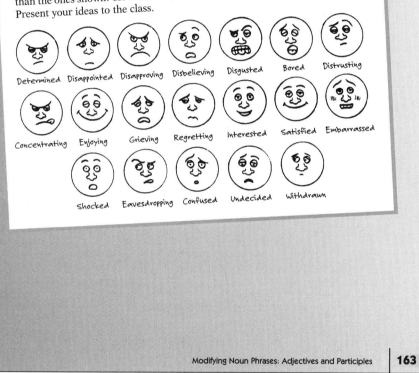

Determined Disappointed Disapproving Disbelieving Disgusted Bored Distrusting

Concentrating Enjoying Grieving Regretting Interested Satisfied Embarrassed

Shocked Eavesdropping Confused Undecided Withdrawn

This activity is more appropriate for advanced classes with a command of more extensive vocabulary. To use this as a diagnostic, ask Ss to write their responses and collect and evaluate as described in Activity 1.

Activities 6 & 7

These work best as discussion topics, rather than as written activities. They can be used well in combination. Use Activity 7 to introduce the general idea and then have Ss label the pictures in Activity 8. Let them use bilingual dictionaries if they don't have sufficient vocabulary to come up with descriptive words by themselves.

Activity 8

This activity can be varied in the same ways as described in Activity 5. *"What things make somebody boring? . . . fascinating?"* etc.

ACTIVITY 7: SPEAKING

On the next page are some other facial expressions. The emotions they portray have been omitted. Choose four or five expressions.

STEP 1 Use adjectives or participles to describe these expressions. Be ready to explain why you have chosen the description that you did.

STEP 2 Compare your answers with those of several other students in the class. Did you interpret any of the expressions differently? Do those differences tell you anything about facial expressions in other cultures?

STEP 3 Report any significant differences or insights to the class.

ACTIVITY 8: WRITING/SPEAKING

What is the difference between an antique and junk? What makes a used item valuable? Make two lists. For each junk item write a description of a similar item you would consider an antique. Think of five examples of each. Compare your list to a partner's. Here's an example.

Junk	Antique
a dirty old cup	a fine, unbroken, hand-painted porcelain teacup

ACTIVITY 9: LISTENING

STEP 1 Listen to these brief conversations, and circle the sentences that best describe the situation.

STEP 2 Compare your answers with a partner's and then listen to the conversations and questions again to check any answers that you disagree on or are unsure about.

Conversation 1

1. (a) The water wasn't cold enough.
   (b) She wanted a glass of water.
2. (a) She wanted iced water.
   (b) She didn't want iced water.
3. (a) The tea was too warm.
   (b) The tea was too small.

Conversation 2

1. (a) The girl's grandmother is the one who teaches physics.
   (b) The girl's grandmother is the one who is retired.
2. (a) He's trying to organize a lecture program for senior citizens.
   (b) He's trying to organize a lecture program for physics.
3. (a) The girl's mother is the one who teaches physics.
   (b) The girl's mother is the one who teaches biology.

Activity 9

Play textbook audio. The tapescript for this listening appears on p. 514 of this book. To save time, process the answers as a whole class rather than in pair discussion.

The test for this unit can be found on p. 456. The answers are on p. 457.

ANSWER KEY

Activity 9
Conversation 1:
1. (a) The water wasn't cold enough.
2. (b) She didn't want iced water.
3. (b) The tea was too small.

Conversation 2:
1. (b) The grandmother is the one who is retired.
2. (a) He's trying to organize a lecture program for senior citizens.
3. (b) The mother is the one who teaches biology.

Unit 10

UNIT OVERVIEW

This unit covers comparatives, equatives, and expressions of similarity and difference. Most students have encountered the basic *more/most* forms before, but this unit focuses on the more complex structures typical of academic writing. For an excellent overview of why these patterns can be difficult for learners, see *The Grammar Book*, Chapter 34 (pp. 717–738).

UNIT GOALS

Review the goals listed on this page so students (Ss) understand what they should be able to do by the end of the unit.

OPENING TASK

Note: The **Opening Task** allows Ss to try using the target structures and allows teachers to notice what kinds of help they may need. For a more complete discussion of the Opening Task, see p. xix of this Teacher's Edition.

UNIT 10

COMPARATIVES

UNIT GOALS:

- To correctly express various degrees of similarity and difference
- To correctly use different complex comparisons of amount
- To understand and use formal and informal statements of comparison

▶ OPENING TASK
Comparing Developing and Developed Countries

Here is some statistical information about four countries that were once British colonies. Use the information to discuss the following questions with a partner or in a small group.

- What are some things that Bangladesh and Pakistan have in common? What are some differences?
- What are some things that Canada and the United States have in common? What are some differences?
- What are some differences between developed and developing countries? Are there similarities? What are they?

People's Republic of Bangladesh

area:	55,600 square miles
population:	127 million
growth rate:	2.7%
density per square mile:	2230
languages:	(national) Bangla; (official) English
religion:	Muslim 83%, Hindu 16%
literacy rate:	38%
GNP:	$155 billion
per capita GNP:	$1,260 per year
politically independent since:	1947 from Britain/1971 from Pakistan

Islamic Republic of Pakistan

area:	307,000 square miles
population:	135 million
growth rate:	2.9%
density per square mile:	440
languages:	(national) Urdu, (official) English, (regional) Punjabi, Sindhi,Pashtu, Baluchi
religion:	Sunni Muslim 77%, Shi'a Muslim 20%, other 3%
literacy rate:	38%
GNP:	$297 billion
per capita GNP:	$2,300 per year
politically independent since:	1947 from Britain

Canada

area:	3.8 million square miles
population:	30 million
growth rate:	0.8%
density per square mile:	8
languages:	English, French
religion:	Protestant 41%, Catholic 47%, Jewish 1%, other 11%
literacy rate:	97%
GNP:	$721 billion
per capita GNP:	$25,000 per year
politically independent since:	1867 from Britain

United States of America

area:	3.6 million square miles
population:	270 million
growth rate:	0.7%
density per square mile:	74
language:	English
religion:	Protestant 56%, Catholic 38%, Jewish 4%, other 2%
literacy rate:	97%
GNP:	$7,662 billion
per capita GNP:	$28,600 per year
politically independent since:	1776 from Britain

This particular Task can be done in a variety of ways:

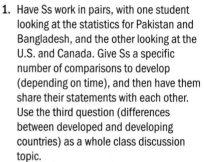

1. Have Ss work in pairs, with one student looking at the statistics for Pakistan and Bangladesh, and the other looking at the U.S. and Canada. Give Ss a specific number of comparisons to develop (depending on time), and then have them share their statements with each other. Use the third question (differences between developed and developing countries) as a whole class discussion topic.

2. For more advanced classes, divide the class into groups of four and go directly to having them discuss the third question as a group. Explain that they need to use the statistics to support their opinions.

3. To use this as a diagnostic, have Ss write individual answers to the third question based on their small group discussions.

Note: Focus boxes explain and give examples of each structure. For a more complete discussion of focus boxes, see p. xx of this Teacher's Edition. This chart and others in this unit are designed for individual study and will appeal to students who are reflective observers or who enjoy concept formation.

This chart and the one for Focus 2 are organized in order of greater to lesser (more→equal→less). They are best used as pre-lesson, individual study, or post-lesson review and follow-up.

S U G G E S T I O N :

Try changing the example sentences to refer to physical differences of Ss in your class.
For example:
(a) *Juan is much taller than Bettina.*
(b) *Frederika is somewhat taller than Beauregard.*
(c) *Morris is just as intelligent as Boris.*
Make sure that Ss can identify the comparative structures, and after you have underlined (or had Ss underline them for you), have Ss turn to the chart to review the format. They can study the focus box at home as review.

FOCUS **1**

Comparisons of Degree: Adjectives and Adverbs

FORM MEANING

EXAMPLES	MEANING	FORM
	MORE X > Y	X *is* (intensifier) { adjective + *er* / *more* + adjective / *more* + adverb } *than Y.*
(a) Pakistan **is much larger than** Bangladesh is. **(b)** Bangladesh is growing **somewhat more quickly than** Pakistan is. **(c)** The people of Pakistan are **slightly more literate than** the people of Bangladesh.	large difference ↕ small difference	*much* / *considerably* / *substantially* } intensifiers *somewhat* / *slightly/a bit*
(d) Pakistan's post-colonial history is **just as recent as** Bangladesh's is.	**THE SAME X = Y**	X *is* (intensifier) *as* { adjective / adverb } *as Y.* *exactly* / *just* } intensifiers
(e) Bangladesh's literacy rate is **nearly as high as** Pakistan's.	**LESS X < Y** small difference˙	X *is* (intensifier) *as* { adjective / adverb } *as Y.* *almost* / *nearly* } intensifiers
(f) Pakistan is **not quite as crowded as** Bangladesh is. **(g)** Bangladesh is **not nearly as large as** Pakistan.	small difference large difference	X *is not* (intensifier) *as* { adjective / adverb } *as Y.* *quite* / *nearly* } intensifiers
(h) Bangladesh is growing **slightly less rapidly than** Pakistan. **(i)** Bangladesh is **substantially less prosperous than** Pakistan is.	small difference ↕ large difference	X *is* (intensifier) *less* { adjective / adverb } *than Y.* *slightly/a bit* / *somewhat* / *substantially/* / *considerably* / *much* } intensifiers

EXERCISE 1

In the following chart, write statements of comparison about the United States and Canada. Use the information on page. 167 Use intensifiers to make accurate statements.

Meaning	Form	Comparative Statement
MORE	. . . er than more . . . than	The area of Canada is slightly larger than the area of the United States. _____
THE SAME	as . . . as	_____
LESS	nearly as . . . as not as . . . as less . . . than	_____ _____ _____

EXERCISE 2

Read the paragraph on the next page comparing Pakistan and Bangladesh and fill in the chart. For each feature listed, note whether it is greater in Pakistan or in Bangladesh, and whether the difference is large or small.

Feature	Greater in Pakistan or Bangladesh?	Small or large difference?
population	Bangladesh	small
area	Pakistan	large
population density		
standard of living		
population growth		
GNP		
educational development		
prosperity		

Exercises 1 & 2

Note: The exercises following each focus box provide meaningful practice with the grammar item presented in that particular box. For a more complete discussion of how to use the exercises, see p. xxi of this Teacher's Edition. Exercises 1 & 2 can be done either individually or as pair work. Exercise 1 stresses production; Exercise 2 practices correct comprehension of these structures. Depending on the needs of your class, you can stress correct decoding of complex comparatives or give your class additional practice at constructing such comparisons themselves.

ANSWER KEY

Exercise 1

Answers will vary. Possible answers include:
MORE: The U.S. is **considerably more populous** than Canada. Canada's population is growing **a bit more quickly than** the U.S.'s.
THE SAME: Winters in Canada are just **as cold as** winters in the northern U.S. Most English-speaking Canadians **speak English as well as** English-speaking Americans.
LESS: America's literacy rate is almost as high as Canada's. The population of the U.S. is increasing **nearly as quickly as** Canada's.

Exercise 2

Answers are given for the feature listed, the country where that feature is greater, and whether the difference is large or small.
population: Bangladesh/small
area: Pakistan/large
population density: Bangladesh/large
standard of living: Pakistan/large
population growth: Pakistan/small
GNP: Pakistan/large
educational development: Pakistan/small
prosperity: Pakistan/not stated

(1) Although the population of Bangladesh is slightly larger than that of Pakistan, its land area is considerably smaller. (2) This means that the population density of Pakistan is not nearly as great as that of Bangladesh, and as a result, the general standard of living is substantially higher. (3) Although the population of Bangladesh is not growing quite as quickly as Pakistan's, its GNP is quite a bit lower, and as a result, it will be a very long time before the standard of living for Bangladeshis becomes as high as for Pakistanis. (4) While educational development is almost as high in Bangladesh as in Pakistan, economic development is substantially lower, and people in Bangladesh are generally less prosperous.

Exercise 3
VARIATION:

Shorten this exercise by assigning a third of the class to compare Brunei and Bulgaria, a third to do the same for Jamaica and Japan, etc. Allow for multiple answers in your whole class processing. Ss can read their answers aloud or write them on the board.

EXERCISE 3

Make comparative statements about the countries below using the information provided. Use appropriate intensifiers to describe whether the difference is large or small. Compare your statements to those of a partner.

▶ **EXAMPLE:** The literacy rate in Brunei is substantially lower than in Bulgaria.

Brunei's per capita income is considerably higher than Bulgaria's.

	Brunei	**Bulgaria**
per capita GDP	$15,800	$4,630
population density	142 per square mile	192 per square mile
literacy rate	88%	98%

	Jamaica	**Japan**
per capita GDP	$3,260	$22,700
population density	621 per square mile	863 per square mile
literacy rate	85%	100%

	South Korea	**Turkey**
per capita GDP	$14,200	$6,100
population density	1,221 per square mile	214 per square mile
literacy rate	98%	82%

ANSWER KEY

Exercise 3

Answers will vary. Possible answers include:
The per capita income of Bulgaria is not nearly as high as Brunei's. The literacy rate in Bulgaria is quite a bit higher than in Brunei. The population density is somewhat lower in Brunei than in Bulgaria. The literacy rate in Jamaica is somewhat lower than in Japan. The per capita GDP in Japan is much higher than in Jamaica. Turkey doesn't have quite as high a literacy rate as Korea. Korea has a much higher population density than Turkey.

EXERCISE 4

Interview a partner to obtain the following information, and then make statements that compare you and your partner.

▶ **EXAMPLE:** *My partner is substantially older than I am.*

I am much younger than my partner.

QUESTIONS	YOUR PARTNER	YOU
how old	37	18
how long studying English		
when he/she usually goes to sleep		
how often he/she goes to the movies		
how quickly he/she thinks English skills are improving		
how big his/her family?		

Exercise 4

If your class does not enjoy the "statistical" nature of the previous exercises, skip them and do this exercise in their place. Be sure to allow more processing of different answer patterns to make sure that Ss get sufficient practice using and reviewing the structures.

Workbook Exs. 1–2, pp. 71–72. Answers: TE p. 498.

ANSWER KEY

Exercise 4

Answers will vary. Possible answers include: My partner has been studying English about as long as I have. I don't usually stay up as late as my partner. My partner goes to the movies much more often than I do. My English skills are improving just as quickly as my partner's. My partner's family is a bit smaller than mine.

FOCUS 2

This chart, like the one used in Focus 1, is designed for individual study and is organized in order of greater to lesser (more→equal→less). Use it for pre-lesson individual study or post-lesson review and follow-up.

SUGGESTION:

Try changing the example sentences to refer to physical differences of Ss in your class.
For example:

(a) *Juan has a much larger family than Bettina does.*

(b) *Juan has slightly more relatives than Beauregard.*

(c) *Juan's family has as much love for each other as Euridyce's does.*

(d) *Morris has just as many nephews as Boris.*

(e) *Beauregard has almost as many cousins as Frederika does.*

(f) *Frederika doesn't have quite as many cousins as Beauregard.*

(g) *Bettina doesn't have nearly as many relatives as Juan does.*

(h) *Bettina's family doesn't have nearly as much free time as Juan's does.*

(i) *Beauregard has slightly fewer cousins than Frederika does.*

(j) *Bettina's family has much less money than Juan's does.*

Make sure that Ss can identify the comparative structures. After you have underlined them (or had Ss underline them for you), have Ss turn to the chart to review the format. They can study the focus box at home as review.

▶ Comparisons of Amount: Noun Phrases

FORM · MEANING

EXAMPLES	MEANING	FORM
(a) Pakistan has **much more land area than** Bangladesh does. **(b)** Bangladesh has **slightly more people than** Pakistan.	**MORE X > Y** large difference ↕ small difference	X + VP + (intensifier) + *more* NP *than* Y (*does*) *much /many* *considerably/* *substantially* } intensifiers *slightly* *somewhat*
(c) One has **as much representation as** the other. **(d)** Pakistan sends **just as many representatives** to the U. N. **as** Bangladesh does.	**THE SAME X = Y**	X + VP + (intensifier) + *as much/many* NP *as* Y (*does*)* *exactly* } intensifiers *just*
(e) Pakistan has **almost as many people as** Bangladesh. **(f)** Pakistan does not have **quite as many people as** Bangladesh does.	**LESS X < Y** small difference	X + VP + (intensifier) *as much/many* NP *as* Y (*does*)* *almost* } intensifiers *nearly*
(g) Bangladesh doesn't have **nearly as much land area as** Pakistan.	small difference large difference	X + *not* + VP + (intensifier) *as much/many* NP as Y (*does*)* *quite* } intensifiers *nearly*
(h) Pakistan has **slightly fewer people than** Bangladesh. **(i)** Bangladesh has **much less land than** Pakistan does.	small difference ↕ large difference	X + VP + (intensifier) *fewer/less* NP *than* Y (*does*)* *slightly* *somewhat* *substantially/* } intensifiers *considerably* *much/many*

*NP = Noun Phrase   VP = Verb Phrase

EXERCISE 5

In the following chart, write statements of comparison about the United States and Canada. Use the information on pages 167. Use intensifiers to make accurate statements.

Meaning	Form	Comparative Statement
MORE	*more . . . than*	The United States had substantially more people than Canada.
THE SAME	*as much/many . . . as*	_____
LESS	*almost as much/many . . . as*	_____
	not + VERB + as much/ many . . . as	_____
	fewer/less . . . than	_____

EXERCISE 6

Read the paragraph comparing Pakistan and Bangladesh on pages 173 and 174. Underline the first comparison statement in each sentence and rewrite it. Then say whether the difference is big or small.

▶ **EXAMPLE:** **1.** Bangladesh has <u>somewhat more people than Pakistan.</u>
Bangladesh's population is greater than Pakistan's. It is a small difference.

2. _____
_____
3. _____
_____
4. _____
_____
5. _____
_____
6. _____
_____

   (1) Although Bangladesh has somewhat more people than Pakistan, it has considerably less land area. (2) This means that Pakistan does not have nearly as many people per square mile as Bangladesh does, and as a result, there is much less pressure on basic resources such as roads and water supply. (3) As

Comparatives **173**

Exercises 5 & 6

These exercises can be done individually or as pair work. Exercise 5 stresses production; Exercise 6 practices correct comprehension of these structures. Depending on the needs of your class, you can stress correct decoding of complex comparatives or give your class additional practice at constructing such comparisons themselves.

a rule, people in Bangladesh have somewhat fewer opportunities for economic improvement than people in Pakistan. (4) Bangladesh has just about as many literate people as Pakistan, but it has fewer people living above the poverty line, and so there is somewhat less political and economic stability in Bangladesh than there is in Pakistan. (5) However, Pakistan has more regional ethnic groups than Bangladesh does, and there are more incidents of ethnic unrest in Pakistan than there are in Bangladesh. (6) Thus, Bangladesh has fewer extreme political conflicts than Pakistan.

EXERCISE 7

Make comparative statements about the countries below using the information provided. Use appropriate intensifiers to describe whether the difference is large or small. Compare your statements to those of a partner.

▶ **EXAMPLES:** Luxembourg has considerably less agricultural land than Libya.
    Libyans don't make nearly as much money as people in Luxembourg.

	Luxembourg	Libya
per capita income	$13,988	$7,130
number of official languages	3	1
GNP	$4.9 billion	$27 billion
amount of land used for agriculture	210 square miles	40,772 square miles

	Switzerland	Swaziland
per capita income	$14,030	$740
number of official languages	4	2
GNP	$97.1 billion	$490 million
amount of land used for agriculture	4,144 square miles	540 square miles

	Taiwan	Thailand
per capita income	$8,750	$800
number of official languages	1	1
GNP	$72.8 billion	$44 billion
amount of land used for agriculture	3,335 square miles	75,413 square miles

Follow the same procedures as suggested for Exercise 3. Shorten this exercise by assigning a third of the class to compare Luxembourg and Libya, a third to do the same for Switzerland and Swaziland, etc. Allow for multiple answers in your whole class processing. Ss can read their answers aloud or write them on the board.

ANSWER KEY

Exercise 7

Answers will vary. Possible answers include: Luxembourg has two more official languages than Libya does. Libya has considerably more agricultural land than Luxembourg. People in Luxembourg make substantially more money than people in Libya. Libya has much more GNP than Luxembourg. Swaziland has fewer official languages than Switzerland. People in Switzerland make substantially more money than people in Swaziland. Switzerland has somewhat more agricultural land than Swaziland. Swaziland doesn't have nearly as much GNP as Switzerland. People in Taiwan make substantially more money than people in Thailand. Taiwan has considerably less agricultural land than Thailand. Thailand doesn't have quite as much GNP as Taiwan.

EXERCISE 8

Interview a partner to obtain the following information, and then make statements that compare you and your partner.

▶ **EXAMPLE:** My partner has taken the TOEFL several more times than I have.
I have taken the TOEFL fewer times than my partner.

QUESTIONS	YOUR PARTNER	YOU
times he or she has taken the TOEFL	5	1
rooms in your partner's house or apartment		
languages your partner understands		
number of children he or she would like to have		
countries he or she has visited		
family members		

As with Exercise 4, if your class does not enjoy the "statistical" nature of the previous exercises, skip them and do this exercise in their place. Be sure to allow more processing of different answer patterns to make sure that Ss get sufficient practice using and reviewing the structures.

Workbook Exs. 3–4, pp. 73–74. Answers: TE p. 498.

ANSWER KEY

Exercise 8

Answers will vary. Possible answers include: My partner has taken TOEFL several more times than I have. My partner's apartment has somewhat fewer rooms as mine does. My partner doesn't understand as many languages as I do. I don't want to have nearly as many children as my partner does. I haven't visited as many countries as my partner has. I don't have quite as many family members as my partner does.

This chart, like the others in this unit, is designed for individual study and will appeal to Ss who are reflective observers or who enjoy concept formation. This one, unlike the previous two, is organized in order of **increasing** difference (identical→similar→different). It is best used as pre-lesson individual study or post-lesson review and follow-up.

S U G G E S T I O N S :

1. Do this focus on another class day than Focuses 1 and 2.
2. Review comparisons of amount and degree (adjective and noun phrases) and then explain that we can also compare things in terms of similarity and difference. Ask if Ss can define "similar" or "similarity."

3. Try changing the example sentences to refer to similarities and differences of students in your class. **For example:**

(a) *Juan speaks the same first language as Beauregard.*

(b) *Juan and Beauregard speak the same first language.*

(c) *People from the U.S. speak very much the same kind of English as people from Canada.*

(d) *People from the U.S. and Canada speak very much the same kind of English.*

(e) *Beauregard doesn't have quite the same course of study as Frederika does.*

(f) *Frederika and Beauregard don't have quite the same course of study.*

(g) *Bettina has a slightly different course of study from Beauregard.*

(h) *Bettina and Brunhilde have very different plans for the future.*

Make sure that Ss can identify the comparative structures, and after you have underlined them (or had Ss underline them for you), have Ss turn to the chart to review the format. They can study the focus box at home as review.

FOCUS **3**

FORM MEANING

Comparisons of Similarity and Difference: Noun Phrases

Comparisons can also be made in terms of **similarity** and **difference,** in addition to amount and degree.

EXAMPLES	MEANING	FORM
(a) Pakistan uses **exactly the same official language as** Bangladesh. **(b)** Pakistan and Bangladesh use **the same official language.**	**IDENTICAL** **X = Y**	X + VP + (intensifier) + *the same* NP *as* Y (*does*).* *X and Y* + VP + (intensifier) + *the same* NP* *exactly* *precisely* } intensifiers
(c) Pakistan has **very much the same literacy rate as** Bangladesh (does). **(d)** Pakistan and Bangladesh have **almost the same growth rate.**	**SIMILAR** **X ~Y** great similarity ↕ small similarity	X + VP + (intensifier) *the same* NP* *as* Y (*does*). *X and Y* + VP + (intensifier) *the same* NP.* *very much* *basically* *almost* *somewhat* } intensifiers
(e) Bangladesh does**n't** have **quite the same population as** Pakistan (does). **(f)** People in Pakistan and Bangladesh do **not** have **at all the same culture.**	**DIFFERENT** **X ≠ Y** small difference ↕ large difference	X + *not* + VP + (intensifier) + *the same* NP *as* Y (*does*).* *X and Y* + *not* VP + (intensifier) *the same* NP.* *quite* *nearly* *at all* } intensifiers
(g) Bangladesh has a **slightly different growth rate from** Pakistan. **(h)** People in Pakistan and Bangladesh have **very different cultures.**	small difference ↕ large difference	X + VP + (intensifier) + *different* + NP *from/than* Y.* *X and Y* + VP + (intensifier) + *different* + NP* *slightly/a bit* *somewhat* *substantially/* *considerably* *much/very* } intensifiers

*NP = Noun Phrase   VP = Verb Phrase

EXERCISE 9

Underline the statements of similarity and difference in the following passage. For each comparative structure you find, (a) identify the things that are being compared, and (b) decide whether the comparison describes things that are identical, similar, or different. The first two sentences have been done for you as an example.

▶ **EXAMPLE:** 1) (a) different kinds of English; (b) similar
2) (a) things like vocabulary and pronunciation; (b) different

---

REGIONAL VARIETIES OF ENGLISH

(1) Although English is spoken in many countries, <u>English speakers don't all speak quite the same kind of English.</u> (2) <u>Things like vocabulary and pronunciation are often substantially different.</u> (3) The differences between some varieties of English are easy to identify. (4) No one would mistake Indian English for Australian English. (5) The pronunciation features of these two "Englishes" are quite different. (6) British English is substantially different from American English, not only in terms of accent, but also spelling and vocabulary—especially slang.

(7) But the differences between some regional varieties are more subtle. (8) For example, many people think that Canadian and American varieties of English are exactly the same, but in fact, there are some differences, and not all words are pronounced alike. (9) In America the vowel sound in the word "out" is pronounced differently from that in *boot*. (10) But in Canada many people pronounce *shout* basically like *shoot*. (11) To most people Canadian English and American English seem very much alike. (12) But the careful listener will be able to find a number of examples of the ways Americans speak the language differently from their northern neighbors.

EXERCISE 10

Based on your own knowledge and the statistical information you read about in the Opening Task, make statements about general similarities and differences between developing countries and developed countries. Describe one characteristic of developing countries that is likely to be (a) identical, (b) similar, (c) somewhat different, and (d) very different from developed countries.

EXERCISE 11

Interview a partner about how she or he typically likes to spend a vacation. Identify two things about your partner's vacation likes and dislikes that are (a) identical, (b) similar, (c) somewhat different, and (d) very different from yours.

Comparatives | **177**

Exercise 9

Exercises 9, 10 and 11 can be done individually or as pair work. Like other exercises, this one emphasizes correct comprehension of these structures. Depending on the needs of your class, you can stress correct decoding of statements of similarity and difference or give your class additional practice at constructing such comparisons themselves by doing Exercise 10. If you feel the class has had enough of statistics, omit Exercise 10 and use Exercise 11 for the production practice.

Exercise 10
V A R I A T I O N :
Present Exercise 10 as a series of simple general discussion questions. Ask the class:
1. *What are some characteristics of developing countries that are likely to be identical to developed countries?*
2. *What are some characteristics that are likely to be similar?*
By keeping the tone "conversational" you can give Ss an opportunity to use those target patterns without making it appear too much like previous exercises.

Exercise 11
E X P A N S I O N :
Have Ss report their partners' vacation preferences orally or in writing.

Workbook Ex. 5, p. 75. Answers: TE p. 498.

Exercise 9

These structures should be underlined in the following sentences:
(5) The pronunciation features of these two "Englishes" are quite different.   (6) British English is substantially different from American English. . . .   (8) many people think that Canadian and American varieties of English are exactly the same . . . and not all words are pronounced alike.   (9) In America the vowel sound in the word "out" is pronounced differently from that in *boot*.   (10) *shout* basically like *shoot.*   (11) To most people Canadian English and American English seem very much alike   (12) Americans speak the language differently from their northern neighbors.

Things being compared and degree of similarity:
(5) (a) pronunciation features of these two Englishes (b) different   (6) (a) British English/American English (b) (quite) different   (8) (a) Canadian and American varieties of English (b) the same   (9) (a) the pronunciation of the vowel sound in "out" and *boot* (b) different   (10) (a) the pronunciation of *shout* and *shoot*; (b) very similar/almost the same   (11)(a) Canadian English and American English (b) very similar/almost the same   (12) (a) the ways Americans and Canadians speak the language (b) different

Exercise 10

Answers will vary. Possible answers include: Developed countries can have the same land area as developing countries. Developing countries can have almost the same GNP as developed countries. Developing countries can have almost as much agricultural land as developed countries. Per capita income in developing countries are usually substantially different from those in developed countries.

Exercise 11

Answers will vary. Possible answers include: (a) My partner enjoys exactly the same kind of vacations I do. (b) My partner and I like to spend our vacations at the same kinds of places. (c) My partner's idea of the perfect vacation is rather different from mine. (d) My ideal vacation is considerably different from my partner's.

Teacher's Edition: Unit 10   **177**

If possible, present this focus on the same day as Focus 3 and in a similar manner.

Try changing the example sentences to refer to similarities and differences of students in your class.

For example:

(a) *Japanese prepare rice just the same as Koreans do.*

(b) *Japanese and Koreans prepare rice very much the same.*

(c) *Japanese prepare rice almost the same as Koreans do.*

(d) *Japanese and Korean rice taste very much alike.*

(e) *Mexican tamales and Guatemalan tamales aren't prepared exactly alike.*

(f) *Mexican cooking and Korean cooking don't taste at all alike.*

(g) *Japanese do not cook rice quite the same as Koreans (do).*

(h) *Thais and Laotians don't cook at all the same.*

(i) *Chinese like their chicken cooked a bit differently from Americans.*

(j) *Italians and Chinese prepare their rice quite differently.*

Make sure that Ss can identify the comparative structures. After you have underlined them (or had Ss underline them for you), have Ss turn to the chart to review the format. They can study the focus box at home as review.

FOCUS **4**

FORM MEANING

▶ **Comparisons of Similarity and Difference: Verb Phrases**

EXAMPLES	MEANING	FORM
(a) Canadians pronounce most words **just the same as** Americans (do).	**IDENTICAL OR SIMILAR**	X + VP* + (intensifier) + *the same as* Y (*does*). X *and* Y + VP + (intensifier) + *the same*
(b) Canadians and Americans pronounce most words **very much the same.**		X + VP (intensifier) *like* Y (*does*). X *and* Y + VP + (intensifier) *alike*.
(c) Canadian English sounds **almost like** American English (does).	identical ↕ similar ↕ less similar	exactly/just almost very much } intensifiers quite/much somewhat
(d) American and Canadian English sound **very much alike.**		
(e) Some Canadian words aren't pronounced **exactly like** American words (are).	**DIFFERENT**	X + *not* + VP + (intensifier) *like* Y (*does*). X *and* Y + *not* + VP (intensifier) *alike*.
(f) Australian English and Indian English do **not sound at all alike.**	small difference ↕ large difference	exactly quite } intensifiers much at all
(g) Canadians do **not** pronounce *"out"* **quite the same as** Americans (do).		X + *not* + VP + (intensifier) *the same as* Y (*does*) X *and* Y + *not* + VP + (intensifier) *the same*.
(h) Americans and Canadians don't pronounce *"out"* **at all the same.**	small difference ↕ large difference	quite a bit } intensifiers at all
(i) Canadians pronounce English **a bit differently from** Americans.		X + VP + (intensifier) *differently from/than* Y. X *and* Y + VP + (intensifier) *differently*.
(j) Australians and Americans pronounce English **quite differently.**	small difference ↕ large difference	a bit somewhat } intensifiers quite

*VP = Verb Phrase

EXERCISE 12

Use the information you read in Exercise 9 and your own experience to make statements of similarity and difference using these cues. Use intensifiers to indicate whether these differences are large or small.

▶ **EXAMPLES:** Indians/Australians/pronounce English/like

Indians don't pronounce English at all like Australians.

Canadians/Americans/pronounce English/alike

Canadians and Americans don't pronounce English quite alike.

1. British/American/use slang expressions/differently
2. No two countries/speak a common language/the same
3. Spanish in Spain/in Latin America/differently from
4. The word color/in Britain/in America/is spelled/not alike
5. Many Canadians pronounce "shout"/"shoot"/the same as
6. grammar/in regional varieties of English/alike

FOCUS **5**

Informal Usage of Comparisons

There are differences between formal (written) and informal (spoken) English when making comparative statements.

LESS FORMAL/ CONVERSATIONAL STYLE	MORE FORMAL/WRITTEN STYLE
(a) The culture of Pakistan is **different than** Bangladesh.	(b) The culture of Pakistan is **different from** that of Bangladesh.
(c) Canadians pronounce certain words **differently than** Americans.	(d) Canadians pronounce certain words **differently from** Americans.
(e) Pakistan had **much the same** colonial history **that** Bangladesh **did.**	(f) Pakistan had **much the same** colonial history **as Bangladesh.**

EXERCISE 13

Change these informal comparisons to their more formal variations.

1. Canadian English follows the same grammatical rules that American English does.
2. My partner usually spends his vacations differently than me.

Comparatives | **179**

ANSWER KEY

Exercise 12

1. British and American speakers of English use slang expressions quite differently. 2. No two countries speak a common language exactly the same. 3. Spanish in Spain is spoken differently from Spanish in Latin America. 4. The word "color" is not spelled alike in Britain and in America. 5. Many Canadians pronounce "shout" basically the same as "shoot." 6. The grammar in regional varieties of English is all basically alike.

Exercise 13

1. Canadian English follows the same grammatical rules **as** American English does. 2. My partner usually spends his vacations differently **from** me. 3. My writing teacher doesn't put the same emphasis on accuracy **as** my mathematics teacher does. 4. The social values of Korea are quite different **from those of** Kuwait. 5. Many people developing countries have a different per capita income **from** many people in developed countries. 6. Cultural conflicts happen when people in one culture feel differently about certain social values **from** people in another culture. 7. My brother eats almost the same food **as** I do. 8. The English spoken in New Zealand is slightly different **than that** spoken in Australia.

---

3. My writing teacher doesn't put the same emphasis on accuracy that my mathematics teacher does.
4. The social values of Korea are quite different than Kuwait.
5. Many people in developing countries have a lower per capita income than many people in developed countries.
6. Cultural conflicts happen when people in one culture feel differently about certain social values than people in another culture.
7. My brother has almost the same hobbies that I do.
8. The English spoken in New Zealand is slightly different than in Australia.

USE YOUR ENGLISH

Note: The activities on these "purple pages" at the end of each unit contain communicative activities designed to apply what Ss have learned and help them practice communication and grammar at the same time. For a more complete discussion of how to use the Use Your English activities, see p. xxii of this Teacher's Edition.

Activity 1
EXPANSION:

To use this as a contact exercise for Ss to interview Americans outside of class, structure it a bit more by creating a worksheet:

Name of person interviewed_____
Example of difference _____

Expand the number of people to be interviewed and differences to be identified as required by the needs of your class. You might lead the discussion on generic differences yourself.

Activity 2

1. This activity can also be done in small groups.
2. Ss may need some additional guidance and discussion on the differences between *stereotypes* and *generalizations*. Teachers who are uncomfortable with classroom controversy should probably choose another activity from this unit.

Use Your English

ACTIVITY 1: SPEAKING

How can you tell if someone is from another country? What are some things people do differently when they come from another culture?

STEP 1 Working with a partner from another culture talk about how you know when someone is a foreigner. If you can, be sure to ask two or three Americans how they know when someone is from another country.

STEP 2 Identify some general or universal differences in behavior, dress, etc. that are true for all cultures. Some examples of generic differences are: speaking with an accent, clothing styles, and so on.

ACTIVITY 2: SPEAKING/WRITING

What are the similarities among people of a particular group?

STEP 1 Decide on a particular group of people. The group could be determined by nationality, culture, age, political beliefs, religion, or some other characteristic like Boy Scouts, people with blue eyes, teachers, tourists—the choices are unlimited!

STEP 2 As you think about things that define a particular group of people, make sure to avoid stereotypes in making your generalizations. **Generalizations** are statements of observation; for example: *Many people in culture X usually take a nap in the afternoon.* **Stereotypes** are statements of judgment; for example: *People of culture X are lazy.* A stereotype is an incorrect assumption that all members of a group share some characteristic.

STEP 3 Write a paragraph describing things that members of this group have in common.

ACTIVITY 3: WRITING

The Opening Task in Unit 12 on page 202 describes the true story of two identical twins who were separated at birth. Refer to the information on page 202 and write a paragraph that describes some similarities and differences between the twins.

ACTIVITY 4: WRITING/SPEAKING

Have you ever met someone who reminds you of someone else? What characteristics and actions were similar? In what ways were the two people different? In a brief essay or oral presentation, tell about two people who reminded you of each other.

ACTIVITY 5: LISTENING

Listen to the following conversation between Kim and Bob about a class in Anthropology. See if you can get enough information to answer the questions on the quiz that Professor Jordan gave them the next day. If necessary you can listen to the conversation more than once.

Anthropology 112: Cultural Geography
Quiz #3

1. Define "language family."

2. Define "culture family."

3. What two examples of culture families were mentioned in the lecture?

4. What is the relationship between culture and economic and political problems in developing countries?

ACTIVITY 6: READING/SPEAKING

In this unit you have examined some information on the economic differences between developing and developed countries. Based on the information in this unit as well as your own knowledge discuss the questions below in a small group.

- Which do you think is a more common source of conflict between nations: economic differences or cultural differences? Can you give examples to support your opinion?
- What do the differences and similarities between developed and developing countries mean for world peace and global development?

Comparatives **181**

ANSWER KEY

Activity 5

Answers to the quiz may vary slightly in form. The basic content is outlined here.

1. **language family:** groups of languages that have somewhat the same linguistic structure
2. **culture family:** groups of cultures that have more or less the same basic values, attitudes, and beliefs
3. **two examples of culture families mentioned in the lecture:** European culture, Latin culture

4. **relationship between culture and economic & political problems in developing countries:** Many developing countries were founded by colonial powers as political unions, not cultural ones. No matter how much their economic and political interests may be alike, cultures that *think* quite differently from one another may choose to *act* quite differently as well. The study of geography shows that political boundaries change much more frequently and more rapidly than cultural boundaries do.

Activity 3

This can be used as an additional exercise to practice the patterns presented in Focuses 3 and 4.

VARIATION:

For advanced classes, assign this as a follow-up to the Opening Task to assess how well your Ss already understand these structures.

Activity 4

For variety, have Ss list similarities and differences for any other category you can think of: cities (*San Francisco and Paris are similar because . . .*), styles of cooking (*Thai and Cambodian cooking are similar because . . .*), clothing, behavior.

VARIATION:

To use as a testing or diagnostic activity, have Ss write their responses as comparison/contrast paragraphs or essays.

Activity 5

Play textbook audio.
The tapescript for this activity appears on pp. 514–515 of this book.
Allow for multiple listenings of the lecture if necessary.
1. Ss listen for the general idea.
2. Ss follow along with the questions and note information needed for answers.
3. Ss listens for specific information they still need.
4. Ss verify their final answers.
To process, go over the answers, and replay portions of the tape as needed to settle differences of interpretation.

Activity 6

This activity probably works best with more "mature" classes that have shown an interest in political and economic topics. You can also assign these topics for written responses which you can then evaluate for accuracy of comparative forms.

The test for this unit can be found on p 458
The Answers are on p. 459 of this book.

TOEFL Test Preparation Exercises for Units 8–10 can be found on pp. 79–81 of the Workbook.
The answers are on p. 499 of this book.

Teacher's Edition: Unit 10   **181**

Unit 11

UNIT OVERVIEW

This unit provides an overview of coordinating conjunctions and logical connectors. These features are particularly important for producing and understanding extended text-length passages typical of academic reading and writing tasks. Since coordination and subordination are often covered in basic writing classes, this unit focuses more on the semantic and syntactic issues surrounding their use. For a comprehensive treatment of the issues surrounding coordination and subordination, see *The Grammar Book,* Chapters 24 and 26 (pp. 461–490, 519–544).

UNIT GOALS

Review the goals listed on this page so students (Ss) understand what they should be able to do by the end of the unit.

OPENING TASK

This task, with its focus on accuracy, may not be palatable to teachers who strongly believe in process writing. If you wish, substitute an editing activity of the next-to-final draft of the Ss' own writing, focusing on use of connectors. Most Ss, however, appreciate a systematic correction of form, and find this task helpful. Additionally, if the general topic of culture shock and adjustment is not appropriate for your class (where, for example, students are still in their home cultures, or have been living in the new culture for a long time), substitute Activity 1 as the Opening Task. Then use this text in combination with Exercise 1.

UNIT 11

CONNECTORS

UNIT GOALS:

- To correctly understand and use different coordinating conjunctions
- To correctly understand and use different sentence connectors
- To correctly understand and use different subordinating conjunctions.

OPENING TASK
Improving Your Writing

My experience with culture shock

Every person has experience with culture shock. However I am no exception. And I have experience with culture shock. Although I have lived in the United States for almost 1 year. I still often feel FRAG homesick and I miss my family. When I first came to the U.S., I was RUNON very comfortable and because everything was new everything was RUNON interesting for me. I enjoyed my independence from my parents. I enjoyed to experience new food and making new friends. Everything was strange, nevertheless I enjoyed the new experiences. RUNON

Soon I got used to many differences. Even though I was used to FRAG them. Still I wasn't comfortable. Little by little I grew tired of the differences. Because the things in America weren't new to me FRAG anymore. The differences weren't interesting they were boring. RUNON However I began to miss things in Indonesia. For example, food, my friends, the warm climate. I became depress and homesick. I stayed in my room, because I was tired of speaking English all the time. Even though I studied however my grades weren't so good.

So I visited my advisor. He told me about culture shock. I learned that every person has this kind of experience and it can't be avoid RUNON I learned that this culture shock is temporary but universal. My advisor told me I must to keep busy and talk about my culture shock with my friends. This was good advice, as a result, my culture shock became less and in spite I sometimes still miss my life in RUNON Indonesia. I don't feel depression the same as before.

Bambang Soetomo asked his English teacher to point out grammatical problems in his essay about culture shock.

STEP 1 With a partner, go over the essay and the teacher's comments. What suggestions would you give to Bambang in order to improve his writing? Can you correct his essay?

STEP 2 Compare your corrected essay to one possible corrected version in Exercise 1 on page 187.

SUGGESTIONS:

1. Have Ss review the essay individually or in pairs before going on to Step 2. If you choose individual review, consider assigning it as homework the night before beginning this unit.
2. This general procedure of teacher correction and student revision can be used throughout the course with any of the writing topics suggested in activities or tasks. If you are using the text in connection with a writing class, consider integrating the topics in the writing class with some of the topics in this book.

1. You may want to use the first part of this focus (on this page) in place of the Unit Goal review at the beginning of the unit. If the class is more advanced, ask why we use these kinds of words in writing and what the purpose for providing them is.

2. Ask Ss if they can define or provide a synonym or a typical word used to express that particular meaning category.
Some examples:
addition: *and, more*
emphasis: *moreover, and furthermore*
contrast: *but, however*
concession: *yes, but, even so . . .)*
reason: *because*
result: *so*
Don't spend too much time on this stage; it's just to get a general conceptual framework for a particular category.

3. Refer the Ss to the correct section of the focus box for additional examples of other logical connectors in that particular category.

4. End the discussion by asking Ss if they can think of other examples in that category. Don't worry if they cannot at this point. Additional connectors are introduced throughout the unit.

FOCUS **1**

FORM MEANING

Overview of Connectors

Connectors show logical relationships between clauses in a sentence, between sentences within a paragraph, or even between paragraphs.

EXAMPLES	EXPLANATIONS
(a) Matt grew up in Kansas, **but** he now lives in San Francisco. **(b)** Bambang **not only** misses his family, **but** he **also** wishes a few friends were in America with him.	There are three categories of connectors: **Coordinating conjunctions** connect two similar grammatical structures, such as noun phrases, prepositional phrases or independent clauses.
(c) Matt grew up in Kansas. **However,** he now lives in San Francisco. **(d)** Bambang misses his family. **In addition,** he wishes that a few friends were in America with him.	**Sentence connectors** show the logical connection between sentences.
(e) **Although** Matt grew up in Kansas, he now lives in San Francisco. **(f)** **In addition to missing** his family, Bambang wishes that a few friends were in America with him.	**Subordinating conjunctions** connect a dependent noun clause or a gerund phrase with the main clause.

The logical relationships that these connectors express can be divided into four general categories: **additive, contrastive, cause and effect,** and **sequence.** See the chart on pages 185–186.

Spread out the categories over more than one lesson, or introduce the first two categories, and preview the meanings of the others before assigning them for homework.

MEANING	FORM		
	COORDINATING CONJUNCTIONS	SENTENCE CONNECTORS	SUBORDINATING CONJUNCTIONS
addition	(a) Bambang misses his family, **and** they miss him.	(b) Bambang misses his family, **too**. He **also** misses his friends. **In addition,** he is having culture shock. **Besides,** he's homesick.	(c) **In addition to** missing his family, Bambang misses his friends.
emphasis/ intensifying	(d) **Not only** does Bambang miss his family, **but** he is **also** experiencing culture shock.	(e) **Furthermore,** he's not doing well in school. **In fact,** he failed two midterms. **Actually,** he's quite depressed. **Indeed,** he's thinking about going home.	(f) **Besides** being depressed, he's having trouble in school, **not to mention** feeling lonely all the time.
contrast	(g) Everyone experiences culture shock, **but** it eventually passes	(h) Some people have severe culture shock. Others, **however,** just feel a mild depression. Bambang's culture shock is almost over; yours, **on the other hand,** may just be beginning. Mild culture shock is a universal experience. Deep depression, **in contrast,** is not.	(i) Some people have severe culture shock, **while** others just feel a mild depression. **Whereas** some people have severe culture shock, others just feel a mild depression.
concession. . . (yes. . .but)	(j) The advisor told him culture shock can't be avoided, **yet** it is fortunately temporary.	(k) Bambang feels homesick. **Even so,** he will stay until he finishes his studies. Bambang studies hard. **Nevertheless,** he isn't getting good grades. **In spite of this,** he is still trying to improve.	(l) **Although** he feels homesick, Bambang will stay until he finishes his studies. He isn't getting good grades, **even though** he studies hard. **In spite of** experiencing culture shock/**In spite of the fact that** he still experiences culture shock, Bambang has decided not to go home.

Continued

Continued

MEANING	FORM		
	COORDINATING CONJUNCTIONS	**SENTENCE CONNECTORS**	**SUBORDINATING CONJUNCTIONS**
reason	(m) Bambang went to see his advisor, **for** he was worried about his grades.	(n) Bambang was worried about his grades. **With this in mind**, he went to see his advisor.	(o) He found it difficult to concentrate, **due to** being depressed. **Because/Since** Bambang was worried about his grades, he went to see his advisor.
result	(p) He was depressed, **so** he went to see his advisor.	(q) Bambang was worried about his grades. **Accordingly**, he went to see his advisor. His advisor told him that culture shock is universal. He **consequently** felt much better about his depression. **As a result**, he decided not to go home early. He **therefore** canceled his plane reservation.	(r) **As a result** of feeling depressed, he decided to talk with his advisor. He made an appointment **so that** he could find out about leaving school early. **In order to** find out more about culture shock, he decided to read some articles about it.
conditional	(s) The advisor told Bambang to keep busy, **or (else)** he would become more depressed.	(t) Bambang didn't want to go home early. **Then** he would feel that he had failed. **Under such circumstances**, he might even feel worse than he had in America.	(u) His advisor told him to get a lot of exercise, **providing/if** he could do that without neglecting his studies.
sequence	(v) He made an appointment, **and** he went directly to see his advisor.	(w) **First**, one must recognize culture shock. **Then** one must deal with it. **Eventually** everyone gets over it. **Soon** they start to feel more comfortable in the new culture.	(x) Bambang felt much better **after** he talked with his advisor. **When** he found out about culture shock, he was glad he hadn't decided to leave **before** talking with his advisor.

EXERCISE 1

Identify the form and meaning of the highlighted connectors. The first sentence has been done for you as an example.

▶ **EXAMPLE:** *and: form: coordinating conjunction; meaning: additive*

since: form: subordinating conjunction; meaning: reason

My Experience with Culture Shock

(1) Every person who has lived in a new culture has had some experience with culture shock, **and** I am no exception, **since** I, too, have had an experience with culture shock. (2) **Although** I have lived in the United States for almost one year, sometimes I still feel homesick, and still miss my family. (3) When I **first** came to the U.S., I was very excited. (4) **Because** everything was new, everything was interesting. (5) I enjoyed my independence from my parents; I **also** enjoyed experiencing new situations and making new friends. (6) **Although** everything was a little strange, I **nevertheless** enjoyed these new experiences. (7) **Eventually** I got used to many of the differences, **but even though** I was used to them, I still wasn't comfortable. (8) **In fact,** little by little I grew tired of the differences. (9) **Because** the things in America weren't new to me anymore, the differences weren't interesting. (10) **Indeed,** they had **actually** become boring. (11) **As a result,** I began to miss things about Indonesia, such as food, friends, and the warm tropical climate, more and more. (12) I **soon** became depressed and homesick. (13) I stayed in my room, **because** I was tired of speaking English all the time. (14) **Even though** I studied hard, my grades weren't good. I wanted to go home.

(15) **Because of** these feelings, I decided to see my advisor, **so that** I could get some advice about returning home without finishing my studies. (16) He told me two important things about culture shock. (17) **First,** I learned that any person in a new culture has a similar kind of experience, **and** that culture shock can't be avoided. (18) **Furthermore,** I learned that culture shock is not only universal, but also temporary. (19) **As a result of** his advice, I realized that I should be patient, and that I shouldn't go home just yet. (20) My advisor **also** suggested that I try to keep busy and talk about my culture shock with my friends. (21) I followed this good advice, **and as a result,** my culture shock has become less troublesome. (22) **In spite of the fact that** I sometimes still miss my life in Indonesia, I don't feel as depressed as I did. (23) **Moreover,** I no longer want to return home before I finish my studies. I know that I can adjust to this new life.

Exercise 1

This exercise should be assigned as homework or follow-up for the presentation and study of Focus 1. For in-class work, assign Ss to read the passage the night before, then have them work through the exercise in pairs.

VARIATION:

To save time, have half the class do the first paragraph and the other half do the second.

ANSWER KEY

(1) **and**—form: coordinating conjunction, meaning: additive/ **since**—form: subordinating conjunction, meaning: cause and effect (2) **although**—form: subordinating conjunction; meaning: contrastive (3) **first**—sentence adverbial; meaning: sequence (4) **because**—form: subordinating conjunction: meaning: cause and effect (5) **also**—form: sentence adverbial; meaning: additive (6) **although**—form: subordinating conjunction; meaning: contrastive/ **nevertheless**—form: sentence adverbial; meaning: contrastive (7) **eventually**—form: sentence adverbial; meaning: sequence/**but**—form: coordinating conjunction; meaning: contrastive/**even though**—form: subordinating

conjunction; meaning: contrastive (8) **in fact**—form: sentence adverbial; meaning: additive (9) **because**—form: subordinating conjunction; meaning: cause and effect (10) **indeed**—form: sentence adverbial; meaning: additive/**actually**—form: sentence adverbial, meaning: additive (11) **as a result**—form: sentence adverbial; meaning: cause and effect (12) **soon**—form: sentence adverbial; meaning: sequence (13) **because**—form: subordinating conjunction; meaning: cause and effect (14) **even though**—form: subordinating conjunction; meaning: contrastive (15) **because of**—form: subordinating conjunction; meaning: cause and effect/**so that**—

form: subordinating conjunction; meaning: cause and effect (17) **First**—form: sentence adverbial; meaning sequence/**and**—form: coordinating conjunction; meaning: additive (18) **furthermore**—form: sentence adverbial; meaning: additive (19) **as a result of**—form: subordinating conjunction; meaning: cause and effect (20) **also**—form: sentence adverbial; meaning: additive (21) **and**—form: coordinating conjunction; meaning: additive/**as a result**—form: sentence adverbial; meaning: cause and effect (22) **In spite of the fact that**—form: subordinating conjunction; meaning: contrastive (23) **moreover**—form: sentence adverbial; meaning: additive

Exercise 2

SUGGESTIONS:

Make sure Ss read the entire passage before doing the Exercise.

1. If time is short, assign pairs to do one of these paragraphs.
2. If you have access to an OHP, a good way to process exercises like this is by making a transparency of this page to show to the whole class.

Exercise 3

Assign this exercise as homework or have pairs do it in class.

Workbook Exs. 1& 2, pp. 82–83. Answers: TE p. 499.

EXERCISE 2

Circle the appropriate connector from the options in parentheses. There may be more than one correct choice.

Both Canada and the United States have large minorities that speak languages other than English. Canada has a large French-speaking minority. The United States, (1) (*on the other hand, furthermore, consequently, yet*) has a large Spanish-speaking minority. (2) (*But, However, So*) the way the two countries deal with this fact are rather different.

Canada has adopted a policy of bilingualism and has two official languages. All students study both languages in school. (3) (*Moreover, Nevertheless, Therefore*) all official government activities are conducted in both languages.

However, in the United States there is a movement to make English the only official language. (4) (*So, So that, As a result*), some people may be officially discouraged from using languages other than English at work. In some parts of the country, there are very few facilities available to people who can't speak English, (5) (*and, but, yet, so*) (6) (*under such circumstances, on the other hand, in addition to*) Spanish speakers may be required to provide their own translators in such places as hospitals or government offices. (7) (*In spite of, Even though, Consequently*) all students in the public schools are taught English, (8) (*but, and, for, no connector*) English-speaking students are not usually required to study Spanish.

These differences in bilingualism may result from geography. In Canada, the French speakers are actually a majority in certain parts of the country, primarily in the Province of Quebec. In the United States, (9) (*however, on the other hand, in spite of this, therefore*) Spanish-speaking communities are spread around the country. Large numbers of Spanish speakers are found in New York, Florida, New Mexico, and California. (10) (*As a result, Under such circumstances, In addition, Besides*) there are substantial numbers in many other large cities. (11) (*Although, However, In spite of*) they do not constitute a majority in any single region.

EXERCISE 3

Complete these sentences using information provided in Exercises 1 and 2.

1. In addition to missing his family, Bambang . . .

   _____

2. In spite of sometimes still missing his family, . . .

   _____

3. Before he talked to his advisor about culture shock, . . .

   _____

ANSWER KEY

Exercise 2

(1) on the other hand   (2) But/However
(3) Moreover   (4) As a result   (5) and, so
(6) under such circumstances
(7&8) Even though, no connector/
Consequently, but   (9) however, on the other hand   (10) In addition, Besides
(11) However

Exercise 3

Answers will vary. Possible answers include:
1. also missed things about Indonesia.

2. Bambang doesn't feel as depressed as before.   3. he was thinking about returning home.   4. . . . he no longer is thinking about going home.   5. he studies hard.
6. studying hard   7. doesn't.   8. all students study both languages in school.
9. . . . all official government activities are conducted in both languages.   10. there's a lot of support for the policy there.   11. all students study both languages in school.
12. . . . Canada can be said to have two official languages.

4. Bambang now understands that his depression was the result of culture shock. Because of this, . . .

_____

5. Bambang sometimes does poorly on tests, even though . . .

_____

6. Bambang sometimes does poorly on tests, in spite of . . .

_____

7. Canada has an official policy of bilingualism. The United States, however, . . .

_____

8. Canada has an official policy of bilingualism. Consequently, . . .

_____

9. As a result of Canada's official policy of bilingualism, . . .

_____

10. Canada's French-speaking minority is concentrated in a particular part of the country. Consequently, . . .

_____

11. Canada's French-speaking minority is concentrated in a particular part of the country. Nevertheless, . . .

_____

12. Since all government business is conducted in both languages, . . .

_____

For more advanced classes, you may be able to skip the first part of this focus and go directly to a presentation of parallelism.

1. Introduce this concept by writing examples k and l on the board, or other incorrect variants about individual Ss in the class. **(For example:** *Yanti likes neither the TOEFL nor studying. Morris was born in Russia, but now here).*
2. Ask Ss to identify what is wrong with these sentences.
3. Circle the coordinating conjunctions and explain that they must be used to connect parallel structures.
4. Have Ss look at the example sentences (a–h) for examples of the different kinds of structures that are being connected in correct usage. Use the first paragraph of Exercise 4 for additional examples.

Exercise 4

Make sure Ss read the entire passage before starting the exercise.

SUGGESTIONS:

1. If time is short, assign pairs to do one of these paragraphs.
2. If you have access to an OHP, a good way to process exercises like this is by making a transparency of this page to show to the whole class.

Workbook Exs. 3–4, pp. 83–84. Answers: TE p. 499.

FOCUS **2**

> ## Using Coordinating Conjunctions to Connect Parallel Forms

Unlike other connectors, coordinating conjunctions (*and, but, or, nor,* and *yet*) can join any parallel grammatical structures.

EXAMPLES	STRUCTURES BEING JOINED
(a) **Jeff** and **Matt** are **roommates** and **best friends.**	nouns
(b) They **live** and **work** in San Francisco.	verbs
(c) They are **poor** but **hard-working** young men.	adjectives
(d) Every Saturday they clean their apartment **quickly** but **thoroughly.**	adverbs
(e) They hurry **down the street** and **around the corner** to do their shopping.	prepositional phrases
(f) They're always in a hurry **to go bike riding** or **to take their dog to the park.**	infinitives
(g) On Saturday nights they like **dancing at discos** and **going to nightclubs** to meet friends.	gerunds
(h) They enjoy living together because **they have many common interests** and **it's cheaper than living alone.**	clauses

EXAMPLES	EXPLANATIONS
(i) Jeff likes neither **dancing** nor **swimming.** **(j)** Matt **is** originally from Kansas but now **lives** in San Francisco.	**Parallel Structure (correct):** In formal written English, structures joined by coordinating conjunctions should have the same grammatical form.
(k) NOT: Jeff likes both **vacations** and **working.** **(l)** NOT: Matt **is** originally from Kansas, but now **living** in San Francisco.	**Nonparallel Structure (not correct)**

EXERCISE 4

Circle the coordinating conjunctions in this passage and underline the elements that each one connects. The first paragraph has been done for you as an example.

(1) <u>Matt (and) Jeff</u> first came to San Francisco in 1980, after they had graduated from college. (2) Both of them had grown up in small towns. (3) <u>Jeff was from Wisconsin, (and) Matt grew up in Kansas</u>, but neither one enjoyed living in a small town. (4) There wasn't enough <u>freedom (or) excitement</u> for their tastes. (5) Each one decided to move to San Francisco because he had heard <u>that it was a beautiful city, (and) that it was filled with interesting people.</u>

(6) When they first met, they were surprised and delighted to discover how many things they had in common and how similar their interests were. (7) Jeff liked weightlifting, and so did Matt. (8) Matt loved opera, and Jeff did too. (9) Jeff wasn't entirely comfortable with "big-city" life, nor was Matt, but neither one missed living in a small town at all. (10) They both liked dogs and wanted to have one for a pet, so they decided to look for an apartment and live together. (11) They both thought it would be cheaper and more fun to have a roommate.

(12) However, when they moved in together and began living with each other, they found that there were also a lot of differences between them. (13) Jeff was very neat, but Matt wasn't. (14) He preferred to let the dirty dishes pile up until there were "enough" to bother with, and he did not pick up his clothes or keep things neat. (15) Jeff, on the other hand, always wanted things to be washed immediately, even if there were only one or two dishes. (16) Matt liked staying out late every Friday night, but Jeff always wanted to get up early on Saturday mornings to clean the house and to finish chores so they could spend the afternoon relaxing or playing with their new puppy in the park. (17) They soon realized that they would either have to start making compromises or start looking for separate apartments, which neither Matt nor Jeff wanted to do. (18) Fortunately, their similarities outweighed their differences, and they settled into a pleasant life together.

ANSWER KEY

Exercise 4

Parts to be underlined are given; coordinating conjunctions are in **bold.**
(6) surprised **and** delighted . . . how many things they had in common **and** how similar their interests were. (7) Jeff liked weightlifting, **and** so did Matt. (8) Matt loved opera, **and** Jeff did too. (9) Jeff wasn't entirely comfortable with "big-city" life, **nor** was Matt, **but** neither one missed living in a small town at all. (10) liked dogs **and** wanted to have one for a pet, . . . look for an apartment **and** live together. (11) cheaper **and** more fun (12) moved in together **and** began living with each other (13) Jeff was very neat, **but** Matt wasn't. (14) He preferred to let the dirty dishes pile up until there were "enough" to bother with, **nor** did he pick up his clothes or keep things neat. (16) Matt liked staying out late every Friday night, **but** Jeff always wanted to get up early on Saturday mornings to clean the house, **and** to finish chores . . . relaxing **or** playing with their new puppy (17) **either** have to start making compromises **or** start looking for separate apartments, . . . **neither** Matt **nor** Jeff (18) their similarities outweighed their differences, **and** they settled into a pleasant life together.

FOCUS **3**

If you are pressed for time, assign Focus 3 for individual study and have Ss hand in Exercises 6 and 7 for you to check and verify that they have understood and studied the information presented in this focus. Otherwise, present the four different problems one at a time by focusing on the "incorrect" examples (sentences a, c, e, h, & k) first and asking Ss to identify the problem and correct it.

S U G G E S T I O N :

Point out that native speakers also make mistakes with these kinds of conjunctions.

► **Problems Using Coordinating Conjunctions**

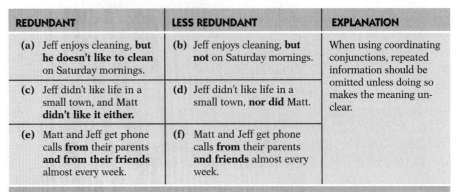

REDUNDANT	LESS REDUNDANT	EXPLANATION
(a) Jeff enjoys cleaning, **but he doesn't like to clean** on Saturday mornings.	**(b)** Jeff enjoys cleaning, **but not** on Saturday mornings.	When using coordinating conjunctions, repeated information should be omitted unless doing so makes the meaning un-clear.
(c) Jeff didn't like life in a small town, and Matt **didn't like it either.**	**(d)** Jeff didn't like life in a small town, **nor did** Matt.	
(e) Matt and Jeff get phone calls **from** their parents **and from their friends** almost every week.	**(f)** Matt and Jeff get phone calls **from** their parents **and friends** almost every week.	

EXAMPLES	EXPLANATIONS
(g) Bambang Soetomo studies **hard, but** he sometimes has trouble understanding assignments. **(h)** NOT: Bambang Soetomo studies **hard but** he sometimes has trouble understanding assignments.	When coordinating conjunctions connect independent clauses, they must be preceded by a comma. Without a comma such sentences are called run-on or run-together sentences. They are considered incorrect in formal written English.
(i) Jeff doesn't plan to leave San Francisco, **nor does Matt want** him to. **(j)** **Not only do** the two **have** similar interests, but they also have similar personalities.	When clauses are joined with negative coordinating conjunctions (*nor, neither, not only*), the clause with the negative coordinating conjunction at the beginning must take question or inverted word order.
(k) AWKWARD: I began to miss my family, **and** I was getting more and more depressed, **so** I decided to talk with my advisor.	In formal written English, using coordinating conjunctions to connect independent clauses is often considered to be awkward or poor style. Other kinds of logical connectors—sentence connectors and subordinating conjunctions—are more frequently used.
(l) BETTER: **In addition to** missing my family, I was getting more and more depressed. **As a result,** I decided to talk with my advisor.	

EXERCISE 5

Combine these pairs of sentences to make them less redundant. There is more than one way to combine most of the sentences, so compare your answers with a partner's.

▶ **EXAMPLE:** Jeff lives in San Francisco. Matt lives in San Francisco.

Jeff lives in San Francisco, and so does Matt.

Both Jeff and Matt live in San Francisco.

1. Jeff likes cleaning. Matt doesn't like cleaning.
2. Jeff may go home for a visit on his vacation. Jeff may travel to France on his vacation.
3. Matt doesn't plan to return to his hometown to live. Jeff doesn't plan to return to his hometown to live.
4. Jeff likes getting up early. Matt doesn't like getting up early.
5. Jeff always wanted to have a dog. Matt always wanted to have a dog.
6. Matt might take the dog to the park this afternoon. Jeff might take the dog to the park this afternoon.
7. Matt likes dancing at nightclubs. Matt likes meeting friends at nightclubs.
8. Matt comes from a small town in Kansas. Jeff comes from a small town in Wisconsin.

EXERCISE 6

Connect the numbered pairs of sentences in one of these paragraphs with coordinating conjunctions. Make any necessary changes to remove redundancy or to correct word order.

Paragraph 1

(1) My mother doesn't smoke. My father doesn't smoke. (2) My father gave up smoking years ago. My mother only quit last year. (3) My mother had wanted to quit for a long time. She knew it was bad for her health. (4) She wasn't able to smoke only one or two cigarettes. She had to give it up entirely. (5) My mother sometimes still wants a cigarette. My mother won't smoke a cigarette no matter how much she wants to. (6) My father is proud of her for quitting. My father gives my mother a lot of praise for quitting.

Exercise 5

VARIATION:

To shorten the time needed for Ss to work on this exercise in class, assign each pair one or two to do and then process as a whole class.

Exercise 6

VARIATION:

To shorten the time needed for Ss to work on this exercise in class, assign half the class to do paragraph 1 and the other half to do paragraph 2. Then pair up paragraph 1 students with paragraph 2 students to discuss the changes that they made. Monitor individual discussions or process as a whole class.

ANSWER KEY

Exercise 5

Answers may vary. Possible answers include:
1. Jeff likes cleaning, but Matt doesn't. 2. Jeff may either go home for a visit or travel to France on his vacation. 3. Neither Matt nor Jeff plans to return to his hometown to live. 4. Jeff likes getting up early but Matt doesn't. 5. Jeff always wanted to have a dog and Matt did too/. . . and so did Matt. 6. Either Matt or Jeff might take the dog to the park this afternoon. 7. Matt likes dancing and meeting friends at nightclubs. 8. Both Matt and Jeff come from small towns in Kansas and Wisconsin respectively.

Exercise 6

Paragraph 1: (1) My mother doesn't smoke and my father doesn't either./and neither does my father/Neither my mother nor father smokes. (2) My father gave up smoking years ago, but my mother only quit last year. (3) My mother had wanted to quit for a long time, for she knew it was bad for her health. (4) She wasn't able to smoke only one or two cigarettes, and had to give it up entirely. (5) My mother sometimes still wants a cigarette, but she won't smoke no matter how much she wants to. (6) My father is proud of her for quitting and gives my mother a lot of praise for quitting.

Paragraph 2: (1) Canada has a large French-speaking minority, and the U.S. a large Spanish-speaking minority. (2) Many people in Canada speak French, and all government publications are printed in both languages. (3) Canada has two official languages, but the United States discourages the use of languages other than English for official purposes. (4) In Canada, the French-speaking minority is found primarily in the Province of Quebec, but in the United States, Spanish-speaking communities are found in New York, Florida, New Mexico, and California.

Exercise 7

Have Ss do this individually and then use a partner for peer correction. You will still need to do a whole class processing to make sure that everyone knows the range of possible answers.

Workbook Exs. 5 & 6, pp. 85–86. Answers: TE p. 499.

Paragraph 2

(1) Canada has a large French-speaking minority. The United States has a large Spanish-speaking minority. (2) Many people in Canada speak French. All government publications are printed in both languages. (3) Canada has two official languages. The United States discourages the use of languages other than English for official purposes. (4) In Canada, the French-speaking minority is found primarily in the province of Quebec. In the United States, Spanish-speaking communities are found in New York, Florida, New Mexico, and California.

EXERCISE 7

Correct these run-on sentences from Bambang's essay. You can correct the punctuation or make two sentences using a sentence connector of similar meaning. Compare your solution to other students' solutions.

1. I still often feel homesick and I miss my family.

2. Everything was strange nevertheless I enjoyed the new experiences.

3. The differences weren't interesting, they were boring.

4. I learned that every person has this kind of experience and it can't be avoided.

5. This was good advice, as a result, my culture shock became less but in spite of this I still miss my life in Indonesia.

ANSWER KEY

Exercise 7

Answers will vary. Possible answers include:
1. I still often feel homesick. **In addition,** I miss my family.   2. Everything was strange. **Nevertheless,** I enjoyed the new experiences.
3. The differences weren't interesting. **In fact,** they were boring.   4. I learned that every person has this kind of experience. **Not only that,** it can't be avoided.   5. This was good advice, **and,** as a result, my culture shock became less. However, **in spite of this,** I still miss my life in Indonesia.

FOCUS 4

▶ **P**roblems Using
Sentence Connectors

EXAMPLES	EXPLANATIONS
(a) I was getting more and more depressed. **As a result,** I decided to talk with my advisor. **(b)** I was getting more and more depressed; **as a result,** I decided to talk with my advisor. **(c)** NOT: I was getting more and more depressed, **as a result,** I decided to talk with my advisor.	Sentence connectors are used with sentences or independent clauses connected with a semicolon. Do not use them with commas to connect clauses. This produces run-on sentences.
(d) Jeff grew up in Wisconsin. **However,** Matt comes from Kansas. **(e)** Jeff grew up in Wisconsin. Matt, **however,** comes from Kansas. **(f)** Jeff grew up in Wisconsin. Matt comes from Kansas, **however.**	Sentence connectors normally occur at the beginning of a sentence, but some can also appear in the middle or at the end. See the chart in Appendix 4 (p. A-8) for more information.
(g) Living together has saved both boys a lot of money. **Besides,** Matt likes having a roommate. **(h)** NOT: Matt **besides** likes having a roommate. **(i)** NOT: Matt likes having a roommate **besides.**	Other sentence connectors cannot occur in the middle and/or end of a sentence. See the chart in Appendix 4 (p. A-8) for more information.
(j) Carmen had a lot of money in her bank account. **Therefore,** she was able to pay cash for her new car. **(k)** She was **therefore** able to pay cash for her new car. **(l)** NOT: She was able to pay cash for her new car **thus.**	

This focus can be presented in a straightforward way, or can be made more inductive in the following way.

1. With Ss books closed, write the example sentences (a, b, and c) on the board and identify that (c) is considered awkward or "bad style." Then ask Ss if they can use that information to generate their own "rules." Have them work in pairs or small groups to do this. If you need to guide them with questions, you can use the following: *How many clauses are in these sentences? What punctuation is used to join the clauses? Can the clauses stand alone as separate sentences?*

2. Follow the same procedure for sentences d, e, and f and then g–l. Ss will probably not be able to generate a rule for the second two groups of examples. Explain that certain connectors must occur in certain places in the sentence. Refer Ss to the chart in Appendix 4. Have them study the charts and then allow time for questions.

3. Do Exercise 8 as an immediate follow-up and practice of the points you have presented.

Exercise 8

While Ss should be able to identify the specific problem, the ways used to correct the problem may vary.

Workbook Exs. 7 & 8, p. 87. Answers: TE p. 500.

EXERCISE 8

These sentences have problems with sentence connectors. Identify the problems and correct them.

1. Every person has experience with culture shock. However, I am no exception.

2. Even though I studied however my grades weren't good.

3. In Canada all official government activities are conducted in both French and English. Under such circumstances, students also study both languages in school. Nevertheless, in the United States, there is no official bilingual policy in government operations. Besides, some local governments have policies that prohibit the use of any language other than English for official business.

ANSWER KEY

Exercise 8

1. Wrong meaning for the logical connector. The situation requires additive rather than contrastive meaning. *Every person has experience with culture shock, and I am no exception.*   2. Too many logical connectors. *Even though I studied, my grades weren't good. I studied. However, my grades weren't good.*   3. **Also** is not needed. Wrong meaning for **under such circumstances, nevertheless,** and **besides.** *In Canada all official government activities are conducted in both French and English. Accordingly, students study both languages in school. In the United States, on the other hand, there is no official bilingual policy in government operations. In fact, some local governments have policies that prohibit the use of any language other than English for official business.*

FOCUS 5

Problems Using Subordinating Conjunctions

CORRECT SUBORDINATION	SENTENCE FRAGMENT	EXPLANATION
(a) **Because** things were no longer new to Bambang, **he** began to miss his friends and family back home.	**(b)** NOT: **Because** things were no longer new to Bambang. **He** began to miss his friends and family back home.	Subordinating conjunctions are used with dependent clauses, gerunds, or noun phrases. They cannot be used with sentences. This produces a **sentence fragment,** which is considered grammatically incorrect.
(c) **Even though** Bambang Soetomo studies **hard, he** sometimes has trouble understanding assignments.	**(d)** NOT: **Even though** Bambang Soetomo studies **hard. He** sometimes has trouble understanding assignments.	

EXAMPLES	EXPLANATION
(e) NOT: **Besides Bambang misses his family,** he also misses his friends. **(f)** **Besides missing his family,** Bambang also misses his friends. **(g)** NOT: Bambang sometimes doesn't do well on tests, **in spite of he studies carefully.** **(h)** Bambang sometimes doesn't do well on tests, **in spite of studying carefully.** **(i)** Bambang sometimes doesn't do well on tests, **in spite of the fact that he studies carefully.**	Some subordinating conjunctions cannot be used with dependent clauses. They function as prepositions and are used with gerund or noun phrases instead. Common subordinating conjunctions of this type are: *besides, in spite of, despite, regardless of, due to, as a result of.* Adding *the fact that* to *in spite of* makes **(g)** grammatically correct.

FOCUS 5

If you are doing this focus immediately after the previous one, you can assign it for study at home. If you have used that procedure for Focus 4, you might present this one in a manner similar to the one described above.

1. With Ss books closed, write the example sentences (a and b) on the board and explain that (b) is considered awkward or "bad style."
2. Repeat this process with examples c and d. If you prefer, make up your own sentences about Ss in the class. (**Some other examples of incorrect subordination:** *Because Yanti has passed the TOEFL Test. She no longer needs to come to English class. Yanti still comes to English class even though she passed the TOEFL Test.*)
3. Ask Ss if they can use that information to generate their own "rules." Have them work in pairs or small groups to do this. If necessary, guide them by asking: *How many clauses are in these sentences? What punctuation is used to join the clauses? Can the clauses stand alone as separate sentences?*

SUGGESTIONS:

1. The other examples discussed in this focus can be treated as discrete "vocabulary" items. Remind Ss that certain subordinators can only be used with gerunds or noun phrases.
2. Do Exercise 9 immediately following this presentation.

This exercise can be done individually, in pairs or in small groups.

VARIATION:

To save time, assign one or two items for each student/pair/group. Process as a whole class.

UNIT GOAL REVIEW

Ask Ss to look at the goals on the opening page of this unit again.

1. For whole class discussion: Review the main meaning categories by asking Ss to name them and give an example of one of the connectors that expresses that meaning. For each correct example, ask Ss to identify whether it is a coordinator, subordinator, or sentence connector.

2. For pair or small group processing: Have Ss fill out a matrix similar to the one below (with their books closed, in pairs or small groups) and then have groups compare answers. Process as a whole class by asking Ss to write examples of individual connectors they have identified on the board.

meaning	coord. conj.	sentence conn.	subord. conj.
addition	and	also	in addition to
.			

Put the matrix on an OHP transparency and fill it out as a whole class.

EXERCISE 9

Here are some problems with the form, meaning, or use of subordinating conjunctions that appeared in Bambang's essay. Identify the problems and correct them.

1. Although I have lived in the United States for almost one year. I often feel homesick and miss my family.

   _____

2. Even though I was used to them. Still I wasn't comfortable.

   _____

3. However I began to miss things in Indonesia. For example food, my friends, the warm climate.

   _____

4. In addition to he told me about culture shock, my advisor suggested that I should be patient.

   _____

5. Besides I was homesick, I was also having trouble getting used to the way classes are taught in the U.S.

   _____

6. In spite of the fact that being homesick, I didn't want to go home without completing my education.

   _____

7. As a result of my conversation with my advisor. My culture shock got a little better.

   _____

8. Despite I was having problems, I didn't stop doing my best.

   _____

ANSWER KEY

Exercise 9

While Ss should be able to identify the specific problem, the ways used to correct the problem may vary.

1. **Although** is a subordinating conjunction, and can't be used with an independent clause. *Although I have lived in the United States for almost 1 year, I often feel homesick and miss my family.* 2. **Even though** is a subordinating conjunction, and can't be used with an independent clause. *Even though I was used to them, I still wasn't comfortable.* 3. **However** and **for example** are

sentence adverbials. They should be followed by commas, and used with independent clauses: *However, I began to miss things in Indonesia. For example, I missed the food, my friends, and the warm climate.* 4. **In addition to** must be used with a noun phrase or a gerund phrase, not with a clause. *In addition to telling me about culture shock, my advisor suggested that I should be patient.* 5. When **besides** introduces contrastive clauses, it should be used with gerunds or noun phrases. *Besides being homesick, I was also having trouble getting used to the way classes are taught in the U.S.*

6. **In spite of** is used with gerunds or noun phrases, in spite of the fact that it is also used with clauses. *In spite of the fact that I was homesick, I didn't want to go home without completing my education./In spite of being homesick.* 7. **As a result** introduces clauses, as a result of noun phrases. *As a result of my conversation with my advisor, my culture shock got a little better.* 8. **Despite** is used with gerund and noun phrases. *Despite having problems, I didn't stop doing my best./Despite my problems, I didn't stop doing my best.*

Use Your English

ACTIVITY 1: WRITING

Give your teacher a piece of your writing. This may be something that you have written for this class or another class. Ask your teacher to indicate places where there are grammatical problems. Follow the same procedure that you used for the Opening Task to analyze your problems and correct your mistakes.

ACTIVITY 2: WRITING

Write a brief essay describing your own personal experience with culture shock. Be sure to connect your ideas with logical connectors and avoid run-on sentences or sentence fragments.

ACTIVITY 3: SPEAKING

What are some common connectors in your native language? How does "good style" affect their use? In this unit we learned that although it is grammatically possible to join sentences with coordinating conjunctions, it is not always considered to be "good writing." Think about the words you use to join ideas in your native language. Identify two situations where "good writing" may be different in your first language than it is in English. Present your ideas to the rest of the class.

USE YOUR ENGLISH
Activity 1

This basic format can be used with any of the written activities in this book, either for diagnosis or testing. For this particular activity, mark problems with logical connectors either by using the system in the Opening Task, or by highlighting/circling/underlining problematic sentences.

Activity 2

This activity represents a logical topic for Activity 1, but it may not be appropriate for all classes. If your Ss are not going through "cultural adjustment," choose some other topic. Other possible topics: choosing roommates, the compromises necessary to living with someone, bilingualism, or giving up a bad habit.

Activity 3

This can be done as a whole class or small group discussion. Although this topic may be a bit sophisticated for less advanced classes, the discussion often is a useful one to have with Ss. Arabic speakers, for example, often carry their language's stylistic preference for coordination into English. Japanese speakers may overuse topic markers (*as for* . . . etc.) You may have already noticed some of these features in previous samples of your student writing.

Activity 4

Step 1: Answers will vary. Possible interpretations include:

1. (a) . . . **and** I love it. *That's why I love it.*
   (b) **but** I love it. *Even so, I love it anyway.*
   (c) . . . **so** I love it. *That's the reason why I love it.*
2. There is a difference in emphasis. In the sentence **(a)**, the fact that I love Indian food is the most important. In sentence **(b)**, the fact that Indian food is spicy is the most important.
3. **(a)** The two ideas don't share a strong logical cause-and-effect relationship.
   (b) The emphasis is on the cause-and-effect relationship.

Step 2: Answers will vary. Possible explanations include:

1. The logical connector doesn't give information about the way these two ideas are related. Most teachers would consider this to be a run-on sentence.
2. This logical connector indicates result rather than cause.
3. This logical connector indicates cause rather than result.

Activity 5

Play textbook audio. The tapescript for this listening appears on p. 515 of this book. Do this activity for fun. It might be more lively to read the script yourself with much appropriate dramatic emphasis, inviting student guesses as you go along.

The test for this unit can be found on pp. 460. The answers are on pp. 461 of this book.

ACTIVITY 4: SPEAKING

Examine the different meanings that are implied by choosing one connector instead of another.

STEP 1 With a partner or in a small group, discuss these three groups of sentences. What are the differences in implied meaning?

1. (a) Indian food is spicy, and I love it. (b) Indian food is, spicy, but I love it. (c) Indian food is spicy, so I love it.	2. (a) Although Indian food is spicy, I love it. (b) Although I love Indian food, it's spicy.	3. (a) Not only is Indian food spicy, but I also love it. (b) Because Indian food is spicy, I love it.

STEP 2 The following sentences are illogical. With a partner or in a small group, discuss how the incorrect use of a logical connector makes the meaning of these sentences strange or unclear.

(1) I love Indian food, and it is spicy.
(2) I love Indian food, so it is spicy.
(3) Since I love Indian food, it is spicy.

ACTIVITY 5: LISTENING

Listen to this story about **Silly Sally.** Silly Sally likes and dislikes various things. There is one single, simple reason for all the things she likes or doesn't like. The purpose of the game is to discover this simple reason.

STEP 1 As you listen to the description of her preferences, follow along on the chart on the next page, and put a check in the appropriate column.

STEP 2 Compare your answers with another student's and try to figure out the secret of her likes and dislikes.

STEP 3 With your partner come up with one additional example of something she likes and dislikes for each category. Your teacher will tell you if your examples are correct or not. If you think you know the secret of the game, don't tell other students. Just give more examples of the things that Silly Sally likes and doesn't like. Your teacher will tell you if you're correct.

ANSWER KEY

Activity 5

Silly Sally only likes things that have double letters. She dislikes things without double letters. Hence she likes cooking, Greek food, Moroccan, etc., but dislikes eating, Chinese, Brazilian, and Japanese cuisine.

Silly Sally's Likes and Dislikes

Category	Like	Dislike?	Category	Like?	Dislike?
styles of food			**movie stars**		
cooking	—	—	Johnny Depp	—	—
eating	—	—	Meryl Streep	—	—
Greek food	—	—	Marlon Brando	—	—
Chinese cuisine	—	—	Elizabeth Taylor	—	—
Brazilian	—	—	Denzel Washington	—	—
Japanese	—	—	Whoopi Goldberg		
Moroccan	—	—	_____	X	
_____	X		_____		X
_____	—	X			
			dating		
sports			restaurants for dinner	—	—
tennis	—	X	restaurants for lunch	—	—
baseball	—	—	art gallery	—	—
skiing	—	—	museum	—	—
horseback riding	—	—	kisses	—	—
hockey	—	—	hugs	—	—
jogging	—	—	marriage	—	—
walking	—	—	engagement	—	—
_____	X		_____	X	
_____	—	X	_____	—	X
people			**vacations**		
queens	—	—	Greece	—	—
princesses	—	—	Italy	—	—
kings	—	—	inns	—	—
princes	—	—	hotels	—	—
Matt and Jeff	—	—	Philippines	—	—
Peter and Denise	—	—	Indonesia	—	—
John and Mary	—	—	travel in the summer	—	—
_____	X		travel in winter	—	—
_____	—	X	_____	X	
			_____	—	X
fruits and vegetables			**animals**		
beets	—	—	sheep	—	—
carrots	—	—	goats	—	—
apples	—	—	cats	—	—
potatoes	—	—	dogs	—	—
oranges	—	—	puppies	—	—
cauliflower	—	—	kittens	—	—
_____	X		_____	X	
_____	—	X	_____	—	X

Unit 12

UNIT OVERVIEW

This treatment of relative clauses may be review for some students (Ss), but many intermediate Ss, who may understand adverbial clauses, have more difficulty producing correct relative clauses or recognizing and accurately decoding reduced relative clauses in complex prose. For an extended discussion of these issues, see *The Grammar Book,* Chapters 28 and 29 (pp. 571–610).

OPENING TASK

1. Assign the reading for this task the night before, followed by a brief post-reading discussion regarding the content. Use your preferred method of pre-reading discussion when you make the assignment, and begin this class by asking Ss for a paraphrase or summary of the article.
2. Have Ss write individual answers for the questions in Step 2 or assign pairs to work together to develop the answers in class.
3. Process as a whole class asking for alternative answers for each of the questions.

UNIT 12

RELATIVE CLAUSES

UNIT GOALS:

- To understand restrictive and non-restrictive modification
- To correctly form subject and object relative clauses in different parts of a sentence
- To correctly use or delete relative pronouns in different kinds of relative clauses
- To use **whose** in relative clause

OPENING TASK
Which One is Which?

STEP 1 Read this article about twins who were separated at birth.

In 1943 two identical male twins were born in Ohio. Their mother was very young, so she gave the children up for adoption. They were separated the day after they were born, and grew up in different parts of the country. One grew up in Ohio and the other grew up in Oregon. Neither one knew he had a twin brother until the one twin moved back to Ohio, where the other twin was living. Then friends of the Ohio twin began to tell him that they had seen a man who looked exactly like him. The Oregon twin met several people who acted as if they knew him, even though he had never met them before. The two men each began doing research, and discovered their backgrounds and the fact that they were twins. They finally met each other in 1989, and the case was even reported on national television news programs.

Many researchers have been interested in this case because they want to see if the two men have any similarities even though they were raised in completely different environments. The researchers have found that there were, of course, many differences between the two men, but there are also some very interesting similarities: They had both married women with blonde hair and had three children. They had both painted their houses yellow. They both had dogs and shared similar interests and hobbies. They both had jobs that called for a lot of travel.

STEP 2 Look at this list of differences between the twins, and use the information to answer the questions that follow.

▶ **EXAMPLE:** Which twin is married to Bernice?

The twin who <u>has an old-fashioned home is married to Bernice</u>

Here is some information about one twin:	**Here is some information about the other twin:**
His nickname is "Rosey."	His nickname is "Red."
He has a modern home.	He has an old-fashioned home.
He is married to a woman named Betty.	He is married to a woman named Bernice.
He has three children—all boys.	He has three children—all girls.
His children knew that he had been adopted.	His children didn't know that he been had been adopted.
He sells plumbing supplies.	He sells advertising space in magazines.
He has a large dog named Prince.	He has a small dog named King.
His favorite sport is football.	His favorite sport is basketball.
He likes to listen to classical music.	He likes to listen to jazz.

1. Which twin has children that are all girls?

   The twin who _____.

2. Which twin owns a dog named Prince?

   The twin who _____.

3. Which twin sells plumbing supplies?

   The twin whose _____.

4. Which twin likes classical music?

   The twin whose _____.

5. Which twin prefers basketball?

   The twin who _____.

6. Which twin lives in a modern home?

   The twin who _____.

7. Which twin is married to a woman named Betty?

   The twin whose _____.

8. Which twin's children didn't know that he had been adopted?

   The twin who _____.

ANSWER KEY

Step 2

Answers for Step 2 will vary. Some possible answers are listed below.

1. The twin who is married to Bernice has children that are all girls.
2. The twin who likes to play football owns a dog named Prince.
3. The twin who has a modern home sells plumbing supplies.
4. The twin who sells plumbing supplies likes classical music.
5. The twin whose nickname is Red prefers basketball.
6. The twin who sells plumbing supplies lives in a modern home.
7. The twin whose nickname is Rosey is married to a woman named Betty.
8. The twin who has three daughters.

Use the examples in the book or alternative sentences for a presentation of these concepts. Alternative sentences should contain real information about Ss in the class.

Possible examples:

Restrictive Modification: *The student who is sitting in the corner is from Japan.*

Nonrestrictive modification: *Shizu, who is sitting in the corner, is from Japan.*

Exercise 1

Make sure Ss read the entire passage before staring the exercise.

S U G G E S T I O N S :

1. If time is short, assign pairs to do one of these paragraphs.
2. If you have access to an OHP, a good way to process exercises like this is by making a transparency of this page to show to the whole class and mark together.

Workbook Ex. 1, p. 88. Answers: TE p. 500.

Restrictive and Nonrestrictive Relative Clauses

EXAMPLES	EXPLANATIONS
(a) Which book do you want? The one **that's under the dictionary.** (b) What kind of food do you like? I like food **that's not too spicy.**	Restrictive relative clauses answer the question "what kind" or "which one."
(c) Nitrogen, **which is the most common element on earth,** is necessary for all life.	Nonrestrictive relative clauses just provide additional information about noun phrases. They do not identify what kind or which one.

EXERCISE 1

Underline each relative clause in this passage and circle the noun phrase it modifies. The first two have been done for you as an example.

(1) My friend Charlie has fallen madly in love. (2) He told me he has finally met (the woman) that he has been looking for all his life. (3) He has always been attracted to (women) that are intelligent and independent and that have a good sense of humor and a love of adventure. (4) The woman that he has fallen in love with has all those things and more, according to Charlie. (5) Even though physical appearance isn't the most important characteristic that Charlie is looking for, he is quite happy his new friend is attractive and athletic. (6) She not only runs and skis, but also goes scuba-diving, and has several other interests that Charlie also shares.

(7) Charlie was never completely happy with the women that he used to go out with. (8) There was always something that he wasn't satisfied with. (9) I used to tell him he was too choosy. (10) The "perfect woman" that he was looking for didn't exist. (11) No real person can equal the picture that someone has in his or her imagination. (12) But I'm glad he has found someone that he thinks is perfect. I've never seen him happier.

A N S W E R   K E Y

Exercise 1
The antecedents of the relative clauses are shown in bold.
(4) **The woman** that he has fallen in love with
(5) . . . **the most important characteristic** that Charley is looking for . . . (6) . . . **several other interests** that Charley also shares.
(7) . . . **the women** that he used to go out with. (8) . . . **something** that he wasn't satisfied with. (10) **The "perfect woman"** that he was looking for . . . (11) . . . **the picture** that someone has in his or her imagination. (12) . . . **someone** that he thinks is perfect.

Forming Restrictive Relative Clauses

EXAMPLES	EXPLANATIONS
(a) I read a book [Charlie really liked ~~the book.~~] last week. *that*	The relative pronoun [*that* in Example (a)] replaces the noun phrase in a relative clause in order to avoid repetition.
(b) I read a book [**that** Charlie really liked ⬈] last week.	When the relative pronoun is in the object position, it is moved to the front of the relative clause.

Relative pronouns can replace any noun phrase within the relative clause.

RELATIVE CLAUSE	UNDERLYING SENTENCE	FUNCTION
(c) I read the book **that** was published last year.	**(d)** **The book** was published last year	subject
(e) I read the book **that** your professor wrote.	**(f)** Your professor wrote **the book.**	object
(g) I met the person **that** Charlie gave flowers to.	**(h)** Charlie gave **the person** flowers.	indirect object
(i) I met the person **that** Lin told me about.	**(j)** Lin told me about **the person.**	object of a preposition
(k) I read the book **that** was published last year. **(l)** NOT: I read the book that **it** was published year.	Remember that the replaced noun or pronoun of the underlying sentence does **not** appear in the relative clause.	

---

1. Use the board to graphically demonstrate how the bracketed sentence in Example a is moved (and transformed) in Example b.
2. Examples c–i can be assigned for review or covered briefly, but the concept introduced in Examples k & l is important because it represents a common mistake that many students make. Be sure to present this point explicitly and follow it up with a second example that is based on the real information about your Ss' lives.

   Additional examples: *The lesson that we studied appeared on the TOEFL Test we took yesterday. (***NOT:** *The lesson that we studied it appeared on the TOEFL Test we took yesterday.) The student that I told you about is over there. (***NOT:** *The student that I told you about she is over there.)*

Exercise 2

Make sure Ss read the entire passage before starting the exercise.

SUGGESTIONS:

1. If time is short, assign pairs to do one of these paragraphs.
2. If you have access to an OHP, a good way to process exercises like this is by making a transparency of this page to show to the whole class and mark per directions.

Workbook Exs. 2 & 3, pp. 88–89. Answers: TE p. 500.

EXERCISE 2

In the following article underline the relative clauses. Then restate each relative clause as an independent sentence. The first three have been done for you as examples.

▶ **EXAMPLES:** (1) A new study may interest many people.

(2) They conducted a survey with several thousand American women all around the country.

(3) These women have common attitudes about men.

Scientists Identify Today's "Prince Charming"

(1) Sociologists at Mills College have released a new study <u>that may interest many people</u>, especially men. (2) They reported the results of a survey <u>that they conducted with several thousand American women all around the country</u>. (3) They wanted to examine common attitudes <u>that these women have about men</u>, so that they could identify important characteristics that women think are necessary in a good husband or boyfriend. (4) The study found a number of interesting results, which will probably not surprise most women, but may surprise some men.

(5) The women in the survey generally seem to prefer men who can express their feelings. (6) Most women prefer husbands who they can talk to easily and that they can share their problems with.

(7) There were also several other things that women consider important in a partner. (8) A man's character or personality is more important to many women than the job that he does for a living or the salary that he brings home. (9) Not surprisingly, most women want a husband that will take on an equal share of housekeeping and childraising duties.

(10) But the most important characteristic is this: Women want boyfriends who they can trust and husbands that they can depend on. (11) Unfortunately, more than 70% of the women who answered the questionnaires said they had husbands or boyfriends who lacked one or more of these important characteristics.

ANSWER KEY

Exercise 2
Relative clauses that should be underlined:
(1) that may interest many people, (2) that they conducted with several thousand American women all around the country. (3) that these women have about men/. . . that women think are necessary in a good husband or boyfriend. (4) which will probably not surprise most women, but may surprise some men. (5) who can express their feelings. (6) who they can talk to easily/that they can share their problems with. (7) that women consider important in a partner. (8) that he does for a living/. . . that he brings home.

(9) that will take on an equal share of housekeeping and childraising duties.
(10) who they can trust . . . that they can depend on. (11) who answered the questionnaires . . . who lacked one or more of these important characteristics.
Restatements of those relative clauses:
1. A new study may interest many people.
2. They conducted a survey with several thousand American women all around the country. 3. These women have common attitudes about men. Women think important characteristics are necessary in a good husband or boyfriend. 4. A number of interesting results

will probably not surprise most women, but may surprise some men. 5. Men can express their feelings. 6. They can talk to their husbands easily. They can share their problems with their husbands. 7. Women consider several other things important in a partner. 8. He does the job for a living. He brings the salary home.
9. A husband will take on an equal share of housekeeping and childraising duties.
10. They can trust boyfriends. They can depend on husbands. 11. The women answered the questionnaires. Husbands or boyfriends lacked one or more of these important characteristics.

FOCUS **3**

▶ Relative Pronouns

The relative pronouns are *who, whom, which,* and *that.*

EXAMPLES	EXPLANATIONS
(a) The man **who** told me about you last week is over there. **(b)** The man **whom** you mentioned last week is here today. **(c)** The man **whom** you told me about yesterday is here to see you.	Use *who* and *whom* to refer to humans. In formal written style, use *who* to refer to subjects in relative clauses and *whom* to refer to objects.
(d) I read the **book which** Kevin had recommended.	Use *which* to refer to nonhumans.
(e) The **man that** wrote this book is a teacher. **(f)** The **man that** you told me about is a teacher. **(g)** I read the **book that** Kevin had recommended.	Use *that* for humans or nonhumans, but only with restrictive relative clauses.
(h) Abraham Lincoln, **who** was the 16th president of the United States, died in 1865. **(i)** NOT: Abraham Lincoln, **that** was the 16th president of the United States, died in 1865. **(j)** San Francisco, **which** is on the Pacific Ocean, has a very cool climate. **(k)** NOT: San Francisco, **that** is on the Pacific Ocean, has a very cool climate.	Do not use *that* as a relative pronoun in nonrestrictive relative clauses. Use only *who, whom,* and *which.*

FOCUS 3

This focus may be review for some intermediate Ss. If so, omit it, but be sure Ss understand the *that/which* distinction for nonrestrictive relative clauses.

SUGGESTION:

Again, to explain these ideas you may choose to use original sentences that refer to actual Ss or situations in the class, such as: *Yumi, who is a student in this class, just wrote a perfect journal. (***NOT:** *Yumi that is a student in this class just wrote a perfect journal.)*

Exercise 3

This is a good exercise to assign for written homework for you to collect and evaluate.

Exercise 4

V A R I A T I O N :

For a more interactive approach, have Ss use these questions to interview each other and report their findings to the class. Process by asking questions such as: *"Yumi, what kind of person does Kenching want to marry?"*

EXERCISE 3

Combine these pairs of sentences by using a relative clause with *that, who, whom,* or *which*.

▶ **EXAMPLE:** I finally met the woman. Charlie has fallen in love with the woman.

I finally met the woman that Charlie has fallen in love with.

1. Last month Charlie fell in love with a young woman. He had been introduced to the woman by some friends.
2. She had a number of positive characteristics. Charlie found these characteristics quite attractive.
3. She has a responsible position in a company. The company produces computer programs.
4. That's a fast-growing field. Charlie is also interested in that field.
5. Hobbies involve athletics and being outdoors. Both of them like these hobbies.
6. Charlie introduced the woman to his parents. He had been dating the woman for several weeks.
7. She has a wonderful sense of humor. This makes their times together relaxing and enjoyable.
8. From the first time they met, Charlie felt there was a "special understanding" between them. He was unable to explain this understanding.

EXERCISE 4

Answer these questions using a relative clause ("I like people who . . ."; "People who I like . . ."). Compare your answers to those of a classmate.

1. What kind of people do you like?
2. What kind of people like you?
3. What kind of food do you like?
4. What kind of leisure activities interest you?
5. What kind of person do you want to marry?
6. What kind of person will want to marry you?
7. What kind of practice is useful in learning languages?
8. What kind of government is the best?

A N S W E R   K E Y

Exercise 3

1. Last month Charlie fell in love with a young woman that he had been introduced to by some mutual friends. 2. She had a number of positive characteristics which Charlie found quite attractive. 3. She has a responsible position in a company that produces computer programs. 4. That's a fast-growing field that Charlie is also interested in. 5. Both of them like hobbies which involve athletics and being outdoors. 6. Charlie introduced the woman that he had been dating for several weeks to his parents. 7. She has a wonderful sense of humor that makes their times together relaxing and enjoyable. 8. From the first time they met, Charlie felt there was a "special understanding" between them which he was unable to explain.

Exercise 4

Answers will vary. Sample answers include:
1. I like people who are outgoing. 2. People who are fun loving like me. 3. I like food that is spicy. 4. Activities that don't require a lot of money interest me. 5. I want to marry a person who is honest and kind. 6. Someone who doesn't expect to be rich will want to marry me. 7. Practice that involves using English outside of class is useful in learning languages. 8. That government is best which governs least.

EXERCISE 5

The following sentences are incorrect. Identify the mistakes and correct them.

1. I read a book that it was published last year.
2. I saw an article which your professor wrote it.
3. Jeff and Matt have been living in the city of San Francisco, that is located in California, since 1985.
4. This is the person whom Charlie gave her flowers.
5. I met the person who Charlie told me about her.
6. The teacher that I studied with her has become quite famous.
7. The money which you loaned me some last week is there on the table.
8. The resort that we read about it in the newspaper is becoming more and more popular.
9. The people whom I visited them last year are coming here for a visit.
10. My father, that lives in San Diego, loves sailing.

Exercise 5

V A R I A T I O N :

To save time, have Ss work on these sentences in small groups. Assign two or three sentences to each group and process as a whole class.

Workbook Ex. 4, p. 90. Answers: TE p. 500.

A N S W E R   K E Y

Exercise 5

1. antecedent of the relative pronoun has not been omitted. *I read a book that was published last year.* 2. antecedent of the relative pronoun has not been omitted. *I saw an article which your professor wrote.* 3. *Which* must be used for nonrestrictive relative clauses (not *that*). *Jeff and Matt have been living in the city of San Francisco, which is located in California, since 1985.*
4. antecedent of the relative pronoun has not been omitted. *This is the person whom Charlie gave flowers.* 5. antecedent of the relative pronoun has not been omitted. *I met the person who Charlie told me about.* 6. antecedent of the relative pronoun has not been omitted. *The teacher that I studied with has become quite famous.* 7. antecedent of the relative pronoun has not been omitted. *The money which you loaned me last week is there on the table.*
8. antecedent of the relative pronoun has not been omitted. *The resort that we read about in the newspaper is becoming more and more popular.* 9. antecedent of the relative pronoun has not been omitted. *The people whom I visited last year are coming here for a visit.* 10. *Who* must be used for nonrestrictive relative clauses (not *that*). *My father, who lives in San Diego, loves sailing.*

1. Explain that sometimes relative clauses are "hidden" in English because we can delete certain portions of the relative clause. Present the example pairs, or variants such as: **(a)** *I ate the cookies that Marianna brought to class.*
(b) *I ate the cookies Marianna brought to class.* **(c)** *The cookies that Marianna brought to class made everyone sick.*
(d) *The cookies Marianna brought to class made everyone sick.*
2. Follow a similar procedure to introduce the concepts outlined in examples g–p. It may not be necessary to go into such detail for your in-class presentation. Just present an example with the *be-form* deleted—for example: *I called on the student who is sitting by the door. I called on the student sitting by the door*—and ask Ss to study the examples as homework later.

FOCUS **4**

▶ Deleting Relative Pronouns

You can delete relative pronouns that function as objects in restrictive relative clauses.

EXAMPLES	FUNCTION OF RELATIVE PRONOUNS
(a) I read the book **that** your professor wrote. **(b)** I read the book your professor wrote.	direct objects
(c) The lady **that** Charlie sent flowers to is on the phone. **(d)** The lady Charlie sent flowers to is on the phone.	indirect objects
(e) I read the book **that** Charlie was so excited about. **(f)** I read the book Charlie was so excited about.	objects of prepositions

You can only delete relative pronouns that function as subjects in restrictive relative clauses that contain *be* (either as a main verb or an auxiliary). In such cases both the relative pronoun and *be* are deleted.

EXAMPLES	EXPLANATIONS
(g) I want a book **that was written** by an expert. **(h)** I want a book **written** by an expert.	relative clauses with passive verbs
(i) I think I know that woman **who is carrying** the blue suitcase. **(j)** I think I know that woman **carrying** the blue suitcase.	relative clauses with progressive verbs
(k) I tried to get an autograph from the baseball player **who is beside** the fence. **(l)** I tried to get an autograph from the baseball player **beside** the fence.	relative clauses with prepositional phrases
(m) Anyone **who is foolish enough** to use drugs should be free to do so. **(n)** Anyone **foolish enough** to use drugs should be free to do so.	relative clauses with adjective phrases
(o) Have you read the book **that made** Darryl Brock famous? **(p)** NOT: Have you read the book **made** Darryl Brock famous?	You cannot delete relative pronouns if they are subjects of a relative clause without *be*.

EXERCISE 6

Underline all the relative clauses in this passage. Make sure that you also include the ones that have deleted relative pronouns. The first paragraph has been done for you as an example.

The War to End All Wars

(1) When World War I, <u>which was fought in Europe from 1914 to 1917</u>, was finally over, it was called "the war to end all wars." (2) It was the most destructive war <u>the world had ever fought until then</u>. (3) Over ten million young men <u>sent to battle from both sides</u> were killed or permanently disabled.

(4) The war introduced powerful new weapons the world had never before seen. (5) The use of the airplane enabled armies on both sides to drop bombs with an effectiveness and precision that had been previously impossible. (6) Heavy casualties were also caused by the wide-scale use of a poison gas, called mustard gas, which permanently damaged the lungs of soldiers caught without gas masks.

(7) There were more than 8.5 million deaths. (8) Many people fighting this terrible war were killed in battles. (9) But many others died from intestinal diseases caused by the unsanitary conditions on the battlefield, or by infections which developed in lungs damaged by mustard gas, which was used by both sides.

(10) The peace established by "the war to end all wars" lasted less than a generation. (11) The most destructive war the world had ever known, like most wars, didn't solve the political and economic problems facing European governments at that time. (12) Less than twenty-five years after the conflict everyone hoped would bring world peace, Europe was again at war.

Exercise 6

Make sure Ss read the entire passage before starting the exercise.

SUGGESTIONS:

1. If time is short, assign pairs to do one of these paragraphs.
2. If you have access to an OHP, a good way to process exercises like this is by making a transparency of this page to show to the whole class and marking it together.

ANSWER KEY

Exercise 6

These clauses should be underlined:
(4) the world had never before seen.   (5) that had been previously impossible.   (6) called mustard gas, which permanently damaged the lungs of soldiers caught without gas masks.
(8) fighting this terrible war   (9) caused by the unsanitary conditions on the battlefield/. . . which developed in lungs damaged by mustard gas, which was used by both sides.
(10) established by "the war to end all wars"
(11) the world had ever known/. . . facing European governments at that time.
(12) everyone hoped would bring world peace

Exercise 7

Process this according to your preferred method, making sure that you use variety in your processing styles: if you have done the last couple of exercises as pair work, do this one individually. Be sure to include a variety of activities in each class period.

Exercise 8

Have one student in the pair report his or her partner's answers. Ask the whole class to determine common likes and dislikes from the report and write them on the board.

Workbook Ex. 5, pp. 90–91. Answers: TE p. 500.

EXERCISE 7

Wherever possible, delete the relative pronouns in these sentences and make any other necessary changes.

▶ **EXAMPLE:** The kind of people ~~that~~ I like are usually people **who** have a good sense of humor.

1. I like people **who** think about other people's feelings.
2. I like people **who** are working to make the world a place **that** we can all share.
3. I like people **who** don't take the work **that** they do too seriously.
4. I don't like people **who** have no sense of humor.
5. I like people **who** don't worry about things **that** other people say about them.
6. I dislike people **who** try to hurt other people's feelings.
7. I dislike people **who** are very concerned with power and position.
8. I like people **who** question the things **that** they have been taught and the teachers **who** have taught them.
9. I like people **who** are like me.
10. I like people **who** like me.

EXERCISE 8

Write five sentences that describe the kind of people you like and five sentences that describe the kind of people you don't like. Compare your sentences with those of a classmate. Describe any common likes and dislikes.

ANSWER KEY

Exercise 7
1. no deletion possible 2. I like people working to make the world a place we can all share. 3. I like people **who** don't take the work they do too seriously. 4. no deletion possible 5. I like people **who** don't worry too much about the things other people say about them. 6. no deletion possible 7. I dislike people very concerned with power and position.

8. I like people **who** question the things they have been taught and the teachers **who** have taught them 9. I like people like me. 10. no deletion possible

Exercise 8
Answers will vary. Possible answers include: The kind of people that I like are usually people who have a good sense of humor. I like people who are actively involved in making the world a better place. I like people who think about important issues. I like people who are like me, and who also like me in return. I dislike people who intentionally try to hurt other people's feelings. I dislike people who try to take power from other people by making them appear or feel bad.

Whose in Relative Clauses

When a relative clause contains a possessive form, *whose* + *noun* can be used in the same way as relative pronouns.

EXAMPLES	UNDERLYING SENTENCE	EXPLANATIONS
(a) I met a man **whose house** was destroyed in the earthquake.	(b) I met a man. **His house** was destroyed in the earthquake.	*Whose* can be used with: • the subject of a relative clause
(c) I got a letter from the man **whose house** we visited last week.	(d) I got a letter from a man. We visited **his house** last week.	• the object of a relative clause
(e) I spoke to the man **whose party** we got an invitation **to.**	(f) I spoke to a man. We got an invitation **to his party.**	• the object of a preposition
(g) I got a letter from the man **whose house** we visited last week. (h) NOT: I got a letter from a man **house** we visited last week.		You can never delete *whose* from a relative clause. It must always be used with a noun.

EXERCISE 9

Combine these sentences using *whose*.

▶ **EXAMPLE:** I got a letter from a man. We visited his house last week.

I got a letter from the man whose house we visited last week.

1. Samira met a man. His twin brother is a well-known geneticist.
2. Jeff and Matt are roommates. Matt's nickname is "Akbar."
3. People may have similar personalities. Their genetic make-ups are similar.
4. Nicole took a class from a teacher. She knew his wife in college.
5. Mary Rae would like to go to the lecture by the mountain climber. She read about his latest climb in *Adventure Magazine*.
6. My friend has a dog. Its eyes are different colors.
7. I keep getting phone calls for some stranger. His last name is apparently the same as mine.
8. Hans finally succeeded in meeting the artist. He had been admiring her work for years.

FOCUS 5

Try introducing this focus in a more inductive way. **1.** Write two "class-relevant" sentences up on the board and ask if anyone can make them into one sentence. **For example:** Hold up a notebook. Say "*I gave this student an A for the day. His/her notebook is in my hand.*" Write the sentences on the board. **2.** Ask for volunteers to combine the two. Ss may answer "*I gave the student who this is her notebook.*" If so, write that response on the board and ask for alternative versions. If no one supplies it, then write a correct version "*I gave the student* **whose** *notebook is in my hand . . .*" Ask Ss to volunteer other examples that follow this pattern.

Exercises 9 & 10

These exercises can be assigned for homework and collected and corrected to review whether Ss have mastered **whose** clauses.

S U G G E S T I O N S :

Start doing them as a whole class, but don't finish the entire exercise if they present no major difficulty.

A N S W E R   K E Y

Exercise 9
1. Samira met a man whose twin brother is a well-known geneticist.   2. Jeff and Matt, whose nickname is "Akbar," are roommates.
3. People whose genetic make-ups are similar may have similar personalities.   4. Nicole took a class from a teacher whose wife she knew in college.   5. Mary Rae would like to go to the lecture by the mountain climber whose latest climb she read about in *Adventure Magazine*.   6. My friend has a dog whose eyes are different colors.   7. I keep getting phone calls for some stranger whose last name is apparently the same as mine.   8. Hans finally succeeded in meeting the artist whose work he had been admiring for years.

Exercise 11

VARIATION:

For a more interactive way to do this exercise, have one student in the pair report his or her partner's answers. Ask the whole class to determine common likes and dislikes from the report and write them on the board.

Workbook Exs. 6 & 7, pp. 91–92. Answers: TE pp. 500–501.

UNIT GOAL REVIEW

Have Ss work in pairs to look over the goals on the opening page of the unit again. Have Ss summarize their understanding of the principles involved with each goal to one another and to identify one question they still have based on this discussion.

Process the questions with the whole class by either:

1. asking pairs to state their question and then asking other pairs if they can answer it or explain the relevant rule in their own words. or,

2. conducting a general review of points of confusion, based on what you hear while listening to the Ss pairs formulate their explanations or develop their questions.

EXERCISE 10

Combine these numbered pairs of sentences in this paragraph using relative pronouns or *whose*.

(1) Charlie wants to make some changes in his life. These changes involve both his lifestyle and his social activities. (2) Charlie wants to find a new place to live. The place has to have enough room for a dog. (3) He's looking at a new apartment. The apartment has a balcony, so he can grow some flowers. (4) Charlie also wants to get married to someone. Her political beliefs are similar to his own. (5) He hasn't found anyone yet. No one seems to share his interest in politics and sports. (6) He's thinking of putting a personals ad in a paper. A lot of people advertise in that paper in order to meet others with similar interests and backgrounds.

EXERCISE 11

Answer these questions, using relative clauses. Compare your answers with one of your classmate's.

▶ **EXAMPLE:** What kind of food do you like?

I like food that is not too spicy.

1. What kind of person do you want to marry?
2. What kind of person should be the leader of a country?
3. What kind of person makes the best teacher?
4. What kind of television programs do you like to watch?
5. What kind of place is the best for a vacation?
6. What kind of house or apartment would you like to live in?
7. What kind of books do you enjoy reading?
8. What kind of students get the best grades?

ANSWER KEY

Exercise 10

(1) Charlie wants to make some changes in his life which involve both his life style and his social activities. (2) Charlie wants to find a new place to live which has enough room for a dog. (3) He's looking at a new apartment that has a balcony, so he can grow some flowers. (4) Charlie also wants to get married to someone whose political beliefs are similar to his own. (5) He hasn't found anyone yet who seems to share his interest in politics and sports. (6) He's thinking of putting a personals ad in a paper which a lot of people advertise in, in order to meet others with similar interests and backgrounds.

Exercise 11

Answers will vary. Possible answers include:
1. someone who is rich. 2. someone who is honest. 3. someone who cares about her students 4. a program that teaches me something 5. a place that has a good beach 6. an apartment that has a nice view 7. books that have a lot of action 8. students who work hard

Use Your English

ACTIVITY 1: SPEAKING

STEP 1 In Exercise 2 you read about some of the things that American women consider important in a husband. Divide into same-gender groups of men and women. In your group discuss the characteristics of "the ideal life partner." Prepare a list of five to ten statements like these.

The ideal partner is someone who takes an equal responsibility for raising the children.

The ideal partner is a person who is able to maintain a good sense of humor.

What ideals do you all agree on? Are there ideals that are controversial?

STEP 2 Present your statements to the other groups. Compare the ideals presented by women's groups and the ideals presented by men's groups.

STEP 3 Discuss these questions as a whole class or in mixed gender groups.

- What are the important similarities and differences between the statements of the two kinds of groups?
- Are there some ideals that all men share, no matter what culture they come from?
- Are there some ideals that all women share, no matter what culture they come from?
- Are there some ideals that both genders share?

ACTIVITY 2: WRITING

Write a brief essay describing personal characteristics in people that you like and dislike. You may wish to look at Exercise 7 for some ideas about the kinds of characteristics other students have identified. Here are some questions you should try to answer in your essay.

- What kind of people do you like most?
- What personal characteristics do you appreciate and respect in other people?
- What personal characteristics do you find distasteful?

ACTIVITY 3: SPEAKING/WRITING

The word *daffy* means silly. A *daffynition* is a made-up definition for a word that doesn't really exist. In fact the word *daffynition* is, itself, a made-up word.

Activity 1

This activity works best when you follow the directions in the student book exactly. It always generates lively and spirited discussion. Teachers who feel they don't know how to handle Ss comments with which they personally disagree are advised to choose a different activity.

Activity 2

Use this activity to generate a written text that you can correct and evaluate following the same procedures as outlined in the Opening Task for Unit 11.

Activity 3

A good activity for a Friday afternoon. Just relax and have fun! Do it in small groups or as a whole class.

EXPANSION:

Have Ss (or groups) write their own "Weird Dictionaries."

STEP 1 Try to invent daffynitions for these made-up words.

EXAMPLE: Who or what is a **murphler**?

A *murphler is someone who makes a lot of noise when he eats.*

- What do **parahawks** do?
- What does **chemicophysiologicalistic** mean?
- What do **flurps** and **mompsquats** have in common?
- What are **quatchels?**
- Define **hypervoraciosity.**

STEP 2 Share your daffynitions with the rest of the class. Which one is the most believable? Which one is the most amusing daffynition for each term?

STEP 3 Make up some of your own imaginary words and provide definitions for them.

Activity 4

Play textbook audio.
The tapescript for this listening appears on pp. 515–516 of this book.

1. Play this tape once for Ss for general comprehension. Ask Ss for a brief summary of the topic.
2. Play a second time for Ss to listen for the specific definitions.
3. Play a third time for Ss to confirm and complete their answers.
4. Play a fourth time, if necessary, for Ss to identify where the specific information was that they needed for correct answers.

ACTIVITY 4: LISTENING

Listen to the following lecture about "hawks" and "doves," and write definitions for the following terms based on the information you heard.

What is a pacifist? _____

_____

What is a "hawk" ?_____

_____

What is a "dove"?_____

_____

What is the difference between a war and a revolution?_____

_____

_____

Activity 5

Like Activity 1, you can easily vary the amount of structure that you apply to this activity, ranging from a free classroom discussion to an organized debate with formal statements and rebuttals. Also, like Activity 1, this topic can generate some controversial opinions on the part of both teachers and Ss.

ACTIVITY 5: SPEAKING

Organize a debate between "hawks" and "doves" to consider the following questions:

- Is there a difference between a **war** and a **revolution?**
- Give some examples of armed conflicts that you feel were or were not justifiable.

216 UNIT 12

ANSWER KEY

Activity 4

pacifist: someone who doesn't believe in fighting wars ; "*hawk*": a person who is in favor of a particular war "*dove*": a person who is opposed to a particular war; *difference*

between a war and a revolution: A war is a conflict which involves two different countries, and a revolution is a war between the people of a single country and their unjust government.

- Under what circumstances is it acceptable to take up arms against your own government, other countries, or other groups of people within your own country?

You may wish to discuss wars in general, or a specific conflict that you are familiar with.

ACTIVITY 6: WRITING/SPEAKING

In English we often make a "dramatic introduction" in certain formal situations. A dramatic introduction lists a person's characteristics and accomplishments and ends with the person's name.

Here's an example of a "dramatic introduction":

> "Ladies and gentlemen, it is my great pleasure to introduce an individual whose honesty and sincerity are well-known, whose commitment to education is serious and wide-reaching, whose work in the field of linguistics has helped many students understand English better, and whose wit and kindness make working together a pleasure. Ladies and gentlemen, I give you our English teacher, Rebecca Buckley."

Make a dramatic introduction for one of your classmates or for a real person whose life and accomplishments you are familiar with.

ACTIVITY 7: SPEAKING

"Nicknames" are additional names that are given to people to describe some physical characteristic or aspect of their personality.

STEP 1 Here is a list of some common American nicknames. Working with a partner, decide what characteristics would be likely for someone whose nickname is one of these:

Blondie	Doc	Sport	Cowboy	Tubby
Sugar	Gramps	Tiger	Honey	

STEP 2 Report your ideas by using sentences like these:

We think that someone whose nickname is **Red** is probably a person who has red hair.

We think that someone whose nickname is **Curly** is probably a person who has curly hair (or perhaps someone who is bald).

We think that someone whose nickname is **Sunny** is probably a person who has a cheerful, outgoing personality.

STEP 3 Discuss how nicknames are used in other countries. Do you have a nickname? Why do people call you that name?

Activity 6

Such introductions are often written ahead of time, even by native speakers, so allow Ss that same opportunity.

VARIATION:

Have Ss guess who the speaker is introducing based on the introduction before the speaker finally announces the name of the person.

Activity 7

Another "Friday Fun" activity. Do any part of this activity as a whole class.

SUGGESTIONS:

1. If you wish to add a step, have Ss make nicknames for everyone in the class, but be sure that this doesn't devolve into name-calling or insulting references.
2. Have everybody choose their own nickname and explain why they chose it to the rest of the class.

The test for this unit can be found on p. 462. The answers are on p. 463 of this book.

TOEFL Test Preparation Exercises for Units 11–12 can be found on pp. 93–95 of the Workbook.
The answers are on p. 501 of this book.

Unit 13

UNIT OVERVIEW

This unit reviews some of the information introduced in Unit 2, Focus 3 concerning the meaning differences communicated by simple present and present progressive tenses, as well as stative verbs and the general uses of present time frame. For advanced classes, this review may not be needed, so choose and present only the focus boxes that you feel are important for your class.

UNIT GOALS

Review the goals listed on this page so students (Ss) understand what they should be able to do by the end of the unit.

OPENING TASK

This task provides an extended context where the difference between simple present and present progressive is important.

Assign Step 1 for individual homework the night before and go directly to Step 2 after a brief general discussion of the content.

UNIT 13

PRESENT TIME FRAME

UNIT GOALS:

- To distinguish the use of progressive aspect from simple present
- To understand and use non-progressive stative verbs
- To understand common uses of the present time frame

▶ OPENING TASK
Outward Bound

WHAT IS OUTWARD BOUND? Outward Bound participants come from ordinary jobs and spend two weeks in the wilderness. The program is physically exhausting, but most people find it deeply satisfying. People go to Outward Bound programs in order to challenge themselves and test the limits of their physical and mental strength. Most people are surprised to learn that they are much braver, stronger, and more capable than they originally thought.

STEP 1 Mary Rae is in Florida, participating in a program called Outward Bound. Use the information in the two charts below to write a paragraph that describes at least five differences between Mary Rae's normal life and her life at Outward Bound. Here are some examples:

> Mary Rae normally spends her day as an account executive in a busy advertising firm, but at Outward Bound, she is spending twelve to fourteen hours a day in vigorous physical activity. In New York she supervises twenty-five employees, but in Florida, she is only supervising herself. . . .

MARY RAE'S LIFE IN NEW YORK	MARY RAE'S LIFE AT OUTWARD BOUND
Occupation: advertising account executive; visits clients, supervises a 25-person office	Occupation: program participant; rows, hikes, climbs trees, builds fires
lives in a small apartment	sleeps in a tent, lives in a canoe
often eats take-out Chinese food	cooks all her own food, catches fish, and picks wild fruit
worries a lot about her career	doesn't think about her career at all
doesn't get much exercise	hikes or rows 12–14 hours each day
doesn't spend much time outdoors	doesn't spend any time indoors
often has trouble falling asleep	falls asleep almost instantly
doesn't feel challenged by her daily routine	feels very challenged by each day's activities
is somewhat bored with life	is excited about growing stronger and more capable
feels that she is not learning anything new	feels that she is learning something new every day
finds making new friends difficult	finds making new friends easy

STEP 2 Compare your paragraph with a classmate's. Did you use the same verb tenses to describe Mary Rae's life in New York and Florida?

STEP 3 Based on Mary Rae's experience, would you ever consider going to an Outward Bound Program? Why or why not?

VARIATIONS:

1. Assign pairs to work together to generate the sentences and then process as a whole class asking pairs to read one difference to the rest of the class. Examples of the kinds of sentences Ss should write have been provided in the task.
2. This task can easily be used for testing or diagnosis by having Ss turn in their paragraphs, rather than comparing them with another student's.
3. Omit Step 3 if you are pressed for time, although most Ss have strong opinions on the subject and enjoy a brief discussion. Try having Ss "vote" and then choose one or two Ss from either position to explain their reasons to the class.

FOCUS 1

With Ss books closed, present one meaning difference at a time.

1. Present the sentences in contrastive pairs (a and d, b and e, c and f). Write the pairs on the board (or the alternative examples listed below) and ask questions such as: *Which sentences describe an action that is happening now and which sentences describe an action that happens more than once or again and again?*
   Alternative examples a–f: *Some students in this class <u>speak</u> (Spanish) with their classmates. Good students in this class <u>speak</u> English with their classmates. All students <u>are speaking</u> English right now.*
2. Follow the same procedure for the other meaning differences described in this focus, using the sentences in the book or alternative examples that refer to real situations in your Ss' lives.
   timeless fact vs. in progress: *The sun <u>rises</u> in the east, but it <u>isn't rising</u> now; <u>it's setting</u>.*

   permanent vs. temporary situations: *John <u>is living</u> with his uncle for the summer. John <u>lives</u> with his family.*

   states vs. actions: *You <u>are</u> a nice person. You <u>care</u> about others. You <u>are being</u> rude. Please stop talking.*
3. Have Ss read the examples in the focus box either in class or as homework and allow time for questions.

Exercises 1 & 2

Use your preferred method for assigning and correcting these exercises. They work equally well as individual homework, class work, pair work, or even group work.

VARIATION:

To save time with Exercise 1, assign one or two questions for each student/pair/group and then process the entire exercise as a whole class, asking others to agree or disagree with the first response.

FOCUS **1**

▶ # Using Simple Present Versus Present Progressive

USE SIMPLE PRESENT TO DESCRIBE	USE PRESENT PROGRESSIVE TO DESCRIBE
• **General statements about recurring habits and skills** (a) My friend **speaks** Spanish. (b) I **study** every night after dinner. (c) The children **sleep** in the upstairs bedroom.	• **Actions in progress at the time of speaking** (d) He **is speaking** Spanish. He must be talking with Carlos. (e) Please turn down the TV. I**'m studying.** (f) Don't make too much noise. The children **are sleeping.**
• **Timeless facts** (g) Baking soda **works** well as a cleaner.	• **Situations in progress around the time of speaking** (h) The refrigerator **is working** well. I just had it repaired.
• **Permanent situations** (i) I **live** in Texas.	• **Temporary Situations** (j) I**'m living** with my uncle for the summer.
• **States and conditions** (k) I **think** you're right. (l) We **have** three dogs at home.	• **Actions** (m) Be quiet! I'm **thinking.** (n) We**'re having** fun!

EXERCISE 1

Choose the correct verb tense (simple present or present progressive) for these sentences. More than one answer may be correct.

1. Don't turn on the TV. I _____ (talk) to you!
2. My brother _____ (speak) a little Spanish. Let's ask him to help us read this letter from Mexico.
3. Tamar _____ (study) for a biology quiz, so I don't think she can come to the party.
4. I _____ (leave) for work about 7:30 every morning.
5. Peter _____ (make) a big mess in the kitchen. Please go help him.

220 | UNIT 13

ANSWER KEY

Exercise 1
1. am talking   2. speaks   3. is studying
4. leave   5. is making   6. is doing   7. am

trying   8. are discovering   9. is getting
10. gets

---

220   Grammar Dimensions, Platinum Edition

6. Ed _____ (do) his best, but he still can't run as fast as the others.

7. I _____ (try) to understand you, but you will have to speak more slowly.

8. Scientists _____ (discover) that many forms of mental illness are caused by chemical imbalances in the brain.

9. The traffic situation _____ (get) worse every year.

10. Learning a language _____ (get) easier when you practice outside of class.

EXERCISE 2

Write the correct form of the verb in parentheses (simple present or present progressive).

Luis (1) _____ (not take) a vacation this summer, because he (2) _____ (not think) that he (3) _____ (have) enough money. He (4) _____ (teach) high school chemistry, so he (5) _____ (get) three months of vacation, but teachers (6) _____ (not make) much money. So he (7) _____ (look for) a temporary job, since he can't afford to go anywhere. He (8) _____ (try) to find work as a computer programmer. But most companies only (9) _____ (hire) workers on a permanent basis. Luis (10) _____ (find) that it is difficult to locate short-term employment. He (11) _____ (get) depressed about the prospects of three months of nothing to do and nowhere to go. No matter how hard he (12) _____ (search), he (13) _____ (begin) to realize that he may have to take a vacation, whether he (14) _____ (want) one or not.

EXERCISE 3

Describe your typical day starting from the time you wake up and ending with going to sleep at night. Write at least eight sentences about things you do on a regular basis. Now describe three things that you are currently doing differently from normal, and why you have changed your routine.

▶ **EXAMPLE:** I'm living in a dormitory, because I have moved to a new city to go to school.

Present Time Frame | **221**

Exercise 3

This is a good exercise to assign for homework to be processed/corrected in class the next day. You can collect and evaluate the responses or have Ss interview each other's in pairs and report their findings to the class.

Workbook Ex. 1, p. 96. Answers: TE p. 501.

ANSWER KEY

Exercise 2
(1) isn't taking   (2) doesn't think   (3) has
(4) teaches/is teaching   (5) gets   (6) don't
make   (7) is looking for   (8) is trying
(9) hire   (10) is finding   (11) is getting
(12) searches   (13) is beginning   (14) wants

Exercise 3
Answers will vary. Possible answers include:
I wake up at 7:00. I have breakfast and read the paper. I take a shower and get dressed. I drive to work. I usually exercise during my lunch hour, and I leave the office around 4:30 or 5:00. I usually go to bed around 10:30 or 11:00 and read for a while before I fall asleep. I'm not eating breakfast these days, because I'm trying to lose weight. I'm not driving to work because my car is being repaired. I'm not exercising at lunch because I'm so busy.

For an inductive approach, try this demonstration:

1. Hold up a brown bag with something in it.
2. Say: "*I'm smelling the contents of this bag*." (Teach the class "Mmmmm!" for a good smell.)
3. Repeat with a second bag (and teach the class "oooh!! or Yuck!" for a bad smell).
4. Then hold up the two bags saying "*This bag smells good. That bag smells bad! What's in them?*"
5. Asian students often find the smell of cheese bad, while European students find the same smell good. This may be a fruitful subject for some cross-cultural discussion.
6. Ask Ss to turn to p. 222 and look at the list of verbs that are commonly "stative" (smell) vs. active "smelling."
7. Give Ss an opportunity to ask about the meaning of the verbs on the list that they do not know.

FOCUS **2**

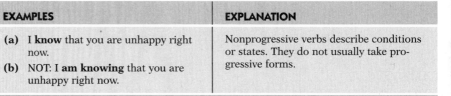

Nonprogressive (Stative) Verbs

EXAMPLES	EXPLANATION
(a) I **know** that you are unhappy right now. **(b)** NOT: I **am knowing** that you are unhappy right now.	Nonprogressive verbs describe conditions or states. They do not usually take progressive forms.

Common Nonprogressive Verbs

SENSORY PERCEPTION	KNOWLEDGE & BELIEF	FEELING & ATTITUDE	LOGICAL RELATIONSHIP	
see	*agree/disagree with*	*love*	**Cause and Effect**	**Measurement**
hear	*believe*	*like*	*results in*	*weigh*
feel	*doubt*	*hate*	*requires*	*cost*
appear	*feel (believe)*	*dislike*	*depends on*	*measure*
look	*imagine*	*appreciate*	*means*	*equal*
seem	*intend*	*prefer*		
smell	*know*	*want*	**Possession**	**Inclusion**
sound	*recognize*	*need*	*belong to*	*contain*
taste	*realize*	*mind*	*possess*	*consist of*
resemble	*remember*		*have*	*include*
look like	*suppose*		*own*	
	think (believe)		*owe*	
	understand			
	consider			

222 | UNIT 13

EXERCISE 4

Work with a partner and ask W*h*-questions for the cues given. Your partner should give true answers, and then ask the same questions of you.

▶ **EXAMPLE:**   which parent/resemble most

   Which parent do you resemble most?

   I resemble my mother more than my father.

1. what kind of fruit/taste best
2. what way/think/most effective to learn a foreign language
3. how/a sick person/appear
4. what/your notebook/contain
5. what/a handshake/mean
6. what activity/your family appreciates/your doing
7. what/learning another language/require
8. how many _____/you/own
9. who/that _____/belong to
10. what/not understand/American culture

EXERCISE 5

Report your partner's answers from Exercise 4 to the rest of the class.

▶ **EXAMPLES:**   Yoshiko resembles her mother more than her father.

Exercises 4 & 5

To use these exercises as diagnostic or testing activities, have Ss write their responses.

Workbook Exs. 2 & 3, pp. 96–98. Answers: TE p. 501.

ANSWER KEY

Exercise 4

Answers will vary. Possible answers include:
1. What kind of fruit tastes best with ice cream? Fruits that aren't too sweet taste best with ice cream.   2. What way do you think is most effective to learn a foreign language? The most effective way to learn a foreign language is to use it whenever possible.   3. How does a sick person often appear? Sometimes he might just appear tired.   4. What does your notebook contain? It contains lists of all the things I'm supposed to do.   5. What does a handshake mean in your culture? It means that two people have reached an agreement about something.   6. What activity do your parents appreciate your doing? They appreciate my studying hard.   7. What does learning another language require? It usually requires a lot of hard work.   8. How many neckties do you own? I only own 5.   9. Who does that Mercedes belong to? I know it doesn't belong to our teacher.   10. What don't you understand about American culture? I don't understand how people become close friends in this country.

Exercise 5

Answers will vary. See the preceding exercise for possible answers.

If you do this focus as a follow-up to the previous focus during the same class period, you can assign it as homework for Ss to study.

V A R I A T I O N :

Assign Ss (individually or in pairs) to think of (and present the next day in class) a context that demonstrates both the action and stative meanings of the verbs listed in this focus. To make it easier for them, assign Ss specific verbs to present.

FOCUS **3**

Verbs with Both Nonprogressive and Action Meanings

Some nonprogressive verbs can also be used to describe actions.

VERB	NONPROGRESSIVE MEANING	ACTION MEANING
have	**(a)** I **have** three brothers. **(possess)**	**(b)** We're **having** a great time. **(experiencing)**
mind	**(c)** I **don't mind** smoke. **(object to)**	**(d)** He's **minding** the children now. **(taking care of)**
see	**(e)** I **see** your point. **(understand)**	**(f)** Yuji **is seeing** a specialist about his back. **(consulting)**
think	**(g)** I **think** you're right. **(opinion)**	**(h)** Be quiet! I'm **thinking.** **(mental activity)**
consider	**(i)** I **consider** money to be the cause of many problems. **(opinion)**	**(j)** I'm **considering** going to Hawaii for vacation. **(mental activity)**
depends on	**(k)** Athletic ability **depends on** strength and practice. **(requires)**	**(l)** I'm **depending on** Yuji to help me move next week. **(relying upon)**
be	**(m)** Mei **is** a teacher. **(identity)**	**(n)** Those children **are being** very noisy. **(behaving)**
feel	**(o)** I **feel** that you're the best choice. **(believe)**	**(p)** I'm **feeling** a little sick today. **(experiencing)**

Other nonprogressive verbs can indicate the **act** of perception or measurement, or the perceptions or measurements themselves.

VERB	PERCEPTION/MEASUREMENT (NONPROGRESSIVE MEANING)	ACT OF PERCEPTION/MEASUREMENT (ACTION MEANING)
smell	**(q)** The flowers **smell** wonderful.	**(r)** The dog **is smelling** the clothes of the missing boy.
taste	**(s)** That cake **tastes** delicious.	**(t)** Our host **is tasting** the soup to make sure it's not too salty.
feel	**(u)** My arm **feels** broken!	**(v)** The doctor **is feeling** my arm to see if it is broken.
weigh	**(w)** Joe **weighs** almost 100 kilos.	**(x)** The butcher **is weighing** that piece of meat.

EXERCISE 6

Decide whether the verbs indicated express an action meaning or a nonprogressive meaning and write the simple present or present progressive tense in the blanks. In some cases both answers may be correct.

1. This cloth _____ (feel) really nice.
2. I _____ (consider) applying to go to Outward Bound.
3. Why did you ask that question? You _____ (be) really rude!
4. I _____ (believe) that Mary Rae _____ (have) a good experience at the Outward Bound program.
5. I don't like this coffee. It _____ (taste) bitter to me.
6. I like people who _____ (mind) their own business and don't try to tell others what to do.
7. Bambang _____ (doubt) that he will be able to pass the TOEFL next week.
8. It _____ (look) as if we will get some rain later this week.
9. John _____ (feel) a little guilty about leaving Mary for so long. But I'm sure he'll get over it.
10. Learning a new language _____ (require) a lot of hard work.
11. These days the government _____ (require) people to take drug tests in order to get a government job.
12. Those children _____ (be) so naughty. I wish someone would make them stop teasing that poor kitten!

Present Time Frame | **225**

Exercise 6

Assign this exercise as a follow-up homework task for the self-study of Focus 3. It can also be done in class individually or in pairs.

Workbook Ex. 4, pp. 98–99. Answers: TE p. 501.

---

1. If you have access to an OHP, make a transparency of the examples of this focus, without the explanations, and ask Ss why the author has used simple present tense.
2. Prepare Ss for this discussion by asking them to review Unit 2 of this book for homework the night before.
3. If you are doing this unit as an immediate follow-up to Unit 2, omit this step and do this unit as soon after your presentation and practice of Unit 2 Focus 2 as possible.
4. With advanced classes, assign different groups or pairs to find examples of the uses listed in the EXPLANATIONS column from local newspapers or popular TV shows.

FOCUS **4**

Uses of the Present Time Frame

EXAMPLES	EXPLANATIONS
(a) Supply **affects** demand in several ways. If supply **exceeds** demand, the cost of the commodity generally **decreases.** When cost **increases,** demand often **drops.** Decreased demand eventually **results** in decreased supply.	Use present time frame • to state general truths and relationships in scientific and technical writing
(b) Here's how we **make** cookies. First we **mix** a cup of flour and two eggs together in a bowl. Next, we **mix** in some sugar. A cup-and-a half **is** probably enough, but if we **want** sweeter cookies, we **add** at least 3 cups of sugar.	• to describe actions as they are performed in live demonstrations
(c) Shimazu **throws** the ball. Martinez **hits** it. He **passes** first base. He's **making** a run to second base. He's out!	• for reporting in radio and television broadcasts such as sporting events
(d) One day I'm **walking** down the street. I **see** this guy talking on a pay phone. I **know** he's mad about something because I **can hear** him screaming all the way down the block. So, anyway, when I **get** next to the pay phone, he **stops** shouting and **asks** me if I have an extra quarter. I **tell** him, "Sorry, man," and all of a sudden . . .	• to tell stories orally in informal situations

EXERCISE 7

Here are reports of two scientific experiments. Change them into present time so that they are statements of general scientific principles, rather than accounts of specific experiments.

▶ **EXAMPLE:** *when baking soda is added to vinegar, a chemical reaction occurs.*
  . . .

Experiment 1

(1) When baking soda was added to vinegar, a chemical reaction occurred. (2) The baking soda bubbled and CO_2 was produced by the combination of elements. (3) When a candle was put next to the container while the chemical reaction was taking place, the flame on the candle went out.

Experiment 2

(1) We wanted to determine whether gravity affected the rate of acceleration of objects falling through space. (2) Two objects of similar size and shape, but substantially different weights—a cannonball and a volleyball—were dropped from the same height. (3) We found that both objects hit the ground at the same time. (4) This indicated that the attraction of gravity was constant.

EXERCISE 8

Tell this story aloud, as if you were Mary Rae describing her own experience. Tell it in present time to make it more vivid and less formal. The first two sentences have been done as examples.

▶ **EXAMPLE:**   There I am, standing in dirty swamp water as deep as my waist, but I'm having a wonderful time! The canoe we're rowing has gotten stuck on a log, so somebody has to get into the water and try to lift one end of it.

There I was, standing in dirty swamp water as deep as my waist, but I was having a wonderful time! The canoe we were rowing had gotten stuck on a log, so somebody had to get into the water and try to lift one end of it. I looked into the water. It looked really dark and dirty. I knew there were a lot of poisonous snakes in this area. I knew there were also alligators. All of a sudden, I realized that I wasn't afraid of any of these things. I had complete confidence in my ability to free the canoe and to avoid getting eaten or bitten. Without another thought, I jumped into the water and started to pull at the canoe. At that moment I knew that there was nothing that I was afraid to do, and nothing that I couldn't do if I put my mind to it.

Present Time Frame | **227**

Exercise 7
SUGGESTIONS:

1. To save time, assign half the class to do one experiment and half the class to do the other.
2. This exercise works well as a written assignment or an oral in-class exercise.

Exercise 8
SUGGESTION:

Have Ss read the passage silently first and then read aloud several sentences at a time. Correct tense choice as needed.

Workbook Ex. 5, p. 99. Answers: TE p. 501.

UNIT GOAL REVIEW

1. Ask Ss to look at the goals on the opening page of this unit again. Review the major differences in meaning that are communicated by simple present and present progressive. Ask Ss what the difference in meaning is between "*Juan speaks Spanish*" and "*Juan is speaking Spanish*," between "*John weighs 200 pounds*" and "*John is weighing 200 books.*"
2. Ask Ss to review pp 220–227. Allow time for this in class and then ask Ss to ask any remaining questions.

Activity 1

VARIATION:

This activity can be made more formal by assigning it as a "how-to" speech assignment. Prepare Ss by giving a demonstration of your own such as How to Make a Peanut Butter and Jelly Sandwich.

Activity 2

To save time, this useful cross-cultural topic can be done as a whole class discussion. It will not be as useful for single-culture classes, and teachers of such classes may wish to use another activity.

Activity 3

This is a useful diagnostic or testing activity. Collect Ss responses to check for form.

Activity 4

Like Activity 2 this may not be useful for single-culture classrooms. Choose another activity.

Use Your English

ACTIVITY 1: SPEAKING

Give the class a demonstration of how to do something. This could be how to prepare a favorite food, how to perform some physical activity, or how to make some simple object. While you are demonstrating the activity, tell how it is done.

ACTIVITY 2: SPEAKING

"How much does that cost?" "How much money do you earn." "How much do you weigh?" "How old are you?" Most Americans think that these would be rude questions to ask anyone who is not a very close friend. In other cultures, people don't consider these to be rude questions but they might hesitate to ask other kinds of questions, such as "How many daughters do you have?" "What do you do—what kind of job do you have?" or even "What kind of house do you live in?" Form a group and talk about what are considered to be rude questions in other cultures that you are familiar with. Present your findings to the rest of the class.

ACTIVITY 3: WRITING/SPEAKING

Describe some of the things that are happening in the drawings on page 218.

ACTIVITY 4: WRITING/SPEAKING

We all learn our basic cultural values when we are very young. A first step in learning about different cultures is learning to identify some of these basic cultural values.

STEP 1 Write down at least five things your parents told you that were general truths when you were growing up. Make sure that these things are not orders or requests (*My parents told me to clean my room*), but rather, statements about things that are always true (*Big boys don't cry. Good manners are important.*)

STEP 2 Compare your list to the lists of several other students. Are any of the statements the same on all your lists? Are there any interesting similarities or differences based on different cultures? What does this tell you about the values your parents tried to teach you?

STEP 3 Report your ideas to the rest of the class.

ACTIVITY 5: LISTENING

STEP 1 Listen to Professor Freemarket's lecture for his Introduction to Economics class, and take notes. You may want to listen to the lecture a second time to make sure you understand the information he describes.

STEP 2 Use your notes to answer the questions that he asked the class on his weekly quiz.

STEP 3 Compare your answers to another student's to check the accuracy of your information, and the grammatical correctness of what you wrote.

Economics 101—Dr. Freemarket
Weekly quiz #5
(Twenty-five points possible)

1. (ten points) Define the Law of Supply and Demand.

2. (ten points) How does transportation affect the Law of Supply and Demand?

3. (five points) What other forces affect the Law of Supply and Demand?

Activity 5

Play textbook audio. The tapescript for this listening appears on p. 516.
As with other "lecture" activities, follow this procedure for extra practice:
1. Play the tape once for general comprehension. Ask for a brief summary of the topic.
2. Play a second time for Ss to listen for the specific answers.
3. Play a third time for Ss to confirm and complete their answers.
4. Play a fourth time, if necessary, for Ss to identify where the specific information was that they needed for the correct answers.

✔

The test for this unit can be found on pp. 464. The answers are on pp. 465 of this book.

ANSWER KEY

Activity 5
Answers will vary. Here is an example of one possible response:
1. According to classical economic theory, the Law of Supply and Demand says that increase in demand raises prices, and increase in supply lowers prices. In classical economics this law is considered to be <u>the</u> major driving force in a free market economy.
2. Transportation has a fundamental impact on the Law of Supply and Demand.

Transportation means that the available supply of something can be moved around the country, and not just kept it in one place. If there is too much in one area, the surplus can be sent someplace else. If there isn't enough, the supply can be increased from other places.
3. advertising, government regulations, and monopolies

Unit 14

UNIT OVERVIEW

This unit reviews some of the information introduced in Unit 1, concerning the meaning differences communicated by basic choice of present or past time frame in the context of choosing present perfect or past tense to describe actions that happened in the past. Even for relatively advanced classes, this review can be very helpful. See *The Grammar Book* (pp. 124–125) for a discussion of this issue if you did not review it in connection with Units 1 and 2.

UNIT GOALS

Review the goals listed on this page so students (Ss) understand what they should be able to do by the end of the unit.

OPENING TASK

This Opening Task is an "academic" topic that may not be appropriate for your specific class. If your Ss are not preparing for academic study in a college or university, you may wish to use one of the activities instead.

U N I T 14

PRESENT PERFECT

Describing Past Events in Relation to the Present

UNIT GOALS:

- To use the present perfect to understand and express past actions that are related to the present moment by time
- To use the present perfect to understand and express past actions that are related to the present moment by logical relationship or present result
- To understand and express meaning differences with present perfect progressive instead of present perfect tense

▶ OPENING TASK
Identifying What Makes You Special

North American Institute of International Studies
Application for Admissions

Applying for: _____ SPRING _____ SUMMER _____ FALL _____ WINTER 20_____

Degree Objective: Undergraduate _____ Graduate _____

Major _____ Minor _____

Personal Data: Name _____

Address _____

Telephone _____ Birthdate _____ Sex _____ Ethnic Background _____

Educational Background:
List all secondary and post-secondary schools attended, including language programs.
Name and location of school   dates of attendance   degree granted   GPA
_____
_____
_____
_____

Personal Essay / Writing Sample:
All applicants must provide a writing sample. On another sheet of paper, write at least 200 words on the following topic. It must be handwritten, and written *only* by the applicant.
What are some characteristics that make you different from other people you know?
How have your experiences in life shaped you as a person? What are some achievements
that you have accomplished that you feel particularly proud of?

Signature _____ Date _____
All applications must be accompanied by official transcripts in English, proof of finances,
and a nonrefundable $40 application fee.

When American students apply to colleges and universities, they often have to write a personal essay about their individual character and achievements. Below are the ideas that Aliona Fernandez used for her successful application to the North American Institute of International Studies. (Her personal essay has been reprinted in Exercise 1 on page 233.)

STEP 1 Think of some of your own special characteristics that might be of interest to a university admissions committee. Identify one special **characteristic,** one **experience** that helped you develop that characteristic, and one **achievement** that this characteristic has enabled you to do. Add your characteristics in the space below.

	Aliona Fernandez	You
Characteristic	flexibility	
Experience	living overseas—Peace Corps volunteer	
Achievement	speak other languages and understand different cultures	

STEP 2 Compare your special characteristic, experience, and achievement with those of another student in the class. Decide whose ideas would be the best to use in a personal essay for a university application. Tell your opinion and your reasons to the rest of the class.

VARIATIONS:
This task can be done in a number of ways in addition to the procedures outlined in the student book.

1. Assign Step 1 for Ss to complete the night before. Ss from some cultures or with lower levels of proficiency may have a difficult time thinking of relevant characteristics, so you may need to prepare them by reading the essay in Exercise 1 together in class first, and then having a general discussion of what kinds of things Ss would put in their own essays.

2. Have Ss work in pairs to find where the concepts listed in Aliona's example occur in her essay (Exercise 1) and then together develop their own entries.

3. Do Step 2 as a small group discussion, and then have Ss do Exercise 1 to hand in.

SUGGESTIONS:

1. A more inductive way to present this information is to use this focus as a follow-up to Exercise 1. Have the Ss read the exercise as homework and then discuss the three questions in pairs or small groups.

2. An alternative method is to do or review Activity 2, Unit 1. Then refer to the focus box for review and a guided discussion of the principle.

3. Assign pairs of sentences (a & b; c & d; e & f) to different student pairs. Ask them to discuss the meaning differences and present their notion of what the different tense choice "means," or a paraphrase of each sentence, to the rest of the class.

Exercise 1

Assign the first part of this exercise for homework. If you do the whole exercise in class, make sure that Ss read the entire exercise first.

FOCUS **1**

► Choosing Past Time Frame or Present Time Frame

We can use both past time frame and present time frame to talk about things that happened in the past.

PAST TIME FRAME	PRESENT TIME FRAME
Use past time frame (in the form of the simple past tense) to show that **a past event has no direct, ongoing relationship to the present.** The event was fully completed in the past or happened at a specific time in the past.	Use a present time frame (in the form of present perfect tense) to show that **a past event is directly related to the present.** The event happened in the past, but **continues to influence the present in some way.**
(a) I **went** to Disneyworld three times while I was living in Florida. Now that I live in Ohio, it's too far away to visit.	**(b)** I **have gone** to Disneyworld three times, so I'm not really anxious to go again so soon after my last visit.
(c) I worked as a limousine driver during college. I **had** many opportunities to meet famous people.	**(d)** As a limousine driver, I **have had** many opportunities to meet famous people. It's one of the things I like about my job.
(e) I started that book, but I **didn't finish** it. It was too boring.	**(f)** I **haven't finished** that book yet. I've been reading it for several hours, and I hope to finish it soon.

EXERCISE 1

Read the following personal essay written by a successful applicant to the North American Institute of International Studies. Underline the verb phrases and identify the tenses that are used. Then discuss these questions with a partner.

- Why did the author use present time in the first paragraph?
- Why did the author use past time in the second paragraph?
- Why did the author use present time in the third paragraph?

ANSWER KEY

Exercise 1

(1) <u>makes/is</u> (2) <u>am</u> (3) <u>is/have had</u> (4) <u>has given</u> (5) <u>was</u> (6) <u>taught</u> (7) <u>was</u> very (8) <u>was/was</u> (9) I <u>have been/have traveled has been</u> (10) <u>speak/understand</u> (11) I <u>have learned/are/have</u> (12) <u>have learned</u> (13) <u>have learned/doesn't/mean</u> (14) <u>have made/has allowed</u> *Why did the author use present time in the first*

paragraph? She is talking about characteristics that she has now and where they came from. *Why did the author use past time in the second paragraph?* She is referring to a time that ended in the past. *Why did the author use present time in the third paragraph?* She is describing how she is today as a result of her previous experiences.

Personal Essay

by Aliona Fernandez

(1) One of the characteristics that makes me different from many people is my adaptability. (2) I am flexible and comfortable in new or unusual situations. (3) I think this is because I have had a lot of experience living in foreign countries. (4) This has given me a lot of opportunities to face unfamiliar situations and to learn about unfamiliar customs and beliefs.

(5) My first experience in a foreign country was as a Peace Corps volunteer. (6) I taught English in a small town in a rural area. (7) Life in my town was very simple. (8) Because there was no electricity and rather little contact with the outside world, my life was a lot like living in an earlier century. (9) I have been to other countries since that first experience, and everywhere that I have traveled has been interesting and educational.

(10) As a result of my experiences in other countries, I speak other languages and understand other cultures. (11) I have learned that relationships between people are very much the same, whether they have modern, busy lives, or old-fashioned, more peaceful lives. (12) I have learned to understand different ways of doing things and different ways of looking at the world. (13) Most of all, I have learned that "new" doesn't necessarily mean "better." (14) My experiences have made me adaptable, and this adaptability has allowed me to understand other people and cultures.

Present this focus in a straightforward way, either using the contrasting sentences in the book or writing variations of your own on the board that refer to real situations in your students' lives.

For example: *Buxtehude has studied English for three years. She is really improving a lot. Quasimodo studied Esperanto for 12 years, but finally gave up when he realized that English was now the international language.*

Exercise 2

Assign this exercise for homework to save time.

Workbook Ex. 2, pp. 100–101. Answers: TE p. 501.

FOCUS **2**

Relationship to the Present: Still True (Present Perfect Tense) Versus No Longer True (Past Tense)

One common way that past events relate to the present is if they are **still true.**

EXAMPLES	EXPLANATIONS
(a) I **have worked** in a factory for three years. I **have learned** how to operate three different kinds of machines so far.	**Present Perfect Tense:** Use the present perfect tense to show that something is **still true now.**
(b) I **worked** in an automobile factory for three years. I **did good work** on the assembly line, but they closed the factory.	**Past Tense:** Use the past tense to talk about something that is **no longer true now.**

EXERCISE 2

Choose past tense or present perfect tense for the verbs in parentheses. More than one answer may be correct, so be prepared to explain why you chose the form you did.

Bambang Soetomo (1) _came_ (come) to the United States last January to get a degree in mechanical engineering. Since he (2) _____ (be) in the United States, he (3) _____ (have) many new experiences. At home in Jakarta, servants (4) _____ (cook) all his food. But here in the United States, Bambang (5) _____ (have) to prepare food for himself. In Indonesia, a lot of his university classes (6) _____ (require) the ability to memorize large amounts of information. But here, Bambang (7) _____ (find) that memorization is not considered to be a very important skill in many of his classes. Of course, he (8) _____ (be) ready for obvious differences in things like food and social customs, but he (9) _____ (not/adjust) to the subtle differences. He (10) _____ (learn) that knowing about differences and dealing with them are two different things. In fact, he (11) _____ (be) rather homesick. In Jakarta he (12) _____ (have) a large group of friends, but here in the States he (13) _____ (meet) only a few other Indonesian students, and none of them are in his department. When he (14) _____ (be) planning his trip to America, he (15) _____ (plan) to go home for a vacation after his sophomore year, but he (16) _____ (change) his mind since he (17) _____ (get) here. He (18) _____ (speak) with his father about the possibility of coming home during his first summer vacation. His father (19) _____ (not decide) whether that's a good idea or not.

234   UNIT 14

A N S W E R   K E Y

Exercise 2
(1) came (2) has been (3) has had
(4) cooked (5) has had (6) required
(7) has found (8) was (9) has not adjusted (10) has learned (11) has been

(12) had (13) has met (14) was
(15) planned (16) has changed
(17) got/has gotten (18) has spoken/spoke
(19) hasn't decided

FOCUS 3

Relationship to the Present: Until Now

Present perfect is used to describe things that began in the past but continue up to the present moment.

EXAMPLES	EXPLANATIONS
(a) Matt and Jeff **have seen** *The Wizard of Oz* over **a dozen times.** (b) **I've ridden** a motorcycle **once,** but I'll never do it again!	Use present perfect to describe: • the number of times something has happened
(c) The doctor **has just left** the office. Maybe you can catch him if you hurry to the parking lot. (d) **We've just been talking about** your suggestions. Won't you join us?	• very recent events with *just*
(e) **I've known** Stephanie **since** we were in high school (f) **I've never eaten** snake meat. **Have you ever tried** it?	• sentences with *ever, never,* or *since*

EXERCISE 3

Work with a partner. Take turns asking each other these questions. Ask at least ten questions. You can use the suggested topics or make up questions of your own.

1. Have you ever . . . (ridden a horse, been in love, seen a flying saucer . . .)
2. How many times have you . . . (eaten Chinese food, taken the TOEFL, driven a motorcycle . . .)
3. Name three things you have never done, but would like to do.
4. Name three things you have done that you don't want to do again.

Then tell the rest of the class about your partner. The class should decide who has asked the most interesting or unusual questions.

FOCUS 3

This focus presents distinctions that are a little more subtle than "still true" vs. "no longer true."

SUGGESTIONS:

1. As in Focus 1, make the presentation more inductive by assigning pairs of sentences (a&b; c&d; e&f) to different pairs of students. Ask them to discuss why the author chose to use present perfect instead of simple past in the examples and to present their ideas to the rest of the class.

2. Use alternative examples that refer to real Ss and situations in your class, such as: **number of times:** *Osama has fallen asleep in class three times this week. Maybe he isn't getting enough sleep.* **just, ever never, since:** *We've just finished Focus 2, and now we're starting Focus 3. I have never seen such a great class. We have been studying present perfect since yesterday.*

Exercise 3

VARIATION:

Make this a diagnostic/evaluation activity by having Ss write their responses. Ss then read their partners' sentences and use the information to write a paragraph about their partner. Collect both papers for review and evaluation.

Exercise 4

If Ss need additional practice with the principles introduced in Focus 3, do this exercise before you do Exercise 3.

Workbook Ex. 3, p. 101. Answers: TE p. 501.

FOCUS 4

1. Present this information in a straightforward manner by asking Ss to read the situations and their present results (examples a–i).

2. Ask pairs or groups to develop sentences for other class-related situations (see example below) that reflect the same kind of past action with present results. Let them decide whether the present result should be directly stated or implied. If it is implied, have them let the class guess what the present result is.
   Examples: *You've given us homework three times this week, so please don't make us do homework tonight. (implied result: The teacher has assigned more homework.)*

EXERCISE 4

Choose past tense or present perfect tense for the verbs in parentheses. More than one answer may be possible. The first sentence has been done for you as an example.

My friend Bob is a very happy man. He just (1) ____found out____ (find out) that he (2) _____ (win) a free trip to Hawaii.
He (3) _____ (buy) raffle tickets for years, but he never
(4) _____ (win) anything until six months ago, when he
(5) _____ (win) an electric toaster. Since then, apparently, his
luck (6) _____ (change). He (7) _____ (get)
more than a dozen prizes from various contests. Most of the
prizes (8) _____ (be) small until last month, when he
(9) _____ (win) a video cassette recorder and a color TV. I
wonder if he (10) _____ (think about) sharing his good fortune with his friends.

(above (1): has)

FOCUS **4**

Relationship to the Present: Present Result (Present Perfect Tense)

Another common way that past events relate to the present is if the past event **continues to affect the present situation in some way.** Use present perfect tense to describe past events that cause a result in the present.

The present result can be stated directly.

PAST ACTION	STATED PRESENT RESULT
(a) I **have** already **seen** that movie,	so I **suggest** we go see a different one.
(b) He **has been wasting** so much money	that I **don't think** we should give him any more.
(c) I **have** always **felt** that teachers were underpaid,	so I **think** we should suggest that our teacher ought to get a raise.

236 · UNIT 14

A N S W E R   K E Y

Exercise 4
(1) just found out/ has just found out
(2) has won/won   (3) has bought   (4) has

never won/never won   (5) won   (6) has changed   (7) has gotten   (8) have been/ were   (9) won   (10) has thought about

---

The present result can be implied.

PAST ACTION	IMPLIED PRESENT RESULT
(d) You **have spilled** juice all over my new tablecloth!	The tablecloth is dirty.
(e) John **has obviously forgotten** about our meeting.	He is not at the meeting.

The present result can also be the speaker's/writer's attitude.

NOT CONNECTED TO THE PRESENT (PAST TENSE)	CONNECTED TO THE PRESENT (PRESENT PERFECT TENSE)	EXPLANATIONS
(f) **Did you find** the article you were looking for?	**(g)** **Have you found** the article you were looking for? Because if not, I think **I know where you can find it.**	The event is connected to the present in the speaker's mind.
(h) The White House **released** new figures **yesterday** concerning the economy.	**(i)** The White House **has released** new figures on the economy in the last quarter. These figures **show** that imports continue to exceed exports by more than 20%.	Reporters often introduce news stories with the present perfect tense to emphasize the connection with the present.
(j) The historian Toynbee **often observed** that history repeats itself.	**(k)** The historian Toynbee **has observed** that history repeats itself, and **I believe that he is correct.**	A writer may mention a past event that has a connection to a point she or he is about to make.

EXERCISE 5

Choose the sentence that reflects the most logical continuation of the ideas expressed in the first sentence, based on the tense used in the first sentence. Both sentences are formed correctly.

1. I have told you that I don't like the color green.
   (a) My brother didn't like that color either.
   (b) So why did you buy me a sweater in that color?

Exercise 5

Ss may find this exercise challenging, since both sentences are grammatically possible. The more logical answer is the one using the same time frame as the cue sentence. Do this exercise quickly as a class to prepare for the more analytical examination in the next exercise.

Exercise 5

(1) (b)   (2) (a)   (3) (a)   (4) (b)   (5) (a)

2. Jeff met Matt at a party.
   (a) They soon became the best of friends.
   (b) They share an apartment in San Francisco.

3. Bambang Soetomo arrived in America about eight months ago.
   (a) He has been adjusting to American life ever since.
   (b) He is living by himself in an apartment.

4. I have been trying to get in touch with my math professor since last week.
   (a) I didn't do well on the last exam.
   (b) Whenever I go to her office, she isn't there.

5. I don't think that Denise likes Peter very much.
   (a) Have you ever noticed that she avoids looking at him when she speaks?
   (b) Did she say anything about her feelings to you at the meeting last week?

EXERCISE 6

Discuss these questions about the short passages below with a partner and compare your ideas with other students'.

- Why do you think the speaker chose to use the present perfect tense instead of simple past tense in these sentences?
- How is the past action related to the present: by time relationship, by present result, or by a combination of both?

1. Scientists have discovered a number of interesting similarities between the atmosphere on Earth and on Titan, one of the moons of Jupiter. They have found significant concentrations of water vapor and other chemicals common on Earth. As a result, they are hoping to send another space probe to the planet later this year.

2. If I have told you once, I've told you a hundred times: I hate broccoli!

3. Guess what? We've been invited to Liz's wedding. What should we get her for a gift?

4. Conservative politicians have often stated that welfare payments to poor families do not help reduce long-term poverty, but recent statistics show that this may not be true.

5. Shakespeare's reputation as a psychologist has grown in recent years. His plays have always reflected a deep understanding of human motivations.

6. Has Jill found a summer job? I was talking with my aunt, and she said her office might need a temporary computer programmer.

Exercise 6

This is an open-ended activity, designed to provoke analysis and discussion. It works well as a pair work or group work exercise.

V A R I A T I O N :

Use it as a whole class follow-up and comprehension check of your presentation of Focus 4. If you use it in this way, be sure to allow Ss adequate time to analyze and construct their explanations.

Workbook Ex. 4, p. 102. Answers: TE p. 501.

ANSWER KEY

Exercise 6
Possible explanations include:
1. There is a logical relationship to the present. The passage connects past discoveries with the current fact that they are planning another space probe in the future.   2. There is an implied logical relationship. This suggests that the speaker has just been offered broccoli.
3. There is a chronological relationship with this moment. The listener is now hearing the news for the first time.   4. Like the first passage, previous information is relevant to the current situation   5. This seems to be connected with the present in the writer's mind. Perhaps the writer is going to make a new point about Shakespeare's understanding of psychology.
6. Connected with the present in the speaker's mind. She has a job possibility for Jill at this moment.

FOCUS **5**

▶ **Present Perfect Progressive Tense**

EXAMPLES	EXPLANATIONS
(a) He **has been living** with his parents, but he hopes to move out now that he has found a job. **(temporary)** **(b)** He **has lived** with his parents since he dropped out of college. **(permanent)**	Use the present perfect progressive tense (*have/has been* + verb + *-ing*) instead of present perfect to describe something that is: • temporary rather than permanent
(c) I **have been talking** to everyone about the problem, but I don't have a solution. Do you have any ideas? **(repeated occurrence)** **(d)** I **have thought** about the problem, and I have a solution. **(single occurrence)**	• repeated rather than a single occurrence
(e) It **has been snowing constantly** for the last three hours. I hope it stops soon! **(continuous)** **(f)** It **has snowed several times** since we got here, but there's still not enough snow for skiing. **(repeated)**	• continuous rather than repeated or recurring
(g) I **have been writing** my term paper. I still have to proofread it and staple it together. **(uncompleted)** **(h)** I **have written** my term paper Let's go celebrate! **(completed)**	• uncompleted rather than completed
(i) Living in foreign countries **has required** a lot of flexibility. **(j)** NOT: Living in foreign countries **has been requiring** a lot of flexibility.	Remember that nonprogressive verbs do not occur with the progressive aspect even when they refer to continuous states.

EXERCISE 7

Choose the correct form, present perfect or present perfect progressive, for the verbs. More than one answer may be possible.

1. I (a) _____ (read) about the development of early forms of

   photography, and I (b) _____ (learn) some very interesting

   facts about it. I would like to continue my research next semester.

FOCUS 5

Ss may already be familiar with these distinctions from studying previous units (Unit 13, Focus 1 and Unit 2), but if additional review is needed:

1. Present this focus with Ss books closed, one meaning difference at a time. Present the sentences in contrastive pairs (a & b, c & d, e & f, g & h). Write the pairs on the board (or alternative examples about the Ss and class-related topics like the ones listed below):

   permanent vs. temporary situations (a & b): *John has lived with his uncle since 1992. John has been living with his uncle since he came here to study.*

   repeated rather than one time occurrence (c & d): *John has been dating Mary ever since they met. He has dated Hortense, and never intends to repeat that experience.*

   continuous rather than repeated (e & f): *The students have laughed at all three of the teacher's jokes. The students have been laughing for the last hour. Their teacher must be really funny.*

   uncompleted rather than completed (g & h): *Juan hasn't been studying for the TOEFL because he has passed it.*

2. Have Ss read the examples in the focus box. Allow time for questions.

Exercise 7

Assign and correct this exercise according to your preferred method, taking into account the principles of variety and efficiency suggested throughout this manual.

ANSWER KEY

Exercise 7
1. have been reading; have learned   2. has been crying   3. has resented   4. have been trying   5. have tried   6. have been working/have worked   7. has been expecting   8. has told   9. has been trying; have called   10. has dreamed/has been dreaming; has become

2. That baby _____ (cry) constantly since we got here. I wish its parents would do something to make it be quiet!

3. Bob's brother _____ (resent) his winning that free trip to Hawaii ever since he heard the news.

4. I _____ (try) to explain that for ten minutes. Aren't you listening?

5. I _____ (try) to explain that every way I know how. I give up!

6. I _____ (work) on this problem all afternoon. It's time for a break.

7. Rebecca _____ (expect) the police to call about the accident. That's why she wants to stay home this afternoon.

8. Bob _____ (tell) the office that he doesn't want to take a summer job until after he returns from Hawaii.

9. The newspaper (a) _____ (try) to contact Bob about some contest. They (b) _____ (call) at least five or six times.

10. Bob (a) _____ (dream) about visiting Hawaii ever since he read a book about volcanoes. He (b) _____ (become) an expert on them.

Exercise 8

This exercise practices all the tenses presented in this unit. Use it as review, as a class quiz, or even as a diagnostic at the beginning of the unit to determine whether your Ss need to study this unit in the first place.

Workbook Ex. 5 & 6, pp. 102–103. Answers: TE p. 501.

UNIT GOAL REVIEW

Review the unit goals by writing these sentences on the board: "*I did it,*" "*I have done it,*" and "*I've been doing it.*" In pairs or as a class have Ss discuss the possible differences in meaning communicated by these tense choices. They can provide paraphrases or a context for possible use. Be sure to review the concept of relation to the present if they don't raise it in their discussions.

EXERCISE 8

Decide whether the verbs in parentheses should use simple present, present progressive, present perfect, present perfect progressive, or the past tense. More than one answer may be correct.

Bambang Soetomo (1) _____ (speak) English quite fluently. I wonder where he (2) _____ (learn) it. He (3) _____ (study) mechanical engineering. He (4) _____ (plan) to go to graduate school once he (5) _____ (get) his B.S. degree. Bambang (6) _____ (live) by himself for the last few months. But he (7) _____ (think) about getting a roommate. He (8) _____ (miss) his friends back home a great deal, and this (9) _____ (affect) his studies. He (10) _____ (hope) that his father will let him come home during the summer, but his father (11) _____ (not decide) yet.

Exercise 8
(1) speaks   (2) learned/ has learned
(3) is studying/studies   (4) is planning/ plans   (5) gets   (6) has been living
(7) is thinking   (8) misses/is missing
(9) is affecting/has affected/has been affecting   (10) is hoping/hopes
(11) hasn't decided

Use Your English

ACTIVITY 1: WRITING

Use the ideas you developed in the Opening Task on page 230 to write a personal essay like the one required for the application to the North American Institute of International Studies.

ACTIVITY 2: READING/SPEAKING

Bring in the front page of a daily newspaper and examine the articles with a partner or in a group. Find examples of sentences written in present time and past time. In what tense are headlines usually written? In what tense are the introductory paragraphs usually written? In what tense is the main part of the article generally written? Can you find a pattern? Why do you think the author chose one time frame rather than another? Discuss your ideas with your partner or group, and present them to the rest of the class.

ACTIVITY 3: SPEAKING

Experts in cross-cultural communication have found that most North Americans tend to believe that most changes in life result in improvement. This is not necessarily true in other cultures.

STEP 1 Find out what important changes your classmates have made in their lives. Interview three other classmates. Ask them the following questions:

- Have you changed any habits or routines recently?
- Describe the changes.
- Why have you made the changes?
- How have the changes affected you?

STEP 2 Based on the changes your group has experienced, decide whether you agree that changes in life are generally for the better. Present your group's ideas and reasons to the rest of the class.

USE YOUR ENGLISH

Activity 1

Use this activity as a follow-up of the Opening Task. Ss can refer to the essay in Exercise 1 for some ideas as to form.

VARIATION:

Have Ss write a preliminary essay and then, based on the work they have done in this unit, revise it for both content and structural correctness.

Activity 2

This is an open-ended activity. The process of careful observation and hypothesis formation is the important part of the activity.

VARIATION:

Bring in articles for Ss to look at or have them choose articles on subjects of interest.

Activity 3

The first part of this activity can be used for diagnosis or testing by having Ss write their classmates' responses as full sentences. For example: *My partner has stopped eating rice, because she doesn't like the kind they serve in the cafeteria. As a result she's lost a little bit of weight.* Check for correct use of present perfect.

Activities 4 & 5

These activities work best with more advanced Ss who are studying in an English-speaking environment and undergoing cultural transition themselves. Use them as out-of-class interview/contact activities. If such an approach is not feasible, try discussing the topics in a general way in a whole class discussion of cross-cultural differences.

ACTIVITY 4: SPEAKING

Experts in cross-cultural communication have found that North American culture tends to value individualism. As a result, many young children are taught to look for ways that they are different from other people. Most Americans can easily identify several personal experiences and characteristics that make them unique. What about people from other cultures?

STEP 1 Interview three or four people from various cultures and ask them these questions:
- What experiences have you had that most other people haven't?
- What things make you different from most other people?

STEP 2 Of the people you interviewed, who was able to think of the greatest number of individual differences?

ACTIVITY 5: SPEAKING

How do North Americans, as a group, compare to the students you interviewed for Activity 3 and 4?

STEP 1 Work with three other students. Two of you should interview three or four North Americans, asking the questions that you used for Activity 3. The second pair should ask the questions you used for Activity 4.

STEP 2 Compare the responses of the North Americans to the responses of the students you interviewed in those activities.

STEP 3 Discuss these questions with your group and summarize your ideas for the rest of the class.
- Were there differences between the answers given by North Americans and those of your classmates?
- Were North Americans able to identify their individual differences more readily than people from other cultures?
- Did North Americans feel differently about change than people from other cultures?
- What do the similarities and differences between the answers of various cultural groups tell you about cultural differences?

ACTIVITY 6: LISTENING/SPEAKING

Which of these two people is most qualified to be accepted for admission to the North American Institute of International Studies?

STEP 1 Listen to the interviews with each candidate. Using the chart below, identify what the candidates say about their most important accomplishment, their background and experience, and their special abilities.

INTERVIEW QUESTIONS	CANDIDATE 1 NAME: _____ PROGRAM:	CANDIDATE 2 NAME: _____ PROGRAM:
What makes you different from other candidates?		
What relevant experience do you have?		
What is an achievement that you're proud of?		

STEP 2 Compare your chart with another student's, and listen to the interviews a second time to make sure you have heard all the important information.

STEP 3 You and your partner should decide which student is a better candidate for admission. Tell your choice and your reasons to the rest of the class.

Present Perfect: Describing Past Events in Relation to the Present | **243**

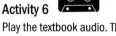

Activity 6

Play the textbook audio. The tapescript for this listening appears on pp. 516–517 of this book.

Follow the instructions in the student book, letting Ss listen a third time, if necessary.

The test for this unit can be found on p. 466. The answers are on p. 467 of this book.

ANSWER KEY

Activity 6

Candidate 1: **Name** *Aliona Fernandez* **Program:** *Masters Program in Teaching English and a Foreign Language.* **What makes you different?** *more actual teaching experience overseas than some of the others.* **What relevant experience?** *been in the Peace Corps and worked in Taiwan and Japan.* **an achievement that you're proud of?** *speaks three languages; lived in other cultures; written a grammar book.*

Candidate 2: **Name** *John Tealhome* **Program:** *International Business.* **What makes you different?** *just returned from spending a year studying in Paris.* **What relevant experience?** *worked in a book store in college* **an achievement that you're proud of?** *high school class president; captain of the football team; received a scholarship to study in France.*

Teacher's Edition: Unit 14 **243**

Unit 15

UNIT OVERVIEW

This unit presents a general overview of the structures used to describe actions and activities that we traditionally conceive of as "the future." Related topics (the differences between prediction and inference—Unit 16; and describing future events in past time—Unit 24, Focus 5) provide additional details about aspects of future time.

UNIT GOALS

Review the goals listed on this page so students (Ss) understand what they should be able to know by the end of the unit.

OPENING TASK

Note: The Opening Task allows Ss to try using the target structures and allows teachers to notice what kinds of help they may need. For a more complete discussion of Opening Tasks, see p. xix of this Teacher's Edition.

UNIT 15

FUTURE TIME

Using Present Tenses, Using *Will* Versus *Be Going To* Versus *Shall* ; Adverbial Clauses in Future

UNIT GOALS:

- To understand and use different verb tenses to express actions and states in future time
- To correctly use, *will, be going to* and *shall* and other modals to express future time
- To correctly express future time in adverbial clauses

▶ OPENING TASK
Thinking About the Future

STEP 1 Write a short paragraph about the following question: **Do you think that life one hundred years from now will be better or worse than it is today? Why?** You can mention some of the current trends and issues listed below.

POSITIVE TRENDS	NEGATIVE TRENDS
Technological improvements, new medical treatments, longer life spans, better food crops, political changes, better communication, more rapid transportation, equal status for women, more education	Environmental problems (pollution, acid rain, global warming), population increase, new diseases, increased traffic, increasing government debt, changing family structures, decreasing natural resources, increasing economic inequality

STEP 2 Exchange paragraphs with a partner, and decide which one of you is more of an optimist (someone who generally expects good things to happen) and which one is more of a pessimist (someone who generally expects bad things to happen) about the future of the world.

STEP 3 Report your decision and some of the reasons to the rest of the class.

Opening Task

This particular task can be done in a number of ways:

1. Follow the instructions in the Ss book. The paragraph called for in this task can be collected and used as a diagnostic to determine whether Ss are having trouble with these forms and whether additional practice with future time, prediction or inference is necessary.
2. Just let Ss have a general discussion about their ideas about the future. Prepare them by previewing the trends listed on this page, making sure that they understand the vocabulary and concepts there before discussing the issues in small groups.
3. With either method, make sure that Ss self-identify as being optimists or pessimists if you intend to do Activity 5 as a follow-up to this unit.

If you have covered Unit 1 and discussed how future time can be indicated by present tenses and modals, skip this review, or do it as a summary follow-up to Exercise 1.

additional examples:

Simple present: *We take the TOEFL tomorrow at 9:00 AM.*

present progressive: *We're spending next Sunday at the beach.*

modals: *Someday I will finish this project.*

Exercise 1

S U G G E S T I O N S :

1. If you have access to an OHP, make a transparency and underline the appropriate verb phrases as part of your whole class correction/discussion.

2. To save time, have half the class do the first passage and half the second.

3. If Ss have no questions concerning your presentation of Focus 1, or are not having trouble recognizing future time, skip this exercise.

Workbook Ex. 1, p. 104. Answers: TE p. 502.

FOCUS **1**

▶ Recognizing Future Time

We use simple present, present progressive, and modals to talk about future time.

EXAMPLES	EXPLANATIONS
(a) Luis **leaves** for work at 7:00 every day.	Simple present can describe present time.
(b) John **leaves** for Europe in three weeks.	It can also describe future time.
(c) Luis is **having** problems with his car, so he's taking the bus to work this week.	Present progressive can describe present time.
(d) We're **having** a test next Tuesday.	It can also describe future time.
(e) There's someone at the door. It **should** be Mehmet.	Modals can describe present time.
(f) When I am fifty years old, I **will have** a big party.	They can also describe future time.

EXERCISE 1

Do the verbs in these passages refer to future time or present time? Underline the verb phrases. Mark verb phrases that refer to future time with (F). Mark verb phrases that refer to present time with (P). The first sentence of each passage has been done for you as examples.

(P)

1. (a) School always <u>begins</u> in September in the United States. (b) This coming year, school begins on September 12. (c) Janet's going to start her third year of high school. (d) She's taking chemistry, history, English, and advanced algebra. (e) She might take a theater class, if she can fit it into her schedule.

(F)

2. (a) We<u>'re having</u> a class picnic in just a couple of weeks. (b) As you know, school ends on June 15, and the picnic will be on the next day, so we're already making plans. (c) Most people are being really cooperative. (d) For example, Lucia makes great potato salad, so she's bringing some to the picnic. (e) There should be enough for everyone to have some. (f) But George is being difficult. (g) He says he will come, but he won't bring anything. (h) Will you explain something to me? (i) Will you tell me why George is so stubborn? (j) He really should be more cooperative. (k) Everyone else is bringing something. (l) Why won't he?

A N S W E R   K E Y

Exercise 1
The following verb phrases should be underlined:
1. (a) begins (P) (b) begins (F) (c) 's going to start (F) (d) 's taking (P) (e) might take (F) . . . can fit (F)   2. (a) 're having (F) (b) ends (F) . . . will be (F) . . . 're already making (P) (c) are being (P) (d) makes (P) . . . 's bringing (F) (e) should be (F) (f) is being (P) (g) says (P) . . . will come (F) . . . won't bring (F/P) (h) Will you explain (P) (i) Will you tell (P) . . . is (P) (j) should be (P) (k) is bringing (F) (12) won't (F)

Present Tenses for Future Planned Events

EXAMPLES	EXPLANATIONS
(a) My birthday **comes** on a Sunday next year. (b) John**'s leaving** for France in a week. (c) Next year **is** my parent's fiftieth anniversary.	Use simple present and present progressive tenses to describe future activities that are **already scheduled or planned** to take place in the future.
(d) We **will** go shopping if they have a big Spring Sale. (e) There **might** be a surprise quiz on Friday.	For future events that are **not already scheduled,** use *will* or other modals of prediction (*may, could, might*).

EXERCISE 2

Make at least five questions about things that will happen in this class at a future time and have already been scheduled. Ask your questions to another student.

▶ **EXAMPLE:** When are we having our next grammar test?

EXERCISE 3

Choose the best tense (present, present progressive, or a modal of prediction) for the verbs in the following sentences. Both forms may be grammatically correct, so be prepared to explain your choice.

▶ **EXAMPLE:** John*'s leaving*_____ (leave) for France in a week.

1. The boat _____ (sail) at dawn. Don't be late.
2. Filipe _____ (have) a party on Friday. Have you been invited?
3. John doesn't know when he _____ (return) from France.
4. Peter is hoping that Denise _____ (stop) demanding that everyone work so hard.
5. Marta's birthday _____ (be) Friday, so we'd better buy her a gift.
6. Perhaps there _____ (be) a test next Friday.
7. There definitely _____ (be) a test next Friday.
8. I _____ (graduate) next June.

Like Focus 1, present this focus as a review, if needed. Otherwise, just begin your discussion of the various ways to describe future events by doing Exercise 3 and then covering the main points of this focus as a follow-up/review.

Exercise 2

If your class is not good at creating sentences without cues, provide a few to get them started, such as *quizzes, midterm grades, conferences, graduation,* etc.

Exercise 3

Do this exercise in your preferred manner, paying attention to the general principles of variety and efficiency outlined throughout this manual.

Workbook Exs. 2, p. 105. Answers: TE p. 502.

ANSWER KEY

Exercise 2
Answers will vary. Possible answers include: What time do classes start next Tuesday? When are we having our next grammar test? When does the semester end? Which unit do we study next? When do we have to make our speeches?

Exercise 3
1. sails/ is sailing 2. is having 3. will return 4. stops/ will stop 5. is
6. is/ will be 7. is will be 8. graduate/ am graduating/ will graduate

FOCUS 3

1. Write two example sentences on the board: *We will have a test next Friday. We are going to have a test next Friday.* Ask Ss if they mean the same thing or different things. They should say *"the same."* Explain that in many situations we can use both forms, but sometimes we must use one rather than the other.

2. Present the uses in the order they appear in the focus box. You can have Ss follow along in the book or use alternative examples as board work (see below),

3. Have Ss review the focus in the text as homework.

Additional examples:

Will:

requests: *Will you open the window, please?*
willingness or unwillingness: *Mary won't answer the question, but John will.;* **promise:** *I'll be there at 5:00.;* **general truths:** *A TOEFL score of 600 will be sufficient for most universities.*

Be going to:

intentions: *I'm going to relax today, no matter what!;* **immediate future:** *This class is going to end in 3 more minutes.;* **plans made earlier:** *I can't go to the movies on Saturday. I'm going to be working on this project all weekend.*

Note: Using *going to* to introduce a topic is a point that is appropriate for more advanced levels, so you may choose to skip it.

FOCUS **3**

USE

Will Versus *Be Going To*

Will

EXAMPLES	EXPLANATIONS
(a) I'm having trouble with my homework. **Will** you help me?	Use *will*: • for requests
(b) I need some milk from the store. Oh, **I'll** get it for you. **(c)** Denise **won't go** with us, no matter how much we ask her.	• to express willingness or unwillingness
(d) I'm sorry I forgot the book. **I'll bring** it tomorrow, I promise.	• to make a promise
(e) Plants **will die** if they don't get enough water.	• to express general truths

Be Going To

EXAMPLES	EXPLANATIONS
(f) **I'm going to go** to the party, whether you're there or not.	Use *be going to:* • to talk about intentions
(g) We shouldn't go hiking this afternoon. It**'s going to** rain any minute!	• to talk about the immediate future
(h) Are you going to Marta's party? I can't. **I am going to be** out of town that weekend.	• to talk about plans that have been made earlier

Will and *Be Going To*

EXAMPLES	EXPLANATIONS
(i) The weather **will be** fine for Reiko's wedding, and everyone**'s going to have** a wonderful time!	Use *will* and *be going to* to make predictions. When *be going to* is pronounced *"gonna"*, it is usually more informal than *will.*
(j) I'm going to paint my apartment. First, **I'll get** the paint and some brushes. Then **I'll get** to work. I **might** paint the walls green, but I haven't decided yet.	*Be going to* usually introduces a topic. Following sentences often use *will* and other one-word modals.

248 UNIT 15

EXERCISE 4

Decide which form, *will* or *be going to*, should be used in the following sentences. In some cases both answers may be correct.

1. I've got an extra ticket to the opera. (a) _____ (you go) with me? It (b) _____ (be) a great performance. Pavarotti (c) _____ (sing) the part of Falstaff. I'm sure he (d) _____ (be) wonderful.

2. I don't know what to do for my vacation. Maybe I (a) _____ (go) to Mexico. I know the plane ticket (b) _____ (be) expensive. Perhaps I (c) _____ (take) the bus to save some money. Your brother's taken the bus before, hasn't he? (d) _____ (you ask) him how the trip was?

3. Lin (a) _____ (finish) her assignment tonight, even if she has to stay up until dawn. It (b) _____ (not be) easy. She has to finish reading W*ar and P*eace, and then write a ten-page paper. She (c) _____ (probably be) up all night. Maybe her roommate (d) _____ (make) some coffee for her and do the dishes, so that Lin (e) _____ (not have) to worry about anything else.

4. Different plants need different amounts of water. Too much water (a) _____ (kill) certain kinds of plants. Other kinds require daily watering, and they (b) _____ (die) if they don't get it. Setting out a garden (c) _____ (require) some advanced planning to make sure that plants with similar water requirements (d) _____ (be) planted in the same areas.

Exercise 4

Do this exercise in your preferred manner, paying attention to the general principles of variety and efficiency outlined throughout this manual.

Workbook Ex. 3, p. 105. Answers: TE p. 502.

A N S W E R   K E Y

Exercise 4
1. (a) will (b) is going to/will (c) will (d) will
2. (a) will (b) is going to/will (c) will (d) will

3. (a) will/ is going to (b) won't/isn't going to (c) will/is going to (d) will (e) won't
4. (a) will (b) will (c) will (d) will

Many students have been taught "strange" notions about the use of shall (for example: "*Shall* is used with *I*, but *will* with *he, she, it*," etc.). In American English, we generally only use *shall* for offers and invitations. You can skip this focus if Ss don't have questions, or if they aren't overusing *shall*. Otherwise, present sentences e–j (or variants like the ones listed below) and then use the first focus box (sentences a–d) as a summary.

Additional examples:

offers: *Shall I give you the answer?*
Should I wash the dishes?

suggestions of mutual activity: *Shall we go on to the next unit? Let's begin with Focus 1.*

Exercise 5

Do this exercise as an immediate whole class follow-up of your presentation of Focus 4.

Workbook Ex. 4, p. 106. Answers: TE p. 502.

FOCUS **4**

Using *Shall*

EXAMPLES	EXPLANATIONS
(a) I'll go to the store. (b) (?) I **shall** go to the store. (c) I **won't** do it. (d) (?) I **shan't** go.	*Shall* is not usually used in American English. Using *shall* to talk about future actions sounds quite formal and old fashioned to Americans. The negative contracted form (*shan't*) is almost never used.
(e) **Shall** I peel you a grape? (f) **Should** I answer the phone? (g) **May** I help you?	Use *shall*: • To make offers *Should* or *may* are often used in this context.
(h) **Shall** we dance? (i) **Shall** we begin with the first exercise? (j) **Let's go out** for dinner.	• To suggest activities that both speaker and listener will participate in. *Let's* is less formal and more common.

EXERCISE 5

Decide whether *will, be going to,* or *shall* is a better form to use in these sentences.

1. _____ we go to a movie tonight?
2. When _____ you graduate?
3. _____ I tell you the answer to the question?
4. He _____ not do it, even though his mother wants him to.
5. Water _____ not flow uphill.

ANSWER KEY

Exercise 5
1. shall 2. will/are you going to
3. shall 4. will 5. will

FOCUS **5**

▶ **O**ther Modals in Future Time

Modals (*will, should, may, might, could*) that describe future events also tell about the **probability** of the event. See Unit 16 for more information and practice with predictions about future events.

EXAMPLES	MEANING	FORM
(a) We **will** arrive in an hour.	**certain** 100% probability	*will*
(b) Aunt Emily **should** like this movie.	**probable** 65%–80% probability	*should*
(c) I **may** be a little late to the meeting, because I **may not** be able to find a taxi at that hour.	**quite possible** 35%–65% probability	*may* *may not*
(d) Peter **might** know the answer, but he **might not** be in his office right now. **(e)** It **could** rain before we get there.	**somewhat possible** 5%–35% probability	*might* *might not* *could*
(f) I **won't** be at the concert next week.	**certain** 0% probability	*will not*

EXERCISE 6
Use a modal to give your opinion about the following questions. Give a reason.

▶ **EXAMPLE:** What will life be like one hundred years from now?

Life should be more complex one hundred years from now, because of so many technological developments.

1. Will there be enough coal and oil?
2. Will there be a decrease in air pollution?
3. Will the overall climate grow warmer?
4. Will the rate of population growth be greater?
5. Will there be increased use of automobiles?
6. Will there be political stability?
7. Will there still be large differences between developing and developed countries?
8. Will there be cures for cancer, AIDS, and other diseases?

Future Time: Using Present Tenses, Using Will Versus Going To Versus Shall Be; Adverbial Clauses in Future   **251**

FOCUS 5

Skip this focus if you plan to teach Unit 16 immediately after this one. If you present it, try using sentences that relate to real events and situations in the class, such as: *We will have a test tomorrow. It should take about 30 minutes to complete. Some students may get good grades, but others may not. The quiz might be hard for those who haven't studied. They could fail the quiz. That won't help their grade in this class.*

Exercise 6

You can use this exercise to predict how much "detail" will be necessary for your presentation of Focus 1 in Unit 16.

Workbook Exs. 5, pp. 106–107. Answers: TE p. 502.

ANSWER KEY

Exercise 6
Answers will vary. Possible answers include:
1. There won't be enough coal and oil, because we haven't developed alternative energy sources. **2.** There could be a decrease in air pollution if we stop using fossil fuels. **3.** The overall climate may grow warmer, because we keep producing CO_2. **4.** The rate of population growth might be lower, because it seems to decrease when society becomes more industrialized. **5.** There may be an increased use of automobiles if the government continues its lack of support for public transportation.

6. There might be political stability if the world economy stabilizes. **7.** There might not be large differences between developing and developed countries if a global economy continues to develop. **8.** There will probably be cures for cancer and AIDS, but there will also probably be new diseases that mankind hasn't yet encountered. **9.** People will probably face the same kind of problems in the twenty-first century. **10.** There won't be any more wars, because we will have a single global government.

1. Present this focus by writing the wrong sentences (sentences b, d, & f)—or variants that are relevant to the Ss in your class (see below)—on the board. Tell Ss that there is a problem with each of these sentences. Ask what is wrong. If possible, elicit the corrections and correct the examples on the board by erasing or crossing out the incorrect modals.

Additional examples: *Juan will visit his uncle tomorrow when he will get (gets) home from school. Ali will watch TV as soon as he will have (has) finished his homework. Danita will visit her relatives in Viet Nam while she will be (is) traveling there.*

Exercise 7

Do this exercise according to your preferred method taking into account the general principles of variety and efficiency outlined throughout this manual.

Workbook Exs. 6 & 7, pp. 107–108. Answers: TE p. 502.

UNIT GOAL REVIEW

1. Ask Ss to look at the goals on the opening page of this unit. Ask the whole class or pairs to provide a rule and give an example for: when we use *will*, when we use *shall*, and when we use *going to*.

2. If you wish, write these three questions up on the board and then allow Ss to look through the unit silently as they formulate their answers.

3. Ask when we can use present tense to talk about future time. Be sure Ss mention both scheduled future activities and future adverbial clauses in their answers. To elicit more responses, ask general questions about example sentences such as: *"What about We have a quiz on Friday?"; "What about I'll do that after we have a quiz?"*

---

9. What will be the problems that people face in the twenty-first century?

10. Will there still be wars between countries?

Make up three questions of your own and ask them to a partner. Compare your ideas about the future to those of your partner. Who is more optimistic about the future?

▶ Future-Time Adverbial Clauses

In future time, adverbial clauses always use present tenses, and not modal auxiliaries.

(a)	I'll do it tomorrow, **when I finish school.**	**(b)**	NOT: I'll do it tomorrow, **when I will finish school.**
(c)	I'm going to watch TV **as soon as I have finished my homework.**	**(d)**	NOT: I'm going to watch TV **as soon as I will have finished** my homework.
(e)	Hani is planning to have party **while his parents are visiting relatives in Canada.**	**(f)**	NOT: Hani's planning to have a party while his parents **will be visiting relatives in Canada.**

EXERCISE 7

Join the second sentence in each of these pairs to the first sentence using the linking word in parentheses. Make sure to change nouns to pronouns where necessary.

▶ **EXAMPLE:** I'll go to the movies. I will finish my homework. (after)

I'll go the movies after I finish my homework.

1. All my friends will be relieved. The semester will end in a couple of weeks. (when)

2. I'm going to go to the movies every day. I will have finished all the household chores that have been postponed all semester. (after)

3. It will be almost three weeks after the last day of class. Lin will finally get her research paper completed. (by the time)

4. I'm going to read that novel. I'll have some time after the exams. (when)

5. Bob's going to spend every day at the beach. The weather will be sunny. (while)

6. Matt and Jeff will be really tired. They are going to finish their ten-mile hike from the beach. (by the time)

7. Mark and Ann are leaving for Europe. They'll finish their last exam. (as soon as)

8. Doug and Elena are going to get married. They will be on vacation in Mexico. (while)

9. Even our teacher's going to take some time off. She will have finished grading the final papers and correcting the exams. (when)

252 | UNIT 15

ANSWER KEY

Exercise 7

1. All my friends will be very relieved, when the semester ends. 2. I'm going to go to the movies every day after I have finished . . . 3. It will be almost three weeks after the last day of class by the time Lin finally gets . . . 4. I'm going to read that book about magic when I have . . . 5. Bob's going to spend every afternoon at the beach while the weather is . . . 6. Matt and Jeff will be really tired by the time they finish . . . 7. Mark and Ann are leaving for Europe as soon as they finish . . . 8. Doug and Elena are going to get married while they are . . . 9. Even our teacher's going to take some time off when she has finished.

Use Your English

ACTIVITY 1: SPEAKING/WRITING

What day and time is it at this moment? Imagine what you will be doing **at this exact moment** ten years from now twenty years from now, fifty years from now. Describe these activities to a partner or write a brief essay about them.

ACTIVITY 2: SPEAKING

STEP 1 Tell several other students about your vacation plans. Listen to their plans.

STEP 2 Then answer these questions as a group.
- Whose plans sound like the most fun? Why?
- Whose plans sound like the most boring? Why?
- Whose plans sound like the easiest to arrange? Why?
- Whose plans sound like the best opportunity to practice English?

Decide on one additional category of your own.

STEP 3 Report your answers to the rest of the class.

ACTIVITY 3: WRITING

Choose one of these three questions and write a paragraph or make a presentation expressing your ideas.
- What major **political and economic changes** are going to take place in your lifetime? Describe them and explain why you think they are going to happen.
- What major **social changes** are going to take place in your lifetime? Describe them and explain why you think they are going to happen.
- What major **scientific advances** are going to take place in your lifetime? Describe them and explain why you think they are going to happen.

USE YOUR ENGLISH

Note: The activities on these "purple pages" at the end of each unit contain communicative activities designed to apply what Ss have learned and help them practice communication and grammar at the same time. For a more complete discussion of how to use the Use Your English activities, see p. xxii of this Teacher's Edition.

Activity 1

Use this as a testing or diagnostic activity by having Ss write paragraphs the night before. Have Ss work in pairs to correct each other's paragraphs (in different color ink), and then collect to evaluate both the original paragraph and the partner's corrections.

Activity 2

This works best as an oral activity, especially a few days before actual vacation periods. Sometimes Ss are lonely and bored during vacation times, and this activity can help them strategize activities to keep busy.

Activity 3

Use this as a testing or diagnostic activity by following the same procedures outlined in Activity 1.

VARIATION:

Use it as a pre-listening discussion to prepare Ss for the ideas discussed in Activity 4.

Activity 4

Play textbook audio. The tapescript for this listening appears on pp. 517–518 of this book.

Follow the same basic procedure of allowing for multiple listenings (if needed) that have been outlined in other units.

VARIATIONS:

If you plan to do Activity 5, omit Step 2 or, alternatively, use it as a first step in having Ss organize their arguments.

ACTIVITY 4: LISTENING/ SPEAKING

STEP 1 Listen to these two speakers talk about the future. As you listen, note the speaker's predictions and the reasons for those predictions in the chart below. Based on those predictions and reasons, decide whether the speaker is optimistic or pessimistic about the future.

Speaker 1

Optimistic or Pessimistic?	Speaker's Prediction	Speaker's Reasons
public health and population		
life expectancy and nutrition		
energy and pollution		
political and economic stability		

Speaker 2

Optimistic or Pessimistic?	Speaker's Prediction	Speaker's Reasons
public health and population		
life expectancy and nutrition		
energy and pollution		
political and economic stability		

ANSWER KEY

Activity 4

Speaker 1: Optimistic
PUBLIC HEALTH AND POPULATION
Speaker's Prediction: Most of the diseases that are common today will be wiped out. There will be more people and they will be leading healthier lives.
Speaker's reasons: Scientists are already making progress in finding cures for AIDS, Alzheimer's disease, heart disease, and cancer.
LIFE EXPECTANCY AND NUTRITION
Speaker's Prediction:
People in the next century will be living longer and healthier lives.

They will have been eating more nutritiously for several generations, so human beings will, on the whole, be larger, stronger than they are today.
Speaker's Reasons: We are already seeing this in countries like Japan and Thailand.
ENERGY AND POLLUTION
Speaker's Prediction: Scientists will have discovered nonpolluting ways to produce cheap, clean energy. There will be much less pollution: no smog, no acid rain, and no fears about global warming.
Speaker's Reasons: There are already alternative energy sources such as water power and solar energy. As fuels such as gas, oil, and coal become

scarcer and more expensive, these clean sources of energy will become cheaper to produce.
POLITICAL AND ECONOMIC STABILITY
Speaker's Prediction: Greater political and economic stability; Global communication and global economic progress will improve the political situation and will remove forever the threat of nuclear war. It will no longer even be necessary to have passports.
Speaker's Reasons: Changes such as the Internet are already making global communication available to everyone and will lead to increasing international cooperation. Important political changes started in the late 1980s.

254   Grammar Dimensions, Platinum Edition

STEP 2 Imagine that you are one of the speakers. Using the notes you took above, try to give a speech in your own words to a partner explaining why you are optimistic or pessimistic about the future. Your partner should do the same with the other speech. If you wish, add some ideas and reasons of your own.

ACTIVITY 5: SPEAKING

Organize a debate between optimists and pessimists.

STEP 1 Using the Opening Task on page 245, decide whether you are an optimist or a pessimist. Form groups of four or more. Try to have an equal number of optimists and pessimists in each group.

STEP 2 As a group, choose one category of world affairs (see Opening Task for examples). Discuss the current trends related to that category. Add one or two significant additional trends of your own. Optimists will then give reasons why they think the world will be better one hundred years from now. Pessimists will give reasons why they think the world will be worse one hundred years from now.

STEP 3 Present both sets of predictions to the other groups. As a whole class, decide who has presented the most persuasive reasons, the optimists or the pessimists.

Activity 5

Debates need to be prepared and structured to be most effective. This particular topic works best if you let Ss choose sides, but you can also assign people to a particular position. This format requires some extensive pre-debate discussion, so this activity might need to take place over a couple of days. As suggested in Activity 4, letting Ss use their oral paraphrases of their notes in Activity 4 is a good way to prepare for this activity.

The test for this unit can be found on p. 468. The answers are on p. 469 of this book.

TOEFL Test Preparation Exercises for Units 13–15 can be found on pp. 109–111 of the Workbook.
The answers are on p. 502 of this book.

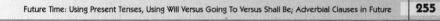

ANSWER KEY

Activity 4

Speaker 2: Pessimistic
PUBLIC HEALTH AND POPULATION
Speaker's Prediction: Population will continue to grow uncontrollably and poor nutrition will affect more and more people. **Speaker's reasons:** The population is increasing at a very rapid rate. Resources for health care, economic development and even food can not keep up with the enormous increase in population. Many governments do not support birth control research or family planning programs.
LIFE EXPECTANCY AND NUTRITION
Speaker's Prediction: There will be more and more shortages of food as the population

continues to grow uncontrollably and poor nutrition will affect more and more people. Lack of sufficient vitamins will make people weaker and less able to resist disease. The growth of new diseases such as AIDS and Ebola Virus will continue, and all diseases will become harder to control. **Speaker's reasons:** Such diseases as malaria and tuberculosis are already increasing. Common antibiotics have begun to lose their effectiveness against infectious diseases like pneumonia.
ENERGY AND POLLUTION
Speaker's Prediction: An increased reliance on nuclear power will result in more nuclear accidents like Chernobyl.

There will be an increase in air pollution.
Speaker's reasons: Supplies of coal, oil, and gas are almost finished, but governments are not supporting programs to develop alternative energy sources, such as solar power or wind-generated electricity. Massive deforestation is changing the world climates and increasing air pollution.
POLITICAL AND ECONOMIC STABILITY
Speaker's Prediction: Small local wars in places will become more widespread. War and revolution will be common in the next century.
Speaker's reasons: Countries like the former Yugoslavia or the former Soviet Union are breaking apart. The economic gap between the rich and the poor is increasing.

Teacher's Edition: Unit 15 **255**

Unit 16

UNIT OVERVIEW

This unit provides practice using modals to make predictions (guesses about the future) and inferences (guesses about the present or past). Many Ss have trouble expressing or distinguishing logical inference as opposed to prediction or possibility. There is a helpful discussion of the these concepts in *The Grammar Book*, pp. 142–144. All modal structures in English, being so dependent on context to determine correct meaning, tend to be challenging for Ss, and therefore even relatively advanced Ss can usefully review this chapter.

UNIT GOALS

Review the goals listed on this page so Ss understand what they should be able to do by the end of the unit.

Opening Task

1. Do this task in pairs or small groups. If time allows, let Ss work on all three mysteries.
2. Let Ss discuss the mysteries for a while, and then go around to each group and whisper the additional clue (from p.428) to each group.

U N I T **16**

MODALS OF PREDICTION AND INFERENCE

UNIT GOALS:

- To understand and use different modals to express predictions in future time
- To understand and use different modals to express logical inferences in present time
- To correctly express predictions and logical inferences in past time

▶ OPENING TASK
Solving a Mystery

MYSTERY #1

A man lives on the fortieth floor of a very tall building. Every day he rides the elevator down to the ground floor. When he comes home he rides the elevator to the twentieth floor, but he has to walk the rest of the way.

Why does he do this?

MYSTERY #2

In a room, a dead woman is hanging by a rope, more than three feet above the floor. There are no windows, and the door has been locked from the inside. The room is empty: no furniture, no ladder. The only thing in the room is a single piece of paper.

What happened to the woman?

MYSTERY #3

A police officer receives an emergency phone call about a terrible automobile accident. A boy and his father have both been very badly injured. The officer has to fill out the report and figure out what happened. The police officer takes one look at the boy and his father, and says "You'll have to find someone else to deal with this. I'm too upset. This boy is my son!"

How can the boy have two fathers?

STEP 1 Work with a partner. Choose one of the mini-mysteries above to try to solve.

STEP 2 Think of five possible explanations. Decide which ones are likely and which ones are not very likely.

STEP 3 Turn to page A-12 and read the additional clues. Then try to solve the mysteries.

1. Present example sentences in order from 100% probability to 0% probability. Use example sentences from Unit 15, Focus 5 as possible alternatives, especially if you omitted that focus from your presentation of Unit 15.
2. Once the meanings are clear, present the last part of the focus (sentence k)

S U G G E S T I O N :

Many teachers have found that explicit treatment of negative predictions and inferences is also useful, but if your students are not having trouble, you can omit this information. These examples can be used if you decide to present negative predictions and inferences. Such a presentation can follow Focus 1 or Focus 2. If you are not sure, do it after Focus 2 (and Exercises 5 & 6). This will give you enough time to see whether or not Ss need explicit presentations of this information.

Negative modals generally occur in either full form or contracted form but not both.

1. _may not/might not_ is preferred. _mayn't/mightn't_ are not standard American English
   (a) _I may not/might not_ be on time
   (b) _(NOT) I mayn't/mightn't_ be there.
2. _shouldn't_ is preferred over _should not_ for predictions
   (c) The test _shouldn't_ be too difficult. (prediction)
   (d) The teacher _should not_ be giving us a test! (negative advisability)
3. _must not_ is preferred over _mustn't_ for negative inferences.
   (e) He _must not_ care about his grade. (negative inference)
   (f) You _mustn't_ forget your homework. (negative necessity)
4. _can't/couldn't_ is preferred over _can not/could not_ to express impossibility.
   (g) That _couldn't_ be John. (impossible)
   (h) He _could not_ be here, after all. (negative ability)

▶ Modals of Prediction

Modals of prediction refer to future time. Use them to indicate how likely or possible it is that some future event will happen. (See Focus 3 for information about making predictions in the past time frame.)

EXAMPLES	FORM	MEANING/USE
(a) We **will** leave in an hour.	_will_	It will **certainly** happen. We can also use simple present or present progressive to describe these events.
(b) We **should** be able to get a good price for Andy's car.	_should_	It is **likely** to happen. Using _should_ for predictions sometimes sounds like advisability. If you aren't sure, use _will probably_ to make your meaning clear.
(c) They **will probably** be here in a couple of hours.	_probably will_	
(d) I **may** be late tonight.	_may_	It will **possibly** happen.
(e) You'd better take an umbrella. It **could/might** rain tonight.	_might_ _could_	
(f) We **may not** have to wait.	_may not_	It will **possibly not** happen.
(g) We **might not** get there in time.	_might not_	
(h) This **shouldn't** hurt.	_shouldn't_	It is **not likely** that this will happen. Using _shouldn't_ for predictions sometimes sounds like advisability. If you aren't sure, use _probably won't_ to make your meaning clear.
(i) This **probably won't** take too long.	_probably won't_	
(j) We **won't** leave before Tuesday.	_won't_	It will **certainly not** happen.

EXAMPLES	EXPLANATION
(k) **Will** they be here by 5:00? Mary **should be** on time, but John **might** be a little late.	To ask for predictions about future events, use only _will_, not other modal forms.

EXERCISE 1

Make sentences from these cues using modals.

▶ **EXAMPLE:** certain: Andy/drive to New York for a vacation.

   Andy will drive to New York for a vacation

1. likely: Andy/decide what to do about his car next week.
2. certainly not: The car/work well enough for his trip to New York.
3. possible: Andy/get it repaired, if it can be done cheaply.
4. not likely: He/have trouble selling it.
5. likely: He/be able to get a good price.
6. possible: Andy's friend Paul/want to buy it.
7. possibly not: Andy/sell the car to Paul.
8. possibly not: The car/be in very good condition.
9. possible: Paul/expect a refund if he has troubles with the car.
10. certain: Andy/need the money to buy a plane ticket if he doesn't drive.

EXERCISE 2

How likely is it that you will be doing the following activities next Saturday night at 8:00 P.M.?

doing English homework	taking a bath
watching TV	speaking another language
thinking about personal problems	sleeping
sitting in a movie theater	writing letters to my family
reading a magazine	having a good time with friends

Work with a partner. Ask questions with *will*. Answer questions with the appropriate modal of prediction.

▶ **EXAMPLES:** At 8:00 P.M. next Saturday do you think you will be doing English homework?

   I won't be doing homework on a Saturday night. I might be at a party.

Exercise 1
Assign this exercise for homework, or use it as a diagnostic before presenting Focus 1 to find out how much Ss already know.

Exercise 2

Process as a whole class by asking follow-up questions involving the reasons for their partners' predictions. For example: *Why did Yanti think she might not be doing homework? She said she won't be doing it? Why not?* etc.

ANSWER KEY

Exercise 1

1. Andy **should** decide . . .   2. The car **won't** work . . .   3. Andy **may/might** get . . .   4. He **shouldn't** have . . .
5. He **should** be able to get a good price.
6. Andy's friend Paul **might/may** want . . .
7. Andy **might/may** not . . .   8. The car **may/might** not be . . .   9. Paul **could/might** expect . . .   10. Andy **will** need . . .

Exercise 2

Answers will vary. All modals are possible in most situations, but likely answers include: I won't be doing English homework. I could/may/might/should be watching TV. I could/may/might/should be sitting in a movie theater. I could/might/be speaking another language. I won't/shouldn't be sleeping. I could/shouldn't be writing letters to my family. I will be having a good time with friends.

Exercises 3 & 4

If Ss have trouble thinking of sentences, try putting them in pairs for Exercise 3 or small groups for Exercise 4. Alternatively, assign one or both of these exercises for homework for you to collect and evaluate.

Workbook Ex. 1, pp. 112–113. Answers: TE p. 502.

EXERCISE 3

Write twelve true sentences about your plans for your next vacation using modals of prediction.

two things that you will certainly do

_____

two things that you will likely do

_____

two things that you will possibly do

_____

two things that you possibly won't do

_____

two things that you won't likely do

_____

two things that you certainly won't do

_____

EXERCISE 4

Write twelve sentences about how you think life will be at the end of the next century using modals of prediction.

two things that will certainly be true

_____

two things that will likely be true

_____

two things that will possibly be true

_____

two things that possibly won't be true

_____

two things that won't likely be true

_____

two things that certainly won't be true

_____

ANSWER KEY

Exercise 3
Answers will vary. Possible answers include: I will go someplace warm. I should have a good rest. I might go with friends. I may not have enough money to fly there. I shouldn't have trouble finding a cheap airplane ticket. I won't stay anyplace really expensive.

Exercise 4
Answers will vary. Possible answers include: Life will be more complex. Communication between countries should be easier. Life may be better. Things may not have improved much compared to life today. People's personal worries shouldn't be too different from the ones they have today. My parents won't be alive.

▶ **M**odals of Inference

Modals of inference refer to the present time frame. Use them to express a logical conclusion, based on evidence. (See Focus 3 for information about making inferences in the past time frame.)

EXAMPLES	FORM	MEANING
(a) That **must** be John. I've been expecting him.	*must*	There is no other possible conclusion from the evidence.
(b) John **should** be here somewhere. He said he was coming.	*should*	This is a logical conclusion, based on the evidence we have, but it is possible that there is another conclusion.
(c) She **may** be unhappy. **(d)** They **might** have some problems. **(e)** John **could** be here.	*may* *might* *could*	This is one of several possibilities.
(f) She **may not** be here. I don't see her anywhere. **(g)** We'd better turn down the music. The neighbors **might not** like rap.	*may not* *might not*	This is one of several possibilities.
(h) They **shouldn't** arrive for several more hours. There's a delay at the airport.	*shouldn't*	This is not a logical conclusion, based on the evidence we have, but it could be possible.
(i) I've looked everywhere for Mary. She **must not** be here.	*must not*	This is not a possible conclusion, based on the evidence we have.
(j) That **couldn't** be John. I know he's still out of town. **(k)** He **can't** be in two places at the same time.	*couldn't* *can't*	This is impossible.

The difference between a prediction and an inference is a subtle but important one.

1. The Opening Task focuses on this issue, so start your presentation with a review of the statements that were made, or use alternative examples that refer to that task. Unlike your presentation of predictions, move from possibility "outward" to impossibility or inescapable conclusion following the examples of one of these mysteries.
   (a) *The elevator <u>might be</u> broken. It <u>might not</u> be working.*
   (b) *The elevator <u>should be</u> able to go up to the fortieth floor, since he is able to ride down. He <u>shouldn't have to</u> walk the rest of the way because of the elevator.*
   (c) *The top button <u>must be</u> too high for him to reach. He <u>must not be</u> able to reach the top button.*
   (d) *The officer <u>might be</u> mistaken. The boy's mother <u>might not be</u> married to the boy's biological father.*
   (e) *The officer <u>should be</u> able to recognize his child. He <u>shouldn't</u> mistake the child for someone else.*
   (f) *The boy <u>can't have</u> two fathers. The officer <u>must be</u> the boy's mother.*
2. Assign the chart on this page for review in pairs or for self-study at home.

Exercise 5

SUGGESTION:

1. Do the first two passages as a whole class, focusing on the "evidence" regarding modal choice. In #1, **should** is preferred because it is followed by the "evidence" *I've been expecting him.* In # 2, **can't/couldn't** is correct because it is followed by the "evidence" *he has a key.* **shouldn't** because it is followed by the "evidence" *he doesn't usually ring the bell.* **shouldn't** is followed by the "evidence" *all my friends think I'm still in New York.* **must** therefore becomes the only possible conclusion.

2. Follow a similar process in processing the other choices.

EXERCISE 5

Make logical conclusions by filling in the blanks with an appropriate modal of inference. Decide whether the logical conclusion you express is:

- the only one possible (*must*) or impossible (*must not/can't/couldn't*),
- more likely than other possible conclusions (*should*) or less likely (*shouldn't*),
- or one of several possibilities (*could/may/might/may not/might not*).

There may be more than one correct answer, so be prepared to explain why you chose the form you did.

1. There's someone at the door. That (a) _____ be my brother; I've been expecting him. But it (b) _____ be the postal carrier, or it (c) _____ even be a salesperson.

2. Someone is ringing the doorbell. It (a) _____ be my brother; he has a key. It (b) _____ be the postal carrier; he doesn't usually ring the bell. It (c) _____ be a friend; all my friends think I'm still in New York. It (d) _____ be a salesperson. Let's not answer it!

3. I hope I can go to the movies with you tonight, but I (a) _____ (not) have enough money. I (b) _____ have enough, because I cashed a check yesterday. But I won't be 100% sure until I buy groceries and see how much money I have left. I really hope I can go. Everyone who has seen that movie says it's really good. It (c) _____ be very funny.

4. Martha looks pretty unhappy. She and George (a) _____ be having another one of their fights. I don't know what the problem is this time. It (b) _____ be because George is always working on his car. It (c) _____ be because Martha wants them to spend every weekend at her mother's house. It (d) _____ (not) be about money, though. That's the fight they had last week. They (e) _____ (not) have a very happy marriage.

5. Where have I put my wallet? It (a) _____ be somewhere! It (b) _____ just disappear by itself. It (c) _____ be on my desk, since that's where I usually put it. But it (d) _____ be in my briefcase, too. I sometimes forget to

---

ANSWER KEY

Exercise 5

1. (a) should (b) could/may/might be (c) could/may/might   2. (a) can't/ couldn't (b) shouldn't (c) shouldn't (d) must
3. (a) might/may not (b) should (c) should/ must   4. (a) must (b) could/may/might (c) could/may/might (d) can't/couldn't/ shouldn't (e) must not/can't   5. (a) must (b) can't/couldn't (c) should/could/ may/might (d) could/ may/might
6. (a) must not (b) must   7. (a) should (b) might/could/may (c) must not

take it out when I get home.

6. Naomi (a) _____ (not) need money. She's always eager to
pay when we go out for a night on the town. She never seems to have a
job. It (b) _____ be nice to have enough money without
having to work.

7. Frank (a) _____ have no trouble finding a job when he
moves to California. It (b) _____ take a while, but I know
he'll find a good position. He seems unhappy in New York. He
(c) _____ (not) like living there very much.

EXERCISE 6

Decide whether the following sentences are predictions or inferences and
choose an appropriate modal. Compare your choices with a partner's.

▶ **EXAMPLES:** It <u>shouldn't</u> (not) be very difficult to find a parking
place today, because it's Sunday, and usually there aren't
many people downtown.

Jack <u>must not</u> (not) have much money, because he
drives a fifteen-year-old car.

1. Traffic is getting heavy; rush hour _____ be starting.

2. Commuters _____ be getting really tired of driving to
work in such awful traffic.

3. Experts tell us that traffic _____ get worse every year
unless we do something about the problem.

4. Some people think that traffic _____ flow more
smoothly if we increase the number of highways.

5. But most experts feel that the problem _____ (not) be
solved by building more highways.

6. That _____ just increase the number of cars on the
roads.

7. The traffic problem _____ begin to improve, once we
have increased public transportation.

8. This city _____ (not) have a very efficient public transportation system, because people seem to drive everywhere.

Exercise 6

Like Exercise 5, Ss should focus on the
"evidence" to determine the likelihood or
probability of inference. You can do the
exercise by following the instructions, or have
Ss work in pairs from the start.

Workbook Exs. 2 & 3, pp. 113–114. Answers:
TE p. 502.

ANSWER KEY

Exercise 6
1. must/ should   2. must   3. will
4. might/ could   5. won't/ shouldn't/ can't
6. will/ should   7. will/ should/ might
8. must

FOCUS 3

This focus can be presented in several ways.

1. With books open, have Ss examine the pairs of sentences (a & b, c & d, etc.). Draw attention to the time contexts in the examples.

2. Write the present/future time inferences about students (Yanti must be tired. Juan Carlos must not have his homework, etc.) on the board. Then elicit the past time forms from Ss, saying *"The same thing happened last week. How can we say that in English?"*

3. Replicate your discussion of the mysteries in Focus 2, using past time forms.

   a. *The elevator <u>might have been</u> broken. It <u>might not have been</u> working.*

   b. *The elevator <u>should have been</u> able to go up to the fortieth floor, since he is able to ride down. He <u>shouldn't have had to</u> walk the rest of the way because of the elevator.*

   c. *The top button <u>must have been</u> too high for him to reach. He <u>must not have been</u> able to reach the top button.*

FOCUS **3**

Modals of Prediction and Inference in Past Time

You can make predictions and inferences about things that happened in the past time frame by using **perfect modals**.

MODAL + *HAVE* + PAST PARTICIPLE

| Alice | might | have | | seen | | that movie. |

MODAL	EXAMPLES WITH PRESENT/FUTURE TIME	EXAMPLES WITH PAST TIME
must	(a) That **must be** John. I've been expecting him.	(b) Who left this note? It **must have been** Stephanie.
should	(c) Peter **should be** here somewhere. He said he was coming.	(d) Let's ask Peter what happened at the meeting. He **should have been** there.
may *might* *could*	Why is Martha crying (e) She **may be** sad. (g) She **might be** having problems. (i) George **could be** the reason.	Why was Martha crying? (f) She **may have been** sad. (h) She **might have been** having problems. (j) George **could have been** the reason.
may not *might not*	(k) She **may not be** here. I haven't seen her yet. (m) She **might not get** invited to the party.	(l) She **may not have been** there. I didn't see her. (n) She **might not have gotten** an invitation to this party.
shouldn't	(o) They **shouldn't be** here until tomorrow morning.	(p) That **shouldn't have been** the reason why Ali didn't come.
must not	(q) I've looked everywhere for Mariko. She **must not be** here.	(r) They don't know what happened at the meeting. They **must not have been** there.
couldn't *can't*	(s) That **couldn't be** John. I know he's still out of town. (u) We **can't take** a test on Friday! I'm not ready.	(t) You **couldn't have forgotten** my name. (v) I **can't have lost** it!

EXERCISE 7

Change this passage to the past time frame.

▶ **EXAMPLE:** Denise might not have enough time to finish the project today. That must be the reason why she isn't at the boss's birthday party.

Denise might not have had enough time to finish the project yesterday. That must have been the reason why she wasn't at the boss's birthday party.

(1) Frank might change jobs. (2) He should have no trouble finding a new job. (3) It might take a while, but he has excellent qualifications and lots of experience. (4) He must be really unhappy to want to move to a brand new company. (5) He must not like working in such a big company very much.

EXERCISE 8

Write the appropriate modal form in the blank. There may be more than one correct answer.

1. Someone called me up in the middle of the night. They hung up before I could answer the phone. It (a) _____ (not be) my brother; he doesn't have a telephone. It (b) _____ (be) someone I know, but why would they call in the middle of the night? It (c) _____ (be) a wrong number.

2. Where were you last night? I thought you were going to join us at the movies. You (a) _____ (have) enough money to go with us, because the tickets weren't that expensive. It's too bad you didn't come. I (b) _____ (be) able to lend you the money. Or perhaps Peter (c) _____ (pay) for your ticket. He's so generous. The movie was really funny. You (d) _____ (be) disappointed to miss all the fun.

3. Janet looked really unhappy as she was leaving Professor Brown's office. She (a) _____ (failed) another exam. I know she's already failed one midterm, and she had two more last week. It (b) _____ (be) her chemistry test. I know she was really nervous about it. But it (c) _____ (be) her calculus exam. She's really good at mathematics, and I know she studied a lot for it.

Modals of Prediction and Inference **265**

Exercise 7

Have Ss do this exercise individually and then process as a whole class.

Exercise 8

Follow the same basic procedure you used for Exercise 5. Have Ss explicitly compare their responses on the two exercises to highlight the basic form differences between the two time frames.

ANSWER KEY

Exercise 7
(1) Frank might have changed. . . . (2) He should have had. . . . (3) It might have taken . . . had . . . (4) He must have been . . . (5) He must not have liked . . .

Exercise 8
1. (a) can't/couldn't/ must not have been (b) could/might/may have been (c) must have been 2. (a) should have had (b) should/ could/might have been (c) should/could/might have paid (d) must have been 3. (a) must have failed (b) could/ may/might have been (c) couldn't/ shouldn't have been
4. (a) couldn't have disappeared (b) may/ might/ could have been (c) may/might/could have been (d) must have left 5. (a) couldn't have been (b) could/may/might have been (c) could/may/might have been (d) must have been

4. Luis looked everywhere for the missing documents. They
(a) _____ (disappear) by themselves. He thought they
(b) _____ (be) on the desk, where he usually put things
he was working on, or they (c) _____ (be) in his briefcase, too. But when he looked, they weren't in either place. Then he
remembered working on them at the office. He (d) _____
(leave) them there.

5. Who killed Judge Clarence? It (a) _____ (be) his wife.
She was in Switzerland learning how to ski. It (b) _____
(be) his accountant. Apparently there was some trouble with money.
But nobody thought his accountant would do such a thing. There
were a few clues. His wallet was missing. His brother's fingerprints
were found on the candlestick that was used to kill the judge. The
murderer (c) _____ (be) his brother. But Detective Nancy
Mann was not convinced. It all seemed too simple. The brother was
rich and didn't need the money. The murderer (d) _____
(be) someone else, someone who was actually trying to get the
brother in trouble with the law.

EXERCISE 9
Use modals of prediction and inference to give possible or probable reasons
for these situations.

▶ **EXAMPLES:** The window was open. The TV was gone.
A thief must have broken into the apartment.

The students are quiet. They're listening carefully.
They might be taking a test.
The teacher could be telling them about their final examination.

1. The parents are laughing. They're looking at a picture.
2. Mary's waiting at the corner. She's looking at her watch.
3. Ahmad was smiling. A doctor was congratulating him.
4. The men were digging holes. They were looking at an old map.
5. A woman was crying. She had just received an envelope in the mail.
6. Denise stays late at the office every night. She tells her boss about it.
7. That man wears old clothes. He doesn't have enought to eat.
8. The police ran to their car. They drove quickly to the house.

Exercise 9

This exercise works well as pair or group work. Have Ss determine their individual explanations first and then compare answers, or have them work with others from the start.

Workbook Exs. 4–6, pp. 114–115. Answers: TE p. 503.

UNIT GOAL REVIEW

1. Ask Ss to look at the goals on the opening page of this unit. Help them understand how much they have accomplished by writing the words *prediction, guess, inference,* and *logical conclusion* on the board.

2. Ask Ss as a whole class or in pairs or groups to decide which terms are synonyms for each other and to compose (or find in the book) one example of each type (prediction/guess and inference/logical conclusion). Allow time for Ss to look over the focuses individually and ask questions according to your preferred method. Some Ss may prefer to write questions in the form of the grammar journal outlined in Unit 5 Activity 1 (p. 11).

ANSWER KEY

Exercise 9
Answers will vary. Possible answers include:
1. It must be a cute picture of their baby.
2. She might be waiting for someone to arrive.
3. He must have gotten some good news about his medical exam.   4. They might have been searching for treasure.   5. She must have gotten some bad news.   6. She must be trying to get a raise.   7. He must be a homeless person.   8. A house must have been robbed.

Use Your English

ACTIVITY 1 : WRITING

STEP 1 Watch a television program (comedy or drama) for a few minutes without turning on the sound. You should be able to see, but not to hear, what's going on.

STEP 2 Describe at least five interactions between characters. Describe exactly what happened, your interpretation of what happened, and your reasons for thinking so.

Description of What Happened—Who did what?	Interpretation of Action—What was the character's reason or purpose?	Reason for Your Interpretation—Why do you think so?
Example: One man kept poking the other man in the chest with his finger.	He was trying to start a fight.	The other man's expression became more and more angry.
Interaction 1		
Interaction 2		
Interaction 3		
Interaction 4		
Interaction 5		

STEP 3 Write a paragraph that describes what you saw and what you think was happening. Be sure to distinguish between things that **might** have been going on versus things that **must** have been going on. Give reasons for all of your interpretations.

Modals of Prediction and Inference **267**

Activity 1

You may want the class to all watch the same program, so that you can compare their interpretations. This activity can be used for testing or diagnosis by having Ss write their descriptions. You will need to specify which time frame they should use in their description, or have them write the descriptions first in present and then in past time.

Activity 2

This is a simpler potential diagnostic activity than Activity 1.

SUGGESTIONS:

1. Ask Ss to distinguish between guesses (they might be . . .) and inferences (it's midnight in my country, so they must be . . .)
2. For less advanced classes, use this distinction to frame all the responses and process as a whole class.

Activity 3

This works best as a speaking exercise. Direct Ss to use the frame *"This object might have been used to . . ."* to give additional practice with past predictions.

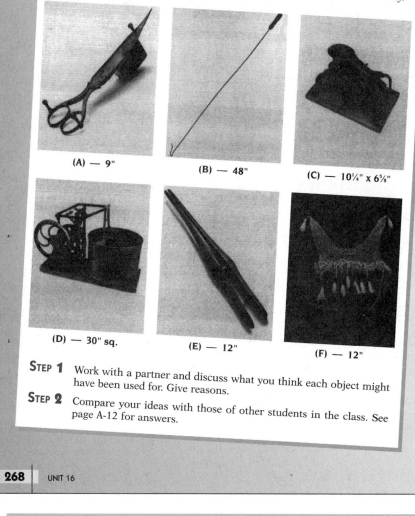

ACTIVITY 2: SPEAKING/WRITING

Do you have friends or family living in another country? What time is it at this moment in that country? Talk or write about what you think they are doing at this moment.

ACTIVITY 3: SPEAKING

Look at these pictures of six household items that are no longer used today.

(A) — 9"

(B) — 48"

(C) — 10¼" x 6⅝"

(D) — 30" sq.

(E) — 12"

(F) — 12"

STEP 1 Work with a partner and discuss what you think each object might have been used for. Give reasons.

STEP 2 Compare your ideas with those of other students in the class. See page A-12 for answers.

ANSWER KEY

The pictures show the following inventions:
Picture A: A candle snuffer
Picture B: A hook to catch chickens
Picture C: A cherry-pit remover
Picture D: A mechanical vegetable chopper
Picture E: A glove dryer/stretcher
Picture F: An ear-protector for carriage horses

A C T I V I T Y   4 :   S P E A K I N G

Do you know how to predict people's future by looking at their palms? Here is a diagram of some of the important "lines" of the palm. If the line is deep and strong, the person should have favorable developments in those areas. If the line is weak or broken, this indicates that the person may have trouble in that area. Using this reference guide, choose a partner examine his or her palm and make predictions about his or her future. Try to make at least two predictions about what will happen to your partner in the future and two inferences about his or her character or personality.

Number of Children
Love and Romance
Health
Wealth

A C T I V I T Y   5 :   L I S T E N I N G / S P E A K I N G

STEP 1 Listen to this conversation about a mystery. Decide whether each person listed below is a possible suspect, a probable suspect, or not a possible suspect.

Suspect	Likelihood of Guilt	Evidence
Mom	could not be guilty	she discovered the cookies were missing
Dad		
Nancy		
Eric		
Diane		

STEP 2 Work with a partner to decide who the criminal is. Give reasons to support your decision.

THE THIEF MUST HAVE BEEN _____.

Modals of Prediction and Inference **269**

Activity 4

Ss love this activity. You can poll the class to find out what other important additional signs and features of palm reading they are familiar with. It can be used as a diagnostic by having Ss write their predictions, but it might be more enjoyable just to relax and let them have fun.

Activity 5

Play textbook audio.
The tapescript for this activity appears on p. 518 of this book. Play the tape more than once, as necessary, directing Ss to listen for general ideas, specific information, verification, etc., as outlined in previous units.

✓

The test for this unit can be found on p. 470. The answers are on p. 471 of this book.

A N S W E R   K E Y

Activity 5
Suspect Dad; **Likelihood of Guilt:** could be guilty; **Evidence:** he's still full; there are crumbs on his mustache

Suspect: Nancy; **Likelihood of Guilt:** might be guilty; might not be guilty; **Evidence:** she likes sweets; she was really hungry after school; she's been dieting

Suspect: Eric; **Likelihood of Guilt:** could not be guilty; **Evidence:** he hasn't been home at all

Suspect: Diane; **Likelihood of Guilt:** could be guilty; might not be guilty **Evidence:** she once ate a whole chocolate cake; her mom was with her the whole afternoon

The thief must have been Dad

Unit 17

UNIT OVERVIEW

Hypothetical meaning often causes difficulty for students (Ss) from non-Indo-European language backgrounds. The forms are relatively straightforward, and speakers of French, Spanish, or Persian should have no difficulty understanding the basic concept. However, speakers of Chinese, Indonesian, and many other languages do not have the same notions of hypothetical meaning in their own languages, and so therefore often find the meaning and use extremely difficult, even if their control of the forms is relatively accurate. Since hypothetical speech is extremely common in English, used for strategies of politeness, indirection and to indicate imaginary or hypothetical ideas, it is important that Ss master the fundamental meaning and use dimensions as well as just the formal "contrary-to-fact" manipulations taught in most grammar texts. See *The Grammar Book,* pp. 548, 551, 555–556 for additional discussion.

UNIT GOALS

Review the goals listed on this page so Ss understand what they should be able to do by the end of the unit.

OPENING TASK

This task provides an opportunity for an important cross-cultural discussion, but if you are teaching overseas, it may have less relevance for your Ss. For such classes, substitute Activity 3.

UNIT 17

HYPOTHETICAL STATEMENTS

UNIT GOALS:

- To correctly identify and understand sentences describing hypothetical or contrary-to-fact situations
- To correctly form hypothetical and contrary-to-fact statements in present, future, and past time frames
- To recognize and use various hypothetical constructions

▶ OPENING TASK
Differences in Educational Values

STEP 1 What are some important differences between educational values in the United States and in other countries? Here is a list of possible ways that teachers and students might behave. Think about the result of these behaviors in the United States and in your own country. Use the chart below to organize your ideas.

Situation	Result in USA	Result in the country you come from
Teacher Behavior: sitting on a desk		
wearing jeans to school		
saying "I don't know"		
making a lot of jokes in class		
hitting a student		
making a mistake		
not giving students homework		
Student Behavior: coming late to class		
asking a question		
making jokes in class		
not doing homework		
copying another student's answers		
making a mistake		

STEP 2 Explain your ideas to a group of three or four other students. (For example: In the United States if a student came late to class, the teacher would probably be annoyed. In Indonesia if a teacher said "I don't know," the students might think she was a bad teacher.) Compare the differences between what is expected of teachers and students in the United States and in other countries. Decide on the one or two important differences between the United States' educational system and the systems of other countries you are familiar with.

There are a variety of ways to do this task in addition to the ways outlined in the student book.

1. Focus on the content of the discussion, and do this as a class. Identify at least three or four generalizations about American cultural assumptions that your Ss should be explicitly aware of (such as, expectations that Ss will take individual initiative, that teachers strive for an informal, nonhierarchical relationship with Ss, etc.).

2. Use this task to check your Ss' ability to use hypothetical meaning in this exercise by seeing whether they frame their responses in hypothetical or nonhypothetical speech. Do Step 1 in pairs or small groups. Circulate around the class and listen in on different groups.

3. If you are pressed for time, skip this task and have Ss do Exercise 1 in pairs. Most Ss will have difficulty deciding on the correct answers initially, so you should review the exercise again after the material in the unit has been presented and practiced.

How you present the information in this unit and how much detail you need depends on your Ss' backgrounds. See the Unit Overview for an explanation of why this unit may be extremely challenging for some Ss and relatively easy for others.

1. If your class has Indo-European language speakers, start by asking them about "subjunctive" (most Ss have heard this term), and explain that this unit deals with how we use subjunctive in English.
2. This approach will not work for non-Indo-European language speakers. For them, start by explaining that in English we must make a special distinction about sentences that are not true or that are imaginary.
3. Then, for both sets of Ss, examine the examples of hypothetical meaning and their implied actual meaning in the focus boxes on this page.

V A R I A T I O N :

1. Write some class-related examples on the board. *If Nita came to class on time I would be amazed. If Joaquin didn't bring his homework to class, I would know that there was something wrong.*
2. Then ask nonhypothetical processing questions to the whole class: *"Did Joaquin bring his homework? Of course! Am I surprised? No! Is there something wrong? No!"* etc.

Exercise 1

Integrate this exercise into your presentation of Focus 1 for additional examples of hypothetical statements and their implied actual meaning. Additional examples in the workbook are also useful.

Overview of Hypothetical Meaning

There is an important difference between **hypothetical** and **actual** meaning.

HYPOTHETICAL STATEMENTS	IMPLIED ACTUAL MEANING	EXPLANATIONS
(a) If I had a million dollars, I would buy a nice house.	I don't have a million dollars, so I probably won't be able to buy a nice house.	Hypothetical statements describe conditions that aren't true or are impossible.
(b) If we were in Hawaii right now, we wouldn't have to study grammar. We could by lying on the beach.	We're not in Hawaii—we're in English class. We can't lie on the beach because we're studying grammar.	
(c) You should be happy with your life. If I were you, I wouldn't feel so sorry for myself!	You aren't happy with your life. I am not you, but I think you feel too sorry for yourself.	We use hypothetical statements to imply that the opposite situation is actually true.
(d) You could have done a better job on your homework. You should have avoided a lot of these careless mistakes.	You didn't do a very good job on your homework. You made a lot of careless mistakes.	

EXERCISE 1

Here are some more hypothetical statements. Choose the sentence that expresses their implied meaning:

1. If you had done your homework, you would have gotten an A.
   (a) You didn't get an A because you didn't do your homework.
   (b) You did your homework, so you got an A.
2. You could have brought a friend to the party.
   (a) You had permission, but you came alone.
   (b) You brought a friend.

Exercise 1
1. (a)   2. (a)   3. (b)   4. (b)   5. (b)
6. (a)   7. (a)

3. You could have been more careful with your homework.

    (a) You did your homework carefully.

    (b) You were careless with your homework.

4. You should have seen the doctor before you got so sick.

    (a) You followed my advice.

    (b) You didn't follow my advice.

5. I would have been here early, but the traffic was terrible!

    (a) I arrived early.

    (b) I arrived late.

6. I wish you had come to the lake last weekend.

    (a) You didn't come.

    (b) You were there.

7. Let's pretend that we had a new president.

    (a) We don't have a new president.

    (b) We have a new president.

SUGGESTIONS:

1. Do the questions one by one as a whole class.

2. Alternatively, pair students from Indo-European language backgrounds with those from non-Indo-European backgrounds to make initial choices, but still process as a whole class.

3. If you use this exercise as an attention focus instead of the Opening Task, review this exercise again after the material in the unit has been presented and practiced.

Workbook Ex. 1, p. 116. Answers: TE p. 503.

Use Focus 2 to continue reinforcing the difference between hypothetical and nonhypothetical meaning. Present the sentences in contrastive hypothetical/non hypothetical pairs (a & b, c & d, e & f) or elicit class-related examples like those suggested for Focus 1.

For example: *Do we have time for a review before the test? No. Is everybody nervous about the test? Yes! If we had time for a review before the test everybody wouldn't be nervous.*

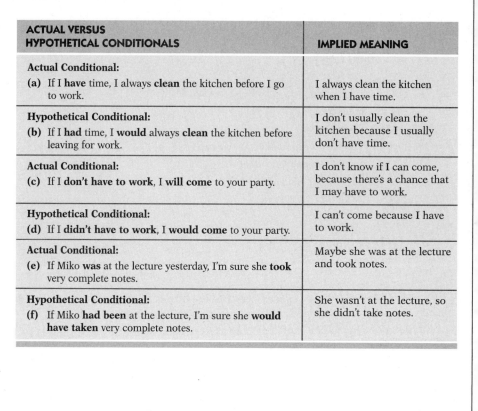

FOCUS **2**

Actual Versus Hypothetical Conditionals

ACTUAL VERSUS HYPOTHETICAL CONDITIONALS	IMPLIED MEANING
Actual Conditional: (a) If I **have** time, I always **clean** the kitchen before I go to work.	I always clean the kitchen when I have time.
Hypothetical Conditional: (b) If I **had** time, I **would** always **clean** the kitchen before leaving for work.	I don't usually clean the kitchen because I usually don't have time.
Actual Conditional: (c) If I **don't have to work**, I **will come** to your party.	I don't know if I can come, because there's a chance that I may have to work.
Hypothetical Conditional: (d) If I **didn't have to work**, I **would come** to your party.	I can't come because I have to work.
Actual Conditional: (e) If Miko **was** at the lecture yesterday, I'm sure she **took** very complete notes.	Maybe she was at the lecture and took notes.
Hypothetical Conditional: (f) If Miko **had been** at the lecture, I'm sure she **would have taken** very complete notes.	She wasn't at the lecture, so she didn't take notes.

EXERCISE 2

Match the statements in column 1 with their correct implied meaning in column 2.

STATEMENT

1. If John has the money, he always stops for a cup of coffee on his way to class.
2. If John had the money, he would always stop for a cup of coffee on his way to class.
3. If I had to work, I wouldn't be helping you with your homework.
4. If I have to work, I won't be able to help you with your homework.
5. If Bambang took the TOEFL yesterday, I'm sure he did very well.
6. If Bambang had taken the TOEFL, I'm sure he would have done very well.

IMPLIED MEANING

(a) He doesn't usually do this, because he usually doesn't have the money.
(b) He always does this whenever he has the money.
(c) I may have to work.
(d) I don't have to work.

(e) Bambang didn't take the TOEFL.
(f) Maybe Bambang took the TOEFL.

EXERCISE 3

Are these sentences hypothetical statements or statements about actual events? If they are hypothetical statements, state the implied meaning.

▶ **EXAMPLES:** Those two are always together, so if she attended the meeting, he did, too. **statement about an actual event**

If the weather hadn't been so cold yesterday, the picnic would have been a lot more fun. **hypothetical statement. Implied meaning: The weather was cold yesterday, so the picnic wasn't much fun.**

1. I would come to your party if I didn't have to work.
2. If Juan went to Hawaii on vacation, he must have spent a lot of money.
3. If Nancy could afford to retire, I'm sure she would have done so by now.
4. I wouldn't tease that dog if I were you.
5. Suppose you had your own private jet. You could take me to Las Vegas for lunch.
6. If they left when they had planned, they should be here any minute.
7. If my brother needed money, he always asked to borrow it from me.
8. If I cook a big casserole for the party, do you think there'll be enough food?

Exercises 2 & 3

These exercises provide additional practice with correctly interpreting hypothetical meaning. Work through them systematically, if your class is very advanced or, demonstrates that these concepts present no great challenge, move ahead to the more "productive" exercises (5–8) that follow Focus 3.

Workbook Exs. 2 & 3, pp. 117–118. Answers: TE p. 503.

ANSWER KEY

Exercise 2
1. (b)   2. (a)   3. (d)   4. (c)   5. (f)
6. (e)

Exercise 3
1. *hypothetical;* I can't come to your party because I have to work.   2. *prediction about a real event*   3. *hypothetical;* Nancy can't afford to retire, so she hasn't done so by now.
4. *hypothetical;* Its not a good idea to tease that dog!   5. *hypothetical;* I know you don't have your own jet, but let's imagine that we do. In our imaginations, we can go to Las Vegas for lunch. (*Notice that it's difficult to think of a way to restate this idea in nonhypothetical speech. That's how "ingrained" the pattern is in English.*)   6. *prediction about an actual event*
7. *statement about a recurring situation in the past*   8. *prediction about an actual event*

1. If your class is not having trouble with these concepts, you can combine your presentation of this focus with Focus 2. Use the examples from Focus 2 that you selected and underline the relevant features (past tense in the *if*-clause, *could/would* + *verb* in the result clause).

2. If your class needs more practice with hypothetical meaning, generate your examples following the same procedure that was suggested for Focus 2.

3. For both kinds of Ss, identify the relevant features (past tense in the *if*-clause, *could/would* + *verb* in the result clause) before moving on to the use of *were* and inverted hypotheticals. Substitute class-related examples for these sentences, or use the ones in the book.

Additional examples: *If today were Friday, we would have a quiz. Were today Friday, we would have a quiz.*

Hypothetical Conditionals in Present and Future Time Frames

EXAMPLES		EXPLANATIONS
Conditions	Results	
(a) If I **had** time,	I **would** always **clean** the kitchen before leaving for work.	Use past-tense verb forms to describe present and future hypothetical conditions. Use *would/could/might* + verb to describe present and future results.
(b) If I **didn't have to work,**	I **would come** to your party.	
(c) If I **won** the lottery,	I **would give** you a million dollars.	
(d) If I already **spoke** English perfectly,	I **wouldn't need** to read this chapter.	
(e) If we **didn't have to go** to school tomorrow,	we **could stay up** all night tonight.	
(f) If John **didn't plan to spend** next year in France,	Mary **might not be** so annoyed with him now.	

Using *were* in hypothetical statements

EXAMPLES		EXPLANATIONS
(g) If my mother **were** here, she would want us all to wash our hands.	**(h)** If Mary **were** coming to the party, she could bring the potato salad.	*If* clauses in hypothetical conditionals use *were* (rather than *was*) for singular subjects in formal English. *Was* is often used in informal situations.

Inverted Hypotheticals

EXAMPLES		EXPLANATIONS
Inverted Form	Regular Form	
(i) **Were** I in charge of this business, I would make big changes.	(j) **If I were** in charge of this business, I would make big changes.	In formal English, in clauses with a *were* auxiliary, we can indicate hypothetical conditions by omitting *if* and using question word or inverted order.

EXERCISE 4

Change these statements of actual condition and result into hypothetical conditionals.

▶ **EXAMPLE:** Actual: (Condition:) I'm not the teacher. (Result:) We have too much homework.

Hypothetical: *If I were the teacher, we wouldn't have so much homework.*

1. I don't have a million dollars. I can't afford to buy you a new car.
2. I don't yet speak English perfectly. I still have to study grammar.
3. Doctors have to spend so many years in medical school. Medical care is quite expensive.
4. My mother doesn't know how I am living now. She's not worried about me.
5. I am not president of my country. I don't have influence on world events.
6. I have many good friends. My life is busy and rewarding.
7. The TOEFL is a difficult examination. Many people can't pass it on the first try.
8. There aren't enough places in universities in other countries. Many students come to North America for university study.

EXERCISE 5

Here are some hypothetical conditions. Add hypothetical results that are true for you.

▶ **EXAMPLE:** If I could be anywhere in the world at this moment, . . .

I would be home in bed.

1. If I were going to attend any American university tomorrow, . . .
2. If I were president of the United States, . . .

Hypothetical Statements **277**

Exercise 4

Have Ss write their answers individually (as homework or in class) and then compare them to a partner's.

V A R I A T I O N :

Shorten time needed for in-class composition by assigning each Ss only two or three to work on and then process as a whole class.

Exercise 5

S U G G E S T I O N S :

1. Have Ss write their answers individually as homework.
2. If Ss have trouble coming up with creative answers, have them develop answers in pairs.
3. To shorten the time needed for the pair work option assign each pair only one or two to work on and then process as a whole class.
4. Do in pairs as structured conversation practice.

A N S W E R   K E Y

Exercise 4

There may be slight variations in phrasing, but the basic meaning should be as follows:
1. If I had a million dollars, I could afford to buy you a new car.   2. If I spoke English perfectly, I wouldn't have to study grammar.   3. If doctors didn't have to spend so many years in medical school, medical care wouldn't be so expensive.
4. If my mother knew how I am living now, she would worry about me.   5. If I were president of my country, I would have a lot of influence on world events.   6. If I didn't have many good friends, my life would be dull and frustrating.
7. If the TOEFL Test weren't a difficult examination, many people could pass it on the first try.   8. If there were enough places in universities in other countries, many students wouldn't come to the United States for university study.

Exercise 5

Answers will vary. Possible answers include:
1. I would be happy.   2. I would reduce military spending.   3. She would worry about whether I was getting enough to eat.   4. I would never give homework.   5. I wouldn't be studying in this class.   6. I would bring everyone in my family a present.   7. I wouldn't have to find a part-time job.   8. I would probably have a child.

3. If my teacher knew how I was studying now, . . .

4. If I were the teacher of this class, . . .

5. If I didn't have to worry about the TOEFL, . . .

6. If I went home next week, . . .

7. If I had all the money I needed, . . .

8. If I were the same age as my parents, . . .

Exercise 6

Follow the same procedures you used for Exercise 5. Use structured conversation practice in pairs or small groups.

EXERCISE 6

Here are some hypothetical conditions. Add hypothetical results that are true for you.

▶ **EXAMPLE:** I would take a vacation . . .

if I *didn't have to pass the TOEFL.*

1. I wouldn't need to work . . .

2. I would bring my family here for a visit . . .

3. We wouldn't come to school . . .

4. We wouldn't need umbrellas . . .

5. I wouldn't be studying English . . .

6. I wouldn't have to take the TOEFL . . .

7. The world would be a much better place . . .

8. I would give my English teacher a thousand dollars . . .

Exercises 7 & 8

If you need time, omit these pair work exercises.

Workbook Exs. 4 & 5, pp. 118–119, Answers: TE p. 503.

EXERCISE 7

Work with a partner. Choose five sentences that your partner wrote for Exercises 5 and 6 and rewrite them in nonhypothetical language.

▶ **EXAMPLES:** If I had a million dollars, I would give you a new car.

My partner *doesn't have enough money to give me a car.*

I would take a vacation if I di'nt have to finish this project.

My partner *has to finish this project, so she can't take a vacation.*

My partner *can't tke a vacation because she has to finish this project.*

EXERCISE 8

Look over the sentences that you and your partner wrote in Exercises 5 and 6. Which sentences can be rewritten as inverted hypotheticals?

FOCUS

Hypothetical Conditionals in Past Time Frame

EXAMPLES		EXPLANATIONS
Conditions	Results	
(a) If Miko **had been** at the lecture,	I'm sure she **would have taken** very complete notes. She **wouldn't have minded** sharing them. She **would have let** you borrow them.	Use past-perfect verb forms to refer to past hypothetical conditions. Use *would have/could have/might have* + verb to refer to past hypothetical results.
(b) If William the Conqueror **hadn't invaded** England in 1066,	the English language **would probably have** many fewer words of French origin.	Use *would/could/ might* + verb to refer to present or future hypothetical results.
(c) If I **had been born** in 1890,	I surely **wouldn't be** alive today.	
(d) If we **hadn't saved** enough money last year,	we **wouldn't be able to take** a vacation next summer.	

Inverted Hypotheticals

EXAMPLES		EXPLANATION
INVERTED FORM	REGULAR FORM	
(e) **Had I known** that you were coming so late, I wouln't have waited.	**(f)** **If I had known** that you were coming so late, I wouldn't have waited.	In formal English, in clauses with a *had* auxiliary, we can indicate hypothetical conditions by omitting *if* and using question word or inverted order.

Hypothetical Statements **279**

1. Use the examples (or similar sentences) from Focus 3 that you selected and provide a context concerning past time. For example: *"Let's pretend that it's last week that we're talking about."* Explain that since hypothetical statements for present and future time use past tense forms and past modals, that when we talk about past time frame we have to make the forms even "more" past (past perfect tense in the *if*-clause, *could have/ would have* + *verb* in the result clause).
2. Underline the relevant features in your past time example.
3. Repeat the process by eliciting another class-related example in present time, which you then transform to past time. **Additional examples:** *If today were Friday, we would have a quiz. If yesterday had been Friday, we would have had a quiz.*
4. Present inverted hypotheticals with a related example: *Had yesterday been Friday, we would have had a quiz.*

Exercise 9

Do this as a whole class. Have Ss read all six sentences before deciding. In processing their choices, identify the additional information that helps Ss decide the meaning (for example: #1 *He's too cheap.* #5 *It's pretty careless.* # 6 *It's unlocked.*)

Exercise 10

Have Ss write their answers individually as homework. To shorten the time needed for in-class writing, assign each student or pair only one or two to work on and then process as a whole class.

EXERCISE 9

Do these sentences indicate statements of past possibility, or hypothetical events that did not actually happen?

▶ **EXAMPLES:**   I didn't see him, but he could have been there. *past possibility*

   If John had been at the concert, he would have been able to explain how the composer was able to get those effects. *hypothetical event.*

1. My brother could have loaned me the money, but he's too cheap.

2. Assuming that the plane was on time, it should have landed a little while ago.

3. I don't know what the problem is. They should have been here by now.

4. You should have asked for a receipt when you bought those clothes.

5. Tiffany might have worked a little harder on this report. It's pretty careless.

6. The thief might have gotten in through the window. It's unlocked.

EXERCISE 10

Change these nonhypothetical statements of condition and result to hypothetical conditionals.

▶ **EXAMPLE:**   I wasn't alive one hundred years ago. I have been able to fly all over the world.

   If I had been alive one hundred years ago, I wouldn't have been able to fly all over the world.

1. My parents didn't speak English when I was a baby. I have to learn it in school.

2. English became a language of international business after World War II. Most developing countries require students to study it in high school.

3. Modern English developed from several different languages: French, German, Latin, Dutch, and even Norwegian. As a result, the grammar and spelling rules are very irregular.

4. England was invaded by France in 1066. Many French words replaced the traditional Anglo-Saxon ones.

5. English society changed a great deal after the French invasion. Modern English grammar is more similar to French grammar than to German grammar.

ANSWER KEY

Exercise 9
1. hypothetical event   2. past possibility
3. hypothetical event   4. hypothetical event
5. hypothetical event   6. past possibility

Exercise 10
1. If my parents had spoken English when I was a baby, I wouldn't have had to learn it in school.
2. If English hadn't become a language of international business after World War II, most developing countries wouldn't require students to study it in high school.   3. If modern English hadn't developed from several different languages: French, German, Latin, Dutch, and even Norwegian, the grammar and spelling rules would have been less irregular.   4. If England hadn't been invaded by France in 1066, many French words would not have replaced the traditional Anglo-Saxon ones.
5. If English society hadn't changed a great deal after the French invasion, modern English grammar would be less similar to French grammar than to German grammar.

EXERCISE 11

Complete these sentences with past-time hypothetical results that are true for you.

▶ **EXAMPLE:** If I had been born one hundred years ago, . . .

     I wouldn't have had a chance to travel.

1. If my family had used English at home when I was growing up, . . .
2. If World War II had ended differently, . . .
3. If the grammar of English hadn't developed from so many different languages, . . .
4. If advanced computer technology hadn't been developed, . . .
5. If I had never studied English, . . .

EXERCISE 12

Add present or future time results to the following sentences.

▶ **EXAMPLES:** If I had been born one hundred years ago, . . .

     I probably wouldn't be alive today.

     my great-grandchildren might be entering the univerity in the next few years.

1. If I had been born in this country, . . .
2. If World War II hadn't ended over fifty years ago, . . .
3. If my parents hadn't wanted me to learn English, . . .
4. If computers hadn't become so inexpensive and widely available, . . .
5. If I had already gotten a score of 650 on the TOEFL, . . .

EXERCISE 13

Here are hypothetical results. Add appropriate past-time conditions.

▶ **EXAMPLE:** I wouldn't have had a chance to travel . . .

     if I had been born one hundred years ago.

1. I wouldn't have asked you to join us . . .
2. I would not be studying English now . . .
3. English grammar would be much more regular . . .
4. Fax machines wouldn't be so popular . . .

Hypothetical Statements   **281**

Exercises 11–13

S U G G E S T I O N S :

1. Have Ss write their answers individually as homework.
2. If Ss have trouble coming up with creative answers, have them develop answers in pairs.
3. To shorten the time needed for the pair work option, assign each pair only one or two to work on and then process as a whole class.
4. Do these exercises in pairs or small groups as structured conversation practice.

A N S W E R   K E Y

Exercise 11

Answers will vary. Possible answers include:
1. I wouldn't have had to study it in high school. 2. The history of the twentieth century would have been very different. 3. the verb system would have been easier to learn. 4. companies like IBM or Microsoft would never have gotten so big. 5. I wouldn't have had to buy this book.

Exercise 12

Answers will vary. Possible answers include:
1. I wouldn't be studying English. 2. there wouldn't yet be such a high level of prosperity in Europe. 3. I wouldn't have come to America. 4. life wouldn't be as convenient as it is. 5. I wouldn't be in this class.

Exercise 13

Answers will vary. Possible answers include:
1. if I hadn't wanted you to be here. 2. if it hadn't been required for my education. 3. if the language hadn't developed from so many different languages. 4. if they hadn't become so inexpensive and easily available. 5. if I had been elected president. 6. if communications satellites hadn't been put into orbit. 7. if the USSR hadn't collapsed 8. if scientists hadn't first developed penicillin. 9. if progress hadn't been made in most technological areas. 10. if I had stayed home and not come to class.

5. America wouldn't be spending so much money on the military . . .

6. Transoceanic telephone calls wouldn't be possible . . .

7. There wouldn't have been such major political changes in Eastern European countries . . .

8. Modern antibiotics might not have been discovered . . .

9. Life today would be much more difficult . . .

10. I wouldn't have to answer this question . . .

Exercises 14 & 15

If you need time, omit these pair work exercises.

Workbook Exs. 6 & 7, pp. 119–121. Answers: TE p. 503.

EXERCISE 14

Look over the sentences that you and your partner wrote in Exercises 11, 12, and 13. Choose five sentences to rewrite as inverted hypotheticals.

EXERCISE 15

Work with a partner. Choose five sentences that your partner wrote for Exercises 11, 12, and 13 and rewrite them in nonhypothetical language.

▶ **EXAMPLES:** I wouldn't have asked you to join us, if I had known you were going to be so rude.

I asked you to come because I thought you would be more polite.

If I had been born one hundred years ago, I wouldn't have had a chance to travel widely.

A hundred years ago people like me didn't have a chance to travel widely.

ANSWER KEY

Exercises 14 and 15
Answers will vary.

FOCUS **5**

▶ **Mixing Hypothetical and Actual Statements**

USE

We sometimes mix actual conditions and hypothetical results.

ACTUAL CONDITION	HYPOTHETICAL RESULT
(a) I had to work last night.	**Otherwise** I would have come to your party.
(b) Peter brought a doctor's excuse to explain his absence.	**Otherwise** Denise would have accused him of being irresponsible.
(c) It's going to rain tomorrow.	**Otherwise** we could have the luncheon outside.

HYPOTHETICAL RESULT	ACTUAL CONDITION
(d) I would have come to your party last night,	**but** I had to work.
(e) Denise would have accused Peter of being irresponsible,	**but** he brought a doctor's excuse to explain his absence.
(f) We could have the luncheon outside,	**but** it's going to rain tomorrow.

EXERCISE 16

Here are some actual conditions. State a hypothetical result by using *otherwise* or *but*.

▶ **EXAMPLE:** I'm not rich.

I'm not rich. Otherwise I would loan you the money you asked for.

I would loan you the money you asked for, but I'm not rich.

1. I don't have a million dollars.
2. I don't yet speak English perfectly.
3. Doctors have to spend many years in medical school.
4. My mother doesn't know how I am living now.
5. My father is not the leader of my country.
6. I have many good friends.
7. Many students come to the United States for university study.
8. The weather forecaster has predicted heavy rain for tomorrow afternoon.

Hypothetical Statements | **283**

FOCUS 5

1. Present this focus in a straightforward manner by leading Ss through the sentences in the book or by "transforming" a class-related example hypothetical conditional into the two mixed variants.
   For example: *If today were Friday, we would have a quiz. Today isn't Friday. Otherwise we would have a quiz. We would have a quiz, but today isn't Friday.*
2. For extra practice use some past time frame examples as well.
   For example: *If the weather had been like last month, we would have canceled class because of the big snowstorm. The weather isn't like last month. Otherwise we would have canceled class. We would have canceled class, but the weather isn't like last month.*

Exercise 16

Do this exercise as part of (or as an immediate follow-up to) your presentation of Focus 5.

1. Having presented some examples on the board, write up these cues and have one student complete the sentence with an *otherwise* sentence.
2. Have another student transform the first S's response using *but*.

Workbook Ex. 8, pp. 121–122. Answers: TE p. 503.

Focuses 6, 7, and 8 deal with additional uses of hypothetical statements. You may decide to skip them unless your class is advanced and ready for these other uses.

VARIATIONS:

1. These focuses work well as self-study activities assigned for homework to be followed up by class processing through discussion of the related exercises.
2. Have Ss work in groups of three, with each student assigned a particular focus to read, internalize, and then explain to the other Ss in his or her group. Walk around the room as the groups are working and assist those who need it, or monitor and clarify Ss' explanations as needed. Follow up with a brief final whole class discussion like: *"Why do we use hypothetical?"*
   - To indicate things that are not true/contrary to fact
   - To discuss unlikely possibilities
   - To discuss sensitive topics
   - To imply **the opposite.**

Additional examples:

unlikely possibilities: *If everybody understood this unit completely, we might be able to have a movie instead of a quiz.*

sensitive topics: *Would you ever change your religion?* See Activity 5 for more

---

Using Hypotheticals for Unlikely Possibility and for Sensitive Topics

Use hypothetical statements to indicate unlikely possibilities.

STATEMENT	IMPLIED MEANING
Likely Possibility (Nonhypothetical) (a) If we **get** some free time, we **can go** to the movies.	There is a strong possibility that we may get free time.
Unlikely Possibility (Hypothetical) (b) If we **got** some free time, this weekend, we **could go** to the movies. (c) If I **had** free time, I **would go** to the movies.	The possibility of free time is not strong, but we are discussing it anyway. There is no possibility of free time, but this is what would happen if there were a possibility.

Use hypothetical statements to discuss potentially "sensitive" topics more easily and diplomatically.

STATEMENT	IMPLIED MEANING	EXPLANATION
Nonhypothetical (d) **Will** you ever leave your husband?	I think you might do this.	
Hypothetical (e) **Would** you ever leave your husband?	This is not a real situation, just an example. I don't really think that you would do this.	Using hypothetical indicates that the speaker does not believe the listener would actually consider doing the thing being discussed.

EXERCISE 17

Decide whether these statements are likely or unlikely possibilities for you, then make a hypothetical or nonhypothetical sentence that reflects that.

▶ **EXAMPLE:** marry someone from another country

(likely possibility)—something that might actually be possible for me

If I marry someone from another country, I will probably become a citizen of that country.

(unlikely possibility)—something that I don't think will ever be possible for me

If I married someone from another country, my parents would be very disappointed.

1. go to Las Vegas for the next vacation
2. pass the TOEFL the next time I take it
3. become president of your country
4. have eight children
5. buy a new car within the next three months
6. join the army
7. get sick later today
8. look for a new place to live
9. have free time before class tomorrow
10. win the lottery
11. be on television sometime in my life

Hypothetical Statements | **285**

sensitive topics.

Exercise 17

VARIATION:

This exercise also works well as a paired discussion activity.

1. Have Ss discuss how possible these situations are for them.
2. Have Ss work together to construct sentences where there is a contrast between their individual lives.

Workbook Ex. 9, pp. 122–123. Answers: TE p. 504.

ANSWER KEY

Exercise 17

Answers will vary. Possible answers include:
1. Real possibility: If I go to Las Vegas for the next vacation, I'll be sure to bring you a present when I come back. Theoretical possibility: If I went to Las Vegas for the next vacation, that would mean that I had already been admitted to the university.   2. Real possibility: If I pass the TOEFL the next time I take it, I will begin my university studies right away. Theoretical possibility: If I passed the TOEFL the next time I took it, I would be the happiest person in the world.   3. This is probably a theoretical possibility for all your students. If I became

president of my country, I would make my grammar teacher the minister of education.
4. Real possibility: If I have eight children, I will probably need to have two jobs to earn enough money. Theoretical possibility: If I had eight children, my family would be very happy.
5. Real possibility: If I buy a new car within the next three months, I will have to renew my driver's license. Theoretical possibility: If I bought a new car in the next three months, I would need to get automobile insurance.
6. Real possibility: If I join the army, I hope I won't have to fight any battles. Theoretical possibility: If I joined the army, I would be the

oldest recruit in boot camp.   7. Real possibility: If I get sick later today, I won't come to class tomorrow. Theoretical possibility: If I got sick later today, I would know that this tuna sandwich has been sitting in the sun too long.
8. Real possibility: If I look for a new place to live, I will consider living with a roommate. Theoretical possibility: If I looked for a new place to live, I would start by checking the newspaper want ads.   9. Real possibility: If I have free time before class tomorrow, I'll write a letter to my parents. Theoretical possibility: If I had free time before class tomorrow, I wouldn't have to do my homework tonight.

See the general comments regarding this focus in the suggestions for Focus 6. Be sure to point out the use of past modals (*could have*, *might have*, *should have*) to communicate the implication of an opposite reality.

Additional examples: *You <u>could have</u> <u>brought</u> your teacher a present. You <u>might have paid</u> better attention to my explanation.*

Exercise 18

This exercise works well as an extension of your presentation of Focus 7. Treat this as a comprehension check of your discussion of the sample sentences.

Workbook Ex. 10, p. 123. Answers: TE p. 504.

▶ **U**sing Hypotheticals to Imply that the Opposite Is True

Use hypothetical statements to talk about things that didn't actually happen.

STATEMENT	IMPLIED MEANINGS
(a) You could have brought a friend.	You had permission, but you came alone.
(b) You could have been more careful with your homework.	You had the ability to be careful, but you didn't do it.
(c) You should have seen the doctor.	You didn't see the doctor.
(d) You might have cleaned the house before my mother got here.	The house was still dirty when she arrived.

EXERCISE 18
Restate these sentences in nonhypothetical language. Compare your answers with those of a partner.

▶ **EXAMPLE:** You should have been there.

　　　　　You weren't there.

1. You shouldn't have gone to so much trouble!
2. We could have been seriously injured in that bus accident.
3. You might at least have invited her to the party.
4. You should be happy that I was able to come at all.
5. She wouldn't have gone even if she had been invited.

286 UNIT 17

ANSWER KEY

Exercise 18
Answers will vary. Possible answers include:
1. You went to too much trouble. 2. It's lucky that we didn't get hurt in that bus accident. 3. Why didn't you invite her to the party? 4. Why aren't you happy that I'm here? 5. It doesn't matter that you didn't invite her.

▶ **U**sing Hypotheticals
with *Wish* and Verbs
of Imagination

We use hypothetical statements with *wish* to talk about situations that are not
true or not likely to become true.

STATEMENT	IMPLIED MEANING
(a) I **wish** you **had come** to the lake last weekend.	You didn't come.
(b) I **wish** you **liked** Chinese food.	You don't like it.
(c) I **wish** you **would come** to my party.	You refuse to come.

We use hypothetical statements with verbs that indicate imagination.

STATEMENT	IMPLIED MEANING
(d) **Let's imagine** that we **had** a new president.	We know this is not a real possibility.
(e) **Pretend** that you **could** fly. Do you think you **would** still own a car?	This is an impossible situation.
(f) **Suppose** we **went** to Europe next summer. How much do you think it **would** cost?	We are only talking about it now; we're not making an actual plan.

See the general comments regarding this
focus in the suggestions for Focus 6. Be sure
to point out the use of specific verbs (*wish,
pretend, suppose*) to indicate unreal or
contrary-to-fact situations.
Additional examples: *I wish I were done with
this project. Let's imagine that it was
finished. Suppose I could take the day off
and go out into the sunshine.*

Exercise 19

1. Assign this exercise for homework and process briefly as part of a general review of hypotheticals before beginning the activities.
2. Have Ss read the entire passage first; then, if you have access to an OHP, use a transparency and underline the examples together in class.
3. Assign different groups to rewrite the sentences and write their paraphrases on the board or on their own transparencies.

Workbook Exs. 11 & 12, pp. 123–124.
Answers: TE p. 504.

UNIT GOAL REVIEW

1. If you are teaching in an English-speaking environment, assign Ss to bring to class one example of a hypothetical statement that they have heard someone say in the last 24 hours. Ask Ss to report the statement and correctly interpret it.
2. As you discuss their examples, try to categorize the meaning and use (to imply that the opposite is true, to discuss a sensitive topic, to be more polite). The pattern is so prevalent in English that no one should have trouble finding an example.

VARIATION:

Review some of the more memorable examples Ss have come up with in doing the exercises.

EXERCISE 19

Read the following paragraph. Underline the hypothetical statements. Rewrite the sentences using nonhypothetical language. The first hypothetical statement has been done for you as an example.

▶ **EXAMPLE:** (3) For example, Sir Isaac Newton decided to take a nap under an apple tree, and as a result he was hit on the head by a falling apple.

(1) Many important scientific developments have happened by accident. (2) Discoveries have often been made because someone was in the right place at the right time, or because someone made a mistake and got an unexpected result. (3) For example, <u>if Sir Isaac Newton hadn't decided to take a nap under an apple tree, he wouldn't have been hit on the head by a falling apple.</u> (4) It was this event that gave him the idea about the Law of Gravity. (5) If Sir Alexander Fleming hadn't left a sandwich on a windowsill of his laboratory and forgotten about it, he wouldn't have discovered the fungus or mold that contains penicillin. (6) Had Christopher Columbus correctly calculated the actual size of the earth, he would never have tried to reach Asia by sailing west. (7) If that hadn't happened, the European discovery of the New World might have occurred in 1592, instead of 1492.

Exercise 19

(3) if Sir Isaac Newton hadn't decided to take a nap under an apple tree, he wouldn't have been hit on the head by a falling apple. (5) If Sir Alexander Fleming hadn't left his sandwich sitting on a laboratory window sill and forgotten about it, he wouldn't have discovered the mold that contains penicillin. (7) Had Christopher Columbus correctly calculated the actual size of the earth, he would never have tried to reach

Asia by sailing west. (8) If that hadn't happened, the European discovery of the New World might have occurred in 1592, instead of 1492.

Possible nonhypothetical paraphrases:
(3) For example, Sir Isaac Newton decided to take a nap under an apple tree and was hit on the head by a falling apple. (5) Sir Alexander Fleming left his sandwich sitting on a window sill and forgot about it. That was how he

discovered the mold that contains penicillin. (6) Christopher Columbus incorrectly calculated the actual size of the earth, and therefore tried to reach Asia by sailing west. (7) Because that happened, the European discovery of the New World occurred in 1492, instead of 1592.

Use Your English

ACTIVITY 1: SPEAKING

Should drugs be legalized?

STEP 1 Form a group with three other students in the class to discuss your opinions on these issues:
- What three things might happen if the government legalized the use of drugs?
- What three things might happen if drugs remained illegal?
- Should drugs be legalized? Why or why not?

STEP 2 Based on your discussion, your group should answer these two questions:
- What is the strongest reason in favor of legalization?
- What is the strongest reason against legalization?

Present these reasons to the rest of the class.

ACTIVITY 2: WRITING

Think about some things that you would have done differently if you had known then the things that you know now. Identify:
- Things you wish you had done that you didn't do. For example: *I wish I had studied harder when I was in high school.*
- Things you wish you hadn't done that you did do. For example: *I wish I hadn't spent all my time watching television instead of exercising.*

Write a short essay about this topic or make a presentation to the rest of the class.

ACTIVITY 3: WRITING/SPEAKING

If you could have three wishes, what would they be, and why would you wish for them?

STEP 1 Write down your three wishes.

STEP 2 Compare your answers to those of someone else in class. What do someone else's wishes tell you about his or her life? What do your wishes tell someone else about you?

STEP 3 Make one statement about why you think your partner made the wishes that he or she did. Tell that statement to your partner, but not to the rest of the class.

USE YOUR ENGLISH

Activity 1
EXPANSION:

Turn this activity into an out-of-class contact assignment to poll Americans outside of class. Have Ss use the three questions in Step 1 to interview people and report their findings.

Activity 2

This activity can be used for testing and diagnosis by having Ss write their responses for you to correct.

SUGGESTIONS:

1. Brainstorm some example responses as a whole class before you assign individual writing tasks.
2. Use the paragraphs as opportunities for peer correction. Collect and evaluate both original writing and the corrections for accuracy.

Activity 3
VARIATION:

Use the questions in Step 2 as topics for general whole class discussion after Ss have shared some of their wishes. Omit Step 3.

Activity 4

SUGGESTIONS:

1. For less advanced classes, have Ss explicitly frame their replies in the sentence *"If I were President of the Entire World, I would . . ."*

2. If your class has trouble thinking and expressing creative ideas, have two or three Ss work together in each area.

Activities 5 & 6

These activities can be used for both written and oral practice.

1. For oral practice, assign them as group discussion topics, or do a whole class discussion. Be sure to point out that native speakers would likely use hypothetical statements to discuss the sensitive issues raised in these activities.

2. To save time, omit Step 2 of Activity 6.

ACTIVITY 4: SPEAKING/WRITING

Suppose that you had just been made President of the Entire World. What actions would you take to:

- end world hunger
- develop renewable energy sources
- control population growth
- protect the environment
- abolish war
- ensure political stability
- maintain economic growth

Choose one of these areas and make a plan for things you would do if you had the power and resources to accomplish them. Report your plan to the rest of the class. The class will decide who they would like to choose as President of the Entire World.

ACTIVITY 5: WRITING/SPEAKING

Identify some things you would and wouldn't do for ten million dollars, and compare them to those of other people in class. Ideas to consider: Would you tell a lie? Would you betray a friend? Would you give a child up for adoption? Would you become a citizen of another country? Would you leave your family? What would you refuse to do, even if you were offered ten million dollars?

ACTIVITY 6: SPEAKING

STEP 1 Think about what you would do if you were faced with the following problems.

- Your parents don't approve of the person you want to marry.
- Your friend and you both work at the same company. You feel very loyal to the company, but you discover your friend has stolen some of the company's money.
- You have fallen in love with the husband or wife of your best friend.
- Your best friend needs to borrow some money "for a serious emergency"—but he won't say what that emergency is. You had been planning to use that money to buy a birthday present for your boyfriend or girlfriend. Your friend needs the money right away, and the birthday celebration is also today. You can't get any more money: only what you have now.

STEP 2 Discuss your solutions in a small group. Together decide on one or two suggestions for what people can do if they are faced with any kind of difficult problem.

ACTIVITY 7: LISTENING

Listen to the following conversation between Peter and Denise. Then choose the sentence that correctly describes the situations that they talked about.

1. (a) Peter didn't hear the announcement because he wasn't at the meeting.
   (b) He heard the announcement because he was at the meeting.
2. (a) The meeting wasn't important.
   (b) The meeting was important.
3. (a) Peter thinks Denise did good work.
   (b) He thinks she was careless.
4. (a) Peter finished the project in plenty of time.
   (b) He didn't finish it in plenty of time.
5. (a) Denise told Peter that she hadn't gone over the figures.
   (b) Denise didn't tell Peter that she hadn't gone over the figures.
6. (a) She didn't check the figures.
   (b) Maybe she checked the figures.
7. (a) There were many mistakes.
   (b) There weren't many mistakes.
8. (a) Denise said that she wanted to get Peter fired.
   (b) Denise said that she didn't want to get Peter fired.

ACTIVITY 8: WRITING

Write two to three paragraphs on the differences between what is expected of students in North America and students in another country with which you are familiar. Use your ideas from the Opening Task when they are appropriate.

Play textbook audio. The tapescript for this listening appears on p. 518 of this book.

Allow for multiple listenings of the conversation if necessary.

1. Have Ss listen for the general idea.
2. Have Ss listen for answers to the questions.
3. Have Ss listen for specific information that they still need.
4. Have Ss verify their final answer choices.
5. Go over the answers and replay portions of the tape as needed to settle differences of interpretation.

Activity 8

Although this activity may be more useful for developing cross-cultural awareness than for providing structured practice with hypotheticals, make it more structured by telling Ss to be sure to use hypothetical structures in their writing. Tell Ss to select three behaviors for both teachers and Ss that would definitely <u>not</u> occur in their own countries, and write about what *would happen* if such behaviors *occurred*.

VARIATION:

If you are not teaching in an English-speaking environment, use another activity such as Activity 5 or 6 to generate text-length writing practice.

The test for this unit can be found on p. 472.
The answers are on p. 473 of this book.

ANSWER KEY

Activity 7
1. (a) 2. (b) 3. (b) 4. (b) 5. (b)
6. (b) 7. (a) 8. (b)

Unit 18

UNIT OVERVIEW

This unit examines some "exceptions" to the rules for gerund/infinitive complementation that were presented in Units 6 and 7. You may want to do this unit as an immediate follow-up to those units, since students' attention will still be focused on verb complements. *The Grammar Book* discusses these issues of complementation in Chapter 31 (pp. 629–661).

UNIT GOALS

Review the goals listed on this page so Ss understand what they should be able to by the end of the unit.

UNIT 18

SENSORY VERBS, CAUSATIVE VERBS, AND VERBS THAT TAKE SUBJUNCTIVE

UNIT GOALS:

- To correctly understand and use sentences with sensory verbs
- To correctly understand and use sentences with causative verbs
- To correctly understand and use sentences with verbs followed by subjunctive *that*-clauses

▶ OPENING TASK
Parenting Techniques

STEP 1 Think about the way your parents raised you. How did they reward your good behavior or punish your bad behavior? What kind of responsibilities did they give you? Complete the chart on the next page to identify some of the parenting techniques your parents used. Decide whether their techniques were effective, and whether you would use (or are using) them to raise your own children. Examples have been provided.

Parenting Techniques Your Parents Used	Effective? Yes/No	Would/Do You Use This Technique? Yes/No/Why
Discipline/Punishment 1. sent to my room 2. 3.	1. no 2. 3.	1. No. My children have toys in their rooms so it's not really an effective punishment. 2. 3.
Responsibilities 1. take care of younger sister 2. 3.	1. yes 2. 3.	1. Yes. It was good practice for being a parent myself. 2. 3.
Rewards/Motiviations 1. ice cream and candy 2. 3.	1. yes 2. 3.	1. No. I don't want to use food as a reward for good behavior. 2. 3.

STEP 2 Form a small group with three or four other students, and compare the information you have written in your charts. Based on your discussion, your group should make ten recommendations for parents.

Start five of them with **"Parents should . . ."**

Start five recommendations with **"Parents shouldn't . . ."**

STEP 3 Compare your group's recommendations to those of other groups. Compile a list of recommendations that the entire class agrees upon. Begin your recommendations with **"Good parenting requires that . . ."**

You may want to do this overview as an immediate follow-up to your discussion of gerunds and infinitives, since Ss' attention will still be focused on verb complements. Present these patterns as "exceptions" to the basic infinitive and gerund patterns that you have been studying.

VARIATIONS:

1. Preface this overview with a quick review of the various gerund and infinitive complement patterns. Try reviewing the materials in Appendix 3.
2. If you are pressed for time, skip this overview, or assign it as an end-of-chapter review.

Exercise 1

Make sure Ss read the whole passage before doing the exercise.

SUGGESTIONS:

1. Assign the reading as a follow-up to the Opening Task.
2. If you have access to an OHP, make a transparency of this exercise and underline the complements as part of your whole class processing/correction.

FOCUS **1**

> ## Overview

The verbs that are dealt with in this unit are followed by simple verb forms or present participles that describe a second action.

TYPES OF VERBS	EXAMPLES
Sensory Verbs (*see, hear*, etc.)	(a) I **saw** the mother **spank** her child. (b) I **heard** the child **crying**.
Causative Verbs (*make, let*, etc.)	(c) My parents **made** me **go** to bed at 8:00 on school nights. (d) They **let** me **stay** up late on Fridays and Saturdays.
Subjunctive *That*-Clause Verbs (*demand, recommend*, etc.)	(e) Good parenting **demands that** parents **be** consistent with discipline. (f) Educators **recommend that** a parent **try** to explain the reasons for punishment to children.

EXERCISE 1

Underline the simple verb form or participle that follows the highlighted verbs in the following passage. The first one has been done for you as an example.

Ideas about the best way to raise children differ a great deal from culture to culture. In some cultures, if a mother **hears** her baby crying, she will immediately go to pick it up and **try** to **get** it to stop. But in other cultures people **insist** that a mother ignore her child, because they feel that if you don't **let** a baby cry, it will become spoiled. In some cultures, any adult who **sees** a child misbehaving will **make** the child stop, but other cultures **prefer** that only the parent be allowed to discipline a child. In some cultures, people **have** slightly older children **help** take care of their younger brothers and sisters, but in other cultures people rarely **let** children be responsible for their brothers and sisters unless they are at least twelve or thirteen years old.

In the United States, most parents prefer to **get** a child to behave by persuasion rather than force. You rarely **see** parents spank their children in public, and schools don't usually **let** teachers use physical punishment as discipline. Parents who are **seen** hitting their children may even be reported to the police. American child-care experts **recommend** that children be given responsibility from a relatively early age. As a result, many parents **let** their small children make their own decisions about what kind of clothes they want to wear, or what they want to eat. They prefer to **get** children to obey instead of **making** them obey.

ANSWER KEY

Exercise 1

get it to stop. . . . **insist** that a mother ignore her child, . . . **let** a baby cry, it will become spoiled. . . . **sees** a child misbehaving . . . **make** the child stop, . . . **prefer** that only the parent be allowed to discipline a child. . . . **have** slightly older children **help** take care of their younger brothers and sisters, . . . **let** children be responsible for their brothers and sisters . . . **get** a child to behave . . . **see** parents spank their children . . . **let** teachers use physical punishment . . . **seen** hitting their children . . . **recommend** that children be given responsibility from a relatively early age. . . . **let** their small children make their own decisions . . . **get** children to obey . . . **making** them obey.

▶ **Sensory Verbs**

EXAMPLES	EXPLANATIONS
(a) Mary **heard** us laughing. (b) I **saw** the dog jump into the water.	Sensory verbs use either a **present participle (verb + *ING*)** or the **simple form** of a verb to express the second action. Depending on which is chosen, the meaning differs.
(c) Bob heard the thieves **breaking** into the house, so he called the police. (d) I saw Mary **leaving** school, **so I ran to catch her.** (e) We saw the fireworks **going off** on New Year's Eve. (f) The police watched the demonstrators **overturning trucks** and **setting them** on fire.	Use a Present Participle to describe actions that are: in progress (c) unfinished (d) repeated (e & f)
(g) Bob saw the thieves **load** the TV into the car and **drive** away. (h) I saw Mary **leave** school, so **I'm sure she's not coming to the teachers' meeting.** (i) We saw the fireworks **go off** at midnight. (j) The police watched the demonstrators **overturn a truck** and set **it** on fire.	Use the simple form of a verb to describe actions that are completed (g & h) or happen just once (i & j)
(m) I saw the bicycle **lying** by the side of the road. (n) **NOT:** I saw the bicycle **lie** by the side of the road.	Use present participles with verbs of position (*lie, stand, sit,* etc.), if the thing that performs the second action cannot move by itself.
(o) We **caught** the thief **taking** money out of the cash register. (p) **NOT:** We caught the thief **take** money out of the cash register. (q) We **found** the security guard **sleeping** at his desk. (r) **NOT:** We found the security guard **sleep** at his desk.	Use present participles with verbs of interception (*find, catch, discover,* etc.), where the second action is interrupted or not completed.

FOCUS 2

Using present participles instead of simple verbs conveys the same meanings as progressive aspect (unfinished, in progress, or repeated actions).

1. Present example sentences in contrastive pairs (c & g; d & h; e & i; f & g).
2. Alternatively, use class-related examples such as: *The teacher heard the two students <u>whispering</u> to each other so she told them to stop talking. The teacher heard one student <u>whisper</u> the answer to another student, so she gave them both bad grades on the test.*
3. Present other parts of the focus (participles with verbs of position and interception) after the first basic distinction outlines above have been presented and perhaps practiced. Alternative class-related examples are: *Where's my grade book? I saw it lying here a minute ago. If I catch you copying another student's homework, I will give you an F.*
4. Alternatively, assign this focus for self-study at home after doing Exercises 2–4 in class.

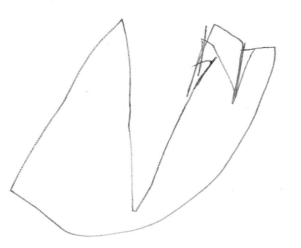

Exercise 2

SUGGESTION:

You can do this exercise more "naturalistically" by having Ss respond with books closed while you ask the class these questions. Elicit multiple responses with cues like "What else can you hear/see?"

Exercise 3

VARIATION:

Shorten this exercise by assigning only one paragraph per Ss or pair/group, according to your preferences.

EXERCISE 2

Answer these questions by using sensory verbs with a second action.

▶ **EXAMPLE:** What can you see at a disco?

You can see people dancing.

1. What can you hear at a concert?
2. What can you see at a skating rink?
3. What can you smell at a bakery?
4. What can you hear at the beach?
5. What can you see at a shopping mall?
6. What can you hear at a playground?
7. What can you hear in an English class?
8. What can you see at a gym?

EXERCISE 3

Restate the lettered sentences in these paragraphs as sensory verbs followed by a participle or simple form of a verb.

▶ **EXAMPLE:** Here is what Tom saw: (a) Three boys were swimming in the river. (b) They were splashing and playing. (c) One of them shouted that it was time to go. (d) They picked up their towels and left.

(a) *Tom saw three boys swimming in the river.* (b) *He watched them splashing and playing.* (c) *He heard one of them shout that it was time to go.* (d) *He watched them pick up their towels and leave.*

1. Here is what Doris observed: (a) A man came into the bank. (b) He got in line. When he reached the teller's window, he handed her a piece of paper and a brown paper bag. (c) The teller was putting money in the bag, when a loud alarm began to ring. (d) Guards rushed in, but the man had escaped through the side entrance.

2. When Mrs. McMartin looked out the window, this is what she saw: (a) There were a few children playing on the swings. (b) Others were climbing on the monkey-bars. (c) One little boy was running very fast around and around the playground. (d) Suddenly he fell down. (e) He screamed in pain. (f) All the other children looked around to see where the noise was coming from. (g) One child ran toward Mrs. McMartin's office.

296 UNIT 18

ANSWER KEY

Exercise 2
Answers will vary. Possible answers include:
1. You can hear musicians play music.
2. You can see people skating. 3. You can smell bread baking. 4. You can hear the waves break. 5. You can see people shopping. 6. You can hear children playing.
7. You can hear people practicing sensory verbs. 8. You can see people lifting weights.

Exercise 3
Answers will vary slightly. These are possible restatements: 1. (a) Doris observed a man come into the bank. (b) She saw him get in

line. (c) When he reached the teller's window, she saw him hand her a piece of paper and a brown paper bag. (d) She observed the teller putting money in the bag, when a loud alarm began to ring. (e) She saw the guards rush in, but the man had escaped through the side entrance. 2. (a) Mrs. McMartin looked out the window and saw a few children playing on the swings. (b) She saw others climbing on the monkey-bars. (c) She watched one little boy running very fast around and around the playground. (d) Suddenly, she saw him fall down. (e) She heard him scream in pain.

(f) She saw all the other children looking around to see where the noise was coming from. (g) She saw one child running toward her office. 3. (a) During the hurricane I hear the wind growing louder. (b) I felt the windows and doors shaking. (c) I saw the trees swaying in the garden outside. (d) I heard a tree crash against the house. (e) I heard the sound of breaking glass upstairs. (f) I saw rain pouring through the broken window. (g) I felt a strong wind blowing into the room. (h) I heard the wind howling louder and louder.

3. Here is what I saw, heard, and felt during the hurricane. (a) The wind grew louder. (b) The windows and doors shook. (c) The trees swayed in the garden outside. I thought the house was moving. (d) A tree crashed against the house. (e) There was a sound of breaking glass upstairs. I went upstairs. (f) Rain was pouring through the broken window. (g) A strong wind blew into the room. (h) The wind howled louder and louder.

EXERCISE 4

Decide on which form of the verb to use, based on the context. In some sentences both forms may be correct.

▶ **EXAMPLE:** I saw smoke (come/ⓒoming) from the storeroom, so I called the fire department.

1. I hear the phone (ring/ringing), but I'm not going to answer it.

2. Brian heard the phone (ring/ringing), but by the time he reached it, the person at the other end had hung up.

3. The principal watched the students (take/taking) the test, so she was sure there had been no cheating.

4. Matt felt himself (get/getting) angry as he and Jeff argued about who should do the dishes.

5. On my way to the store I saw Morris (ride/riding) his new bike.

6. As Mary listened to the radio (play/playing) her favorite song, she began to cry and hurried out of the room.

7. I heard the workers (leave/leaving) earlier today. I'm sure they haven't returned yet.

8. We could all smell something (burn/burning). Apparently somebody had tossed a lighted cigarette into the waste paper basket.

9. As the hurricane grew stronger, they heard many branches of the big oak tree (snap/snapping) and (fall/falling) to the ground.

10. John was relieved when he saw his lost wallet (sit/sitting) next to his checkbook on the shelf.

11. Deborah heard Evan (cry/crying), so she went in to see what was wrong.

12. When we arrived we found the dog (wait/waiting) at the door for us.

Exercise 4

Do this exercise in a "traditional" way: as a whole class, calling on individual Ss to read the sentence and to indicate the correct choice. As with most exercises in this book, be sure to allow opportunity for Ss to volunteer other potentially correct responses as part of your correction process.

Workbook Exs. 2–5, pp. 125–127. Answers: TE p. 504.

ANSWER KEY

Exercise 4

Where both answers are possible, the preferred answer is first:

1. ringing / ring   **2.** ring   **3.** take
4. getting / get   **5.** riding   **6.** playing
7. leave   **8.** burning   **9.** snapping, falling
10. sitting   **11.** crying / cry   **12.** waiting

Present this material in a straightforward manner since the examples in the book also set up some semantic contexts for some of the subsequent exercises and activities.

V A R I A T I O N :

Substitute class-related examples for the ones listed in the focus boxes.
Additional examples: (a) *Teachers should force students to do their homework.* (b) *Teachers should make students do their homework.* (c) *Teachers should get students to read for pleasure.* (d) *Teachers should employ tutors to help students with homework.* (e) *Teachers should have tutors help students with homework.* (f) *Teachers should allow students to talk with each other about anything.* (g) *Teachers should let students talk with each other about anything.* (h) *Teachers should help their students to understand grammar.* (i) *Teachers should help their students understand grammar.*

Exercise 5

Make sure Ss read the whole passage before doing the exercise. This can be assigned as homework or done in class. For in-class correction, if you have access to an OHP, make a transparency of this exercise and circle and underline the elements as directed in the instructions.

FOCUS **3**

Causative Verbs

Many causative verbs are followed by infinitives. But a few common causative verbs (*make, let, have, help*) are followed by the simple form of the verb. Causative verbs show how much force or persuasion is necessary to cause a person to perform an action.

CAUSATIVE VERB + INFINITIVE	CAUSATIVE VERB + SIMPLE FORM OF THE VERB
(a) Parents should **force** naughty children **to stand** in the corner.	(b) Parents should **make** naughty children **stand** in the corner.
(c) Parents should **get** their children **to read** instead of watching TV.	*no synonym for this form*
(d) Parents should **employ or hire** a doctor **to examine** their children at least once a year.	(e) Parents should **have** the doctor **examine** their children at least once a year.
(f) Good parents should **allow** their children **to play** outside on sunny days.	(g) Good parents **let** their children **play** outside on sunny days.
(h) Good parents **help** their children **to learn** good manners.	(i) Good parents **help** their children **learn** good manners. (*help* can occur with either form)

EXERCISE 5

Underline the causative verbs and circle the infinitive or base form of the verb that follows.

(1) Kilroy hated his life in the army from the very first day. (2) When he arrived at Fort Dix for basic training, a drill instructor had him (join) all the other new recruits on the parade ground. (3) The officers made them stand in the hot sun for several hours, while clerks filled out forms. (4) They wouldn't allow the new recruits to joke, or talk to each other, or even to move their

---

A N S W E R   K E Y

Exercise 5

The causative verbs are indicated by boldface and the infinitive or base form of the verb that follows has been underlined.
(2) **had** him join   (3) **made** them stand
(4) **allow** the new recruits to joke, or talk to each other, or even to move their heads.

(5) **had** Army barbers cut their hair
(6) **ordered** Kilroy to report   (7) **had** each man choose a bed.   (8) **let** them put   (9) **helped** the man in the next bunk make his bed, . . . **helped** Kilroy to do the same thing.
(10) **required** the recruits to sweep the floors and clean

---

heads. (5) Then they had Army barbers cut their hair so short that Kilroy felt like he was bald. (6) An officer ordered Kilroy to report to a long building called Barracks B, along with about twenty other men. (7) The sergeant at Barracks B had each man choose a bed. (8) He let them put their personal possessions in lockers next to each bed. (9) Kilroy helped the man in the next bunk make his bed, and that man helped Kilroy to do the same thing. (10) The sergeant then required the recruits to sweep the floors and clean the bathrooms. (11) Kilroy had wanted to join the army to learn how to be a soldier, but now he was beginning to worry that the army would only teach him how to be a janitor.

EXERCISE 6

Decide whether you think the policies suggested below are good ideas or not. Make statements with *should* or *shouldn't*. Then give a reason with *because*.

▶ **EXAMPLE:** Parents should let their kids play actively every day, because vigorous physical exercise is important for growing bodies.

causer	caustive verb	doer of action	action
EXAMPLE: *parents*	*let*	*kids*	*play actively*
1. parents	make	children	go to bed at 6:00
2. teachers	help	students	learn things by themselves
3. police	allow	people	break laws
4. people	have	a dentist	examine their teeth regularly
5. dog owners	let	pets	run around freely
6. a government	require	all citizens	take drug tests
7. a good manager	allow	employees	do whatever they like
8. a good manager	motivate	employees	do their best

EXERCISE 7

Match the verbs listed in Group A with the verbs in Group B which have the same or similar meaning.

Group A		Group B		
let	get	convince	assist	employ
help	make	hire	encourage	force
have		require	permit	allow

Sensory Verbs, Causative Verbs, and Verbs that Take Subjunctive **299**

Exercise 6

This works well as in-class pair or small group discussion. To save time, assign one or two items per each pair/group and then process as a whole class.

Exercise 7

Use as a whole class review or omit if you are pressed for time.

ANSWER KEY

Exercise 6
Answers will vary. Possible answers include:
1. Parents shouldn't make their children go to bed at 6:00, because that's too early.
2. Teachers should help students learn things by themselves, because then they will know how to learn independently.   3. Police shouldn't allow people to break laws, because that will make the society a bad one to live in.
4. People should have a dentist examine their teeth regularly, because that's a good way to prevent tooth decay or gum disease.   5. Dog owners shouldn't let their pets run around freely, because that might annoy people who don't like dogs.   6. A government shouldn't require all citizens to take drug tests, because this violates individual privacy.   7. A good manager shouldn't allow her employees to do whatever they like, because not everyone is a responsible worker.   8. A good manager should motivate his employees to do their best, because that's the best way to get people to do things.

Exercise 7
let—permit, allow; help—assist; have—employ, hire; get—encourage, convince; make—require, force

Exercises 8 & 9

These exercises can also be used for small group or whole class discussions or as structured pair-conversation practice activities.

Workbook Exs. 6 & 7, pp. 128-129. Answers: TE pp. 504-505.

EXERCISE 8

What should a teacher do in order to help students learn to speak English?

Make sentences stating your opinion, using the causative verbs in Focus 3. Be careful to use the right form (infinitive or base form of the verb).

▶ **EXAMPLES:** Teachers should have students do homework every night.

Teachers should help students guess the meaning of unfamiliar vocabulary.

EXERCISE 9

Use this chart to make sentences about what governments should expect citizens to do and what citizens should expect governments to do. Choose three actions from each category and make sentences that express your real opinion. Write two sentences that express your opinion: one with a causative verb followed by a simple verb and one with a verb + infinitive.

▶ **EXAMPLE:** **causer:** government **doer:** citizens **action:** vote in regular elections

Governments should let their citizens vote in regular elections.

Governments should allow their citizens to vote in regular elections.

causer	doer	action
government	citizens	pay taxes read any books and magazines they wish be of service to the nation meet national goals defend the country
citizens	government	be responsive to their wishes work without corruption establish national goals maintain law and order provide for basic defense

ANSWER KEY

Exercise 8

Answers will vary. Possible answers include: Teachers should **have** students do homework every night. Teachers should **help** students guess the meaning of unfamiliar vocabulary. Teachers should **let** students talk about their lives in class. Teachers should **get** the students to talk as much as possible.

Exercise 9

Answers will vary. Possible answers include:
The government should: make citizens pay/require citizens to pay taxes. let them read/allow them to read any books or magazines they wish. get them to be/encourage them to be of service to the nation. help them meet/assist them to meet national goals. have them defend/require them to defend the country.
Citizens should: get the government to be/require the government to be responsive to their wishes. make the government work/require the government to work without corruption. let the government establish/allow the government to establish national goals. have the government maintain/expect the government to maintain law and order. help the government provide/assist the government to provide for basic defense.

FOCUS **4**

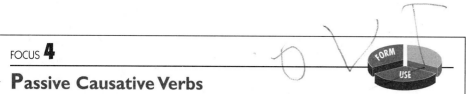

Passive Causative Verbs

The causative verbs *make* and *help* can be made passive, especially when the causer or agent of the action is obvious or not stated, or is a law or an institution. When the verbs *make* and *help* are passive, they must be followed by an infinitive, not the base form of the verb.

PASSIVE CAUSATIVE VERBS	ACTIVE CAUSATIVE VERBS
(a) Children should **be made to brush** their teeth before bedtime.	(b) Parents should **make** their children **brush** their teeth before bedtime.
(c) Children should **be helped to learn** good table manners.	(d) Parents should **help** their children **learn** good table manners.

Other causative verbs (*get, have, let*) cannot appear as passive verbs in causative sentences. If the agent is unknown or unimportant, we must express the passive sentence with another causative verb + infinitive that has the same meaning.

(e)	NOT: Children should **be gotten** to read.	(f)	Children should **be inspired** to read not forced.
(g)	NOT: Teachers should **be had** to teach.	(h)	Teachers should **be employed** to teach, not baby-sit.
(i)	NOT: Children shouldn't **be let** to stay up too late.	(j)	Children shouldn't **be allowed** to stay up too late.

EXERCISE 10

Decide whether the causative verbs in these sentences can be made passive without omitting important information or being ungrammatical. If so, write the passive version of the sentence.

▶ **EXAMPLES:**   The law requires parents to send their children to school.

Parents are required to send their children to school.

The doctor got the patient to take the bitter tasting medicine.

No change possible

1. Tradition doesn't allow people to smoke in church.
2. Lack of time forced Kilroy to return to the barracks before the movie was over.
3. The law requires everyone who works to pay some income taxes.
4. People shouldn't let their dogs run free around the neighborhood.
5. We had the janitor clean up the mess.
6. When I was a child my mother didn't allow me to play in the street.

Sensory Verbs, Causative Verbs, and Verbs that Take Subjunctive | **301**

FOCUS 4

SUGGESTIONS:

1. If you are pressed for time, skip this focus, or assign it for study at home.
2. For more advanced classes, combine the special features of *make* and *help* when you present the causatives in your discussion of Focus 3.

Additional examples:
make: *Students should <u>be made</u> to obey their teacher.*
help: *Students should <u>be helped</u> to understand English grammar.*

Exercise 10

Do this exercise in your preferred way, taking into account the principles of variation and efficiency discussed throughout this Teacher's Manual.

Workbook Exs. 8 & 9, pp. 129–131. Answers: TE p. 505.

ANSWER KEY

Exercise 10
1. People aren't allowed to smoke in church.
2. Kilroy was forced to return to the barracks before the movie was over.   3. Everyone who works is required to pay some income taxes.
4. No change possible   5. No change possible   6. When I was a child I wasn't allowed to play in the street.

FOCUS 5

Like Focus 4, these specific verbs can be treated as "vocabulary" items.

1. Present the focus in a straightforward way, by telling Ss that as there are certain verbs that require infinitive complements, gerund complements, etc., there are also some verbs that require an uninflected *that*-clause.

2. Use the examples in the book or make up class-related variations, such as: *I require that every student bring his or her book to school.* (not *brings*) *Hamid insists that Ahmed not ask questions about his sister.* (not *doesn't ask*)

Exercise 11

This exercise can be used for individual, pair, or small group work. For individual work, assign as homework and then either collect Ss' papers or process as a whole class. For pair or small group work, assign each pair/group two or three sentences and then process as a whole class.

Workbook Ex. 10, p. 131. Answers: TE p. 505.

UNIT GOAL REVIEW

1. Ask Ss to look at the goals on the opening page of this unit again. Help them understand how much they have accomplished in each area by asking for an example of each kind of verb-type in a full sentence. Write their examples on the board.

2. Alternatively, refer back to Focus 1 and ask Ss to summarize their understanding of the differences between the two complements for sensory verbs (participles vs. simple form) and to provide additional example sentences for the ones listed as causatives.

FOCUS **5**

Verbs of Urging Followed by Subjunctive *That* Clauses

EXAMPLES	EXPLANATION
(a) The doctor **suggested** that John **lose** fifteen pounds. (b) NOT: The doctor **suggested** that John **loses** fifteen pounds. (c) The children **demanded** that their father **give** them candy. (d) NOT: The children **demanded** that their father **gives** them candy.	Certain verbs of urging (*advise, ask, demand, desire, insist, propose, recommend, request, require, suggest, urge*) are followed by a *that* clause. The verb of the *that* clause must appear in simple form.

EXERCISE 11

Are these sentences correct or incorrect? For incorrect sentences, identify the mistake and fix it.

1. The students were got to do their homework.
2. The sergeant made the recruits to march for several hours.
3. A tailor was had to shorten my pants.
4. Parents shouldn't let their children watch too much television.
5. I had the waiter to bring the food to the table.
6. They encouraged all their children be independent.
7. We heard the protesters come closer and closer, so we left the area.
8. Companies should be required to provide their employees with health insurance.
9. The baby sitter made the children to fall asleep by singing quietly.
10. Kilroy had his hair to be cut.
11. The judge demanded that he was punished.
12. The army requires that every new soldier gets his hair cut very short.
13. My parents heard our coming in late from the party.

ANSWER KEY

Exercise 11
Ways to correct problems may vary.
1. incorrect—**got** can't be made passive. The teachers got the students to do their homework.
2. incorrect—**made** doesn't require **to**. The sergeant made the recruits march for several hours. 3. incorrect—**had** can't be made passive. I had a tailor shorten my trousers.
4. correct 5. incorrect—**had** doesn't require to. I had the waiter bring the food to the table.
6. incorrect—**encouraged** requires **to**. They encouraged all their children to be independent. 7. incorrect—unfinished

actions should be described with V + ing. We heard the protesters coming closer and closer.
8. correct 9. incorrect—**made** has the wrong meaning for this sentence. The baby sitter **got** the children to fall asleep by singing quietly.
10. incorrect—**to be** is not correct. Kilroy had his hair cut. 11. incorrect—**demand** requires subjunctive. The judge demanded that he be punished. 12. incorrect—**require** requires subjunctive. The army requires that every new soldier get his hair cut very short.
13. incorrect—wrong pronoun form. My parents heard us coming in late from the party.

Use Your English

ACTIVITY 1: WRITING/SPEAKING

Seeing is the sense that we rely on most. But when we are deprived of sight, our other senses become sharper. Test your other senses through the following activity.

STEP 1 Go to a place you know well. It could be this classroom, or a favorite room in your house, or someplace outdoors. Close your eyes and keep them closed for three minutes. Listen for the sounds that you can hear, both inside and outside. Are there any smells that you notice? Are they pleasant or unpleasant? What can you feel? Is it hot, cold? Make a list of things you have noticed about this place that you never noticed when your eyes were open. Try to think of at least three things for each of these categories:

I heard . . .   I smelled . . .   I felt . . .

STEP 2 Compare your list with several other people's lists. As a group, decide what other kinds of things escape your attention when you can rely on eyesight for information about the world around you. Present your ideas to the rest of the class.

ACTIVITY 2: SPEAKING/WRITING

In the previous activity you had an opportunity to experience the world as a blind person does. How are blind people able to move around independently? In what ways do they compensate for lack of sight? How do they get information about where they are and where they are going? Consider deaf people, who cannot hear. How are they able to communicate with each other and the rest of the world?

In a small group discuss ways that people with sensory handicaps can compensate for those handicaps. Use your experience in the previous activity, and any other experiences you have had with people who are blind or deaf. Present your ideas in a written or oral report.

ACTIVITY 3: SPEAKING/WRITING

There is a proverb in English that says. "You can catch more flies with honey than you can with vinegar." What do you think are the best ways to get someone to do something? Support your ideas by describing a situation when someone convinced you to do something you didn't want to do. How did that person convince you? Were you glad you did it or not?

Activity 1

This can be done orally or written, or used as a diagnostic by having the Ss write their responses to hand in for you to evaluate. If you choose the "written variation" skip Step 2, or do it as a brief whole class discussion as you collect Ss' responses.

Activity 2

This activity is a good follow-up for the experience in Activity 1.

Activity 3

Try using this topic as a general discussion for the whole class. Start by asking if it is better to **get** someone to do something or to **make** someone do something. Ask for individual examples. If your class is not good at open-ended discussion, use the topic to generate a writing sample.

Activities 4–6

If needed, use these as additional follow-up exercises for your presentation and practice of causatives (Focuses 3 & 4, Exercises 6–10) rather than waiting until the end of the unit.

Activity 4

Notice that you can practice both causatives and hypothetical constructions by having Ss write their responses for Step 1 following the same structure as provided in the example.

VARIATION:

Preview some of the proverbs listed in the Opening Task of Unit 19 and ask Ss to observe people's behavior in order to confirm or deny the validity of the saying.

Collect and correct, as suggested in Step 2, or just ask people to bring examples to class and discuss.

ACTIVITY 4: LISTENING/WRITING

Here are some general statements about human nature.

- People are usually in too much of a hurry.
- Children are spontaneous.
- Teenagers like to spend time together in groups.
- Older people are usually slower than younger people.

Do you think such generalizations are true or not? Test the validity of such generalizations by doing the following:

STEP 1 Choose a generalization that you want to test. It could be one of the statements listed above, or some other generalization. You may want to test a generalization that involves cultural differences, such as *North Americans are very outgoing* or *Asians are studious.*

STEP 2 Go to a place where you can watch lots of people. A shopping mall, a cafeteria, a busy corner—these are all good places. Watch how people behave. Look for examples of behavior that reflect the generalization you are testing. Find as many examples as you can that either support or contradict the generalization, and write a paragraph describing what you have observed. Here's an example:

They say that most people are friendly, and I have found that this seems to be true. At the mall yesterday I saw many people smiling at each other, I saw two people meet by chance. They must have been old friends because I saw them hug each other. I heard many people laughing and joking. I heard many of the salespeople say "Have a nice day" to customers. I saw one family arguing with one another, but strangers tended to be polite.

ACTIVITY 5: SPEAKING

What routine jobs do you hate? Pretend that you don't have to worry about money. What things would you have other people do for you?

STEP 1 Decide on five to ten personal tasks that you would have someone else do, if money were no problem. (For example: *If money were no problem, I would have somebody else do my homework.*)

STEP 2 Compare your list to those of other students in class. Based on your discussion, decide what the three most unpopular tasks are that people have to do.

ACTIVITY 6: SPEAKING

If you were the leader of the country, what things would you change?

- What laws would you establish for people to follow?
- What would you require people to do?
- What privileges would you allow people?
- What things would you not allow them to do?
- How would you get people to support you?

Think of at least three answers to each of these questions. Then tell the class why they should let you be their leader. Take a vote to see who is the most convincing candidate.

ACTIVITY 7: LISTENING/ SPEAKING/WRITING

In the radio, TV, and movie business they use the term "sound effects" to refer to the noises that are added to make the program or movie seem more real.

STEP 1 You will hear some common sound effects that are used in radio and TV broadcasts or movies. After you hear each sound, write a description of what you heard. Here's an example.

▶ **EXAMPLE:** I heard a dog barking.

STEP 2 Once you have identified all the sounds, compare you descriptions to those of another student to make sure you both interpreted the sound effects in the same way. Together, use your descriptions to write the story that the sounds tell you.

ACTIVITY 8: LISTENING

Listen to this conversation between Matt and his doctor, and answer the following questions. You may need to listen to the conversation more than once. The first question has been answered for you as an example.

1. What does Dr. Wong recommend that Matt do?
   She recommends that ___he change his eating habits.___

2. How does she suggest that Matt do this?
   She suggests that _____

3. What is the problem Matt has with following her advice?
   His roommate Jeff, _____

4. How does Jeff insist that food be cooked?
   He insists that _____

5. What does Dr. Wong urge that Matt demand?
   She urges that _____

6. What other solution does Dr. Wong suggest?
   She suggests that _____
   _____

Sensory Verbs, Causative Verbs, and Verbs that Take Subjunctive **305**

ANSWERS

Activity 7
Sound 1: car driving up and stopping
Sound 2: car door slam
Sound 3: footsteps slowly climbing stairs
Sound 4: knocking at a door
Sound 5: creaky door opening
Sound 6: woman's scream
Sound 7: gunfire
Sound 8: rapid footsteps running away
Sound 9: car door slam, start up and drive away
Sound 10: police sirens in the distance growing louder

Activity 8
Answers will vary slightly:
2. he start eating foods that are low in fat.
3. does all the cooking.   4. food be cooked with lots of butter.   5. Matt demand Jeff to start cooking in a healthier way.   6. Jeff take over the cooking a couple of nights a week.

Activity 6

This activity adapts well to small group discussion. Have Ss agree within the group to a specific number of changes they would make. (Decide on fifteen things everybody in your group thinks are good ideas.)

Activity 7

Play textbook audio. There is no tapescript for this particular listening, but the "answers" are listed below. This is a good activity to do for fun. Set the stage by telling Ss that they are the witnesses to a crime, but they are blind and cannot see what happened. All they can use is their hearing. This procedure makes it a natural follow-up to Activities 1 and 2 in this unit.

Activity 8

Play textbook audio. The tapescript for this listening appears on p. 519. Follow the same procedure for allowing for multiple listenings for general idea, specific information, and verification of answers.

VARIATION:

Treat this like one of the "lecture" sections of the TOEFL Test, as part of the TOEFL practice exercises in the Workbook.

The test for this unit can be found on p 474. The answers are on p. 475 of this book.

TOEFL Test Preparation Exercises for Units 16–18 can be found on pp. 132–134 of the Workbook.
The answers are on p. 505 of this book.

Unit 19

UNIT OVERVIEW

This unit provides an overview of the different categories of determiners and a detailed treatment of a system for choosing articles for noun phrases in particular sentences. Students (Ss) can use this system to generate the correct choice in the majority of cases. Make sure you have an understanding yourself of the "process" for determining the correct article based on form (count or noncount) and reference (generic or particular and specific or nonspecific) by reviewing the information summarized in the chart in Appendix 5. A comprehensive discussion of articles and an introduction to concepts that may be new to Ss such as the null article (ø) can be found in *The Grammar Book*, Unit 15 (pp. 271–296).

UNIT GOALS

Review the goals listed on this page so Ss understand what they should be able to do by the end of the unit.

OPENING TASK

All Ss at this level will probably find this task challenging. It works best as an out-of-class writing assignment for you to collect and evaluate.

1. Start with a brief general discussion of proverbs. Ask Ss to paraphrase the proverbs on this page and, if possible, to provide similar proverbs from their own countries. Keep this discussion brief if you intend to use Activity 1 as a follow-up to the unit.
2. Assign Ss to write paragraphs according to the instructions in the book.
3. Follow up with peer correction, general discussion, or other activities that you prefer.

UNIT 19

ARTICLES IN DISCOURSE

UNIT GOALS:

- To correctly distinguish generic and particular statements
- To correctly understand and distinguish specific and nonspecific reference in particular statements
- To use correct articles with specific, non-specific and unique nouns

▶ OPENING TASK
Proverbs

Common American Proverbs

A *dog* is man's best friend.

Time is money.

A *fool* and his money are soon parted.

Experience is the best teacher.

An *idle mind* is the devil's playground.

Absence makes the heart grow fonder.

The *leopard* cannot change its spots.

Actions speak louder than words.

Beauty is only skin-deep.

Every *cloud* has a silver lining.

Time heals all wounds.

Money is the root of all evil.

You are known by the company you keep.

STEP 1 Proverbs are well-known sayings that express general truths. On the previous page are some common American proverbs. Choose one that you agree with, and think of an example from your own life (or the life of someone that you know) that proves the truth of that proverb.

STEP 2 Write a paragraph about that example. Show why the proverb is true from your own experience. The first proverb has been done for you as an example.

VARIATION:

For a more interactive task, or in countries where dogs are viewed as unclean animals and not as household pets, substitute Activity 6.

A DOG IS MAN'S BEST FRIEND.

I once had a dog named Poppy. She was a very faithful friend. Every afternoon when I came home, the dog would greet me with kisses and a wagging tail. I liked the wagging tail, but I didn't enjoy the kisses very much. Even so, she was always glad to see me, and I was happy to see her, too. There was a time in my life when I was feeling very lonely. I didn't think I had any friends. Every day I came home to an empty house with an empty heart. But Poppy was always at the door waiting for me. She seemed to know whenever I was sad or lonely, and at those times she would be extra friendly. One time she even gave me a "gift": an old bone. Somehow she knew that I was especially sad. She must have thought the bone would cheer me up. Those bad times passed eventually, but they would have been a lot more difficult without my faithful companion, Poppy. She proved to me that a dog really is a wonderful friend.

---

1. Since Ss at this level have probably been introduced to determiners and count/noncount nouns before, omit a formal presentation if you are pressed for time.

2. Alternatively, treat this focus as a review by having Ss do Exercise 1 first as a diagnostic and then referring them to the focus box for study at home.

3. If you want to do a formal presentation, have Ss open their books and cover the explanations column with a piece of paper, or put the page on an OHP. Then ask if anyone knows what we call the boldfaced structures as you lead them through sentences a–d. Don't worry if students don't know the formal grammatical terminology, but someone usually does.

4. You can postpone discussion of nouns that have both count and noncount meanings until after you've done Exercise 1.

FOCUS **1**

▶ **Overview of Determiners**

FORM

Most noun phrases in English require a determiner.

EXAMPLES	EXPLANATIONS
(a) We need **this** pen. **That** pen is out of ink.	Determiners can be: • **Demonstratives** (see Unit 20 for more information)
(b) **Peter's** information surprised us more than **his** appearance.	• **Possessives** (see Unit 21 for more information)
(c) Denise has **few** friends. She doesn't make **much** effort	• **Quantifiers** (see Unit 22 for more information)
(d) Denise has **a** new position. She has **some** work to do. She feels **the** work is quite important.	• **Articles** (see Focus 2 for more information)
(e) NOT: Here is **a this** pen. **(f)** NOT: **That my** pen is green.	There is only one determiner of these types in each noun phrase.

The form of most determiners depends on whether the noun is count or noncount, singular or plural.

EXAMPLES	EXPLANATIONS
one bottle/two bottles one dollar/two dollars one man/two men one chair/two chairs	Count nouns can be counted and must indicate singular or plural.
water (one liter of water/two liters . . .) money (one dollar/a hundred yen . . .) furniture (two pieces of furniture)	Noncount nouns cannot be counted without using words that tell a unit or amount. They usually have no plural form.

Many nouns can have both a count and a noncount meaning.

NONCOUNT MEANING	COUNT MEANING
(g) There is **much beauty** in nature.	**(h)** There were **many beauties** at the beach.
(i) They grow **coffee** and **tea** in Sumatra.	**(j)** We ordered **two coffees** and **a tea** in addition to dessert.

EXERCISE 1

Underline and identify the determiners in the sample paragraph of the Opening Task. Are they demonstratives, possessives, quantifiers, or articles? Are the nouns count or noncount, singular or plural?

Exercise 1

If you have access to an OHP, make a transparency of the sample paragraph on p. 307, and underline and identify as a whole class. If you have chosen to do another activity in place of the Opening Task, be sure the Ss read the entire paragraph before doing this exercise.

Workbook Ex. 1, p. 135. Answers: TE p. 505.

ANSWER KEY

Exercise 1

A dog . . . a dog . . . a very faithful friend. . . . the dog . . . a wagging tail. . . . the wagging tail, . . . the kisses . . . a time in my life . . . any friends. . . . an empty house . . . an empty heart. . . . the door . . . those times . . . One time . . . a "gift": an old bone. . . . the bone . . . Those bad times *a lot* **(NB. an intensifier, not a noun phrase)** . . . my faithful companion, . . . a dog . . . a wonderful friend.

1. Prepare for presenting this focus by reviewing (for yourself) the chart in Appendix 5, which outlines the basic organization of this unit, and the sequence of questions that Ss must ask as they decide which article to use with any given noun phrase.
2. The overview of definite and indefinite articles is assumed to be review. Ask the class if they can tell you the rule for choosing *a* vs. *an*. If they cannot, write some examples on the board (or use the OHP with the explanation side covered, and elicit an explanation).
3. What will probably **not** be review is the notion that, in some cases, *some* can be considered a determiner, and the concept of ø (no article or "null article") as a possible "determiner choice."
4. Since much of this focus is review, you can choose to do Exercise 2 first as a diagnostic/attention focus, and then explain the portions of the focus that Ss ask about or do not understand.

FOCUS **2**

Overview of Articles

There are two kinds of articles: definite and indefinite.

Definite Articles

EXAMPLES	EXPLANATIONS
the pencil/**the** pencils **the** rice **the** information	There is only one form for definite articles: *the*. *The* can be used with any kind of noun: count, singular and plural, and non-count.

Indefinite Articles

EXAMPLES		EXPLANATIONS
a book **a** church **a** hotel	**a** shiny apple **a** university	*a/an*: Used with singular count nouns. *A* precedes nouns (or their modifiers) that begin with a consonant sound.
an apple **an** honest man **an** easy lesson	**an** uncomfortable situation **an** hour	*An* precedes nouns (or their modifiers) that begin with a vowel sound.
(a) Please get me **some pencils.** (b) I've invited **some friends** for dinner. (c) I have **some ideas** about the party. (d) Would you like **some rice?** (e) **Some water** got on my notebook. (f) I'm looking for **some information.**		*some*: Used with plural count nouns and noncount nouns. *Some* indicates a nonspecific quantity or amount.
(g) Everyone needs **friends.** (h) **Teachers** want **students** to succeed. (i) **Ideas** can come from anywhere. (j) **Rice** is eaten all over Asia. (k) **Water** is necessary for life. (l) I'm looking for **information** about public transportation.		No article (ø): Used with plural count nouns and noncount nouns. Use ø to make generic statements (see Focus 3) and statements that do **not** refer to a quantity or amount. (See Focus 4 for other rules regarding *some* versus ø.)

NOTE: See Appendix 5 on page A-9 for a chart that reviews the process for deciding how to choose the correct article for most situations in English.

310 UNIT 19

EXERCISE 2

Decide which articles (*a, an, the, some, ø*) can **NOT** be used with the following noun phrases.

1. pencils
2. water
3. apple
4. university professor
5. hourly employee
6. motherhood
7. bread
8. fast food
9. test

Exercise 2

This exercise is a logical review/recap of your presentation of Focus 2. Do this as a whole class exercise or as pair work.

FOCUS **3**

Using Articles in Generic and Particular Statements

There are different rules for using articles depending on whether we are making a **generic** statement or a **particular** statement.

GENERIC STATEMENTS	PARTICULAR STATEMENTS
Generic statements describe concepts and ideas. They refer to general categories of things.	Particular statements describe real situations. They refer to individual members of a category.
(a) **Bicycles** are an excellent means of transportation. (a category)	**(b)** They went shopping for **bicycles** yesterday. (particular things they wanted to buy—they didn't buy all the bicycles in the world)
(c) **An angry customer** is a frightening sight. (a category of person)	**(d)** We saw **an angry customer** complaining about the high price of tickets. (a particular person—not all customers are angry)
(e) **The lion** is found throughout Africa. (a category of animal)	**(f)** I saw **the lion** at the circus. (a particular animal—not all lions are in the circus)

Articles in Discourse | **311**

ANSWER KEY

Exercise 2
1. a, an   2. a, an   3. a, ø, some   4. an, ø, some   5. a, ø, some   6. the, an   7. a, an   8. a, an   9. an, ø, some

FOCUS 3

This focus introduces key concepts of generic and particular statements. An understanding of these categories is crucial to being able to select articles correctly.

SUGGESTIONS:

1. Present this focus with books open or closed. In either case, provide the context of why these categories are important.

Introduce these concepts by writing the words *generic* and *particular* on the board, and saying there are two kinds of categories for all statements in English: (1) statements about concepts, ideas, and categories and (2) statements about real situations or individual members of a category.

2. If you choose to present this with books open, have Ss refer to the pairs of sentences. Point out the contrast between a category and an individual member of a category. Remind Ss that the rule for selecting determiners for each of these categories is different.

3. If you want to have books closed, write some alternative class-related sentences on the board like these additional examples: *Students hate homework. The students in this class love homework. Schools can be difficult places to learn, but our school makes learning easy.*

4. You may want to skip the last part of this focus, since Book 3 deals primarily with articles in particular statements. Book 4 of this series deals more specifically with use of articles in generic statements.

(g) **Some people** never fall in love. (a category of people)	**(h)** **Some people** are joining us for dinner. (particular people, not a class of people)
(i) **Information** is increasingly communicated by electronic rather than printed media. (a category of things that are communicated electronically)	**(j)** Please give me **some information** on medical treatments for heart disease. (particular written or spoken facts)

Both definite and indefinite articles can be used to express generic statements. The following examples are listed from most common to least common.

EXAMPLES	EXPLANATIONS
(k) **Lions** are mighty creatures. **(l)** **Rice** is eaten throughout Asia.	ø **with plural count or noncount nouns** is the most common way to make generic statements.
(m) **A** lion is a mighty creature.	A/*an* **with singular count nouns** is less common, but also acceptable.
(n) **The** lion is a mighty creature.	T*he* **with singular count nouns** is also possible, but sounds very formal to most native speakers.

NOTE: Article usage in particular statements is explained in the rest of the focus boxes of this unit.

EXERCISE 3

Decide whether these sentences are generic statements (describing classes or categories) or particular statements (describing members of a category).

▶ **EXAMPLES:** **Computers** are cheaper now than they were ten years ago. *generic*

Computers for the new lab are being donated by a company in San Jose. *particular*

1. I wanted to buy **some mangoes** for the fruit salad, but they were too expensive!

2. **Mangoes** are a fruit found in most tropical places.

3. I saw **a doctor** about my cough.

4. **A doctor** is someone who has received training in medical science.

5. **Computers** have completely changed the way we live.

6. Don't go to that store for **computers.** They're cheaper at Radio Hut.

7. **Many people** don't like spicy food.

8. There weren't **many people** at Reiko's party.

9. If you really want to know how John is feeling, don't ask the **doctor,** ask the **nurses.** They will have better information.

10. There is a shortage of **nurses** in American hospitals today.

11. Many people in this country can't afford to go to **the doctor** when they are sick.

12. Raul is starting **a new company.**

13. **A company** needs to make sure that it is earning a profit.

EXERCISE 4

Write one generic statement and one particular statement for each of the cues listed here. The first one has been done for you as an example.

▶ **EXAMPLES:** **Generic:** *Bicycles are a cheap and efficient means of transportation.*

Particular: *Both Billy and his sister got bicycles for Christmas.*

1.	bicycles	6.	salespeople
2.	a new car	7.	books
3.	the English language	8.	hard work
4.	transportation	9.	Chinese food
5.	tea	10.	trouble

Articles in Discourse | **313**

Exercise 3

If the class is having trouble understanding this distinction, do this exercise as a whole class, allowing plenty of time for discussion and questions after each item. If the concepts are less problematic, do the exercise according to your preferred method, taking into account the principles of variety and efficiency outlined throughout this Teacher's Edition.

Exercise 4

1. If your class has trouble with exercises that require the creation of sentences, do this exercise in pairs or small groups. Circulate around the room and provide prompts or alternative examples as needed.

2. Even though you can save time by assigning each group/pair/Ss only one or two exercises to prepare, this is a challenging and important concept, so it may be better to allow for the additional practice of having everyone do all ten items.

Workbook Ex. 2, pp. 135–136. Answers: TE p. 505.

ANSWER KEY

Exercise 3
1. particular   2. generic   3. particular
4. generic   5. generic   6. particular
7. generic   8. particular   9. particular
10. generic   11. generic   12. particular
13. generic

Exercise 4
Answers will vary. Possible answers include:
1. *particular:* The store just got a new shipment of bicycles. *generic:* Bicycles provide cheap and efficient transportation.   2. *particular:* My Dad just bought a new car. *generic:* A new car needs to be developed that doesn't use gasoline.   3. *particular:* We're studying the English language in school. *generic:* The English language is spoken all over the world.   4. *particular:* Can you tell me where I can find transportation to the airport? *generic:* We won't solve our pollution problems until we solve our transportation problems.   5. *particular:* Please pass the tea. *generic:* Do you prefer tea or coffee?   6. *particular:* If you want to know where the sale items are, you should ask the salespeople over there. *generic:* Salespeople are not well paid in this country.   7. *particular:* There are books all over this desk. *generic:* Books always make good presents at Christmas.   8. *particular:* Doing this exercise is hard work. *generic:* Hard work is good for you.   9. *particular:* There was a lot of delicious Chinese food at the picnic. *generic:* Chinese food is delicious and healthful.
10. *particular:* I had some trouble doing this exercise. *generic:* Many people have trouble deciding what they want to major in at college.

SUGGESTIONS:

1. Throughout this unit you may want to keep a large chart or OHP projection of Appendix 5 to use as a way of keeping Ss oriented to the principles of article choice. You are now focusing on the concepts necessary to understand the rules that govern article selection for particular statements only.

2. As with the concepts of "generic" and "particular" statements, there are two other logical categories that are crucial to making correct article choices: "specific" and "nonspecific" reference. Without understanding these categories, Ss will not be able to develop an independent ability to choose the correct forms.

3. This focus is best done with books open, reading together the implied meaning communicated by article choices. Contrast examples a & c and b & d.

4. Put a table on the board with speaker/listener on the left side and knows/doesn't know on top.

	KNOWS	DOESN'T KNOW
Speaker		
Listener		

Categorize sentences a–m according to who knows and or doesn't know. If you wish, use class-related examples in place of the ones in the book.
Additional examples: speaker knows listener doesn't (Examples e–g): *A student in this class got a perfect score on the last quiz.*
listener knows but speaker doesn't: (Examples h–j): *Juan has a question?*
neither speaker or listener know: *Do you have any questions, class?*
both speaker and listener know (Examples a & b): *The test is tomorrow.*

5. Emphasize that only the last category (both speaker and listener know) uses definite articles.

Specific Versus Nonspecific Nouns

In particular statements, article use is determined by whether a noun is specific or nonspecific.

SPECIFIC NOUNS	IMPLIED MEANING	EXPLANATION
(a) Please give me **the** red pen.	There is only one red pen.	Specific nouns require definite articles. Specific nouns refer to an identified object. **Both** the speaker and the listener know specifically which object is being talked about.
(b) Please pass **the** tea.	There is a teapot right here.	

NONSPECIFIC NOUNS	IMPLIED MEANING	EXPLANATION
(c) Please give me **a** red pen.	There are several red pens. Any red pen is O.K.	Nonspecific nouns require indefinite articles. A noun is nonspecific when **either** the speaker or the listener or both do **not** know specifically which object is being referred to.
(d) Let's go to **a** restaurant and have **some** tea.	We don't know which restaurant it will be, or what kind of tea we will have.	

EXAMPLES	IMPLIED MEANING	EXPLANATIONS
(e) I bought **a new car.**	You haven't seen it yet.	Use indefinite articles (*an/an, ø, some*) when: • the speaker has a specific mental image of the noun, but the listener doesn't.
(f) I had **some cookies** with lunch today.	I know which cookies I had, but you don't.	
(g) There are **students** in my class who always do their homework.	I know which ones they are, but you don't.	

(h)	I hear you bought **a new car.** What kind is it?	You know, but I don't.	Use indefinite articles (*an/an, ø, some*) when: • the speaker doesn't have a specific mental image or idea, but the listener does.
(i)	You said you were holding **some mail** that came for me.	You know what kind and how much mail there is, but I don't.	
(j)	Mary tells you **secrets** that she never tells me.	You know which secrets, but I don't.	
(k)	I hope you have **a wonderful time** on your vacation.	We don't know what events will make it a wonderful vacation.	• neither the speaker nor the listener has a specific mental image.
(l)	Let's get **some spaghetti** when we go out tonight.	We don't know what kind of or how much spaghetti we're going to get.	
(m)	We're supposed to bring **dessert** to the picnic	We haven't been told a specific kind of dessert to bring.	

EXERCISE 5

Decide whether the nouns in the sentences below are specific or nonspecific. Is the noun phrase identified for the speaker, the listener, or both? Write the number of the sentence on the appropriate line below. The first two have been done for you.

Listener and speaker know which one: _____

Listener knows which one, but speaker doesn't: _____

Speaker knows which one, but listener doesn't: ___#2_____

Neither listener nor speaker know which one: ____#1_____

1. Do you want to go to **a movie** tonight?

2. The Jordans just bought **a beautiful new house.** You really ought to see it. I'm sure you'll think it's wonderful.

3. I want you to meet **a friend** of mine. You both have the same interests.

4. Did you have fun at **the party?**

5. Let's have **some friends** over for dinner on Saturday.

6. I heard Ali has **a new girlfriend.** What's she like?

Exercises 5–7

If Ss are having trouble with these concepts, do these exercises as a whole class, question by question, allowing for plenty of time for discussion and further questions. Otherwise, do them according to your preferred method.

Workbook Exs. 3 & 4, pp. 136–137. Answers: TE p. 505.

ANSWER KEY

Exercise 5
Listener and speaker know which one #4
Listener knows which one, but speaker doesn't: #6

Speaker knows which one but listener doesn't: #2 &3
Neither speaker nor listener know which one: #1 & 5

EXERCISE 6

Choose the correct implied meaning for each of these sentences. (*I* refers to the speaker. *You* refers to the listener.)

1. The student from Japan is here to see you.
   (a) There are several students from Japan who had appointments.
   (b) There is only one student from Japan who had an appointment.

2. Let's go to a restaurant.
   (a) We've already decided which restaurant to go to.
   (b) Let's choose a restaurant.

3. Some friends are coming to dinner.
   (a) You know who's coming to dinner.
   (b) You don't know who's coming to dinner.

4. Let's invite the neighbors to dinner.
   (a) You know which neighbors will be invited to dinner.
   (b) You don't know which neighbors will be invited to dinner.

5. You should see a doctor about that cough.
   (a) I am thinking about a specific doctor.
   (b) Any doctor should be able to help you.

EXERCISE 7

Add the appropriate article (*a/an, the, some,* or *ø*) in the blanks. There may be more than one correct answer.

1. I didn't bring _____ roses that you asked for. I completely forgot them.

2. Sally wanted to buy _____ new dress, so she's gone out to find one.

3. _____ teacher was here to see you. I think it was your English teacher.

4. Did you give _____ musicians a nice tip? They certainly played beautiful music for your party.

5. Would you like _____ cold iced tea?

6. How did you enjoy _____ Chinese food last night?

7. I have _____ problems that I don't want to talk about.

8. John sent Mary _____ card for her birthday, but she says she never received it.

9. (a) _____ bank where Dora works was robbed by

   (b) _____ masked man with (c) _____ gun.

   By the time (d) _____ police officer arrived, it was too

   late. (e) _____ robber had disappeared.

ANSWER KEY

Exercise 6
1. (b) 2. (b) 3. (b) 4. (a) 5. (b)

Exercise 7
1. the 2. a 3. A 4. the 5. some/ø/a
6. the 7. some/ø 8. a 9. (a) The (b) a
(c) a (d) the/a (e) the

FOCUS **5**

▶ **U**sing Articles in Discourse

A noun is usually used with an indefinite article the first time it is mentioned because it is nonspecific: It is the first time the listener has encountered it. In later sentences the same noun is used with a definite article because it has become specific; both the speaker and the listener now know exactly which noun is being talked about.

EXAMPLES	EXPLANATIONS
(a) There once was **a** little old man who lived in **a** house by **a** river. **The** shack was rather dirty, and so was **the** man. **(b)** I once had **a** big black dog and **a** little white dog. **The** black dog kept itself very clean, but **the** white dog loved to roll in mud.	A noun is usually used with an indefinite article the first time it is mentioned because it is nonspecific: it is the first time the listener has encountered it. In later sentences the same noun is used with a definite article because it has become specific; both the speaker and the listener now know exactly which noun is being talked about
(c) I had **a dog** named Poppy. Every afternoon when I came home **the dog** would greet me with **kisses** and **a wagging tail**. I liked **the wagging tail**, but I didn't enjoy **the kisses** very much.	A noun becomes specific • **by direct reference.** (The noun is repeated.)
(d) If you have **a dog** as **a pet**, you can always look forward to going home because of **the kisses** and **the wagging tail** that are there to greet you when you arrive. **(e)** I read **an interesting book. The author** suggested that all life came from visitors from another planet. **The first chapter** tells stories of visitors from outer space that are found in many different cultures.	• **by indirect reference.** (The noun itself is not repeated, but the reference is still clear from the context.)

This focus outlines the basic rule that nouns are generally nonspecific for the listener/reader the first time they are mentioned and therefore tend to appear with indefinite articles.

1. You can present this more inductively by asking Ss in pairs to look at examples a and b (on the OHP or written on the board) and explain why the articles change in the second sentence. Then have each pair compare their explanations with another pair. You can have them discuss the same example or match a pair that looked at example a with a pair that looked at example b.
2. Introduce the concepts of direct and indirect reference by having Ss look over examples (c–e).

V A R I A T I O N :

Use class-related examples such as:
There is a student in this class who took a test. The student got a perfect grade on the test. [direct reference] As a result, the teacher and the class [indirect reference] were very happy for the student.

Exercise 8

There are many ways to do this exercise:
1. Assign it for homework the night before and go over in class.
2. Assign it as an in-class activity, either for pairs or individually. To save time, assign each Ss/pair one passage, but process as a whole class. If you have access to an OHP, make a transparency and write the possible article choices in the blanks as you go over the answers.

Workbook Ex. 5, p. 137. Answers: TE p. 505.

EXERCISE 8

Write articles (*a/an, ø, some, the*) in the spaces. More than one answer may be correct.

1. I have (a) _____ foolish friend who is really careless with (b) _____ money. He has (c) _____ good-paying job, but he doesn't even have (d) _____ bank account. He says he doesn't need one because he spends his salary right away. He gets (e) _____ paycheck once (f) _____ week. (g) _____ money is always gone before (h) _____ week is over. I can't tell you what he spends it on. And you know what? Neither can he!

2. I saw (a) _____ interesting play last night.
   (b) _____ actors were excellent, and
   (c) _____ set was beautiful. However,
   (d) _____ play itself was unfortunately not very well written.

3. Would you like (a) _____ cake? (b) _____ frosting is (c) _____ special recipe from
   (d) _____ friend of my mother's. I made
   (e) _____ cake and (f) _____ frosting myself.

4. Little Billy doesn't like (a) _____ school. He says
   (b) _____ teachers are boring. He doesn't like doing
   (c) _____ homework. He much prefers to watch
   (d) _____ cartoons on TV. As (e) _____ result, his teachers aren't very happy with (f) _____ way he performs in class. If he doesn't take (g) _____ responsibility for doing (h) _____ assignments, he may have to repeat (i) _____ same grade next year.

318 | UNIT 19

▶ Repeating the Indefinite Article

There are certain situations in which the usual rule of replacing an indefinite article with a definite article after the first time it is mentioned is not followed.

EXAMPLES		EXPLANATIONS
(a)	There once was **a** little old man who lived in **a** house by **a** river. **The** house was rather dirty, and so was **the** man. Although **there was a river** right next to **the** house, **the** old man had to walk quite far to get clean drinking water.	• sentences with *there is/there are*.
(b) I once had **a** dog. Her name was Poppy. She was **a** good dog.	**Implied Meaning:** She was a member of the category "good dogs."	• sentences that identify someone or something as a member of a category.
(c) You know John. He's **a** teacher.	He's a member of the category "teachers."	
(d) John is **a** teacher. John and Fred are teachers. **(e)** NOT: John and Fred are **some** teachers. **(f)** Paris is **a** city. Paris, Rome, and Munich are cities. **(g)** NOT: Paris, Rome, and Munich are **some** cities.		Do not use *some* for plural nouns that identify things as part of a group.

EXERCISE 9

Add the correct article to the blank spaces in these sentences.

I once had (1) _____ experience that proved to me that (2) _____ idle mind is (3) _____ devil's playground. Miss Kersell was my eighth grade science and math teacher. She was (4) _____ very strict teacher, and wouldn't allow any misbehaving in class. To my friend Billy this presented (5) _____ irresistible challenge. He found math and science very easy, so he was

ANSWER KEY

Exercise 9
Alternative answers have been indicated:
(1) an   (2) an/the   (3) a/the   (4) a
(5) an   (6) a   (7) ø   (8) a/the   (9) an
(10) an   (11) a   (12) the   (13) a   (14) a
(15) a/ø   (16) the   (17) ø/some
(18) ø/some   (19)   (20) a   (21) a/the
(22) a/the

FOCUS 6

This focus should be presented as an exception to the general rule outlined in Focus 5. Tell the class there are three situations where the rule does not apply and then ask them to turn to the chart in the book, or present the three exceptions as class-related examples.
Additional examples: there is: *A student knew the answer to the question. But even though there was a student who knew the answer, the teacher explained it herself.*
members of a category: *Students in this class are great. Juan is a student in this class.*
If you wish, omit a formal presentation of examples d–g and assign Ss to look over the chart for homework.

Exercise 9

This exercise is another comprehensive review of article use. Follow the same suggestions as outlined in Exercise 8, taking into account the general principles of efficiency and variety outlined throughout this Teacher's Edition. Make sure Ss read the entire passage before choosing the articles for the blank spaces.

Workbook Ex. 6, p. 138. Answers: TE p. 505.

frequently bored in class. As (6) _____ result, he would try to play (7) _____ tricks on her without getting caught. It was (8) _____ challenge that he could never resist, especially when he didn't have anything else to do. One day we were taking (9) _____ arithmetic quiz. It was (10) _____ easy quiz, but I have never been good at arithmetic, so it was taking me (11) _____ long time. But Billy had finished (12) _____ quiz in just (13) _____ few minutes. I heard (14) _____ strange noise coming from the back of the room. It was (15) _____ noise like no other I had ever heard. Someone in (16) _____ front of the class began to giggle. Then there were (17) _____ giggles in the back. Soon there was (18) _____ laughter everywhere. Miss Kersell was furious and looked everywhere to find out where (19) _____ noise was coming from. Billy had found (20) _____ way to make (21) _____ strange noise by rubbing his foot against (22) _____ leg of his chair.

FOCUS **7**

► Unique Nouns

There are certain nouns that are specific for both the speaker and the listener the first time they are mentioned. These are called unique nouns.

EXAMPLES			EXPLANATIONS
(a) I hear someone knocking at **the** door.			Unique nouns are used with definite articles. We do not need to "introduce" them in a specific context.
(b) **The** sun is too hot. Let's sit in **the** shade.			
Unique Nouns	**Implied Meaning**		A noun can be unique:
(c) We were all having dinner. We were sitting around **the table,** and I asked my brother to pass **the butter.**	There was only one table and one dish of butter.		• because of a particular situation or setting.
(d) "How did you do on **the exam** yesterday?" "Terrible! **The questions** were really difficult!"	The speakers both know which test is being discussed.		
(e) I hope you remembered to ask **the neighbors** to pick up **the mail** while we're on vacation.	We've previously decided which neighbors we will ask to pick up the mail.		
(f) **The sky** is so beautiful tonight. **The moon** is bright.			• because it is a universal reference (there is only one)
(g) **The street that John lives on** is lined with trees.			• if it is immediately identified by a relative clause or prepositional phrase
(h) First we went to a hotel where **the man at the desk** told us we had no reservations.			
(i) **The book the teacher told us about** is available at **the bookstore across the street.**			

Introduce unique nouns as a second exception to the basic rule of indefinite article with first mention and definite article with second mention. Have Ss study the chart or present it more inductively by writing examples on the board.
Additional examples: unique because of context: *How do you like the teacher in the class?*
universal reference: *I always like to go to the ocean for my vacations.*
immediately identified reference: *The lesson of this focus is that some nouns are unique.*

Exercise 10

This exercise works well as a paired activity. To save class time, assign each pair three sentences, and then process as a whole class, asking other pairs who worked on the same question to confirm the first pair's answer or to provide alternative answers.

Exercises 11–13

These exercises provide comprehensive practice with choosing articles in discourse. There are many ways to do them.

1. Assign them for homework and go over in class or collect and evaluate.
2. Go over in a traditional item-by-item manner. Have Ss look over each passage before they start the exercises.
3. Break the class up into three groups and assign each group one of the exercises to prepare.

EXERCISE 10

Why do you think the highlighted nouns in the following sentences are unique? Decide whether they have been specified:

   (a) by being mentioned previously by direct or indirect reference (identify the reference)
   (b) by a specific context/situation (identify the context or situation)
   (c) by a universal context or situation
   (d) by being immediately identified by a relative clause or prepositional phrase (identify the modifier)

   1. An idle mind is **the devil's** playground.
   2. I saw a great movie last night. **The camera work** was fantastic.
   3. **The newspaper** said it was going to rain tonight.
   4. **The tallest mountain** in **the world** is on **the border** between Nepal and China.
   5. **The place** we went last year is great for a vacation.
   6. Let's go to **the club** for dinner tonight.
   7. **The teacher** said we have to finish **the assignment** before Friday.
   8. **The town** that I grew up in was quite small.
   9. **The noise** Billy made was like no other noise I had ever heard before.
   10. What did **the doctor** say about **the medicine** you've been taking?

EXERCISE 11

Write the appropriate article (*a, an, the,* or ø) in the blanks. There may be more than one correct choice.

   Peter Principle believes that every cloud has (1) _____ silver lining. He is (2) _____ very optimistic person. He thinks that (3) _____ problem is really (4) _____ opportunity in disguise. As (5) _____ result, he is always happy and reasonably content with (6) _____ things that (7) _____ life has given him. (8) _____ people like being around him, because he's (9) _____ cheerful, positive person.

   Denise Driven is just (10) _____ opposite. She always looks on (11) _____ dark side of (12) _____ things. If she encounters (13) _____ problem, she sometimes blames it on

---

ANSWER KEY

Exercise 10

1. (c)   2. (a) (a great movie)   3. (b) (there's only one newspaper in town)   4. (d) (in the world); (b) (there is only one border between the two countries)   5. (d) (we went last year)   6. (b) (we both know which club) 7. (b) (we both know which teacher and assignment)   8. (d) (that I grew up in) 9. (d) (Billy made)   10. (b) (doctor); (d) (you've been taking)

Exercise 11

Alternative answers have been indicated:
(1) a   (2) a   (3) a   (4) an   (5) a (6) the/ø   (7) ø   (8) ø   (9) a   (10) the (11) the   (12) ø   (13) a   (14) the   (15) a (16) a   (17) the   (18) a   (19) ø/some (20) an   (21) the/some   (22) a   (23) a (24) a

---

(14) _____ fact that she is (15) _____ woman in

(16) _____ man's world. She believes that (17) _____

world isn't (18) _____ fair place, and she in particular has always

had (19) _____ bad luck. Although she's not (20) _____

optimistic person, she doesn't spend much time feeling sorry for herself.

She rarely has time to listen to anyone's troubles or tell you about

(21) _____ troubles she is facing. But whenever

(22) _____ friend does something nice for her, she always

suspects that the person actually has (23) _____ hidden motive.

She believes that every silver lining has (24) _____ cloud.

EXERCISE 12

Write the appropriate article in the blanks. There may be more than one correct choice.

The tall person in this picture is one of (1) _____

most beautiful people I know: (2) _____

woman by (3) _____ name of Big Sue.

She proves (4) _____ truth of

(5) _____ saying "Beauty is only skin

deep." Perhaps people who don't know her well would

say that she is not (6) _____

beautiful person. I guess that compared to (7) _____

movie star or (8) _____ fashion model

she isn't that attractive. But anyone who knows her

well thinks that she has (9) _____ beautiful and courageous spirit.

Her beauty is in her personality. She has (10) _____ deep,

booming laugh that makes other people laugh with her. She's not self-conscious

about her size. She makes (11) _____ jokes about it. She

was (12) _____ person who invented (13) _____

name "Big Sue." She says there are plenty of Sues in (14) _____

world, but only one Big Sue. If she gains (15) _____ few pounds

she doesn't worry. She just says "There's more of me to love." She is

(16) _____ incredible dancer, and moves around (17) _____

dance floor with (18) _____ grace and style. She is

ANSWER KEY

Exercise 12
Alternative answers have been indicated:
(1) the   (2) a   (3) the   (4) the   (5) the
(6) a   (7) a   (8) a   (9) a   (10) a   (11) ø
(12) the   (13) the   (14) the   (15) a
(16) an   (17) the/a   (18) ø   (19) a
(20) ø   (21) a   (22) ø   (23) ø   (24) the
(25) ø   (26) a   (27) a

(19) _____ wonderful comedian. She can tell (20) _____ stories in (21) _____ way that has (22) _____ people falling down with laughter. She has (23) _____ friends all over (24) _____ world. She has turned down (25) _____ dozens of proposals for marriage. People can't help falling in love with her, once they get to know her well. But she's not in (26) _____ hurry to find (27) _____ husband. She says "I'll wait till I'm old and skinny. Right now I'm having too much fun."

EXERCISE 13

Write the appropriate article in the blanks. There may be more than one correct choice.

When I first went to (1) _____ university I learned the truth of the proverb "Absence makes (2) _____ heart grow fonder." It was (3) _____ first time I had lived away from home. I was surprised to discover how homesick I got, even after just (4) _____ few days. When I lived with my family, my brother and I used to fight about everything. He wanted to watch one TV program and I wanted to watch another. We fought about whose turn it was to do certain chores like feeding (5) _____ dog, sweeping (6) _____ garage, cutting (7) _____ grass, and taking out (8) _____ garbage. We argued about whose turn it was to use (9) _____ car on Saturday night. (I was allowed to use it one week, and then he was allowed to use it on (10) _____ other.)

But when I moved away, I realized that there were (11) _____ lot of things about my brother that I missed. I began to forget about all (12) _____ tricks he used to play on me. I started to remember only (13) _____ happy times we had spent together. By (14) _____ time (15) _____ year ended and I went back to spend (16) _____ summer at home, I was really anxious to see him again.

UNIT GOAL REVIEW

Use the chart in Appendix 5 to review articles. As you walk through the process of deciding on the form and the reference, ask Ss to provide examples of count and noncount nouns, a generic statement and a particular statement, and an example of specific and nonspecific reference. Finally, ask Ss to give you some examples of unique nouns.

Use Your English

ACTIVITY 1: SPEAKING

Every country has different proverbs. In America we say "Don't bite off more than you can chew," to remind people not to be too ambitious or try to do too many things at once. In Afghanistan the same idea is expressed by this proverb: "You can't hold two watermelons in one hand."

STEP 1 Work with a partner from a different cultural background, and come up with three pairs of proverbs. Each pair should express the same idea in two different ways.

STEP 2 Share each message and its two different proverbs with the rest of the class.

ACTIVITY 2: SPEAKING/WRITING

Describe an object that you found once, and what you did with it. Compare your story with the stories of other people in the class. Can you create a proverb that talks about finding objects, and what should be done with them? (For example, "Find a penny, pick it up, all day long you'll have good luck.")

ACTIVITY 3: SPEAKING

A time capsule is a metal or concrete box (usually about one cubic meter) that is sometimes built into the floor or walls of a building. The designers of the time capsule fill it with objects that they think are important, or interesting, or characteristic of the time when the building was built.

STEP 1 Imagine that you are organizing a time capsule to be placed in a skyscraper being built today. The building is expected to remain standing for several hundred years. What objects would you place in the time capsule, and why would you choose those particular objects?

STEP 2 Work with several other people and decide on the contents of a time capsule that will not be opened for at least 500 years. Present your list of items and your reasons for choosing them to the rest of the class.

USE YOUR ENGLISH

Activity 1

This activity is meant as a thematic follow-up of the Opening Task. However, because many proverbs will involve generic rather than particular statements, this may not be the best activity to use for testing or diagnostic purposes.

Activity 2

Use this activity as a diagnostic by asking Ss to write their stories and then hand them in for you to evaluate. Activities 1 and 2 work well together, with Ss first identifying proverbs, and then creating a "proverb" of their own.

Activity 3

Use this activity as a small group discussion activity rather than as a way to diagnose problems with articles. You can structure responses by asking Ss to use the following pattern: "*Our time capsule would include an X. We chose the X because it . . .*"

Activities 4 & 5

These are good opportunities to check student writing for errors in form, meaning, or use. Follow the procedure outlined in the Opening Task of Unit 11 in correcting/discussing Ss' errors with articles.

Activity 6

This activity adapts well to use as a paired or small group fluency circle exercise. Once the story has been "rehearsed," listen for correct article use, with "*a* dog . . . *a* bone" *followed by* "*the* dog . . . *the* bone . . . *the* water."

ACTIVITY 4: WRITING

Write a short paragraph about a discovery or invention that has changed the course of history.

ACTIVITY 5: WRITING

What are three things that everybody needs? Write a short composition describing your three choices and why you think everyone should have them. Start your essay with: "*There are three things everyone needs: . . .*"

ACTIVITY 6: SPEAKING

Here are four pictures. What story do you think they tell? Tell your story to a partner or write it down for your teacher to correct

ACTIVITY 7: LISTENING

Listen to the following short conversations and then choose the statement from the pairs listed below that can be correctly implied from the conversation.

Conversation #1

_____ There is one ACME sales representative.

_____ There are several ACME sales representatives.

_____ There is one vice president.

_____ There are several vice presidents.

Conversation #2

_____ There is only one snack bar in the building.

_____ There are several snack bars in the building.

_____ John has already decided what he is going to eat.

_____ John hasn't decided what he is going to eat yet.

_____ Mary already knows what snack John will bring her.

_____ Mary doesn't know what John will bring her from the snack bar.

Conversation #3

_____ This is the first time Bob and Betty have discussed the idea of having a party.

_____ They've discussed the party before.

_____ They have already decided who they are going to invite.

_____ They haven't decided who they are going to invite.

_____ They have already decided which restaurant to go to.

_____ They haven't decided which restaurant to go to.

Activity 7

Play textbook audio. The tapescript for this listening appears on p. 519 of this book. Play these conversations one at a time, allowing for multiple listenings as needed.

✓ The test of this unit can be found on p. 476. The answers are on p. 477 of this book.

ANSWER KEY

Activity 7

These statements can be correctly implied from the conversation:

Conversation #1
There is one ACME sales representative.
There are several vice presidents.

Conversation #2
There is only one snack bar in the building.
John has already decided what he is going to eat.
Mary doesn't know what John will bring her from the snack bar.

Conversation #3
This is the first time Bob and Betty have discussed the idea of having a party.
They haven't decided who they are going to invite.
They haven't decided which restaurant to go to.

Unit 20

UNIT OVERVIEW

This unit covers the use of demonstratives in discourse. Most students (Ss) have encountered these forms before, but are puzzled by their use as referential forms, especially when they are used in place of pronoun reference to indicate subtle differences in inference or presupposition. *The Grammar Book* (pp. 307–309) contains a very helpful explanation of these issues.

UNIT GOALS

Review the goals listed on this page so Ss understand what they should be able to do by the end of the unit.

OPENING TASK

Note: The **Opening Task** allows Ss to try using the target structures and allows teachers to notice what kinds of help they may need. For a more complete discussion of the Opening Task, see p. xix of this Teacher's Edition.

The primary purpose of this particular task is to give Ss an opportunity to observe, analyze, and hypothesize in an open-ended way. Ss should always be encouraged to make hypotheses, even ones that may not be correct. They will have opportunities to test the validity of their hypotheses in the rest of the chapter.

UNIT 20

DEMONSTRATIVES IN DISCOURSE

UNIT GOALS:

- To correctly understand and use determiners and demonstrative pronouns
- To correctly understand and communicate differences in reference by using determiners
- To correctly understand and communicate differences in focus and emphasis by using determiners

▶ OPENING TASK
This, That, or It?

STEP 1 Read the following dialogue and look at how the words *it, this,* and *that* are used. What is being referred to each time one of these forms is used? Can you substitute other forms? Does this change the meaning? What can you say about when to use *it* instead of *that*?

> **Denise Driven:** Mr. Green has informed me that you're not going to be here this afternoon. **That's** outrageous, Peter! What about the Davis contract? **It's** due first thing Monday morning.
>
> **Peter Principle:** Well, my son's in a play at school. **It's** his first big role. He's one of the Three Wise Men.
>
> **Denise Driven:** He certainly didn't learn **that** role from his father! Is some stupid school play more important than your job?
>
> **Peter Principle:** You'd better believe **it!** Besides, I spoke with Mr. Green. I told him **it** would get done sooner or later.
>
> **Denise Driven:** If he believes **that,** he'll believe anything. **That's** what makes me so annoyed, Peter. **This** isn't the first time you've left work early. You're always asking for permission to take time off, and I get left having to do all the work. I'm getting real tired of **it,** Peter. **It's** all I can do to keep this office running professionally!
>
> **Peter Principle:** I'm sure Mr. Green would be happy to give you time off, too. Just ask for **it,** Denise. **That's** all you have to do.
>
> **Denise Driven:** **That's** not the point. **It's** true that most of us would probably rather be playing instead of working. But some of us have a sense of responsibility and a respect for hard work.
>
> **Peter Principle:** **That's** true. My responsibility is to my son, and I respect the hard work he's put into learning his lines. **It's** not easy when you're only six years old.
>
> **Denise Driven:** Don't give me **that** nonsense, Peter. I don't much fancy **it.**
>
> **Peter Principle:** **That's** your trouble, Denise. You need a little nonsense in your life.
>
> **Denise Driven:** My personal life is none of your business!
>
> **Peter Principle:** Denise Driven has a personal life? Fancy **that!**
>
> **Denise Driven:** **That's it!** I'm leaving. I'm making a formal complaint about **this** with Mr. Green.
>
> **Peter Principle:** Well, **that's that,** then, isn't **it?** I guess there's nothing I can do to calm you down. I may as well leave a little early for the play. **It's** important to get there early if you want to get a good seat.

STEP 2 Discuss your ideas with a partner. Together decide on two things you have noticed about how *this, that,* and *it* are used in English and report them to the rest of the class.

---

1. This first part of the focus should be review for just about everybody. Elicit the information by putting sample sentences a & b on the board and asking: *"What are the grammatical differences between the two underlined words? [What are the words called?]"* (one is a pronoun, one a determiner) and *"What are the meaning differences between the forms?"*

2. The next part of the focus (nonphysical distance and avoiding repeated use of demonstratives) will probably <u>not</u> be review, and so should be presented more formally. Present sentences k–o, followed by sentence p, followed by q–u.

V A R I A T I O N S :

Assign specific groups of Ss to study the above portions of the focus and then present them to the rest of the class.

If possible, refer back to some of the hypotheses they made for the Opening Task and ask if this information has helped them change or omit some of the statements they or other Ss made.

▶ **O**verview of Demonstratives

Demonstratives can be used as determiners or as pronouns.

EXAMPLES	EXPLANATIONS
(a) Does **this** pencil belong to you?	Demonstrative determiner
(b) Yes, **that** is mine.	Demonstrative pronoun

The form of the demonstrative depends on whether the thing being referred to is singular or plural, and near or far.

	NEAR	FAR
singular	**(c)** You should read **this book.** **(e)** **This** is delicious.	**(d)** Does **that pencil** belong to you? **(f)** Is **that** yours?
plural	**(g)** **These problems** aren't so serious. **(i)** If you like peaches, try **these.**	**(h)** **Those people** live down the street from my parents. **(j)** **Those** are the cutest puppies I have ever seen!

EXAMPLES	EXPLANATIONS
(k) Please sit in **this** chair **(by me.).** **(l)** **That** chair **(over there)** is broken.	Near and far distinctions can be determined by: • physical distance.
(m) I've been to two parties in the last week, but **this** one (today) is much more enjoyable than **that** party Denise had (a few days ago) at the club.	• time distance.
(n) What are we going to do about **this** budget deficit? **(o)** I don't know. **That's** for you to worry about, not me!	• whether the speaker feels involved with the situation or distanced from it

EXAMPLE	EXPLANATION
(p) There once was **a** wicked king who live in **a** castle. Every day **this king** would go to **a** secret room. **This** room was where he liked to count this money.	Use demonstratives with nouns that have been specified by being mentioned previously (see Unit 19 for more information).

A demonstrative is not usually repeated to refer to the same item. A personal pronoun (*he, it*, etc.) or a definite article (*the*) is used instead.

(q)	Have you tried **these** pears? **They** are quite delicious.	**(r)**	NOT: Have you tried **these** pears? **These** are quite delicious.
(s)	**This** is the problem Denise was talking about. **It** will continue to get worse if we don't find a solution.	**(t)**	NOT: **This** is the problem Denise was talking about. **This** will continue to get worse if we don't find a solution.
(u)	I bought **that** pen and notebook at a drug store. **The** pen was a little expensive, but **the** notebook was cheap.	**(v)**	NOT: I bought **that** pen and notebook at the drugstore. **That** pen was a little expensive, but **that** notebook was cheap.

EXERCISE 1

Add appropriate demonstratives (*this, those*, etc.), personal pronouns (*he, it*, etc.), or articles (*a/an, the*) in the blanks. More than one answer may be possible. The first one has been done for you as an example.

1. When Denise came to Mr. Green with her complaints about Peter, he realized that they had talked about (a) __these/those__ issues before. He told her there was no point in discussing (b) __them__ any further.

2. I got these new skirts and blouses on sale. I'd like you to take a look at (a) _____. Which of (b) _____ dresses do you like better, (c) _____ red one or (d) _____ green one? What about (e) _____ blouses? Which do you prefer? (f) _____ one or (g) _____ one?

3. I got a new bike for my birthday. (a) _____ was a gift from my parents. I'm glad they got (b) _____ bike instead of another kind. (c) _____ will be much more practical.

Demonstratives in Discourse | **331**

Exercise 1

This Exercise can be assigned for homework, done in class individually, or in pairs. To save time assign individuals/pairs to prepare one or two passages and then correct as a whole class.

Workbook Ex. 1, p. 140. Answers: TE p. 506.

4. The essay that John wrote didn't receive a passing grade.

(a)_____ didn't contain any of the guidelines Dr. Montaigne had explained when she had first assigned (b) _____ essay. (c) _____ guidelines were not simple, but (d)_____ had to be followed in order to get a passing grade on (e) _____ essay.

(f) _____ grade made John rather upset, but Dr. Montaigne had made (g) _____ guidelines quite clear.

5. Where did you get (a) _____ ring? (b) _____ is really beautiful. (c) _____ looks like (d) _____ came from Mexico. Is (e) _____ silver?

FOCUS 2

1. Start this focus by linking it to the previous one where the class learned that we usually do not repeat demonstratives for reference, but rather use pronouns (it) for subsequent reference. Introduce this focus as another "rule" for helping to decide when to use *this, that,* or *it.*

2. Present the focus in a straightforward way, using the examples in the book or class-related examples such as:
   backward pointing reference: *It's only three days until vacation. That/this must be why everyone is daydreaming.*
   forward pointing reference: *These (not those) chapters are going to be on the test: 20–25.*

3. Follow-up by doing Exercise 2 in class.

FOCUS **2**

Demonstratives for Reference

EXAMPLES	EXPLANATIONS
(a) Everyone started laughing. **This** made John very angry **(b)** I knew it was going to rain! **That's** why I didn't want to come to this picnic in the first place.	There are two kinds of demonstrative reference: • **backward-pointing reference:** where demonstratives refer to information that has been previously mentioned
(c) **This** is why I can't come to your party: I don't have the time, I don't have the clothes, and I have no way to get there. **(d)** I like **these** kinds of Asian food: Chinese, Japanese, Indian, and Thai.	• **forward-pointing reference:** where demonstratives refer to information that is about to be introduced.

Using a particular demonstrative form depends on whether it refers forward or backward in the text.

EXAMPLES	EXPLANATIONS
(e) **This** is why I wasn't at your party: I had a terrible case of the flu. **(f)** I had a terrible case of the flu. **This** is why I wasn't at your party.	*This/these* can be used to point both forward or backward.
(g) I had a terrible case of the flu. **That** is why I wasn't at your party. **(h)** Paris is a beautiful city. **That** is why everyone wants to go there.	*That/those* are usually only used for backward pointing reference (except with modifiers that follow a noun—see Focus 4).

EXERCISE 2

What do the demonstratives refer to in these sentences? Circle the demonstratives in these passages, and draw an arrow to what each one refers to. Is it an example of forward-pointing or backward-pointing reference? The first passage has been done for you as an example.

1. Most people find it difficult to sleep during the day and work at night. This is why people who work "swing shift" (as that work schedule is called) are usually paid a higher wage than those who those work during the day.

2. We hold these truths to be self-evident, that all men are created equal, and have a right to life, liberty, and the pursuit of happiness.

3. Let me make this perfectly clear: No new taxes!

4. Frank said that he wanted to leave New York because he was tired of big city life. But I don't think that was the real reason for his move to California. The real reason was that his wife wanted to live in a place with warmer winters. At least, this is what Stuart told me.

5. These soldiers must report to Barracks B: Private Rebecca Adams, Private Mary Collins, and Corporal Marsha Powell. These soldiers have been assigned to patrol duty: Sergeant Kitty Westmoreland and Corporal Mary MacArthur. Those are your orders, soldiers.

6. The causes of the American Civil War were not very different from those of other wars that have taken place between different regions of any country. This is one of the things that can be learned by studying history.

7. The chemical composition of baking soda is similar to that of any compound containing sodium. This is what allows baking soda to enter into a chemical reaction with any compound containing acid, such as those found in vinegar or even orange juice.

Demonstratives in Discourse **333**

Exercise 2

If you have access to an OHP, make a transparency of this exercise and mark it in your class processing as instructed in the student book. To save time, assign individuals/pairs to prepare one or two questions, and then correct as a class.

Workbook Ex. 2, p. 141. Answers: TE p. 506.

ANSWER KEY

Exercise 2

Demonstratives have been boldfaced and the things they refer to have been underlined:

2. We hold **these** truths to be self-evident, that all men are created equal, and have a right to life, liberty, and the pursuit of happiness.

3. Let me make **this** perfectly clear: No new taxes!

4. Frank said that he wanted to leave New York because he was tired of big city life. But I don't think **that** was the real reason for his move to California. The real reason was that his wife wanted to live in a place with warmer winters. At least, **this** is what Stuart told me.

5. **These** soldiers must report immediately to Barracks B: Private Rebecca Adams, Private Mary Collins and Corporal Marsha Powell. **These** soldiers have been assigned to patrol duty: Sergeant Kitty Westmoreland and Corporal Mary MacArthur. **Those** are your orders, soldiers. Troops dismissed!

6. The causes of the American Civil War were not substantially different from **those** of other wars that have taken place between different regions of any country. **This** is one of the things that can be learned by studying history.

7. The chemical composition of baking soda shares a number of similarities with **that** of any compound containing sodium. **This** is what allows baking soda to enter into a chemical reaction with any compound containing acid, such as **those** found in vinegar or even orange juice.

8. Management techniques of many American companies now tend to resemble **those** used in Japan much more than they did a few years ago. **This** is due to the success **those** techniques have had in raising worker productivity.

8. Management techniques of many American companies now tend to resemble those used in Japan much more than they did a few years ago. This is due to the success those techniques have had in raising worker productivity.

This/That Versus *It*

EXAMPLES	EXPLANATIONS
"Did you hear the news? Scott is in jail?" **(a)** "I knew **it**! That boy was always a trouble-maker!" (*Implied Meaning:* I'm not surprised!) **(b)** "I knew **that**. His mother told me last week." (*Implied Meaning:* I'd already heard that news.)	Both demonstrative pronouns (**this/that**) and personal pronouns (**it**) refer back to ideas or items in previous sentences, but there is often a difference in emphasis or implied meaning.
They say that Mary is getting married to Paul. **(c)** Has John heard about **this**? (*Implied Meaning:* Has this important information been told to John?)	Using *this/that* emphasizes that the idea being referred to is the most important information in the new sentence.
They say that Mary is getting married to Paul. **(d)** I don't *believe* **it**! (*Implied Meaning*: That's unbelievable!)	Using *it* indicates that some other part of the sentence (the subject or verb) is the most important information. We do not generally use pronouns to talk about significant new information.

In some cases we **must** use *that* instead of *it*.

(e) Don't leave your keys in the car. Someone might steal **it**. **(f)** Don't worry. I'm smarter than **that**. **(g)** (**NOT**) I'm smarter than **it**.	This is especially true in cases where *it* could refer to a physical object (*the car* or *the dog*) rather than the general idea or situation.
(h) Aunt Martha is planning to bring her dog when she visits us. **(i)** I was afraid of **that**! No wonder she was asking if we had cats. **(j)** (**NOT**) I was afraid of **it**!	

S U G G E S T I O N S :

1. The distinctions in this focus are more subtle and may be harder for your Ss to grasp. Be sure to give a "dramatic" oral rendition to the example sentences, since the stress will never fall on the pronoun (it).

2. Help Ss by giving them other examples of the difference. Try looking at the examples in the book where the use of *that* is obligatory and then supply a few more orally delivered examples that refer to things in the class.

   Additional example 1:

   "Kyoko told Mari that we we're going to have a quiz tomorrow, and what did she say? I was afraid of . . ." Let the class supply the correct reference for *that*.

   Another example: *"Our teacher told us that she was going to give us two hours worth of homework tonight! Can you believe . . . ? (it?) She must think we have nothing else to do."*

3. Do Exercise 3 in class as part of your presentation. Ss' understanding of this feature will continue to "develop" as you work through the additional examples there.

EXERCISE 3

Decide which form, demonstrative pronoun (this/that) or personal pronoun (it), to put in the blanks. In most sentences, both forms are possible, but native speakers would tend to choose one form instead of the other to indicate a particular emphasis. Compare your choices with those of other students and your teacher.

1. Someone took your wallet? I was afraid _____ would happen!

2. I'm glad Sunyoon hasn't had her baby yet. She was afraid _____ would happen while her husband was out of town.

3. I'm sorry you had to spend such a beautiful, sunny day in the library. _____ isn't really fair, is it?

4. I assume you have all heard the news about Ali. _____ is why I have asked you here to this meeting.

5. I love the wonderful California climate. _____ is why I moved here.

6. Did you say George's son is involved in another financial scandal? Are you completely sure of _____?

7. I just know Mary's dating someone else. I'm sure of _____!

8. If you don't take advantage of this great opportunity, I know you'll regret _____ in the future.

9. Don't worry about making such a mess. _____ really doesn't matter.

10. Don't worry about making such a mess. _____ is why I put newspapers over everything.

11. A: You said "seventeen." Don't you mean "seventy"?
    B: Oh yes, _____ 's what I meant.

12. Don't complain to me. _____ is why we have a complaint department.

Exercise 3

Do this exercise immediately after your presentation of Focus 3.

1. Work through it as a whole class, sentence by sentence. Allow plenty of time for multiple right answers and questions.

2. It can also be used as an open-ended pair or small group exercise. Ss can compare their answers with the ones listed here and reevaluate the hypotheses they made in the Opening Task.

Workbook Ex. 3, p. 141. Answers: TE p. 506.

ANSWER KEY

Exercise 3

While in most questions all three are grammatically possible, the **best** answer (based on native speaker responses) has been indicated. In some cases, more than one choice is equally acceptable.

1. that 2. it 3. That/It 4. This/That
5. That 6. that 7. it 8. it 9. It
10. That/This 11. that's 12. That/This

FOCUS 4

1. This use of *this/that* for forward-pointing reference is more straightforward and easier for Ss to grasp. Present the focus as written or use class-related examples such as the following:
   Relative clauses: <u>Those</u> who do their homework will get good grades in this class, but <u>those</u> who don't will probably fail.
   Prepositional phrases: Compare your paragraph to <u>that</u> of another student.
2. Alternatively, assign this and the focus that follows for self-study at home.

Exercise 4

Do this exercise question by question as a class. If Ss can easily identify the structure, only do a few and move on to the next focus.

Workbook Ex. 4, p. 142. Answers: TE p. 506.

FOCUS **4**

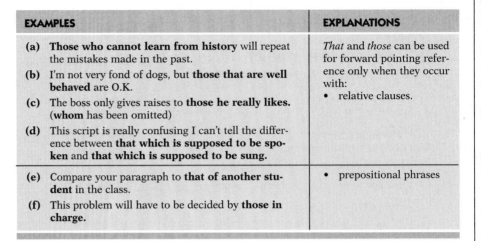

That/Those with Forward-Pointing Reference

EXAMPLES	EXPLANATIONS
(a) **Those who cannot learn from history** will repeat the mistakes made in the past. (b) I'm not very fond of dogs, but **those that are well behaved** are O.K. (c) The boss only gives raises to **those he really likes.** (**whom** has been omitted) (d) This script is really confusing I can't tell the difference between **that which is supposed to be spoken** and **that which is supposed to be sung.**	*That* and *those* can be used for forward pointing reference only when they occur with: • relative clauses.
(e) Compare your paragraph to **that of another student** in the class. (f) This problem will have to be decided by **those in charge.**	• prepositional phrases

EXERCISE 4

Identify the demonstratives that are followed by modifying clauses or phrases in these passages. Not all sentences contain these structures.

1. There is an old proverb that says fate helps those that help themselves.
2. Please put those in the refrigerator.
3. My brother is very fussy about eating certain vegetables. He won't touch these, but those he likes won't stay on his plate for very long.
4. Those in the stock brokerage business think that this is a bad time to invest.
5. One must learn to distinguish between that which is necessary and that which is only desirable.
6. Those who can't tell the difference between the colors teal and aquamarine shouldn't become interior decorators.
7. That is not my responsibility. You'll have to speak to those in charge of that part of the operation.
8. I read about that in the newspapers.

ANSWER KEY

Exercise 4
Sentences 2 and 8 do not contain the structure.
1. . . . those that help themselves . . .
3. . . . those he likes . . . 4. Those in the stock brokerage business . . .
5. . . . that which is necessary . . . that which is only desirable. 6. Those who can't tell the difference between teal and aquamarine . . . 7. . . . those in charge of that part of the operations.

► **Special Uses of Demonstratives**

Using *This/These* with Nonspecific Nouns

EXAMPLES	EXPLANATIONS
(a) I'm walking down the street and I see **this** man on the corner. He's talking with **these** two other guys.	In very informal speech or written narratives we can use *this* and *these* in place of indefinite determiners to introduce nouns for the first time.

Using *That* to Refer to Humans

EXAMPLES	EXPLANATIONS
(b) **That** man over there is married to **that** woman in the red dress.	**That** is not usually used to refer to humans, except when the speaker is pointing to the person.
(c) Were you talking to **that** boy again? I told you not to speak to him!	When it is used in other kinds of reference, it usually indicates the speaker is annoyed, or is insulting the person being referred to.

EXERCISE 5

Make this paragraph more informal by replacing the underlined articles with demonstratives. Decide which demonstratives are appropriate for the blanks.

I went to (1) <u>a</u> party where I met (2) <u>some</u> rather strange people. They had all read (3) <u>an</u> article in the newspaper about (4) <u>a</u> new invention that was supposed to help people lose weight. Mary, the hostess, was the strangest of all. She went around the room, asking all the guests to put on (5) <u>some</u> very dark glasses. Apparently (6) _____ is supposed to help people eat less. Now I ask you: Why does a person go to all the trouble of giving (7) <u>a</u> party if she doesn't want her guests to eat? (8) _____'s Mary for you! She'll believe anything she reads in the paper.

Demonstratives in Discourse | **337**

FOCUS 5

To save time, assign this focus for self-study at home, or briefly point out that there are two "details" that people should probably remember. You can skip it entirely (and Exercise 5) if you are pressed for time.

UNIT GOAL REVIEW

1. If you saved some of your Ss' hypotheses from the Opening Task discussion, show that transparency (or post that flip chart or write those samples on the board) and ask Ss now to refine, reject, or correct the previous hypotheses based on their study of this unit. This process can be done as a class or in groups or pairs.
2. If you have not saved the hypotheses, ask Ss to review the Opening Task and reflect on one notion that has changed as a result of studying the unit. Have Ss report those changes to the rest of the class.

ANSWER KEY

Exercise 5
(1) this   (2) these   (3) this   (4) this (5) these   (6) this   (7) a   (8) That's

USE YOUR ENGLISH

Note: The activities on these "purple pages" at the end of each unit contain communicative activities designed to apply what Ss have learned and help them practice communication and grammar at the same time. For a more complete discussion of how to use the Use Your English activities, see p. xxii of this Teacher's Edition.

Activity 1

This is a "Friday fun" kind of activity. If your class is serious or has not enjoyed other such puzzles, skip this exercise. Be sure that Ss don't just turn to the answer in the book. The correctly punctuated sentences are: **That that is, is. That that is not, is not. Isn't that it? It is!**

Activity 2

You can use this activity to see if Ss can use *that, this,* and *it* correctly, but it might just be better to relax and let them have fun with it.

Activity 3

Ss should have no trouble finding examples in most popular sitcoms, but you may wish to assign a particular program or use a clip in class to be sure that there actually are examples of *that* and *it.* The open-ended discussion can be done in pairs, small groups, or as a class.

Activity 4

Make this a writing assignment to provide a context for evaluating Ss' mastery of the reference forms discussed in this unit.

Use Your English

ACTIVITY 1: SPEAKING/WRITING

Here is a puzzle. Can you punctuate this so that it makes sense?

that that is is that that is not is not isn't that it it is

There are four sentences in the correct answer. The solution is on page A-12.

ACTIVITY 2: WRITING/SPEAKING

STEP 1 Write a dialogue like the one in the Opening Task on page 329. Work with a partner. First, decide what the argument will be about. Then write your dialogue. Try to use some of the phrases that Peter and Denise used.

STEP 2 Perform your dialogue for the rest of the class.

ACTIVITY 3: LISTENING

Listen to an argument on a television comedy or drama. Write down the examples you hear using *that* or *it.* Why do you think the speakers used a particular form?

ACTIVITY 4: WRITING/SPEAKING

Compare two products from different countries or people from two different settings. For example: How does the coffee of Guatemala differ from that of Sumatra? How do students in high school differ from those in college? Present your comparison in either written or spoken form.

ACTIVITY 5: SPEAKING

Tell a story in informal spoken English. Use the present time frame and demonstratives (*this* and *these*) instead of indefinite articles. See Exercise 5 for an example to get you started.

ACTIVITY 6: LISTENING

STEP 1 Denise and Peter are arguing again. Listen to their conversation and write answers to the questions below. You may need to listen to the conversation more than once. Use *it* or *that* in your answers. The first question has been answered for you as an example.

1. When did Denise finish the Davis contract?
   She finished it late last night.

2. What did Denise think of Peter's offer to help?

3. When did Denise write her official complaint to Mr. Green?

4. How does Denise react when Peter offers to show her pictures of his son's play?

5. What does Denise threaten to do with the computer terminal if Peter doesn't stop telling her to be less serious about work?

6. Why does Peter decide to leave the office to take his children to the beach?

7. What effect does Denise think that firing Peter would have on the office?

STEP 2 When you have finished, compare your answers to those of another student in the class.

Activity 5

See comments for Activity 2.

Activity 6

Play textbook audio. The tapescript for this listening appears on p. 519 of this book. Allow for multiple listenings as needed: once for general comprehension, once for answers to specific questions, once for clarification and confirmation, and once to check answers.

The test of this unit can be found on p. 478. The answers are on p. 479 of this book.

TOEFL Test Preparation Exercises for Units 19–20 can be found on pp. 143–145 of the Workbook.
The answers are on p. 506 of this book.

ANSWER KEY

Activity 6

Answers will vary slightly:

2. She thought it was too little and too late.
3. She wrote it before she finished the Davis contract.   4. She doesn't like it.   5. She threatens to throw it at him.   6. Denise told him to leave and said that she really meant it.
7. It would make this office so much more business-like.

Unit 21

UNIT OVERVIEW

This unit covers the use of possessives in discourse. Most students (Ss) have encountered possessive pronouns and determiners before, but have not studied the more complex issues of when to use one form rather than another or what actual "nonpossessive" meaning might be communicated by a particular possessive. Helpful information concerning these issues of meaning and use of possessive forms is contained in *The Grammar Book* (pp. 311–317).

UNIT GOALS

Review the goals listed on this page so Ss understand what they should be able to do by the end of the unit.

OPENING TASK

The primary purpose of this task is to give Ss an opportunity use a variety of possessive forms in an entertaining context. It can be done in a variety of ways.

1. Do it as a class discussion, writing the possessive forms on the board.

2. Have Ss do it in pairs or small groups. Introduce an element of competition by doing a variation of Activity 3. Allow them to look at the picture for a limited period of time and then have them make a list of anomalies with books closed. The pair or group with the most complete list wins the game.

3. Use it as a diagnostic by having Ss write their responses for you to collect and evaluate.

UNIT 21

POSSESSIVES

UNIT GOALS:

- To correctly identify and use possessive forms (possessive determiners, possessive pronouns, possessive phrases and possessive nouns)

- To know when to use possessive nouns and when to use possessive phrases

- To correctly understand the various meanings of possessives

OPENING TASK
What's Wrong with this Picture?

How observant are you? There are at least ten strange things about the picture on the next page. For example, the legs of the table seem to be a person's legs. Find as many other strange things as you can and write descriptions of them on the next page.

Strange Things

1. _____
2. _____
3. _____
4. _____
5. _____
6. _____
7. _____
8. _____
9. _____
10. _____
11. _____
12. _____

ANSWER KEY

Strange things about the picture:
The flowers of the plant are cups and saucers. The man's shoes are swim fins. The top of the table appears to be grass. The legs of the table appear to be human legs. The fringe of the sofa appears to be fingers. The door knob appears to be a tomato. The hands of the clock are carrots. One of the drawers in the dresser looks like a mouth. The knobs of the TV are happy faces. The wheels of the child's tricycle are not round. The child's hair looks like snakes. The dog's tail is very, very long. The cover of one of the books has a bite taken out of it.

This focus may be review for most students.

SUGGESTIONS:

1. Ask *"What forms do we use to talk about who something belongs to"* or write a sentence on the board such as *"Whose book is this?"* and elicit various possessive structures. *("It's Juan's book. It's Juan's. It belongs to Juan. It's his book. It's his. It belongs to him." etc.)*
2. Optional follow-up: Ask Ss to provide the grammatical labels (possessive determiner, possessive pronouns, etc.).

Pronunciation Note: Write sentences containing the examples below and ask if anyone can pronounce the possessive form or tell you the rule of how to pronounce it.

Pronunciation of *-'s* or *-s'* in possessive nouns varies according to the last sound of the word it is added to.
After voiceless consonants:
it is pronounced /s/
Rick's, Mac's, aunt's, Chip's
After voiced consonants & vowels:
it is pronounced /z/
Mary's, Sam's, mother's, Joe's
After sibilants:
it is pronounced /iz/
Grace's, church's, judge's, Dennis'

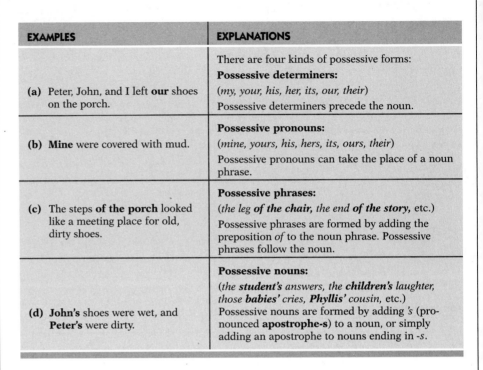

FOCUS **1**

▶ **Possessive Forms**

EXAMPLES	EXPLANATIONS
(a) Peter, John, and I left **our** shoes on the porch.	There are four kinds of possessive forms: **Possessive determiners:** (*my, your, his, her, its, our, their*) Possessive determiners precede the noun.
(b) **Mine** were covered with mud.	**Possessive pronouns:** (*mine, yours, his, hers, its, ours, their*) Possessive pronouns can take the place of a noun phrase.
(c) The steps **of the porch** looked like a meeting place for old, dirty shoes.	**Possessive phrases:** (*the leg of the chair, the end of the story,* etc.) Possessive phrases are formed by adding the preposition *of* to the noun phrase. Possessive phrases follow the noun.
(d) **John's** shoes were wet, and **Peter's** were dirty.	**Possessive nouns:** (*the **student's** answers, the **children's** laughter, those **babies'** cries, **Phyllis'** cousin,* etc.) Possessive nouns are formed by adding *'s* (pronounced **apostrophe-s**) to a noun, or simply adding an apostrophe to nouns ending in *-s*.

342 UNIT 21

EXERCISE 1

Underline and identify all the possessive structures in the following passage. Are they: (a) possessive determiners, (b) possessive pronouns, (c) possessive phrases, or (d) possessive nouns? The first paragraph has been done for you as an example. Do all the structures you identified describe possessive relationships?

(1) Have you ever tested (*a*) <u>your</u> memory? (2) There have been many studies of (*d*) <u>people's</u> ability to remember things. (3) These studies have found that there are two types (*c*) <u>of memory</u>: short-term memory and long-term memory.

(4) Short-term memory depends on the "length" or number of items that someone needs to remember. (5) A person's ability to remember a series of numbers for more than a minute is limited to about twelve or fourteen digits. (6) An individual's ability to remember strings of unconnected words seems to average about eight items. (7) Most people's performance on such memory tests will drop quickly if they are tested again, even after only a few hours' time.

(8) Long-term memory seems to be determined by the item's usefulness to the person being tested. (9) For example, people do a better job of remembering one of Shakespeare's sonnets if they can apply the "message" of the poem to some part of their own lives. (10) The more important a piece of information is to a person's life, the longer and more accurately it can be retained.

Exercise 1

Ss can discuss the "meaning" of the possessive structures as part of this exercise or in connection with Focus 3.

SUGGESTIONS:

1. Many of the structures do not have possessive meanings. Point out such examples in sentences 5, 6, 9, and 10.
2. Preview the concept of quantifiers (*one of . . .*) which is treated in Unit 22.
3. If you have access to an OHP, make a transparency of the passage and underline the possessives.

Workbook Ex. 1, p. 146. Answers: TE p. 506.

ANSWER KEY

Exercise 1
(1) (a) your   (2) (d) people's   (3) (c) of memory: (4) (c) of items   (5) (d) person's (c) of numbers   (6) (c) of unconnected words s
(7) (d) people's (d) hours'   (8) (d) item's
(9) (c) of remembering (c) of (d) Shakespeare's sonnets (c) of the poem (a) their   (10) (c) of information is to a (d) person's

1. Refer back to the *"Whose book is this?"* question you asked in the previous focus. Write *"the student's book"* and *"the book of the student"* on the board. Ask Ss if the meaning is the same. (They should answer "yes".) Then ask if we use them in the same situations. (The answer should be "no".)

2. Present the examples in the book in a straightforward way, writing them in two columns, one under "−'s" the other under "of + −".

3. Do Exercise 2 immediately as follow-up.

FOCUS **2**

Possessive Nouns Versus Possessive Phrases

EXAMPLES	EXPLANATIONS
(a) **The tall man's** face appeared in the window. **(b)** The face **of the tall man** appeared **in the window.**	Possessive noun (-'s) mean the same thing as nouns with a possessive prepositional phrase (*of . . .*), but one form is usually preferred over the other in specific situations.
(c) the **boy's** cap NOT: the cap **of the boy** **(d)** the **horse's** mouth NOT: the mouth **of the horse**	Use possessive nouns (with -'s) for: • most animate (living) nouns
(e) the **razor's** edge **(f)** the **train's** arrival	• objects that perform an action
(g) the **moon's** orbit **(h)** the **river's** mouth **(i)** the **earth's** atmosphere	• natural phenomena
(j) the back **of the chair** NOT: the **chair's** back **(k)** the roof **of the house** NOT: the **house's** roof **(l)** the cause **of the problem** NOT: the **problem's** cause	Use possessive phrases (with *of* + noun phrase): • for most inanimate (nonliving) nouns
(m) the daughter **of a well-known local politician** NOT: **a well-known local politician's daughter**	• when the possessive noun phrase is very long
(n) the that **of Mary's tall old-fashioned mother** NOT: **Mary's tall old-fashioned mother's** hat	• when a multiple possessive is long

EXERCISE 2

For each noun + possessive, write the best possessive form in the blank in the sentence. Add articles where necessary.

▶ **EXAMPLES:**   hat/boy: _The boy's hat_____ blew into the sea.

cover/*Time* magazine: Being on _the cover of Time magazine_ made Elvis Presley even more famous.

1. results/investigation: _____ were reported in the newspaper.
2. restaurant/Alice's mother: We had dinner at _____.
3. ability/individual: _____ to remember something depends on how important the information is.
4. rights/women: Suffragettes were early activists in the battle for

   _____ .
5. opening/novel: _____ begins with the famous words, "Call me Ishmael."
6. take-off/rocket: _____ was quite an amazing spectacle.
7. music/Elvis Presley: _____ has been heard all over the world.
8. discovery/penicillin: Sir Alexander Fleming was responsible for

   _____ .
9. children/a very famous American movie star: I went to school with

   _____ .
10. rotation/earth: _____ is what causes night and day.

EXERCISE 3

Change the cues in parentheses to the correct possessive constructions. Add articles where necessary.

Last week Matt went shopping. It was (1) _____ (his roommate Jeff/birthday), and he wanted to buy a really "unusual" gift. He drove (2) _____ (Jeff/car) downtown. When he got there he realized that the (3) _____ (shopping district/center) was already quite crowded, and most (4) _____ (stores/the parking lots) were already full. He was in a hurry, so he decided to park in front of a hotel. He thought the (5) _____ (hotel/doorman) looked annoyed, but he wasn't really paying much attention. He visited several stores. In (6) _____ (one of the stores/window) he saw the perfect gift: a statue of a cowboy. In (7) _____ (cowboy/

Possessives | **345**

Exercise 2

Go through these one at a time as a class to follow up your presentation of Focus 2. If you wish, assign individuals or pairs to prepare three or four and then process as a class.

Exercise 3

Assign as homework. Review briefly in class the next day.

Workbook Exs. 2 & 3, pp. 147–148.
Answers: TE p. 506.

hand) there was a container for toothpaste, toothbrush, and razor. He thought that the statue would look perfect in (8) _____ (their apartment/bathroom). He bought it and hurried back to where he had parked. The car was gone! At first Matt thought it had been stolen, but then he realized that it had probably been towed away. He called the police, and they verified that the car was at the station. When he got there, he found that (9) _____ (the car/front fender) had a dent, and there was a big scratch on (10) _____ (the car/side). Matt had to pay for the (11) _____ (repair/cost) and the towing charges. Jeff got a very expensive birthday present, and Matt got a long-overdue lesson about traffic laws and parking regulations.

Meanings of Possessive Forms

EXAMPLES	EXPLANATIONS
(a) Please give me ten **dollars'** worth of unleaded gasoline. **(b)** That leather coat cost me a **week's** pay. **(c)** This book represents three **years'** work.	Possessive forms can be used to describe other kinds of meaning besides belonging to someone or something. We also use possessive forms to indicate: • amount or quantity
(d) The **index of a book** is the best place to start when you're looking for specific information. **(e)** The **team's captain** scored the goal.	• part of a whole
(f) Scientists are still trying to discover **the cause of cancer.** **(g)** **The streets of New York** can be dangerous at night. **(h)** **Margaret's friend** is blind.	• a general relationship or association
(i) We learned about **the exports of Australia** in our international business class. **(j)** **Joan's conversation** with the doctor caused her some concern.	• origin or agent

346 | UNIT 21

FOCUS 3

1. Remind the class that you have discussed the form of possessives, and the use. Now you are turning your attention to meaning.
2. If you have access to an OHP, make a transparency of the example sentences, covering up the explanation side, and ask Ss if they can identify what meaning is communicated by the structure. You many need to help them by asking questions like *"In sentence B does the pay belong to the week?" "In sentence H does the blind friend belong to Margaret?"*
3. Show the explanation side of the focus chart and ask Ss if they can generate other examples of that particular meaning difference (see below for other possible examples).

V A R I A T I O N :

1. Use class-related examples such as: **amount or quantity:** *I'm assigning three hour's homework for you all to night.;* **part of the whole:** *Half of the class will do question three. A few of the students will fail this course.* **general relationship:** *The purpose of this class is to improve your grammar.* **origin or agent:** *Our teacher's assignment helped us improve quickly.*
2. Do Exercise 4 as an immediate follow-up or use it as a source for more examples.

EXERCISE 4

By yourself: Read the following article about Elvis Presley and underline all the possessives.

With a partner: Compare your answers. Find at least two examples of possessives that convey each of the following meanings, and write those examples in the space next to the meanings listed.

(a) quantity or amount   _____

(b) part of a whole   _____

(c) general relationship or association   _____

(d) origin or agent   _____

(e) actual possession   _____

(f) phrases with *of* that should   _____

    not be considered possessive

THE KING OF ROCK AND ROLL

(1) The most-visited residence in the United States is, <u>of course</u>, the White House, in Washington, D.C., the home <u>of the President of the United States</u>. (2) But the second most-visited residence may surprise you. (3) It is Graceland Mansion in Memphis, Tennessee, the home <u>of Elvis Presley</u>, the "King" <u>of Rock and Roll</u>. (4) Presley's influence on the popular music <u>of America</u> was profound. (5) He was one <u>of the first blues artists</u> to make rock and roll popular with the middle class <u>of the United States</u>. (6) And <u>Elvis'</u>

swinging hips and sexy voice made him the dream boyfriend <u>of an entire generation of teenage girls.</u>

(7) Presley's historic appearance on a 1958 broadcast of "The Ed Sullivan Show" caused an uproar. (8) His singing could not be heard because of the screams of his adoring fans. (9) And Presley's famous swinging hips were not seen at all, because of the objections of TV broadcasters, who felt his wild movements weren't suitable for family television. (10) Presley rapidly became America's most popular male singer of all time. (11) He made dozens of records and many films. (12) Everywhere he went crowds of screaming, adoring fans showered him with gifts, love, and devotion.

(13) But his personal life was marked by tragedy. (14) By the time he died in 1977, everyone had heard the rumors of his troubles with alcohol and drugs. (15) They had read about his failed marriage in the movie magazines. (16) His suspicions about his friends' loyalties and motivations had made a "living nightmare" of his life. (17) He died a prisoner of his own popularity.

(18) In spite of his death, Elvis is still called "The King of Rock and Roll." (19) Graceland Mansion is visited by hundreds of adoring fans every day. (20) His

Possessives **347**

Exercise 4

1. Do this exercise as an immediate whole class follow-up to your presentation of Focus 3.

2. Follow the instructions, or do items one by one, calling on individual Ss. To save time, assign two or three sentences for each individual (or pair) to prepare, and then process as a class.

ANSWER KEY

Exercise 4

The following possessives should be underlined. The possessive meaning for each has been indicated.

(1) of course, (f) of the President, (e) of the United States. (c)   (3) of Elvis Presley, (e) of Rock and Roll. (c)   (4) Presley's (d), of America (c)   (5) of the first blues artists (b), of the United States. (b)   (6) Elvis' (e), of an entire generation (e), of teenage girls. (b)   (7) Presley's (c) of the Ed Sullivan Show (c)   (8) His (e), of the screams (f) of his adoring

fans. (c/d)   (9) Presley's (e/b), of the objections (f) of TV broadcasters (d) his (d/e)   (10) America's (c), of all time (c).   (11) of records (a)   (12) of screaming, adoring fans (a)   (13) his (e)   (14) of his (e) troubles (15) his (e)   (16) His (e), his friends' (e), of his life. (X)   (17) of his own popularity. (c) (18) of his death, (f) of Rock and Roll". (c) (19) of adoring fans (a)   (20) His (d), Presley's (d)   (22) his (e), of his (e), fame (c) . . . his fans' (e).   (23) his (e/b)   (24) of letters (a), "The King's" (e/c).

Exercise 5

If you have access to an OHP, make a transparency of the exercise and underline the possessive forms as part of your group processing of the exercise.

EXERCISE 5

Underline the possessive forms in the following sentences. There may be more than one possible interpretation. With a partner, discuss which of the following meanings the possessive forms indicate:

(a) an amount or quantity   (d) an origin or agent

(b) a part of a whole   (e) actual possession

(c) a general relationship/association

▶ **EXAMPLE:** The streets of San Francisco are famous for their steep hills.
                             (b)   (c)

1. Scientists are studying the effects of alcohol on an individual's memory.
2. The wines of France are among the best in the world.
3. The teacher's assistant will hand back the homework.
4. That concept was introduced in the book's first chapter.
5. Chicago is four days' drive from Los Angeles.
6. An investigation of short-term memory has shown that items of personal importance are more easily remembered.
7. The steps of the porch looked like a meeting place of old, dirty shoes.
8. Matt's roommate likes ice cream.
9. Beethoven's symphonies still thrill listeners.

EXERCISE 6

Are these sentences correct or incorrect? If they are incorrect, identify the problem and correct it.

1. The fame of Elvis Presley spread across America.
2. The table's top was covered with newspapers.
3. The child of Bambang's classmate was sick with the flu.
4. Gladys' well-known next-door neighbor's dog's barking annoyed the entire neighborhood.
5. The scientists' studies' results indicate that memory is affected by such things as weather and time of day.
6. Memory's investigations have shown that the ability of people to remember things declines with age.
7. Rock and Roll's King died in 1977.
8. Elvis' death's circumstances are somewhat mysterious.

EXERCISE 7

Ask a classmate for his or her opinions on these topics, and the reasons for those opinions. Report your partner's answers to the rest of the class.

▶ **EXAMPLE:** best place to sit in a classroom

> **You:** Where's the best place to sit in a classroom?
>
> **Your partner:** The front of the class is better if you're a good student, but the back of the class is better if you want to sleep.

1. most important part of the semester (beginning, end, or middle)
2. favorite object that belongs to someone else
3. most important period of history
4. favorite piece of music

Ask two additional questions of your own that use possessive forms.

Possessives | **349**

Exercises 6 & 7

UNIT GOAL REVIEW

1. Ask Ss to look at the goals on the opening page of this unit and, as a class or in pairs, to provide a rule and give an example for: when we use 's, when we use *of* + *NP*.

SUGGESTION:

Write these two questions up on the board and then allow Ss to look through the unit for awhile silently as they formulate their answers.
2. Ask if using possessive forms always indicates a possessive meaning. (Students will hopefully answer "no.")
3. Repeat the process of having Ss find an example of these other kinds of possessive meaning, allowing them to look through the unit as needed.

ANSWER KEY

Exercise 6

1. Better to use possessive noun with animate nouns: *Elvis Presley's fame spread across America.* 2. Better to use possessive phrase with inanimate nouns: *The top of the table was covered with newspapers.* 3. OK. 4. The possessive phrase is very long: *The barking of the dog of Gladys' well-known next-door neighbor annoyed the entire neighborhood.* 5. **Studies** is inanimate: *The results of the scientists' studies indicate that memory is affected by such things as weather and time of day.* 6. **Memory** is inanimate: *Investigations of memory* have shown that the ability of people to remember that things decline with age. 7. **Rock and Roll** is inanimate: *The King of Rock and Roll died in 1977.* 8. **Death** is inanimate: *The circumstances of Elvis' death are somewhat mysterious.*

Exercise 7

Answers will vary. Possible questions and answers include:

1. What is the most important part of the semester—beginning, end, or middle?/ The beginning of the semester, because you want the teacher to get a good impression of you right away. 2. What is your favorite object that belongs to someone else?/My favorite object is my brother's car. I wish I had one too. 3. What is the most important period of history?/I think that the present day is the most important period of history, because there have been so many changes in the forms of government and the kinds of economic structures. 4. What is your favorite piece of music?/My favorite piece of music is "Mathis der Mahler" by Paul Hindemith.

Activity 1
VARIATION:

Use this activity as a written check by asking Ss to write descriptions of the differences between the two sets of diagrams to hand in for evaluation.

Activity 2

Remind Ss of Exercise 5 (the description of Elvis) as an example of the kind of description that they may want to write.

Activity 3

This activity is best used as a "Friday fun" pair work change of pace. Do not use it if you already integrated this "short-term memory aspect" into your treatment of the Opening Task.

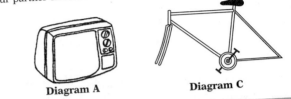

Use Your English

ACTIVITY 1: SPEAKING

Work with a partner to fill in the missing parts of the diagrams. Student A, look at diagrams A and C below. Student B, look at Diagrams B and D on page A-12. Diagram A contains elements not contained in Diagram B. Help your partner complete Diagram B correctly. Your partner should help you complete Diagram C, which is incomplete. You should not look at Diagrams B and D. Your partner should not look at Diagrams A and C.

Diagram A   **Diagram C**

ACTIVITY 2: WRITING

Write a short description of a famous person. What are the things that made him or her famous? Here are some things you might mention in your description: his or her accomplishments, childhood, important experiences, influence on society.

ACTIVITY 3: SPEAKING

Check your short-term memory. Study the picture at the beginning of this chapter for thirty seconds. Then close your book and describe it to a partner. Your partner should look at the picture while you describe it and check your description for accuracy.

ACTIVITY 4: WRITING/SPEAKING

Oh no! There's been an automobile accident! Look at the picture and describe what has happened to the car and its passengers. After you have written your description, check the accuracy of your use of possessive forms.

ACTIVITY 5: LISTENING/SPEAKING

STEP 1 As you listen to the following talk, use the information to draw the diagram that is described by the speaker. Once you have finished, listen to the lecture again to check that you have completed your diagram correctly.

STEP 2 Compare your diagram with two or three others. As a group, decide on the correct answer to the two questions the speaker asks at the end of the lecture.

Possessives | **351**

Activity 4

The self-monitoring and correction suggested in this activity is a useful technique that can be applied to any of the written activities in this unit or elsewhere in the book.

Activity 5

Play textbook audio. The tapescript for this listening appears on p. 520 of this book. Allow for only two listenings, as described in the instructions.

Allow time for Step 2, and process as a whole class by having an individual or group draw the diagram on the board. Then, as a class, count the actual number of squares and triangles.

The test for this unit can be found on p. 580. The answers are on p. 581 of this book.

ANSWER KEY

Your completed diagram should look like this:

There are larger and smaller shapes, with the larger shapes being made up of groups of smaller shapes:

number of triangles: 40
number of squares: 10

Unit 22

UNIT OVERVIEW

This unit examines two areas that sometimes cause students difficulty, particularly in the area of subject-verb agreement: quantifiers and collective nouns and adjectives: The unit can be studied sequentially or as two separate (though related) topics. Quantifiers are covered in Focuses 1–5 and collectives in Focuses 6 and 7. There is a helpful discussion of these concepts in *The Grammar Book, Chapter 17,* especially pp. 328–335.

UNIT GOALS

Review the goals listed on this page so students (Ss) understand what they should be able to do by the end of the unit.

OPENING TASK

The task can be done in pairs, small groups, orally or written. You can elicit additional use of quantifiers by asking specific questions about the graphs. For example: *"Do most students study art and literature? No, they don't. Only a few study those subjects. Most students study . . ."* etc. See Exercise 5 for possible statements that can be made in connection with the statistics presented in these graphs.

UNIT 22

QUANTIFIERS, COLLECTIVE NOUNS, AND ADJECTIVES

UNIT GOALS:

- To correctly understand and use affirmative and negative quantifiers
- To correctly understand and use collective nouns
- To correctly understand and use collective adjectives

▶ OPENING TASK
Statistics About International Education

The Institute for International Education publishes statistical information about international educational exchange. Work with a partner. Examine these charts on the enrollment of international students in educational institutions in the United States. Using that information and your own knowledge, answer these three questions:

- What fields of study do international students pursue in the United States?
- How do they finance their education?
- Where do most students study?

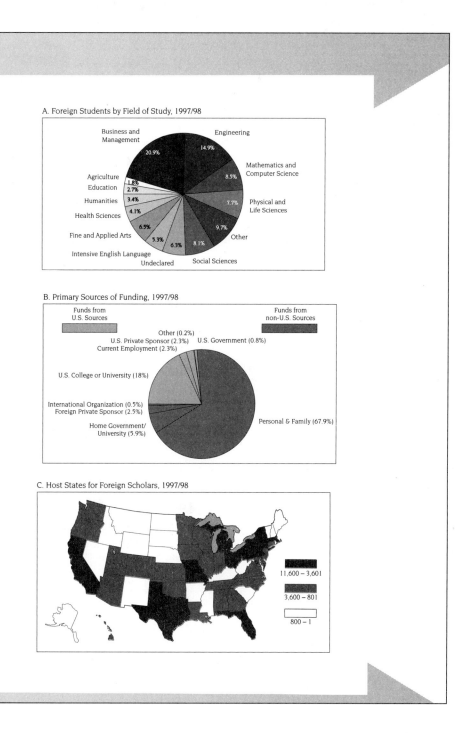

A. Foreign Students by Field of Study, 1997/98

Business and Management 20.9%
Engineering 14.9%
Mathematics and Computer Science 8.5%
Physical and Life Sciences 7.7%
Other 9.7%
Social Sciences 8.1%
Undeclared 6.3%
Intensive English Language 5.3%
Fine and Applied Arts 6.5%
Health Sciences 4.1%
Humanities 3.4%
Education 2.7%
Agriculture 1.8%

B. Primary Sources of Funding, 1997/98

Funds from U.S. Sources
Funds from non-U.S. Sources

Other (0.2%)
U.S. Private Sponsor (2.3%)
U.S. Government (0.8%)
Current Employment (2.3%)
U.S. College or University (18%)
International Organization (0.5%)
Foreign Private Sponsor (2.5%)
Home Government/University (5.9%)
Personal & Family (67.9%)

C. Host States for Foreign Scholars, 1997/98

11,600 – 3,601
3,600 – 801
800 – 1

FOCUS 1

Much of this should be review for your Ss, so this focus adapts well to being assigned as homework for self-study.

1. Follow up your discussion of the Opening Task by writing some of the student-generated sentences on the board, underlining the quantifiers.
2. Ask if anybody knows what we call these kinds of structures. If Ss do not know, say, *"We call the structures quantifiers,"* and write the word on the board.
3. Have Ss turn to the chart on this page, and say, *"Here is a list of all the quantifiers in English. I want you to study this tonight for homework."*

SUGGESTIONS:

1. You may need to review the notions of count and noncount—especially if you have not already done Unit 19.
2. Call attention to the two categories of quantifiers (affirmative and negative) and preview the fact that they are important categories that you will be studying.

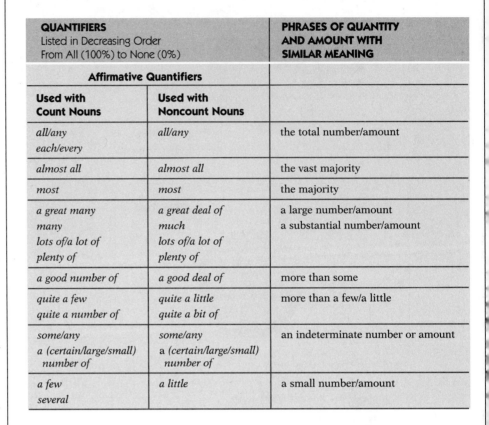

▶ **O**verview of Quantifiers in English

QUANTIFIERS Listed in Decreasing Order From All (100%) to None (0%)		PHRASES OF QUANTITY AND AMOUNT WITH SIMILAR MEANING
Affirmative Quantifiers		
Used with Count Nouns	**Used with Noncount Nouns**	
all/any *each/every*	*all/any*	the total number/amount
almost all	*almost all*	the vast majority
most	*most*	the majority
a great many *many* *lots of/a lot of* *plenty of*	*a great deal of* *much* *lots of/a lot of* *plenty of*	a large number/amount a substantial number/amount
a good number of	*a good deal of*	more than some
quite a few *quite a number of*	*quite a little* *quite a bit of*	more than a few/a little

some/any
*a (certain/large/small)
   number of*
	some/any
	*a (certain/large/small)
	   number of*
		an indeterminate number or amount

a few *several*	*a little*	a small number/amount

Negative Quantifiers		
Used with Count Nouns	**Used with Noncount Nouns**	
not all/every	*not all*	an unspecified number are not/do not
not many	*not much*	a small number/amount
few	*little*	an insufficient number/amount
hardly any almost no/none	*hardly any almost no/none*	the vast majority are not/do not
no/none/not any	*no/none/not any*	the total number/amount are not/do not

EXAMPLES	EXPLANATIONS
(a) **Most international students** study scientific or technical subjects.	You can use quantifiers: • as determiners with noun phrases
(b) **A few** study humanities or fine arts.	• in place of noun phrases to describe number or amount

EXERCISE 1

STEP 1 In the following passage, underline the quantifiers and circle the noun phrases they modify. The first sentence has been done for you as an example.

STEP 2 Are there quantifiers that do not appear with noun phrases? What sentences do they appear in, and what do they refer to?

▶ **EXAMPLE:** Clause 1 of the first sentence has a quantifier that does not appear with a noun phrase: **many.** It refers to **people** or **experts.**

Medical Education in the United States

(1) Even though American medical education is considered by <u>many</u> to be the best in the world, (2) there are relatively <u>few</u> (spaces) in American medical schools, and <u>a substantial number of</u> (Americans) are forced to go overseas to get their basic medical training. (3) As a result, not all the doctors practicing in the United States have received their training from American medical schools. (4) In fact, quite a few

---

Exercise 1

1. Have Ss read the entire passage before doing the exercise.
2. If you have access to an OHP, make a transparency of this exercise and mark it according to the instructions in the book as part of your whole class processing of the exercise.

Workbook Ex. 1, p. 150. Answers: TE p. 507.

ANSWER KEY

Exercise 1
Step 1: Quantifiers are underlined and noun phrases have been indicated in bold. (3) <u>not all</u> **the doctors** (4) <u>quite</u> **a few** (5) <u>all</u> **physicians** (6) <u>Most</u> **doctors** (7) <u>Every</u> **hospital** . . . <u>a few</u> **recently-graduated medical students** (8) <u>many</u> **foreign medical schools.** (9) <u>some</u> **popular hospitals** . . . <u>a great many</u> **applications** . . . <u>each</u> **available space** (10) <u>a number of</u> **hospitals** . . . <u>only</u> <u>a few.</u> (11) <u>most</u> (12) <u>A few</u> . . . **some** (13) <u>Many</u> **doctors** (14) <u>No</u> **doctor** . . . <u>every</u> **area** . . . <u>some</u> **doctors** (15) <u>Each</u> **area**

Step 2: (1) many (people/experts) (4) quite a few (doctors practicing in the U.S.) (10) only a few (applications for residency) (11) most (periods of residency (12) a few, some (residencies)

---

have been educated in other countries. (5) However, all physicians must have clinical experience and pass qualifying examinations in order to receive a license to work in the United States.

(6) Most doctors currently working in the United States have completed their practical training in an American hospital or clinic. (7) Every hospital in this country accepts a few recently graduated medical students each year, (8) including graduates from many foreign medical schools. (9) While some popular hospitals receive a great many applications for each available space, (10) a number of hospitals in rural areas may receive only a few. (11) This period of practical training is called a "residency," and most last for two years. (12) A few are longer; some are shorter, depending on the specialization of the doctor.

(13) Many doctors study for an extra year before they begin their residency in order to become a specialist in a particular area of medicine. (14) No doctor is an expert in every area of medicine, but some doctors have more than one specialty. (15) Each area of medicine has its own period of residency and its own qualifying examinations.

Exercise 2

1. If your class is not good at creating answers, put Ss in pairs or small groups. Do the second part of the exercise for homework.
2. Alternatively, have them make statements about their own countries first.

EXERCISE 2

Based on the information you read in Exercise 1, write sentences that describe the training of medical doctors in the United States. Then write another set of sentences that describes medical training in another country that you are familiar with.

1. Most doctors . . .
2. Not all doctors . . .
3. All doctors . . .
4. A few doctors . . .
5. No doctors . . .
6. Many doctors . . .

Exercise 3

V A R I A T I O N :

To make this exercise a review or even a quiz of the meanings outlined in the chart of Focus 1, do it with books closed. No matter how you present it, make sure that Ss are not just reading the chart.

EXERCISE 3

Use quantifiers to paraphrase the highlighted phrases of quantity or amount.

▶ **EXAMPLE:** **The vast majority of students** pass their qualifying examination on the first try.

Almost all students pass their qualifying examination on the first try.

1. **The vast majority of medical students** in the United States already have bachelor's degrees.

2. **An indeterminate number of students** have more than one major.

ANSWER KEY

Exercise 2
Answers will vary: Possible answers include:
1. study both theoretical and applied topics.
2. are familiar with Western medicine.   3. try to cure patients as quickly as possible.
4. have advanced degrees from the U.S.
5. are children.   6. have private practices.

Exercise 3
1. Almost all medical students . . .
2. Some students . . .   3. There are a few scholarships . . .   4. It takes a great deal of money . . .   5. A few students . . .
6. Some applicants . . .   7. Most international students . . .   8. Many students . . .

3. There are **a small number of scholarships** for international students.

4. It takes **a large amount of money** to fund a university education.

5. **A small number of students** apply to only one university for admission.

6. **An unspecified number of applicants** don't pass the qualifying exams such as TOEFL, GRE, or GMAT.

7. **The majority of international students** apply for admission to more than one university.

8. **A large number of students** study English before they begin their academic studies.

FOCUS **2**

Affirmative and Negative Quantifiers

EXAMPLES	EXPLANATIONS
(a) Do **all** foreign students have similar educational backgrounds? **(b)** **Many** have different backgrounds, but **most** have graduated from high school, although **a few** haven't.	Affirmative quantifiers can usually be used in both affirmative and negative statements and questions.
(c) NOT: **Few** doctors **don't** have medical degrees. **(d)** BETTER: **Almost all** doctors **have** medical degrees.	Negative quantifiers have a negative meaning, and usually do not occur in sentences with negative verbs.

Negative quantifiers often imply that the amount or number is insufficient.

AFFIRMATIVE QUANTIFIERS (A SMALL AMOUNT)	NEGATIVE QUANTIFIERS (NOT ENOUGH)
(e) **A few** doctors have studied nonwestern medicine. (**Some** doctors have studied it.)	**(f)** **Few** doctors have studied nonwestern medicine. (**An insufficient number** have studied it.)
(g) There's **a little** money left after the bills are paid. (There is still **some** money for other things.)	**(h)** There's **little** money left after the bills are paid. (There is **not enough** money for other things.)

This focus can be presented in several different ways.

1. Refer back to the chart in Focus 1 and tell Ss that negative quantifiers are called that because they already have a negative meaning, and as a result do not typically appear in negative sentences.

2. With Ss books closed, write sentences e and f on the board (or class-related alternatives—see below) and ask if they have the same meaning. Point out the implication inherent in negative quantifiers: that "not enough" is part of the implied meaning.

3. Follow up by looking at sentences g & h or class-related alternatives like the following: *Few students in this class need to work harder.* (Almost everyone is doing a good job.) vs. *A few students in the class need to work harder.* (Some students are not doing a good job.)

4. If necessary, present the noncount variant (little and a little) in the same way.

5. Do Exercise 4 as an immediate in-class follow-up to your presentation.

Exercise 4

Do this exercise as directed, or do it as a class immediately following your presentation of Focus 2.

Exercise 5

If your class is not good at creating answers, put Ss in pairs or small groups to do this exercise.

Workbook Exs. 2–4, pp. 150–152. Answers: TE p. 507.

EXERCISE 4

Decide whether to use *few* or *a few, little* or *a little*. Compare your answers to those of a partner.

1. The students were discouraged because _____ people passed the examination.
2. Even very good students sometimes have _____ difficulty gaining admission to a good university.
3. I can loan you some money, but I've only got _____ dollars.
4. They were working in the laboratory for so long that now there's _____ time to get ready for the quiz.
5. There are _____ scholarships available for first-year medical students, so a medical education is expensive.
6. He put _____ effort into studying for examinations, and as a result, didn't pass on the first try.
7. The average medical student usually applies to at least _____ places for residency.
8. Bambang had _____ trouble finding a university. Several schools were willing to accept him.

EXERCISE 5

Using the following negative quantifiers, make true statements about the statistics on international education that you studied in the Opening Task.

1. few
2. not all
3. little
4. hardly any
5. no

FOCUS 3

▶ Singular and Plural Quantifiers

EXAMPLES	EXPLANATIONS
(a) **All doctors know** basic first-aid techniques. **Most have** studied them in medical school. **(b)** **Every doctor knows** basic first-aid techniques. **Each has** studied them in medical school.	Most quantifiers are used with plural count nouns, but a few have a singular form.
(c) **Each student was** asked a question. **(d)** **Every student wants** to do **his or her** best in this class.	*Each* and *every* are only used with singular count nouns.
(e) **No student has** ever taken this test more than once. **(f)** **No doctors** in this country **are** allowed to practice without a license.	*No* can be used with both singular and plural nouns.
(g) When Bambang and Yanti took the TOEFL, **both students** passed on **their** first try. **(h)** **Both were** worried about doing poorly on the exam, but **neither has** to take it again. **(i)** They applied to the same two universities; **both universities have** accepted Yanti, and Bambang is willing to go to **either university** that **accepts** him.	*Both, either,* and *neither* are used in situations where there are only two nouns being described. *Both* is considered plural, but *either* and *neither* are considered to be singular.

EXERCISE 6

Change these statements with plural count nouns to statements with *any, each,* or *every.* Remember to make any other necessary changes to preserve the meaning of the original sentence. More than one answer may be correct.

▶ **EXAMPLE:** All doctors know basic first aid.
    Every doctor knows basic first aid.
    Any doctor knows basic first aid.

1. All doctors must complete their residencies within two years.
2. All parents want their children to succeed in life.
3. Yanti spends all free weekends at the beach.
4. All the people who came to the examination brought calculators.
5. A wise student takes advantage of all opportunities to gain practical experience.

Quantifiers, Collective Nouns, and Adjectives **359**

FOCUS 3

1. Write sentences a & b (or class-related variants—see below) on the board and asking if the subjects are singular or plural. If Ss cannot answer, direct them to the verb and ask whether it is singular or plural.
   Alternative examples: *All students in the class are studying English. Most are working really hard. Every student needs to do the homework. Each student is responsible for making up missed work.*
2. Present sentences e & f and follow the same procedure:
   No student likes to take tests.
   No students failed the last one.
3. Present the final section (*both, either,* and *neither*) in a similar fashion, or assign for homework.

Exercise 6

Do this exercise as a whole class immediately following your presentation of Focus 3.

Assign both exercises for individual homework the night before, and then do as a pair work/peer review follow-up in class.

V A R I A T I O N :

If your Ss have trouble with creative exercises, have the initial composition take place in pairs, followed by comparison with another pair's answers and/or a whole class examination of sentences on the board.

FOCUS 4

If you have not done Unit 19, it is probably better to skip this focus. If you have done the unit:

1. Begin with a brief review of specific and nonspecific references by asking what structures in examples b, d, & f identify the nouns. (Answers: (b) . . . *that stop here*, (d) *who Donna teaches*, (f) *at the police station*.) Point out that the specific noun phrases are marked with *the* and use *of* after the quantifier. In place of the examples in the book, use sentences like these alternative class-related examples: *Any student should be able to answer this question. Any of the students who answer this question will get an A in the class.*
2. Present the exceptions involving *all* and *no/none*.
3. If pressed for time, skip this focus and Focus 5 and tell Ss to review them at home.

EXERCISE 7

Complete these sentences with true information.

1. Each student in this class . . .
2. Every teacher I have had . . .
3. Any English class . . .
4. No student . . .
5. No teachers . . .

EXERCISE 8

Use each of the following quantifiers—*both, either, neither*—to make true statements about similarities between each of the following categories.

1. two students in your class
2. two other people that you know
3. you and a good friend

FOCUS **4**

Using Quantifiers with *Of*

Quantifiers usually refer to nonspecific nouns (nouns that describe how many or how much, rather than identifying a specific item). But you can also use quantifiers with specific noun phrases, by adding *of* to the specific noun phrase. (See Unit 19 for more information and practice with specific and nonspecific reference.)

GENERIC/NONSPECIFIC REFERENCE	SPECIFIC REFERENCE
(a) **Any bus** will take you downtown.	(b) **Any of the buses** that stop here will take you downtown.
(c) **Most students** want to get good grades.	(d) **Most of the students** who Donna teaches have college degrees.
(e) **Several cars** have passed.	(f) **Several of the cars** at the police station had been stolen.

360 UNIT 22

A N S W E R   K E Y

Exercise 7
Answers will vary. Possible answers include:
1. . . . is learning about English grammar.
2. . . . has taught me something.
3. . . . will have students of different abilities.
4. . . . likes homework.   5. . . . sleep in class.

Exercise 8
Answers will vary. Possible answers include:
1. Both Abdul and Chen like to study grammar.
2. Neither student has passed the TOEFL but both of them hope to by the end of the semester.   3. Either my roommate or I will do the dishes before the party.

Note the exception for *all* and *no*.

(g) **All students** hate to take tests.	**(h)** **All the students** in this class hate tests.
	(i) **All of the students** in this class hate tests.
(j) **No buses** run after midnight.	**(k)** **None of the buses** that run after midnight stop here.

EXERCISE 9

Decide whether to use a *quantifier* or *quantifier + of* for these sentences.

1. (All) _____ laboratory equipment on this table should be sterilized before use.

2. (Almost all) _____ plants require sunlight to survive.

3. (Most) _____ coffee served in restaurants contains caffeine.

4. You won't need (much) _____ your warm clothing if you go to medical school in the Philippines.

5. (A great deal) _____ the population still believes in traditional medicine.

6. (Some) _____ the information in your report was incomplete.

7. I don't need (any) _____ your help.

8. Bob wasted (little) _____ the money he won on frivolous things.

9. (No/None) _____ students came to the party

Exercise 9

Do this exercise as an immediate follow-up to your presentation of Focus 4.

Workbook Exs. 5–8, pp. 152–154. Answers: TE p. 507.

ANSWER KEY

Exercise 9
1. All   2. Almost all   3. Most   4. much of
5. A great deal of   6. Some of   7. any of
8. little of   9. No

FOCUS **5**

Quantifiers: Special Cases

EXAMPLES	EXPLANATIONS
(a) **Much of the financial support** for study in the United States comes from the students themselves. **(b)** How **much** money do you have? **(c)** **Not much.** We'd better stop at the bank and get a little. Are there any banks around here?	*Much* is **not** usually used in affirmative statements unless it is a specific reference (used with *of*). *Much* is used in questions and negative sentences.
(d) NOT: I'm having **much** trouble with finding a school. **(e)** I'm having **a lot of** trouble with finding a school.	*A lot* (*lots*) *of* is usually preferred in affirmative sentences.
(f) Is it true that **no students** failed the test? **(g)** That's correct. **None** did.	*No* cannot be used in place of a noun. *None* is used instead.
(h) Did **every** student pass the exam? **(i)** Yes, **every one** did. **(j)** NOT: Yes, **every** did.	*Every* cannot be used to replace a noun phrase without using *one*.

Exercise 10

This is a good exercise to assign for written homework or to review in class.

V A R I A T I O N S :

1. Use it as a structured pair work question and answer exercise.
2. For more variety, assign a third student to each pair to record answers and to write them on the board.

EXERCISE 10

Using the information in the article in Exercise 1, answer these questions with complete sentences, using quantifiers in place of noun phrases.

▶ **EXAMPLE:** Where are most doctors trained?
> *Most are trained here in America, but some study medicine overseas.*

1. Do all doctors in the United States have to pass qualifying examinations?
2. How much money does it take to get a medical education in the United States?
3. How much competition is there for admission to American medical schools?
4. How many doctors have more than one specialty?
5. How many residency positions do most medical students apply for?

A N S W E R   K E Y

Exercise 10
Answers will vary. Possible answers include:
1. Yes they do. All have to pass.   2. It takes quite a bit to get a medical education in the U.S.   3. There's a great deal.   4. A few have more than one specialty.   5. They usually apply for several.   6. Many study overseas.
7. Some are enrolled in the U.S., but not many.   8. No doctor is an expert in every area of medicine.

6. How many Americans study at medical schools overseas?

7. How many foreign students are enrolled in American medical schools?

8. How many doctors are experts in every area of medicine?

EXERCISE 11

Choose the correct form in these sentences.

1. I feel sorry for Albert. He's so shy and he has (few/a few/quite a few) friends he can talk to if he has problems.

2. Hardly any people (came/didn't come) to the meeting.

3. Ivan went to (quite a bit of/a bit of/only a bit of) trouble to get those tickets, so you must remember to thank him.

4. (Not every/Not all/None of) people like to go dancing on Saturday nights.

5. Do you have (many/much/every) time to help me?

6. Sure I do. I've got (a lot/lots of).

7. Why are Albert and Britta so sad? (Both/Neither/None) passed the chemistry exam.

8. Learning English takes (several/a certain amount of/any) practice.

FOCUS **6**

FORM

▶ Collective Nouns

One category of collective nouns refers to groups of people or animals.

EXAMPLES		EXPLANATION
a **troupe** of dancers two **teams** of ball players several **committees** of experts a **delegation** of officials	a **flock** of birds that **herd** of goats **packs** of dogs a **swarm** of insects a **school** of fish	These collective nouns function like other count nouns. You can use them alone or with *of + a noun phrase*. They can have both singular or plural forms.

Quantifiers, Collective Nouns, and Adjectives | **363**

Exercise 11

1. This reviews the whole range of issues involving quantifiers, and probably should be done as a whole class. Do it in your preferred way, but be sure to process the answers so the entire class can check their work.
2. Follow up by asking Ss why they chose the answer that they did. If possible, have Ss refer to the focus that explains the principle involved.

FOCUS 6

1. Begin this focus on another day from your discussion of quantifiers. Have Ss open their books to the focus box and follow along as you present the two categories.
2. Present the second category (on the next page) as a contrast to the first, stressing the fact that the nouns in the second category only occur in singular form. Make sure Ss understand the meaning of the collectives listed.

(Notes continued on next page.)

ANSWER KEY

Exercise 11
1. few 2. came 3. quite a bit of/a bit of
4. Not all 5. much 6. a lot 7. neither
8. a certain amount of

A second kind of collective nouns refers to social or political categories.

EXAMPLES		EXPLANATION
the government the middle class the media the opposition the arts community	the administration the aristocracy the public the establishment	They always occur with *the*. Their grammatical form is singular: **NOT: a** public, **a** media. **NOT:** the **publics** of the United States

Although the form of this kind of collective noun is singular, it can be used with either singular or plural verbs and pronouns.

SINGULAR	PLURAL
Using singular verbs and pronouns usually implies that the group operates as a whole. American English tends to use singular forms with singular collective nouns.	Using plural verbs and pronouns focuses on the individual behavior of the members of the group. British English tends to use plural forms with singular collective nouns.
(a) **The committee** of experts **has** decided to release **its** findings next week.	**(b)** **The committee** of experts **have** decided to release **their** findings next week.
(c) **The aristocracy has** opposed any challenge to **its** economic privileges.	**(d)** **The aristocracy have** opposed any challenge to **their** economic privileges.
(e) **The middle class** in America **has** begun to protest the accelerating decline in **its** standard of living.	**(f)** **The middle class** in America **have** begun to protest the accelerating decline in **their** standard of living.

EXAMPLES	EXPLANATION
(g) The beginning class **likes its** teachers to give **it** lots of homework. **(h)** The beginning class **like their** teachers to give **them** lots of homework. **(i)** NOT: The beginning class **likes their** teachers to give **them** lots of homework.	Although either singular or plural can be used, it is bad style to change from singular to plural within a single sentence or single reference.

3. Present the point about the second category (although always singular) being used with singular or plural verb agreement. Work through the examples (sentences a–f) provided in the focus box.
4. Point out that the class can be considered as an example of this second kind of collective (refer to examples g–h).

EXERCISE 12

In the following sentences, underline each collective noun and any pronouns and verbs which refer to it. Decide why the author chose to consider the collective noun singular or plural.

▶ **EXAMPLE:** The French Revolution was caused in part by the refusal of <u>the aristocracy</u> to give up <u>its</u> social privileges.

Reason: Reference to a single social class—not a collection of individuals.

1. The victorious team all waved to their supporters while the crowd roared its approval.

2. The media is aware of the important role it plays in American presidential elections.

3. The herd of sheep bleated nervously to its shepherd as a pack of wolves made their way through the forest.

4. The military continues to fight further reductions in its funding.

5. The middle class is facing a greater tax burden than it has ever faced before.

6. A rash of new developments have made a great change in the government's priorities, and it is just beginning to respond to them.

EXERCISE 13

Decide whether the collective nouns in these sentences should be used with singular or plural verbs and pronouns, and choose the correct form. Although both choices may be grammatically correct, there may be a clear preference for one form instead of the other, so be prepared to explain why you have chosen the forms you did.

1. The staff took a vote about what kind of holiday party (it/they) (want/wants). (It/They) decided to rent a hall and hire a band.

2. The college administration (want/wants) a basketball team that (is/are) able to win enough games to place (itself/themselves) in the final play-offs.

3. The rowing team raised (its/their) oars as (its/their) boat crossed the finish line.

4. The advanced grammar class never like to turn in (its/their) homework right after a long vacation. (It/They) prefer(s) to finish all assignments before (it/they) leave(s) for vacation.

5. The crowd showed (its/their) approval by letting out a deafening roar.

6. The opposition voiced (its/their) disapproval of the policies the government had released in (its/their) latest report, by making more than three dozen speeches in Parliament.

Quantifiers, Collective Nouns, and Adjectives | **365**

Exercises 12 & 13

These open-ended exercises can be used for pair work or group work discussion, or for individual assignment and subsequent correction or comparison. Process the answers as a class to allow for full discussion and clarification.

Workbook Exs. 9–11, pp. 154–155. Answers: TE p. 507.

ANSWER KEY

Exercise 12

Likely reasons have been indicated:
1. The victorious <u>team</u> all waved to <u>their</u> supporters while <u>the crowd</u> roared <u>its</u> approval. (team members wave in different ways, the crowd behaved as a single entity)   2. <u>The media is</u> aware of the important role <u>it plays</u> in American presidential elections. (an abstract single entity)   3. <u>The herd of sheep</u> bleated nervously to <u>its</u> shepherd as <u>a pack of wolves</u> made <u>their</u> way through the forest. (The sheep behaved more as a group, and the wolves behaved as individuals.)   4. <u>The military continues</u> to fight further reductions in <u>its</u>

funding. (Focus on the whole group, not individual members of the group.)   5. <u>The middle class is</u> facing a greater tax burden than <u>it has</u> ever faced before.(an abstract single entity)   6. <u>A rash of new developments have</u> made a great change on <u>the government's</u> priorities, and <u>it is</u> just beginning to respond to <u>them</u>. (The author wants to keep the pronoun reference clear: developments—plural; government—singular.)

Exercise 13

The most likely reasons have been indicated in parentheses.

1. . . . **they want. They** (Singular sounds very British.)   2. **wants** . . . **is** . . . **itself** (The team and the administration are each a single entity.)   3. **their** . . . **their** (Oars in plural implies that we will talk about the members of the team, since each one has an oar.)
4. **their** . . . **They** . . . **they** (It might be preferable for the first sentence since it's the advanced grammar class, rather than "students in the advanced grammar class." However, the following sentences seem more natural with plural forms.)   5. **its/their** (Both are possible.)
6. **its** . . . **their** (By making "government" plural, pronoun reference is clearer.)

1. Have Ss look at the examples in the book.
2. Do Exercise 14 immediately afterward as a class for a follow-up/application.
   Additional examples: *Only the stupid or the lazy expect their books to be so comprehensive.*

Exercise 14

Do Exercise 14 immediately afterward as a whole class follow-up to your presentation. As an alternative, have Ss frame their restatements as rewrites of the full original sentences.

Workbook Ex. 12, p. 155. Answers: TE p. 507.

Exercise 15

1. This exercise practices all the collective noun forms in an integrated way. It can be done as homework, as an in-class quiz, or as additional practice and review.
2. If you have access to an OHP, make a transparency of the passage and circle the correct answers as you work though the passage.

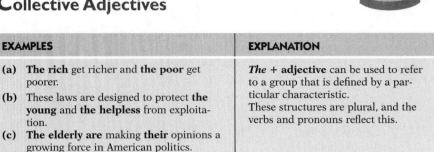

FOCUS **7**

Collective Adjectives

EXAMPLES	EXPLANATION
(a) **The rich** get richer and **the poor** get poorer.	***The* + adjective** can be used to refer to a group that is defined by a particular characteristic.
(b) These laws are designed to protect **the young** and **the helpless** from exploitation.	These structures are plural, and the verbs and pronouns reflect this.
(c) **The elderly are** making **their** opinions a growing force in American politics.	

EXERCISE 14

Rewrite each *the* + adjective construction below as a noun + relative clause.

▶ **EXAMPLE:** The French aristocracy didn't care about the poor.
   The poor = people who were poor.

1. Elvis Presley was very popular with the young.
2. Dear Abby writes an advice column in the newspaper for the lonely and the confused.
3. Nelson Mandela is an important hero for the oppressed.
4. Albert and Florence became doctors so they could help the sick.
5. The government should establish more comprehensive programs to help the underprivileged.

EXERCISE 15

Circle the correct form of the underlined phrases below.

The Problem of Homelessness in America

(1) The homeless <u>are/is</u> an increasing problem in most American cities. (2) The homeless <u>consist/consists</u> of several different categories of people. (3) The first category <u>consist/consists</u> of the mentally disabled. (4) In the early 1980s the Reagan administration ended most of <u>its/their</u> funding for treatment programs for the mentally ill. (5) As a result, quite a few mental hospitals were closed, and many of the mentally ill <u>was/were</u> released, and left to make <u>its/their</u> own way. (6) A substantial number <u>have/has</u> been unable to establish normal lives, and, as a result, <u>it/they</u> <u>has/have</u> ended up living on the streets.

ANSWER KEY

Exercise 14
1. the young = people who were young
2. the lonely and the confused = people who are lonely and confused   **3.** the oppressed = people who are oppressed   **4.** the sick = people who are sick   **5.** the underprivileged = people who are underprivileged

Exercise 15
(1) are   (2) consist   (3) consists   (4) its
(5) were; their   (6) have; they   (7) is/are
(8) are   (9) them; have; their; they
(10) they   (11) have; their   (12) are
(13) are; are   (14) represents   (15) are; has; its; their .

(7) A second category of the homeless <u>is/are</u> the unemployed. (8) Typically, the unemployed <u>is/are</u> part of the homeless for a relatively short period of time—usually less than a year. (9) Some of <u>it/them</u> <u>have/has</u> lost <u>its/their</u> jobs; or the factories where <u>it/they</u> worked were closed without warning. (10) As a result, <u>it/they</u> didn't have enough money to pay rent. (11) Many of the unemployed <u>has/have</u> also ended up living on the streets or sleeping in <u>its/their</u> automobiles. (12) But the majority of the people in this category of the homeless <u>is/are</u> able to find housing again, once they have found other jobs.

(13) A third category of the homeless <u>is/are</u> the people who <u>is/are</u> addicted to drugs or alcohol. (14) Like the mentally ill, this category of homelessness <u>represent/represents</u> a persistent social problem. (15) The unemployed can hope for better times, and <u>is/are</u> usually able to escape from poverty and life on the streets, but the government <u>has/have</u> been very slow in giving <u>its/their</u> support to programs that help the mentally disabled or the addicted work on <u>its/their</u> recovery.

EXERCISE 16

Are these sentences correct or incorrect? If they are incorrect, identify the problem and correct it.

1. None of doctors are allowed to practice without a license.
2. I watched the flock of birds as it landed in the field across the road.
3. Few students never pass their qualifying exams.
4. The rich is always trying to avoid giving its money to pay taxes.
5. Quite a bit of time that doctors spend in their residencies is clinical training.
6. Students usually apply to several of universities for admission.
7. The herd of sheep was frightened by a pack of wolves, and it bleated nervously in their pen.
8. We had much trouble with the examination this morning.
9. A great many of traditional medicines are still used in rural areas.
10. No unlicensed physicians are allowed to practice in the United States.
11. Foreign students need lots of opportunities to get used to American educational techniques.
12. A few doctors don't stay up-to-date, but a lot of do.
13. Few students don't take their studies seriously.

Quantifiers, Collective Nouns, and Adjectives **367**

Exercise 16

This exercise practices all the collective noun forms in an integrated way. It can be assigned as homework, as an in class quiz or done by the class sentence by sentence for additional practice and review.

UNIT GOAL REVIEW

1. Have Ss work in pairs to look over the goals on the opening page of the unit again. Have them summarize their understanding of the principles involved with each goal to one another and to identify one question they still have based on this discussion.
2. Process the questions with the whole class by asking pairs to state their question and then asking other pairs if they can answer it or explain the relevant rule in their own words.

ANSWER KEY

Exercise 16

1. No doctor is allowed . . .   2. correct
3. correct, but awkward: Most students pass their qualifying exams.   4. The rich are always trying to avoid giving their money . . .
5. correct   6. . . . to several universities
7. . . . and they bleated nervously in their pen.   8. We had a lot of trouble with the examination this morning.   9. A great many traditional medicines are still used in rural areas.   10. correct   11. correct
12. . . . but a lot do.   13. correct, but awkward: Most students take their studies seriously.

Use Your English

Activity 1

This activity is for more advanced classes. It is intended to be used for fun, not for serious vocabulary development. Follow the pair work instructions in the student book or use it as a topic for whole class or small group discussion.

Activity 2

Even a few sentences on each topic will allow you to evaluate whether or not Ss have mastered collective nouns.

ACTIVITY 1: SPEAKING

English used to have many different collective nouns to refer to specific animals. These nouns usually indicated a quality or characteristic that these animals had.

• a pride of lions (because lions are proud)
• a parliament of owls (because owls are wise)
• a leap of leopards (because leopards leap)

Such collective words are rarely used in modern English. But sometimes for humorous reasons, people will invent collective words to apply to a particular group of people. Here are some examples:

• a sweep of cleaning ladies
• a hustle of salesmen
• a splash of swimmers

Working with a partner, decide on some humorous collective terms for some of these categories of people:

flight attendants	English teachers	puppies
lawyers	magicians	computer programmers
accountants	kittens	real estate agents

ACTIVITY 2: WRITING

Write a brief paragraph on one of these topics:

(a) Compare two athletic teams that play a sport you are familiar with. Why do you think one team is better than the other?

(b) Discuss one or more famous performing troupes (opera, drama, circus, dance, orchestra). Why are they famous, and do you feel that reputation is justified?

(c) What lessons can the old teach the young?

ACTIVITY 3: SPEAKING/WRITING

There is a joke that says, "A camel is a horse that was designed by a committee." Some management experts think that committees result in a product that is better than one made by a single individual. Others feel that committees tend to be inefficient and badly organized.

Based on your experience, identify the strengths and weaknesses of working in a committee. What are the advantages of having a group work together on a single task?

What are the disadvantages? Present your ideas to the rest of the class as a list of pros and cons.

▶ **EXAMPLE: Pro:** *A committee is able to assign tasks to each member, so the work can be divided.*

Con: *A committee doesn't reach decisions quickly, because each member has to agree about the issue before they can take action.*

How are you going to do this activity? By yourself or in a group?

ACTIVITY 4: SPEAKING

Should the rich pay more taxes or higher penalties (for traffic tickets, etc.) than the poor? Why do you think so? Discuss your ideas in a small group, and present a report on your group's opinion to the rest of the class. Your report should use phrases like "Our group feels that . . ."

ACTIVITY 5: WRITING/SPEAKING

Have you ever seen a political demonstration? Where and when did it occur? What was the demonstration about? What did the crowd do? What did the police do? Write a description of what happened.

Activity 3

Use this as a preparatory activity before doing Activity 6. Do it as directed, letting Ss decide whether they want to work independently or collectively. Alternatively, use it as a whole class discussion topic.

Activities 4 & 5

Even a few sentences on each topic will allow you to evaluate whether or not Ss have mastered these two categories of collectives.

Activity 6

SUGGESTIONS:

1. If you like to use a lot of small group work in your classes, you may wish to use this activity early in the semester to "set the tone" for working together and establish ways to make the group process more effective

2. Follow up the group presentations by generating a list of effective techniques for group work and "traps" to avoid that you want small groups to use throughout the course.

Activities 7 & 8

These are related activities. Activity 7 provides a good "rehearsal" for doing Exercise 8. Obviously, Exercise 8 works best when Ss' out-of-class environment is also English-speaking. Depending on how much guidance is necessary, this activity might take up to three class periods: one to formulate the questions (and rehearse them), a second to share responses and devise the graphic representations, and a third for groups to deliver their presentations.

ACTIVITY 6: SPEAKING

What is a good way to organize a complicated group project? Business managers have found that certain organizational techniques can make any group or committee run more smoothly and efficiently. Bad organization can result in a few people doing all the work, duplication of effort, or wasted time and energy. Here's an opportunity for you to explore techniques for streamlining group processes and decision-making.

STEP 1 Suppose the class has decided to all take a weekend trip together. In a small group, decide on the best way to organize such a complex project to make sure that work is done efficiently and everyone is involved in the process.

- Decide on the **tasks** that need to be done in order to organize and carry out such a trip.
- Establish a list of **committees** to accomplish these tasks, and specify the duties and members of each committee. Make sure that the work is evenly distributed, and that no single committee has too much to do.

STEP 2 When you have decided on your organizational plan, make a report to the rest of the class. Describe your plan. Tell what committees you have established, what responsibilities each committee has, and who each committee has as members.

STEP 3 Report on the decision-making process of your group. Identify any problems you had working as a committee. Present any techniques you used that helped you work together more efficiently.

STEP 4 The class should decide who has the best-organized plan for the trip.

ACTIVITY 7: SPEAKING

STEP 1 Conduct a poll of your classmates to find out about their educational backgrounds.

- How many years of school do they have?
- What subjects have they studied?
- Did most of them enjoy school?
- Decide on two more questions to ask them.

STEP 2 Present your information by constructing charts similar to the ones in the Opening Task of this unit.

ACTIVITY 8: SPEAKING

Conduct a public opinion poll on some aspect of current events.

STEP 1 In a group, choose some topic of current interest from the news, and develop a list of five to eight questions to determine how people feel about this issue.

STEP 2 Poll your classmates, and also interview ten to fifteen people outside of class.

STEP 3 Devise a graphic representation of your results similar to the charts in the Opening Task of this unit.

STEP 4 Using your charts, make a presentation of your findings to the rest of the class. Report any interesting differences between the opinions of your classmates and the people you interviewed outside of class.

ACTIVITY 9: LISTENING

STEP 1 Listen to the following brief news reports and answer the following questions. You may need to listen to each report more than once.

Report 1
1. What happens every year on March 19th?
   _____
2. Who provides publicity about this event?
   _____
3. Who else arrives on March 19th besides the swallows?
   _____

Report 2
1. What did the Canadian government ask the committee to do?
   _____
2. What is being anxiously awaited by the press and the public?
   _____

Report 3
1. What is different about the theater company described in this report?
   _____
2. When was it founded?
   _____
3. What effect has the company had?
   _____

STEP 2 Compare your answers with a classmate's.

Quantifiers, Collective Nouns, and Adjectives | **371**

Activity 9

Play textbook audio. The tapescript for this listening appears on p. 520 of this book.

Allow for multiple listenings of each report if necessary. The first time, have Ss listen for the general idea. The second time, follow along with the questions and choose answers. The third time, listen for specific information that is still needed, and the fourth time verify final answer choices. Go over the answers and replay portions of the tape as needed to settle differences of interpretation.

The test for this unit can be found on p. 582. The answers are on p. 583 of this book.

TOEFL Test Preparation Exercises for Units 21–22 can be found on pp. 157–159 of the Workbook.
The answers are on p. 507 of this book.

ANSWER KEY

Activity 9
Answers may vary slightly:
Report 1: 1. A large flock of swallows returns to San Juan Capistrano Mission in Southern California. 2. The city government in San Juan Capistrano 3. Flocks of tourists arrive at the Mission as well.
Report 2: 1. To look into the effects of acid rain on the forests of North America 2. The release of the committee's report
Report 3: 1. Most of the company cannot hear, and many members can only "speak" by using sign language. 2. Nearly 30 years ago 3. The troupe has played an important role in involving the disabled in the arts.

Unit 23

UNIT OVERVIEW

This unit reviews some of the information introduced in Unit 2, concerning the meaning differences communicated by simple and perfect and progressive aspect, in the context of past time. You may want to teach this as a follow-up to Unit 2, as a more detailed survey of the entire system of tense and time in English. It also works well as a review lesson. For advanced classes, it may not need to be presented in its entirety, but only as a response to errors or questions coming out of the students' writing or reading of more complex academic prose. If so, choose and present only the focus boxes that you feel are important for your particular class.

UNIT GOALS

Review the goals listed on this page so students (Ss) understand what they should be able to do by the end of the unit.

OPENING TASK

This task works best as a written diagnostic. By focusing on a particular "unforgettable" moment you can structure the response so that it is necessary to talk about time before, time during, and time after that particular memorable moment.

UNIT 23

PAST TIME FRAME

Using Adverbs and Aspect to Indicate Time Relationships

UNIT GOALS:

- To use correct sequence of tenses in past time to indicate time relationships
- To correctly understand and use clauses with *when* and *while* in past time
- To correctly understand and use progressive and perfect aspect in past time

▶ OPENING TASK
I'll Never Forget . . .

Write a paragraph or tell a partner about an experience that you will never forget. You can tell about a time when you heard about an important world event (for example, *"I will never forget the moment I heard that Yitzak Rabin had been assassinated,"* or *"I will never forget the moment I heard that the Berlin Wall was being torn down."*), or it could be something more personal (*"I will never forget the day my mother told me that I was going to have a new baby brother or sister."*). Your description should include what you were doing at the time, what you had been doing, and how you reacted. See the example on the next page.

Anyone living in San Francisco on October 17, 1989, can tell you exactly what he or she was doing when the earthquake occurred at 5:08 P.M. Here is Jeff's story about his experience in that earthquake.

(1) I will never forget the moment the earthquake struck San Francisco. (2) I was still in my office. (3) I had been trying to finish a project before I left for the day. (4) Suddenly, the building began to sway. (5) Books fell off their shelves. (6) People were screaming. (7) It seemed like things were moving for several minutes, but I guess the actual time was pretty short. (8) As soon as the building had stopped moving, I tried to get out as quickly as possible. (9) This wasn't easy, because I work on the seventeenth floor, and of course the electricity went out the moment the earthquake struck, so no elevators were working. (10) I ran down the emergency stairs in darkness and got out to the street. (11) Hundreds of people were just standing around, wondering what to do. (12) Pretty soon someone appeared who had a radio, so we all gathered around and heard about what had happened and what was happening. (13) After about twenty minutes, I realized that, of course, all public transportation had stopped, and if I wanted to get home, I'd have to walk, so I did. (14) When I finally got home, there was no electricity, but the apartment was O.K., and my roommate Matt and the dog were both sitting outside talking to the neighbors, watching the news broadcasts on a portable battery-operated TV. (15) We all sat around and told each other about our experiences.

SUGGESTION:
Use the reading as a model paragraph. Have Ss underline and identify the tenses in the example paragraph and tell whether actions happened before, during, or after the unforgettable moment at 5:08. Passage 3 of Exercise 1 is a variant of this passage and asks Ss to make the same kinds of observations in a more structured way.

VARIATION:
Start with a general discussion of "unforgettable moments." Allow Ss to generate ideas and important details in pair discussions before writing the assigned paragraph at home.

FOCUS 1

This focus is a good review/reminder of all the ways we can indicate time relationships <u>other than</u> tense. Non-native English speakers tend to "over-use" past perfect in situations where simple past might be preferred by native speakers because there is already enough adverbial information, or the sequence is clear from previous sentences. This initial discussion of alternative methods to indicate time relationships provides background for the later treatment of Focuses 2–4.

1. Present the example sentences of this focus as a single paragraph, either written on the board, projected on an OHP, or as a handout. Have Ss read it and decide the order of events.

2. Lead a class discussion by asking questions like: *"In the first two sentences (a & b) what tells us about which thing happened first?" "In the next three sentences (b)?".* Have Ss identify the specific structures that provide the adverbial information (highlighted in the student book).

3. Have Ss refer to the actual focus box and go directly into the example for Exercise 1 to solidify their understanding. Allow for questions before moving on to Passages 2 & 3 of Exercise 1.

Exercise 1

1. The suggestions for Focus 1 explain ways to integrate Passage 1 with your presentation of Focus 1.

2. Assign Passages 2 and 3 for Ss to work on in pairs or small groups. Allow class time for them to discuss the passages and determine the time sequence.

3. Process as a whole class, so the half of the class that worked on Passage 2 can also briefly review how Passage 3 was put together, and vice versa.

FOCUS **1**

▶ **Overview of Time Relationships in Past Time Frame**

USE

EXAMPLES	EXPLANATIONS
(a) He **walked** up the stairs. He **turned** the knob, and **opened** the door.	Time relationships in past time can be indicated by: • sequence Things happened in the order they are mentioned.
(b) **As he entered the room,** he realized something was different. **Before he had a chance to turn around,** he knew something was missing. **In a moment,** he realized what it was.	• adverbial information Adverbial clauses and phrases describe the order in which things happened.
(c) The television **had disappeared.** The antenna wires **were hanging** from the wall. He **had been watching** TV a few hours ago, but now there **was** nothing there.	• perfect and progressive aspect Choice of a particular verb tense and aspect describes the order in which things happened.

EXERCISE 1

Work with a partner to examine how time relationships are indicated in these passages. Passage 1 has been done for you as an example.

STEP 1 Place the highlighted verbs on a timeline in the order that they occurred.

STEP 2 Tell how you think that the order was indicated (by sequence, adverbials, or using perfect or progressive verb tenses). Sometimes there is more than one indication.

Passage 1

As he **entered** the room, he realized something was different. Before he **had** a chance to turn around, he **knew** something was missing. In a moment, he **realized** what it was. The television **had disappeared.** The antenna wires **were hanging** from the wall. He **had been watching** TV a few hours ago, but now there **was** nothing there.

STEP 1 Timeline

1. he **had been watching** TV	2. the TV **had disappeared**	3. the wires **were hanging** from the wall	4. there **was** nothing there	5. he **entered** the room	6. he **knew** something was missing	7. he **had** a chance to turn around	8. he **realized** what it was

STEP 2 How is the order of events indicated? (Example from #1)

1. perfect progressive; adverbial (a few hours ago) aspect
2. perfect aspect
3. progressive aspect
4. adverbial (now)
5. adverbial (as) aspect
6. sequence aspect
7. adverbial (before) aspect
8. sequence, adverbial (in a moment) aspect

Passage 2

Police reported yesterday that they **had uncovered** a large amount of stolen property from a warehouse in the southern part of the city. The warehouse **had been** under surveillance for some time. A suspiciously large number of people **had been seen** going in and out of the building. Once the police **had obtained** a search warrant, they **entered** the warehouse in the middle of the night and **discovered** large amounts of electronic equipment and other supplies. Police **announced** that this discovery **may lead** to the solution of a number of robberies.

Passage 3

1.	2.	3.	4.	5.	6.	7.	8.	9.

At the time of the earthquake Jeff **was** still in his office. He **had been trying** to finish a project before he left for the day. Suddenly, the building **began** to move. Books **fell** off their shelves. People **were screaming.** Although it seemed as if things were moving for several minutes, the actual time was just fifteen seconds. Even before the building **stopped** moving, people were trying to get out as quickly as possible. This wasn't easy for people who **had been working** on the higher floors of the building. The electricity **had gone off** the moment the earthquake struck, so no elevators **were working.** Most people **ran** down emergency strains in darkness and **got** out to the street.

1.	2.	3.	4.	5.	6.	7.	8.	9.	10.	11.

Past Time Frame: Using Adverbs and Aspect to Indicate Time Relationships | **375**

SUGGESTION:
If possible, give pairs transparencies so they can write the sequence of events in an actual timeline like the example shown in the student book for Passage 1.

ANSWER KEY

Exercise 1

Passage 2:

Step 1: (in this order)
1. The warehouse had been under surveillance. 2. A suspiciously large number of people had been seen going in and out of the building. 3. The police had obtained a search warrant. 4. They entered the warehouse in the middle of the night. 5. Discovered large amounts of electronic equipment and other supplies 6. They had uncovered a large amount of stolen property. 7. Police reported yesterday 8. Police announced that this discovery 9. This discovery may lead to the solution of a number of robberies.

Step 2: (how indicated).
1. aspect, adverbial (for some time)
2. aspect 3. aspect, adverb (once)
4. sequence 5. sequence 6. aspect
7. adverb (yesterday) 8. sequence
9. future time.

Passage 3:

Step 1: (in this order)
1. people **had been working** on the higher floors 2. He **had been trying** to finish a project 3. Jeff **was** still in his office 4. the building **began** to move 5. The electricity **had gone off** 6. People **were screaming.**
7. Books **fell** off their shelves 8. people **were trying** to get out 9. the building **stopped** moving, 10. no elevators **were working.** 11. Most people **ran** down emergency stairs and got out.

Step 2: (how indicated)
1. aspect 2. aspect 3. adverbial (at the time of the earthquake) 4. aspect, adverbial (at the moment the earthquake struck)
5. sequence 6. aspect 7. sequence
8. aspect 9. sequence, aspect,
10. adverb (before) 11. sequence

Teacher's Edition: Unit 23 **375**

FOCUS 2

Many students have trouble with *when* and *while* because of the different kinds of additional information that are required to indicate sequence. *While* carries the notions of "in progress" and "duration" in a way that *when* does not.

SUGGESTION:

Have Ss look at sentences a & b and then discuss the different sequences implied.

VARIATION:

Use this class-related contrast:
With *when* these two sentences have a distinct meaning difference: *The students* <u>were laughing</u> *when the teacher entered the room.* (They had started laughing already, and perhaps they stopped when the teacher arrived.)
The students <u>laughed</u> *when the teacher entered the room.* (They began laughing after the teacher came in, and they continued to do so.)
Using *while* instead of *when* gives both sentences roughly the same meaning.

When, While, and Progressive Aspect in Past Time

Using *When*

EXAMPLES	TIME SEQUENCE	EXPLANATIONS
(a) When the books **fell** off the shelf, Jeff **hid** under his desk.	First the books fell off the shelf; then Jeff hid under his desk.	If you use *when* to connect two clauses with simple past tense verbs, the action described in the *when*-clause happened before the action in the main clause.
(b) When the books **fell** off the shelf, Jeff **was hiding** under his desk.	First Jeff hid under his desk; then the books fell off the shelf.	Use past progressive with the main clause to describe situations where the action described in the main clause happened before the action described by the *when*-clause.

Using *While*

EXAMPLES	EXPLANATIONS
(c) While the books **fell** off the shelf, Jeff **hid** under his desk.	*While* indicates that the action was **in progress at the same time** as the action described by the verb in the main clause.
(d) While the books **were falling** off the shelf, Jeff **was hiding** under his desk.	We can use either past progressive or simple past, since *while* makes the meaning clear.

EXERCISE 2

Answer these questions about the example passage in the Opening Task on page 373.

1. What was Jeff doing when the building started to sway?
2. What did he do when the building stopped swaying?
3. What happened to the elevators when the earthquake struck?
4. What was happening when Jeff reached the street?
5. What happened when Jeff reached the street?
6. What was happening when Jeff finally got home?
7. What happened when Jeff finally got home?

FOCUS **3**

▶ # Other Uses of Progressive Aspect

EXAMPLES	EXPLANATIONS
(a) In 1997, while I **was researching** the economic consequences of the American Civil War, I found a fascinating piece of information.	Use progressive aspect to express: • actions that were in progress or uncompleted
(b) During the last few years of his life, Mozart **was constantly trying** to borrow money from anyone who would loan it to him.	• actions that were repeated or continous
(c) Before John found an apartment in Paris, he **was staying for a short while** at the house of a shopkeeper and his family.	• temporary situations

EXERCISE 3

Identify all the past progressive verb forms in the example passage of the Opening Task and tell why you think the author chose to use past progressive.

Exercise 2

If you did not have Ss read the example paragraph as part of doing the Opening Task, be sure that they read the entire passage first for general comprehension before doing this exercise. Process it like a series of reading comprehension questions. Make sure that answers are in complete sentences so you can check for correct verb tense.

FOCUS 3

This focus reviews the basic meanings of progressive aspect that were first presented in Unit 2 of this book. You may be able to skip a formal presentation and go directly to Exercise 4. Refer Ss back to this focus if they had trouble with that exercise or feel that they need additional review.

Exercise 3

1. Have Ss identify the verb phrases individually, but the follow-up discussion can be done in pairs or as a class.
2. Omit this exercise if Ss have demonstrated that they have no trouble identifying verb phrases or identifying the meaning inherent in aspect choice.

ANSWER KEY

Exercise 2

Answers may vary slightly:
1. He was trying to finish a project that he had been working on. 2. He tried to get out as quickly as possible. 3. They stopped working. 4. People were standing around, wondering what to do. 5. Someone appeared who had a transistor radio. 6. Matt and the dog were sitting outside. 7. He and Matt told each other about their experiences.

Exercise 3

(3) I had been trying (6) were screaming
(7) I were moving (9) were working
(11) were standing around (14) were both sitting
In most cases progressive aspect indicates "already in progress" or "duration over time."

Exercise 4

Do this exercise individually or in pairs. If you have access to an OHP, process the correct answers by making a transparency of this passage and circle the correct choices. Make sure Ss read the whole passage before selecting the correct tenses.

Workbook Exs. 1 & 2, pp. 160–161.
Answers: TE p. 508.

FOCUS 4

1. If necessary, review the different ways time relations are indicated. Native speakers tend to avoid past perfect except in the situations outlined in examples d–g.
2. The best way to present this focus is with the whole class reading through the examples and the explanations together.

EXERCISE 4

Circle the appropriate form of the verbs in parentheses. There may be more than one correct choice. The first sentence has been done for you as an example.

The Search for the Northwest Passage

(1) The St. Lawrence Seaway, the waterway that (links/is linking) the Great Lakes of North America with the Atlantic Ocean, was discovered by explorers who (looked/were looking) for the Northwest Passage. (2) Geographers at that time (believed/were believing) that there was a water course that (connected/was connecting) the Atlantic and Pacific oceans. (3) Throughout the sixteenth and early seventeenth centuries, both England and France constantly (sent/were sending) one expedition after another to attempt to find the passage. (4) Early explorers (investigated/were investigating) every large inlet and river along the entire eastern coast of North America.

(5) Even though they never (found/were finding) the Northwest Passage, these early explorers (made/were making) a valuable contribution to the knowledge of North American geography. (6) While they (explored/were exploring) the coast they (made/were making) many other very useful discoveries. (7) Not only the St. Lawrence Seaway, but also Hudson Bay, Chesapeake Bay, the Hudson River, and the Delaware River all (were discovered/were being discovered) by explorers who actually (looked/were looking) for something else.

FOCUS **4**

Using Perfect Aspect in Past Time Frame

You can use both adverbials and perfect aspect to indicate that a particular action happened before others.

ADVERBIALS	PERFECT ASPECT
(a) **Before** we left on the trip, we checked the car thoroughly. (b) **After** we checked the oil, we made sure the tires had enough air.	(c) But we **hadn't gotten** more than a few miles when we realized that we **had forgotten** something: We **had left** our suitcases on the front porch. We **had been worrying** so much about the mechanical condition of the car that we left without thinking about its contents.

We don't usually use both adverbials and perfect aspect in the same sentence, and tend to avoid the past perfect tense if the time sequence is clear from other information.

EXAMPLES	EXPLANATIONS
	In general, we indicate time relationships with perfect aspect only when it is necessary:
(d) He **had seen** the movie, and **therefore** didn't want to go with us.	• to communicate a logical connection between the two events
(e) They only **started** the project when I **arrived,** but they **had finished** it when I **left.**	• to clarify a time relationship
(f) I **had finished** all my homework before I went to Jane's party.	• to describe an action that was fully completed
(g) They **told** me that the doctor **had just left.**	• to change the time frame in reported speech.

EXERCISE 5

With a partner, examine how adverbials and aspect are used to indicate time relationships in these passages.

• For each sentence, identify the verb phrases that happened **before** the verb phrases listed in the first column of the chart, and write them in the "Time Before" column.
• Then decide whether each time relationship is indicated by adverbials, by aspect or by both. Record that information in the "How Indicated" column.
• Compare your answers with another pair of students.

The first two sentences in each passage have been done for you as examples.

1. (1) Before we left on the trip, we checked the car thoroughly. (2) After we checked the oil, we made sure the tires had enough air. (3) But we hadn't gotten more than a few miles when we realized that we had forgotten something: We had left our suitcases on the front porch. (4) We had been worrying so much about the mechanical condition of the car that we left without thinking about its contents.

	TIME BEFORE	HOW INDICATED
1. we left on the trip	we checked the car	adverb (before)
2. we made sure the tires had enough air	we checked the oil	adverb (after)
3. we realized that . . .		
4. we left without thinking about its contents		

Past Time Frame: Using Adverbs and Aspect to Indicate Time Relationships | **379**

Exercise 5

SUGGESTIONS:
1. Make sure that Ss read the entire passage before doing the exercise.
2. Passage 2 may be more appropriate for advanced classes.
3. Alternatively, have half the class work on the first passage and the other half the second.

Workbook Exs. 3 & 4, pp. 161–162. Answers: TE p. 508.

ANSWER KEY

Exercise 5
Passage 1. (3) **time before:** we hadn't gotten more than a few miles/we had forgotten something/ we had left our suitcases; **how** indicated: aspect (past perfect)   (4) **time before:** we had been worrying so much; **how indicated** aspect and adverb (so/that)

Exercise 6

Be sure to stress the "only if it is necessary" part of the instructions. That is the point of this particular focus. Do the exercise individually or in pairs.

2. In the fifteenth century, a new social and economic order was born in Europe. (1) By the end of the fourteenth century, the population of Europe was about a third smaller than it had been at the beginning of the century. (2) It was one of the few times in history when the population had actually decreased. (3) This smaller population was caused by repeated outbreaks of bubonic plague which had swept through the continent several times during the century, (4) and by the time the century had ended, this disease had caused some fundamental changes in society. (5) So many people had died that the traditional feudal landlords were forced to intermarry with wealthy merchant families, instead of the aristocracy. (6) People who had previously only had the opportunity to make a living as farmers or serfs were able to become craftsmen and artisans. (7) The plague had killed so many people that the traditional social boundaries were wiped out, and this created a period of great social mobility and economic change.

	TIME BEFORE	HOW INDICATED
1. the population was one third smaller	than it had been at the beginning of the century	adverbial (By the end of the fourteenth century) aspect
2. it was one of the few times in history	the population had actually decreased	aspect
3. the smaller population was caused by repeated outbreaks of plague		
4. the disease had caused some fundamental changes in society		
5. landlords were forced to intermarry with wealthy merchants		
6. people were able to become crafsmen and artisans		
7. this created a period of great social mobility and economic change		

EXERCISE 6

Use past perfect in these sentences only if it is necessary to the meaning of the sentence. Otherwise use simple past or past progressive.

1. Peter (a) _____ (went) to talk with Mr. Green about the fight he (b) _____ (have) with Denise earlier in the day.

Exercise 5 (Continued)
Passage 2. (3) **time before:** which had swept through the continent several times during the century; **how indicated:** aspect (4) **time before:** the century had ended; **how indicated:** adverbial (by the time) aspect (5) **time before:** So many people had died; **how indicated:** aspect/adverbial (so/that) (6) **time before:** who had previously only had the opportunity to make a living as farmers or serfs; **how indicated:** aspect/adverbial (previously) (7) **time before:** The plague had killed so many people that the traditional social boundaries were wiped out; **how indicated:** aspect/adverbial (so/that)

Exercise 6
1. (a) went; (b) had 2. (a) stopped moving; (b) tried; (c) had stopped working 3. had grown 4. (a) looked; (b) didn't find; (c) had disappeared 5. (a) went; (b) had left 6. (a) was; (b) had not received

2. As soon as the building (a) _____ (stop moving), Jeff
   (b) _____ (try) to call Matt, but the telephones
   (c) _____ (stop working).

3. It was too late to put out the fire because it _____
   (grow) too big for anything to control.

4. I (a) _____ (look) everywhere for my wallet, but I
   (b) _____ (not find) it anywhere. It (c) _____
   (disappeared).

5. Denise (a) _____ (go) to Peter's office to complain about
   his attitude, but he (b) _____ (leave) early to take his
   children to the circus.

6. Mary (a) _____ (be) extremely worried about John
   since she (b) _____ (not receive) any letters from him
   in over a month.

FOCUS **5**

▶ **Perfect Progressive Aspect
in Past Time Frame**

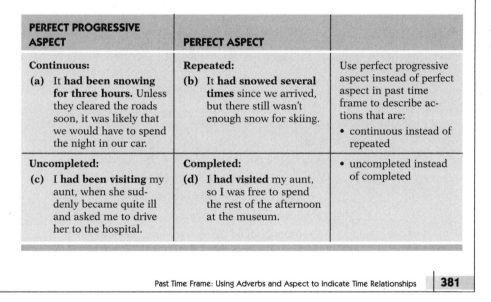

PERFECT PROGRESSIVE ASPECT	PERFECT ASPECT	
Continuous: (a) It **had been snowing for three hours.** Unless they cleared the roads soon, it was likely that we would have to spend the night in our car.	**Repeated:** (b) It **had snowed several times** since we arrived, but there still wasn't enough snow for skiing.	Use perfect progressive aspect instead of perfect aspect in past time frame to describe actions that are: • continuous instead of repeated
Uncompleted: (c) I **had been visiting** my aunt, when she suddenly became quite ill and asked me to drive her to the hospital.	**Completed:** (d) I **had visited** my aunt, so I was free to spend the rest of the afternoon at the museum.	• uncompleted instead of completed

FOCUS 5

This focus reviews the basic meanings of perfect progressive aspect that were first presented in Unit 2 of this book. You may be able to skip a formal presentation and go directly to Exercise 7. Refer Ss back to this focus if they had trouble with that exercise or feel they need additional review.

Exercise 7

This review can be done as a whole class, calling on individuals one sentence at a time. If you feel your class needs more practice, do it as pair work.

Exercises 8 & 9

These exercises practice all the meaning differences discussed in this unit. Use them for class review, for a pop quiz, or for more systematic pair work with comparison and discussion if your class is still having trouble with these concepts. Ss typically enjoy the content of **Exercise 9** a great deal. If yours do, consider the thematic connection in Activity 3 as a logical follow-up activity.

EXERCISE 7

Fill in the blanks with the appropriate form of the verbs in parentheses (past perfect or past perfect progressive).

1. When the earthquake struck, Jeff was still in the office because he _____ (try) to finish a project before he left for the day.

2. Denise _____ (look) for a reason to complain about Peter even before he took time off from work to see his son's school play.

3. By the beginning of the fifteenth century, the bubonic plague _____ (cause) some fundamental social and political changes.

4. The police _____ (keep) the warehouse under surveillance for some time when they finally obtained a search warrant and investigated.

5. They first became suspicious because so many people _____ (go) in and out of the warehouse at strange hours of the day and night.

EXERCISE 8

Fill in the blanks with the appropriate form of the verbs in parentheses (simple past, past perfect, or past perfect progressive). More than one answer may be correct.

1. I (a) _____ (work) on my homework for about twenty minutes when I (b) _____ (overhear) the TV broadcast announcing Rabin's assassination.

2. Jeff (a) _____ (experience) several minor earthquakes, but he (b) _____ (be) still surprised by the strength of this one.

3. Nancy (a) _____ (be) not really happy with what she (b) _____ (do) so she (c) _____ (decide) to look for another job.

4. European explorers (a) _____ (try) to reach Asia, when they (b) _____ (land) in the New World "by accident."

5. When Jeff (a) _____ (get) to the street, he (b) _____ (see) that hundreds of other people (c) _____ (leave) their offices and (d) _____ (stand) out on the street wondering what to do.

ANSWER KEY

Exercise 7
1. had been trying 2. had been looking
3. had caused 4. had kept/had been keeping 5. had been going

Exercise 8
1. (a) had been working; (b) overheard
2. (a) had experienced; (b)was 3. (a) was; (b) had been doing; (c) decided 4. (a) had been trying; (b) landed 5. (a) got; (b) saw; (c) had left; (d) were standing

EXERCISE 9

Fill in the blanks with the correct forms of the verbs in parentheses (present, present perfect, simple past, past perfect, past progressive, or past perfect progressive). There may be more than one correct answer.

George Washington (1) _____ (be) the first President of the United States, and (2) _____ (serve) as the leader of American troops during the War of Independence. According to a famous story, when George (3) _____ (be) a young boy, and (4) _____ (learn) how to use farming tools, his father (5) _____ (give) him a hatchet for his birthday. George (6) _____ (be) anxious to use the hatchet, so he (7) _____ (run) out of the house and (8) _____ (chop) down a cherry tree in his father's garden. When his father (9) _____ (discover) that someone (10) _____ (chop) down the tree, he (11) _____ (be) very angry. He (12) _____ (demand) to know who (13) _____ (chop) down his cherry tree. When little George (14) _____ (hear) his father's angry shouting, he (15) _____ (go) to his father and (16) _____ (tell) him that he (17) _____ (do) it with his new hatchet. He said, "I (18) _____ (be) sorry you (19) _____ (be) angry, and I (20) _____ (know) you will punish me, but I must admit my crime, because I cannot tell a lie." George's father (21) _____ (be) so impressed with his honesty, that he (22) _____ (decide) not to punish the boy after all, and, in fact, (23) _____ (reward) him, by giving him a silver dollar.

This incident actually never (24) _____ (happen), but millions of American children (25) _____ (read) this story in school. Parents and teachers (26) _____ (think) that it is a good way to teach children to always tell the truth.

UNIT GOAL REVIEW

1. Ask Ss to look at the goals on the opening page of the unit again. Help them understand how much they have accomplished in each area. You can use this to review some of the common meaning distinctions communicated by aspect choice covered in the Units 2, 3, 13, and 14 that you think your Ss might still be having trouble with.

2. Alternatively, ask Ss to identify which areas they would like more practice with. Point out that these aspect differences are covered in more detail in other units of the book.

ANSWER KEY

Exercise 9
(1) was   (2) served   (3) was   (4) was learning   (5) gave   (6) was   (7) ran
(8) chopped   (9) discovered   (10) had chopped   (11) was   (12) demanded
(13) had chopped   (14) heard   (15) went
(16) told   (17) had done   (18) am   (19) are
(20) know   (21) was   (22) decided
(23) rewarded   (24) happened   (25) read
(26) think

Activity 1

Ss can find an example of the kind of paragraph they should write in the Opening Task of Unit 19. If you have already done that task, you may want to use one of the other activities.

Activity 2

Use this "write-around" for a "Friday fun" activity, since there is not much opportunity to check each individual's mastery of verbs in past time frame.

VARIATION:

As a somewhat more structured alternative, have Ss rewrite the selected story from their group individually, paying particular attention to correctly communicating the various time relationships. Collect and evaluate.

Use Your English

ACTIVITY 1: WRITING

Write a paragraph about an experience that happened to you or to someone you know that supports the truth of one of the following proverbs.

- An idle mind is the devil's playground.
- Too many cooks spoil the broth.
- Two heads are better than one.
- If at first you don't succeed, try, try again.
- Never count your chickens before they have hatched.

ACTIVITY 2: WRITING

Form groups of three to five people. You are going to write a group story.

STEP 1 Each person should take a piece of paper and start a story with this sentence: "It was a dark and stormy night. Suddenly, (your teacher's name) heard a terrible scream."

Then each person in the group should write for three minutes. When the three minutes is up, fold the paper so that only the last sentence or two can be read.

STEP 2 Pass your story to the person on your right, and take the paper of the person on your left. Then each person should write for three minutes to continue that person's story. Repeat the process until the papers have gone completely around the group.

STEP 3 Unfold the papers and read the resulting stories to each other. Which story is the funniest? Which story is the clearest? Choose the story you like best to read aloud to the rest of the class.

ACTIVITY 3: SPEAKING/WRITING

Every country has famous stories in its history that all children learn about when they are growing up. In the United States, for example, all school children have heard the story of George Washington and the cherry tree (Exercise 9).

Do you know any similar kinds of famous stories about real people that you were told as a child? Write down the story or tell it to a partner or the rest of the class.

ACTIVITY 4: SPEAKING

Listen to other people tell their stories of their unforgettable experience from the Opening Task. Compare your account to other people's stories. In a group decide an answer to this question:

• Are there any common feelings or reactions that all or most people share in situations when they hear about or experience some very important or surprising event?

Present your list of shared reactions to the rest of the class.

ACTIVITY 5: LISTENING

Listen to this story of one person's unforgettable experience and answer the questions below.

1. What was the speaker doing when she heard the news about John F. Kennedy (JFK)?

_____

2. What did the speaker do when she heard the news about JFK?

_____

3. What were her classmates doing when they heard the news about JFK?

_____

4. What did they do when they heard the news about JFK?

_____

Activity 3

If you decide to have your Ss tell their stories orally to the rest of the class, use a basic "fluency circle" technique to help them develop and express their ideas.

Activity 4

Use the same approach as was suggested in Activity 3. The post-story discussion topic is more suitable for advanced Ss.

Activity 5

Play textbook audio. The tapescript for this activity appears on p. 520 of this book. Play the tape more than once, as necessary, directing the Ss to listen each time for a specific purpose (i.e., for the general idea, to identify specific information, to verify their answers).

The test for this unit can be found on p. 484. The answers are on p. 485 of this book.

ANSWER KEY

Activity 5
Answers will vary slightly:
1. She had been (was) studying in the library.
2. She left the library. 3. They were taking a test. 4. People began crying and all normal activities came to a halt.

Unit 24

UNIT OVERVIEW

This unit focuses on using modals to express ability, habitual action, and predictions about future events in past time. You should probably have presented the following other units before this one: Unit 5 (a general review of one-word modal meaning and uses in earlier volumes of the *Grammar Dimensions* series, as well as the meaning and use of phrasal modals); Unit 16 (prediction and inference); Unit 17 (hypothetical constructions); and, perhaps, Unit 15 (future time). This unit discusses problematic past time modal constructions such as *could/was able to, would/used to,* as well as the more difficult issue of how to express future events in past time frame. See *The Grammar Book,* Chapter 8 (pp. 137–160) for a more detailed overview of modals.

UNIT GOALS

Review the goals listed on this page so students (Ss) understand what they should be able to do by the end of the unit.

UNIT 24

MODALS IN PAST TIME

UNIT GOALS:

- To correctly use *could* versus *was able to* to describe abilities in past time
- To correctly use *would* versus *use to* to describe habitual actions in past time
- To correctly use *would* versus was *going to* to describe future events in past time

▶ OPENING TASK
Identifying the Benefits of Growing Older

STEP 1 Think about these questions:

- In what ways are you different than you were in the past?
- What are some things that you used to do but don't do anymore?
- What are some things that you do now, but you couldn't or wouldn't do five or ten years ago?
- How do people change as they grow older?

STEP 2 Discuss your ideas with two or three other students in the class. Your group should decide on two general ways that people's lives change for the better as they grow older, and present those ideas to the rest of the class. You can read the paragraph below as an example of the kind of changes you may want to consider.

GROWING OLDER

Growing older makes people less worried about what other people think. In high school I used to be really shy. I would avoid talking to people, and I couldn't express my ideas in class without feeling very uncomfortable. I guess I was afraid that people were going to laugh at me, or that they would think I was strange. In high school people were supposed to "fit in." They weren't allowed to be different. So I used to wear the same kind of clothes and try to behave the same way as everybody else. I felt I had to be "one of the crowd." Now that I am older, I can stand up in front of other people and tell them what I think. I certainly couldn't do that in high school. I wear clothes because I like them, not because other people like them. I think I'm much more independent and self-confident than I used to be in high school.

OPENING TASK

Like most **Opening Tasks** in this book, this task can be used to diagnose your Ss' control of modal constructions to describe abilities or habitual actions in past time. Whether you use it for that purpose or as an introductory communicative context where command of these structures is necessary, you can do it in several possible ways:

1. As an alternative to the way described in the student book, have Ss read the sample paragraph first and then discuss the more general questions in Step 1.

2. Either way, be sure Ss make statements about their own individual past habits and abilities as well as statements about how they thought things would be when they were younger that are different than they thought.

3. Combine this Opening Task with the topic in Activity 1. You can have half of the class write on one topic and the other half on the other. Let Ss choose the topic they prefer, or you can have each write on both.

Overview of Modals in Past Time Frame

FORM | **USE** | **MEANING**

1. If you presented Unit 5 well before this unit, review the social uses of modals outlined in Unit 5 Focus 2 (pp. 68–70) as part of your presentation. Assign this review as homework the night before, or review it briefly in class. Make sure Ss review the past time ways of expressing the modals meanings of necessity, permission, and advice.

2. Since this is an overview, present the entire focus by having Ss look at the examples in the book as you cover them in your presentation.

3. For an inductive approach, ask some general questions from the Opening Task such as *"Tell me something you couldn't do in English two months ago that you can do now." "Tell me a mistake that you used to make in English that you don't make anymore." "Tell me something that you thought you would be able to do in English by the end of this course that you still can't do."* Follow up their responses by asking them to look at the focus for the kinds of structures we use to talk about such ideas.

MEANING/ USE	ONE- WORD MODALS	EXAMPLES	PHRASAL MODALS	EXAMPLES
necessity			had to	**(a)** I **had to** do my homework before we went to the movies.
permission	*(No one-word modals for these uses.)*		was allowed to	**(b)** John **was allowed to** bring a guest.
advice/ obligation			was supposed to	**(c)** You **were supposed to** be at the doctor's office at 2:00.
ability	could couldn't	**(d)** John **could** speak French when he was younger.	was able to	**(e)** I **was able to** get tickets to the concert.
habitual actions	would wouldn't	**(f)** When he lived in France he **would** always have his meals at a bistro.	used to	**(g)** He **used to** play tennis, but he doesn't anymore.
future events in past time	would wouldn't might might not	**(h)** Naomi hoped that she **would** have the kind of vacation where she **might** meet someone and fall in love.	was going to was about to was to	**(i)** Nora **was about to** leave for the airport She **was going to** spend a couple of months in Japan.

EXERCISE 1

Decide whether the modals in these sentences are requests in present time or questions about past habits and abilities.

1. Could you tell me how to get to Carnegie Hall?
2. Would you cry when your mother punished you?
3. Could you ride a bicycle when you were five?
4. Would you mind putting out that cigar?
5. Do you think you could tell that joke without laughing?
6. When you were little, would you always do everything your parents wanted?

FOCUS **2**

Expressing Necessity, Permission, and Advisability in the Past Time

EXAMPLES	EXPLANATION
	Use phrasal modals in the past time frame to describe:
(a) When I was a child my brothers and sisters and I **had to** do a number of chores.	• necessity
(b) If we didn't, we **weren't allowed to** watch TV.	• permission
(c) I **was supposed to** wash the dishes on Mondays.	• advisability

EXERCISE 2

Make five statements about things you **were allowed to do** when you were a child. Make five statements about things you **weren't allowed to do.**

EXERCISE 3

Work with a partner, and ask if he or she was allowed to do the things you talked about in Exercise 2.

▶ **EXAMPLE:** When you were a child, were you allowed to stay out after dark?

Identify one privilege that was the same for both of you, and report it to the rest of the class.

Modals in Past Time **389**

Exercise 1

Modals use both past (*could, would, might*) and non-past (*can, will, may*) forms regardless of time reference. Therefore, it's useful to make sure that Ss can distinguish the meaning (actual time reference) in spite of the particular form being used. (*could* vs. *can* in requests, *would* for future requests, etc.) Do this exercise as an immediate follow-up to your review of modals used to talk about past time.

Workbook Ex. 1, p. 164. Answers: TE p. 508.

FOCUS 2

This focus replicates the first part of the overview in Focus 1. Therefore, you may wish to include this as part of your "overview" presentation of the last focus. Use the examples in the book or class-related examples such as these: **necessity:** *We had to do homework five times last week. Please give us a night off.* **Permission:** *We weren't allowed to copy each other's homework.* **Advisability:** *We were supposed to keep our grammar journal up to date.*

V A R I A T I O N :

If you have done a recent review of Unit 5, ask Ss to come up with examples of statements of advisability, permission, and necessity. Together, transform them into past time variations.

Exercises 2 & 3

If your class has difficulty making up sentences, combine these exercises by putting Ss in pairs or small groups to develop the initial statements called for in Exercise 2.

Exercises 4 & 5

If your class has difficulty making up sentences, combine these exercises by putting Ss in pairs or small groups to develop the initial statements called for in Exercise 4.

Workbook Exs. 2-6, pp. 164-167. Answers: TE pp. 508.

Exercise 5

EXPANSION:

Have Ss circulate, talk to other Ss in the room. Try to find two other Ss with similar responsibilities.

FOCUS 3

The notions of general ability and specific ability, while somewhat abstract, are critical to understanding which form to use. Other examples of this difference: *Martin couldn't speak Spanish (general ability) so he wasn't able to understand the conversation between Lupe and Conchita. Mary couldn't cook, so she wasn't able to bring the soufflé that we had requested.*

EXERCISE 4

Make five statements about things that you **had to do** when you were a child. Make five statements about things that you **were supposed to do** when you were a child but didn't always do.

EXERCISE 5

Work with a partner, and ask if he or she had to do the things you talked about in Exercise 4.

▶ **EXAMPLE:** When you were a child, did you have to come home before dark?

When you were a child, were you supposed to do your home-work before you could watch TV?

Identify one responsibility that was the same for both of you, and report it to the rest of the class.

FOCUS **3**

Ability in Past Time: *Could* Versus *Was Able To*

EXAMPLES	EXPLANATIONS
(a) John **could speak** French. (b) John **was able to speak** French.	In statements of general ability (skills that exist over time), there is no difference in meaning or use between *could* and *was able to*.
(c) I **was able to** get two tickets to the concert. (d) NOT: I **could** get two tickets to the concert.	In statements of specific ability (specific events or actions), use *was able to*.
(e) I stood in line for over an hour, but **I couldn't** get tickets. (f) I stood in line for over an hour, but **I wasn't able to** get tickets.	In negative statements of specific ability both *couldn't* and *wasn't able to* can be used.

390 UNIT 24

EXERCISE 6

Fill in the blanks with *could* or *be able to*.

▶ **EXAMPLE:** <u>Were you able to go</u> to Joan's party?

No, I <u>couldn't/wasn't able to</u>. But I <u>was able to</u> send her a birthday card.

1. George (a) _____ get tickets to the play. However, he (b) _____ (not) find them when it was time to go to the theater.

2. Peter (a) _____ convince his boss to let him do anything he wanted. As a result, he (b) _____ stay home from work last week.

3. Professor Katz (a) _____ speak Russian. Because of this, she (b) _____ translate the ambassador's speech to the United Nations.

4. Bambang (a) _____ (not) pass the TOEFL, so he enrolled in an English course. He still (b) _____ (not) pass the TOEFL last semester, but he succeeded this semester.

EXERCISE 7

1. Which of the following activities were you able to do ten years ago? Use complete sentences to identify things that you could do ten years ago and things that you couldn't do.

2. Describe two other things not listed below that you could do ten years ago and two other things that you couldn't do.

ride a bike	run a mile in eight minutes
speak fluent English	drive a truck
understand American films	support my family
play a musical instrument	shop for food in a foreign country
read and write English	swim
speak a second language	play soccer
drive a car	translate things into English

Exercise 6

Do this exercise as a class, calling on individuals to answer the questions, as an immediate follow-up to Focus 3.

Exercise 7

Do this exercise as a written homework assignment to collect and correct or use it as a topic for structured pair discussion or even small group work.

ANSWER KEY

Exercise 6

1. (a) was able to; (b) couldn't 2. (a) could; (b) was able to 3. (a) could/was able to; (b) was able to 4. (a) couldn't/wasn't able to; (b) couldn't/wasn't able to

Exercise 7

Answers will vary. Possible answers include: Ten years ago I could ride a bike. Ten years ago I couldn't read and write English. Ten years ago I could run a mile in eight minutes.

Exercise 8

This is an open-ended exercise to be done in pairs or in small groups, or as a class. Be sure Ss read each passage first.

EXERCISE 8

Underline the structures that describe past abilities in these short passages. Why do you think the author decided to use the form he did?

1. (a) Matt stood in line for four hours, but he wasn't able to get tickets for the concert. (b) When he got home, Jeff could tell that he was frustrated and a little angry. (c) He wanted to cheer Matt up, but he couldn't do much to improve Matt's mood.

2. (a) Nigel was a genius. (b) He was able to do many things that other children his age couldn't do. (c) He could solve complicated mathematical equations. (d) He could write poetry and quote Shakespeare. (e) He was even able to get into college when he was only fourteen years old. (f) But he couldn't make friends with other children his own age.

FOCUS 4

1. Approach this focus from the common student confusion between *used to + verb* and be *used to + verb + -ing* (present participle). Write example sentences on the board such as: *Tetsu used to forget* to bring his homework, but now he *is used to bringing* it every night. Ask if there is a difference in meaning. *"In the past did Tetsu do his homework?"* (no) *"Does he do it now?"* (yes)
2. Once you have made that meaning distinction clear, introduce *would* as a variant of *used to*.
3. Like the difference between general vs. specific ability, habitual actions vs. states is another crucial "abstract" principle that is fundamental to the understanding of basic issues of form, meaning, and use. If necessary, review the concepts concerning stative verbs that were introduced in Unit 13, Focus 2.

FOCUS **4**

Habitual Actions in Past Time: *Would* Versus *Used To*

EXAMPLES	EXPLANATIONS
(a) I **used to** live in Washington, D.C. (b) Every day I **would** go jogging past all the famous monuments. (c) No matter how hot or cold it was, I **would** run around the Tidal Basin and along the Mall.	Habits and regular activities in the past are described by using *used to* and *would*. *Used to* is often used in the first sentence to establish the topic. *Would* is used in other sentences to supply the details.
(d) When I was a child I **would wait** at the bus stop for my father to come home. (e) When I was a child I **used to wait** at the bus stop.	Habitual **activities** can be expressed by both *would* and *used to*.
(f) When I was a child I **used to have** lots of toys. (g) When I was a child I **had** lots of toys. (h) NOT: When I was a child I **would have** lots of toys.	Habitual **states** must be expressed by *used to* or simple past tense. We do not use *would*.

Exercise 8

1. (a) wasn't able to get (b) Jeff could tell (c) couldn't do   2. (a) was able to do (b) couldn't (c) could solve (d) could write (e) was even able to get into (f) couldn't make

EXERCISE 9

Below is a list of things many children do.

1. From this list choose five things that you used to do when you were a child.

2. Choose five things that you didn't use to do.

3. Think of three additional examples for each category.

4. Describe these activities in complete sentences. Be sure to use the correct form for verbs that describe habitual states rather than activities. You should have eight sentences describing things you used to do as a child and eight sentences about things you didn't used to do.

believe in ghosts	have a secret hiding place
be afraid of the dark	play with dolls
eat vegetables	like going to the doctor
play "cops and robbers"	enjoy going to school
pretend to be able to fly	obey older brother or sisters
ride a bicycle	cry when hurt
spend the night at a friend's house	

EXERCISE 10

Work with a partner, and ask questions about the things you described in Exercise 9.

▶ **EXAMPLE:** *When you were a child, did you ever pretend that you could fly?*

Report some of your partner's answers to the rest of the class.

Exercise 9

This exercise is structured for you to assign as homework to collect and correct. In class, have people do Exercise 10 in pairs from memory.

Exercise 10

You may need to provide a structured example for the class to follow, such as: *When you were a child did you use to/ did you ever play cops and robbers? Yes, I did. We used to play it every day after school.* Consult the answer key for another possible example conversation to use.

Workbook Ex. 9, p. 168. Answers: TE p. 509.

ANSWER KEY

Exercise 9
Answers will vary. Possible answers include:
I didn't believe in ghosts./I used to be afraid of the dark./I would eat vegetables./I would play cops and robbers with my friends./I would pretend to be able to fly./I wouldn't ride a bicycle, because I was afraid./I used to cry when I was hurt./I used to spend the night at a friend's house./I had a secret hiding-place./I didn't play with dolls./I didn't like going to the doctor./I would enjoy going to school./I wouldn't obey my older brother.

Exercise 10
Answers will vary. Possible answers include:
When you were a child did you ever pretend that you could fly? No, I didn't. But I pretended my bed could fly. When she was a child, Graziella used to pretend that her bed could fly.

1. Make sure that Ss understand the concept of "future in the past" by providing some additional examples that clearly identify class-related future in the past events that have already passed: *Nora didn't know that we <u>were going to have</u> a quiz yesterday, so she didn't study. Boris hoped that <u>I would forget</u> to collect the homework, but I <u>didn't</u>, and he got a zero because he didn't do it.*

2. Explain that all past time one-word modals (*might could would*) can be used for future in the past (example sentence c).

3. Review the uses for *was going to* vs. *would* briefly in class or assign for individual study and review homework.

Future in Past Time Frame

EXAMPLES	EXPLANATIONS
(a) My parents got married almost fifty years ago. In 1937 my father first met the woman that he **would marry** a few years later. From that very first day my father knew that he **was** eventually **going to marry** her.	The past time-frame often includes references to future events. The actual time of these events may be in the past (in relation to **now**), but it is in the future in relation to our moment of focus. The moment of focus in Passage (a) is "that very first day" in 1937.
(b) Although Lincoln **wasn't to become** president until 1860, he started running for political offices quite early in his career. At that time he had no idea that he **was going to have** three unsuccessful attempts before he **would** finally **win** his first election.	In passage (b) the moment of focus is when Lincoln "started running for political offices." We use the one-word and phrasal modals for future activity in their past tense forms (*would, was/were going to,* and *was/were to*). See Unit 15 for more practice with these modals in the present and future time frames.
(c) Naomi hoped that she **would** have a vacation where she **might** meet someone and fall in love. Perhaps it **could** even become a more permanent romance.	"Past tense" one-word modals (*might, would, could*) of future activity can be used to talk about future events in the past time frame.

EXAMPLES	EXPLANATIONS
(d) Elizabeth didn't have much time to get ready for the dance She **was going to** do all her errands in a single afternoon. First she **would** pick up her dress. Then she **would** get her hair done. That **would** leave her the rest of the afternoon to get ready.	*Was going to* is preferred over *would*: • to introduce a topic
(e) Yuri didn't want to leave the house It **was going to** rain any minute.	• to indicate immediate future
(f) At first my parents **weren't going to** let me stay up late but I convinced them to let me do it. **(g)** Oh, here you are! I **was going to** call you. But now I don't have to. **(h)** We **were going to** go skiing tomorrow, but there's no snow, so we'll just stay home instead.	• to describe unfulfilled intentions—intended actions that did not actually take place

EXERCISE 11

Underline all the modal structures that refer to future events or intentions in these paragraphs. The first sentence of each passage has been done for you as examples.

1. (a) When I was a child I used to dream that I <u>would have</u> a bright future. (b) I thought I was going to be a doctor or a movie star. (c) I would have a university medical degree. (d) I would have a job where I could do what I wanted, and wouldn't have to go to an office every day. (e) I was going to be famous, and I was definitely going to have lots of money. (f) I would have a big house in Hollywood and ten children.

2. (a) Nora <u>was going to spend</u> a month in Japan before she started her new job, which <u>was to begin</u> in six weeks. (b) She was going to fly to Japan last Monday, but a strange thing happened as she was about to leave for the airport. (c) Suddenly she had a strong sensation that she shouldn't get on the plane. (d) She had a strange feeling that there might be an accident or that there would be some other problem. (e) She knew that she could take a flight later in the week, so that's what she decided to do.

EXERCISE 12

Do these sentences describe unfulfilled intentions or future activities in the past time frame? In sentences that describe future activities, substitute *would* for *was/were going to*.

▶ **EXAMPLE:** Nora and Jim aren't here right now. They said they **were going to** be studying at the library.

If describes future activity. They said they would be studying at the library.

1. I **wasn't going to** mention the money you owe me. But since you brought it up, I guess we should talk about it.

2. My teacher **wasn't going to** postpone the test, so we studied for the entire weekend.

3. The committee organized the refreshments for the party. Mary **was going to** bring cookies. John **was going to** take care of beverages.

4. I'm not finished painting the house. Jim **was going to help,** but I guess he had something else to do.

5. **Were you going to** send me a check? I haven't received it yet.

6. I never thought this party **was going to** be so much fun.

7. We **weren't going to** extend our vacation, but the weather was so nice that we decided to stay for a few more days.

Exercise 11

To save time, assign half the class the first passage and the other half the second. The passages are short enough that you do <u>not</u> need to make a transparency for the correction process. Asking individual Ss to identify the modal structures in a given sentence should be sufficient.

Exercise 12

This exercise can be done question by question as a class, in pairs, or even in small groups. Take into account the general principles of variety and efficiency outlined throughout this manual.

ANSWER KEY

Exercise 11

1. (a) would have (b) was going to be (c) would have (d) would have . . . could do . . . wouldn't have to go (e) was going to be . . . I was definitely going to have (f) would have

2. (a) was going to spend . . . was to begin (b) was going to fly . . . was about to leave (c) shouldn't get (d) might be . . . would be (e) could take

Exercise 12

1. unfulfilled intention   2. My teacher **wouldn't** postpone the test   3. Mary **would** bring cookies. John **would**   4. unfulfilled intention   5. unfulfilled intention   6. the party **would**   7. unfulfilled intention

Exercise 13

To save time, assign one or two passages to each individual, pair, or group. Make sure that Ss read the entire passage before filling in the blanks.

Workbook Exs. 10–12, pp. 169–170.
Answers: TE p. 509.

UNIT GOAL REVIEW

1. Ask Ss to look at the goals on the opening page of this unit. Ask Ss in pairs or as a class, to provide a rule and give an example for: when we use *could* vs. *was able to, would* vs. *used to,* and *would* vs. *was going to.*

2. If you wish, write the above three questions up on the board and then allow Ss to look through the unit for a while silently as they formulate their answers.

3. Ask how we can discuss future events in past time frame. Be sure Ss mention past modal forms (both one-word modals—*would, could, might*—and phrasal modals—*was to, was going to*). To elicit more responses, establish a basic past time context (*100 years ago . . . before you came to America . . .*) and ask general questions about future activities: *"A hundred years ago what did people think would be happening today?"* *"Before you came to America how did you think you would spend your Saturday nights?"*

EXERCISE 13

Decide which form, *would* or *was/were going to,* should be used in the following sentences. In some cases both answers may be correct.

1. As soon as Charlie heard about Maria's party he decided that he (a) _____ (not go). Sofia (b) _____ (be) there, and she and Charlie didn't get along. He was afraid that she (c) _____ (probably) to tell everyone about how they used to be engaged to be married.

2. Last week Jeff stood in line for five hours to get a ticket to the opera, but he knew it was worth the long wait. It (a) _____ (be) a great performance. Pavarotti (b) _____ (sing) the part of Falstaff. Jeff had heard him before so he was sure it (c) _____ (be) wonderful.

3. Naomi didn't know what to do for her vacation. Perhaps she (a) _____ (go) to Mexico. The plane ticket (b) _____ (be) expensive, but she didn't want to travel by herself on the bus.

4. When I talked to Lin last Sunday night she wasn't planning on getting much sleep. Her project was already a week late, and she couldn't ask the professor for another extension. She (a) _____ (finish) her assignment, even if she had to stay up until dawn. It (b) _____ (not be) easy. She had to finish reading *War and Peace* and then write a ten-page paper. She (c) _____ (probably be) up all night.

5. We performed a very difficult experiment in our chemistry class the other day. I was very nervous because we had to put just the right amount of chemicals into a solution in order for the reaction to occur. Too much phosphorous (a) _____ (cause) the wrong reaction. If there was too little, nothing (b) _____ (happen) at all. If I (c) _____ (do) the experiment correctly, it (d) _____ (be) necessary to measure very, very carefully.

Use Your English

ACTIVITY 1: WRITING/SPEAKING

In the Opening Task on page 387 you read about ways in which people change for the better as they grow older. Now think about ways that people change for the worse.

STEP 1 Make a list of things that you can no longer do that you used to be able to do. These may be activities or privileges. If you wish, compare your list to those of other students in the class.

STEP 2 Write a paragraph or give a short speech to the rest of the class describing one general way that people's lives change for the worse as they grow older. Be sure to provide examples to support your ideas.

ACTIVITY 2: SPEAKING

In 1989 political changes in Eastern Europe resulted in important changes in worldwide economics, politics, and military alliances. In 1991 the outbreak of war in the Middle East caused similar unexpected changes in world affairs.

STEP 1 What predictions did people make about world events before these changes occurred? What things are happening now that seemed impossible a few years ago? With other students develop two lists:

- Things people thought were going to happen that no longer seem likely to happen.
- Things that are happening now that people never thought would happen.

STEP 2 Make a presentation to the class about other great surprises in history.

USE YOUR ENGLISH

Activities 1–3

These activities adapt equally well either to spoken discussion/presentation or to written responses for you to collect and evaluate/correct. Check responses for accuracy of form, meaning, and use. You may wish to follow the procedure outlined in the Opening Task of Unit 11 in correcting/discussing Ss' errors.

Activity 4

Play textbook audio.

The tapescript for this activity appears on p. 521 of this book.

Allow for multiple listenings of the lecture if necessary.

1. Have Ss listen for the general idea.
2. Ask Ss to follow along with the questions and note information needed for answers.
3. Have Ss listen for specific information that they still need.
4. Have Ss verify their final answer choices.
5. To process, go over the answers, and replay portions of the tape as needed to settle differences of interpretation.

ACTIVITY 3: WRITING

Write a short paragraph about one or more of these topics:

- bad habits that you used to have, but don't have anymore.
- things you would do as a child when you were unhappy.
- a time when you were going to do something but weren't allowed or weren't able to do so.
- how your life has turned out differently from your expectations (things you thought were going to happen that didn't, and vice versa).

ACTIVITY 4: LISTENING

Listen to the following short lecture on science fiction and match the predictions listed below to the authors who imagined them, by writing the initials of the author (JV—Jules Verne; HGW—H.G. Wells; GO—George Orwell; or AH—Aldous Huxley) next to the prediction Then put a check by those predictions which have actually come true, and compare your answers with a partner's.

_____ The government will control all aspects of people's lives.

_____ Anyone who tries to disagree with the government will be put in prison.

_____ Many people will own airplanes.

_____ There will be exploration of the moon.

_____ People will be able to travel through time.

_____ Children will be raised in state-run nurseries, instead of in individual families.

_____ There will be a single world language.

_____ People will use solar power to get energy.

_____ Aliens from Mars will invade and conquer the Earth but will eventually die from common bacterial infections.

_____ Scientists will discover a way to make people invisible.

_____ People will be watched by police, by hidden cameras and microphones.

_____ Children will be born through artificial means.

_____ There will be movies that are so realistic that people will think they are actually happening.

_____ There will only be three or four huge governments, and they will constantly be at war with each other.

_____ The use of mind-altering drugs will be widespread, and encouraged by the government.

398 | UNIT 24

ANSWER KEY

Activity 4

GO ✔ The government will control all aspects of people's lives.

GO ✔ Anyone who tries to disagree with the government will be put in prison.

JV Everyone will own an airplane.

JV ✔ There will be exploration of the moon.

HGW People will be able to travel through time.

AH ✔ Children will be raised in state-run nurseries, instead of in individual families.

JV There will be a single world language.

JV ✔ People will use solar power to get energy.

HGW Aliens from Mars will invade and conquer the Earth but will eventually die from common bacterial infections.

HGW Scientists will discover a way to make people invisible.

GO ✔ People will be watched by police, by hidden cameras and microphones.

AH ✔ Children will be born through artificial means.

AH There will be movies that are so realistic that people will think they are actually happening.

GO There will only be three or four huge governments, and they will constantly be at war with each other.

AH ✔ The use of mind-altering drugs will be widespread, and encouraged by the government.

ACTIVITY 5: SPEAKING

Based on the information you learned from the lecture in Activity 4, discuss the following question in a small group and present your opinion and your reasons to the rest of the class.

- Which writer did the most accurate job of predicting the future?

ACTIVITY 6: WRITING/SPEAKING

Think about these questions:

- How has the social role of women changed?
- What things were your grandmothers not allowed to do, simply because they were women?
- What things wouldn't women consider doing fifty years ago that are commonplace today?

Write a paragraph or make a presentation to the rest of the class discussing the five biggest differences between women's lives fifty years ago and today.

Activity 5

Use this activity as a follow-up to Activity 4, if desired, either in a structured pair discussion as directed or as a general class follow-up to the taped lecture.

Activity 6

Like Activities 1–3, this activity adapts equally well either to spoken discussion/presentation or to written responses for you to collect and evaluate/correct.

The test for this unit can be found on p. 486. The answers are on p. 487 of this book.

Unit 25

UNIT OVERVIEW

Reported speech is a very high-frequency grammatical phenomenon in academic writing. It is extremely common in both written and spoken contexts, used for both summarizing and paraphrasing. It is therefore important that students (Ss) master the whole range of referential changes involved in its meaning and use dimensions as well as just the formal "tense" manipulations taught in most grammar texts. Chapter 33 of *The Grammar Book* (pp. 687–715) contains a comprehensive review of both the structural and "sociological" ramifications of this important area.

UNIT GOALS

Review the goals listed on this page so Ss understand what they should be able to by the end of the unit.

OPENING TASK

1. You may want to review some of the things Ss discussed about nonverbal communication before doing this task. The content of some of the exercises and activities in Unit 9 deals with these topics.
2. Otherwise, discuss as a whole class what the pictures tell us about the two people and their relationship before you have people do the assignment.
3. This task can also be done easily (and successfully) as is. Have Ss save their conversations for use with the Unit Goal Review at the end of the unit.

U N I T 25

R E P O R T E D   S P E E C H

UNIT GOALS:

- To restate direct quotations and indirect thought by using reported speech
- To know when to make necessary changes in verb tenses and reference forms
- To correctly report questions and commands when using reported speech

▶ O P E N I N G   T A S K
What Are They Saying?

Look at this series of pictures. It is the photographic record of a conversation between Jack and Jean.

STEP 1 What do you think these people are talking about? Write down the exact conversation that you think occurred between them.

Photo 1:

Jack: _____

Jean: _____

Jack: _____

Jean: _____

Photo 2:

Jack: _____

Jean: _____

Jack: _____

Photo 3:

Jean: _____

Jack: _____

Jean: _____

Photo 4:

Jack: _____

Jean: _____

Jack: _____

Jean: _____

STEP 2 Compare your conversation with that of another student. Discuss what you thought they were talking about in each picture and why you thought that. Your discussion might be something like this:

> **You:** In the first picture I thought that Jack was telling Jean that he had something important to tell her.

> **Your partner:** Oh really? I thought that he was trying to introduce himself for the first time. Why did you think he already knew her?

> **You:** Because they're sitting rather close together.

STEP 3 Report the three most interesting differences between your two conversations (and your reasons for thinking so) to the rest of the class.

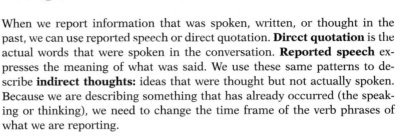

This basic feature of reported speech (switching time frames to "more past") is a fundamental characteristic of reported speech. There are a number of ways to present this important focus, depending on the personality of your class.

1. For a straightforward, comparative approach, have Ss read this focus along with you in the book. Alternatively, make transparencies of the sample sentences of the direct quotation and reported speech versions of the same utterances.

2. Assign the focus box for self-study as homework and then ask Ss to paraphrase what they learned the next day in class.

Note: Because reported speech does not typically make the required time frame shift when reporting very recent speech (*She said she can't hear you*), having Ss report other Ss' utterances is not an effective way to introduce and practice this basic feature.

Reported Speech and Change of Time Frame

When we report information that was spoken, written, or thought in the past, we can use reported speech or direct quotation. **Direct quotation** is the actual words that were spoken in the conversation. **Reported speech** expresses the meaning of what was said. We use these same patterns to describe **indirect thoughts**: ideas that were thought but not actually spoken. Because we are describing something that has already occurred (the speaking or thinking), we need to change the time frame of the verb phrases of what we are reporting.

To refer to Present Time Frame:

DIRECT QUOTATION	REPORTED SPEECH
(a) Jack thought, "**I'm** really sick. I **am having** terrible headaches. **I'm going to try** to see my doctor this afternoon, if I **can get** someone to drive me to her office."	**(b)** Jack thought that he **was** really sick. He **was having** terrible headaches. He **was going to try** to see his doctor yesterday afternoon, if he **could get** someone to drive him to the doctor's office.

To refer to Past Time Frame:

DIRECT QUOTATION	REPORTED SPEECH
(c) Yesterday I spoke to Jack on the phone. Here is what he said: "My headache **was getting** worse all the time, so I **went** to the doctor yesterday. She **took** my temperature. She **prescribed** some pills. My condition **has improved**, but I still **haven't gone** back to work yet."	**(d)** Yesterday I spoke to Jack on the phone. He told me that his headache **had been getting** worse, so he **had gone** to the doctor the day before yesterday. She **had prescribed** some pills. Jack felt that his condition **had improved**, but when I spoke to him he still **hadn't gone** back to work.

EXERCISE 1

Denise Driven had a meeting with her boss, Mr. Green, to complain about Peter Principle's work in the office. Here are some of the complaints that Denise made about Peter. Change these direct quotations to reported speech, using the cue given.

▶ **EXAMPLE:** "I've been getting more and more annoyed by Peter's behavior."
Denise reported that . . .

Denise reported that she had been getting more and more an-noyed by Peter's behavior.

1. "Peter needs to be more serious about work."

Denise felt that . . .

2. "Peter came to work fifteen minutes late for the second time in a month."

Denise was angry that . . .

3. "Peter is going to leave the office early to see his child perform in a school play."

She complained that . . .

4. "He is always whistling in the office."

She didn't like the fact that . . .

5. "He has made rude comments about my personal life."

She was upset that . . .

EXERCISE 2

Here are other complaints Denise had about Peter. How do you think she stated her complaints? Restate them as direct quotations, using "Denise said."

▶ **EXAMPLE:** She reported that she had been getting more and more annoyed by Peter's behavior.

Denise said, "I have been getting more and more annoyed by Peter's behavior."

1. She was annoyed that he didn't always finish projects on time.

2. She was unhappy that he told so many jokes at staff meetings.

3. She didn't like the fact that he refused to come into the office on Saturdays.

4. She was upset that he was going to miss an important meeting be-cause he had promised to take his children to the circus.

5. She was angry that he constantly allowed his personal life to inter-fere with his work obligations.

Reported Speech | **403**

Exercise 1

For more advanced classes, do this exercise in a lively whole-class way, reading the direct quotations aloud as cues.

Exercise 2

Try doing this exercise as a whole class. For a more "natural" elicitation of the answers, ask *"What did she say?"* and have Ss supply the direct quotation.

Workbook Ex. 1, p. 171. Answers: TE p. 509.

ANSWER KEY

Exercise 1

1. Peter needed to be more serious about work. 2. Peter had come to work fifteen minutes late 3. Peter was going to leave the office early 4. He was always whistling in the office. 5. He had made rude comments . . .

Exercise 2

1. She said, "I am annoyed that he doesn't always finish projects . . ." 2. She said, "I am unhappy that he tells so many jokes . . ." 3. She said, "I don't like the fact that he refuses to come . . ." 4. She said, "I am upset that he is going to miss . . . 5. She said, "I am angry that he constantly allows . . ."

SUGGESTIONS:

1. The changes outlined in Focuses 2, 3, and 4 all follow as a logical extension of the basic shift introduced in Focus 1. If possible, structure your presentation so all three of these focuses are covered in a single lesson.

2. Present this focus in a straightforward fashion by writing the sample sentence, or a class-related example, on the board. *(What did I say yesterday? "There will be a quiz on Friday." I told you that there would be a quiz on Friday.)*
3. Do Exercise 3 as an immediate follow-up.

Exercise 3

This is a good exercise to assign as homework to be collected and corrected.

Workbook Exs. 2–4, pp. 172–173. Answers: TE p. 509.

FOCUS **2**

Modal Changes in Reported Speech

Change present modals to past modals in reported speech.

DIRECT QUOTATION	REPORTED SPEECH
(a) "I **will try** to see my doctor this afternoon, if I **can** get someone to drive me to her office."	**(b)** He said that he **would try** to see his doctor yesterday afternoon, if he **could** get someone to drive him to the doctor's office.

may *can* *shall* *will*	**changes to** ⟶	*might* *could* *should* *would*

EXERCISE 3

Here is the response Mr. Green made when he talked with Denise. Change his direct quotation to reported speech. Start your paragraph with *Mr. Green said that. . . .* Use *Mr. Green suggested that . . .* and *Mr. Green thought that*
. . . later in the paragraph.

Mr. Green said, "The personnel officer will be asked to speak to Peter. If Peter can't get to the office on time, he will just have to take an earlier bus. He may not be crazy about getting up at 5:30, but he will have to do it if he wants to keep his job. Personnel won't talk to Peter about the other problems he may be having, though. One of Peter's friends in the office can deal with him directly about his lack of responsibility. Peter probably won't change much, but he may be more willing to listen to the complaints if he can get the information from someone he likes and respects."

ANSWER KEY

Exercise 3
Precise wording of the rewrites will vary, but the necessary changes in verbs and modals have been highlighted.
. . . the personnel officer **would** be asked to speak . . . **He also said** that if Peter **couldn't** get to the office . . . he **would** just have to take . . . He **might** not be crazy about getting up at 5:30, but he **would** have to do it if he **wanted** to keep his job. Personnel **wouldn't** talk to Peter . . . he **might** be having, though. **Mr. Green suggested that** one of Peter's friends . . . **could** deal with him . . . **Mr. Green thought that** Peter probably **wouldn't** change much, but he **might** be . . . if he **could** get . . . he **liked** and **respected**.

FOCUS **3**

Changes in Pronouns and Possessive Determiners in Reported Speech

In reported speech we must change pronoun forms in order to keep the same meaning.

EXAMPLES	IMPLIED MEANING
(a) Jack said, "**I** am sick."	Jack is sick.
(b) Jack told me that **I** am sick.	I am sick—not Jack.
(c) Jack told me that **he** was sick.	Jack is sick.

Compare the pronouns in these two passages.

DIRECT QUOTATION	REPORTED SPEECH
(d) Jack said, "**You** will be happy to know that **my** condition has improved, but **I** still haven't gone back to **my** office yet."	**(e)** He said that **I** would be happy to know that **his** condition had improved, but **he** still hadn't gone back to **his** office yet.

If there is some confusion about what the pronoun or possessive determiner refers to, it may be necessary to substitute the actual noun.

DIRECT QUOTATION	REPORTED SPEECH
(f) Jack said, "I asked **my** brother Peter to bring **his** wife to the party."	**(g)** Jack asked **his** brother Peter to bring **his**—Peter's—wife to the party.

Reported Speech | **405**

SUGGESTIONS:

1. The changes outlined in Focuses 2, 3, and 4, all follow as a logical extension of the basic shift introduced in Focus 1. If possible, structure your presentation so all three of these focuses are covered in a single lesson.
2. Present this focus in a straightforward fashion by writing the sample sentence, or a class-related example on the board. *(What did Yoko say yesterday?" She said she left <u>her</u> homework on the bus.)*
3. Do Exercise 4 as an immediate follow-up.

Teacher's Edition: Unit 25   **405**

Do this exercise as a whole class follow-up of your presentation of Focus 3 by doing the questions one by one, calling on individual Ss and allowing for alternative answers and questions for clarification.

FOCUS 4

S U G G E S T I O N S :

1. The changes outlined in Focuses 2, 3, and 4, all follow as a logical extension of the basic shift introduced in Focus 1. If possible, structure your presentation so all three of these focuses are covered in a single lesson.
2. Present this focus in a straightforward fashion by writing the sample sentence, or class-related examples, on the board. *(Last Monday I said, "There will be a quiz tomorrow". I said there would be a quiz on the following day.)*
3. Follow up immediately with Exercise 5.

EXERCISE 4

Change these direct quotations into reported speech.

▶ **EXAMPLE:** Peter said, "My kids have an invitation for your kids."

Peter said that his kids had an invitation for my kids.

1. Peter said, "My kids are having a birthday party at my house on Saturday."
2. Peter told me, "My kids have invited your kids to come their party."
3. Peter said, "I've asked my friend to bring her three girls."
4. Peter said, "I've hired a clown to entertain all our kids."
5. Peter said, "While our kids are watching the clown, my wife and I can prepare the cake and ice cream for your kids."
6. Peter said, "I asked Denise's secretary to tell her about the party, because she wanted me to work all weekend."
7. Peter said, "My family is more important to me than Denise's project."

FOCUS **4**

▶ **Changes in Demonstratives and Adverbials in Reported Speech**

You may also need to change demonstratives and adverbials to keep the same meaning.

DIRECT QUOTATION	REPORTED SPEECH
(a) On Saturday Maria said, "Please come **here** for lunch **this afternoon**."	(b) On Saturday Maria asked me to go **there** for lunch **that afternoon.**
(c) Jack said, "I went to the doctor **yesterday**."	(d) Jack told me that he had gone to the doctor **(on) the previous day.**

A N S W E R   K E Y

Exercise 4

1. Peter said that his kids were having a birthday party at his house that weekend.
2. Peter told me that his kids had invited my kids . . . 3. Peter said that he had asked his friend to bring her . . . 4. Peter said that he had hired a clown . . . 5. Peter said that while their kids were watching the clown, his wife and he could prepare . . . for his kids.
6. Peter said that he had asked Denise's secretary to tell Denise . . . because Denise had wanted him . . . 7. Peter said that his family was more important to him than . . .

Here are some examples of common changes in reference that are required in reported speech:

this/these		*that/those*
here		*there*
today/tonight		*(on) that day/that night*
yesterday	**changes to**	*(on) the day before/the previous day*
tomorrow		*the next day*
two days from today		*two days from then*
two days ago		*two days earlier*

EXERCISE 5

Change these direct quotations into reported speech:

▶ **EXAMPLE:** Ali said, "I came here to get some groceries, but the store's closed until tomorrow."

Ali said that he had gone there to get some groceries, but the store was closed until the next day.

1. Yesterday morning Peter said, "I am coming to the meeting this afternoon."

2. When I saw Petra last week, she told me, "My father may be able to take this letter directly to the Immigration Office later today."

3. Last week my brother told me, "I have already completed all the assignments I have for my classes this week."

4. Two days ago I spoke to the doctor, and he said, "The results of your test will be here by tomorrow morning."

5. Yesterday my mother promised me, "Tomorrow when you come here, I'll give you some of my delicious fudge."

Exercise 5

Do this exercise as a whole class follow-up of your presentation of Focus 4 by doing the questions one by one, calling on individuals, and allowing for alternative answers and questions for clarification.

Workbook Exs. 5 & 6, pp. 173–174. Answers: TE p. 509.

ANSWER KEY

Exercise 5

1. . . . Peter said that he was coming . . . that afternoon   2. . . . she told me that her father might be able to take that letter . . . later that day.   3. . . . told me that he had already completed all the assignments he had for his classes that week.   4. . . . he said that the results of my test would be there by the next morning.   5. . . . promised me that today when I came there, she'd give me some of her . . .

FOCUS 5

If you are pressed for time, combine your presentation of Focuses 5 and 6 into a single contrastive treatment. Ss have probably already internalized the notion of quotation marks, so you may be able to skip the first part of this focus.

Statements in Reported Speech

In direct quotation, the same markers—quotation marks ("...")—are used for statements, questions, and imperatives.

EXAMPLES	EXPLANATIONS
(a) The doctor told me, "I'm afraid we'll have to do more tests."	Direct quotation of a statement
(b) "The doctor asked me, "Have you been having these headaches for a long time?"	Direct quotation of a question

In reported speech, different patterns are used for statements and questions. *That* is used for statements.

EXAMPLES	EXPLANATIONS
(c) The doctor told me **that** he was afraid we would have to do more tests.	*That* introduces reported statements.
(d) The doctor told me he was afraid we would have to do more tests.	*That* is often omitted in informal contexts and conversation.

Exercise 6

Ss usually really enjoy this exercise. Make sure they read the whole passage first before doing the exercise.

S U G G E S T I O N S :

1. If you have access to an OHP, make a transparency and underline the reported speech patterns together as a class.
2. For adult classes, follow with a brief discussion of where people thought babies came from when they were children.

Workbook Ex. 7, p. 175. Answers: TE pp. 509-510.

EXERCISE 6

Underline the reported speech patterns in the following passage that tell what the narrator heard or thought. Restate each one as a direct quotation. The first paragraph has been done for you as an example.

▶ **EXAMPLES:** His parents told him, "We found you under a cabbage leaf."

He thought, "That probably isn't true."

He thought, "There are lots of new babies in my neighborhood and no cabbage plants at all."

(1) When I was a child I had some very strange ideas about where babies come from. (2) My parents always told me <u>that they had found me under a cabbage leaf.</u> (3) I knew <u>that probably wasn't true,</u> since I realized

---

A N S W E R   K E Y

Exercise 6

These structures should be underlined:
(2) that they had found me under a cabbage leaf. (3) that probably wasn't true, . . . there were lots of new babies in my neighborhood and no cabbage plants at all. (4) . . . my parents had actually bought my younger sister at the hospital. (5) . . . hospitals were places that sold babies to any couple that wanted one. (6) he had to be sure to pay the bill before that week was over. (7) my father would forget to pay and that the hospital would decide to take her back and sell her to someone else. (8) babies were neither bought nor found.

Direct quotation restatements:

2. His parents told him, "We found you . . ."
3. He thought, "That probably isn't true, since there are . . ." **4.** He thought, "My parents actually bought my younger siste . . ." **5.** He figured, "Hospitals are places that sell . . . wants one." **6.** His mother said to his father, "You have to be sure/ Be sure to pay the bill before this week is over." **7.** He hoped, "Maybe my father will forget to pay and the hospital will decide . . ." **8.** Here is what he found out: Babies are neither bought nor found.

---

there were lots of new babies in my neighborhood and no cabbage plants at all.

(4) For several years I thought my parents had actually bought my younger sister at the hospital. (5) I figured hospitals were places that sold babies to any couple that wanted one. (6) This was because when my mother came back from the hospital after giving birth to my sister, I heard her remind my father that he had to be sure to pay the bill before that week was over. (7) I was a little jealous of my new sister, and I hoped that my father would forget to pay and that the hospital would decide to take her back and sell her to someone else. (8) It wasn't until several years later that I found out that babies were neither bought nor found.

FOCUS **6**

▶ **Questions in Reported Speech**

Changes in Word Order: All reported speech occurs in statement word order, whether it is a statement or a question.

DIRECT QUOTATION	REPORTED SPEECH
(a) "Am I late?"	**(b)** Yuri asked **if he was late.**
(c) "Do you need money?"	**(d)** Paolo wanted to know **whether I needed money.**
(e) "How much do you need?"	**(f)** He asked **how much I needed.**

Adding Question Markers: We use different patterns depending on whether the question being asked is a *yes/no* question or *Wh*-question.

EXAMPLES	EXPLANATIONS
(g) He wanted to know **if** I could bring my notes to the meeting.	*Yes/no* **Questions**
(h) He wanted to know **whether** I could bring my notes to the meeting.	We can use either *if* or *whether (or not)* to report *yes/no* questions. *If* is preferred for *yes/no* questions.
(i) He wanted to know **whether or not** I could bring my notes to the meeting.	

FOCUS 6

Reported questions are a little more complex than reported statements. So even if you are presenting this focus in connection with Focus 5, be sure to clearly distinguish between reported *yes/no* questions and reported *Wh*-questions. You will also need to explicitly present the statement word order that is common to either kind of reported question.

Present this focus in a straightforward way.
1. After you have made the basic contrast between statement and question, have Ss read the examples in the book or read them aloud yourself with Ss following along. If you wish, use class-related examples like these: **Yes/no question:** *My parents keep asking if I have passed the TOEFL.* **Wh-question:** *They want to know when I can begin my university study.* **Imbedded question:** *Can you tell me if I will ever be done with this project?*
2. Do Exercise 7 as an immediate follow-up to your presentation. If you have combined Focuses 5 and 6, do Exercises 6 and 7 together in the same class period.

(j)	I applied for a job. They wanted to know **where I had worked, when I worked there, how many years of experience I had,** and **what kind of previous experience I had had** in sales.	**Wh-Questions** We use a *Wh*-question word to report *Wh*-questions.
(k)	Can you tell me **what your zip code is?**	**Embedded Questions** Direct *yes/no* and *Wh*-questions sound more polite if they are embedded in a conversational frame such as "Do you know . . . ," or "Can you tell me . . . ," or "I wonder . . . ." It is not necessary to change the tense of the questions from present to past.
(l)	Do you know **what time the store opens?**	
(m)	I wonder **if Dr. Tang is able to come to the phone.**	

Exercise 7

This exercise can be assigned as homework to be written in a single paragraph. It can also be done as a general discussion, calling on individual Ss to report the questions. The final discussion question should be done in class as follow-up no matter which way you choose to do it.

EXERCISE 7

Here is a list of interview questions that were common in American businesses thirty or forty years ago. Some of them are no longer asked by employers these days. In some cases the law prohibits asking such questions.

Restate the questions as statements about old-fashioned hiring practices by adding such reporting phrases as "A number of years ago employers used to ask . . . ," "They wanted to know . . . ," "They often asked prospective employees to tell them . . . ," and other similar phrases you can think of.

Which questions do you think are still being used?

1. Are you married or single?
2. Does your wife work outside the home?
3. How many children do you have?
4. Are you a Communist?
5. Do you go to church?
6. How old are you?
7. Why do you want to work for this company?
8. Do you use drugs?
9. What is your racial background?
10. How much experience do you have?

EXERCISE 8

Change this report of a job interview into the list of questions that the interviewer actually asked.

▶ **EXAMPLE:** *Where did you graduate from high school?*

(1) Bob applied for a summer job as a computer programmer in a large company. (2) The head of the Personnel Office interviewed him. (3) <u>She wanted to know where he had graduated from high school</u>, and if he had ever studied in a college or university. (4) She wanted to know if he had ever been arrested, or whether he had ever needed to borrow money in order to pay off credit card purchases. (5) She wanted to know how fast he could type and what kind of experience he had had with computers, and whether he was more proficient in COBOL or BASIC. (6) She asked him what companies he had worked for in the past. (7) She wanted to know what his previous salary had been. (8) She wanted to know why he was no longer working at his previous job. (9) She asked him if he would voluntarily take a drug test. (10) He began to wonder if he really wanted to work for a company that wanted to know so much about his private life.

EXERCISE 9

Change these direct questions into more polite forms by making them embedded questions using phrases such as "Do you know," "Can you tell me," or "I wonder."

1. What time does the train leave?
2. Is the bookstore open yet?
3. Can Sunyoon come with us to the party?
4. How do I get to Carnegie Hall?
5. Where can I find a cheap apartment?

Exercise 8

This is another exercise that works equally well as an individual homework assignment or as a paired in-class activity.

Exercise 9

EXPANSION:

Have Ss role-play situations where a tourist or newcomer to a city asks directions. Encourage them to use and listen for embedded questions.

Workbook Ex. 8, p. 176. Answers: TE p. 510.

ANSWER KEY

Exercise 8

Where did you graduate from high school? Have you ever studied in a college or university? Have you ever been arrested? Have you ever needed to borrow money in order to pay off credit card purchases? How fast can you type? What kind of experience have you had with computers? Are you more proficient in COBOL or BASIC? What companies have you worked for in the past? What was your previous salary? Why aren't you still working at your previous job? Will you voluntarily take a drug test? Do I really want to work for a company that wants to know so much about my private life?

Exercise 9

The frames will vary, but the reported questions should be:
1. . . . what time the train leaves 2. . . . if the bookstore is open yet 3. . . . if Mary can come with us to the party 4. . . . how I get to Carnegie Hall 5. . . . where I can find a cheap apartment

This focus can be presented as a follow-up to reported questions or independently on its own. It's probably better not to assign it for homework.

1. Demonstrate the example sentences or just have Ss follow along as you present the various explanations directly from the book.

2. Do Exercise 10 as an immediate follow-up.

Exercise 10

Do this exercise orally in class by having Ss say the direct quotation.

Workbook Ex. 9, p. 176–177. Answers: TE p. 510.

FOCUS **7**

Commands and Requests in Reported Speech

EXAMPLES	EXPLANATIONS
(a) Teacher to student: "Do the homework." **(b)** The teacher **told me to do** the homework.	To report commands, use verbs like *tell* or *order* + infinitive.
(c) Roommate: "Can you help?" **(d)** My roommate **asked me to help** with the dishes.	To report requests or invitations, use verbs such as *ask* or *invite* + infinitive.
(e) The teacher told me **not to joke** with other students. **(f)** My roommate asked me **not to play** my stereo too loud.	Negative commands and requests are reported with *not* + infinitive.

EXERCISE 10

Rewrite these indirect commands and requests as direct quotations.

▶ **EXAMPLE:** On his first day in the army, Kilroy was told to report to the drill field by the master sergeant.

The master sergeant told Kilroy, "Report to the drill field."

1. Another officer assigned him to clean the area for nearly an hour.
2. The officers ordered all the new recruits not to talk to each other.
3. They were told to stand at attention until their papers had been processed.
4. Kilroy asked to go to the bathroom, but this request was denied.
5. Finally the processing was over, and they were ordered to return to their barracks.
6. Several other recruits invited Kilroy to join them in a game of cards.
7. He told them he was too tired, and asked them not to be too noisy since he wanted to sleep.

ANSWER KEY

Exercise 10

Answers will vary slightly. Possible answers include:

1. Another officer ordered, "Clean the area for the next hour." 2. The officers commanded "Don't talk to each other." 3. Someone said, "Stand at attention until your papers have been processed." 4. Kilroy asked, "Can I go to the bathroom?" But they told him, "No!" 5. The officer said, " Return to your barracks." 6. Several other recruits asked Kilroy, "Would you like to join us in a game of cards?" 7. He told them, "I'm too tired. Would you please not be too noisy, since I want to sleep."

When No Tense Changes Are Required in Reported Speech

FOCUS 8

This is the one focus in this unit that can be effectively assigned as self-study outside of class. Review briefly which categories require no changes in class the next day.

In certain situations, English speakers do not always make the tense and modal changes we have practiced here. These situations occur when we are reporting:

CATEGORY	DIRECT QUOTATION	REPORTED SPEECH
• things that are always true	**(a)** My father always told me, "Time **is** money."	**(b)** My father always told me that time **is** money.
• things that are still true	**(c)** Jean told me, "Jack **is still living** with his parents after all these years."	**(d)** Jean told me (that) Jack **is still living** with his parents after all these years.
• hypothetical statements	**(e)** Peter said, "If I **had** the money, I **would make** a donation to the club, but I **am** a little short on cash this month."	**(f)** Peter said that if he **had** the money, he **would make** a donation to the club, but that he **is/was** a little short on cash this/last month.
• statements that were made only a very short time ago	**(g)** Bambang told me, "I **can't** understand a word you're saying"	**(h)** He **just** said that he **can't** understand a word **I'm** saying.
• future events that have not yet occurred	**(i)** Diane said, "I **am going** to Hawaii next month."	**(j)** Diane said that she **is going** to Hawaii next month.

Exercise 11

Assign this exercise as part of the self-study of Focus 8 and review the reasons the next day to make sure that Ss understand the concepts.

Workbook Exs. 10 & 11, pp. 177–178.
Answers: TE p 510.

UNIT GOAL REVIEW

1. Start by asking briefly what kinds of forms must be changed when we report speech. Jot a list down on the board. If items are not mentioned, you can cue the class by asking questions like *"What about pronouns? Do we need to change those?"*
2. Have Ss take out their conversations written in Step 1 of the Opening Task and trade with a partner. Each should rewrite the conversation using reported speech. Walk around and monitor the rewrites individually, reminding Ss of the various forms that need to be changed.
3. At the end summarize and review common areas of difficulty.

EXERCISE 11

Decide whether tense changes are required in the following sentences when they are changed to reported speech. If a tense change is not required, state the reason.

▶ **EXAMPLE:**   Shakespeare once observed, "Love is blind."

No change. Timeless truth—still true

Last week our teacher reminded us, "Do your homework before you come to class tomorrow."

Last week our teacher reminded us to do our homework before we came to class the next day.

1. A student in my geography class reported, "Not all the people who live in China speak Chinese as their first language."
2. My brother told me, "I wouldn't need to borrow money from you all the time if I had a better paying job."
3. It was only a minute ago that I asked, "Are you paying attention?"
4. Jae told me, "I couldn't get any tickets for the concert."
5. Yesterday Denise said, "If I were you, I would plan things a little more completely before you leave for vacation next week."
6. This morning Peter told me, "I'm still having problems with Denise, but I'm trying extra hard to get along with her."
7. Bob said, "We're all going to go skiing the second week in January."

ANSWER KEY

Exercise 11

1. No change—timeless truth   2. No change—hypothetical statement   3. No change—statements occurred a very short time ago   4. No change—tense change would result in a change of meaning   5. No change—hypothetical statement   6. This morning Peter told me that he **was** still having problems . . . **he was** trying . . .   7. Bob said that we were all . . .

Use Your English

ACTIVITY 1: SPEAKING/WRITING

Work with a different partner from the one with whom you worked on the Opening Task. Together, write a conversation that matches the photos in the Opening Task. Act out your conversation for the rest of the class. Other students should write a paraphrase of your conversation.

ACTIVITY 2: LISTENING/SPEAKING/WRITING

To *eavesdrop* means to secretly listen to someone else's conversation. Go to a public place, like a restaurant, a shopping mall, or a bus station, and eavesdrop on someone's conversation. It's important not to let people know what you're doing, so pretend to read a book, or study your English grammar, or read a magazine in another language (people might think that you don't understand English), or pretend to write a letter.

Report what the people were talking about, and tell or write two or three things that they said to each other. Did you learn anything interesting about their lives, or about English, as a result of this experience?

ACTIVITY 3: LISTENING/SPEAKING/WRITING

Listen to a news broadcast on television. Report one story that you heard on that broadcast to the rest of the class. Start with some sort of statement like this: *I heard on the news that. . . , It was announced that. . . ,* etc.

ACTIVITY 4: LISTENING/SPEAKING

Play a game of "Telephone." Here's how to play:

Form two or more teams of ten people each. Student #1 should make a statement to Student #2 very quietly, so that only Student #2 can hear what was said. Student #2 then reports what was said to Student #3 using reported speech (*Student #1 told me that . . .*). Student #3 tells Student #4 and so forth. When the last student receives the report, he or she should announce the message to the rest of the class. Compare how close that message is with what was originally said by Student #1. The team that has the closest, most accurate report wins a point. Student #2 starts the next round.

USE YOUR ENGLISH

Activity 1

If you wish, substitute this activity for the pair work described in the Unit Goal Review, being sure to preserve the pre- and post-discussion of categories of things that change.

Activity 2

This is a good activity to do in connection with cross-cultural discussions on body language and nonverbal communication or with Activity 4 in Unit 18. Make sure that you explicitly review eavesdropping "strategies" so that Ss can listen in on conversations unnoticed—this is not intended to be a "contact" assignment!

Activity 3

This activity can be done in written form as a diagnostic. You can give all the Ss a recording of the same broadcast.

Activity 4

Use this activity for fun, not for serious practice, since you won't be able to evaluate individual restatements.

Activity 5

This activity can also be used as the topic for small group discussion.

Activity 6

Have Ss compare the direct speech patterns of their story with the indirect speech patterns of what they learned.

Activity 7

Play textbook audio. The tapescript for this listening appears on p. 521 of this book. Allow for multiple listenings as needed: once for general comprehension, once to develop the probable direct-quotation versions, and once to clarify and confirm the direct quotations they have written. Omit Step 2 if you are pressed for time.

The test of this unit can be found on p. 488. The answers are on p. 489 of this book.

TOEFL Test Preparation Exercises for Units 23–25 can be found on pp. 179–181 of the Workbook. The answers are on p. 510 of this book.

ACTIVITY 5: WRITING

Write a paragraph discussing some of the misconceptions about life that you had when you were a child. Describe what you thought, and why you thought it. See Exercise 6 for an example.

ACTIVITY 6: WRITING

Tell about a time when you had an important conversation with someone. Perhaps you learned some important information about yourself or someone else. Perhaps you found out about a decision that had a big effect on your life in some way. Perhaps you got some valuable advice.

STEP 1 First, tell the **story** of the conversation. Write down who it was with, where, and when it took place. Then try to write the conversation word-for-word.

STEP 2 Next, write a paragraph telling what you learned from this conversation, and why it was important for you. You may want to begin your paragraph with *When I was . . . , I learned that . . . .*

ACTIVITY 7: LISTENING

STEP 1 Based on the short news broadcast you hear, complete the following sentences with the actual words that were probably used by the speaker.

1. The Police Department representative announced, "_____."

2. He admitted, "_____."

3. He predicted, "_____."

STEP 2 Use the sentences you have written to perform the announcement.

ANSWER KEY

Activity 7
1. "The rate of violent crime has decreased significantly over the last five months."
2. "There has been a slight increase in thefts and burglaries, and the Department will continue frequent patrols in all neighborhoods."
3. "The budget will be finalized by the end of this week, and the accelerated hiring program may begin as soon as next Wednesday."

Appendices

Appendix 1A

Present Time Frame: Use Present Time to talk about general relationships. Most scientific and technical writing is in Present Time. Anything that is related to the present moment is expressed by Present Time, so newspaper headlines, news stories, and spoken conversations, jokes, and informal narratives are often in Present Time.

Form	Meaning	Use	Example
SIMPLE PRESENT *I/you/we/they* + simple form of verb *he/she/it* + *-s* form of verb	true in the past, present and future	general relationships and timeless truths permanent states	**(a)** Time **changes** the way people live. **(b)** Bob **has** two brothers and one sister.
		habitual and recurring actions	**(c)** Bob **works** in the library every afternoon.
PRESENT PROGRESSIVE *am/is/are* + present participle (verb + *-ing*)	already in progress now or around this time	actions in progress	**(d)** Bob **is studying** for a midterm at this moment.
		repetition or duration	**(e)** Bob **is taking** a biology class this semester.
		temporary states and actions	**(f)** Bob's brother **is living** with his father for the summer.
		uncompleted actions	**(g)** **He is** still **looking** for a cheap apartment.

A-1

Form	Meaning	Use	Example
PRESENT PERFECT *have/has* + past participle (verb + *-ed* or past participle of irregular verbs)	began in the past but related in some way to the present	past events related to now by time past events related to now by logical relationship	**(h)** Bob **has visited** Canada twice, so he won't join the tour to Quebec. **(i)** Bob **has gotten** very good at the computer, so he doesn't need to take another class.
PRESENT PERFECT PROGRESSIVE *have/has* + *been* + present participle (verb + *-ing*)	in progress before and including the present	repeated and/or continuous actions	**(j)** Bob **has been spending** his weekends at home since he started living in the dorm. **(k)** Bob **has been singing** in a chorus ever since he was in high school.

Appendix 1B

Past Time Frame: Use Past Time to talk about things that are not directly connected to the present moment. Most fiction, historical accounts, and factual descriptions of past events are in Past Time.

Form	Meaning	Use	Example
SIMPLE PAST verb + *-ed* or irregular past form	at a certain time in the past	states or general relationships that were true in the past habitual or recurrent actions that took place in the past specific events that took place in the past	**(a)** Tuberculosis **was** a common cause of death 50 years ago. **(b)** Robert Lee **worked** 12 hours a day for low wages. **(c)** Robert Lee **went** to work in a factory at age 14.

Form	Meaning	Use	Example
PAST PROGRESSIVE *was/were* + present participle (verb + *-ing*)	in progress at a certain time in the past	interrupted actions	**(d)** Robert **was studying** in high school when his father died.
		repeated actions and actions over time	**(e)** Robert **was** always **trying** to get promotions at the factory.
PAST PERFECT *had* + past participle (verb + *-ed* or past participle of irregular verbs)	before a certain time in the past	actions or states that took place before other events in the past	**(f)** His father **had been** dead for several weeks when Robert quit school and started working to help his mother.
PAST PERFECT PROGRESSIVE *had been* + present participle (verb + *-ing*)	in progress until a certain time in the past	continuous versus repeated actions	**(g)** Robert **had been working** for 12 hours when the foreman told him to go home.
		uncompleted versus completed actions	**(h)** Robert **had been hoping** to complete school when he had to find a job to help his family.

Appendix 1C

Future Time Frame: Use Future Time for anything that is scheduled to happen or predicted to happen in the future. Notice that two tenses (simple present and present progressive) that are used in Present Time Frame can also be used to talk about future plans or scheduled events.

Form	Meaning	Use	Example
SIMPLE PRESENT	already scheduled or expected in the future	schedules	**(a)** The plane **leaves** at 6:30 tomorrow.
PRESENT PROGRESSIVE		definite future plans	**(b)** I **am spending** next summer in France.
SIMPLE FUTURE one-word (*will/might*/etc.) or phrasal modals (*be going to*) + simple verb	at a certain time in the future	predictions about future situations	**(c)** Roberta is **going to take** a vacation on the moon. **(d)** She **will** probably **get** there by space shuttle, and she **might stay** on an observation platform.
FUTURE PROGRESSIVE future modal + *be* + verb + *-ing*	in progress at a certain time in the future	future events in progress	**(e)** 100 years from now Roberta **will be living** on the moon.
FUTURE PERFECT modal + *have* + past participle (verb + *-ed* or past participle of irregular verbs)	before a certain time in the future	events happening before other future events	**(f)** Scientists **will have visited** the moon long **before** tourists **will be** able to.
FUTURE PERFECT PROGRESSIVE modal + *have* + *been* + verb + *-ing*	in progress until a certain time in the future	repeated and/or continuous actions	**(g)** When Roberta retires on Earth she will probably not be used to the earth's level of gravity because she **will have been living** on the moon for several years.

A-4   APPENDICES

ASPECT:	Simple	Progressive	Perfect	Perfect Progressive*
TIME:	**TENSES:**			
Present	is/are studied	am/is/are being studied	has/have been studied	has/have been being studied
	is/are given	am/is/are being given	has/have been given	has/have been being given
Past	was/were studied	was/were being studied	had been studied	had been being studied
	was/were given	was/were being given	had been given	had been being given
Future	will be studied	will be being studied	will have been studied	will have been being studied
	will be given	will be being given	will have been given	will have been being given

*Although perfect progressive passive forms are theoretically possible in English, such forms are **very** rarely found in speech or writing.

Verb Patterns that Are Followed by Infinitives

(a) Norman **decided to specialize** in African stamps when a friend **offered to give** him some stamps from Ghana.	Pattern 1: verb + infinitive
(b) A friend **advised Norman to order** rare stamps from commercial companies, and **encouraged him to be** persistent.	Pattern 2: verb + noun phrase + infinitive
(c) Norman **likes to send** stamps to other people, and also **likes other people to send** stamps to him.	Pattern 3: verb (+ noun phrase) + infinitive

Verb Patterns that Are Followed by Gerunds

(a) Charlie **can't help falling** in love with a new woman every week. **(b)** The doctor told me that I've got to **quit smoking.**	Pattern 1: verb gerund
(c) Doctors **advise reducing** fats in one's diet. (It's good advice for everyone.) **(d)** The doctor **advised me to reduce** fats in my diet. (She gave this advice to me specifically.)	Pattern 2: verb { + gerund + noun phrase + infinitive
(e) I **don't mind sleeping** late when I get the chance, and **I don't mind other people doing** it either.	Pattern 3: verb (+ noun phrase) + gerund

Verbs that Are Followed by Infinitives			Verbs that Are Followed by Gerunds		
Pattern 1	**Pattern 2**	**Pattern 3**	**Pattern 1**	**Pattern 2**	**Pattern 3**
appear	advise	expect	can't help	advise	appreciate
refuse	remind	arrange	keep on	encourage	anticipate
seem	persuade	want	recommend	urge	dislike
agree	urge	intend	suggest	forbid	don't mind
claim	encourage	consent	deny	allow	enjoy
care	convince	ask	consider	permit	resent
deserve	force	need	admit	invite	consider
decide	forbid		give up	cause	delay
demand	command		avoid	teach	postpone
pretend	order		quit		excuse
hesitate	allow		practice		imagine
offer	permit		include		miss
tend	invite		resist		tolerate
learn	trust				understand
neglect	cause				
wait	tell				
	warn				
	teach				
	hire				

Meaning Categories	Beginning of the Clause	Middle of the Clause	End of the Clause
ADDITION	additionally also in addition	also in addition	also in addition too as well
EMPHASIS/ INTENSIFYING	actually as a matter of fact besides furthermore indeed in fact moreover	actually as a matter of fact furthermore indeed in fact moreover	as a matter of fact indeed in fact
CONTRAST	despite this however on the other hand	however on the other hand	despite this however on the other hand
CONCESSION	despite this even so in spite of the fact nonetheless	nonetheless	despite this even so in spite of the fact nonetheless regardless though
REASON	with this in mind for this reason therefore	therefore	therefore with this in mind for this reason
RESULT	accordingly as a result consequently thus	accordingly as a result consequently therefore thus	accordingly as a result consequently t
CONDITIONAL	providing if then under such circumstances		under such circumstances
SEQUENCE	next then first, second, etc.	and next then first, second, etc.	next first, second, etc.

1. What is the form of the noun? Noncount or count? Singular or plural?
2. Is the noun used to make a generic reference or particular reference?
   Does it describe a class of things or does it refer to a particular item?
3. If it refers to a particular thing, is the reference specific or nonspecific?

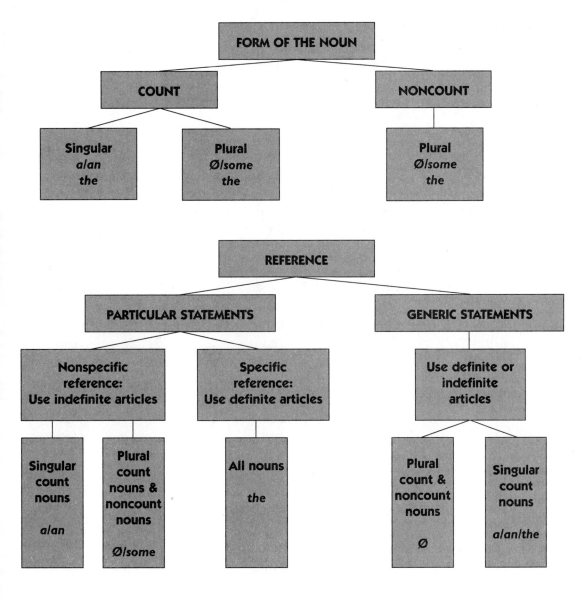

Simple Form	Past Tense Form	Past Participle	Simple Form	Past Tense Form	Past Participle
become	became	become	grow	grew	grown
begin	began	begun	hang	hung	hung
bend	bent	bent	have	had	had
bet	bet	bet	hear	heard	heard
bind	bound	bound	hide	hid	hidden
bite	bit	bit	hit	hit	hit
bleed	bled	bled	hold	held	held
blow	blew	blown	hurt	hurt	hurt
break	broke	broken	keep	kept	kept
bring	brought	brought	know	knew	known
build	built	built	lead	led	led
buy	bought	bought	leave	left	left
catch	caught	caught	lend	lent	lent
choose	chose	chosen	let	let	let
come	came	come	make	made	made
cost	cost	cost	mean	meant	meant
cut	cut	cut	meet	met	met
dig	dug	dug	put	put	put
do	did	done	quit	quit	quit
draw	drew	drawn	read	read	read
drink	drank	drunk	ride	rode	ridden
drive	drove	driven	ring	rang	rung
eat	ate	eaten	rise	rose	risen
fall	fell	fallen	run	ran	run
feed	fed	fed	say	said	said
feel	felt	felt	see	saw	seen
fight	fought	fought	seek	sought	sought
find	found	found	sell	sold	sold
fit	fit	fit	send	sent	sent
fly	flew	flown	set	set	set
forbid	forbade	forbidden	shake	shook	shaken
forget	forgot	forgotten	shine	shone	shone
forgive	forgave	forgiven	shoot	shot	shot
freeze	froze	frozen	shut	shut	shut
get	got	gotten	sing	sang	sung
give	gave	given	sink	sank	sunk
go	went	gone	sit	sat	sat
grind	ground	ground	sleep	slept	slept

Simple Form	Past Tense Form	Past Participle	Simple Form	Past Tense Form	Past Participle
slide	slid	slid	swing	swang	swung
speak	spoke	spoken	take	took	taken
speed	sped	sped	teach	taught	taught
spend	spent	spent	tear	tore	torn
split	split	split	tell	told	told
spread	spread	spread	think	thought	thought
spring	sprang	sprung	throw	threw	thrown
stand	stood	stood	understand	understood	understood
steal	stole	stolen	wake	woke	woken
stick	stuck	stuck	wear	wore	worn
sting	stung	stung	weave	wove	woven
strike	struck	stricken	weep	wept	wept
swear	swore	sworn	win	won	won
sweep	swept	swept	wind	wound	wound
swim	swam	swum	write	wrote	written

Answer Key (for puzzles and problems only)

UNIT 11

Answer to Activity 5 (page 201)

Secret: Silly Sally only likes things with double letters.

UNIT 16

Additional Clues for Opening Task (page 256)

Mystery 1	Mystery 2	Mystery 3
The man is very, very short.	There's a big puddle of water in the room, and the paper is a delivery bill from an ice company.	The police officer is a woman.

Answer to Activity 3 (page 268)

(A) Candle snuffer; **(B)** Hook to catch chickens; **(C)** Cherry pit remover; **(D)** Mechanical vegetable chopper; **(E)** Glove dryer/stretcher; **(F)** Ear protector for carriage horses

UNIT 20

Answer to Activity 1 (page 338)

That that is, is. That that is not, is not. Isn't that it? It is!

UNIT 21

Activity 1 (page 350)

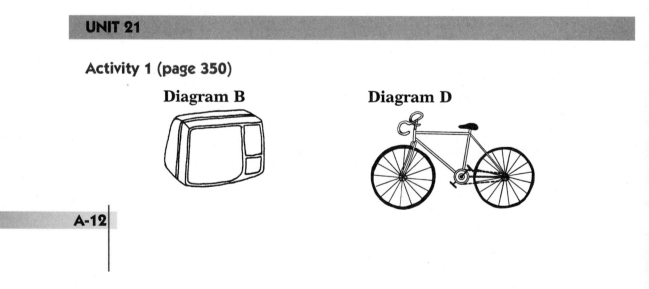

Diagram B   Diagram D

Index

and, 185, 186, 190, 192
apostrophes, 344–346, 346–349
articles, 306–327
    definite, 310–311
    demonstratives and, 308
    determiners and, 308
    direct and indirect reference using, 317–318
    in discourse, 306–327, 317–318
    generic statements using, 311–312
    indefinite, 310–311
    indefinite, repetition of, 319–320
    modifying phrases for noun phrases, 148
    no article use, 310
    particular statements using, 311–312
    possessives and, 308
    quantifiers and, 308
    specific vs. nonspecific nouns and, 314–317
    unique nouns and, 321–324
as a result, 186, 192, 195, 197
as soon as, 252
ask, 412
aspect of infinitives, 90
aspect of verbs, 2, 4, 12–28,
at all, 176, 178
attitude, nonprogressive (stative) verbs and, 222–223
awfully, 128

backward-pointing demonstrative references, 332–334
basically, 176
be
    in passive form, 48
    phrasal modals with, 66
    in relative clauses, deleting, 210
    modals in, 48, 66
be able to, 73, 80, 82
be going to, 73, 82, 248–249
because/because of, 186, 197
before, 186, 378
besides, 185, 195, 197
both, 359
but, 185, 190, 192, 283
by phrase, 48
    passive verb use of, 53

can/can't/could/couldn't, 66, 68, 69, 72, 79, 82, 404
    common meanings of, 68, 69
    in social interactions, 68
    as modal of inference, 261
    as perfect modal, 264
causative verbs, 292, 298–300
    active and passive, 301
cause-and-effect
    connectors, 184
    nonprogressive (stative) verbs and, 222–223
changing time frame within a passage, 7–8
clauses
    adjective clauses, 30
    adverbial, 28–45
    dependent, 30

    independent, 30
    relative, 30
collective adjectives, 366–367
collective nouns, 352, 363–365
    plurals and, 364
commands in reported speech, 412
comparatives, 166–181
    amount, 172–175
    degree, 168–171
    informal usage of, 180
    similarity and difference, noun phrases for, 176–177
    similarity and difference, verb phrases for, 178–179
complements of degree, 124–144
    enough, 134–135
    so, 140–142
    such, 140–142
    too, 134–135
conditional statements, 274–275
conditionals
    future time, 276–278
    past time, 279–282
    present time, 276–278
conditions, present tense in, 220
connectors, 182–201
    additive relationships and, 184
    cause-and-effect relationships and, 184
    contrastive relationships and, 184
    coordinating conjunctions as, 184, 185
    coordinating conjunctions to connect parallel forms, 190–191
    coordinating conjunctions, problems of usage, 192–194
    sentence connectors and, 184, 185, 186, 192
    sentence connectors, problems of usage and, 195–196
    sequence and, 184
    subordinating conjunctions as, 184, 185, 186, 192
    subordinating conjunctions, problems of usage and, 197–198
consequently, 186
considerable/considerably, 168, 172
contrastive relationships and connectors, 184
coordinating conjunctions
    connectors, 184, 185, 186
    to connect parallel forms, 190–191
    problems of usage, 192–194
could/couldn't, 68, 69, 72, 73, 79, 247, 251, 258, 261, 264, 276, 279, 386, 388, 390, 394, 404
    common meanings of, 72
    as modal of inference, 261
    as modal of prediction, 258
    as modal of probability, 251
    as past tense modal of future activity, 394
    as perfect modal, 264
    for social interactions, 68, 69
    was able to vs., 390
could have, 279, 286
count nouns, 308

TESTS AND ANSWERS

Grammar Dimensions Book 3

Name _____

Unit 1 Overview of the English Verb System

Score _____
100

Time and Tense

A. Complete the passage with the correct form of the verb in parentheses. (5 points each)

I _____ (1. never be) interested in sports but I _____ (2. be)

very excited nine years ago when I _____ (3. get) a chance to meet

Mohammed Ali. I _____ (4. always, consider) him a personal hero of

mine even though I _____ (5. never see) him box. I _____

(6. hate) boxing then and I _____ (7. hate) boxing today. I just

_____ (8. not understand) the romance of watching two grown men

_____ (9. hit) each other. At any rate, when I _____ (10.

teach) at Columbia in the 1980's I _____ (11. take) every class of mine

on a walking tour of Harlem. I always _____ (12. end) the tour at

Patsy's. It _____ (13. be) the best soulfood restaurant in New York and

it still _____ (14. be). One day I _____ (15. finish) a tour

and we _____ (16. eat) lunch when Mohammed Ali

_____ (17. walk) into the restaurant.

B. Write a logical, grammatical sentence with the phrase in parentheses. (5 points each)

18. (everyday last year) _____

19. (a year from now) _____

20. (since) _____

UNIT 1 ANSWERS

A.
1. have never been
2. was
3. got
4. had always considered
5. had never seen
6. hated
7. hate
8. don't understand
9. hit
10. was teaching/taught
11. took
12. ended
13. was
14. is
15. had just finished
16. were eating
17. walked

B.
18. past tense (We went everyday last year.)
19. will or be going to (He'll still be here a year from now.)
20. present perfect 1 past (They haven't called since they had the accident.)

Grammar Dimensions Book 3

Name _____

Unit 2 Overview of the English Verb System

Score _____
100

Aspect

A. Rewrite the incorrect sentences. (5 points each)

1. While I was waiting for you to call, I was deciding to wash my hair, so now it's still wet.

   _____

2. Tina wanted to go to the movies but by the time she had finished her work, her friends left.

   _____

3. We've often left him alone in the park, and he has never run away before.

   _____

4. The Boyce family will only be here until Janice returned from Europe.

   _____

5. We're going to be seeing them next week, so I can ask them to call you.

   _____

B. Complete the paragraph with the correct form of the verb in parentheses. (5 points each)

When I first _____ (6. meet) Maria, we both _____ (7. live) in

the dormitory at school. I _____ (8. notice) her because we always

_____ (9. eat) lunch at the same time and I _____ (10. think)

she was very attractive. One day, while we _____ (11. have) lunch, I

_____ (12. decide) to go and talk to her. I _____ (13. study) very

hard for a Spanish exam and _____ (14. want) to ask her for some help.

After we _____ (15. get) to know each other, she _____

(16. admit) that she _____ (17. notice) me in the cafeteria, too. On that day

we _____ (18. begin) a friendship that _____ (19. last) for many

years. Maria and I _____ (20. celebrate) our twentieth wedding

anniversary last month.

UNIT 2 ANSWERS

A.
1. I decided
2. her friends had left
3. correct
4. Janice returns
5. correct

B.
6. met
7. were living
8. noticed / had noticed
9. ate
10. thought
11. were having
12. decided
13. had been studying/was studying
14. wanted
15. got
16. admitted
17. had noticed
18. began
19. has lasted
20. celebrated

A. Unscramble the sentences and rewrite them in the correct order. More than one order may be possible. (7 points each)

1. at the parking lot / often / gather / the teenagers / on Friday nights

   _____

2. for the summer / she went to Mexico / in order to fulfill her language requirement / to study Spanish

   _____

3. immediately / I plan to rent out his room / for a long time / since he's going to be away

   _____

4. out of the building / we ran / as fast as we could / when the emergency light went on

   _____

5. exactly at 8 / we leave / because we don't want to be late for class / every morning

   _____

B. Write questions for the answers given below. (6 points each)

6. _____?
   Until spring.

7. _____?
   About four pounds.

8. _____?
   The tall one.

9. _____?
   To see if they were home.

10. _____?
   Incredibly well.

C. Add three adverbials to each sentence. Do not use an adverbial more than once. You do not have to use all of them. (7 points each)

everyday	as fast as possible	to get the medicine
because its fun	together	by training hard
in the afternoon	near the factory	occasionally
often	on the street	once a week
outdoors	yesterday	to improve her spelling
to the store	with considerable difficulty	all alone

11. Betsy studies.

_____

12. The workers marched.

_____

13. Bob and Rebecca do the tango.

_____

14. She won the race.

_____

15. I drove.

_____

UNIT 3 ANSWERS

A. 1. The teenagers often gather at the parking lot on Friday nights.
Alternative:

On Friday nights, the teenagers . . .

2. She went to Mexico for the summer to study Spanish in order to fulfill her language requirement.
Alternatives:

In order to fulfill her language requirement, . . .

3. I plan to rent out his room immediately since he's going to be away for a long time.
Alternative:

Since he's going to be away for a long time . . .

4. When the emergency light went on, we ran out of the building as fast as we could.
Alternative:

We ran out of the building as fast as we could when . . .

5. We leave exactly at 8 every morning because we don't want to be late for class.
Alternative:

Because we don't want to be late for class . . .

B. 6. A question beginning with how long

7. A question beginning with how much

8. A question beginning with which or who

9. A question beginning with why

10. A question beginning with how

C. Sample sentences:

11. Betsy studies all alone in the afternoon once a week.

12. The workers often marched on the street near the factory.

13. Bob and Rebecca occasionally do the tango together because it's fun.

14. She won the race yesterday by training hard every day.

15. I drove to the store as fast as possible to get the medicine.

A. Change the active verbs to passive and the passive verbs to active. Add an agent if necessary. Write "no change" if you cannot change them. (5 points each)

1. My purse was stolen out of my car.
2. The committee is considering giving her a scholarship.
3. He was born in 1869.
4. They are picked up by a man in a blue car.
5. The state police have arrested Paul four times.
6. They had a lot of bad luck on their vacation.
7. The mayor will open the new museum next month.
8. I got my house painted last summer.
9. The park can be saved if we all work hard.
10. The two cars collided at the corner of Russell and Oak.

B. Decide whether active or passive forms should be used in these sentences. Write the correct form in the space provided. (5 points each)

Oman, which _____ (11. locate) on the Persian Gulf, is one of the most

fascinating countries to visit. Before oil _____ (12. discover) in 1970 it was

one of the world's poorest nations. However, since that time the Omanis

_____ (13. make) astonishing progress catching up with the rest of the

world. Before 1970 Oman _____ (14. have) only about five kilometers of

paved road, two schools and two hospitals. In the past 25 years, thousands of miles of

paved roads _____ (15. build). And today all Omani children

_____ (16. receive) an education and every citizen

can _____ (17. care for) in a local hospital or clinic. Much of the credit for

this remarkable transformation must _____ (18. give) to Sultan Qaboos,

the leader of Oman. He _____ (19. guide) his country successfully through

a very difficult transition. Oman _____ (20. transform) into a truly modern

state.

UNIT 4 ANSWERS

A.
1. Someone / A thief stole my purse.
2. She is being considered for a scholarship by the committee.
3. no change
4. A man in a blue car picks them up.
5. Paul has been arrested by the state police four times.
6. no change
7. The new museum will be opened by the mayor next month.
8. no change
9. We can save the park if we all work hard.
10. no change

B.
11. is located
12. was discovered
13. have made
14. had
15. have been built
16. receive
17. be cared for
18. be given
19. has guided
20. has been transformed

A. Rewrite the incorrect sentences. (5 points each)

1. I must can learn to swim this summer.

2. You have to be able to leave early.

3. Hadn't Joseph better ask the teacher first?

4. They should to vote in every election.

5. She has got to get there by tomorrow!

6. We haven't to study this evening.

7. All parents have to should help their children with their homework.

8. Used you to jog everyday?

9. You should are allowed to smoke in your own home.

10. He ought to be able to get a recommendation from his boss.

B. Choose the correct response. (5 points each)

11. A: Do we have to learn all these words by tomorrow?
    B: No, we _____ learn them all.
       a. must not   b. don't have to   c. aren't allowed to
12. A: What a lovely meal. You're a wonderful cook, Mrs. Brown.
    B: Thank you. I really love to cook.
    A: May I have some more pie?
    B: _____
       a. Of course, here you are.
       b. No, I think you've had enough.
       c. Yes, you may.
13. A: _____ I open the window?
    B: Thank you. It's hot in here.
       a. Will   b. Would   c. Shall
14. A: Look at this old picture of me.
    B: That _____ be you! You look completely different.
       a. won't   b. shouldn't   c. can't
15. A: Listen to those fire sirens.
    B: There _____ be a fire nearby.
       a. should   b. must   c. can

16. A: Where are you going on vacation this year?
    B: I'm not sure. I _____ go visit my grandparents.
       a. might   b. have to   c. am going to
17. A: What time are you going?
    B: At 7 because we _____ get there an hour early.
       a. would   b. might   c. are supposed to
18. A: Were you an imaginative child?
    B: Oh yes. I _____ always pretend that I was a famous writer or painter.
       a. would   b. will   c. could
19. A: Don't light that cigarette.
    B: Why not?
    A: No one _____ to smoke in a restaurant in this city.
       a. might   b. must   c. is allowed
20. A: You _____ make him angry again.
    B: I know. I don't want to lose my job.
       a. are allowed to   b. had better not   c. are going to

UNIT 5 ANSWERS

A.
1. I must / can learn . . .
2. correct
3. Hadn't Joseph better . . .
4. They should vote . . .
5. correct
6. We don't have to study . . .
7. All parents have to / should help their . . .
8. Did you used to jog . . . ?
9. You should be allowed . . .
10. correct

B. 11. b 12. a 13. c 14. c 15. b 16. a 17. c 18. a 19. c 20. b

A. Restate each sentence by using an infinitive phrase. (5 points each)

1. She hopes that she will finish by the fall.

   She hopes _____.

2. I always tell my children, "Don't talk to strangers."

   I always tell _____.

3. They thought it would be an easy exam.

   They expected _____.

4. The law requires that all citizens pay their taxes by April 15th.

   The law requires _____.

5. I don't like it when I hear people whispering in the movies.

   I don't like _____.

B. Combine these two sentences to make one sentence. Use an infinitive in each new sentence. (5 points each)

6. Sam got angry when he heard the news. His mother didn't expect this.
7. I got a scholarship. My teacher arranged this.
8. The children need to get flu shots. The law requires this.
9. David plans to go to college. His parents have encouraged this.
10. The president will leave tomorrow. He has decided this.
11. I didn't do my homework. I neglected this.
12. Danny is going to quit school. Maria never intended this.
13. The package is being sent by boat. Jack would prefer this.
14. The teachers will not give any more tests. The students have requested this.
15. I have to request my vacation three months in advance. My company requires this.

C. Use the cues to create sentences. Use one infinitive in each sentence. (5 points each)

16. convince / leave _____

17. order / marry _____

18. warn / not cheat _____

19. forbid / see _____

20. urge / invite _____

UNIT 6 ANSWERS

A.
1. She hopes to finish . . .
2. I always tell my children not to . . .
3. They expected the exam / it to be easy.
4. The law requires citizens to pay . . .
5. I don't like to hear people . . .

B.
6. Sam's mother didn't expect him to get angry . . .
7. My teacher arranged for me to get a scholarship.
8. The law requires children to get flu shots.
9. David's parents have encouraged him to go to college.
10. The president has decided to leave tomorrow.
11. I neglected to do my homework.
12. Maria never intended Danny to quit school.
13. Jack would prefer the package to be sent by boat.
14. The students have requested the teachers not to give any more tests.
15. My company requires me to request my vacation . . .

C. Examples:
16. We convinced her to leave.
17. They ordered me not to marry him.
18. I warned you not to cheat on the test.
19. He forbid her to see me.
20. They urged me to invite you.

A. Complete each sentence with a gerund or an infinitive. (5 points each)

1. I intend _____ (enter) to Drake Community College next year.

2. She enjoys _____ (ride) horses all day.

3. They despise _____ (live) there and I don't blame them.

4. She remembers _____ (receive) the letter but doesn't know what she did with it.

5. We stopped _____ (rest) because Mike was tired.

6. I tried _____ (get) him a tutor but even that didn't work.

7. I'm sorry I forgot _____ (call) you last night.

B. Complete these sentences. Use an infinitive or a gerund in each sentence. In some sentences you will have to add a second subject. (7 points each)

8. My sister always avoids _____.

9. He doesn't enjoy _____.

10. They know that they should quit _____.

11. I cannot tolerate _____.

12. We expect _____.

13. _____ makes me sad.

14. The class is looking forward to _____.

15. The teacher refuses _____.

16. She is excited about _____.

17. They've decided _____.

UNIT 7 ANSWERS

A.
1. to enter
2. riding
3. living
4. receiving
5. to rest
6. to get
7. to call

B.
8. My sister always avoids cleaning the house.
9. He doesn't enjoy meeting new people.
10. They know that they should quit leaving early.
11. I cannot tolerate people smoking.
12. We expect to have jobs by June.
13. Listening to Bach makes me sad.
14. The class is looking forward to going on the field trip.
15. The teacher refuses to put up with students who fight.
16. She is excited about getting married.
17. They've decided to go anyway.

A. Choose the correct implied meaning for each sentence. (4 points each)

1. He's quite a dedicated worker.
   a. He works hard.
   b. He doesn't work hard enough.
2. He's somewhat enthusiastic about his job.
   a. He hates his job.
   b. He sometimes likes his job.
3. He just doesn't work hard enough.
   a. He needs to work harder.
   b. He needs to slow down.

4. He works too hard.
   a. He needs to work harder.
   b. He needs to slow down.
5. He's a bit lazy.
   a. He's lazy sometimes.
   b. He's very lazy.

B. Complete the sentences with so, such, too, very, or enough. (5 points each)

6. Chris needs to buy a _____ good car because she travels a lot.

7. He was _____ rude that I got up and left.

8. Sam and Mike are _____ young to drive. They're only 15!

9. He had _____ problems learning English, that he failed the first course four times!

10. I got to the opera _____ late to see the first act. They never let anyone in after the curtain goes up.

11. We had _____ a good time that we didn't want to come home.

12. That car is _____ expensive. Can you really afford it?

13. You have to be 5'10" to be a police officer. I'm not tall _____!

14. It was _____ cold that the pipes froze.

15. She's smart _____ not to get caught.

C. Combine the sentences with statements of degree using too or enough. (6 points each)

16. They have only a little time. They can't get their work finished.
17. There are a lot of children in the class. The teacher can't control them.
18. Teenagers think they know a lot. They don't want to listen to adults.
19. My office is very formal. I can't wear jeans to work.
20. Cindy is wise. She never disagrees with her boss.

UNIT 8 ANSWERS

A.   1. a   2. b   3. a   4. b   5. a

B.   6. very   11. such
       7. so   12. very
       8. too   13. enough
       9. such   14. so
     10. too   15. enough

C. 16. They don't have enough time to get their work done.

     17. There are too many children in the class for the teacher to control.

     18. Teenagers think they know too much to listen to adults.

     19. My office is too formal for me to wear jeans to work.

     20. Cindy is wise enough not to disagree with her boss.

Grammar Dimensions 3

Unit 9 Modifying Noun Phrases

Adjectives and Participles

Name _____

Score _____
100

A. Rewrite the incorrect sentences. (8 points each)

  1. I saw a cotton, triangular, purple, interesting scarf.

  2. She bought wooden, expensive, antique, heavy, chair.

  3. My grandmother gave me a silver, small, old, cigarette case.

  4. Clara is going to wear a striped, nice, blue, new dress.

  5. He lost a Japanese, old, valuable Samurai sword.

B. Complete these sentences with present or past participles which modify the nouns. (6 points each)

  6. I made this bread at home. It's _____ bread.

  7. A lecture that confuses people is a _____ lecture.

  8. The child has blue eyes. He is a _____ child.

  9. A bat that eats fruit is a _____ bat.

  10. A book that many people love well is a _____ book.

C. Complete the sentences with the correct participle form of the verb in parentheses. (6 points each)

  11. The boy _____ (play) with Adam is her son.

  12. The car _____ (destroy) in the fire was a 95 Ford.

  13. She wants to meet the man _____ (play) the saxophone.

  14. A picture _____ (paint) by Picasso is worth millions of dollars.

  15. The child _____ (leave) on the doorstep survived.

UNIT 9 ANSWERS

A.
1. an interesting triangular purple cotton scarf
2. expensive heavy antique wooden chair
3. small old silver cigarette case
4. nice new blue striped dress
5. old valuable Japanese Samurai sword

B.
6. homemade
7. confusing
8. blue-eyed
9. fruit-eating
10. well-loved

C.
11. playing
12. destroyed
13. playing
14. painted
15. left

A. None of these sentences is factually correct. Rewrite them so that the facts are correct. (5 points each)

1. Africa is not quite as big as the United States.

2. England is exactly the same size as the United States.

3. New York City doesn't have nearly as many people as San Francisco.

4. A computer can do complex mathematical calculations slightly faster than a human being.

5. The Middle East has almost as much oil as Italy.

6. A grape is considerably larger than an apple.

7. An adult is somewhat stronger than a baby.

8. A bicycle is almost as fast as a car.

9. Canada's culture is much more different from that of the United States than Japan's is.

10. The average woman has greater physical strength than the average man.

B. Use the information in the chart to compare Singapore with Sweden and Singapore with Grenada. Use intensifiers to make accurate statements when possible. (10 points each)

	Singapore	Sweden	Grenada
population	2,792,000	8,644,119	100,000
area	238 sq. mi	158,830 sq. mi	133 sq. mi
population density (per square mile)	11,574	50	706
GNP	$35 billion	$137 billion	$119 million
per capita income	$12,700	$16,200	$1400
number of official languages	4	1	1
independence	since 1959	since 1527	since 1974

almost   considerably   nearly   somewhat   substantially   slightly

11. _____

12. _____

13. _____

14. _____

15. _____

UNIT 10 ANSWERS

A. Examples:

1. Africa is much larger than the United States. The United States is not nearly as large as Africa.
2. England is much smaller than the United States.
3. San Francisco doesn't have nearly as many people as New York City.
4. A computer can solve complex mathematical problems much faster than . . .
5. The Middle East has much more oil than Italy.
6. A grape is considerably smaller than an apple.
7. An adult is a great deal stronger than a baby.
8. A bicycle isn't nearly as fast as a car.
9. Canada's culture is much more similar to that of the United States than Japan's is.
10. The average woman has less physical strength than the average man.

B. Examples:

11. The population of Singapore is substantially smaller than the population of Sweden.
12. Singapore is nearly the same size as Grenada.
13. Singapore is considerably denser in population than Sweden.
14. The per capita income of Sweden is somewhat larger than that of Singapore.
15. Singapore has been independent slightly longer than Grenada.

Grammar Dimensions Book 3

Name _____

Unit 11 Connectors

Score _____
100

A. Rewrite the incorrect sentences. (5 points each)

1. Even though she was sick however she finished all her work.

2. The teacher besides likes having the time off.

3. We will be getting more students, as a result we will have to find more classroom space.

4. She doesn't like fresh tomatoes. However, she will eat cooked ones.

5. Because it always needed more land. The United States government kept moving Native Americans further and further west.

6. Besides, he has a new car, he also just bought a new condo.

7. Kevin not only missed graduation, he was also unable to go to France with his class.

8. My sister was concerned about her health. Nevertheless, she went to see a doctor that she trusted.

9. Charles hates public speaking. Accordingly, he agreed to make a speech at our next meeting.

10. In spite of the fact that I hate my job, I have decided to quit.

B. Complete the sentences logically and grammatically. (10 points each)

11. We've decided to leave even though _____.

12. I've been given permission to go providing _____.

13. My boss had to go to a meeting. Consequently _____.

14. I'm dissatisfied with my progress in this class. Furthermore, _____.

15. We've always been good friends; on the other hand _____.

UNIT 11 ANSWERS

A. 1. Even though she was sick she finished . . .
2. Besides, the teacher likes . . .
3. We will be getting more students. As a result, we . . .
4. correct
5. Because it always needed more land, the United States . . .
6. In addition to a new car, he has just bought . . .
7. correct
8. My sister was concerned about her health. Therefore / Consequently she went . . .
9. Charles hates public speaking. However, he . . .
10. Because I hate my job, I have decided to quit. (In spite of the fact that I like my job, I have decided to quit.)

B. Examples:
11. . . . even though we enjoy living here.
12. . . . that I provide my own transportation.
13. Consequently, I'll be in charge.
14. Furthermore, it's at a very inconvenient time.
15. . . . on the other hand, all's fair in love and war.

A. Rewrite the sentences correctly. (5 points each)

1. Did you go to the hotel Betty recommended?

2. He would like the book published in 1999.

3. My sister, that lives in Washington, has visited the White House.

4. We saw that the man which car was in an accident.

5. I don't like people which I can't trust.

B. Combine these pairs of sentences with *that, who, whom, which,* or *whose.* (5 points each)

6. She works in a factory. The factory makes computer chips.

7. I gave him some books. He found these books very helpful.

8. He met a woman. Her 11-year-old daughter is a concert pianist.

9. We went to see a movie. I really enjoyed the movie.

10. My father is a person. My father never gives up.

11. She wants to marry a man. The man has a good education.

12. He has the annoying habit of tapping his fingers. This makes me very nervous.

13. Philip wants to find a cheap old car. The car will run perfectly.

14. I had never met a doctor. The doctor's manner was so unfriendly.

15. The car is parked at the corner. The car is mine.

UNIT 12 ANSWERS

A.
1. correct
2. correct
3. . . . who lives in Washington,
4. We saw the man whose car was . . .
5. I don't like people whom I can't trust.

B.
6. She works in a factory which / that . . .
7. I gave him some books which / that . . .
8. He met a woman whose 11-year-old . . .
9. We went to see a movie that / which . . .
10. My father is a person who never . . .
11. She wants to marry a man who has a good . . .
12. He has the annoying habit of tapping his fingers which makes . . .
13. Philip wants to find a cheap old car which / that runs . . .
14. I had never met a doctor whose manner was so unfriendly.
15. The car that is parked at the corner is mine.

Complete this paragraph from a letter with the correct form of the verb in parentheses. (5 points each)

I am so busy these days that at night I _____ (1. feel) too exhausted to do

anything, even watch TV. I normally _____ (2. work) 40 hours a week but

right now we have a big new contract and I _____ (3. work) about 60

hours a week. In addition, right now Raul _____ (4. travel) in Latin

America. He _____ (5. see) all of his company's clients. So, for the

moment, it _____ (6. look like) I'm a single mother.

    The kids are fine. Chelsea isn't at home much. She _____ (7. have) a

job at the local grocery store. She _____ (8. want) to earn money for her

college fund. Raul and I _____ (9. think) that's a good idea. Tommy has

been a big help since his Dad's been gone. He _____ (10. learn) to cook

and he _____ (11. help) out a lot with the housework. He _____

(12. mind) Katie and Ralph when he _____ (13. get) home from school

but it's still difficult.

    In fact, I _____ (14. consider) leaving my job. I _____

(15. not like) working but I _____ (16. have) second thoughts about

working full time. I _____ (17. doubt) that I can do it for much longer. Of

course, I _____ (18. know) things won't be easy if I quit. We

_____ (19. need) two salaries. So, I _____ (20. think) of starting

a business at home.

UNIT 13 ANSWERS

1. feel
2. work
3. am working
4. is traveling
5. is seeing
6. looks like
7. has
8. wants
9. think
10. is learning
11. is helping / helps
12. minds
13. gets
14. am considering
15. don't like
16. am having
17. doubt
18. know
19. need
20. am thinking

A. Rewrite the incorrect sentences. (5 points each)

1. I've waited here for three hours. What took you so long?

2. Barbara hasn't been believing in Santa Claus since she was six.

3. I've read this book for a month and I'm still only halfway through.

4. I learned how to ride a bike a long time ago.

5. When I lived in New York, I've gone to the opera a lot.

6. He has been calling me several times but I've been refusing to speak with him.

7. I've been planning to talk to you. Do you have time now?

8. Janet worked here for almost 50 years and now she's leaving.

9. I think I'm perfect for this job because I have been extremely skilled.

10. Tim has been having a lot of problems with his car lately.

B. Complete the paragraph with the correct form of the verb in parentheses. (5 points each)

My son Jeremy _____ (11. go) to study in England two months ago. At first

he _____ (12. be) very happy. However, lately, he _____

(13. have) some problems. He _____ (14. get) good grades in his classes.

But he _____ (15. feel) socially isolated.

Jeremy _____ (16. be) very athletic. He _____ (17. play)

football and basketball here at home. But in England, all the people he

_____ (18. know) play rugby or soccer. He _____ (19. plan) to

stay for a whole year. But now he _____ (20. decide) to come home after

this semester.

UNIT 14 ANSWERS

A.
1. I've been waiting here . . .
2. Barbara hasn't believed in Santa Claus . . .
3. I've been reading this book . . .
4. correct
5. . . . I went to the opera . . .
6. He has called me . . .
7. correct
8. Janet has worked here . . .
9. . . . I am extremely . . .
10. correct

B.
11. went
12. was
13. has been having
14. is getting / has gotten
15. feels / is feeling / has been feeling
16. is
17. played
18. knows
19. planned / was planning
20. has decided

A. Complete the conversation with *will, might,* or *be going to.*

A: Hi Anita. I need a favor. _____ (1) you give me a ride home?

B: Sure. I _____ (2) meet you in the parking lot at 3:00.

A: Oh, dear. Three's too late for me. Bob _____ (3) call at 2:00. And he's always on time. And he _____ (4) be worried if I'm not there.

B: _____ (5) (not) he call back later if you're not home?

A: I'm not sure. He _____. (6) But I know it _____ (7) be very busy today, so he _____ (8) (not) be able to.

B: I have an idea. I _____ (9) give you my car. Then you can go home and come back to pick me up. Just don't be late. I _____ (10) go to make dinner for Maria and Tomas tonight, so I need to get home.

A: Don't worry. I _____ (11) be back by 3, I promise.

B. Rewrite the incorrect sentences. (5 pts. each)

12. He's finishing it if he has time.

13. Maybe he will coming this afternoon.

14. He's not sure when they are being back.

15. Too much sun and not enough water is going to kill plants.

16. If you want to make the train you are having to leave now.

17. The weather report said it shan't rain tomorrow.

18. As soon as I will have finished, I'll help you out.

19. We're planning to visit my relatives while we are in France.

20. I'll take him tomorrow, when I will have the car.

UNIT 15 ANSWERS

A.
1. Will
2. will
3. is going to
4. will
5. Won't
6. might
7. is going to
8. might not
9. I'll
10. I'm going to
11. will

B.
12. He'll finish it . . .
13. . . . will come . . . .
14. . . . when they will be back / are going to be back
15. . . . will kill plants.
16. . . . you have to leave now.
17. . . . it won't / isn't going to rain tomorrow.
18. As soon as I have finished, I'll . . .
19. correct
20. . . . when I have the car.

Grammar Dimensions Book 3

Unit 16 Modals of Prediction

and Inference

Name _____

Score _____

100

A. Make logical conclusions by filling in the blanks with an appropriate modal of inference or prediction and the correct form of the verb in parentheses. (5 points each)

1. He left at 7. It's a usually a three-hour drive. So, he _____ (be) here by 10.

   However, if the weather is bad, it _____ (take) him longer.
2. **A:** Whose sandwich is this?

   B: Marta's. I made it for her. She _____ (forget) take it with her.
3. **A:** I'm really angry at Frank for not calling.

   B: Don't be upset. He _____ (call) while you were out.

   A: That's true. Or else his brother _____ (not give) him the message.

4. You _____ (like) your job a lot. Every time I call you, you're working.

5. **A:** Tom and Harriet told me that they _____ (not come) because they have a lot of work to do.

   B: I bet they _____ (be) here. Tom never refuses a free meal.
6. **A:** Someone just opened the front door!

   B: Don't worry. That _____ be my roommate. She's the only one with a key.
7. You _____ do well on the test. You certainly studied hard enough.

B. Use modals of prediction and inference to respond to these comments. (10 points each)

8. **A:** Oh no! My car's not in the driveway!

   B: _____
9. **A:** Rebecca is two hours late.

   B: _____
10. **A:** Clarence always looks tired and he rarely does his homework.

    B: _____
11. **A:** I'm very worried about my father. He has to have a heart operation.

    B: _____
12. **A:** Look at that man. He looks just like my kindergarten student Jeffrey.

    B: _____

UNIT 16 ANSWERS

A.

1. should / will / might / may / could be; should / will / might / may / could take
2. must have forgotten
3. might / could have called; might not have given
4. must like
5. might not come; will be here
6. must be
7. should / will

B. Sample responses:

8. It must have been stolen. Someone must have stolen it. Your brother might have borrowed it.
9. She might have left late. / There might be a lot of traffic.
10. He could have a job.
11. Don't worry. He'll be all right.
12. He must be his father.

A. Choose the logical response to each statement. (5 points each)

1. **A:** If I had time, I'd help you with the housework.

   B: _____
   (a) Thanks for your help.   (b) That's okay I can do it myself.

2. **A:** If I'm not working, I'll go.

   B: _____
   (a) Maybe next time.   (b) When can you let me know?

3. **A:** Dave is going to work for me tomorrow. Otherwise I wouldn't be able to go.

   B: _____
   (a) Well that's nice of him.   (b) Sorry, you won't be there.

4. **A:** Will they ever immigrate to the United States?

   B: _____
   (a) No, they won't. Only if their lives were in danger.   (b) Maybe in a few
       years.

5. **A:** I wish you'd reconsider taking that job.

   B: _____
   (a) Of course I'm going to take it.   (b) I'm sorry. My mind is made up.

B. Change these statements of actual condition and result into hypothetical statements. (5 points each)

Example: (condition) He is sick. (result) He won't leave the house.
If he weren't sick, he would leave the house.

6. (result) She won the prize. (condition) She didn't enter the contest.
7. (condition) I'm not rich. (result) I can't buy a new car.
8. (condition) Maria doesn't like my cooking. (result) She won't eat at my house.
9. (condition) Carlos doesn't speak Italian. (result) He can't get a job in Rome.
10. (condtion) Mario didn't arrive on time. (result) They left without him.

C. Complete these statements. (10 points each)

11. You could stay home all day _____

12. If she had given me the key, _____

13. Everyone could have gone _____

14. It's good thing you're here. Otherwise _____

15. If he lets us talk, _____

UNIT 17 ANSWERS

A. 1. b   2. b   3. a   4. a   5. b

B. 6. She wouldn't have won the prize if she hadn't entered the contest.

7. If I were rich I would buy a new car.

8. If Maria liked my cooking, she would eat at my house.

9. If Carlos spoke Italian, he could get a job in Rome.

10. If Mario had arrived on time, they wouldn't have left without him.

C. Examples:

11. . . . if you didn't have a job.

12. . . . I could get in the house.

13. . . . if we'd known sooner.

14. . . . I wouldn't be able to finish the work.

15. . . . I'll help you.

A. Rewrite the incorrect sentences. (5 points each)

1. Your boss cannot require you to be stayed after five.

2. I actually saw the thief to leave when I was walking the dog.

3. Don't let the children to go out without coats.

4. I heard them singing and dancing all night.

5. She got her hair to be cut.

6. The police officer demanded that Bill goes down to the police station.

7. He encourages us all to leave when we like.

8. Why are you just sitting there? Don't you hear the phone ring?

9. He always lets leave early.

10. Why don't you get your friends to help you?

B. Complete the sentences logically and grammatically. (10 points each)

11. A responsible boss should not make her employees _____.

12. Good parents should have their children _____.

13. An effective teacher should allow his students _____.

14. A good army sergeant should help his soldiers _____.

15. A good school requires its students _____.

UNIT 18 ANSWERS

A.   1. . . . you to stay . . .
  2. . . . the thief leaving / leave . . .
  3. . . . children go out . . .
  4. correct
  5. . . . her hair cut.
  6. . . . that Bill go down . . .
  7. correct
  8. . . . the phone ringing?
  9. lets (them/me/us, etc.) leave early.
  10. correct

B. Examples:
  11. work too hard.
  12. do their homework.
  13. to have some free time.
  14. learn the rules.
  15. to behave well.

A. Complete these sentences with the appropriate article (a/an, the, some, or ø). More than one answer may be possible. (5 points each)

1. _____ cars are not an efficient means of transportation.

2. There is _____ food shortage in Africa.

3. I lost _____ wedding ring that my father gave my mother on their wedding day.

4. Would you like _____ coffee with your cake?

5. _____ sun comes up very early in the summer.

6. Could you please answer _____ telephone while I'm out?

7. I live in _____ white house. I hate brightly colored houses!

8. The president lives in _____ White House.

9. He always brings me _____ roses.

10. _____ honest man is hard to find.

11. _____ peacock is a spectacular bird.

12. _____ pineapples don't grow on trees!

13. Don't eat _____ breakfast that they serve in the dorm. It's terrible!

14. Let's go out and have _____ ice cream.

B. Complete this paragraph with appropriate articles. More than one answer may be possible. (5 points each)

I saw _____ (15) children playing near _____ (16) river behind

my house. _____ (17) next day I read that _____ (18) child had

drowned in _____ (19) river. I felt terrible because I could have saved

_____ (20) child's life by telling them to leave.

UNIT 19 ANSWERS

A.
1. ø (Cars)
2. a
3. the
4. some / ø
5. The
6. the
7. a
8. the
9. ø / some
10. An
11. The
12. ø (Pineapples)
13. the
14. some / ø

B.
15. some / ø
16. the
17. The
18. a
19. the
20. the

A. Rewrite the incorrect sentences. (6 points each)

1. This is what she was trying to tell you yesterday. This needs an immediate solution.
2. He gave me that pen for my birthday. That pen is my favorite.
3. This is the reason I refused to tell him. I knew he wouldn't believe me.
4. **A:** Karen is planning to take her clothes when she goes. Then she's going to leave them at her mother's.
   B: I was afraid of them.
5. **A:** David won the contest!
   B: I knew that. I had a feeling he'd win.
6. These who wish to leave may do so now.
7. She only invites those which she really likes.
8. These chairs over there are very inexpensive.
9. **A:** Have you bought those books yet?
   B: Yes, I got those books yesterday.
10. Everyone left early. That made John really angry.

B. Complete the sentences with the correct demonstrative. (4 points each blank)

11. **A:** The dog needs to be walked three times a day.

    B: I was afraid of _____.

12. Compare our lives to _____ of people two hundred years ago.

13. Just check yes and put this card in the mail. _____ all you have to

    do to take advantage of _____ free offer.

14. **A:** Well, if your boss didn't like it when you took the afternoon off,

    _____ will really make him angry.

    B: _____ is why I'm not going to tell him

    about _____ until tomorrow.

15. **A:** _____ children over there are the ones who broke my window.

    B: Really? Is _____ woman with them their mother?

    A: I think _____ is. I suppose I should go talk to her.

UNIT 20 ANSWERS

A.
1. It needs . . .
2. It is . . .
3. correct
4. I was afraid of that.
5. I knew it.
6. Those who wish . . .
7. . . . those whom . . .
8. Those chairs . . .
9. I got them
10. correct

B.
11. that.
12. those
13. That's; this
14. this; That; it
15. Those; that; she / it

Name _____

Score _____
100

A. Combine the elements to make sentences containing a noun + possessive. (6 points each) Sometimes you will need to add articles. (7 points each)

1. He fell over (back / chair)

2. (opening / movie) was very frightening

3. (dog / daughter) is very affectionate.

4. (waterways / state) are very polluted.

5. (noise / the children who live next door) bothers him.

6. Credit for (discovery / new world) is usually given to Columbus.

7. (cover / book) was torn.

8. (music / the Arab world) is not well known in the west.

9. Put the desk at (class / front)

10. (The cries / the baby) were heard by all.

B. Rewrite these sentences using possessive forms. (6 points each)

11. I bought gas. I spent $20.

12. The dress was expensive. It cost $400. That's the amount I earn in a week.

13. Barbara visited the museum. It made her unhappy.

14. The United Nations has many member states. Every state has the right to vote.

15. He has a vacation every year. It lasts for one month.

UNIT 21 ANSWERS

A. 1. . . . the back of the chair.
2. The opening of the movie . . .
3. My daughter's dog . . .
4. The state's waterways . . .
5. The noise of the children . . .
6. For the discovery of the new world . . .
7. The cover of the book . . .
8. . . . the music of the Arab world . . .
9. The front of the class.
10. The baby's cries . . .

B. 11. I bought $20 worth of gas.
12. The dress cost a week's salary.
13. Barbara's visit to the museum made her unhappy.
14. Each member state of the United Nations has the right to vote.
15. He gets a month's vacation every year.

Grammar Dimensions Book 3

Unit 22 Quantifiers, Collective Nouns,

and Adjectives

Name _____

Score _____

100

A. Rewrite the incorrect sentences. (4 points each)

1. None of the chapters I studied was on the exam.
2. Each of the men is here.
3. I didn't think that every house had been robbed but every was.
4. He gave me a lot of informations.
5. Any child could tell you that.
6. What bad luck! I bought five lottery tickets and neither of them one.
7. The football team has elected Tim their captain.
8. He's got much money in the bank.
9. Neither of my sisters are excellent students.
10. The poor never get what it needs.

B. Complete the sentences with correct quantifiers. Some blanks may have more than one possible answer. (4 points each blank)

11. **A:** Does _____ student know about the test?

    B: No. _____ them already know but _____ were not in class yesterday, so they don't know.

12. **A:** Can you lend me _____ money, Jack?

    B: I'm sorry. But I only have _____ money myself. I was going to ask

    you if you could lend me _____.

13. **A:** It's a shame that so _____ people vote on election day.

    B: That's true. I think that _____ citizen should vote.

14. **A:** _____ stores have closed downtown in the last six months.

    B: I know. there just doesn't seem to be _____ business these days.

15. **A:** _____ went to Jackie's party.

    B: Oh dear! That's too bad. I know she made _____ food and spent

    _____ money.

16. **A:** Do you know where almost _____ students who are in my class are from?

    B: No, where?

    A: The United States! I'm very disappointed. I was hoping to meet

    _____ people from other places!

UNIT 22 ANSWERS

A. 1. correct
2. correct
3. . . . but every one was.
4. . . . a lot of information.
5. correct
6. . . . none of them won.
7. . . . its captain.
8. . . . a lot of money . . .
9. . . . is an excellent student.
10. . . . what they need.

B. 11. every; Most of; several/some/a few
12. a little/some; a little; some/a little
13. few; every/each
14. A lot of/Many/Quite a few; much/any
15. Hardly anyone/No one; a lot of/plenty; a lot of/plenty
16. all; a lot of

A. Complete the sentences with the correct forms of the verbs in parentheses (present, present perfect, simple past, past perfect, past progressive or past perfect progressive). (4 points each verb)

1. We _____ (practice) for an hour by the time

   he _____ (arrive).

2. When I _____ (realize) that someone _____ (break into) my

   house, I _____ (start) to shake.

3. Before he _____ (be) able to gain control of the car again, all the

   eggs _____ (break).

4. I _____ (be) unable to find a job that I could do while I

   _____ (study), so I _____ (decide) to quit school.

5. What _____ you _____ (do) when

   I _____ (call) last night? It _____ (sound) like you

   _____ (have) a party.

6. I _____ (leave) the bus terminal when I _____ (see) the

   police cars pull up outside.

B. Complete the sentences logically and grammatically. (9 points each)

7. By the time _____, most people had left.

8. The teacher laughed while _____.

9. As soon as _____, the picture fell off the wall.

10. We had just finished dinner, _____.

11. After I helped her with her homework, _____.

12. When _____, we realized our mistake.

UNIT 23 ANSWERS

A. 1. had been practicing / had practiced; arrived
2. realized; had broken into; started
3. was; had broken
4. was; was studying; decided
5. were you doing; called; sounded; were having
6. had just left / was leaving; saw

B. Examples:
7. By the time I arrived, . . .
8. The teacher laughed while the boys were clowning around . . .
9. As soon as we walked into the room, . . .
10. . . . dinner, when the doorbell rang.
11. . . . homework, we both watched TV.
12. When we got / had gotten to the door, we . . .

A. Complete the sentences with the correct form of a modal from the list below. (5 points each)

be able to	be about to	be allowed to	be going to	be supposed to
be to	could	couldn't	have to	might
might not	used to	would	wouldn't	

Last night I had a really frightening experience. I _____ (1) go to bed,

when I heard someone downstairs. Well, I was really scared because I had left the

door unlocked. Well, actually I _____ (2) leave it unlocked because the

lock was broken. I know that you _____ (3) lock your doors at night. I

always _____ (4) lock it. In fact, I _____ (5) never even go to

bed unless I had checked all the doors and windows. I _____ (6) get the

lock fixed last week but I forgot. Besides, where I live is really safe (or so I thought!).

I knew I _____ (7) go downstairs or else I _____ (8) never be able

to go back to sleep. I didn't dare turn on the light because I was afraid that the burglar

_____ (9) see it. However, I _____ (10) go downstairs unarmed. I

looked for my baseball bat but I _____ (11) find it in the dark. However, I

_____ (12) get a golf club out of my closet without turning on the light.

I _____ (13) start going downstairs when the hall light went on and I

heard my brother's voice calling my name. I had forgotten that he said he

_____ (14) come over after his baseball game. I felt really foolish standing

there in my nightgown with a golf club in my hand. My brother promised that he

_____ (15) fix the lock on my door the next day.

B. Complete the sentences logically and grammatically. (5 points each)

16. When I was young our family always used to _____.

17. I remember my grandfather well. He would never _____.

18. We were going to leave at 7 _____.

19. When my daughter was a baby she would _____.

20. I don't know how he could _____.

UNIT 24 ANSWERS

A.
1. was about to / was going to
2. had to
3. are supposed to
4. used to
5. would
6. was supposed to
7. had to
8. would
9. might / would
10. couldn't
11. couldn't / wasn't able to
12. was able to
13. was about to
14. might / would
15. would

B. Examples:
16. . . . have big Sunday dinners.
17. . . . stop telling jokes.
18. . . . but the baby was sleeping.
19. . . . always talk in her sleep.
20. . . . forget your birthday.

A. Change the following direct quotations to reported speech. (6 points each)

1. "I can't get anyone to help me," Dan complained.

   _____

2. "They'll go if they have to," said Tricia.

   _____

3. "My wife's leaving on a business trip tomorrow," announced Paul.

   _____

4. "Debbie and I went yesterday but the office was closed," said Mike.

   _____

5. "The teacher may ask us to turn in our work early," said Jim.

   _____

6. "Please leave by the side doors," the speaker told the audience.

   _____

7. "I'm sure that you are wondering why I asked you here today," began the detective.

   _____

8. "Can you meet me here tomorrow?" asked Jane.

   _____

9. "Where did you live before you moved here?" asked the interviewer.

   _____

10. "Don't leave until you finish," my mother warned me.

    _____

B. Change the following reported speech statements into direct quotations. (6 points each)

11. The manager told us to come back at 3:00.

    _____

12. Mrs. Thomas asked Hillary why she had gone by train.

    _____

13. I told you to come straight home.

    _____

14. The captain warned them not to lean over the railing.

    _____

15. Dick complained that no one was ever home when he called.

    _____

UNIT 25 ANSWERS

A.
1. Dan complained that he couldn't get anyone to help him.
2. Tricia said that they would go if they had to.
3. Paul announced that his wife was leaving on a business trip the next day.
4. Mike said that he and Debbie had gone yesterday but the office was / had been closed.
5. Jim said that the teacher might ask us / them to turn in our / their work early.
6. The speaker told the audience to leave by the side doors.
7. The detective said that he was sure that we were / I was wondering why he had asked us / me there that day.
8. Jane asked if I / we could meet her there the next day.
9. The interviewer asked where I had lived before I moved here.
10. My mother warned me not to leave until I finished.

B.
11. "Come back at 3:00," the manager said.
12. "Why did you go by train?" asked Mrs. Thomas.
13. "Come straight home," I said.
14. "Don't lean over the railing," warned the captain.
15. "No one is ever at home when I call," complained Dick.

WORKBOOK ANSWER KEY

Unit 1

Overview of the English Verb System: Time and Tense

EXERCISE 1

(1) is   (2) are registering   (3) can't   (4) said   (5) owes
(6) knows   (7) paid   (8) shall/will   (9) has asked/asked
(10) is going to call/will call   (11) hopes/is hoping
(12) keeps/has kept

EXERCISE 2

1. simple present   2. present progressive   3. simple present
4. simple past   5. simple present   6. simple present   7. simple
past   8. simple future   9. present perfect / simple past
10. present progressive / simple future   11. simple present /
present progressive   12. simple present / present perfect

EXERCISE 3

(1) have discovered   (2) tested / has tested   (3) switched /
have switched   (4) remained / have remained   (5) die   (6) is
(7) can occur / occur   (8) do not recommend   (9) focuses
(10) has already changed

EXERCISE 4

1. present   2. past / present   3. past / present   4. past /
present   5. present   6. present   7. present   8. present
9. present   10. present

EXERCISE 5

2. Every day people are discovering new uses for old materials. /
Just yesterday I read a story about using old tire tubes for floating
down the river. The story said that the old tubes could be used for
a year or more. / What will they think of next?
3. For more than 30 years, Dr. Simmons has been treating patients
in the office on the first floor of his home. He has mended broken
bones and delivered babies in this office. / Recently, however, the
county medical association ordered him to move his office to a
separate building. The association insists that the old office doesn't
meet modern standards. / Dr. Simmons will probably retire and
close his medical practice rather than go through an expensive
move. What a loss this will be for the community!
4. I was happy when I opened my mailbox yesterday. The mail
contained a letter from my family and my tax refund check. / What
will I do with the money? / First, I need to repair my car. / Then I will
hire someone to paint my living room. / I really don't like to paint.

EXERCISE 6

2. In the future   3. On January 1   4. The ancient Greeks
5. in 1969   6. Paul Gauguin; Shortly after he turned 40;
today   7. first; later   8. Right now; As soon as she completes
36 units of her major   9. For more than five years   10. before
she left for her research work overseas; for several days afterward.

Unit 2

Overview of the English Verb System: Aspect

EXERCISE 1

(1) a   (2) a   (3) b
4) b   (5) a

EXERCISE 2

1. keeps   2. was delivering; attacked   3. took
4. speaks   5. is still deciding   6. watches   7. proposed
8. remembered; walked   9. snows   10. snowing

(1) has graded **(2)** died **(3)** has visited **(4)** lived **(5)** had never worked **(6)** immigrated **(7)** had traveled only **(8)** took **(9)** flies **(10)** has been

EXERCISE 4

1. In the first sentence, the action was repeated for a finite period of time in the past. In the second, it is part of the actor's professional experience.

2. In the first sentence, the speaker has finished his or her required chores for the week. In the second, the speaker is asserting that over a long period of time, he or she has fulfilled his or her housecleaning duties.

3. In the first sentence, the case is closed. In the second, there is still the possibility that the law will be changed.

4. In the first sentence, Bob keeps trying (and failing) to get a business off the ground. In the second, there is the implication that this is the first new business he has ever started.

5. The activity in the first sentence is an unusual occurrence, while that of the second is a habit.

EXERCISE 5

1. lectured / had lectured / had been lecturing **2.** have eaten **3.** has been trying; has been busy **4.** has increased **5.** have searched / have been searching **6.** have changed **7.** has stopped **8.** will have lived **9.** has been writing **10.** have been studying / have studied

EXERCISE 6

1. have been planning / have planned **2.** learned **3.** has rented / has been renting **4.** convinced **5.** have decided /

decided **6.** finish / have finished **7.** have already selected **8.** have met / met **9.** made **10.** can't / won't be able to **11.** will need / are going to need **12.** are looking

EXERCISE 7

(1) The first sentence talks about something in the past that is now over. The second describes an activity that started in the past and continues in the present. The third describes a habit.

(2) In the first sentence, the activity is happening at the moment of speaking. In the second, it started in the past and is still happening at the moment of speaking. In the third, the activity is a habit.

(3) The first sentence describes something that is happening right now; the second, something that has begun recently and continues into the present; and the third, something that happened in the past (once or numerous times) and is now over.

(4) In the first sentence, Tina tried once, failed, and left the bank, whereas in the second, she is perhaps still in the bank, or she has been back several times to try to cash her check.

(5) In the first sentence, the speaker is still driving. The second sentence describes an activity that ended in the past.

(6) The first sentence is about habit. The second is about a recently acquired habit.

(7) In the first sentence, Ms. Warner still works for IBM, but in the second, her employment has ended (she's probably retired).

(8) The first sentence describes a habit; the second, an activity that is occurring at the moment of speaking.

(9) The first sentence describes something that happened at a specific time in the recent past, whereas the second is about Dr. Lang's experience with a particular patient.

(10) The first sentence describes an ongoing activity. The second describes an action that occurred in the past.

Unit 3

Adverbial Phrases and Clauses

EXERCISE 1

1. How much **2.** Where / How **3.** How long **4.** when **5.** How **6.** Why **7.** How often **8.** How **9.** how long / how much time **10.** When

EXERCISE 2

1. Usually (frequency)... where (place)... when workers can eat (time)... in the office (place).

2. At Argus Word Processing (place)... only in the kitchen area (place)... only at lunchtime (time)... on breaks (time).

3. ...vigorously (manner)... to keep the office machines clean (purpose and reason).

4. once (time)... in the fax area (place).

5. ...right away (time).

6. The next day (time)... on all the walls (place)... clearly (manner).

7. ...only in the kitchen area (place)... only at specified times (time)... in order to reduce accidents (purpose and reason).

8. In the past (time)... often (frequency)... on the manuscript pages (place).

9. Now (time)... always (frequency)... because no food is allowed (purpose and reason)... near the office equipment (place).

10. These days (time)... often (frequency).

EXERCISE 3

Answers may vary. Check students' work for correct positioning of adverbials.

1. Belinda goes to the Bahamas every winter to make sure she gets a tan. / Every winter Belinda goes to the Bahamas to make sure she gets a tan.

2. Every day she swims two miles in the ocean to keep in shape. / To keep in shape, she swims two miles in the ocean every day.

3. Whenever she can, Belinda applies sunscreen to her body. / Belinda applies sunscreen to her body whenever she can.

4. Every day she eats fruit and fish because they are fresh. / She eats fruit and fish every day because they are fresh.

5. To lose weight, she recently stopped eating beef and chicken. / Recently, to lose weight, she stopped eating beef and chicken.

6. When she gets home, she will continue to eat carefully. / She will continue to eat carefully when she gets home.

EXERCISE 4

Spoken skills pair / group work. Answers will vary.

EXERCISE 5

Only incorrect sentences are included below.

1. Jerry eats out in local restaurants on a regular basis. *(Place before time.)*

2. He recently discovered a Thai restaurant in his neighborhood in Hollywood. *(Adverbs can precede the verb if there is no auxiliary; the more specific adverb comes first when there are two of the same kind.)*

4. He will meet them in the lobby at 7 o'clock tonight. *(The more specific adverb comes first when there are two of the same kind.)*

5. Unfortunately, as a result of some confusion, he gave them the wrong directions to the restaurant. *(Adverbials usually come after the verb phrase, which includes direct objects.)*

7. He's sincerely hoping that they look for the correct address in the phone book. *(One-word adverbials usually go between the auxiliary and the main verb; adverbials usually come after the verb phrase.)*

EXERCISE 6

Only incorrect sentences are included below.

1. Benjamin took on a second job so that he could afford to pay his car insurance.

3. The old man died after he entered the hospital.

4. I eat where the truck drivers eat.

6. First he washed the car, then he waxed it.

8. Sally got a job in the computer lab so that she could spend more time using computers.

Unit 4

Passive Verbs

EXERCISE 1

(1) are handed   (2) is collected   (3) are given   (4) was shown   (5) had been performed / was performed   (6) is being compared   (7) can be completed   (8) will be graded   (9) will be excused   (10) will be selected

EXERCISE 2

(1) are processed   (2) are given out   (3) are applied for   (4) is given   (5) told   (6) be filled out   (7) was turned down   (8) had not been completed   (9) had been written / was written   (10) be redone

EXERCISE 3

(1) are aged   (2) are roasted   (3) prefer   (4) are preferred   (5) are used   (6) have been roasted   (7) are cooled   (8) is tested   (9) are placed   (10) sold   (11) shipped

EXERCISE 4

First, the oranges are picked and cleaned. Then, they are cut and the juice is squeezed out. The orange skins are thrown away or used for fertilizer.

Next, most of the liquid is taken out, and the result is that the juice is concentrated. Then, the juice is frozen and shipped to market. In the last step, water is added by the customer to make juice.

EXERCISE 5

Answers will vary.

EXERCISE 6

(2) are sighted (R = They)   (3) are described (R = UFOs)   (4) have been nicknamed (R = UFOs)   (5) was reported (R = saucer; A = a man)   (6) was followed (R = man; A = UFO)   (7) was given off (R = he; A = UFO)

(8) been reported (R = lights; A = others) **(10)** have been abducted (R = people; A = ships) **(11)** were examined (R = they)

1. ~~by the translator~~ 2. by women 3. ~~by a police officer.~~
4. ~~by a surgeon~~ 5. by Dr. Werts 6. ~~by someone~~ 7. by my grandmother 8. ~~by fax machines~~

1. Agent cannot be deleted. 2. Agent cannot be deleted.
3. That car was built in Japan. 4. Agent cannot be deleted.
5. After Richard's car was hit, it had to be repaired. 6. The pictures were taken at the wedding. 7. Agent cannot be deleted. 8. Agent cannot be deleted.

(1) get **(2)** be **(3)** was **(4)** was **(5)** was **(6)** was
(7) was **(8)** was was **(9)** was **(10)** get

Only rewritten sentences are included below. All other sentences are *NC.*

1. The search for the missing child was conducted by the sheriff. 3. The police accused a postal carrier. 6. The sheriff arrested him anyway. 8. The police found the child in another state.
10. The police released the postal carrier from jail. 11. The sheriff arrested the real kidnapper.

1. were donated *agent unknown* 2. were passed *agent obvious* 3. have been reported *emphasize the recipient*
4. is required *emphasize the recipient* 5. should be done *generic statement* 6. was awarded *emphasize the recipient*
7. can be tailored *connect ideas in two clauses* 8. has been made *agent unimportant* 9. can be done *connect ideas in two clauses* 10. has been attempted *agent unknown*

(1) is being built **(2)** is living **(3)** are being hung **(4)** are being painted **(5)** will arrive **(6)** are being installed **(7)** is being tested **(8)** is supervising **(9)** is paid / is being paid **(10)** is doing

(1) translate **(2)** are written **(3)** must think **(4)** will be understood **(5)** must be written **(6)** will be performed **(7)** can perform **(8)** are used **(9)** is interpreted **(10)** will still be needed

(1) was hit **(2)** was **(3)** hit **(4)** shattered / were shattered **(5)** was crushed **(6)** was **(7)** was **(8)** got out **(9)** was trapped **(10)** called **(11)** was told **(12)** got
(13) had begun **(14)** burst **(15)** dropped **(16)** came
(17) discovered **(18)** had broken **(19)** hit **(20)** promised

TOEFL® Test Preparation Exercises Units 1–4

1. C	5. B	9. A	13. A	17. C
2. D	6. A	10. B	14. C	18. C
3. A	7. B	11. C	15. C	19. B
4. C	8. D	12. B	16. B	20. A

Unit 5

One-Word and Phrasal Modals

1. Where is Claudia able to drive? 2. Is Claudia allowed to drive on the highway? No, she isn't allowed. 3. Why can't she drive at night? 4. Is Claudia able to see without her glasses? 5. Should Bob get a driver's license? 6. Did Juan used to drive a truck in his country? 7. Is Martin supposed to have car insurance? 8. Should Martin buy special car insurance for his new sports car? 9. Barbara doesn't have to do housework. 10. Can Martin drive a truck? Yes, he can.

1. making offers Shall I drive tonight? 2. making suggestions We could go to a movie instead. 3. expressing necessity or prohibition He'd better not arrive late for the final exam. 4. making offers Would you like me to fix lunch now?
5. expressing advice You ought to study harder. 6. giving invitations Would you like to come to my graduation?
7. denying permission You're not allowed / supposed to chew gum in church. 8. giving invitations Can you attend our party? 9. expressing intention I'll do it. I'll pick you up later.

10. expressing advice   You don't have to wash paper plates.
11. expressing prohibition   You'd better not drive fast near a police officer.   12. expressing intentions   I'm going to be a millionaire before I'm thirty.   13. making requests   Could you please turn the TV off?   14. expressing advice or obligation We mustn't forget to shut the windows.   15. giving invitations Can you come to my birthday party on Sunday?

EXERCISE 3

(1) impossibility   (2) prediction   (3) habitual actions in the past
(4) ability   (5) prediction   (6) general possibility   (7) future time   (8) habitual actions in the past   (9) logical inference
(10) impossibility   (11) prediction   (12) general possibility
(13) ability   (14) logical inference   (15) future time

EXERCISE 4

(1) necessity   (2) advice   (3) future   (4) inference
(5) permission   (6) ability   (7) past habitual actions
(8) possibility   (9) suggestion   (10) prediction   (11) request
(12) future time   (13) impossibility   (14) invitation   (15) promise

EXERCISE 5

(1) must   (2) should   (3) mustn't   (4) must
(5) shouldn't   (6) must

EXERCISE 6

Part A
You: will   You: must   FOB: should   You: not able to
FOB: should
Part B
Bob: have to, ought to   You: can't   Bob: can't, aren't going to

EXERCISE 7

1. necessity   2. ability, negative   3. necessity
4. inadvisability   5. necessity   6. ability

EXERCISE 8

(1) I   (2) F   (3) F   (4) I   (5) F   (6) I

Unit 6

Infinitives

EXERCISE 1

INFINITIVES: (3) to spend   (4) to make; to prepare   (6) to match; to represent   (7) to organize   (9) to learn; to finish
(10) to be completed   (11) to be named   (12) to prove; to pay
GERUNDS: (3) practicing   (8) Practicing   (13) Building; designing; paying for

EXERCISE 2

1. not to go—negative   2. to stay out—affirmative   3. to live—affirmative   4. not to commute—negative   5. to be cleaned—passive   6. to look—active   7. to be unpacked—passive
8. to unpack—active   9. to have gotten—perfect   10. to be finishing up—progressive

EXERCISE 3

1. is dropped off at a shopping mall   2. had been a princess
3. sign an ethics statement   4. would have done the dishes
5. Type your term papers   6. will be paid   7. are left alone
8. would be waiting

EXERCISE 4

1. Pauline will clean up after the party.   2. Norman will lose 10 pounds by July.   3. We will go to the library.   4. All students must return library books before they can get their semester grades.
5. The city government must resume funding the school lunch program.   6. Michael will pick the flowers in Mr. Johnson's front yard.

EXERCISE 5

Answers can vary. Italicized words are examples of extra information that may be added.
2. He needed to be told about the situation *before it was too late.*
3. We decided to leave earlier *than we had originally planned.*
4. They appeared to be happy.   5. Would you dare to swim during an *electrical* storm?   6. Raphael sometimes hesitates to raise his hand in class.   7. She should never have agreed to send money *to that person.*   8. Sam refused to be nominated *treasurer of his class.*   9. Do you really want to know your future?   10. Bill neglected to pay his rent last month, *and now he's in big trouble with his landlady.*

EXERCISE 6

Spoken pairwork

EXERCISE 7

Only incorrect sentences are included below.
2. He warned *me* not to drive so fast.   3. He allowed *me* to go without giving me a ticket.   5. My mother hired *a gardener* to trim the trees and cut the bushes.   8. Our speech teacher taught *us* how to introduce a topic in a natural way.   9. The state requires *car owners* to have car insurance.

EXERCISE 8

1. someone else will word process it for her   2. Beth to pay for the drinks   3. for someone else to write the invitations   4. someone else to arrange the flowers   5. to buy (herself) a new dress

EXERCISE 9

1. Kate's professor has requested her to keep detailed notes of her research.   2. The government requires Kate to get vaccinations

before she goes.   3. Her professor insisted that she study the language of the Amazon tribe that she will live with. *("Insist" cannot be followed by an infinitive; it takes the English subjunctive.)*
4. Kate has decided to try to learn about Amazon folk medicine.
5. Kate's professor has encouraged her to write a list of research questions.   6. Kate's family expected her to feel a little bit nervous before her trip.

EXERCISE 10

1. Kate was expected to...
2. Kate was asked by her parents...
3. Kate was encouraged by her brother...
4. Martha was selected...
5. Martha was invited...
6. Stanford is considered to be...

EXERCISE 11

1. It can be difficult to cook...   2. It's enjoyable to swim...
3. It's easier to learn...   4. It is my pleasure...   5. It's a good idea for Max...   6. It's a wise idea for...

Unit 7

Gerunds

EXERCISE 1

1. he is being spied on   2. most women are whistled at by men
3. you watered my garden   4. there would be an earthquake
5. I don't have to make the bed when I stay in a hotel

EXERCISE 2

Spoken activity

EXERCISE 3

1. I   2. Pete's   3. we   4. John's   5. Phil's   6. Jack's
7. Jack   8. Charles's

EXERCISE 4

(1) relaxing   (2) enjoying   (3) following   (4) filling
(5) mowing   (6) trimming   (7) painting   (8) feeling
(9) shopping   (10) cleaning   (11) sleeping   (12) having
(13) getting   (14) letting

EXERCISE 5

Verbs that require gerunds (from Exercise 4): *recommend, resist, insist on, avoid, admit, help, try, consider, suggest*

EXERCISE 6

1. to take   2. giving up   3. to join   4. eating   5. to go
6. to sign up

EXERCISE 7

1. Katherine misses eating freshly made bread. / Katherine missed her sister's singing in the shower.   2. Benjamin understands needing time alone. / Benjamin understands his roommate's needing time alone.   3. I won't tolerate receiving torn magazines in the mail. / Patrick won't tolerate his mother's getting poor service.   4. Warren postponed waxing his car. / Mr. Davis postponed his daughter's getting married.   5. Scott denied taking the last piece of cake. / The captain denied Anthony's taking a vacation.

EXERCISE 8

1. Matt's brother doesn't understand Matt's wanting to get a good job right away.   2. Matt wanted to avoid still having two term papers to write in his last semester.   3. Matt won't miss eating dinner in the cafeteria.   4. Matt's roommate Tom resents Matt's talking about returning to Hawaii.   5. Matt's

parents are not looking forward to Matt's getting a new car.
6. Matt didn't anticipate having to pay for his own car insurance.

1. Jogging   2. driving   3. worrying   4. spending
5. Relaxing   6. not smoking   7. Staying   8. watching
9. Collecting   10. not having

(1) to watch   (2) playing   (3) to get   (4) spending   (5) to use   (6) to read   (7) being   (8) watching   (9) selecting   (10) to play / playing   (11) to imagine   (12) to practice / practicing   (13) to unplug   (14) to let

1. a   2. b   3. b   4. a

1. Jack quit smoking.   2. I always remember to lock the front door.   3. The teacher tried to close the window.   4. We tried turning on the heater.   5. I'd forgotten taking these pictures.
6. He stopped to think.   7. Penny stopped drinking coffee.
8. Carl meant to pick up some milk on the way home.

1. talking   2. to do   3. to visit   4. listening   5. to put / putting   6. to answer   7. to explain   8. to read   9. to hurt / hurting   10. talking

TOEFL® Test Preparation Exercises Units 5–7

1. B	5. A	9. B	13. B	17. D
2. C	6. C	10. A	14. D	18. A
3. A	7. D	11. D	15. C	19. B
4. D	8. B	12. C	16. A	20. D

Unit 8

Intensifiers and Degree Complements

(3) His partner told him that his new designs were somewhat <u>hard</u> to understand.   (4) At first, Peter was extremely <u>upset</u> by his partner's observation because he had worked very <u>hard</u>.
(5) Later, he realized that his designs really were too <u>complicated</u> for most city buildings.   (7) First, he made the hallways slightly <u>wider</u> to make it easier to deliver office equipment.   (9) This would provide quite a bit <u>more</u> light.   (11) Peter is quite <u>proud</u> of his new design and is fairly <u>confident</u> that it will be accepted.

(1) too / very   (2) somewhat / rather / pretty / kind of / sort of / fairly   (3) a little / slightly / a bit / a tad   (4) too / way too
(5) a little / slightly / a bit / a tad   (6) very / really   (7) quite / very / extremely / really   (8) kind of / rather / somewhat / sort of
(9) too / way too   (10) a little / a tad / a bit / slightly

1. too   2. very   3. too   4. very   5. too   6. too   7. very
8. too   9. too   10. very

1. a little too / a bit too   2. a little too / really too   3. really too   4. a bit too   5. way too

1. direct   2. softened   3. direct   4. direct   5. direct
6. direct   7. softened   8. direct   9. direct   10. direct

3. This coffee isn't as strong as I'd like.   4. The seats aren't quite big enough.   5. That story was not very short.   6. The soup isn't very spicy.   8. Pauline doesn't really like going to museums.   9. The new delivery person is not very fast.
10. Janice isn't a very good skier.

Intensifiers are in italics.

1. Mr. Green was worried *enough* about delays on the new project to ask everyone to come in on Saturday.   2. Mr. Green is *too* cheap to provide free coffee for the office workers.
3. Mr. Green is *too* busy at work to take a vacation.
4. Mr. Green has *enough* worries to keep him up at night.
5. Mr. Green's employees don't like him *enough* to have a birthday party for him.

1. b.   2. a.   3. b.   4. b.   5. a.

EXERCISE 9

1. Betty has too much pride to ask her friend for a loan.
2. Teresa is too young / not old enough to get married.   3. The office is too noisy for Mr. Addison to concentrate on his work.
4. The cat weighs too much to catch mice.   5. Pedro bought enough photocopier paper to print his project.   6. Sam doesn't like his neighbor enough to water her plants while she is away.
7. The little boy is old enough to go to school.   8. I am too old / not young enough to join the army or police force.   9. Helen always has enough money to buy stocks and bonds.   10. Barbara has too many exams to be able to help me with mine.

EXERCISE 10

(1) so   (2) Such   (3) so   (4) such   (5) Such   (6) such
(7) so   (8) so   (9) Such   (10) so

EXERCISE 11

1. The Harrisons have purchased so many paintings that they can't show all of them at one time.   2. Paul has such an easy job that he can often leave work early.   3. The earthquake caused such heavy destruction that the bridge was no longer usable.
4. Carl ate so much pie that he could hardly get up from his chair.   5. The government had so little success with the anticrime program that the program was canceled.   6. The carpet had become so dirty that it couldn't be cleaned.   7. The rabbits had so few natural enemies in Australia that they multiplied very quickly.   8. The water hyacinth caused such extensive flooding that the river had to be drained and cleared.

Unit 9

Modifying Noun Phrases: Adjectives and Participles

EXERCISE 1

1. a large new multistoried   2. some of that very old French
3. two rather spoiled little   4. six old-fashioned silver serving
5. several really fat wild   6. three slightly broken

EXERCISE 2

(1) blue and white striped   (2) original store   (3) two very expensive wool   (4) old, pajama-style wool   (5) big round white
(6) bright green wool   (7) shabby old hand-me-down   (8) ugly, worn-out   (9) brand-new designer   (10) well-polished Italian leather

EXERCISE 3

Only incorrect sentences are included below.
2. Patricia is planning her next month-long exotic cruise.
5. The entire family was living in a tiny, dark, one-room apartment.   6. The competition was held on the first floor of the brand-new government Department of Justice building.

EXERCISE 4

1. *Pressed*—PAST; *interesting*—PRESENT   2. *Enduring*—PRESENT; *contented*—PRESENT   3. *Interesting*—PRESENT; *revealed*—PAST; *reading*—PRESENT   4. *puzzling*—PRESENT; *exciting*—PRESENT   5. *growing*—PRESENT; *balanced*—PAST
6. *surprised*—PAST; *unexpected*—PAST

EXERCISE 5

1. damaging; damaged   2. embarrassing; embarrassed
3. satisfying; satisfied   4. disappointed; disappointing
5. terrified; terrifying

EXERCISE 6

1. enduring   2. interesting   3. interested   4. fascinating
5. annoying   6. worried   7. surprising   8. surprised
9. upsetting   10. boring

EXERCISE 7

1. a child who is in great need of attention   2. a museum that is visited by a lot of people   3. a salesperson who talks fast
4. a river that flows slowly   5. a fairy tale that is known by many people   6. a house that has been destroyed by fire   7. a millionaire who did not inherit his or her fortune   8. a steak that has been cooked thoroughly   9. a move that happens at a good time   10. food that was frozen quickly

EXERCISE 8

(1) disappointing   (2) expected   (3) worried   (4) frightened
(5) embarrassed   (6) confused   (7) insulting   (8) accused
(9) required   (10) expected   (11) frightened   (12) interested
(13) annoyed   (14) puzzling   (15) mistaken   (16) concerned
(17) uninvolved   (18) surprising   (19) terrified
(20) recommended

Spoken group work

EXERCISE 10

1. The price hike that was announced last week was the second in a year.   2. The reporter who was planning to break the story got a sudden surprise.   3. The criminal who was arrested last week will be tried in federal court.   4. The student who is speaking in front of the class is quite nervous.   5. The project that was mentioned in the first chapter took a year to complete.   6. The prize that will be given at the end of the week will be the largest in the club's history.

Unit 10

Comparatives

EXERCISE 1

1. X = lumber production in Canada
   Y = lumber production in the United States
   X > Y: large difference
   X = lumber use in Canada
   Y = lumber use in the United States
   X < Y: large difference
2. X = the population of the United States
   Y = the population of Canada
   X > Y: large difference
   X = the literacy rate of the United States
   Y = the literacy rate of Canada
   X < Y: small difference

EXERCISE 2

1. The number of castles in the United States is substantially smaller than that in France.   2. The number of castles in France is much higher than in the United States.   3. The land area of New Mexico is somewhat larger than that of Arizona.   4. The land area of Arizona is somewhat smaller than that of New Mexico.   5. The total size of Alaska is considerably bigger than that of Rhode Island.   6. The total size of Rhode Island is considerably smaller than that of Alaska.   7. Alaska achieved statehood slightly earlier than Hawaii.   8. Hawaii achieved statehood a bit later than Alaska.

EXERCISE 3

1. X = California
   Y = Connecticut
   feature: land area
   X > Y: large difference
2. X = Indiana
   Y = Kentucky
   feature: land area
   X < Y: small difference
3. X = Earth
   Y = Jupiter
   feature: number of moons
   X < Y: large difference
4. X = sherbet
   Y = ice cream
   feature: amount of fat in one cup
   X < Y: large difference

EXERCISE 4

1. New York City has many more immigrants than Fargo, North Dakota.   2. New York City has slightly less air pollution than Los Angeles.   3. An elephant is much heavier than a horse.   4. A plane ticket from Los Angeles to Paris is considerably more expensive than one from Los Angeles to San Francisco.   5. Catherine is not quite as tall as Marie.

EXERCISE 5

1. (a) one medicine and another;   (b) similar   2. (a) red wine and white wine;   (b) identical   3. (a) students who don't have to work and those who do have to work;   (b) different   4. (a) the United States and Panama;   (b) identical   5. (a) two ideas;   (b) different   6. (a) his voice and his brother's voice; (b) similar

EXERCISE 6

1. (a) family structures   (b) very different   (c) *from very different family structures*
2. (a) family structures   (b) identical / very similar   (c) *from the same or similar family structures*
3. (a) patterns of behavior   (b) somewhat similar (c) *somewhat similar*
4. (a) a woman and a man   (b) identical   (c) does not like his mother
5. (a) family structure   (b) identical   (c) *the same type*
6. (a) educational levels   (b) somewhat similar   (c) *very different*
7. (a) interests   (b) somewhat similar   (c) *similar*
8. (a) expectations   (b) very different   (c) *completely different*
9. (a) religion   (b) identical   (c) *the same*
10. (a) age range   (b) identical   (c) *the same*

1. The eating habits of France are quite different from those of the United States.   **2.** Charles had much the same experience as Mitchell.   **3.** Europeans drive differently from Americans.   **4.** Patrick's writing style is not very different from mine.   **5.** Washington State has much the same number of rainy days as Oregon.   **6.** Health-conscious people eat differently from other people.   **7.** The societal opinions about raising children in North America are quite different from those in Asia.   **8.** I ate the same lunch as Jeff.

TOEFL® Test Preparation Exercises Units 8–10

1. D	**5.** B	**9.** C	**13.** D	**17.** A
2. D	**6.** B	**10.** B	**14.** C	**18.** D
3. D	**7.** C	**11.** B	**15.** A	**19.** C
4. C	**8.** D	**12.** B	**16.** A	**20.** C

Unit 11

Connectors

EXERCISE 1

Connector: Form, *Meaning*
(2) First: sentence connecter, *sequence*   **(3)** After: subordinating conjunction, *sequence*   **(4)** but: coordinating conjunction, *contrast*
(5) Consequently: sentence connector, *result*   **(6)** (none)
(7) Then: sentence connector, *condition*   **(8)** Eventually: sentence connector, *sequence* and *coordinator addition*   **(9)** As a result: sentence connector, *result*   **(10)** However: sentence connector, *contrast*   **(11)** While: subordinating conjunction, *contrast*
(12) In fact: sentence connector, *emphasis*   **(13)** Besides: subordinating conjunction, *emphasis*   **(14)** (none)   **(15)** Furthermore: sentence connector, *emphasis*   **(16)** If: subordinating conjunction; *condition* and: coordinating conjunction, *addition*

EXERCISE 2

(1) but   **(2)** on the one hand   **(3)** on the other hand / however
(4) In fact   **(5)** if   **(6)** However   **(7)** but   **(8)** Moreover / Furthermore   **(9)** and   **(10)** Besides

EXERCISE 3

Words to be circled are shown in italics.
(3) Janice cleaned her apartment until it was <u>shining</u> *and* <u>spotless</u>.
(4) <u>She was going to get flowers</u>, *but* <u>she didn't have time</u>.   **(5)** On her way to the airport, <u>she thought about making reservations</u> for dinner, *but* <u>she wasn't sure</u> whether her mother would prefer <u>Chinese</u> *or* <u>Thai</u> food.   **(6)** She knew that her mothcr liked *neither* <u>pepper</u> *nor* <u>curry</u>.   **(7)** Once she was on the road, Janice <u>turned on</u> the radio *and* <u>realized</u> that her mother was going to be late.   **(8)** <u>The weather was good in L.A.</u>, *but* <u>snow near Chicago had caused a delay</u>.   **(9)** Janice had time <u>to go shopping</u> *or* <u>to sit</u> in a cafe *and* <u>read</u> a book.
(10) An hour later, <u>Janice again headed toward</u> the airport, *and* <u>she took her time</u>.   **(12)** Her mother had <u>heard about</u> the Chicago snow storm *and* <u>decided</u> to take an earlier flight.   **(13)** <u>She didn't have time</u> to call Janice, *but* <u>she knew</u> that Janice <u>was</u> careful *and* <u>would</u> arrive early to pick her up.   **(15)** <u>Janice could have gotten</u> to the airport earlier, *but* <u>she didn't</u>.   **(16)** <u>Her mother could have called</u> from the plane, *but* <u>she didn't</u>.   **(17)** They were both <u>hungry</u> *and* <u>tired</u>.   **(18)** <u>Janice offered</u> to take her mother to *either* a <u>Chinese</u> *or* a <u>Thai</u> restaurant, *but* <u>her mother</u> just <u>wanted</u> to <u>get</u> to Janice's apartment *and* <u>take</u> a nap!

EXERCISE 4

1. but   **2.** and   **3.** or   **4.** nor   **5.** but
6. or   **7.** but   **8.** and   **9.** nor   **10.** or

EXERCISE 5

1. Karen likes to drink strong coffee, but Margaret doesn't. / Karen likes to drink strong coffee; however, Margaret doesn't.
2. Both Karen and Margaret want to go to Sea World. Karen wants to go to Sea World, and Margaret does too.   **3.** Karen likes water skiing and diving. / Karen likes both water skiing and diving.   **4.** Margaret enjoys water skiing, but not when it's cold on the lake.   **5.** Karen likes getting visits from her friends and relatives every summer.   **6.** Margaret doesn't like meeting her relatives at the airport, and Karen doesn't either. / Neither Margaret nor Karen likes meeting her relatives at the airport.

EXERCISE 6

1. Kate enjoys yoga but not judo.   **2.** Neither Kate nor Mary Jo goes home to change between work and her yoga class. / Kate doesn't go home to change between work and her yoga class, and neither does Mary Jo / Mary Jo doesn't either.   **3.** Kate doesn't eat before her yoga class, but Mary Jo does.   **4.** Both Kate and Mary Jo / Kate and Mary Jo both think that practicing yoga helps them to reduce stress.   **5.** After yoga class, Kate usually wants to eat, but Mary Jo doesn't.   **6.** The instructor wants both Kate and Mary Jo to try the advanced yoga class.

1. Although Pierre wanted to return to his country, he didn't want to leave his job here.   2. Because he made a lot of money in the United States, he was able to send money to his family.   3. As a result of becoming more and more nervous about making a decision, Pierre started smoking again.   4. In addition, he started to drink heavily.   5. He eventually went to the doctor, but he ignored the doctor's advice.

EXERCISE 8

1. Besides I paid for *Besides paying for*   2. pay. Mary *pay, Mary*
3. In spite of she didn't pay *Even though she didn't pay*   4. Due to she is cheap *Because she is cheap* 5. classes. I *classes, I*

Unit 12

Relative Clauses

EXERCISE 1

Relative clause	Word modified
(3) which is in Paris	The school
(4) who are accepted	The students
(6) that attracted the attention of Chef Troisgros	The project
(6) that Michelle made for a wedding	a cake
(7) that was as light and creamy	a cake
(9) that began her career baking for a large restaurant	this invitation
(10) that will fly her to Paris	the plane
(11) that Chef Troisgros attended	the three-month course

EXERCISE 2

1. Michelle is attending the cooking course that she dreamed about.
2. The man whom she is cooking with is an experienced cook.
3. Michelle prefers to learn baking techniques that she can use back in the United States.
4. She met the man who is co-owner of the cooking school.
5. The school, which has received three blue ribbons, has been open since 1926.
6. Michelle was only recently introduced to the family whom she is now living with.
7. She bought the cookbook that was written by her teacher.
8. Every day, the students eat the food that they have prepared.

EXERCISE 3

1. Patrick took a course that is no longer offered at our school.   2. Kate bought a dress that was on sale.
3. Lawrence introduced me to the new friend with whom he had been jogging for two months.   4. Michelle has a friend who owns a restaurant just outside of Paris.   5. I want to visit the beach that was featured on a TV show.   6. The dog that was in my backyard belongs to my neighbors down the street.

EXERCISE 4

1. This is the person to <u>whom</u> David gave flowers.
2. My brother, <u>who</u> runs for two miles each morning, is in good physical shape.   3. Correct   4. The book that I read was interesting.   5. Correct   6. Correct

EXERCISE 5

1. Relative pronoun cannot be deleted.   2. She examined the menus the chef had planned.   3. She wants to return home with a diploma signed by Chef Lyon.   4. The student she had dinner with last night is from Italy.
5. Relative pronoun cannot be deleted.   6. Michelle prefers to make friends with people studying at her school.
7. Chef Lyon tasted each cake baked by his students.
8. The prize awarded to the best student is a white chef's hat.   9. Relative pronoun cannot be deleted.
10. Students near the bottom of the class may need to repeat the class in order to get a diploma.

EXERCISE 6

1. ...whose fur is long.   2. ...whose sister she met in the gym.   3. ...calls for a doctor whose phone. ...
4. ...whose window my son had broken.   5. ...whose grade was ...   6. People whose thinking styles are similar may vote alike.

EXERCISE 7

1. geRund 2. hEr 3. seLf 4. pAst 5. posT 6. actIve
7. neVer 8. sElect 9. Comma 10. deLete 11. dAffy
12. pUll 13. whoSe 14. hEad

Unit 13

Using Present Time

EXERCISE 1

1. plays 2. is speaking 3. is sleeping / sleeps 4. is having 5. goes / is going 6. is doing 7. are waiting 8. gets 9. speaks 10. is popping

EXERCISE 2

1. is doing 2. am living 3. makes 4. is working 5. want, have 6. tries, forgets 7. feels 8. is feeling 9. is searching 10. live

EXERCISE 3

Questions only are listed.
1. Which type of visa does the school require? 2. What don't you like about winter? 3. Who do you resemble most in your family? 4. What does your wallet contain? 5. How many shoes do you own? 6. What does taking the TOEFL require? 7. What kind of food do you prefer? 8. To whom does that child belong? 9. How much does that house cost? 10. When did he realize he had a problem?

EXERCISE 4

1. requires 2. tastes 3. is tasting 4. minds / is minding 5. has / is having 6. are being 7. am depending / depend 8. is weighing 9. weighs 10. is considering 11. are / are being 12. require

EXERCISE 5

(1) I push him back, and he falls down on the sidewalk. (2) When he gets up, he sees that his pants are torn. (3) He's really mad! (4) He goes to get a policeman to arrest me. (5) He crosses the street, and a cop gives him a ticket. (6) The light was / is yellow, and this guy crossed / crosses anyway. (7) Well, he tells his story to the cop, but the cop doesn't believe him. (8) The guy deserved it!

Unit 14

Present Perfect

EXERCISE 1

(3) was–(c) (4) was born–(c) learned–(c) (5) translated–(c); went shopping–(c) (6) has done–(b) (7) has translated–(b) (8) has helped–(b); have been–(b); have thanked–(b) (9) has experienced–(b) (10) has taught–(b)

EXERCISE 2

(1) applied (2) has worked (3) has looked (4) decided (5) planned (6) made (7) reserved (8) didn't have to (9) has worked (10) has wanted (11) was canceled (12) was (13) quit (14) has heard (15) has been (16) has just seen (17) brought in (18) resolved

EXERCISE 3

(1) has just discovered (2) has canceled / canceled (3) has already made / already made (4) just returned / has just returned (5) opened (6) read (7) told (8) has done (9) complained (10) put (11) hasn't changed

EXERCISE 4

1. a 2. b 3. b 4. a 5. a. 6. b

EXERCISE 5

1. has been painting 2. has been charging / has charged 3. has known 4. has been asking 5. has been running 6. has wanted / has been wanting; has called 7. has been trying 8. has resulted 9. has smelled / has been smelling 10. have been dreaming / have dreamed

EXERCISE 6

(1) has been considering / is considering (2) is thinking (3) has been (4) enjoys (5) likes (6) was (7) hasn't had (8) started (9) has begun / is beginning

Unit 15

Future Time

1. return (P)   2. is bringing (F)   3. might take (F)
4. 's having (F)   5. tells (P)   6. get (F); 'll get (F)   7. Look
(P); could rain (F)   8. 's staying (P)   9. starts (F)   10. is
wearing (F); can't (P)

EXERCISE 2

1. might / will graduate   2. is   3. will go   4. might rain
5. is leaving   6. might / could win   7. 're going   8. is

EXERCISE 3

1. (A) will hurt   (B) will do   (C) is going to begin   (D) won't /
isn't going to include   2. (A) are you going to fix   (B) won't run
(C) won't be seen   (D) will buy   3. (A) is going to do   (B) will
end   (C) won't have   (D) is... going to say / will... say

EXERCISE 4

1. will   2. won't   3. Shall   4. are you going to   5. Shall

EXERCISE 5

Answers will vary. Below are possible answers.
1. It will increase because its residents keep reproducing at the
same rate.   2. They should, because technology keeps
advancing.   3. It might if enough citizens lobby for it.   4. I will
have to take them at some other time.   5. I may not always have
the same career.   6. There could be a cure for cancer someday.

7. She should like her present, because it's something she asked
for.   8. The government will never get rid of taxes, because it is
in debt up to its armpits.

EXERCISE 6

1. Paul and Kathy are going to have a good time while they are on
vacation in Montreal.   2. I'm going to go camping for three days
once I finish all of my final exams.   3. Carl and Alicia are leaving
for their new jobs as soon as they sell their house.   4. Even my
boss is going to take time off when he finishes printing and
checking the month-end report.   5. The cruise will be over
before we realize how much money we spent.   6. It will be
almost the next semester by the time Carol finally gets her paper
typed.   7. He's going to go skiing when he gets a book of
discount ski lift tickets.   8. Janet will read her book while the
baby is napping.

EXERCISE 7

(1) is going to / will travel   (2) returns   (3) gets   (4) will
have flown   (5) arrives   (6) will / is going to call   (7) will / is
going to go   (8) leaves   (9) will stop   (10) will be sleeping
(11) ends / will end   (12) touches   (13) will finally be

TOEFL® Test Preparation Exercises Units 13–15

1. B	5. B	9. B	13. C	17. D
2. C	6. C	10. C	14. B	18. B
3. A	7. D	11. C	15. B	19. C
4. D	8. A	12. A	16. A	20. D

Unit 16

Modals of Prediction and Inference

EXERCISE 1

1. Pat should be able to decide where to go on vacation.
2. Pat won't want to take his mother-in-law along.   3. He
might not even tell her about the trip.   4. His wife will tell her
mother.   5. They may ask the mother-in-law to watch their
house.   6. She might look in all of their closets.   7. It
might / could rain heavily tonight.   8. That student won't
be able to finish on time.   9. He shouldn't expect a tax
refund.   10. That sick child will cry all night.

EXERCISE 2

1. (A) could / may / might   (B) may / might / could   (C) might
/ could   2. (A) should   (B) couldn't   (C) must / should
(D) could   3. (A) might / may / could   (B) should   (C) can't
(D) must

EXERCISE 3

1. a   2. b   3. a   4. b

EXERCISE 4

(1) Susan was late to the dinner party.   (2) There may have been traffic on the way.   (3) She could have called from her car phone.   (4) The phone must not have been working.   (5) She must have been frustrated.

EXERCISE 5

1. (A) must have been   (B) may have been   (C) should have arrived   2. (A) should have called   (B) could have given   (C) must have had   3. (A) could have taken   (B) may have left   (C) might have given   (D) must not have been wearing

EXERCISE 6

Across: 1. perfect   11. should   13. must   15. used   16. blank   17. might

Down: 1. past   8. could   12. doubt   14. ok

Unit 17

Hypothetical Statements

EXERCISE 1

1. a   2. b   3. a   4. b   5. b

EXERCISE 2

1. I didn't live in Paris.   2. He didn't pay his share.
3. I won't come to your party.   4. He didn't ask me for help.   5. She didn't try to start the machine.
6. Bob lied.

EXERCISE 3

1. b   2. a   3. a   4. b   5. b

EXERCISE 4

1. If I had $20,000, I would be able to pay next year's tuition.   2. If my mother were here, she would cook for me.   3. If the manager weren't visiting our department, we wouldn't have to wear suits.   4. If my writing teacher returned essays on time, I would know how to improve my writing.
5. If Mary didn't have to study, she could have a part-time job.   6. If Alice were going to graduate next semester, I would need a new roommate.

EXERCISE 5

1. if he didn't smoke.   2. if I had the time.   3. if she had a car.   4. if we already knew English.   5. if I visited them more often.   6. if I had a maid.   7. if people were more peaceful.
8. if people didn't commit violent crimes.

EXERCISE 6

Answers will vary.
PART A: 1. ...I would not have been born.   2. ...he would be able to buy that new bike.   3. ...I would have fixed you something to eat.   4. ...we would all have been blown to smithereens.
PART B: 5. ...I wouldn't be taking it again this semester.
6. ...more people could be studying now.   7. ...I wouldn't be working in a mall.   8. ...I wouldn't be living in a dormitory.

EXERCISE 7

Answers will vary.
1. I can't go back to my county because I have to finish this term paper.   2. I didn't know he was so impolite when I invited him to the party.   3. I didn't attend this college 20 years ago when the tuition was cheaper.   4. Janice didn't pass her exam, so she's retaking the class in summer school.   5. He didn't get the job because he lied on his resume.   6. She doesn't have a third ticket to give you.

EXERCISE 8

Answers will vary.
1. Otherwise I would have gone to the movies with you.
2. Otherwise she wouldn't have given me this album.
3. I would drive the 200 miles to see you, but it's going to snow tomorrow.   4. Otherwise she could take you to the airport.
5. Otherwise they would suffer political persecution and censorship.   6. Catherine wouldn't be so hard on Jack about his grades, but she doesn't know how hard he's studying.
7. Otherwise it would be finished by now.   8. I would go camping with you, but my boss asked me to work this weekend.

EXERCISE 9

PART A: **1.** likely **2.** unlikely **3.** likely **4.** likely
PART B: **5.** hypothetical **6.** nonhypothetical
7. nonhypothetical **8.** hypothetical

EXERCISE 10

1. unlikely event **2.** past possibility **3.** unlikely event
4. past possibility

EXERCISE 11

1. not true **2.** actual possibility **3.** not true **4.** actual
possibility **5.** not true

EXERCISE 12

1. b **2.** a **3.** b **4.** b **5.** b

Unit 18

Sensory Verbs

EXERCISE 1

1. to be let in **2.** to sit **3.** to finish **4.** be let outside

EXERCISE 2

1. SENSORY VERB: *watched*
OBSERVED ACTION: *The children skated on the lake.*
2. SENSORY VERB: *to feel*
OBSERVED ACTION: *The sun shines on Carol's face.*
3. SENSORY VERB: *heard*
OBSERVED ACTION: *The car crashed.*
4. SENSORY VERB: *observed*
OBSERVED ACTION: *The baby was crawling on the floor.*
5. SENSORY VERB: *smell*
OBSERVED ACTION: *The toast is burning.*
6. SENSORY VERB: *listened*
OBSERVED ACTION: *The customer complained about the broken washing machine.*

EXERCISE 3

1. play / playing **2.** fix / fixing **3.** mowing **4.** leave / leaving **5.** burning

EXERCISE 4

(1) I felt the house begin to shake. **(2)** I heard the sound of the movement get louder. **(3)** I saw the dishes fall out of the kitchen cabinet. **(4)** I heard glass breaking. I went under a table. **(5)** I heard the sound grow fainter.

EXERCISE 5

1. fall / falling; break / breaking **2.** stealing **3.** bite
4. burning **5.** playing **6.** arguing

EXERCISE 6

Causative Verb	Infinitive or Base Form
3. made	dial
4. forced	to listen
5. made	say
7. got	to file
8. made	photocopy
9. helped	organize
10. let	start

EXERCISE 7

Answers will vary.
1. CAUSATIVE: *Cat owners shouldn't let their cats scratch guests.*
VERB + INFINITIVE: *Cat owners shouldn't allow their cats to scratch guests.*
2. CAUSATIVE: *Teachers should have students type term papers.*
VERB + INFINITIVE: *Teachers should require students to type term papers.*
3. CAUSATIVE: *A thief should not make a victim give up his watch.*
VERB + INFINITIVE: *A thief should not require a victim to give up his watch.*
4. CAUSATIVE: *Schools should have doctors examine students once a year.*
VERB + INFINITIVE: *Schools should require doctors to examine students once a year.*
5. CAUSATIVE: *Creative teachers should help students learn by example.*
VERB + INFINITIVE: *Creative teachers should get students to learn by example.*
6. CAUSATIVE: *The doctor should make Jack go on a diet.*
VERB + INFINITIVE: *The doctor should require Jack to go on a diet.*

7. CAUSATIVE: *Most people should have an accountant check their taxes.*

VERB + INFINITIVE: *Most people should get an accountant to check their taxes.*

8. CAUSATIVE: *Police officers should make drunk drivers pull over.*

VERB + INFINITIVE: *Police officers should force drunk drivers to pull over.*

EXERCISE 8

1. People are not allowed to drink and drive. **2.** NO CHANGE POSSIBLE. **3.** All adult men are required to go into the army. **4.** NO CHANGE POSSIBLE. **5.** Wilson's report was prepared by his sister. **6.** Children should be helped by their parents to learn good eating habits.

EXERCISE 9

(1) The boss required Patrick to answer the phone for several hours. **(2)** When the phones were slow, he allowed Patrick to read the reports from last month. **(3)** Later, the boss taught him to use the fax machine. **(4)** At noon, he allowed Patrick to go out to lunch. **(5)** But the boss required him to bring back lunch for several people on the phone staff.

(6) He persuaded Patrick to pick up a newspaper and some rubber bands. **(7)** At 5:00, the boss encouraged Patrick to work a few minutes extra. **(8)** At 6:30, he allowed Patrick to go home.

EXERCISE 10

Only incorrect sentences are included below.

1.	—were gotten	*They got the children to be quiet.*
2.	—to redo	omit *to*
4.	—to be	omit *to be*
5.	—be	omit *be*
7.	—to borrow	omit *to*
8.	—was had	*He had a mechanic change the oil.*
9.	—carries	*that every officer carry a gun*
10.	—to write	omit *to*
11.	—was included	*that she be included*
12.	—was given	*that he be given a break*

TOEFL® Test Preparation Exercises Units 16–18

1. A	5. D	9. D	13. C	17. A
2. B	6. B	10. B	14. B	18. C
3. B	7. C	11. A	15. C	19. D
4. B	8. C	12. C	16. B	20. C

Unit 19

Articles in Discourse

EXERCISE 1

1. The (article); his (possessive) **2.** The (article); some (article) **3.** That (demonstrative); the (article) **4.** Few (quantifier); the (article) **5.** Those (demonstrative); her (possessive) **6.** their (possessive); the (article)

EXERCISE 2

1. generic **2.** particular **3.** generic **4.** particular **5.** particular **6.** generic **7.** particular **8.** generic **9.** particular **10.** generic

EXERCISE 3

1. b **2.** a **3.** b **4.** b **5.** a

EXERCISE 4

1. the/some/ø **2.** a **3.** the **4.** ø **5.** The; a **6.** a; the **7.** A/Some **8.** the/a; the/an **9.** the **10.** ø/some

EXERCISE 5

1. (A) a **(B)** the **(C)** The **(D)** the **(E)** the **(F)** Some **(G)** the
2. (A) Some/The **(B)** the **(C)** ø/the **(D)** the **(E)** The **(F)** the / a
3. (A) ø **(B)** a **(C)** the **(D)** ø **(E)** Some

EXERCISE 6

1. a; ø **2.** ø **3.** a; a **4.** a; the **5.** Some **6.** a; a **7.** a; the **8.** a; an **9.** a; a **10.** a; ø

EXERCISE 7

1. the **2.** the; the **3.** a; the **4.** The **5.** an; the **6.** a; the **7.** the; the **8.** the **9.** the; the/an **10.** The; the/a **11.** the **12.** a; a

EXERCISE 8

1. b **2.** a **3.** b **4.** b

Unit 20

Demonstratives in Discourse

EXERCISE 1

1. These/Those; those/these   2. these; They   3. the/those
4. these; the/this; the/this   5. The; the   6. that/this; It; It;
the   7. It; this; the/that; This   8. the; these

EXERCISE 2

2. Let me make (this) clear: No cheating!
3. (These) students are excused from the final exam:
Robert Gonzales, Hosein Arifipour, and Carla Arnold.
4. The manager stated that he had received several expense
reports that were not filled out correctly. (These) will be returned.
5. Louise said that she left her job because she wanted more
free time. (That) doesn't sound correct to me.
6. (These) practices will be stopped immediately: taking long
lunch breaks and leaving early.
7. Smith will write the report and Wilson will word
process it. (Those) are your assignments.
8. Our salaries will be reduced 5%. I don't like (that).

EXERCISE 3

1. that   2. That/It   3. It   4. That   5. that/this   6. it   7. it
8. That

EXERCISE 4

Only sentences that contain a post-modifier are included
below.
1. *that of your partner*   3. *Those who cannot hear the
difference between "t" and "th"*   5. *those who she thinks
know the material*   6. *that which is genuine, that which
is not*

TOEFL® Test Preparation Exercises Units 19–20

1. C	5. B	9. C	13. D	17. B
2. D	6. D	10. B	14. B	18. D
3. C	7. A	11. A	15. D	19. A
4. D	8. B	12. C	16. C	20. A

Unit 21

Possessives

EXERCISE 1

(3) his (a)   (4) of each house (d)   (5) his (a)   (6) Their (a)
(7) of the condo (d); of the last place (d)   (8) of the day (d);
Jerry's (c); Anita's (c)   (9) Their (a); theirs (b)

EXERCISE 2

1. Bob's friend's golf clubs   2. Beethoven's symphonies
3. the child's mouth   4. the child's friend Sally   5. The first
page of a book   6. parking lot of the mall   7. the son of
a well-known French movie director   8. the seat of the chair
9. Susan's cousin's store   10. The cause of the dispute

EXERCISE 3

Spoken pair work.

EXERCISE 4

1. of the common cold–*(c/d)*   2. Karen's–*(e)*   3. of
Freud–*(d)*; Professor Randolph's–*(e)*   4. of Holland–*(d)*;
their–*(c)*   5. of his hikes–*(e)*; of Yosemite–*(c)*   6. the
book's–*(b)*

EXERCISE 5

Only incorrect sentences are included below.
1. The roof of the house was damaged in the storm.
3. He was a prisoner of his own fame when he died.
4. The wool sweaters of England are famous for their quality.
6. The step-daughter of a little-known singer's wife will be
playing the guitar tomorrow night.

Unit 22
Quantifiers and Collective Nouns

Underlined words are listed below.
(2) plenty of colleges; not all of them; every major field of study   (3) quite a few students; one college   (4) Most students   (5) Almost all schools; some assistance
(6) Many counseling departments   (7) Hardly anyone
(8) Quite a bit of the counselors' advice   (9) More than one counselor; most of the time   (10) Not many students
(11) A lot of students; three or four courses   (12) Some people
(13) A few unlucky students

EXERCISE 2

1. There are a few cookies left in the jar.   2. Almost all parents worry about their children.   3. Some teachers work in the summer.   4. Most homeowners in the United States have some kind of home owner's insurance.
5. All children in the United States must have vaccinations before they may start school.   6. It takes a lot of money to buy a house.

EXERCISE 3

Spoken pair work.

EXERCISE 4

1. little   2. a little   3. few   4. a little   5. few   6. little
7. Few   8. a little

EXERCISE 5

1. Every / Any / Each student wants to get a good grade.
2. Every / Each / Any postal carrier is warned about dogs.
3. Jack spends every / each paycheck on his car.   4. Every / Each letter will be answered.

EXERCISE 6

1. Both   2. Both of them   3. Neither   4. both; either
5. either of them

EXERCISE 7

1. Some of my   2. Any   3. A little of the   4. No
5. Almost all   6. Most   7. hardly any   8. Several of the

EXERCISE 8

1. attended   2. every one   3. none   4. much   5. a lot
6. a few   7. a great deal of   8. every one

EXERCISE 9

Underlined words are listed below.
2. groups; a flock of pink birds; a gaggle of geese; a herd of goats; a flock of sheep; a swarm of bees   3. a committee of professors; herds of dairy cows; a delegation of dairy farmers
4. the government; the public; the media; a group of unhappy citizens; a team of media analysts

EXERCISE 10

1. has; its   2. are; their   3. are; their   4. their   5. is; is; its; its

EXERCISE 11

1. drink; their   2. has; its   3. has; its   4. were   5. has; its
6. are; their

EXERCISE 12

1. Fast bicycles and large pizzas are very popular with people who are young.   2. Very few well-paying jobs are open to people who can't read and write.   3. The shelters were opened to prevent people who don't have a place to live from dying.
4. Some hospitals in the United States specialize in diseases of people who are old.   5. Porsches and Ferraris are generally considered to be cars for people who are very wealthy.

TOEFL® Test Preparation Exercises Units 21–22

1. C	5. C	9. D	13. D	17. D
2. A	6. D	10. B	14. B	18. B
3. D	7. C	11. D	15. B	19. A
4. B	8. A	12. D	16. A	20. C

Unit 23

Past Time Frame

2. FIRST ACTION: had been waiting; SECOND ACTION: rang; HOW INDICATED: aspect and adverbial *(when)*
3. FIRST ACTION: returned; SECOND ACTION: picked up; HOW INDICATED: sequence
4. FIRST ACTION: had not yet been deposited; SECOND ACTION: didn't pay; HOW INDICATED: aspect and adverbial *(yet)*
5. FIRST ACTION: had been boiling; SECOND ACTION: turned down; HOW INDICATED: aspect and adverbial *(before)*
6. FIRST ACTION: signed; SECOND ACTION: ended; HOW INDICATED: sequence

EXERCISE 2

1. b   2. a   3. a   4. b   5. a

EXERCISE 3

(1) was constantly looking   (2) was trying; returned   (3) went
(4) were having   (5) was looking; found; needed   (6) helped; left

EXERCISE 4

1. went; had registered   2. destroyed   3. was looking; found   4. heard; had been drafted; called   5. noticed; had chewed / was chewing   6. was; hadn't gotten

EXERCISE 5

1. had been searching   2. had finished   3. had been raining
4. had been using   5. had gotten   6. had been waiting

EXERCISE 6

1. had been trying; discovered   2. wasn't; was running / had been running; took   3. had written; decided   4. had been training   5. got; had left   6. spent   7. went; exchanged
8. had been listening; realized

Unit 24

Modals in Past Time Frame

EXERCISE 1

1. (a)   2. (a)   3. (b)   4. (a)   5. (b)   6. (b)

EXERCISE 2

1. applaud   2. apple   3. wash   4. stay   5. chew
6. stand   7. cob   8. mind   9. type   10. answer

EXERCISE 3

Answers will vary.
ALLOWED: 1. I was allowed to swim in the lake.   **2.** I was allowed to make the campfire.   **3.** I was allowed to stay up later than usual.   **4.** I was allowed to play all day.
NOT ALLOWED: 1. I was not allowed to cut school.   **2.** I was not allowed to go out on school nights.   **3.** I was not allowed to watch TV instead of doing my homework.   **4.** I was not allowed to stay up late.

EXERCISE 4

Answers will vary.
1. I had to fill out a lot of forms.   2. I had to get certain vaccinations.   3. I had to prove that I would be studying here.
4. I had to send my passport to the United States embassy in my country.

EXERCISE 6

Answers will vary.
1. Sabine was supposed to make her bed every day.   2. Sabine was supposed to watch her younger brother when her parents weren't at home.   3. Sabine was supposed to cook for the family once a week.   4. Sabine was supposed to do her homework every night.

EXERCISE 7

1. specific   2. general   3. specific   4. general   5. general
6. general

EXERCISE 8

1. was able to; couldn't   **2.** couldn't   **3.** was able to
4. couldn't

EXERCISE 9

(1) used to/would   (2) used to   (3) used to
(4) used to/would   (5) used to   (6) would/used to
(7) used to

EXERCISE 10

1. (a) wasn't to open   (b) would work; had saved
(c) was... going to be   **2.** (a) ø   (b) would

write up   **(c)** was... going to visit   **(d)** was to
become

EXERCISE 11

1. **(A)** was going to   **(B)** would/was going to   **(C)** would/was
going to   **2.** **(A)** was going to   **(B)** would   **(C)** would
3. **(A)** was going to   **(B)** would   **(C)** would

EXERCISE 12

1. was going to postpone   **2.** Were you going to send
3. correct   **4.** was going to

Unit 25

Reported Speech

EXERCISE 1

1. The teacher told me that my son needed to come to school on
time.   **2.** She didn't like the fact that he often teased other
children.   **3.** Pauline was annoyed that the supermarket cashier
had dropped her eggs.   **4.** The veterinarian explained that my
cat needed more exercise.

EXERCISE 2

1. The manager said, "I am unhappy that we can no longer have
free coffee."   **2.** The manager said, "I don't like the fact that
there will be no more doughnuts at staff meetings."   **3.** The
manager said, "I'm concerned that Mr. Pearson didn't get any new
contracts last month."   **4.** The manager said, "I'm concerned
that two employees have left for other jobs."

EXERCISE 3

1. The teacher commented that Bill would probably need extra
tutoring.   **2.** The bus driver admitted that he could have avoided
the accident.   **3.** Jack's doctor stated that his father shouldn't
continue smoking.   **4.** Patrick mentioned that the reports might
be ready to send this / that afternoon.   **5.** The government
official announced that the new tax rates would be released
tomorrow / the next day.

EXERCISE 4

1. Jack said that his wife and your husband had a lot in
common.   **2.** Jack's wife said that her husband thinks that
she can read his mind.   **3.** Jack's brother said that his brother

(Jack) and he often went fishing on Mary's boat.   **4.** Jack's
mother said that Jack (her son) needed to visit her more often.

EXERCISE 5

1. Last week Mary told me that she had already taken all of the
units she needed for her degree.   **2.** When Max saw his sister,
he promised her that he would definitely be there for her
graduation.   **3.** On Saturday evening, Peter mentioned that he
could go to my concert after all.   **4.** When he stopped me, the
INS agent said that he wanted to see my green card and my
driver's license.

EXERCISE 6

1. When I saw Tomoko last week, she told me that the counselor
had told her that he wouldn't be able to help her get into ESL
classes until the next day.
2. Yesterday the car mechanic said that he wouldn't be able to
get the part he needed to repair my engine until two days from
yesterday.
3. Last week the dormitory manager said that I would have to
move all of my things out of my room by that night. He said that
the plumbers were going to fix the pipes in the room above mine.
4. When I went to the embassy, the official said that those
papers had to be signed and returned by the next day at the
latest.

EXERCISE 7

(2) Her coworker told her that they never chewed gum while sitting
at the front desk.   (3) The woman who sold coffee from the

coffee cart warned her that refills were not allowed.   (4) her boss reminded her that she couldn't leave early.   (5) her mother told her that there was no food in the refrigerator for dinner. RESTATEMENTS: **2.** Janice's coworker said, "We never chew gum while sitting at the front desk."   **3.** The woman who sold coffee from the coffee cart said, "Refills are not allowed."   **4.** On Friday, her boss said, "Remember, you can't leave early." **5.** When Janice got home that evening, her mother said, "There's no food in the refrigerator for dinner."

EXERCISE 8

2. How are your grades?   **3.** Have you had any speeding tickets or other problems with the law?   **4.** How are you planning to pay for your education?

EXERCISE 9

1. Another advisor told her, "Get an American checking account."   **2.** Akiko's new roommate said, "Take the bed near the window."   **3.** Akiko's host family asked, "Would you like to go to the mall with us?"   **4.** Akiko's English professor warned her, "Type all your assignments."   **5.** Akiko's friend asked, "Are you happy in your new school?"

EXERCISE 10

1. Marilyn said that if she had known then what she knows now, her life would be very different.   **2.** Just five minutes ago the child asked if they were there yet.   **3.** Last month my roommate asked me if I minded if she borrowed my chemistry notes.   **4.** Paulette told us that Carol was still in the hospital from complications during / from her surgery.   **5.** Catherine warned her roommate that she would be up late typing her paper.

EXERCISE 11

1. Theresa called me to say that she had been nominated "Engineering Student of the Year." She told me that there were five finalists. She commented that she was the only woman of the five.   **2.** I told my mother that I knew where the North Pole was. I announced that I had written Santa a letter.   **3.** if you know how I can reach Mr. Zoltan; whether he's still teaching history; that I'm getting my M.A. in history.

TOEFL® Test Preparation Exercises Units 23–25

1. B	5. A	9. B	13. C	17. B
2. C	6. C	10. A	14. B	18. D
3. D	7. D	11. D	15. A	19. A
4. B	8. C	12. A	16. C	20. B

TAPESCRIPT

Unit 1 (Activity 2)

Speaker: The foundation for Social Research today announced the winners of this year's Madison Award for distinguished work in the field of sociology. The award, one awarded posthumously, will provide $5000 to fund further research projects. This year's winners are Dr. Deborah Smith and Professor Sally Jones.

Dr. Smith has been a senior researcher at the Institute for Social Change since 1987. She is the author of several books on the welfare system, and has served on the President's Council for Welfare Reform for the last three years. Her research interests include the impact of welfare reform on the urban family and the effect of Head Start programs on later academic performance of school-aged children. This is her first major award, and she says that she will use the prize money to fund further research on the effect of poverty on family structure.

Professor Jones was the chair of the Social Welfare Department at Jordan College. She wrote extensively on economic patterns in rural America, and, in later years, researched the sociological profile of families involved in the home-schooling movement. In the last several months, she had been increasingly interested in the sociological impact of breast cancer. She received numerous awards throughout her long and distinguished career, including the Peabody Award and the Pulitzer Prize. Jordan College, which accepted the prize on her behalf, said that the money would be used for medical research, as Professor Jones had requested.

Unit 2 (Activity 1)

Narrator: Conversation number one. Listen to this conversation between John and Mary.
John: What an interesting apartment. You don't have much space, do you.
Mary: No, not really. But actually it's OK because I live by myself.
John: Hmm. I'm living by myself, too, but it's really too expensive.

Narrator: Conversation number two. Listen to this conversation between Peter and Denise.
Peter: I've looked over the Johnson contract, and everything looks fine.
Denise: Oh really, Peter? I've been looking it over too, and I can see at least three serious errors.

Narrator: Conversation number three. Listen to this conversation between Kathy and Angela.

Kathy: Did the new janitor do an OK job of cleaning up the office?
Angela: Yeah, I think he'll be fine. When I came in this morning he had done the windows and he was washing the floors.
Kathy: What about the trash? Did he empty the trash?
Angela: Yeah, he did it when I got there.

Narrator: Conversation number four. Listen to this conversation between Bob and Dave.
Dave: Hey, Bob. Did you read in the newspaper that they're going to close down the steel mill?
Bob: Yeah, Dave, I saw it all right. I worked there for 15 years, and I must say, I'm not too sorry to hear it.
Dave: That's fine for you, but I've been working there for five years, and I'm not really happy about having to look for another job.

Unit 3 (Activity 6)

Narrator: Broadcast number one.
Speaker 1 (male): An army-led coup on Christmas Eve toppled the two-year-old civilian government of Surinam. The coup was carried off without a single shot being fired, and by today normal holiday activity had resumed in the nation's capital. The leader of the country's military police appeared on national television to announce

the takeover and promised that elections would be held within 100 days. However, the real leader of the coup is widely believed to be chief of the armed forces, General Bouterse. Bouterse was the dictator of the former Dutch Colony from 1980 to 1988, and has served as commander of the armed forces since then. Although General Bouterse announced his own resignation from the army earlier in the day, he is reportedly still in charge of the troops. Bouterse carried out a similar coup in 1980, which toppled the previous civilian-led government. Both the U.S. and Dutch governments vigorously condemned the takeover.

Narrator: Broadcast number two.

Speaker 2 (female): Roosevelt Williams, a well-known educator and AIDS activist in Alameda County, died today from complications caused by AIDS. He was one of the world's longest-surviving AIDS patients. Since he was first diagnosed with the disease in 1980, he had been a tireless promoter of more education, support and under-standing for people with AIDS. He was widely known throughout the Bay Area for his inspirational appearances at local schools and churches, as well as on radio and television. He was a persuasive and eloquent speaker, and his efforts were so successful that a number of private organizations set up free treatment programs for the public. Memorial services will be held in several area churches on Sunday.

Unit 4 (Activity 6)

Officials in the Spanish Ministry of the Interior in Madrid announced today that a previously unknown masterpiece by Diego de Velasquez has been discovered in a storage closet at the Ministry. It seems clear that no one had opened the closet for at least 50 years, and officials have no idea how the painting got there in the first place. Officials believe that the painting, a portrait that was probably painted sometime between 1685 and 1700, had been stored away for safekeeping sometime during the Spanish Civil War, and then forgotten about.

Felipe Velasquez, a spokesman for the Ministry, who, in spite of having the same name, says that he is not related to the famous artist, theorized that officials at the time had no idea that the painting was particularly valuable. It isn't listed on any of the inventories of the Ministry, and, until yesterday, when it was authenticated by experts at the Prado Museum, nobody knew of its existence.

Diego de Velasquez, one of Spain's most famous artists, was very prolific, and painted dozens of portraits of many of the Court Nobility. The discovery of this portrait of a yet-to-be-identified middle-aged nobleman has led experts to wonder if there might not be other undiscovered masterpieces lying around in Ministry closets. "We'll be doing some serious house cleaning," said spokesman Velasquez, "to see what else is hiding in the attic."

The painting has been valued at over 1.5 million dollars.

Unit 5 (Activity 5)

Conversation 1
A (Male): (annoyed) Can you turn down the television? I'm talking on the phone, and I can't hear a thing.
B (Female): (defensive) You don't have to shout. Just ask nicely. You can be so unpleasant sometimes.
A: (sarcastic) You could try sitting in the same room as the TV. That way the rest of us wouldn't have to go deaf.
B: (cold) Sorry, I can't hear you. I'm watching TV.

Conversation 2
Mom: Will you tell Steve to stop teasing Nancy? She's going to cry in a minute.

Dad: Oh relax. Boys will be boys. Besides, she's got to toughen up if she's going to grow up to become a soldier in the army like her mom.
Mom: No she doesn't. Boys have got to become more supportive and caring. Listen, we'd better start teaching them when they're little, or they're never going to learn.
Dad: Look, boys tease each other all the time. Why shouldn't they act that way with girls, too?
Mom: You must be joking. I mean, you can't be serious.
Dad: No, you're right. I was just trying to tease you, too.
Mom: Watch it, buster. You know, I'm about to lose my temper.
Dad: All right, Stevie! Stop teasing your sister!

Unit 6 (Activity 6)

A (male): Were you in English class yesterday? What happened? Did the teacher say anything about the final examination tomorrow?

B (female): Well, he didn't exactly tell us what to study, but he did tell us what not to study. He said we could expect not to be tested on anything in the first half of the book.

A: Hey, that's good news! I was planing on studying all night tonight, but now it looks like I won't have to. I know the second half of the book really well.

B: So where were you yesterday? You missed a good review session.

A: I'm trying to be selected for a position on the student advisory board for the library, so I had an appointment to be interviewed by the head librarian.

B: Student advisory board? That sounds like a chance you couldn't afford to pass up!

A: Well, I want to get a master's in library science and my advisor told me to try to get some practical experience. Successful applicants are expected to have first-hand knowledge of all areas of library operations.

B: Well, why don't you just get a job in the library? That way you have a chance to get paid while you're learning.

A: I don't think I'd have much opportunity to get experience in all areas. I'd probably just be expected to put books on the shelves, and I already know how to do that. The advisory board will give me a chance to learn about a variety of library issues.

Unit 7 (Activity 6)

Narrator: Welcome to this week's edition of "Talk Talk, with our ever popular host, Barry Roast."

Barry: In today's program we'll find out some surprising information about what experts are calling our latest endangered species: Free Time. We'll be hearing today from Doctor Belva Murphy, author of *Free Time: America's Vanishing Resource*. According to her study, Americans are having a hard time holding on to their free time. Dr. Murphy has discovered that the amount of leisure time in the U.S. has decreased by nearly 30 percent in the last 20 years. In a conversation with her in the studio earlier this week, I found out some interesting facts about our latest Vanishing Resource.

Barry: Doctor Davis, you've stated in your book that Americans now have less leisure time than people in any other industrialized country in the world, and this amount will probably continue to decrease in the future. Where is this time going to?

Belva (female): Well, employment practices in the U.S. are one cause. The average American company requires employees to work 40 hours per week. They are allowed to take 11 paid holidays, and have an average of 12 vacation days (about two weeks). Compare that to the Germans. They are required to work a 38-hour week, and get to enjoy a yearly total of 10 holidays and 30 days (six weeks) of paid vacation. Even the hard-working Japanese (who spend an average of 42 hours a week working at the office), are encouraged to take 16 paid vacation days, and have an additional 20 days of holidays. As you can see, the U.S. doesn't stack up too well in the time-off department.

Barry: But Dr. Murphy, work requirements aren't the only reason, are they?

Belva: A second reason for this growing lack of free time comes from changing social patterns. Today, in most American families, both the husband and the wife need to work full-time outside the home. They are forced to postpone doing household chores until the weekend. Eighty-two percent of the people in my study said they need to spend at least one entire day of their weekend doing household chores, such as shopping for food, cleaning house, doing the laundry, and so forth.

Barry: But Dr. Murphy, you say vanishing free time isn't all the boss's fault. A surprisingly important cause of decreased free time is a way more and more Americans are using their free time.

Belva: Yes Barry, there has also been a rapid growth in the popularity of "working vacations." Travel agencies can now arrange for people to work on scientific research projects, or to assist ecologists with collecting and cataloging plant and animal species in the national parks. Other popular "working vacations" include going on digs at archaeological sites, or participating in community development projects in other countries. Still other people enroll in travel-study courses in foreign languages, history, or geography.

Barry: For some Americans, their idea of a relaxing vacation is to take a 300-mile bicycle trip, or to spend a week climbing mountains in South America. But for all Americans one thing is certain: People have less free time than they did a generation ago, and the so-called labor saving technological developments of the last 50 years have only made life faster—not easier! With Dr. Belva Murphy this is Barry Roast of "Talk Talk."

Unit 8 (Activity 7)

In the second half of the twentieth century, there has been such a rapid growth in population that many countries have started to develop lands that only a few years ago were uninhabited, dense tropical rain forest. Now, results of this population growth have had two economic impacts that have contributed to rapid deforestation. These developing countries need foreign exchange, which they can get by selling wood from the trees that grow in the rain forest, and they also need additional land for their growing populations. This need for lumber for export and land for agriculture has become so great that literally hundreds of square miles of tropical rain forest are now disappearing every day.

Now this process of destruction is happening extremely rapidly... so rapidly, in fact, that unless we can slow it down, all the world's rain forests—yes all of them—will be completely gone in just another 20 years!

Now why is this a problem? Why don't we just plant new trees to replace the ones that are being cut down? The problem is, that once the rain forests have been cut down, they don't just grow back. There is too little fertility in the soil of most tropical areas for the jungle to grow back at all. The original forests can never grow back again. This problem is so serious that scientists around the world and international organizations like the United Nations are all getting extremely concerned.

All right, so we can't replace the rain forests. Why should this is a problem? Why should we worry about it? We have many other resources like coal, and oil and minerals that can't be replaced. Why should rain forests be different from those?

Well, there are two primary reasons why the destruction of the rain forests poses a global threat. First, rain forests contain so many plants with possible medical uses that scientists are worried that many valuable species will be destroyed before we can find out how useful they are. But there is a second, more important reason why the destruction of the rain forests is too important to be ignored. There is a clear relationship between rain forests and the climate and weather patterns of the entire world. Rain forests are disappearing so quickly that scientists are afraid that this may already be causing changes in the atmosphere and weather of the planet. There are signs that it may already be too late for us to stop this process of global warming and climatic change. But further destruction of the rain forests will only make matters worse.

Unit 9 (Activity 9)

Narrator: Conversation number one.
Snooty Woman: Oh waiter, please give me a glass of cold water.
Man: Here you go.
Woman: No, I said I wanted cold water.
Man: Oh, I'm sorry. If you want cold water, I'll have to put ice in it.
Woman: Well, I didn't really want ice-water. If you have to add ice, then just make it an iced tea.
Man: I'll have to charge you for iced tea.
Woman: How much is it?
Man: A regular glass is 95 cents, and a tall glass is a dollar fifty.
Woman: Fine, I'll have a tall iced tea.
Man: Here you are.
Woman: You call that tall iced tea? The regular must be really small!
Man: Look, lady, I only work here. Would you like to talk to the manager?

Narrator: Conversation number two.
Young girl: Hello, Jocelyn residence.
Man: I'm trying to reach Dr. Jocelyn.
Girl: Well which Dr. Jocelyn do you want? There are two here.
Man: I'm not sure. I'm calling for the Physics Department and I need to speak to the Dr. Jocelyn who is the retired physics professor.
Girl: Oh, then I think you want to talk with my grandmother, but she's a retired biology professor.
Man: Oh, I think she's the one. I'm calling about setting up a senior citizens lecture series.
Girl: Oh well. Are you sure you don't want to talk with her daughter, the other Dr. Jocelyn? She teaches physics.
Man: No, this is about a senior citizen's lecture series. I think I need to speak to the retired professor.
Girl: OK, I'll get her. Hey grandma! Phone call!

Unit 10 (Activity 5)

Bob: Hi Kim. I had to go to the dentist today. What did Professor Jordan talk about in Anthropology class?
Kim: She talked about culture.
Bob: Hmm. Is that like the "language families" she talked about last time?
Kim: Yeah, she said that just as there are large "language families"—you know . . .
Kim and Bob: (reciting together as if by rote) "groups of languages that have somewhat the same linguistic structure" (they laugh).

Kim: Yeah, well, she said that anthropologists are now trying to define and identify large "culture families," as well.
Bob: So now what are culture families?
Kim: Hold on. Let me look at my notes...Oh here it is. Just as language families are made up of languages that share certain basic linguistic characteristics, culture families might be defined as groups of cultures that have more or less similar values, attitudes, and beliefs.
Bob: There's nothing surprising about that. I've traveled enough to know that one "European" culture—which, by the way, includes

areas outside of geographical Europe, such as Australia and North America—has many of the same basic characteristics as any other European culture.

Kim: Yeah, well, the example she used in the lecture was the countries of Latin America. She said that in spite of being quite different from each other in terms of customs and social structures, people from Colombia probably think more like people from Venezuela than like people from Nepal. And a Nepalese and an Indian will be more alike than a Nepalese and a Viennese.

Bob: I'm confused. If no culture has exactly the same set of values as another culture—which is what she told us last week—how are they going to determine culture families?

Kim: Well, let's see here. According to my notes, she said one important unifying factor is religion. Another factor is a shared historical and political development. Cultures that have a shared historical background tend to have somewhat the same outlook on the world.

Bob: But wait a minute. Any student of geography knows that political boundaries change much more frequently and more rapidly than cultural boundaries. What about places like the former Yugoslavia, or in countries like Rwanda or Burundi?

Kim: Yeah, she mentioned that. She said that many of the problems in newly independent countries today are because these developing countries were founded by the Colonial Powers as political unions, not cultural ones. But it is also important to remember that the differences between cultures can sometimes be more important than the similarities, no matter how much their economic and political interests may be alike, cultures that think quite differently from one another may choose to act quite differently as well.

Bob: Well, it doesn't sound like I missed anything terribly surprising. I think I already knew all that stuff.

Kim: Well, I thought it was pretty interesting, and she said it would definitely be on the midterm.

Unit 11 (Activity 5)

Narrator: Here are Silly Sally's likes and dislikes about styles of food.

Voice 2: Silly Sally loves cooking, but hates to eat. She likes Greek food but not Chinese cuisine. She won't touch anything from Brazil or Japan, but she likes Moroccan cooking a great deal.

Narrator: Now, here are Silly Sally's likes and dislikes about sports.

Voice 2: Silly Sally not only loves tennis and baseball, but also skiing. However, she hates horseback riding and hockey. She doesn't mind jogging, but she hates to walk.

Narrator: Now, here's what she thinks about people.

Voice 2: She likes queens and princesses, but neither kings nor princes. She loves Matt and Jeff, but she likes neither Peter and Denise, nor John and Mary.

Narrator: Now, here are Silly Sally's likes and dislikes about fruits and vegetables.

Voice 2: She's wild about beets, carrots, and apples, but she can't stand potatoes, or oranges, or especially cauliflower.

Narrator: Now, here are Silly Sally's likes and dislikes about movie stars.

Voice 2: She likes films with Johnny Depp and Meryl Streep, but not Marlon Brando or Elizabeth Taylor. She hates Denzel Washington, but loves Whoopie Goldberg.

Narrator: Now, here is what Silly Sally thinks about things to do on a date.

Voice 2: She likes going to nice restaurants for dinner, but not for lunch. She'll go to an art gallery, but not a museum. She loves to kiss, but she hates to hug. She wants to get married, but she doesn't want to get engaged.

Narrator: Now, here are Silly Sally's ideas about places to go for a vacation.

Voice 2: She loves Greece, but hates Italy. She likes inns, but she hates hotels. She'll go to the Philippines, but not to Indonesia. She'll travel in the summer, but not in the winter.

Narrator: And finally, here are Silly Sally's likes and dislikes about animals.

Voice 2: She doesn't mind sheep, but she's not fond of goats. She hates cats and dogs, but is fond of not only puppies, but also kittens.

Unit 12 (Activity 4)

We use the term "pacifist" to describe someone who doesn't believe in fighting wars. But there can be different kinds of pacifists. Most pacifists are opposed to war under any circumstances. They feel that armed conflict should never be used to solve disagreements. However, some pacifists believe that there is a difference between a war and a revolution. A war is a conflict which involves two different countries, and a revolution is a war between the people of a single country and their unjust government. Some pacifists feel that "revolution" is a justifiable conflict, but "war" is not. Whenever there is armed conflict, people will disagree about whether or not such a conflict can be justified.

All the recent examples of U.S. military involvement (such as the Vietnam War, the War in the Persian Gulf, or the war in the former Yugoslavia) have divided public opinion into two camps: "hawks" (the term we use to describe people who are in favor of a particular war) and "doves" (the term we use to describe people who are opposed to it). In American politics, disagreements between the "hawks" and the "doves" have been frequent and serious. Hawks and doves disagree about the role the U.S. military should play around the world, and how much money the government should spend on military purposes. Hawks usually favor a strong army and large amounts of money for military purposes. Doves typically favor a small army and want less money spent on military purposes and more money spent on social programs.

Unit 13 (Activity 5)

Good morning class. Today we're going to continue our discussion of the law of supply and demand. Remember last class, we said that according to classical economic theory, supply and demand—remember that's the law that says increase in demand raises prices, and increase in supply lowers prices—well, this law in classical economics is considered to be THE major driving force in a free market economy. Well, modern economic theory states that there are a number of other forces at work too, so today we're going to take a look at what some of those other forces might be. The first thing we're going to look at is transportation. And in order to understand this, I'm going to tell you a little story. We're going to take a look at what happened about 100 years ago in the Midwestern U.S., OK?

Now, about 100 years ago in the Midwest, there wasn't really a very good system of transportation. There wasn't really a very good way of transporting goods long distances, and getting things to market, so things were pretty much on a very local, region-by-region basis. So corn and wheat—which were the primary agricultural products, just as they are today—the price of corn and wheat were determined by the classic relationship of supply and demand that we talked about yesterday. Supply was determined by how much corn and wheat were available, and demand was determined by how many people needed to buy it. So, during the 1870s and 1880s, as the population increased, the demand for wheat rose, and the price also rose. But then farmers responded to the price increase by producing more wheat, since they could get more profit on their investment of time and effort because of the higher prices. This made more corn and wheat available, so the competition to sell also increased, and the prices dropped.

Now this was really bad news. There were these continuous cycles of boom and bust, boom and bust. Prices would drop and farmers would go bankrupt. Then there wouldn't be enough corn and wheat, because nobody was growing it, and the prices would shoot though the roof. People couldn't by bread or feed their livestock. It was really terrible.

Now what happened to change this? One thing: railroads. There was this explosion of railroad construction in the 1880s and everything changed. Railroads meant that you could move the available supply around the country, and not just keep it in one place. If you had too much in one area, you could send the surplus to someplace else. If you didn't have enough, you could increase the supply from other places. So the development of transportation had a really fundamental and significant impact.

So that's the first factor or force that affects the basic law of supply and demand. Next time we're going to take a look at some of the other forces: advertising, government regulations, and monopolies. Any questions?

Unit 14 (Activity 6)

Narrator: Interview number one.
Interviewer 1: Hi. Thanks for coming. We're glad that you're interested in the North American Institute for International Studies. Could you tell us your name, and which program you've applied for?
Candidate 1: Sure. Hi. My name is Aliona Fernandez, and I'm applying for the Master's Program in Teaching English as a Foreign Language.
Interviewer 2: Great! Well, why don't we get started by having you tell us why you think you'd be a good candidate for our program. I mean, what makes you different from the other candidates?

Aliona: OK. Well, I'm not sure about the other candidates' background, but I suspect that maybe I've had more actual teaching experience overseas than some of the others. I've been in the Peace Corps and I've also worked in Taiwan and Japan.
Interviewer 2: Yes, we saw that on your application. Well, why do you want to go back to school, with so much experience?
Aliona: Well, I think that this experience has been really helpful, but I feel I really need some formal training to help me improve my skills.
Interviewer 1: That makes sense. Well, our time is a bit limited, so

we've only got time to ask you one more question. Can you tell us about an accomplishment that you feel particularly proud of?

Aliona: Gosh. Well, I guess this is not time to be modest, is it? Well, I speak three languages. I've lived comfortably in other cultures. And I've written a grammar book.

Interviewer 2: Really? Where was that?

Aliona: Oh, that was when I was a Peace Corps volunteer.

Interviewer 1: Well, our time's up. Thanks for coming.

Aliona: Thank you!

Narrator: Interview number two.

Interviewer 2: Thanks for coming. We're glad that you're interested in the North American Institute for International Studies. Could you tell us your name and which program you've applied for?

Candidate 2: Sure. Hi. My name is John Tealhome and I'm applying for the International Business Program.

Interviewer 1: Great! Well, why don't we get started by having you tell us why you think you'd be a good candidate for our program. I mean, what makes you different from the other candidates?

John: OK. Well, I've just returned from spending a year studying in Paris, and I'm really interested in using that experience to work in import-export.

Interviewer 1: Oh, a year in Paris, that's interesting. Have you had any experience in international business?

John: Well, not really. But I've made some good contacts that I hope to follow up on once I've gotten a little more training. Oh, and when I was in college here I worked in a book store.

Interviewer 2: Mmmm. Well, our time is a bit limited, so we've only got time to ask you one more question. Can you tell us about an accomplishment that you feel particularly proud of?

John: Let's see. Well, I was class president of my high school. I was captain of the football team. As you probably noticed on my application, I received a scholarship to study in France.

Interviewer 1: Yes, we did. Are you fluent in French?

John: Bien sur! I made some really good friends in France and they taught me a lot.

Interviewer 2: Well, that's terrific, it was really nice to meet you. I'm afraid our time's up. Thank you very much for coming.

John: You're welcome. Nice talking to you.

Unit 15 (Activity 4)

Narrator: Listen to these two speakers talk about the future. As you listen, note that speaker's predictions and the reasons for those predictions in the chart below. Based on those predictions and reasons, decide whether the speaker is optimistic or pessimistic about the future.

Speaker 1:

A hundred years from now will be a wonderful time to be alive. Certain things are already happening that will change human society and make the next century a wonderful time in the history of the world.

A hundred years from now there will be more people and they will be leading healthier lives. Most of the diseases that are common today will be wiped out. Scientists are already making progress in finding cures for AIDS, Alzheimer's disease, heart disease, and cancer. So people in the next century will be living longer and healthier lives.

In a hundred years people will have been eating more nutritiously for several generations; so, as we are already seeing in the countries like Japan and Thailand, human beings will, on the whole, be larger, stronger and more intelligent than they are today.

Another area of progress will be energy resources. Scientists will have discovered nonpolluting ways to produce cheap, clean energy. There are already alternative energy sources such as water power and solar energy, and as fuels such as gas, oil, and coal become scarcer and more expensive, these clean sources of energy will become cheaper to produce. So it is likely that by the end of the next century there will be much less pollution: no smog, no acid rain, and no fears about global warming.

Finally, 100 years from now will see greater political and economic stability. Global communication and global economic progress will improve the political situation. Changes such as the Internet are already making global communication available to everyone and will lead to increasing international cooperation. By the end of the next century, the political changes that started in the late 1980s will remove forever the threat of nuclear war. People will be so used to thinking in global terms, and will have been doing so for so long that it will no longer even be necessary to have passports.

Speaker 2:

A hundred years from now will be a terrible time to be alive unless the governments of the world begin to act now. If certain things don't begin to happen, the next century could be a very unpleasant period in the history of the world.

The population is increasing at a very rapid rate. Resources for health care, economic development, and even food cannot keep up with the enormous increase in population. In spite of this fact, many governments do not support birth control research or family planning programs. There will be more and more shortages of food as the population continues to grow uncontrollably and poor nutrition will affect more and more people. Lack of sufficient vitamins will make people weaker and less able to resist disease.

The growth of new diseases such as AIDS and Ebola Virus will continue, and all diseases will become harder to control. Such diseases as malaria and tuberculosis are already increasing. And common antibiotics have begun to lose their effectiveness against infectious diseases like pneumonia.

Supplies of fossil fuels such as coal, oil, and gas are almost finished, but governments are not supporting programs to develop alternative energy sources, such as solar power or wind-generated electricity. Massive deforestation is changing the world climates and increasing air pollution. And an increased reliance on nuclear power will result in more nuclear accidents like Chernobyl.

In spite of increase global communication, countries are breaking apart. The small local wars in places like the former Yugoslavia or the former Soviet Union will become more widespread. This trend will continue around the world, as the economic gap between the rich and the poor continues to increase. War and revolution will be common in the next century.

Unit 16 (Activity 5)

Mom: John, all the cookies I baked this morning have disappeared. I think one of those kids has been robbing the cookie jar. But which one is it?

Dad: Well, it could be any of them. You know how Nancy likes sweets. She could have eaten them when she came home from school today. But then again, it might have been Diane. Remember what happened to that chocolate cake you cooked for the bake sale? Of course, I suppose it could have been Eric, too. He's not that fond of sweets, but he is a growing boy.

Mom: Well, it couldn't have been Diane, because I was with her all afternoon. I don't think it was Nancy. She's been on a diet, so I don't think she could have done it. It must have been Eric.

Dad: Well, I think it could have been Nancy. She should have been really hungry after school if she's been dieting. She could have done it. Are you sure you were with Diane the whole afternoon? She might have taken them while you weren't looking.

Eric: Hi, Mom, hi, Dad. Sorry I'm late. Basketball practice lasted longer than expected. What's for dinner? I'm starved!

Mom: Well, it must not have been Eric, I guess. He hasn't been home at all. It must have been one of the girls.

Dad: Let's check their rooms. That should tell us something. We might find some cookies still lying around.

Mom: Oh, we can do that later. We're going to have dinner in a minute.

Dad: Dinner already? I'm still full!

Mom: Full? Full from what, honey?

Dad: Um, err, uh

Mom: Wait a minute—are those cookie crumbs I see on your mustache?

Unit 17 (Activity 7)

Peter: Say, Denise, do you know if Mr. Green has announced the new projects?

Denise: Well, Peter, if you had been at the meeting, you would have heard the announcement. You couldn't have chosen a more important meeting to miss.

Peter: Yes, Denise, I know. But I was busy finishing up the contract. You know, you could have been more careful with the figures. I had to change several at the last moment.

Denise: You should have checked them before it got so close to the deadline.

Peter: And you might at least have warned me that you hadn't gone over them.

Denise: I might have gone over them, Peter. What makes you think I didn't?

Peter: If you had gone over them there wouldn't have been so many mistakes. We both know you are a careful worker. I think you left them there on purpose.

Denise: Now why would I do that?

Peter: Well, let's pretend that you wanted to get me in trouble with Mr. Green. What would be an easy way to do that, I wonder?

Denise: Please, Peter. I've got better things to do. If I wanted to get you fired, I would have done it a long time ago.

Unit 18 (Activity 8)

Matt: Hi, Doctor Wong. How did the lab tests turn out?

Dr. Wong: Hi, Matt. I got the results this morning, and I'm afraid your cholesterol level is quite high. You really need to change your eating habits. You need to start eating foods that are low in fat.

Matt: Well, I try to eat healthy foods, but my roommate, Jeff, does all the cooking. He always cooks everything with lots of butter, and he won't do it any other way. He says that butter gives foods more flavor.

Dr. Wong: Well, you could try to take over cooking a couple of nights a week, and then slowly start to introduce your roommate to more healthful ways to prepare foods.

Matt: I'm not sure he'd agree. He really loves to cook.

Dr. Wong: Then just demand that he start preparing foods in a healthier way. That's the best way. Good sensible eating habits require that a person take responsibility for his or her own body and the food that goes into it.

Matt: Well, I guess I could try that. Is there any other way?

Dr. Wong: Well, we could put you on medication to lower your cholesterol, but here might be side-effects. Any way, it's better if we can correct the problem naturally, without having to use expensive drugs.

Unit 19 (Activity 7)

Narrator: Conversation number one is between Denise Driven and her secretary.

Denise: Hi, Dave. Where there any phone calls while I was away at the sales meeting?

Dave: Oh yes, Ms. Driven. The sales representative from ACME Publishing called. And a vice president came by to talk with you. She left something for you on your desk.

Denise: OK, I'd better take care of that one right away.

Narrator: Conversation number two is between John and Mary.

John: I can't concentrate on this any longer. I'm starving! Let's go down to the snack bar.

Mary: But we're almost done. Can't you wait just a little longer.

John: I'm just going to get a quick snack. I promise I'll be back.

Mary: OK. Well, get a snack for me, too.

Narrator: Conversation number three is between Bob and Betty.

Bob: Betty, it's my birthday next week, and I'm thinking about having a party.

Betty: I remembered that it was your birthday. I was thinking about inviting some friends over for cake and ice cream.

Bob: Hmm, I was thinking about going to a restaurant.

Betty: Sounds like fun. Chinese food is the cheapest choice for a lot of people.

Bob: Great! Let's do it.

Unit 20 (Activity 6)

Peter Principle: Good morning Denise. Did the Davis contract get finished?

Denise Driven: It took some doing, but I got it done late last night.

PP: Well, I came in early to help out, just in case you needed it.

DD: That's nice, Peter. Thanks for your concern and support. But, as usual, it's too little and too late.

PP: Gee. I guess you don't need help with your official complaint to Mr. Green either.

DD: No, Peter. That's done, too. In fact, I did it before I finished the Davis contract.

PP: Oh good, Denise. I'm glad you have your priorities straight. Would you like to see pictures of my son's school play?

DD: Don't start that again, Peter. I'm warning you!

PP: Come on, Denise. It won't hurt you to think about something besides work for just a minute.

DD: If you bring that up one more time, Peter, I swear I'll throw this computer terminal at you.

PP: That's very professional, Denise, very professional.

DD: I think you had better leave right now, Peter. I really mean it!

PP: Gee, Denise. Are you giving me the day off? That's really nice of you. I guess I can take my kids to the beach after all. Bye bye, then. Have a nice day. And I really mean that!

DD: That man is going to drive me crazy! If I could only fire him, it would make this office so much more business-like.

Unit 21 (Activity 5)

Speaker: OK class, we're going to play a little game with geometry today. We're going to look at one of Euclid's laws that shows the fundamental relationship of squares and triangles. I would like you all to take out a piece of paper and draw a perfect square. If you need to use a ruler to make sure that all four sides of the square are the same length, go ahead. (pause) Has everybody done that? OK. Now draw a line from the upper left-hand corner of the square to the bottom right-hand corner. (pause) How many triangles do you have? Two, right? OK, now do the same thing from the bottom left-hand corner to the opposite corner of the square. (pause) You should now have a total of four isosceles triangles. All right, now here comes the tricky part: I want you to draw a mirror image of each triangle, with the base of each triangle being the line that you drew as the side of your original square. (Pause) So, your diagram should now look like this: a square with an X inside it, inside another square, which is at a 45 degree angle to the first square. OK, now connect the top and bottom corners and the left and right corners of the new square with lines. (pause) So your original square should now be divided up into eight triangles, and the whole diagram should still be a perfect square. Now, here are my questions: How many triangles are there in your diagram, and how many squares have you drawn? Count carefully, ladies and gentlemen, because there are probably more of both than you think

Unit 22 (Activity 9)

Narrator: Report number one.
Speaker: Every year on March 19 a large flock of swallows returns to San Juan Capistrano Mission in Southern California. No one knows how this flock manages to return every year on exactly the same date, but they have been doing just that for more than 200 years. The city government of San Juan Capistrano has been providing a great deal of publicity on the event for many years, and as a result, March 19 is also the day when flocks of tourists arrive at the Mission as well to watch the swallows return. (pause)

Narrator: Report number two.
Speaker: A committee of scientists has been appointed by the Canadian government to look into the effect of acid rain on the forests of North America. They have been asked to present the results of their study by the end of the year. The press and the public are waiting anxiously for the committee to release its report.

Narrator: Report number three.
Speaker: There is a very unusual company of actors which is based in Washington, DC. Most of the company cannot hear, and many members can only speak by using sign language. The National Theater of the Deaf was founded nearly 30 years ago, and since then they have performed all over the U.S., and in dozens of foreign countries. The troupe has played an important role in involving the disabled in the arts.

Unit 23 (Activity 5)

What was my unforgettable experience? Gosh—(slight pause) I think one has to be the day I heard that John F. Kennedy had been assassinated. I think any American who was alive at the time probably feels the same way. It's just something you can't forget. Even though it was more than 30 years ago, I can still remember everything about that day; it's amazing!

I was a junior in high school. I was studying in the school library at the time. Ordinarily, I would have been in class, but our teacher was giving a make-up examination. Since I had already passed the test, I had been excused from class and given permission to go to the library.

I can remember it just as if it were yesterday! The library door was open, and I heard a radio playing from one of the classrooms across the hall. At first I was kind of bothered by the noise. I wondered why they were playing that radio so loud when people were trying to study. Then all of a sudden I heard the announcer saying, "We have confirmed that President John F. Kennedy has been shot while traveling through Dallas, and that he is now dead. We repeat: President John F. Kennedy is dead." I was shocked. I couldn't believe it! I immediately left the library and returned to class. I was so upset, I had to tell someone!

When I entered the room they were still taking the test. I was about to interrupt when I heard the school principal on the public address system announcing the horrifying news. Even before he finished talking, people began to cry. And when he was finished, all normal activities came to a halt. Of course we forgot about the test. No one could believe it. Our teacher turned on the television and for the rest of the day we watched the news reports instead of studying. (slight pause) Yeah—that definitely has to be one of my most unforgettable experiences, no doubt about it!

Unit 24 (Activity 4)

Science fiction is a kind of literature that describes how things will be in the future. Writers of science fiction have been making predictions about the future for more than 100 years, and several famous writers have described how life would be at the end of the twentieth century.

It is interesting for us today to look at the works of some of these famous science fiction writers to see the sort of future that they predicted, and how accurate those predictions reflect our actual living conditions. There are four writers whose predictions about life at the end of the twentieth century are particularly famous: Jules Verne, H.G. Wells, George Orwell, and Aldous Huxley. Let's take a look at some of the things they expected would happen before the year 2000.

Jules Verne was a popular late nineteenth-century French writer. Although he wrote many novels, his most famous works are probably his science fiction novels, *From the Earth to the Moon*, and *Twenty Thousand Leagues Under the Sea*. The world that he portrayed in those books was surprisingly accurate. He predicted that many people would have their own personal airplanes. He also accurately predicted that there would be scientific exploration of the moon, and that people would use solar power to get energy. He also predicted, less successfully, that there would be a single world language. He undoubtedly thought that that language would be French, although today it seems that English is a more likely candidate for that title.

Our next author is H.G. Wells. Wells was an English writer of the late nineteenth and early twentieth centuries. His most famous books were *The War of the Worlds, The Invisible Man,* and *The Time Machine*. In *War of the Worlds* he described a frightening invasion from Mars, where aliens conquered the earth, but eventually became victims of simple nonserious earth diseases such as the common cold. His other famous novels, as their titles suggest, predicted worlds where scientists created inventions that would allow people to travel through time, or would make people become invisible.

Two more famous English authors wrote in the second half of the twentieth century about times that they thought would be here very, very soon. Instead of writing about the world 100 years later, they wrote about a future that was less than 50 years away.

In the 1930s, George Orwell wrote his most famous novel, *1984*. In it he portrayed a gloomy and frightening world of three or four all-powerful governments that were constantly at war with each other and with their own people. Orwell pessimistically predicted that the government would control all aspects of people's lives, and that people would be watched by secret police, by hidden cameras and microphones. He also feared that anyone who tried to disagree with the government would be put in prison.

Aldous Huxley's predictions in *Brave New World* were somewhat more optimistic, but he hardly expressed the optimism of Jules Verne or H.G. Wells. He portrayed a world where children would be born through artificial means and raised in state-run nurseries, instead of by individual families. He thought that there would be movies that were so realistic that people would think they were actually happening. He also thought that the use of mind-altering drugs would be widespread, and encouraged by the government.

As we can see, all four authors had an intriguing mix of right and wrong guesses about the ways we would actually be living today.

Unit 25 (Activity 7)

At last month's press conference, a representative of the Metropolitan Police Department announced the rate of violent crime had decreased significantly over the last five months. He admitted there had been a slight increase in thefts and burglaries, and that the Department would continue frequent patrols in all neighborhoods. When asked about the budget being discussed with the Mayor's Office, he predicted that it would be finalized by the end of the week, and the accelerated hiring program might begin as soon as the following Wednesday.